"What is provided in this book is a series of speculations about some of the major problems which American Catholicism faces—sex, community, leadership, work, play, celebration, God, priesthood, society, self. These speculations are intended as models for interpretation both of the present condition and the future possibilities of the American Church. But, having set out to write a book about the Catholic condition, I find that I have also written a book to some considerable extent about the catholic condition, for the concerns and problems that face the American Church are no different from those that face the human race, which is, I take it, as it should be. For the problems and the possibilities of the contemporary Church, at least if they are seen at the most general thematic level, are no different than the problems and the possibilities of mankind."

—from the *Introduction*

Books by Andrew M. Greeley

The Church and the Suburbs
Strangers in the House
Religion and Career
*And Young Men Shall See Visions**
*Letters to Nancy**
*The Hesitant Pilgrim: American Catholicism after the Council**
*The Education of Catholic Americans (with Peter H. Rossi)****
*The Catholic Experience**
The Changing Catholic College
Uncertain Trumpet
The Crucible of Change
*A Future to Hope in**
What We Believe (with Martin Marty and Stuart Rosenberg)
Life for a Wanderer
Alumni after Seven Years (with Joe L. Spaeth)
A Profile of Catholic Higher Education
Religion in the Year 2000
Why Can't They Be Like Us? Ethnic Conflict in America

A FUTURE TO HOPE IN

Socio-Religious Speculations

Andrew M. Greeley

IMAGE BOOKS

A DIVISION OF DOUBLEDAY & COMPANY, INC.

GARDEN CITY, NEW YORK

Image Book edition 1970
by special arrangement with Doubleday & Company, Inc.

Image Books edition published September 1970

Lines from *The Path to Rome* by Hilaire Belloc. Reprinted by permission of A. D. Peters & Co.

Excerpt from *The Tasks of Adolescence* by Kenneth Keniston, a report for Task Force III of the Joint Commission on the Mental Health of Children. Reprinted by permission of the author.

Excerpts from *The Theology of Hope* by Jurgen Moltmann. Reprinted by permission of Harper & Row, Publishers and SCM Press Ltd.

Lines from *A Sleep of Prisoners* by Christopher Fry. Reprinted by permission of Oxford University Press.

Excerpts from Psalms are from *The Jerusalem Bible*. Copyright © 1966 by Darton, Longman & Todd, Ltd. and Doubleday & Company, Inc. Used by permission of the publishers.

For H

CONTENTS

We do not know . . . whether this earth of ours will still exist in A.D. 2000 or whether some criminal gamble with nuclear power will have transformed the earth once again into a chaos inimical to all forms of life. Or to express it in more moderate terms, we do not know whether this earth, if it has not yet been turned back into dead landscape, will in A.D. 2000 still be the sort of earth on which one would want to live and on which it makes sense to be alive. And we most certainly do not know whether by A.D. 2000 there will be any point in "inheriting" the earth, i.e. making a responsible contribution to its structure and government. . . . But if there is any hope at all for an earth worth living on . . . one thing is certain: only the meek will inherit this earth.

FRITZ BAADE The Race to the Year 2000

Dark and cold we may be, but this
   Is no winter now. The frozen misery
Of centuries breaks, cracks, begins to move,
   The thunder is the thunder of the floes,
The thaw, the flood, the upstart Spring.
   Thank God our time is now when wrong
Comes up to face us everywhere,
   Never to leave us till we take
The longest stride of soul men ever took.
   Affairs are now soul size.
The enterprise
   Is exploration into God . . .

CHRISTOPHER FRY A Sleep of Prisoners

INTRODUCTION

The focus of most of my writing has been American Catholicism in its present social context. I have tried to examine from a viewpoint that has been more or less sociological such phenomena as the Church's postwar suburban upper middle-class, its young people, its schools, its pastoral problems, and its adjustment to the changes of the second Vatican Council. In the last two years, however, it has become clear to me that I cannot understand these highly specific questions unless I learn to think of them within the framework of more general themes which have characterized the American Catholic tradition. Thus as a companion to the present volume (in *The Catholic Experience*), I tried to draw out what I thought were, from the sociologist's viewpoint, the important themes that have run through the history of the Catholic Church in the United States. In this book I turn from the past to the present and the future, and will try to make some assertions about the opportunities and the dangers that Catholicism faces in the United States, let us say, in the century to come. I do not intend this exercise merely to engage in amusing fantasy divorced from the realities of the present. Future developments in the Catholic condition that I anticipate are but projections from the present and projections that are made in order that I might better understand the present. As my colleague to whom this book is dedicated has pointed out on countless occasions, only the present has reality. The past possesses its reality insofar as it exists in the memory of the present, and the future possesses its reality only insofar as it exists in the expectations of the present. This book, then, is really about the present, but from the perspective of the future, just as *The Catholic Experience* was really about the present, though from the perspective of the past.

In *The Catholic Experience* I attempted to develop a model for interpreting from the sociological viewpoint the data that historians have made available to us about the past of American Catholicism. But we have no data about the future—only projections—and to attempt to find meaning and order in projections, one must go beyond the limits of social science and call on the services of faith and religion. So the present volume is considerably less sociological and much more religious than was its predecessor and can make no serious claim to scientific sociology, but must rather be considered as an essay in religious speculation set in a sociological context. In a dim and vague way, I shall try to do with the social sciences what Teilhard de Chardin did in the geological sciences —use the findings from academic discipline as a basis for speculating about religious evolution. But that I will be less successful than Teilhard is the result not merely of the fact that he was a genius and I am not (though heaven knows this is true), but also of the fact that the geological disciplines are far advanced over the behavioral disciplines.

What is provided in this book, then, is a series of speculations about some of the major problems which American Catholicism faces—sex, community, leadership, work, play, celebration, God, priesthood, society, self. These speculations are intended as models for interpretation both of the present condition and the future possibilities of the American Church. But, having set out to write a book about the Catholic condition, I find that I have also written a book to some considerable extent about the catholic condition, for the concerns and problems that face the American Church are no different from those that face the human race, which is, I take it, as it should be. For the problems and the possibilities of the contemporary Church, at least if they are seen at the most general thematic level, are no different than the problems and the possibilities of mankind. This book, therefore, could probably just as well be called *The Human Condition*, save that Father Teilhard has already pre-empted that title. It could also be called, one supposes, *The Western Condition*, save that disturbing images of John Wayne riding off into the sunset would be brought to mind.

The basic theme of the book is not a particularly new one: The options available to the human race are rapidly decreasing. Because of the technological and cultural advances of the past century, man must learn to live in trust with his fellow men or face the certainty of self-destruction. He must recapture intimacy in the large corporate structures which encompass his life or become the victim of corporate irresponsibility. He must discover new forms of leadership or his society will become ungovernable. He must learn to play with his world or he will convert the world into a rubbish heap. Even his work must become playful, if it is to be done at all. But what such assertions postulate is a major evolutionary leap for the human race. Either mankind will move dramatically beyond its present condition or it will recede toward barbarism. In the next century there will be no alternatives available besides these two.

I will further contend that the Christian Church has a critical role to play in the decisions that mankind must make about these options, both because Christianity has been to some extent responsible for the scientific and cultural progress that has pushed man into his present awkward set of circumstances, and because to the man of faith Christianity has the basic answer to the questions that are at issue, even though it has done its best to obscure these answers frequently, even for itself.

Since the aim of the book is to present general themes, I propose to draw with very broad strokes. The summaries of behavioral-science literature presented in various parts of the book are necessarily sweeping and simplified and based on data of varying quality. For example, while there would be little question among most sociologists about the survival of the importance of the primary group in modern corporate society, the evidence is not yet overwhelming and unquestionable for my contention that the friendship group is the most effective productive unit, though I think it is safe to say that most of the evidence points in this direction. Similarly, the claim that the counseling disciplines are on the way toward a solution of distrust and suspicion in the human personality may seem to many to be premature; for even among those in the population who are willing to be counseled, successes are probably less numerous than failures. In both instances, however, I am dealing with projections of present trends rather than with clearly established events. It "looks like" further and more careful research will confirm the importance of the friendship group for the corporate structure, and it "looks like" rapid progress is being made in dealing with human neurosis, and that the rate of progress is accelerating. One need not be a naïve Lockeian optimist to feel that in both areas progress will continue, albeit haltingly, and this is all that the argument of the present volume requires.

As I read over the chapters of the book, I have the somewhat lonely feeling that it will please rather few. My non-Christian colleagues will probably accept, at least as broad summaries, my statements of the problems Western man faces, but they will not understand, and may not like the religious dimension that runs throughout the book. Since I defended one way or another, celibacy, monogamy, authority, institutions, organizations, ritual, the sacred, prayer, and contemplation, and since these are all, in one way or another, outmoded in the minds of most Catholic "liberals," the "liberals" will continue to be quite upset with me. But since the categories and terms used to defend the traditions, as well as to project the future, are not those to be found in standard religious works, the Catholic "conservatives" will also be deeply offended and will darkly hint that there is something suspicious and possibly heretical about what I am saying, even though what is presented here is not definitive theology or even definitive religion, but merely religious speculation. Certainly the conservatives will not like my criticisms of the Catholic Church or the importance attributed to sex in the second chapter of the volume; and the liberals, on the other hand, will not take the criticisms seriously, because they only take seriously criticisms of the priests who have left the priesthood or left the Church, and they will be highly incensed that a celibate presumes that he is qualified to speak on sex.

Under the influence of the noted irenicist, Daniel Herr,

I refrained for the most part from anticipating the arguments of these critics and fighting with them. However, I gave advance warning to those lay sexologists who argue in principle that a priest is unqualified to write a chapter on sex: I reject out of hand the notion that everyone who has slept with a woman is *ipso facto* qualified to write about sex, and that everyone who has not is *ipso facto* disqualified. If they persist in arguing this point, I will demand from them certification that they and their wives are friends in the light of the position I take in the second chapter.

The H to whom the book is dedicated is the real name of the blithe spirit who otherwise operates under the alias of John F. Hotchkin. His influence on my thoughts about the subjects discussed in this book is so extensive and pervasive that I am quite unable to describe its limits, although he must not be held responsible for any of the ideas herein expressed; we must await publication of his own *Systematic Theology* before we can know his position on these questions in any detail. Anyone who has read the works of Reverend Eugene Kennedy will recognize my intellectual debt to him. And finally, I must also express my gratitude to the aforementioned irenical Mr. Herr, who presides over the rocky land of the extreme center with an eagle eye and a ready lance.

Chapter 1

A PAST TO REMEMBER

This is a book about the future, but because it is about the future, it is not a rejection of either the past or the present. He who wishes to ignore the past and wipe out the present, dreams of a future that will never be because the future is built in the present and built on the past. So this book is a projection into the future of both the strengths and the problems of the present and is based on a profound realization of the benefits we have inherited from the past. My brand of futurism deplores the hatred and rejection of the past that is characteristic of so many of the visionaries and self-styled revolutionaries of our day. It is only the accumulated wisdom of the past that provides us with the insight in the values that makes it possible for us to criticize both the past and the present. He who wants to obliterate the traditional usually wants to do so in terms of, and in the name of, values he has inherited from the tradition. We are where we are in the course of human history only because we stand on the shoulders of those who came before us, and we might as well begin by acknowledging this fact.

Recently I was on a panel with a young college radical—a brilliant and idealistic young man. Most of the discussion on the panel was quite civilized, but it was clear that the young man was keeping his anger under control. Finally it was too much for him, and he burst out: "The past has failed. You can't blame us young people for wanting to start over anew when you see the mess in Vietnam and the mess in the streets of American cities. What have we to learn from a generation which has produced Vietnam and ghettos?"

The answer was simple enough, though I am sure it did

not placate the young revolutionary. He was basing his criticism of American society on two principles: 1) Thou shalt not make aggressive war; and 2) Thou shalt not oppress minority groups. Neither of these principles is self-evident and neither has been honored through most of human history. Mankind came to accept the theoretical truth only after a long process of evolution. If my young college radical friend was not the end product of such a long evolution, he would be proving his masculinity not by proclaiming revolution, but by conquering minority groups in bloody warfare, an activity which, until very recently in human history, was viewed with considerable approbation. He was able to criticize the past from the present only in terms of the value systems which had been formulated in the past and handed on to him in the present by the American value system which he felt completely contemned. To hear him talk, one would have thought that he and his generation had thought up these values by themselves.

We would not, therefore, even be able to criticize the world around us unless there had been generations of revolutionary progress before us through which man slowly and painfully arrived at the value system which we use to make our criticisms. He who rejects the possibility of further evolution and wants to begin anew after a revolution has wiped out the traditions of the past, is destroying the very ground on which he stands. He who thinks he has nothing to learn from the experience of the past contradicts himself, because the very arguments he uses for rejecting the past are arguments which have been derived from the past. Revolutions generally don't work, if only because they ignore the wisdom of the human evolutionary experience. Furthermore, in addition to not working, they lead to evils worse than those they are trying to correct precisely because insofar as they cut themselves off from the traditions of the past, they deny themselves access to the very value systems on which they are basing their protests.

But the revolutionary rhetoric survives just the same, and is currently going through a fashionable phase, demonstrating once again that rhetoric need have no connection with historical reality; if there is one thing that the history of the last fifty years demonstrates, it is that social progress is not accomplished by taking control out of the hands of one elite and giving it over into the hands of another elite. Such a procedure is based on the notion that the socioeconomic "pie" is of a fixed size and that the revolutionary elite will do a better job of dividing it than the elite it has displaced. It may do so at first, but the tendency for a ruling class to behave like a ruling class seems to be irresistible. Progress comes, then, not from redividing the "pie" but from making a bigger and ever growing pie, whether the pie be of economic affluence or decision-making power in the Church. One ends poverty in the world not by redistributing the world's goods but by producing more goods. Similarly, many laity who want to participate in decision-making in the Church start by taking power away from the clergy and hierarchy, whereas they should be cooperating in the creation of new structures in which there will be more power to go around because the structures are more efficient.

The thrust of this book, then, is evolutionary. While it is critical of the past, it does not reject it. As a human institution, the Christian Church has much to be ashamed of. As I will note later on in the book, it has made many mistakes, missed many splendid opportunities, and tolerated far too long the scandal of disunion in itself. Yet almost everything we value in Western society has its roots in the Christian tradition, and it seems highly unlikely that we would have gotten much beyond the scientific or cultural or political achievements of Greece and Rome had it not been for the new life the Church injected into the bloodstream of the human race.

The Christian tradition and its Jewish predecessor, as we shall insist time after time in this book, broke through the cycle of eternal return and persuaded man that life was not a circle but a line, a journey, beginning and then moving ahead toward the goal. Progress and history are essentially Christian notions, as are both the possibility of belief and belief in possibility. And while the notion of the rationality and intelligibility of the universe was a Greek notion before it was a Christian one, it was eagerly welcomed into the Christian tradition and kept alive by it. The exodus myth, Jewish in origin, and preserved by Christianity, is the most powerful dynamic that mankind has ever known. The fact that we Westerners take this dynamic for granted blinds us to how different it has made our lives.

Furthermore, the notions of political, economic, and social freedom are at root Christian notions based on the New Testament's concept of the dignity of the human person; one can find nowhere but in the world as influenced by Christianity (and its Jewish predecessor) a concern for the individual person that one finds in the West. It took the Christian churches a long time to understand the full implications of their own doctrine on the human person. Slavery was eliminated only a short time ago, and the inequality of women is not yet eliminated. But only in societies influenced by Christianity are both these forms of oppression considered objectionable. As in so many other instances we will note in this book, Christian churches have not realized the implications of their own teachings nearly as well as many of those who are outside the churches are unaware of the religious roots of their secular crusades. The role of the churches has been paradoxical; they have kept alive the Christian tradition, but they have impaired its fulfillment.

Finally, if we are to believe many of the historians of ideas (such as Whitehead), it is no accident that the scientific and technological advances in the last three centuries happened in a culture that had been prepared for such advances by over a thousand years of Christianity. Without faith in the intelligibility and rationality of the universe and the possibility of progress, without the intellectual training of the rationalistic medieval tradition, and without the concern about science which kept alive the accomplishments of the Greeks, the technical and industrial revolutions which have made possible the abundance of our time simply could not have occurred. Those who would view the Catholic Church's relationship with science, for example, in terms of the Galileo controversy alone, forget that had it not been for the Catholic Church there would not have been either a science in the modern world or the modern world at all; they confuse an incident, however horrendous, with a tradition. No one can deny that the Christian churches, particularly the Roman Church, have been something less than enthusiastic about the scientific revolution, this strange, unwanted child of theirs. But the objection of the churches to science must be considered merely an incident—a tragic, inexcusable incident—in a tradition without which there very well might not be any science.

As a Christian, then, I am ashamed of the mistakes and failures of the Christian churches and particularly of the Roman Church, but I am all too conscious that I would not even have the values which cause me to feel shame, were it not for the churches, and any criticism that I may utter against them must necessarily be in terms of values they have handed down to me.

Similarly, I am ashamed of the mistakes and inequities of the American Republic in both its domestic and foreign policies. But to be ashamed of mistakes is not to indulge in the "hate America" romanticism which is so popular with our would-be revolutionaries. The United States is not merely a land of plenty, though the physical abundance of our natural resources has surely been a help; it is also the most noble work of polity that man has ever devised. It is based on a philosophy of government and society that is rooted in the Christian past, yet represents in theory a notion of civil discourse more advanced than that achieved by any other nation. As Robert Bellah pointed out in a recent article in *Daedalus*, if the United States is to be truly criticized, it must be criticized not for having efficient ideals, but for not having lived up to its ideals; if the American political structure is to be criticized, it must be criticized not for being a rigid and flexible structure, but for perhaps losing some of the flexibility[1] which has marked it in its past.

It must be remembered, in any judgment of the United States as a polity or a society, that it is still a relatively new nation put together in a very brief period of time by vastly different peoples on a raw and unexplored, if wealthy, continent. It must therefore cope with fantastic divisive forces, and has been able to respond to an acculturation process the like of which the world has never known before and which

[1] And yet if one recalls the preliminaries to the 1968 presidential campaign, one is forced to wonder whether the political structure may not be more flexible than it has ever been.

would have torn apart almost any other society on the face of the earth. France, for example, a much older nation, much more homogeneous, with a much longer cultural tradition, can be governed effectively only by a highhanded autocrat; whereas the United States, a new nation composed of very different kinds of people, subjected to tremendous internal strains, with hardly any cultural tradition at all, elects literally tens of thousands of public officials each year, frequently in fiery electoral campaigns representing strong divergencies of public opinion, without becoming "unstuck." Given the size, origins, and nature of the American Republic, the astonishing thing is not that it has problems, but that it exists at all.

Furthermore, despite the ineptitude of its foreign policy in the last quarter of a century (an ineptitude which might be perfectly understandable given the nation's novice role in foreign policy), it has still been incredibly generous with the rest of the world, pouring hundreds of billions of dollars into aid to other countries, not only without getting much back from such aid, but without even expecting to. The image which many Americans have of their country as the leader in a crusade against Communism, or as global policemen, may be inadequate or even dangerous, but to dismiss the United States as an imperialistic nation is to miss the obvious fact that America's foreign policy represents economic loss and not economic gain, and political liability, not political strength. Inept and misguided American foreign policy may be, but it is an ineptitude based on mistaken generosity and responsibility and not on greed or avarice or ambition.

It is to be wondered whether any country in the world is capable of sustaining such a high level of criticism and dissent as is the American Republic. It is fashionable, of course, for many American dissenters to think of themselves as persecuted, but in fact in almost any other country they would have long since been in jail. No nation in the world would sustain the criticism of its foreign policy that the United States has tolerated about the Vietnam War. One wonders whether any minority group in the history of the human race has had as much support from the majority group as black Americans do from white Americans (even though presently it is fashionable for the blacks to ignore or to contemn this support).

There is much that is wrong with the United States of America—very much indeed—but in a book which purports to offer vision about the future of the Catholic Church in the United States, one must at least acknowledge that most of our criticisms of American society are based on values that are not merely American, but which have been realized in the United States far better than they have in almost any place else in the world.

Finally, I will have no part of what Father Edward Duff has called the "mass masochism" of most American Catholic "liberals." I think that I will, in the course of the present volume, level against the Catholic Church in general, and the American Church in particular, criticisms stronger than most of those uttered by the prophets of the liberal establishment. What I have always failed to see is why those who feel the need to criticize must be compelled to demand destruction. There are many weaknesses, for example, in American Catholic higher education that I daresay I have pointed out in more documentary detail than anyone else, and yet I have not, much to the chagrin of many of the "liberals," demanded a termination of the Catholic involvement in higher education; I have refused to say that the Church-affiliated college or university is a contradiction in terms. In the strange two-toned world of the Catholic "liberal" there is no room for grays; but in the multi-toned world of reality there are Church-related schools which have made a definite contribution to American society and to American higher education. There are also Church-related schools which have become academically presentable and even excellent. Criticism demands, in my judgment, change, growth, renewal, and reform. It does not mean, at least if one is not incurably romantic, a revolutionary wiping the slate clean.

The voluntarism of the American Church, the close relationship between its priests and people, its pragmatic approach to problems of expansion, its fantastic organizational accomplishment, its emphasis on freedom and cooperation, and the high level of religious devotion among its people are all extraordinarily impressive. These accomplishments are not without faults, indeed, but despite the faults, they are still impressive. The vast, complicated, and pluralistic institution that is called American Catholicism must change and grow and renew itself. But to say that it must change is not to say that on next Tuesday morning it should go out of business, or turn the direction of its affairs over to the editorial writers of a certain number of Catholic journals who are the only ones qualified to run the Church because they are laity. American Catholicism has, despite its problems and pains, a tremendous amount of vitality. If it were not for the vast institutional structure that this vitality has spawned, most of its articulate critics would have neither jobs, which provide an institutional base for their criticism, nor the values with which to criticize (values, of course, which they have learned for the most part in the hated Catholic school system).

When I make these points to some Catholic groups the response is that, while my position is undoubtedly a balanced one, not everyone should be expected to seek for balance, and that social change is frequently accomplished only by those who see merely *one side* of the question strongly. Criticism, I am told, is far more effective if it is one-sided rather than balanced.

I must say that I find such assertions highly dubious. I would scarcely deny the utility of the gadfly, but if he is useful, he is not *very* useful, and certainly cannot lay much claim to being an intellectual if he persists in seeing but one side of the question. I would argue, on the contrary, that criticism of American Catholicism which respects its traditions, admires its strengths, acknowledges its accomplishments, is going to be far more effective in the long run, not merely because it is balanced, but also because it is true. In the long run, I should think, accuracy triumphs over militant revolutionary propaganda, though the militants may sell a lot of books and newspapers in the process.

This book, then, is evolutionary, not revolutionary, in its description of the present and the future of the Catholic condition. It respects the past which we all remember, even if we do not want to admit it. It acknowledges explicitly and cheerfully that we build the future in the present and in the terms of the past, and that there is no alternative in the human condition. To those who call for revolution, this volume says that there isn't going to be any revolution, either political or ecclesiastical, and that if there were one, it wouldn't be any good. Rejection of the wisdom and the traditions of the past is silly, foolish, and indeed, impossible. Those who engage in it are children, no matter what their chronological age, and everyone knows that you can't trust anybody under thirty.

Chapter 2

SEX TO LOVE WITH

We hear on all sides that ours is a day of sexual revolution. This is often interpreted as meaning that we have at last entered into a "permissive society" complete with pictures of Jane Fonda on the cover of *Newsweek*. Whether our society is any more permissive than the Paris of Louis XV, the London of the Restoration of the Regency, the Rome of Cesare Borgia or of Nero, or even more permissive than Puritan New England, where the practice of "bundling" was widespread, and where serious divines argued whether sleeping with one's betrothed was indeed sinful, may remain problematic. Furthermore, in the absence of comparative data, it is difficult to establish that sexual behavior or attitudes are appreciably different now than they were twenty-five, fifty, or one hundred years ago. Journalistic comparisons between our age and the Victorian Age betray merely a lack of understanding of what went on in the Victorian Age, which was, if inhibited, something less than chaste.

Nonetheless, there has been a sexual revolution—widespread, profound, and with deep implications for the future of mankind. The Manichaeism which has plagued the human race for at least three millennia is being put aside. Sex is no longer something secret or dirty or obscene. It is, rather, something self-fulfilling and interpersonal. While this changing outlook on sex may still be largely theoretical, and may also be frequently presented in caricaturized form, it nevertheless represents a dramatic leap forward for the human race.

At the risk of considerable historical oversimplification, we can say that much of our present problem can be traced back to the rise of the world religions in the first millennium before Christ. In centers of learning, like India, Persia, and Greece, man became explicitly conscious that there was something in him which transcended his body; that there existed, in addition to the material world, a world of ideas and spirit. Unfortunately, these two worlds were seen as separated, if not divorced, and authentic reality was located in the world of the idea or of the spirit, while the material world was seen either as merely imitative of the world of the spirit or, even worse, as a prison constricting it. It was then but a short step to conclude that sex, which is manifestly and indisputably associated with the human body, was something of which man ought to be ashamed and about which he ought not to talk. It is a long way from Zoroaster, Manes, and Plato to the Jansenist Irish seminaries of the nineteenth century. But the links connecting the two ends of the tradition are clear enough. The Manichaean temptation has been a long one and was not overcome by the frequent outbursts of exactly the opposite temptation which it periodically generated.

It is difficult to find many traces of the temptation, however, in the Jewish or very early Christian traditions, despite attempts to quote St. Paul out of context to establish that he was a sexual puritan. The Jews were hardly personalists in their approach to sex, but neither were they as "hung up" on it as the Gentile world has been for several millennia. Furthermore, in the Jewish description of the relationship between God and his people as a marriage union and in the continuation of this description by St. Paul, can be found roots for Christian sexual personalism, if one but looks for them. Unfortunately, far from responding to the personalist revolution enthusiastically, the Church has been more inclined to be hostile and suspicious, and to persist in its Jansenistic and rigid view of sexuality to the bitter end. The natural law, morality, which was built up to defend the birth-control position (a natural law, by the way, which had little in common with St. Thomas' views on the matter), and the ideology and training which developed around clerical celibacy, combined to make Catholicism, at least until Vatican Council II, quite unable to cope with sexual personalism.

On the other hand, not all has been well with the personalists. Under the influences of Kierkegaard, Freud, Sartre, and the like, they have discovered that sex is an integral part of the human personality and that it cannot be excluded from the personality without serious damage. Sex is, therefore, no longer dirty, but one of the "finest things in life," "maturing" and "self-fulfilling." While there has been general rejoicing over the discovery that sex can be, or at least should be, enjoyed without guilt, it must also be acknowledged that deliverance from guilt and inhibition has been both partial and limited. Sex is out in the open now, but it does not seem to be any less an obsessive "hang-up." Fear and anxiety about sex persist, and it's an open question as to whether doubts about one's masculinity or one's femininity are not much more obsessive in our society than they were in a society where sex was not so explicitly important. Under such circumstances, Marshall McLuhan's suggestion that in the years to come sex will become "cooler" and therefore better, is not without wisdom, but it still seems that there is a long way to go before sex can be so integrated into the rest of man's life that he need not be unduly anxious about it.

It seems to me that if one is to attempt to think through the implications of sex for human life, one must start with the basic biological fact: Man is an animal, and therefore man's sexuality is an animal sexuality. It may well be more than that, but if one attempts to ignore the basic zoological roots of human sexuality, one is likely to get caught in a mysticism, whether it be religious or secular, that can only be self-deceiving.

Man is an animal, a primate, an ape, and his sex is basically a reproduction mechanism oriented toward the continuation of the species, as is sex in any animal. It is curious to note, in passing, how much the older approach of moral theologians has in common with the approach of the biologists, neither group being able to see that the human reproductive process has evolved into something more than just a means of continuing the species.

For man is a very special kind of ape and he has a very special kind of animal sexuality. The most important thing we can say about human sex is that, even from the biological viewpoint, it is relational; that is to say, it bears within itself a straining toward the establishment of a permanent relationship. Man, unlike most of the other apes, is "pair bonded": He has basic biological tendencies toward an enduring relationship with his mate.[1]

The reason for this "pair bonding" is not hard to find. The human offspring requires a long and watchful period of care before it is able to subsist on its own. If the child is to survive even physiologically, it requires sustained protection and nurture from both its parents. Furthermore, the female of the species requires more protection and help before, during, and after childbirth than do most other female animals. If the male human ape was not tied to his mate by powerful emotions rooted in his physical nature, chances of the offspring surviving, and even of the mate lasting very long, would not be great. In the absence of pair bonding, the human species would not have had an impressive expectancy for survival.

Some modern social scientists, such as Talcott Parsons, would further argue that the proper development of the human psyche requires that the human offspring be reared in a pair-bonded atmosphere; that is to say, in a situation in which both the male and the female of the species are present, and where the two are involved in the pair-bonded relationship. Only in such circumstances, argues Parsons, will

[1] Human zoologists debate about the precise nature of this pair bonding, the main differences focusing on how similar it is to that found in other animals. It hardly need be said that neither fidelity nor monogamy are irresistible tendencies in the human animal, and they may have been even less irresistible earlier in the evolutionary process. The present writer is not qualified to comment on this debate; but it suffices to say that both the long period required for child care and the permanent readiness for intercourse—discussed in later paragraphs—indicate some "built-in" tendencies toward pair bonding, and that this fact is all that needs to be insisted on in the context of the present chapter. There are tendencies in the opposite direction which man does not seem to share with other pair-bonded animals, and this presents a complex problem both for those who would understand human behavior and for those who engage in human behavior; but an explanation of these opposite tendencies does not seem to be required for our basic assertions to be valid.

the human offspring be able to work out both his own sexual identity and the interaction skills required for coping with someone of the opposite sexual identity.

There are many manifestations of this rather special form of biological pair bonding to be found in the human ape. First of all, his sexual abilities and inclinations are not limited to specific times. Intercourse is not just a transitory episode when the female is in heat. On the contrary, in the human ape, desire and the ability to satisfy the desire are both pervasive and permanent. Secondly, intercourse is both more complicated and more rewarding physically and psychologically for man than it appears to be for other animals. The act itself takes much longer in the human species, at least if it is to be satisfying to both partners. It also requires more effort and more practice over a sustained period of time if the two partners are to become skillful in providing each other with the most pleasure, and to acquire a repertory of approaches and techniques which will prevent the sexual act from growing dull and routine. However, despite these complications and difficulties which he must endure, man also has far greater rewards, both physically and psychically than do other animals. While strict comparability is impossible until the other animals are able to testify for themselves, it still does appear that both in anticipation, execution, and reaction, human sex is more powerful, explosive, and rewarding than is animal sex. The male lion or the male chimpanzee is hardly capable of spending his working day dwelling on pleasurably lustful thoughts about his mate to whom he will return at night, or of spending the following day in proud and pleasant distractions over the delights that he brought to her and she to him before, during, and after their act of union.

From the biological viewpoint, therefore, it seems reasonable to contend that nature wanted the male and the female of the human species to be "enthralled" with one another even if they themselves were something less than completely pleased with the intense demands of their own emotions. I am not arguing at this point against either divorce or multiple mating, but simply arguing that relationship—that is to say, pair bonding—is a built-in biological mechanism in the human species. Episodic and nonrelational sex (à la *Playboy*), however pleasurable it may be at the moment, seems to have a built-in biological strain toward frustration. Man and woman may resist the strong inclination toward establishing a relationship with one another, but when they do so they do violence to their own biology.

But having said that man is a pair-bonded monkey, we have only given half the biological picture. He is also, as Konrad Lorenz has pointed out, an extraordinarily aggressive animal who finds it extremely difficult to cooperate with other members of his species. Like other apes, he has his own "turf" which he does not want to be invaded by others, though the turf for man tends to be more psychic than purely physical. When anyone gets too close to him, man is threatened; he becomes afraid that he is going to be pushed around, taken advantage of, "chumped." Like other very aggressive animals, he does not trust anyone to get too close to him, which means, if we translate into psychological terms, that man is gravely suspicious about intimacy and builds strong defenses, psychic and occasionally even physical, against intimacy.[2]

We then perceive the dilemma, and indeed the agony, of the human condition in general and of human sex in particular. Man possesses a very special kind of pair bonding, since extremely close cooperation in intimacy is required to feed and protect young children—more so than is required by any other animal. The human family necessarily, therefore, is almost oppressively intimate; but intimacy is something that another of man's biological reactions, the aggressive impulse, strongly resists. Sex, therefore, brings great pleasure —more than to any other animal—but also demands a high price both in terms of skills and obligations—more than is demanded of any other animal. Man is crowded by his wife and children (at times almost unbearably so). (Of course she is crowded by her husband and children, at times almost

[2] Many psychologists are inclined to disagree with Lorenz that aggressiveness is a distinct element in the personality. They argue that it is merely another way of considering man's need to protect and defend himself. They also say that if man does have a "turf," it's more psychic than physical. I am not competent to judge this controversy, but no matter how it might be resolved, the remarks made in the above paragraph still seem to be valid.

unbearably so), and wants desperately to be able to put them away. On the other hand, he is also drawn irresistibly to her and to them and held, if he wishes to obtain anything more than minimum satisfaction from her, to show a great deal of consideration, both physical and psychological, for her (and she for him).

It need hardly be pointed out that this animal ambivalence rooted deeply in man's biology serves as a very adequate description of most marriages in the course of the human race's existence, and probably most marriages today. The two mates are caught in a tug of powerfully ambivalent forces; they are capable of enjoying with each other extraordinarily intense pleasure, both physical and psychic, but on the other hand they are repelled by the insistent demands that the other makes, since these demands are viewed as a threat to one's own independence, dignity, and freedom. The compromise that is usually reached requires that both sides cede that amount of independence which is essential to maintain the minimum relationship and thus assure sufficient pleasure so that the relationship will not be torn apart. It is a compromise which has kept the human race in existence, but it has made men and women feel that they were not "getting out" of the marriage what they ought to, or what they expected. The reaction to this situation is historic. Man blames his wife and she blames him.

But the human race has "stumbled" on an alternative reaction to intimacy. It has discovered that besides responding to another's insistent demands with aggression, one can respond with friendship. The human sexual relationship becomes not only bearable, but also unbelievably pleasurable precisely when aggression is replaced by friendship. To put the matter quite simply, love between a man and woman is sex plus friendship; sex and friendship constantly intermingling with each other and reinforcing each other. In the marriage union sex can easily become dull and uninteresting—save for occasional outbursts of passion—without friendship, and the kind of sacrifices required for such an intimate friendship are not likely to be consistently made unless the overwhelming rewards of sex are present to encourage the sacrifices.

Aggression assumes that he who comes close will take something away and cannot be trusted. Friendship says, "I will give him what he wants before he takes it, because I trust him." It says, "I will open myself to the other and exult in his closeness, in my utter defenselessness before him and his corresponding defenselessness toward me." Trust is putting aside the aggressive barriers and surrendering to the other in confidence that the other will not hurt but enrich.

Can we, for the sake of making a point, imagine a myth of two human apes, a man and his mate, accidentally stumbling into mutual submission? Perhaps the two of them have decided almost fortuitously at the same time that they were profoundly weary of resisting the insistent demands of the other and that the only way to have peace would be to give up all resistance, all aggressive defense against the other. Thus the two apes accidentally discovered trust, and their names were Adam and Eve. When the breath of life was breathed into them they were able to love. To pursue the myth further, one might suggest that the overwhelming experience of love was too much for these two apes; they did begin to trust each other, but they did not trust enough; they lost their nerve and they held back on their giving, refusing to let their trust be complete, and this was the original sin. Distrust—the most painful manifestation of man's sinfulness—was thus passed on to their offspring as a reflection of the distrust and the aggressive defense that their parents had built around themselves. Cain's murder of Abel out of distrust, competition, and fear was but a reflection of the very incomplete love and trust which existed between Adam and Eve.

This is only a myth and is not meant to be either a historical or a theological interpretation, but it does point out two extraordinarily important facts: Man is the only animal in the world capable of trust, and secondly, most, if not all, the problems that face the world today, be they in a marriage or international relations, are ultimately rooted in distrust, fear, and suspicion. The discovery of the possibility of trust and the temptation to distrust could very easily be described as eating the fruit of the tree of the knowledge of good and evil.

For with this discovery, man's life became potentially much more rewarding, but also much more complicated and probably more agonized; now he was not only biologically "hooked" on his spouse, but also found within himself a strain toward being psychologically "hooked" on her. He discovered that in this psychological pair bonding there were more surpassing and ecstatic joys than he had believed possible and that these joys, in their turn, made the sex act itself more powerfully rewarding than it had been before. But the unexpected psychic joys and the intensified physical pleasures also demanded even more intimacy in the union between husband and wife than had appeared necessary previously. The joy of friendship was a burdensome joy because it required work and humiliation. It was necessary to exercise constant effort to keep one's defenses down. One had to commit one's self to ever increasing self-revelation. Physical nakedness was both a joy and a burden in the marriage union, but man came to discover that psychic nakedness was even more rewarding and even more difficult, and that without it physical nakedness quickly became routine and uninteresting. Sacrifice for the other and consideration of the other seemed to know no limits. The other had to be treated as a *self* and not as an *it*. To treat the other constantly as a self demanded more time and energy and dedication than man believed himself capable of. The rewards of friendship and marriage were therefore very great, but the price was high—in many, if not most instances, too high—and hence the line was drawn. One could not give up too much because one might get "chumped"; and if the other was a self, not merely intermittently on the marriage bed, but all the time, one would certainly give up too much and run the constant risk of being chumped. There was also the additional problem that man was only too well aware of his own weaknesses and failures and felt guilty about them. This guilt, in its turn, persuaded him that he wasn't very good, nowhere good enough to make the sacrifices that friendship demanded. So guilt for past failures simply reinforced fear and assured even more failures.

In addition, there has been a special problem with woman becoming another self for her husband. We have argued that man, unlike many other animals, reacts aggressively to an invasion of his physical or psychological territory, even by a member of the opposite sex. Man was therefore afraid of being dominated or "chumped" by woman. Since woman is somewhat weaker physically and in no position to defend herself, particularly in times of pregnancy and lactation, man was able to subjugate woman and turn her into a slave, or at best, a second-class human being (a misbegotten male, as some of the medieval scholastics thought). Even though this subjugation of woman was based on fear and distrust, and made possible by physical weakness, it has been rationalized, dignified, and even sacralized by law, theology, psychology, custom, poetry, and art. The mysticism of "the eternal feminine," for which there is no biological or empirical justification, represents the ultimate attempt to "keep woman in her place." Even the modern feminist revolution is making only slow progress against this subjugation, since women are taught from their very earliest years that to be submissive to men is their proper role. Unfortunately, submissiveness is often submissiveness with a sting in it, since in order to survive, woman has learned many tricks which have enabled her to dominate her male while at the same time appearing to be dominated by him. For all the theoretical power he may have, man frequently finds that fear of the bitchiness of his wife paralyzes him in the exercise of his power, and that she, not he, is really the dominant one in the family. One need not be in a country like Ireland for long to realize that whatever the theorists say, the Irish family and Irish society are dominated by women (and of course, the clergy), while the husband is driven out of the family to find solace for his wounded male dignity in the local public house (at least at such hours as the clergy will permit the public house to be open).

Neither style of dominance, man over woman or woman over man, is conducive to the development of friendship. Woman's fulfillment is not in being a wife and a mother; it is in being a human being. Part of her humanity, of course, involves being a wife and mother, but part of his humanity involves being a husband and father, and short of the joys of childbirth (which may be much more culturally based than

biologically), there is no reason to see any more self-fulfillment for a woman in wifehood and motherhood than there
is for a husband in husbandhood and fatherhood. There may
be some biologically linked sex traits in the human psyche,
but there are not very many and they are not very important,
if they do exist. Because woman has had to submit to man,
the more submissive traits of the human personality have been
reinforced in her personality, so we are told that she is more
given to warmth, sympathy, affection, and the seeing of
things in their concrete, particularistic totality than is man;
and since man's role has tended to be dominating (at least
in theory), men have been encouraged to develop dominating tendencies of the human personality, to be strong, hard,
aggressive, assertive—to see things abstractly, universally, and
analytically. Man, we are told, is the analyzer, woman the
synthesizer: man, the head of the family; woman, the heart
of the family.

Despite all the Cana conferences in which this doctrine
has been preached, we have no choice but to describe it
for what it is—unmitigated rot. The ideal human personality
is androgynous; that is to say, a complex and balanced blending of the so-called masculine and so-called feminine traits,
which the sociologists, by the way, would much rather describe as instrumental and affective traits. To be fully human,
man needs submissiveness and woman needs assertiveness.
Man needs to be affective; woman needs to be instrumental.
Man needs more sympathy, warmth, and gentleness in his
life and woman needs more assertiveness, explicit aggressiveness (to eliminate implicit aggressiveness), and more
viewing of reality in its abstract and universal terms. Furthermore, man needs a more aggressive wife and woman needs
a more submissive husband, not merely so that they may
have more in common and understand each other better, but
even that their sexual union might be more rewarding. If,
in the sexual act, man can blend submissiveness along with
his own assertiveness and woman can blend aggressiveness
along with her own submissiveness, the act itself will be
much richer and more rewarding, as will the social and
psychic context in which it is placed. The limiting of one
half the virtues of the complete human being to a male and

the other half to a female has been a major cultural mistake of the human race, and the termination of this mistake is long overdue.

One cannot, in the final analysis, have a friendship with an inferior. Woman must be a person equal unto oneself, or mutual trust is impossible. Therefore, most marriages in the history of the human race have fallen far short of their potential because the cultural and social structure which elaborated the role of woman minimized the possibility of friendship and reinforced the necessity of distrust. The arranged marriages which have been typical of most human marriages through history have assumed both the inequality of woman and the unimportance of friendship; the attempt of certain Catholic writers to make unfavorable comparisons between the present state of marriage (based as it is, however imperfectly, on equality and friendship) and the past state, displays appalling ignorance. As a matter of fact, it ignores even the obvious historical data. St. Paul's insistence that there was no longer Greek, Roman, Jew or Gentile male or female, but all one in Christ Jesus—may well be the most important source of mankind's belated discovery of the equality of the sexes. Once again it seems that the Church has overlooked and misunderstood its own traditions.

I am not arguing that man's potential for loving friendship did not and does not break through the barriers of distrust and inequality. On the contrary, it frequently did. The potential for friendship between husband and wife was always there. The powerful sex drive which reinforced it would not be obliterated by Manichean training. Culture and social structure created odds against human love that were overwhelming but not insoluble. Man and woman did, on occasion, learn to love one another even though their training, their culture, and their social structure militated against it. And the "battle of the sexes," usually much more humorous in a movie with the late Spencer Tracy and Katharine Hepburn than it is in real life, one very much fears, is far more characteristic of the state of armed coexistence which exists between man and woman than is friendship with someone who is perceived as another self.

Man's sex relationships, therefore, particularly in marriage,

have not been very successful thus far in his history. The beginnings of friendship which are blended with the glow of
physical attractiveness at the start of a marriage are quickly
crushed as the burden of intimacy creates distrust and fear
(and particularly fear of being "chumped" or "being had")
and self-pity (the world's greatest excuse for aggressions).

Does marriage destroy love, as Ignace Lappe has suggested? The answer must be that it does not; rather, the
intimacy of marriage is too strong, too insupportable a burden,
for the incipient friendship at the beginning of marriage to
endure. Man can make the effort required for friendship to
grow and expand and flourish after marriage, but he usually
does not. Marriage does not destroy love, but most married
people are not brave enough to work at the arduous task of
developing their friendship. On the contrary, they permit
the incipient friendship called romance, which exists at the
beginning of marriage, to be destroyed and settle for
ambivalence occasionally underscored by passion, for lustful,
armed coexistence. We are not, after all, so far out of the
jungle as we might have thought.

Dan Sullivan, one of the current "experts" within American Catholicism on the question of sex, has suggested as a
hypothesis that one's view of sex depends on how one responds to the question of whether it is possible for married
love to continue. I should be inclined to go even further than
he and say that one's view of sex ultimately depends on
whether one believes that it is possible for married love to
grow. Or, to put the matter even more strongly: Unless married love is constantly growing and expanding, there is no
friendship, and man's capacity for sexual fulfillment, and
even sexual enjoyment, will atrophy.

It is against this context that we are better able to evaluate
the meaning of the personalist sexual revolution. For the
first time man has a comprehensive and detailed point of
view at the highest theoretical level that reinforces what was
merely romantic poetry or very incomplete theology in the
past. For the personalists say that, in addition to human sex
being relational (something that is obvious, if frequently
ignored), it is also personal. It demands for its fulfillment
friendship, and is frustrated and fails to the extent that it

falls short of friendship. We said before that the nonhuman ape does not, as he goes about his work, look forward with pleasurable eagerness to the conquest of his mate in their sexual union at the end of the day, and that neither does he recall on the following day the multitudinous delights of the conquering union. Neither does the female ape look forward expectantly to the return of her mate to the marriage bed, nor rejoice on the following day over *her* conquest of *him*. In the final analysis, man can do this and the ape cannot, because man can be friends with his mate and the ape cannot. Furthermore, if man and his mate are not friends, then there very likely will be no pleasures either to anticipate or recall, or at least they will not exist either very frequently or very fully. The complex, psychological, and physical interrelational patterns which combine consideration, patience, tenderness, conquest, and seduction are all bound together in one unity that is to be called "married friendship." In the absence of this unity and the slow, careful effort required to achieve and maintain it, man might just as well watch pro-football on television.

Friendship, therefore, ends the dilemma, or at least makes possible the end of the dilemma that mankind has faced of having to choose between a series of instant replays (with different lovers), of the transient joys of early romance *à la* Don Juan, and the frustration of a nagging intimacy of armed coexistence. If man still has much to learn about sex, the ultimate reason is that he still has much to learn about friendship.

We therefore must say more about friendship if we are to understand the context of human sex. Friendship, first of all, is a trust; it is the conviction that you can let yourself be important to another. If we permit ourselves to be important to others, we permit them to make demands upon us, for if someone thinks we are important to them, that someone *wants* us and we must respond by giving ourselves to them. We must trust them not to take advantage of us or exploit us; we must have enough confidence in ourselves to believe that in giving ourself we will not lose ourself. We do not hide from our friends or try to keep some dark corner of our personality secret so that they do not know about it. Neither do we consider self-giving to be the same thing as exhibitionism or the destruction of privacy. It is not necessary that the friend know everything *about* us, but it is necessary that he *know* us. We must be willing to believe that we are so important to the other, despite his occasional signs to the contrary, that he holds us in reverence and will not violate us, save perhaps occasionally, through weakness or mistakes. If we do not have the strength to believe in ourself, we will not have the strength to believe in the other person. But conversely, if we are not willing to make at least a hesitant act of faith in the other person's basic good intentions toward us, it will be terribly difficult to believe in our good intentions toward him.

Secondly, friendship evolves slowly. It cannot be mass-produced; it cannot be created instantaneously. It requires delicacy, tact, prudence, urbanity, and diplomacy (all of which run against the cult of raw honesty that is so popular among the uninformed and the misinformed in the contemporary church). The other person must be given the option of deciding whether we are really important to him and whether he is willing to permit us to think him important. This option must be open, at least in theory, to the whole course of the friendship. We must at all times be ready to permit the other person to get out of the relationship if he wants, although deep in our hearts we are confidently persuaded that he will not want to do so. The base of friendship cannot be forced. There can be no rush—no desperate clinging to the friendship as the only source of our life. It must be free, open, and optional.

It is curious to note that, just as friendship evolves very slowly between a man and a woman, so do the skills and the sophistication of their sexual union. The tremendous and horrendous emphasis on the wedding night that has lurked in the underground of human culture since time immemorial, runs against the basic psychic and physiological facts of human existence. The wedding night is the beginning, but only the beginning and the relevantly unimportant beginning compared to the possibilities for fulfillment if: a) the unnecessary psychic fears which have grown up around the beginning do not do permanent damage to the possibilities of friendship, and b) the newly married couple realizes what ought to be obvious—that the physical and psychological adjustments to marital intimacy necessarily grow slowly as the lock-step progress of friendship and pleasure progress.

One need not be a complete success the first time, especially since such success is almost impossible. Competency in the marriage union and competency in friendship are not attributes born into man; on the contrary, they both evolve slowly, at least if the couple are patient and open and permit this joint evolution to occur.

Thirdly, friendship is patient. It is based on a developing commonality and complementarity—growing out of common interests, values, and commitments, and mutually reinforcing contributions to the emerging pattern of friendship. Commonality is not conformity. It permits the other to be different from the self; to have interests, values, commitments, and relationships which we do not share, personality characteristics we do not like, and friendships of which we are not a part. Friendship does not mean that we and our friend share everything in common, but only that we share each other, learning to put up with, tolerate, and even to enjoy the differences which at first separate us from our friend. It is painful, difficult, and requires constant self-control. The joys of friendship are purchased at a high price, but a price that, paradoxically enough, makes us richer rather than poorer.

Fourthly, friendship is not competitive. There is no need for one friend to surpass the other or to be afraid of being surpassed by the other. On the contrary, friends rejoice over each other's successes and accomplishments because they take nothing from either, but add to each. We are not afraid that a friend's successes and accomplishments will take him away from us, but will merely deepen and enrich our union with one another. Unfortunately, the traditional war between the sexes creates a model which most young people almost unconsciously imitate in their own marriages, a model which creates particular difficulty when the husband, assuming that he is to be the assertive, combative, and aggressive member of the family, discovers that his wife may be more talented than he, or, should she have a career of her own, be more successful than he. How, indeed, can you be a man if your wife is more intelligent than you are, or makes more money than you do? Or, on the contrary, how can you be a woman if you have surpassed your man in competition, if you are both powerfully motivated to prove your superiority to him and powerfully frightened of what might happen when this superiority is indeed accomplished?

The only kind of competitiveness that is possible between friends is the competitiveness of play. Indeed, playful competition between friends may even be necessary because it provides a channel into which repressed competition can be diverted. The channel is safe because man is able, at least if he wants to, to draw a line between the world of play and the real world, and while he may be very serious about his playing when he is in the world of play, he realizes that it is most unwise to transfer the seriousness with which he plays into the real world beyond play. For all this, it is still true, at least in our present state of cultural development, that a woman who plays a better game of golf than her husband is going to be in a bad way.

Fifth, friendship is open-ended; that is to say, it is never perfect, never fulfilled, never incapable of more growth, never offers us reason to relax our efforts; on the contrary, friendship is the basic means of human growth. Man works out his salvation by breaking down the barriers of egoism and fear which are built up around himself. He becomes himself in freedom exactly to the extent that he is willing to sacrifice himself in friendship. It is therefore necessary that man view his friendships as a long series of new beginnings, of painful new awakenings caused by awkward mistakes. In many marriages, unfortunately, the spouses grow weary of beginning anew, particularly as age starts to sap their enthusiasm and energy. Even those marriages which do not end up in hostility and mutual loneliness are frequently marked by a slow drifting apart as the two spouses find that the ever increasing demands of friendship are too difficult to bear and turn aside to find their basic satisfaction in other interests and relationships. A man and woman enter into marriage with different personalities and different interests. These differences represent a constant strain toward separation—a strain which must forever be held in check by and for the sake of the evolving friendship. What many married couples do not realize is that these different interests may very legitimately increase with the passage of the years, and that only persistent efforts to increase simultaneously the friendship will prevent the deadly drift from beginning.

Sixth, friendship is outgoing. It does not close in on the dyadic community of my friend and me as do possessive pseudo friendships which close the personality rather than open it up to the world around. Because friendship enriches us and develops the hidden dimensions of our person—because it enables us to be that which we would really like to be (and fear we never would), it enables us to give more to others. Since the other believes in us and what we wish to be, we are able to become what we want to be. We have quite literally more to give to the other, and together we have much more to give to the world. Furthermore, the joy in our union of friendship is so great that we want to share it with others and not keep it to ourselves, so together with our friend, we go about trying to bring joy to the rest of men. Love, as I believe Paul Claudel said, is not two people looking at each other, but two people looking together in the same direction.

In married love, the primal result of the outgoing nature of the friendship is, of course, the children born of the marriage. But it must be noted that, at least in ordinary circumstances, if husband and wife are not able to give themselves to each other in friendship, it will be very difficult for them to make the gift of friendship to their children. Furthermore, the friendship which limits itself to its immediate surroundings is neither very deep nor very outgoing, and therefore the love between husband and wife which is unable to transcend the boundaries of the nuclear family is not likely to be very strong in love; indeed it is probably not love at all, but merely a somewhat transmuted selfishness, which is but another name for distrust.

Seventh, friendship is playful. We shall say more about play in a later chapter, but it is sufficient to assert at the present that play is one of man's primary obligations and that the people we are most at ease with in our play are, of course, our friends. In playfulness, we let much of our own imp out of the particular little bottle in which we have encased him. Play brings us out of ourselves, enables us to relax, to "let our hair down," and to have fun. In playful activities, we put aside barriers, lower our defenses, cast away inhibitions, and we are able to do this and enjoy it most completely when we know we can trust those with whom we are playing. When we play together with someone, we say, "Look, we are both making fools of ourselves. We are both taking seriously things that are unimportant and refusing to take seriously things that are important." To be a fool together with someone else both requires friendship and deepens it because the shared secrets of play bring two people together in an intimacy which is all the more powerful because its strength is not realized until it has been established.

The relationship between husband and wife, therefore, must have about it a playful dimension. But one can say more. The sexual union is one of those things that is so serious that if man does not approach it playfully, he runs the risk of being destroyed by it. We need only look to the sober and grim narrowness of Jansenism or Puritanism to see what seriousness about sex will do to the human personality. Hugh Hefner's Playboy philosophy is wrong not because it is inaccurate but because it is incomplete. Sexual union must be playful, and in this Hefner is right. But it is also rational and personal, and this the Playboy philosophy ignores. The playmate must be the mate, and if the mate is not a good playmate, then she (or he) is not a good mate. On a priori grounds it's hard to understand how something which obviously was designed to be played with can have been converted by man into something serious, oppressive, and burdensome. The human body very clearly has been carefully designed for the entertainment, amusement, and enjoyment of one's sexual partner and therefore, indirectly, for one's own enjoyment. Our bodies are, in the literal sense of the word, meant to be played with. But the inhibitions, the shame, the fears, the terrors which prevent sex from being playful are immense. Modesty is unquestionably a virtue, though its exact content varies with time and place. But it is quite unaccountable that modesty should have been confused with prudery and, even worse, with a paralyzingly somber and guilt-ridden shame.

We will contend in a later chapter that the world has been designed as a place to play in, but it seems most unlikely, if man and woman cannot joyously and exultantly play with each other, that anyone will be able to play in the world, none of whose physical beauties can be compared with the human body.

Closely related to the playfulness of friendship is what I will call, for lack of a better word, its "seductiveness"—our determination to bring the friend "out of himself"—though the word is more appropriate for married friendship than for other forms of friendship. As we get to know our friend better we begin to probe for the weak links in his armor; if the friendship is exploitive, our goal is to twist him more and more to serve our purposes and goals. But in authentic friendships we probe weaknesses so that we may be able to facilitate our friend's attempts to remove the barriers which separate us. The "weak links" are, in fact, those elements in his personality which are most disposed to break out of the limitations of fear and distrust. As we become more sophisticated in understanding and reinforcing these "break-out" elements, we can become so sensitive to the behavior of our friend that with but a few words we can create a situation in which our friend has almost no choice but to be himself.

In marriage seductiveness is a physical-psychological dimension of behavior which must be both pervasive and playful, covering situations as diverse as cheering a discouraged husband after a frustrating day at work (or a wife after an equally frustrating day at home), or preparing a somewhat reluctant wife (or husband) for intercourse. It must be tender and gentle and yet at the same time powerful and challenging; further, it must be bold and imaginative, and at the same time, demure and reassuring. As the married couple becomes more sensitive to one another, the spouse's insights into the "weak links" of the other's body and personality become so skillful that defense mechanisms are dismantled almost at will and the other, caught in the joyous trap of trust, has no choice but to yield. Indeed, in the ideal marriage, one would suppose that man and wife are so adept at "playing with" each other—body and soul—that openness and surrender are almost a constant.

Unfortunately, in many marriages (and many friendships outside of marriage) "seductiveness" is viewed as an occasional action or series of actions instead of an ongoing condition. It is thought of as appropriate at the beginning of the marriage, or as a prelude (more or less proximate) to love-making but not as a continuous condition that is part of the very essence of the marriage union. Seduction, in the strictest sense of the word, is a preparation for conquest, but conquest is not a single event or even a series of events, but an ever new challenge to the relationship. When the seduction-conquest-celebration cycle goes out of the marriage relationship (or out of any friendship), there is not much excitement or love left. Like every other activity that is required to sustain a marriage (or a friendship), seductiveness requires effort, confidence, and imagination. It also requires bravery, because the seducer runs the risk that the gift he offers will be rejected and he will be humiliated, but to these risks there is no alternative save a narrow, closed loneliness. The most effective form of seduction in any friendship, and probably the one that requires the least risk, is tenderness. For all its fierce exterior, the human ego is remarkably fragile and finds gentleness terribly difficult to resist.

Friendship must be honest, that is to say the two partners must be able to say both the hard and soft things that are necessary to prevent the curse of implicitness and covert rules from taking spontaneity out of their relationship. But honesty does not come easy and cannot afford to take the form of the raw bluntness which frequently poses for honesty in the fans of pop psychology. It takes much practice and care to learn how to tell our friend with affection and tenderness about those things which obstruct his growth and impede our relationship; and it takes equal practice and care to be able to listen to our friend when he speaks honestly to us. The arts of speaking and listening to affectionate criticism are rare in our society, but they must be developed if a friendship is going to become intimate. Even more painful in its own way is learning the arts of speaking and listening to affectionate praise (an activity which the pop psychology enthusiasts never seem to get around to). We can accept criticism from our friend with some embarrassment and some anger, but when he praises us both he and we are embarrassed and do not know how to behave. Yet such moments of honest praise generate extraordinarily powerful emotions (which is why we are embarrassed) and can, if permitted, sustain our mutual pilgrimage into entirely new areas of intimacy.

In married friendship both criticism and praise of sexual behavior are simultaneously awkward and crucial. Here again affectionate criticism comes easier than affectionate praise, though the latter is far more important. Most Americans enter marriage dubious about their sexuality and their abilities to perform sexually. They need frequent reassurance from their partner that their sexual performance is exciting, rewarding, overpowering. Such praise generates a sexual confidence which can easily transform a person's attitude towards himself and his body and in the process actually make him more attractive. It is interesting to watch the subtle change that marriage makes particularly in women. Some whose sexual endowments are not great gradually become profoundly attractive as seemingly minor changes in posture and bearing transform their sexual demeanor; others who are naturally more attractive become dowdy and uninteresting. In the former case it is easy to surmise that the woman has learned from her husband that she is so attractive that he can barely keep his hands off her (even if initially this was something of a rhetorical exaggeration) while in the latter one fears that the absence of explicit and concrete praise is leading to the slow death of sexual attractiveness.

Friendship must therefore also be encouraging; it must make the other so confident of himself that the very best of his talents are summoned into action. But in a performance-oriented society like ours it is difficult for the friend to understand that the demand for performance is not a manifestation of the conditioned love he experienced in his family environment. We will not withhold love if he does not perform, we are not trying to pressure him into performance, we are not forcing him to be something that he does not want to be. We are rather trying to create an atmosphere of affection and assistance where he can be most himself. But such "disinterested" support is hard to give and hard to receive since most of the available models of assistance from our past experience are not at all "disinterested" but rather seek—at least at some level of the psyche—the good of the assister rather than the assisted. A supportive wife can easily become a nagging one because her mother's "support" was mostly nagging as was her mother-in-law's support. Hence neither she nor her husband knows how to behave in a situation where a demand liberates rather than imprisons.

In marriage much of the support and encouragement ought to come from physical affection. A shrewd and sensitive wife comes to know exactly what caresses will reduce her husband to putty in her hands. When she turns from caressing (physical and psychological) to nagging it is because she has lost confidence in her sexuality and resorts to bitchiness as a more certain way of exercising influence. That such influence imprisons her husband and eventually herself in a punitive relationship is a risk she is either unaware of or is willing to take. (Needless to say, the gender of the nouns and pronouns in this paragraph can readily be reversed.)

Friendship cannot last for long if it is not gentle. Almost all of us are far more fragile than we are willing to admit even to ourselves. If we are so fragile we must be prepared to acknowledge that our friend is at least as fragile. He is sensitive, he hurts easily, he is lonely and afraid; he is not really sure that we love him. So we must not only be gentle but perhaps twice as gentle as we think necessary—and even then this may not be enough. Our friend has been hurt and probably hurt badly even if he doesn't realize it; our tenderness and affection must help to heal his wounds and give him new strength and courage. When he is worried we must bring him peace; when he is tense we must help him to relax; when he is hurt we must comfort him. When he is anxious we must capture him with our serenity.

The human sense of touch seems to be made to order for the communication of gentle reassurance; but in our puritanical society we are not able to permit ourselves to understand the depths and the power of its effectiveness. Even the attempts being made to explore the implications of touching as communication seem to us bizarre—and it must be acknowledged that frequently they are, precisely because so little is known about the appropriateness of touch.

Even in marriage where touching is more legitimated than in other relationships, the emphasis is rarely on gentleness and reassurance. While it is obvious that the relaxed human body is more attractive to hold and embrace and more pleasurable to sleep with, the emphasis in the manuals and folklore of marriage is on exciting the partner rather than relaxing him. Yet if the contact of the lovers' bodies does not first bring peace, it suffices poorly for the creation of pleasure and yet more peace. One observer has asked why, if there is so much stress on intercourse in American society, there is so much of a need for tranquilizing drugs; perhaps the answer is that if tranquility does not exist in the bodies of a man and his woman before their bodies are united it cannot come after the union.

We know very little then about how we can communicate peace from our bodies to the bodies of others. The "kiss of peace" is an expectation rather than a reality. As time goes on and we understand our bodies better and respect them more deeply, we will learn how our bodies can radiate peace. For if, as we said before, they were obviously made to be played with, they also clearly were made to spread peace with.

Finally, friendship cannot be pursued directly, nor does it result from mere focus on the nature of the relationship between two people. On the contrary, a direct, self conscious search for friendship is bound to be self-defeating. For just as friendship contributes to an ever greater sharing of efforts, it also develops from shared efforts. We are drawn to someone else because of a common interest, to work on something together. In the increasing openness of the interplay between the two of us as we share our work, the first signals of affection and trust are sent out; if the signals are returned, we, the two of us, realize (in a tremendous burst of joy) that we both love and are loved. We deceive ourselves, however, if we think that this joy and love are anything but transitory and superficial. It is a beginning and perhaps even a good beginning, but we do not realize, if we are young, both the effort that will be required for us to sustain this beginning and the joys that will be bestowed upon us if we are willing to expend the effort.

In our society the kind of openness to commitment which is the beginning of friendship and which results from shared efforts, is not possible for most marriage partners before marriage. They do not marry friends. In fact, many, if not most, marry strangers, and all too many marry people with whom it will be impossible ever to become friends. There is, of course, a strain toward friendship in the beginnings of physical attraction because physical revelation draws one toward psychological revelation. The strain is a powerful one, but so is the opposite strain which inclines us to hold back and not take chances with our "real self." Reasonably well-developed friendship does not exist before marriage because we have yet to develop the techniques for making this friendship possible before marriage. Marriage is not in fact a ratification of love, since friendship takes time and shared efforts to develop, and married love is a combination of sex and friendship. At marriage, in our society, there is present only a very inchoate promise of love, a promise made in the presence of the community to work toward a greater fullness of love. It would seem to me that on purely psychological grounds, the eagerness of many of the proponents of the New Morality to promote premarital sex on the grounds of love is wildly absurd. If love means friendship—and we are arguing in this chapter that it does—there is precious little friendship, at least as we have defined it and described it, in most premarital romances. In the absence of a public commitment to dedicate one's life to the development of friendship, one wonders what human meaning, if any, can be attached to premarital sex.

It will therefore be necessary, as the personalist evolutionary leap in the understanding of sex continues, that society develop more effective ways to promote the development of friendship between a young man and a young woman to a much stronger, more open, and more trusting level of development before they take on the joy and the burden of physical intimacy. The greater the progress in friendship made before marriage, the easier will be the transition to the intimacies of marriage and the more rapid and smoother will be the growth in friendship after marriage. When human society develops that far, one suspects it will be seen not only that married love need never stop growing, but also that the glow and excitement of the weeks immediately before and immediately after marriage need never wear off. In the meantime, it would seem that the counseling of engaged couples as a facilitation of the understanding of the self and understanding of the other is an extremely important function and one that within the Church is not taken care of merely by attending the Cana conference.

Whether one thinks most marriages are happy or unhappy depends, I would suppose, on one's temperament, point of view, and standards. But the point ought not to be happiness versus unhappiness. Rather, it would seem to me that the issue is whether, given the nature of the human condition, it still might not be possible for large numbers of marriages to be much happier than they are with relatively little more effort, relatively little more trust, relatively little more willingness to surrender one's self in confidence to the other.

The myth of the frustrated suburban marriage has, since the Second World War, become enshrined in the American tradition both in fiction and in popular legend. The harassed, frustrated, not quite successful business or professional man who makes casual love to a woman in his office while his bitchy, neurotic and equally frustrated wife permits or seduces another man into their bedroom have become almost stereotypical characters in American life. Jealousy, suspicion, infidelity, neuroticism, excessive drinking (frequently an absolutely necessary precondition for love-making), misunderstanding, loneliness, and occasional mental sickness are all part of the myth. One surely does not want to argue that the myth represents the whole reality, but the mere fact that the myth exists would suggest that the successes of the personalist revolution have thus far been rather meager. Despite the material affluence of American society, despite our allegedly enlightened sexual attitudes, despite the new independence of women, despite our increased understanding of the human psyche, we are still afraid of the total giving which intercourse necessarily implies both in the act itself and in the context of the future relational development which the act demands. For while it may be a simple act in itself, it demands for its success both total giving in the present and total giving in the future or at least mighty efforts in that direction. The care, patience, understanding, sensitivity, realism, and tenderness with which a man and woman must slowly develop their skills at making love to one another are a reflection, a cause, a human effect of the same sort of development of the total friendship which must come to exist between them. Despite the widespread popularity of how-to-do-it marriage manuals, many husbands and wives seem remarkably untuned to the shadings and nuances of each other's passion. Yet without this sort of sensitivity, friendship in marriage cannot grow, because it is a rare marriage that can endure for long the burdens of intimate friendship without the support of a sustained series of exciting delights in the marriage bed. On the other hand, it is simultaneously true that a spouse cannot become sensitively attuned to sexual yearnings of the partner unless he is also becoming sensitively attuned to the yearnings of the whole personality. In the final analysis, one cannot even speak of these two processes as though they were separate because in reality they are so intermeshed that they cannot be separated. We were not exactly accurate when we said earlier that love is a combination of sex and friendship, for in the human animal sex is friendship and friendship is sex.

It is therefore possible to assert that marriage is still in its primitive stages, that the human race has ahead of it physical and psychological joys yet undreamed of as man becomes increasingly conscious of the implications of friendship for sex and sex for friendship, and increasingly sophisticated in eliminating from the world the primal distrust and suspicion which for so many millennia have kept man and his mate tragically separated and unfulfilled.

We have spoken thus far in this chapter of marriage and friendship as though the two of them were identified. It is probably true that friendship came into the human race through the sexual union. But given man's awareness of his personhood and also his awareness that while he cannot separate himself from his body, he can, nonetheless, transcend his body, it became possible to transfer trust and friendship from his relationship to his mate to his relationships with other persons. Love was born in marriage but is not limited necessarily to marriage, and, at least occasionally, seems to have flowered outside of the marriage union, probably because friendship, outside the context of marriage, is less intense and less burdensome. It is possible for man to love intimately a member of his own sex or a member of the opposite sex with whom he does not share the marriage bed, or even a whole community to which he dedicates himself. Although love came to the human race through the marriage union and is deeply rooted in that union, it is by no means limited to it.

A number of conclusions can be drawn for the marital origins of human love. First of all, trusting and surrendering are, at root, sexual activities both in their origins and psychodynamic effects. Man is not sexual merely when he is embracing his wife or when he is eagerly anticipating the pleasures of such an embrace. Man is sexual in all his actions, in all his relationships, because sex is something that pervades him completely, because it is something that he *is* rather than something that he *has*. Therefore, it follows that there is a strong sexual component in his friendships, first of all, with members of his own sex. Homosexuality is a fixation in development, not because it is unnatural for man to enjoy friendship with members of his own sex, but rather because homosexuality precludes the possibility of the development of the personality toward marital union, which, as we have said, is the source of human sexual giving and receiving.

But friendship with members of the same sex, particularly when heterosexuality has been firmly established (either through the beginnings of friendship with a genital partner of the opposite sex, or openness to the possibility of such beginning), enriches the human personality and provides both cement for the social order and the ultimate basis for the end of world conflict. The genital act is ordered toward the family relationship in a biology which cannot be negated, but the possibility of extending a profoundly sexual friendship to others as a substitute for aggression is, after all, the difference between human society and animal societies. Human sexuality is as flexible and plastic as is human love, to which it imparts strength and depth and breadth. Even within the context of the genital union established by marriage, there is a vast richness of possible sexual behavior restricted only by limitations of time and human imagination. But in the area of nongenital human sexuality, the possibilities of relationships of loving friendship stagger the imagination. If marriage is only beginning to emerge from its primitive state, we must affirm that friendship outside of marriage is even further behind and that we only dimly perceive its implications. There is very little in the way of friendship in the world. The conflict between ideologies and ethnic groups which threatens to tear the human race apart and destroy our planet are ultimately based on man's inability to trust his fellowmen—a trust which, as we have noted before, is sexual both in its origins and its dynamics. Furthermore, friendships with members of our own sex, while in some respects less burdensome than marriage, are still limited in their development because of our fear of homosexuality, because of our own lack of sexual identity, and because of our fear of the opinions of others.

Perhaps the least progress of all has been made in developing friendships with members of the opposite sex. Here it must be conceded that we have not gotten far out of the jungle at all and perhaps with reason. For only if there is trust, confidence, and friendship in the marriage union is it possible for the partners to trust each other enough to permit intimate friendship with others who might be potential partners in the marriage bed. A man must have a great deal of confidence in both himself and his wife to say, "She has a deep and intimate friendship with other men and, far from resenting it, I rejoice in it because it makes her a better person and enriches our own relationship." It would be equally difficult for a woman to say, "I do not mind my husband intimately loving another woman because I have great trust and confidence in his love for me and my love for him." Such relationships and attitudes ought to be possible if we are prepared to concede that human friendship can sufficiently transcend biological origins to permit man to develop friendships which are not destined by some sort of gonadic determinism to lead to sodomy or adultery. We also realize that empirically such relationships do occur either in the professional context of psychotherapy or the somewhat less professional relationships of, let us say, a business executive and his secretary. We can also point to a number of historical examples of such relationships, particularly those between saints of the opposite sex. There is, in short, no limitation to the human capacity to love other than sheer time. But cross-sexual friendships abound only when there exists a sufficient number of people with maturity and trust in their genital commitments. These cross-sexual friendships are similar to marriage in that they exist between a man and a woman and are thus profoundly sexual in their origin, in their dynamics, and to some extent, in their manifestation. They are dissimilar, however, in that the sexual energies are not directed toward intercourse or family formation even though both partners are realistically aware of their openness to the possibility of genital sex, a possibility which is restricted by the nature of their relationship and the direction of their friendship.

Not very many such friendships exist in contemporary American society, though perhaps there are more than we may be aware of. Insecurity, jealousy, fear of the "dirty mind" of the washroom humorist, all preclude their possibility. Nonetheless, it does not seem unreasonable to suspect that in years to come such friendships will become increasingly widespread, whether one wishes to consider this an evolutionary leap or merely the development of a new form of sublimation or self-transcendence.

Another form of friendship that, in its own way, represents a major evolutionary development, is celibate love. As Sidney Calahan has correctly observed, the celibate is not a person who rejects sexuality, but rather one who diverts his sexual forces to the direct service of the entire community; whose intimate friendships are precisely more extensive because he has voluntarily relinquished (temporarily or permanently) marital intimacy for another, but no less powerful and sexual, form of human friendship and human giving. As Mrs. Calahan rightly observes, a man may give himself in heroic virtue, but he has no right to demand this of his wife and family.

I have no desire at the present moment to defend the possibility of celibacy or its desirability; Mrs. Calahan, in my judgment, has done this quite well. Much less do I care to become involved in the present (often rather simple-minded) debate on obligatory celibacy for the clergy. I simply want to affirm that both faith and reason (as manifested by no less a person than Dr. Freud) do recognize that celibate service of the community is a valid and valuable form of sexual activity, and those who would deny this are not well-informed either theologically or psychologically.

We may say in conclusion, therefore, that while human love came into the world through sex in marriage, and while it can never separate itself from its powerful sexual component, it need not be limited to the marriage relationship. On the contrary, the great contribution of married sex to human society should teach men the joy and the agony of trusting and loving one another. Friendship between a man and a woman, reinforced by the throbbing union of their bodies and preserved and enriched by the sensitive tenderness of their common life, is the model on which all human relationships must be based. It is to the open-ended friendship of marriage that men must look if they are to learn how to live with one another. We can confidently look forward in years to come to a vast improvement in the quality of the relationship between man and woman as personalist philosophy and advances in psychology and psychiatry enable us to understand more deeply the meaning of sexual union. It would therefore follow that man will become more loving and the world will become a more trusting, open, and peaceful place. The process will not take place overnight, *but it will take place.*

For a church which considers itself the bride of Christ, and which has used the sexual union constantly as an image of its relationship with God, the mandate ought to be clear. The Manichaeism which has plagued us for almost all of our existence is dead. Our Jansenist reaction to the personalist sexual revolution is irrelevant, useless, and false to our own principles. As we shall suggest later in the volume, it is the vocation of the Church to lead mankind through his present crisis. If its vocation is to be exercised primarily by improving the quality of relationships within the Church, then the Church's first concern as it attempts to re-establish its credibility as a guide to the world must be to understand more deeply, explain more fully, and rejoice more vigorously as it stands in the presence of the sexual union between man and his mate.

Chapter 3

A COMMUNITY TO BELONG TO

In the last chapter we suggested that man and woman are caught in a dilemma in their relation to one another—a dilemma of independence versus subjection, and we pointed out that the dilemma can be solved only by redefining the problem and adding the paradox of friendship, the gift of self which enhances freedom by producing more self than that which was originally given. This dilemma is the reflection of a large problem—man's relationship with all of his fellows. He cannot survive without them, and he apparently cannot survive with them, either. The individual wants to be free of society, and yet, once he is excluded from society, he desperately wants to get back into it. The struggle between the individual and society is almost as old as the struggle between man and woman, and is perhaps not much nearer to a solution now than it was in the beginning.

Man is a cooperating animal. Unlike many of his fellow monkeys, he does not play it alone. Desmond Morris has suggested that cooperation among mankind is the result of a mutation of the species brought about to facilitate man's adjustment to the hunting life of the plains when he left behind the food-gathering life of the forests. Be that as it may, man is not only a cooperating animal, but also a suspicious cooperator. He knows he must depend on his fellow men if he is to survive, but rather wishes that his survival was not dependent upon the will of others. Cooperation enables him to become a specialist and to do certain things well, while his fellows also concentrate on their own particular skills. This specialization pleases man very much because he likes the sense of accomplishment that accompanies it, but it also worries him because it makes him even more dependent on the increasingly complicated skills of his colleagues.

In addition to the very simple food-gathering society, there were three basic social forms into which prehistoric man organized himself: hunters, herders, and farmers. While it does not appear that there was any strict line of evolution, it is generally true that a hunting society is the most simple, and an agricultural society the most complex, with the specialization and division of labor required by herding somewhere between the two. There was little time for leisure, for developing special skills in the hunting society, because the balance between population size and available food was always precarious, and man had to hunt most of his waking day if he and his family were to eat. However, the herders, who were able to domesticate animals and keep a ready food supply available, were not required to commit themselves quite so completely to physical exertion, and were able to develop certain specialties of their own and produce more sophisticated art forms than had their predecessors. Finally, the farmers (who apparently appeared on the ridges of the fertile agricultural valleys of the Near East around 12,000 B.C.) were both the most sophisticated and the most leisurely of the primitive societies. The division of labor grew more complicated, and with it there also appeared greater independence. The fact that the gathering of food could be limited to one season of the year and that the planting and cultivating did not consume the rest of the year entirely substantially extended the amount of available leisure time and also, probably for the first time in human history, produced a leisure class which, appropriately enough, was clerical. The religion of the early farming peoples was closely linked with the forces of nature on which they depended for their existence. Ritual was seen as the re-enactment of the great cosmic events as reflected in the cycle of birth, growth, harvest, and death each year in their fields. Religion was, therefore, a link between the cosmic mysteries and the mystery of agriculture, and the men who directed this religion and were the initiates of its mysteries were extraordinarily important people in the agricultural society; hence they were allowed the freedom and leisure to probe more deeply into the meanings of the world.

There also grew up, eventually, among the farming peoples, a military class as warfare became more organized. The hunters and the herders had undoubtedly fought before as roving bands encountered each other, but there was plenty of land in which to flee. Warfare was more occasional than systematic. However, the rise of agricultural communities placed a premium on fertile and well-irrigated land, and the rapid increase in population that abundant harvest made possible led to systematic wars between the various primitive agricultural settlements. Some settlements eventually triumphed over others and reduced their inhabitants to a state of slavery. Unlike the hunters and the herders, conquered farmers had no place to go when defeated in battle, and no choice to make but to remain as slaves to the conquering invaders.

Exactly how primitive society was organized is not clear, since it is assumed today that it is hardly adequate to compare modern primitives with prehistoric tribes. But in all likelihood it was organized in some rough form of democracy of a paternalistic variety where wisdom and strength were both important but where no one was strong enough or wise enough to impose his will on others unless they were willing to collaborate with him. However, with the development of agricultural society, improvement in military organizations, elaboration of more sophisticated weapons, men, and eventually one man, could prove strong enough and rich enough and clever enough to impose their, or his, will on others. Paternalistic democracy of the herdsmen and hunters was replaced by an oligarchy and eventually a dictatorship. Ironically, the social and technical progress that made possible the rise of agricultural society also gave man the power to deny other men their freedom. The balance between individual and community was broken; the individual became subservient to the community, while the community became subservient to a handful of men, and eventually to a single man, who ruled it.

There were, therefore, in the agricultural societies of the Near East, drawn together as they were in primitive cities, four social classes: the king, who was either the president of the ruling body of military leaders or a complete autocrat; the nobles, who were either colleagues together with the ruling king, or merely his military assistants; the priests, who also served as scholars and were, at least in Egypt, frequently able to be a countervailing force against the king and the nobility; and finally, the slaves, the overwhelming majority of the community, who existed entirely for the community and had no rights or freedom of their own. There were many different kinds of slaves, of course—the common laborer who worked in the fields, the artisans who did the more sophisticated labor, and finally the household slaves who waited on the persons of the kings, the nobles and the priests. Some of these two upper classes of slaves occasionally did, in fact, become an emergent middle class, particularly when they were entrusted with responsibilities for commerce and industry. But however much power they had and however comfortable a living they might have earned for themselves, they were still slaves and their basic rights over against the rest of society were minimal.

It is important for us to realize that this basic social organization of mankind has persisted through most of human history from the beginning of agricultural society; that it still exists, at least in attenuated form, in some parts of the world today; and that it has a profound effect on the social structure of many of the most modern nations. For example, the class system of Great Britain is difficult to understand unless we conceive of it as a highly transformed residue of the organization of ancient agricultural societies.

While such agricultural civilizations were growing up in Egypt and the Near and Middle Eastern countries as well as in India and China, they were also rising in other parts of the world, particularly in commercial cities around the rim of the Mediterranean, such as Rome and Athens. These cities were, in all likelihood, founded by tribes of wandering herdsmen who, even though they may have practiced agriculture after they settled down on the shores of the Mediterranean and before they began their commercial ventures, did not, at least initially, organize themselves in the same fashion as the great slave plantations of the Middle East, probably for reasons of geography, climate, and ecology. Therefore, the cities of Greece and Italy reflected in the millennium before the coming of Christ a style of government more appropriate to herdsmen than to owners of large estates. They were free citizens and they governed themselves collegially through a council of elders who were either elected or senior members of the subtribes which constituted the community. But two observations must be made about this Mediterranean democracy. First of all, the family or the tribe (*familia* or *genes*), were far more important than their individual members; as Fustel de Coulanges showed in his analysis of religion and family life in Rome, preservation of the family tradition, the family property, and the family gods was essential, and against these the individual had no rights. Marriage, for example, was thought of as existing to perpetuate the family, and the woman entering into marriage was considered expelled from her own clan and incorporated as a hostile stranger into her husband's clan.

Secondly, while the Mediterranean cities did have free citizens, they also had slaves, and as their commerce spread and their military rule widened, the slaves, whether they lived in the huge tenement *insulae* of Rome or the *latifundia* of the countryside, became the overwhelming majority of the population.

One might well ask why slavery was so widespread in the ancient world and indeed persisted so strongly even into the present century. First of all, it was an economically efficient social organization. Perhaps it was the only way to develop the natural resources of an agricultural community and to protect those resources from foreign invasion. Secondly, mankind did not possess the social skills necessary for other and more sophisticated forms of cooperation. In many countries of the world today—Latin America, Africa, and even, as Edward Banfield has demonstrated, in rural Sicily—man's ability to cooperate beyond the limits of his own nuclear family are extremely limited, and beyond the limits of the extended family, practically nonexistent. Hostility, suspicion, and distrust even today make efficient, complex, human organization extremely difficult outside of the Atlantic community and Japan.

Thirdly, the new technologies which emerged at an increasingly accelerated rate from the development of the first agricultural community enabled some men to concentrate more and more power in their own hands and to use that power to generate greater power, which gave them even more effective control of the community and the individuals within it.

The era after the birth of Christ did not represent any dramatic change from previous social organizations. Feudalism was essentially a continuation of slavery with some amelioration—an amelioration which increased slowly as the Church was able to specify in more and more detail the rights of all men, even serfs. However, it was only with the French Revolution, less than two centuries ago, that European peasants were able to gain land for themselves, and in many European countries and in the southern part of the United States this freedom came even later. Whether the wage contract which still exists for industrial laborers (an admittedly decreasing proportion of society) is anything more than one step removed from slavery (though in the Atlantic community and Japan an increasingly comfortable step), is something that will have to be left to the historians of the future to judge.

The collegial relation of man to his fellow men in the economic community, while it may have grown rapidly in the last two decades, has hardly kept pace with the political collegiality implicit in the democratic revolutions. But then it must be noted that democratic political forms have been successful only in a limited number of countries, and that even in France, the self-acknowledged center of European civilization, there seems to be an inability to cooperate in the maintenance of a reasonably orderly political society. France is governed now by an autocrat precisely because that is the only way, it would seem, that France can be governed. Man's political and economic lot, at least in the North Atlantic community (and in Japan) is far more comfortable than it used to be, but one would hesitate to say that the goals of the British, French, and American revolutions have been realized more than superficially in even these three countries. We are not that far away from slavery yet.

In addition to the gradual and accelerating amelioration of

the lot of the serfs during the Middle Ages, there was also once again the emergence of the trading cities in the late Middle Ages. These cities to a much greater extent than in the Mediterranean Era, represented a decisive turning point in the development of man's relationships with his community. Freedom from the community became functional once again, and for an increasingly large number of people, precisely because the merchant adventurers and the artisans who were the core of the city simply could not perform their work effectively unless there was a maximum of individual discretion in decision-making. The urban commune of the Middle Ages, a combination of the Greek city state, the Teutonic tribe and the Roman legal tradition of the Catholic Church, slowly produced a middle class which, on occasion, aligned with the king, began a campaign that would end half a millennium later in the destruction of feudalism and the emergence of a society which, in theory, was free and democratic. It must be remembered, however, that for a long time the governmental wisdom of John Locke, Thomas Jefferson, and James Madison was not considered self-evident (and is not self-evident in many of the leadership positions in the Roman Catholic Church even today).

Legal systems evolved along with society, both learning from society's experience and also pushing society to further experience. However, for long periods of human history, legal codes were concerned with ensuring maximum privileges for leadership and minimum rights for subjects. The persistence of Anglo-Saxon common law, with its deep roots in the rough democracy of Teutonic tribal paths, must be considered a remarkable event and an astonishing commentary on the continuity of the human experience as well as a sign that respect for the rights and freedoms of the human person are not completely foreign to the human condition and could not be obliterated by several millennia of slavery. On the other hand, Roman law which, for all its capacity to grow and to modify itself and its great wisdom in governing human relationships, does not reveal the same concern for the individual over against the community as does the common law. Perhaps the difference in the way the two traditions developed might be explained by the fact that slavery was far more widespread on the Continent than it was in the British Isles and that Roman law evolved, particularly under the influence of the Byzantine branch of the Empire, to cope with large plantations in a tightly organized and rigidly run society. The British yeomanry were never quite as depressed as the Continental serfs.

Even in England, however, and even with the emergence of the trading cities, the late Medieval and Renaissance worlds were essentially a somewhat transformed feudal society organized according to castes—static, stable, and "organic." These societies were not without certain considerable advantages. In such a society one knew what the dimensions of one's world were; one knew who one was and what was expected. If the society was static and stable, it was also supportive. If caste lines were rigidly drawn, relationships could still be informal and relaxed so long as both sides of the relationship knew their place. If there were not too many decisions to be made, at least there was not much anomy. A man was rooted in the past, understood his traditions, celebrated his joys, perhaps even developed his arts, and worshiped in his churches. It was not a completely closed society, by any means, but the opening end was rather small. Until commerce and industrialism and the population explosion forced people out, there were only a few brave souls who were hardy enough to venture forth.

Sociologists of the nineteenth and early twentieth centuries, such as De Tocqueville, Tonnies, and Weber, were somewhat sentimental about the passing of this organic society, even though it was not that ancient, particularly since the serfs had become peasants only a century previously. Nonetheless, the slowly changing post-feudal society had much to be said for it, though very few readers of this volume, I daresay, would want to live in it since they would find it physically and culturally impoverished and psychologically oppressive. As one who has visited the ancestral acres and carefully inspected them, I must assert that I find no nostalgia for Ballendrehid, County Mayo, Ireland. One of the best things my grandfather ever did was to get out of the place permanently.

It is worth noting in the midst of the contemporary resurgence of nostalgia for "the community" that even in this most recent manifestation of organic community, the dilemma of man versus society was almost always solved in favor of the community, which meant, in practice, in favor of the powerful men in the community (which, in Ireland, meant the British landlords), and that fear and force, either overt or enshrined in custom, dominated human behavior. Furthermore, the family relationships between husband and wife and parent and children were caught up in the tight constrictions of a narrow and oppressive culture and social structure. The openness, trust, friendship and love which we have described in the last chapter could exist in the post-feudal society only with great difficulty, and indeed can exist in the surviving post-feudal societies of the underdeveloped world only with great difficulty even today.

Then came the "big change." One perhaps could make a case on a priori grounds that the human race would have been much better if there had been a slow growth of the post-feudal agricultural society. But another revolution occurred, or rather a whole series of revolutions, comparable with the agricultural revolution of fourteen millennia ago. Industry, science, technology, geography, electronics—all generated their own revolutions, and mankind made a fantastic technological leap forward. As a result of the leap, human living became better, infinitely better, and in the Western community poverty, instead of being practically universal, was limited to small and regrettably rejected subgroups within the society. But just as the agricultural revolution of the twelfth millennium B.C. broke up existing social structures and produced slavery, so the technological revolutions of the eighteenth, nineteenth and twentieth centuries smashed the organized social structure of the post-feudal society and almost revived slavery.

One says "almost" in two senses. The first attempts at industrial slavery in nineteenth-century England and the United States, beginning almost before agricultural slavery was legally eliminated, were defeated partly by the organization of the trade unions and partly by the social legislation of enlightened, or at least politically sophisticated, governments, partly by universal education, and partly by the sheer affluence that industrialism made possible. But a new and more sophisticated form of slavery is not to be ruled out as a possibility as the world becomes increasingly rationalized, bureaucratized, formalized, and computerized; man's modal organization has become a giant corporation, whether it be business, labor, education, government, or church, and he may be entering into a new era of slavery in which man will no longer be slave to his fellow men, but to machines and organizations. These new masters will treat us more graciously and it will be a far more comfortable and pleasant form of slavery than existed in medieval Europe or pre-Christian Egypt, but freedom and control of one's own destiny will be as absent in the new slavery as it was in the old. I do not think that this new slavery will come into being, or at least grow beyond its present state of development, but we would be unrealistic to exclude the possibility that this might happen.

However, a concern of far greater importance to modern man than the emergence of a new slavery is the destruction of the old community, a concern so reinforced by much of the official sociological tradition that it has become an obsession with modern man, and more particularly, with the modern young man in the Catholic Church.

It will be remembered that we have insisted thus far in the present chapter that, in the struggle between man and community for the last thirteen or fourteen millennia, the advantages have all been on the side of community. Man's efforts for self-fulfillment and self-realization, insofar as they were permitted to exist at all, consisted essentially of an attempt to free himself from the bonds of community. We now seem to have come full circle as man finds himself free but isolated by the impersonality and the anomy of urban industrial society. He is seeking once again to create community, though as we will note later in this chapter, it is a different kind of "community" he is trying to create than that which his ancestors left behind. A comparison between the new community and the old is both unhelpful and misleading.

The word "community" is bandied about so much, particularly by enthusiastic, if shallow, Catholic "experts," that we must at this point define the precise sense in which the word is being used in the present chapter. The definition we choose to use is one furnished by Robert Nisbet, who has contributed as much as anyone to the urgency of the present quest for community:

> By community I mean something that goes far beyond mere local community. The word, as we find it in much nineteenth- and twentieth-century thought encompasses all forms of relationship which are characterized by a high degree of personal intimacy, emotional depth, moral commitment, social cohesion, and continuity in time. Community is founded on man conceived in his wholeness rather than in one or another of the roles, taken separately, that he may hold in a social order. It draws its psychological strength from levels of motivation deeper than those of mere volition or interest, and it achieves its fulfillment in a submergence of individual will that is not possible in unions of mere convenience or rational assent. Community is a fusion of feeling and thought, of tradition and commitment, of membership and volition. It may be found in, or be given symbolic expression by, locality, religion, nation, race, occupation, or crusade. Its archetype, both historically and symbolically, is the family, and in almost every type of genuine community the nomenclature of family is prominent. Fundamental to the strength of the bond of community is the real or imagined antithesis formed in the same social setting by the noncommunal relations of competition or conflict, utility or contractual assent. These, by their relative impersonality and anonymity, highlight the close personal ties of community.[1]

Nisbet analyzes brilliantly the treatment of community in the sociological tradition from Comte to Weber, showing how these great forefathers of contemporary sociology repeated many variations on the theme provided by Disraeli: "Modern society acknowledges no neighbour." "The ghost of traditional community," says Nisbet, "hovers over all his [Comte's] sociology as it does, though less obviously, over

[1] Robert A. Nisbet, "The Unit-Ideas of Sociology," in *The Sociological Tradition* (New York: Basic Books, Inc., 1966), pp. 47–48.

the work of Tocqueville, Le Play, and their successors."
While it is not the purpose of this chapter to repeat Nisbet's
analysis of the writings of men like Tonnies, Von Gierke,
Maine, Fustel de Coulanges, we may still point out briefly
that he sees three basic themes being commented on:

> (1) the transition of Western polity from the corporate
> and communal to the individualistic and rational; (2) of
> Western social organization from one of ascribed status to
> contract; and (3) of Western ideas from the sacred-
> communal to the secular-associational.[2]

The *Gemeinschaft* (communal) society of Tonnies was
therefore seen as slowly dissolving under the pressures of
urban industrialism, or, in Weber's word, "rationalization"
(the organization of society in such a way that it operates
most effectively toward achieving its ends—which are generally thought to be economic or productive). Sentiment,
tradition, feeling and the personal touch were going out of
life and being replaced by cruel, efficient, rational, organizational charts. Weber and his predecessors had no doubts
about the inevitability of such a change, but had great fears
about what would happen in the depersonalization and
dehumanization of life as it ceased being "organic" and became "rational." Long before George Orwell, they saw the
possibilities of 1984 and of a new slavery more impersonal
and inhuman, if somewhat less cruel, than the old slavery.

A number of comments are in order about these masters of
the sociological tradition:

1) Their analysis was extraordinarily acute and imaginative, and has yet to be matched by a contemporary work of
equal intellectual stature.

2) They have had a profound influence on the thought of
modern educated man. The use to which the word "community" is put and the concerns which modern educated
young people express have been, to a considerable extent,
shaped by men like Tonnies and Weber, whom most of them
have never read. But a sociologist objects that they are using
a word of his—community—in a sense he finds unacceptable.

[2] Ibid., p. 73.

He is not being as imperialistic as he might first appear, because the whole context in which the word "community" is used has been created by the founders of the sociological tradition, and his use of the word is similar to its use by men like Weber and Tonnies, though without (and this is extremely important) the precision and clarity with which these writers used the word.

3) The founders of the sociological tradition were unduly nostalgic and sentimental about the "organic" community which they saw dying. It was a community but one step removed from slavery; it was stagnant, limited, and immobile. It exercised rigid controls over its members and there was within it much physical poverty and suffering. Something has been lost in the death of *Gemeinschaft* society, but much has been gained, if at a high price, in the rise of *Gesellschaft* (contractual) society. Even if modern man has replaced a specialization of labor with a specialization of relationships; even if relationships rooted in blood, land, and tradition are no longer important; even if the "folk" have been replaced with the "masses," still physical comforts, political freedom and personal mobility are not benefits contemporary man is willing to give up for any resurgence of community. If community is to be reborn in society, it will have to be a community that guarantees affluence, that one may enter and leave freely, or it will be a community of which modern man will want no part for very long.

4) To a much greater extent than any turn-of-the-century analysts would have thought, *Gemeinschaft* has survived. A whole new sociological tradition, beginning with the famous Hawthorne experiments of Elton Mayo and his colleagues of the 1920s, has established that the primary group (the close, intimate, face-to-face friendship relationships which man forms in his neighborhood, office, factory) is of tremendous importance in regulating the operation of our highly rationalized industrial society.[3] Production on the assembly line,

[3] The Hawthorne experiment was carried out in the late twenties, but the finding referred to in the text of Professor Elton Mayo and his colleagues from the Harvard Business School is that the management of the factory had no real power to determine production rate; rather the informal pressures of the friendship

voting decisions, marketing decisions, the choice of professional service in law, medicine, dentistry, undertaking, real estate, construction, and psychiatry, the choice of a career, the purchase of a home, are all profoundly affected by man's primary relationships. The ethnic group and its successor, the religio-ethnic group, has emerged, as E. K. Francis has pointed out, precisely as the result of modern man's determination to keep intimacy, social support, and primordial ties alive in an industrial world.

5) While the masters of the sociological tradition were only occasionally inclined to romanticism, the same cannot be said for all of their enthusiastic nonsociological disciples, whether these disciples damn the infamies or celebrate the glories of the secular city. *Gesellschaft* is not all that pervasive, and *Gemeinschaft* is not all that dead, and the romanticism which subscribes to either mistake is likely to be irrelevant and self-destructive.

However, the social changes created by the revolutions of the last three centuries are real enough, and the dilemma of individual versus community is now more complex than ever. The hold of the old community over the individual was broken by the emergence of contract, democracy, and urbanization. But the result was both affluence (for most) and anomy (in part). Man's life became simultaneously hyperorganized and disorganized. By asserting the value of the individual over the community, and by asserting it for the first time effectively, the political and industrial revolutions of the early middle-class did, indeed, make possible material abundance and a large amount of personal freedom, but they seemed also to have moved social control simply to a higher level, out of the hands of individuals and into the hands of large corporate bodies, and simultaneously cut considerably the ties of personal social support. Man must then ask himself whether, to regain control of his destiny and re-establish

---

groups prevented the rates from becoming too high on the assumption that if production became too high, the payments per unit produced would be reduced. There was no evidence for this, but the accusation of "rate buster" in a friendship group was enough to control a given worker's tendency to produce over what his fellow workers thought was appropriate.

intimate personal relations, he must also give up his freedom and possibly his affluence too? With more than just humor or conscious irony, modern man is saying to himself: It's a great society, but is it a good society? The question is not merely rhetorical, and while it is my conviction that a society can be simultaneously great and good, affluent and personal, it must be emphasized that the question is not phony, and that the contemporary cultist of community should realize the issues at stake.

To put the question more specifically: Can man act as a total person in industrial society, or is he merely a skill in a division of labor so highly specialized that intimate relationships, or to use our more preferred word, friendships, beyond the family are neither required nor possible?

Secondly, can he control the behavior of the larger corporate bodies of which he is a part, or must he settle for a situation of corporate irresponsibility? Since no single man is responsible for everything that happens in a large corporation, is no one responsible? The corporate bodies, having their own ethics, their own momentum, and their own direction, lurch ahead like automobiles driven by an intoxicated driver, completely out of human control. Are friendship and responsibility possible, therefore, save in the interstices of modern society, or are they quite irrelevant in the mainstream of modern living?

The old *Gemeinschaft* organic community was not exactly a community of friendship. It was rigidly structured and inhibited men from stepping outside their roles. Suspicion and distrust were rampant in its highly stylized relationships. Nonetheless, men were in such constant intimate relationship, one with another, that friendships did emerge almost unintentionally, as they did frequently in the marriage relationship also. But the new communities which are evolving in the midst of industrial society tend to be friendship groups precisely because they are voluntary; the built-in strain toward friendship is much stronger precisely because the relationships are between free and equal persons. It is easier for friendship to exist among humans in the interstices of industrial society because the large corporate bodies do not view these "free-time" friendships as interfering with their goals, and indeed, on the contrary, are inclined to think that they may be good for "morale."

Since the family is not a productive unit anymore (and decreasingly even a consumption unit), contemporary society does not at all mind if husband and wife become friends. On the contrary, its ideology encourages this friendship as being the occasion for most of man's happiness and life satisfaction. Nonetheless, when urban industrial society is organized and a division of labor is imposed on man and woman, it tends first of all to separate the husband from his wife for most of his working day (an abuse of human dignity which one presumes will shortly be seen as intolerable), and to preoccupy man and his mate with vastly different interests that make it even more difficult for them to achieve a commonality which is the social and psychological basis of friendship. If urban industrialism is to be humanized, therefore, it must be compelled to organize itself in such a way as to reinforce in practice, as well as in theory, intimacy between man and woman—to permit husband and wife to spend much more time together—to allow a woman to develop the masculine side of her personality while freeing her husband to develop the feminine dimensions of his personality.

But it is equally important to ask whether it can be demanded of industrial society that it respect and reinforce the friendship group in its own corporate organizational structure. The research tradition we mentioned earlier, as established with these groups, are of critical importance in determining the level of productiveness and the cohesiveness of a large corporate body, but another and somewhat newer research tradition has suggested something much stronger: Corporate bodies work most effectively to the extent that they facilitate and utilize the informal quasi-friendship groups as their basic operational units. The combat squad in the military, for example, or the sophisticated electronic teams in complex modern weapon systems, depend for their effectiveness on the extent to which the members of the team know and understand one another. Research evidence that there is a direct relationship between the level of friendship in a unit of a corporate body and that unit's effectiveness is not yet absolutely persuasive; but as the complexities of the issue are separated one from another, and the various intervening factors are isolated, there is increasing reason to believe that a strong relationship exists between the degree of love in a corporate body and that body's effectiveness. The organizational implications of such a finding are yet to be worked out, but the potentiality for human growth and happiness that these findings suggest is astonishing. The impersonality and the rationality that Max Weber and his predecessors feared they saw in the emerging industrial society and to which they reluctantly resigned themselves because they could see no organization surviving by the standards of efficiency, turns out to have been, in fact, inefficient, precisely because it persisted in the horrendous mistake of treating man as a square in an organization chart or a cog in a machine (or, more recently, a computer card).

It seems quite to the contrary, that man works most efficiently when he is permitted to work as a person, relating in friendship and trust to those with whom he works. In thinking it could eliminate friendship and intimacy from its organizational concerns, the large corporate body made a tragic mistake, not merely because it depersonalized human existence, but also because it impaired the maximum effectiveness of its most important component: the skilled, confused human ape with his powerful urge to love and be loved.

To put the matter even more strongly, friendship within castes, and even occasionally across caste lines, was optional in the old preindustrial society. In modern industrial society it is optional no longer. Just as the pressures of the modern world made it no longer optional for man to love his wife more fully, more richly and more pleasurably, so it is no longer optional for friendship to be the basic cement and driving force in a large corporate organization. Not merely to remain human, not merely to insure democratic control, but to prevent chaos and assure a minimum level of satisfactory effectiveness, the modern corporate organization must not only tolerate friendship among its workers but must do all in its power to create a situation where work and friendship mutually reinforce one another. The rationalized urban industrial world needs a lot more love than it presently has merely to continue operating.

We are therefore asserting that the quest for community in which man is engaged since he left behind the comforting if uncomfortable peasant village and which, in the present generation, has become a highly conscious search, is a quest to which urban industrial society must respond if it is to achieve even its own rationalized goals. But it is not, as we have noted before, merely a reincarnation of the old community, clad now in modern dress, that must be created; it is, rather, a different kind of community, into which man is not born but which he builds by serious effort and great maturity. The friendship skills which we said in the last chapter were necessary to the development of a successful marriage are equally imperative in the construction of community beyond the limits of the family, whether this community exists in the interstices of the society or is integrated in the actual "productive" work of the large corporate organizations.

In this context it will be perceived how unfortunate and inept are many of the assumptions of the current discussion about community. The new community cannot be brought into existence by executive fiat any more than the marriage friendship can come into existence merely by spoken wedding vows. In fact, the new community is a slowly evolving web of relationships around a common activity, even if this activity is only recreational. One does not form a community and then do something with it. Rather, one gathers people together for some purpose, and as the people work together for the common purpose, the friendship community, at least occasionally, slowly emerges. There is a sign in a convent where I say mass frequently that announces "Community happens!" I think I understand what the Sisters mean, but, at least as the phrase stands, I must disagree. Community does not happen; neither, despite romantic myths to the contrary, does friendship or love just happen. They emerge slowly and gradually, through constant hard work and shared effort both toward the common goal and against the common barriers which separate us from one another.

We are also told that preaching the word of God creates community. Though one is at a loss to know exactly what this means, one is forced to say, nonetheless, that empirically, the preaching of the Gospel does not usually, in itself, create community. Rather, it is much more likely to infuse and transform an existing community, to which it then gives yet more reason for trust and friendship. Some communities come into being precisely to spread the Gospel, to work for its implementation. But it is not merely preaching the Gospel that brings the community into being; rather, it is the determination of individuals to band together to implement or spread the good news. Moreover, in most instances these communities, in turn, will create other communities, not so much by pulling individuals out of the interpersonal context in which they live, but rather by transforming the context itself.

There is, furthermore, the dilemma of the community of Christians and Christians in the community. The former is liturgical, generally relatively small, and frequently familial in its relationships. In addition, it is usually territorial, or quasi-territorial. The latter is functional, nonritualistic, and often much less personal, depending on the emphasis of the would-be prophet. We are frequently told either that we must form a Christian community or that we Christians must become immersed in *the* community. But prophets of either of these doctrines forget that one of the basic tendencies of the modern world is not disjunctive, but conjunctive, not to see the world in terms of either/or, but rather in terms of both/and. Surely there must be *both* a community of Christians and Christians in the community, and there need be no opposition between the two. On the contrary, the two ought to reinforce each other. The more friendship and love that exists in the world, the better the world will be. As one reads the Scriptures as well as the documents of the Vatican Council II, one is persuaded that the whole purpose of a community of Christians is to deepen and strengthen Christians in their work in *the* community. Those who see opposition between the two and scream "ghetto" whenever a group of Catholics band together, are psychologically, historically, and theologically naïve.

How has the Church reacted, then, in the quest for community, in the refashioning of the old question of individual *versus* society into the new question of individual *and* society? First of all, one must observe that the Church ought to have rejoiced in the rephrasing of the question when social change made it necessary for the question to be rephrased. We ought to have been happy to get rid of much of the excess baggage of feudal and post-feudal culture with which we have been trapped. We ought to be overjoyed that man is freer and more mobile because he is then more ready to respond to the promptings of the spirit. We should sing the praises of personal freedom because this freedom is rooted in and validated by our own doctrine. We should rub our eyes in disbelief as we read that modern organizational research has begun to suggest that charity is indeed the ultimate dynamic of any society because that's what we've been saying all along. We should finally understand that in our own experience of friendship groups, particularly in the religious community, we have arrived at a profound awareness of what King Hal was speaking about in Shakespeare's *Henry V* when he said, "We few, we happy few, we band of brothers."

These are the things that the Catholic Church should have done. In fact, however, we have failed very badly in the face of the new communitarian challenge. In our own structures we have tended to pass from feudalism to giantism (of a monstrously inefficient variety) without ever pausing at the stage of democracy, even though we have anticipated democracy in the organizations of the religious orders of the Middle Ages and in the early structure of the Church itself. We who elected bishops when emperors and kings were chosen by heredity or by force, are now in the peculiar situation of not electing them when most of the rest of the world is convinced that free elections are the only appropriate way to choose leaders. We have let the friendship element in religious orders, irresistibly obvious in the band of brothers that began these communities, turn into juridic and authoritarian rigidity. We have permitted ourselves to be viewed by many in the modern world as opponents of human freedom. And we who, of all people, ought to be protecting the rights of religious liberty, hesitated for four sessions of the Vatican Council about whether we could accept such an idea. We callously ignored the basic human rights of our membership and let the tradition of due process, which we had preserved for centuries, atrophy in our own organizational activities.

We tried to replace love with coercion and authoritarianism

to such an extent that one distinguished churchman made the astonishing claim that authority in the Church had nothing to do with love, and indeed, argued that anyone who held the contrary belief was a heretic. (In other times, one suspects, an ecclesiastic who so manifestly denied the words of Jesus would have been deposed, if not burned at the stake.) We permitted ourselves in this country to become so closely identified with "closed" communities of the old ethnic variety that in large cities we have become identified with the forces of hatred, intolerance and reaction at the very time when our own theories should drive us into the opposite camp. Even now we still are most reluctant to change our structure in order to take advantage of the implications of modern man's quest for community. Or alternately, we engage in mad, enthusiastic attempts to "create community" without understanding the issues. Thus, as we lost, or at least are in the process of losing, a golden opportunity in the new personalist approach to sex, so we are missing an equally great opportunity in failing to react, with the best of our traditional insights, to modern man's quest for community and friendship as the basic dynamics of social interaction.

Why have we failed so completely to understand the meaning of the quest for community? Our leadership has, of course, resisted the signs of the times. This is not new—our leadership usually has done so—as do most leaderships in other organizations. But we have not had, at least until very recently, the kinds of prophetic witness in the rank and file which have, in the past, prodded leadership to face the signs of the times, the sort of witness that in other eras men like Benedict, Bernard, Francis, Ignatius, and Vincent de Paul furnished for the Church. We have become so efficient in repressiveness that we have not tolerated these prophetic voices to speak amongst us and have forced some of them, such as Pierre Teilhard de Chardin, to remain silent most of their lives. However, one cannot look at the contemporary Church without understanding that the Holy Spirit will tolerate obscurantism of leadership and cowardice of followership just so long.

Even now we witness across the length and breadth of Catholic America the emergence of "new communities," or as others somewhat more dramatically call them, "The Underground." One may rail against it, one may fear the chaos it will bring, but one must still face the fact that it is a Catholic reflection of the universal quest for community and quite inevitable. It is not, however, inevitably healthy for productive human growth. This is why there must be an open, positive dialogue between the new communities and an enlightened ecclesiastical leadership. But we will turn to this problem of dialogue in a subsequent chapter.

By what criteria can we determine whether these new ecclesial communities emerging within the Catholic Church (and within many of the other churches too) are healthy responses to the needs and challenges of the age?

First of all, they must be voluntary, for any organization whose membership is not voluntary has no place in a world determined to have freedom. Involuntary servitude is only slowly receding from the human experience, but receding it is, and men do not want it back. Therefore the new ecclesial communities must be both physically and psychologically free. There is no room in them for the more subtle kinds of group manipulations occasionally practiced by inexperienced but enthusiastic leaders.

The new community must be "organic." That is to say, its existence as a group must be as closely related to action as possible, even if the action be only playing golf or water skiing, since man's reasons for coming together are basically to cooperate in *doing something*, and not just because interaction is a good in itself. Therefore, it would seem to be unrealistic to try to create such a community of people who do not have at least some reasonable similarity of interests, concerns, and backgrounds. Friendship is hard enough among people who have much in common. As in marriage, so in the new community, the absence of commonality makes friendship difficult, if not impossible.

The new community of a church must be collegial, and hence relatively unstratified, as we shall discuss in the next chapter.

It also must be, for reasons we will turn to in a later chapter, liturgical.

It must be, above all else, a community of trust, of friendship, of love and openness. "By this shall all men know ye that you are my disciples, that you have love for one another." It therefore will require, if it is to grow strong and vigorous, a long, hard, and powerful effort. We must not grow discouraged in the face of frustrations, misunderstandings, frictions, desertions and obstacles. Just as the marriage bond is preserved by an unending series of new beginnings, so the new community must not lose the courage to write off its losses, forget about its mistakes, and start all over again.

It must be explicit. About this there is little choice, both because of its nature as a voluntary, collegial, and organic association, and because of the ideology of personalism to which so many of its members are committed. Hence, to some extent the new community will be therapeutic as the group helps its members and they help each other to overcome fear and suspicion. There is danger in therapy, of course, because therapy for a group could readily turn into group therapy, and playing psychological games could become an end in itself instead of a means to more effective communication and fuller love.

The new community must be sophisticated about the forces it is playing with. It is engaged with dimensions of the human personality which have been held in check by the old community for a long, long time. As human society emerges to a more personalist phase of its development, it will be faced with problems, difficulties and dangers hitherto undreamed of. As the most basic and elemental of human emotions, such as love, fear, hatred, become conscious and explicit, powerful forces are released, and one must treat these forces with care and respect. When they break through the barriers of distrust that separate them, husband and wife must realize that they, too, are releasing powerful forces which are exciting and joyous, but forces about which they cannot be nonchalant.

The new community must be personalist, as all human communities must be. That is to say, the dilemma of man versus society has now been permanently resolved. Society must exist for the enrichment of the person and not—Hegel, Marx and others to the contrary, notwithstanding—as an end in itself. The person must make sacrifices for the community just as the husband makes sacrifices for his wife in the marriage. But the marriage bond is not a goal in itself. Rather, it exists to serve the two persons who have committed themselves to the goal. Similarly, the community, though it will demand sacrifices from its members, exists merely to facilitate the growth and love of its members.

Finally, the new community must be outgoing. As a marriage, if it is to be happy, must give itself to the service of others, so the new community must not be turned in, separatist or gnostic, for if it is, there will emerge a new anomy, a new isolation, not now of individuals, but of community. The Church must view itself, therefore, not as a community, but rather, as a community of communities, a collection of groups within which there is trust, as groups, that are able to trust other groups.

The greatest single problem the new ecclesial communities face is what sociologists call "the iron law of oligarchy," the tendency of organizations to cease being means and to become ends unto themselves. An earlier generation of sociologists was persuaded that such a development was inevitable, but more recent sociologists, including particularly my friend and colleague Peter Blau, have repealed the iron law of oligarchy and have established conclusively that organizations can build in mechanisms of control, self-criticism, and self-examination that prevent them from growing rigid and hard. The new ecclesial communities must do just this. Otherwise they will become an end, once again, and they will be no different from the old communities they have supposedly replaced. Friendship that is not outgoing, that does not grow, that has no need of new self-revelations and ever increasing trust, is, as we suggested in the last chapter, not friendship, or is at best a dying friendship. When friendship begins to die in a marriage, the whole nature of the sexual union between man and wife begins to disintegrate. Similarly, when a community becomes an end unto itself, friendship either slowly ebbs or is transmuted into a false imitation of itself. Such an organization is, in fact, no longer a community, or at least no longer a new community.

The paradox is exactly the same as in marriage. You become the most when you are the most defenseless; so the ultimate answer of the question of man versus society as it is being discovered in the modern world, and in particular in the new ecclesial communities, is that the more a person serves his friends in freedom, trust, and honesty, the more the community stops being a coercive and restrictive force and rather creates a condition in which each person can be himself. As friendship transforms aggression into love, so it also transforms social control into social support; the old dilemma of whether man can afford to trust his fellow men will finally be resolved by the conclusion that he cannot afford not to.

Chapter 4

AUTHORITY TO LEAD WITH

In the social group we discussed in the last two chapters—
the relationship between man and woman and the relationship among a small group of friends—most decisions are made
by informal consensus. Authority is not absent from these
groups but it is usually informal authority and is distributed
among the members more with respect to their competencies
than to the role they play. The husband is the head of the
family on some occasions, but the wife is the head of it on
other occasions, depending on what decisions are being faced
or problems being resolved. If anyone in the friendship group
or family claims a monopoly on authority, either formally or
informally, considerable stress and friction are bound to arise.
In the normal course of events, however, such authority problems tend to be minimal in smaller groups, if only because the
need for consensus is so obvious in such groups that no one
in his right mind is prepared to deny it. In larger groups the
situation is much different, both because authority has more
power and can become more oppressive and because mankind
has apparently yet to discover that consensus is indispensable
in any human organization.

Until the present time most authority exercised in human
organizations has been mediocre, inept, and only relatively
effective. While problems of authority have grown far more
complex in the pilgrimage from the Teutonic tribe to General
Motors, skills in the exercise of authority have not kept pace.
As a result, authority, both in state and church, is currently in
ill-repute, and one defends even the principle of authority
against the political and ecclesiastical New Leftists at some
peril. To say that authority is in trouble because it has mis-

used its power is not to say that authority is unnecessary. But unfortunately, the distinction between the two assertions is frequently overlooked.

To understand the problems and the necessity of authority in our present condition, one must first of all realize that there are a number of different ways in which man has theorized about the obvious fact that authority exists. One theory which, it must be admitted, has been the most common in recorded history, is that authority is an inherent quality inherited by kings from their fathers and passed on by divine mandate of the church. It is a quality which authorizes one to command, and also imposes on others the demand for obedience. It involves a claim to superior wisdom or skill ex officio, either by blood lines or by the Holy Spirit. If authority is sacred and legitimated by divine powers, it ought not to be questioned or opposed (and according to some now unfashionable spiritual writers—it should not be questioned even intellectually). Furthermore, authority has the right to resort to coercion or force to obtain consent and cooperation if it is not offered, and is rewarded for its superior position in the social system by a variety of rights and privileges. He who holds authority by such sacred mandate comes close to being sacred himself, and a number of times in history emperors have been deified in their lifetimes. Even those holders of sacred authority who would reject as blasphemous such identification with the Deity, are nonetheless careful to insist on the special divine guidance that is theirs, and the obligation of their subjects to reverence this guidance by giving prompt obedience.

Viewed in this perspective, authority does not need to, should not, and indeed cannot, subject its decisions to review, consent, or dialogic examination. It will be judged on how it has discharged its responsibilities, and its responsibilities are its own and no one else's. It could not delegate responsibility even if it wanted to. Authority is therefore viewed by those who possess it as a heavy burden which, they affirm, they would cheerfully renounce if they only could, though it should be noted that most of those who do view their authority as sacred are rarely, in fact, very eager to give it up, no matter how old they become or how much pressure is brought to bear on them to yield to younger or more able successors. In

Lord Acton's words, "Power corrupts, and absolute power corrupts absolutely."

It is not difficult to see why those in authority have made such claims at certain times in history. Their task was extraordinarily difficult. Human life was difficult. Most of their subjects were uneducated and unsophisticated. Respect for law and order was not highly developed. To keep a human grouping together and operating with some degree of effectiveness and consistency required both a great deal of personal wisdom (if of a rather unsophisticated variety) and also the willingness of one's subjects to accept one's wisdom, particularly at times when the wisdom seemed dubious. If authority wished to survive, much less accomplish certain new social goals, it had to appeal to divine sanctions for legitimacy, even though in fact authority had passed into its hands initially for much more pragmatic reasons. Dukes, kings, emperors, held power not by any specific divine mandate, but rather because they or their ancestors had been skillful in battle, and church leaders though they could claim their authority came from God, who had founded the Church, were nonetheless men who were chosen to preside over the community of the faithful by the members of the community and were subject to demand for dialogue from the community. In the Apostolic Church, therefore, Paul could boast that he had resisted Peter even unto his face when Peter was using authority in a way Paul judged illegitimate (imposing Jewish law on Gentile converts) and won the argument. Only as the Church grew larger and more elaborate and began to model itself after the civil society (and in great part substituted for the organs of civil government, as these deteriorated during the early Dark Ages) did the Church begin to claim a special inviolability for authority. Even at the end of the thirteenth century, however, such a famous papal absolutist as Boniface VIII would not have dreamed of making his decision without prior consultation with his college of cardinals. As a matter of fact, absolutism as a papal and episcopal style became extensive only in the Renaissance.

Although authority may have always been viewed to some extent as a sacred power, concern with this sacredness and a desire to push this concept to its logical conclusion can usually be interpreted as a sign that he who possesses authority is either hard-pressed to account for how he has used it, or is trying to consolidate his basic power in order to begin a new adventure toward which he expects his followers to be something less than enthusiastic.

A second kind of authority is that which the German sociologist Max Weber called charismatic. The leader who possesses charisma does not govern in the name of a divine power that he has inherited or that has been mandated to him, but rather by virtue of certain characteristics of his personality which lead people to turn to him for guidance and instruction in matters which are important to them. The charismatic leader may claim he has been sent on a divine mission, or he may appeal to the traditional standards of legitimacy to justify his methods, but in fact, it is the force of his personality that wins him followers, in some instances incredibly loyal and dedicated followers. Whether he be leader of a religious movement or a ghetto street gang, however, the charismatic leader must also be politically adroit if his charisma is not to wear thin very quickly. Even though skillful in balancing the needs and demands of his diverse and often feuding followers, he must become tactful in distributing praise and blame, and must not demand either too much or too little of his admirers. His charisma passes when he passes from the scene, though his successors may claim to share in it, by converting the leader's charismatic power into sacred authority.

In some instances a position itself is thought to have the potential of bestowing a charisma on someone who occupies it. Thus charismatic power has some relationship with bureaucratic power, which we will describe in subsequent paragraphs. It is argued, for example, that the presidency of the United States seems to bring out certain leadership qualities previously invisible in the man elected to the office. Both charismatic authority and sacred authority are rooted in nonrational legitimation, the major difference being that charismatic authority tends to be transitory, not always lasting even to the end of the leader's lifetime, while sacred authority is capable of persisting for generations, centuries, and even millennia.

Charismatic authority has clearly survived in the modern

world, as mention of the names of Roosevelt, Churchill, De Gaulle, Adenauer, Ho, Mao, and John F. Kennedy will readily call to mind. Sacred authority is somewhat less prevalent, even though it is still observable to some extent in the military and in the churches. However, there remains considerable residue of the divine-right approach to authority in many other human organizations, and the attempt to sacralize certain political leaders such as Chairman Mao suggests that we have not yet seen the end of sacral authority.

The third kind of authority, in Weber's treatment of the subject, is called bureaucratic. Since this word is often used in the pejorative sense as indicating something narrow, unimaginative, and mediocre, it is necessary to specify exactly what Weber meant by bureaucratic authority. He saw it as authority based not on personal characteristics, not on some especially mandated sacred power, but rather on competence, training, and access to information. Even though Weber recognized the rise of this kind of authority as an inevitable part of the "rationalization" of society, and conceded that it was a far more intelligent way of organizing human behavior, he still had many fears about the dehumanization of human relationships that such rationalized authority could produce.

A bureaucrat is not a man without power or without the ability to award for cooperation or for punishment. Governmental commissions, professional associations, licensing agencies have immense power over a man's freedom and livelihood, but the extent of their power and the ways in which it is to be used are presumed to be precisely limited by law. The bureaucrat, in words to which Weber returned frequently, rules *sine ira et studio*—without anger and without favoritism. His job is to see that the details of laws and regulations are observed by everyone without regard to who they are or who they know or what problems they may have. He rules by "the book" and is not to be corrupted by money, threats, friendship, compassion, or his own personal wisdom. His training is focused on developing competencies and understanding in applying "the book." When he is faced with problems that exceed his training and responsibility, these problems must be referred to another bureaucratic structure or to a higher level in his own structure. He is not disinterested in the people with whom he interacts, be it at an employment center, a regulatory commission, or a union hiring hall. But he has his own professional standards of work, supervisors who will systematically evaluate the level of his performance, and a conviction that in the last analysis people will be served best by the enforcement of the regulations *sine ira et sine studio.*

The rise of bureaucratic authority was an inevitable response to the technological revolutions of the last three centuries, and it has in turn facilitated even more rapid progress in science and technology, as well as in the various organized services which industrial society needs or demands. Max Weber was not the last one to point out the dangers that may arise when a bureaucracy gets out of hand. As we noted in the last chapter, a primary danger is that bureaucracy and bureaucratic authority will convert themselves from ends to means. The survival of the bureaucratic structure then becomes an end in itself. The ends for which it was called into being, or the people for whose service it allegedly exists, are no longer important. A second problem is the risk of dehumanization, a problem clearly not unrelated to the first. The bureaucratic leader bases decisions on his competencies and on universalistic principles. But such professionalization may lead the bureaucrat to turn his clients into mere cogs in a machine (or, as we have said before, computer cards), and to cede responsibility for his decisions either to higher levels in the structure or to the structure itself. Under such circumstances no one is assumed to have any responsibility for what has happened, and decisions affecting human happiness, and even human life, are made by impersonal forces or communication flows beyond the control of any human agency.

The dilemma of bureaucracy, then, is how to govern humanly and still govern *sine ira, sine studio.* But the dilemma is not as insoluble as Max Weber and his disciples might have thought. The more sophisticated bureaucracies emphasize the competency, training, and impartiality required of those who possess bureaucratic authority; but they also stress that efficiency and effectiveness require human involvement at all levels of the bureaucracy and that bureaucratic

decisions are most likely to serve the purposes for which bureaucracy has been called into existence if wide discretionary
powers are left to the individual bureaucrats. The decisions
then are not merely rigid enforcement of "the book" but
rather intelligent and sensitive application of general principles
to specific circumstances. The sophisticated bureaucrat, in
other words, approaches his book much as a judge in the
common-law tradition approaches legal precedent—looking
for justification to do what he knows ought to be done.

In the complicated organizational structures by which authority is distributed in modern society, the question is
whether technical skill and human skill can be combined; or
more specifically, whether those who are technically competent to make decisions and execute them are also competent
in understanding the human aspects and the human implications of their decisions.

To be a good president of the multiversity, for example,
one must possess not only sophisticated economic skills to
rationalize the finances of the multiversity (or at least be
smart enough to hire someone who does), but one also must
be intelligent enough to realize that an economically viable
university is a waste of time unless its organizational structure takes into account the developmental needs of the
students enrolled in the multiversity.

Similarly, an instructor in freshman English 101, if he is to
be at all effective with his students, must not only know the
rules of good grammar and good punctuation, but also understand the fears and anxieties of the seventeen-year-olds in his
classroom.

It therefore appears that modern society must develop a
postbureaucratic concept of authority. Bureaucratic authority is vastly superior to sacred authority in that it is based
on competency and rationality. Capriciousness and favoritism
are rigidly excluded. But bureaucracy must further understand that legitimacy is based not merely on superior competency or on its position in the bureaucratic structure, but
also on its responsiveness to human needs and problems. It
must understand that it exists not merely to impose a rational
scheme on recalcitrant and emotional creatures, but also to
obtain the maximum possible participation of its clients in

the making of decisions required by the goals for which the bureaucracy exists.

This postbureaucratic authority, therefore, will represent a marriage of competency with democracy, of impartiality with sympathetic understanding, and of rationality with collegiality.

The development of a postbureaucratic concept of authority is not optional. Tasks in which modern organizations are engaged are so complicated and require such sophisticated skills that leadership lacks both the insight and the information to be able to make decisions by itself. The observations, the skills, the talents, the enthusiasms of the members of the organization are imperative if the organization is going to succeed in its mission. The sacred, charismatic, and early bureaucratic authority may have been able to dispense with the full human participation of those who followed. If followers did not consent voluntarily, then they could be coerced. But the kind of participation of followership required in the modern world cannot be coerced. It must be given voluntarily, or it is not given at all. Followers are no longer merely robots who obey commands; they are necessarily colleagues with ideas, understanding, and skills that are essential for the leader to be effective. The leader either obtains their consent or his instructions are, for all practical purposes, a waste of time.

This postbureaucratic use of authority combines elements of both charismatic and bureaucratic authority, for it demands that the bureaucrat be a charismatic leader. The man who occupies a thoroughly rationalized place in the social structure must possess those personality characteristics which inspire trust and confidence in his clients (or subordinates), who now must be called his colleagues. In other words, a bureaucrat with authority is likely to be effective to the extent that his relationship with his colleagues approaches the relationships of a friendship group. We are arguing, in effect, that as society grows more complicated and men's skills in it more sophisticated, the only kind of authority that will really be effective is that which is based upon friendship.

Do we have enough "great men," enough charismatic

leaders, to turn the structures of the polity and the economy into aggregations of friendship groups? Our first inclination would be to respond negatively. Great men, we assume, are born, not made. Winston Churchills and John F. Kennedys are not that plentiful. But a more optimistic view and one to which I am willing to subscribe is that effective, if not great, leaders, can be made, or can at least be trained. It is possible for large numbers of human beings to learn how to create an atmosphere of authentic trust in a group of colleagues. It is not easy to train these men, and several weeks at Bethel Maine are hardly enough time.[1] Nor is it easy for leaders to create an atmosphere of trust and friendship among their colleagues, even if we concede that the trust need not be as profound or the friendship as intimate as in familial or religious groups. But that it is not easy does not mean it is impossible. On the contrary, it is both possible and imperative if the discovery of bureaucratic rationality is not, in the final analysis, merely to lead men from favoritism and capriciousness to stifling impersonality without at any point making it possible for competency in a position of authority to definitively replace mediocrity.

One would have thought it would be possible to look to the Christian Church, which discovered the notion of authority of service long before the rest of the world, for guidance on how to combine efficiency with humanity. But one would surely look to the Church in vain. As the rest of the world strives to move from bureaucratic to postbureaucratic authority, the Church is struggling to emerge from traditional styles of authority to bureaucratic styles. While there are structures in the Catholic Church that look bureaucratic from the outside, and behave internally like many inefficient bureaucracies, there is actually, in fact, rather little bureaucratic authority in the Church in the sense that Max Weber defined it. There is little emphasis on competence in the exercise of authority in the Church, and much on sacred power. Capriciousness and favoritism in appointment and decision-making are still rampant. Demands for unquestioning obedience,

[1] Bethel Maine is the headquarters for the National Training Laboratory in Group Dynamics, the center and capital of the Sensitivity Training Movement.

refusal to delegate power, references to the sanctity of authority and the virtue of obedience, and the absence of a system of due process of appeals seem to indicate that churchmen's view of authority has progressed little beyond the Renaissance.

It is further argued, at least by some, that it is quite impossible for change to take place in the Church's view of authority and power because the power comes from God, is sacred in nature, is sustained and inspired by the Holy Spirit, and is absolutely immutable in its essence. Some theologians have responded to this argument by pointing out that there is little justification in the Scriptures for the present exercise of ecclesiastical authority, since the Scriptures claim that authority in the Church ought to be an authority of service. I have no wish to get into the theological hassle, but to simply point out that what is at issue is not the nature of authority but the way in which it is to be used, and that the Church's styles of leadership have shown a remarkable flexibility through the ages, responding in most instances to leadership styles that were most effective in the secular society in which the Church found itself. The Lord's authority was certainly the most sacred of all authorities, and yet he did not "lord it over" his followers and warned them not to "lord it over" their followers. Only the most naïve observers would contend that the use of authority in the Roman Church today is free from the "lord it over" temptation. Quite the contrary. Despite Jesus' injunctions, the use of authority in the Church is all too frequently arbitrary, dominating, inconsiderate, ill-informed, and incompetent—and on occasion, arrogant too.

If the postbureaucratic style of authority which we have described as a mixture of bureaucracy and democracy, competency and collegiality, turns out to be the most effective way for a human organization to operate in modern society, there is no reason in the world why the Church cannot operate this way too, and there are a number of reasons, to which we will turn in a later chapter, why the Church ought to be leading the way in this development of postbureaucratic authority.

Another way to approach the question of authority is to ask what model of society do the four forms of authority we have discussed in this chapter assume. Charismatic authority assumes a small group of people following a leader with a powerful personality. Traditional, or sacred, authority assumes a simple and stable society with wise leaders, unsophisticated followers, and uncomplicated problems. Bureaucratic authority assumes a society growing in complexity and sophistication in which some men can evolve master plans and other men can be trained in the intelligent application of these master plans, while most men are still expected merely to follow instructions because that is all that is required and all that is possible for them. The postbureaucratic model assumes a society so complicated that every man's understanding and insight are required for that society to operate effectively—so sophisticated that it is able to train men in the style of such cooperation and so filled with trust that men can work together intimately without tearing the social structure apart. Our argument is that the first two assumptions are already valid for the urban industrial world, and that the third assumption ought to be valid for the Christian Church.

The basic issue is whether human society can survive much longer without recognizing that authority and leadership are, in the final critical instance, indistinguishable. In the past it may have been possible to view authority as merely the power to give commands, or the right to reserve all decisions to one's self, or the need to exercise tight control over one's followers, or the obligation to concern one's self with a multitude of petty and trivial administrative details. It is now clear, however, that leadership—that is to say, the ability to move the minds and hearts of men to challenge them, to stimulate them, to obtain their consent and cooperation—is indistinguishable from authority. At one time consent could be obtained crudely by force and fear; at another time, more recently, it could be obtained in a more sophisticated fashion by appeal to the law; but in the society of free men faced with complicated and intricate tasks, consent is quite worthless unless it is free. The leader who is to be effective must respond to the needs and the insights of his followers and also challenge them to respond to the vision of the common good of the organization.

Not all in positions of authority have discovered that the service required of authority is essentially the service of leadership, and that the burden of responsibility is to challenge with vision and to obtain free consent. Yet there is not much time for this discovery to be integrated into the operation of society, for the alternatives are either anarchy or impersonality—the former more popular with the young, the latter more popular with the old and weary. The Hippies and the New Left are in revolt against the authority of government, and the neoliberals on the right seem to argue almost the same case when they advocate as little government as possible. Similarly in the Church, American Catholicism is going through what many have called a revolution because the rank-and-file Catholic has discovered that religious consent is necessarily free and cannot be obtained by force or imposed by coercion. Ecclesiastical leadership may fulminate until it's blue in the face against disobedience and disrespect for authority, but it will no longer obtain consent by so doing. The Catholic layman and the younger Catholic cleric look leadership in the eye and say, "I don't believe you and I don't believe that what you tell me comes from God. I simply refuse to take you seriously as having authority or as a leader." And there is no effective response to such a statement, because the Inquisition went out of fashion long ago. But the Hippies, the New Left, the neoliberals, and the Catholic enthusiast ask a more profound question: Why is it necessary to have authority at all? Cannot the establishment, the power structure, be pulled down and permanently replaced by a system of human relationships based on love? Is not authority necessarily oppressive and coercive? Does it not interfere with authentic human spontaneity and freedom? Cannot man replace authority with loving cooperation? Are not followers more powerful than fear or force?

We have been arguing in this volume that human society has progressed to a point where, unless it is permeated by love and friendship, it may destroy itself. So to some considerable extent, we are in agreement with the Hippies and the New Left and the Catholic enthusiasts. Let there be more flowers rather than less. Yet love, as Bruno Bettelheim has pointed out,[2] is not enough, and one need only look at the new

---

[2] Dr. Bettelheim, a survivor of the Nazi concentration camps and professor at the University of Chicago, is famous for his book, *Love Is Not Enough.*

society that the Hippies have created to see how destructive anarchy can be. Similarly, if one looks critically at the operation of the American Government, one is forced to say that most of its problems cannot be laid to the conspiracies of a power elite or of an establishment, or even to the incompetencies of a bureaucracy. The Kerner Commission report demonstrated that the establishment members who belong to the Commission were acutely sensitive to the nature of the racial problem in America, and the bureaucracy which supported their investigation was able and imaginative. The difficulties in implementing the Kerner report are the same that impede much social development in American society: poor vision at the top leadership levels and ineptitude in a generally antiquated Congress. Any realistic appraisal of the American scene today would conclude that what we need is not less government, but better government. Furthermore, there must be some middle ground between the anarchy of the Hippies and the appalling venality and mediocrity of most state legislatures.

Why, then, do we need authority, leadership, and power in human society? In the Western political tradition, rooted in the Middle Ages and made most explicit by the founders of the American Republic, there are three functions which are seen as justifying authority, functions which can be best exercised in the modern world through a combination of bureaucracy and democracy, competency and collegiality:

Authority protects the rights of those who need protection, and at some time or other almost all of us do, in fact, need protection.

Authority coordinates, stimulates, challenges the members of the organization to focus on group concerns and goals and refuses to permit its membership to become so involved in its respective individual concerns that it forgets about the common good.

It furnishes a climate of stability and cooperation where the sharing of resources and talent are facilitated rather than impeded in order that the maximum development of the individual members may take place.

The Western political tradition argues that in the absence of an authority that serves these functions the result will be chaos—not merely, as Thomas Hobbes would have it, because there is evil in man and he must be coerced into cooperation, but rather because man is limited—he cannot think of two things simultaneously—and will be most unlikely to focus on the problems of the common good unless there is someone who demands that he concern himself with the common good. In the present state of human development, authority must still be more or less coercive, though at least in the Western tradition this coercion is kept to the bare minimum necessary for the protection of human rights. But as man grows more sophisticated in his interactions with his fellow men, and hopefully more friendly in his relationships with them, coercion ought to become increasingly less important—though one may wonder whether it will ever vanish completely. However, even in a society where love is far more developed than it is today, human beings would still need authority, not because they were deficient in love, but because they were limited in their vision and perspective, and because they need leadership to inspire them.

The goal, then, of social reform, ought not to be to eliminate authority, but to make it more flexible, more fully human, and more responsive to human needs. Even though some Catholics are unaware of it, the debate about authority and freedom has gone beyond Thomas Hobbes and Jean Jacques Rousseau. Hobbes argued that authority was needed to coerce man to be virtuous. Rousseau responded that if man were left alone he would indeed be virtuous. The main stream of the Western political tradition, particularly as it was filtered through John Locke and Americans such as Jefferson and Madison, has consistently responded that authority is rather to protect the common good and to promote the general welfare. In such a tradition the state is neither a monstrous leviathan essential to maintain society lest man's vices tear it apart, nor a tyrannical oppressor that hopefully will wither away, but rather an agency to which men concede certain powers in order that they might more effectively interact with each other.

If authority becomes too oppressive it must be resisted, although the Western tradition is prepared to concede to authority the right to make a certain number of mistakes, and even the right to be annoying and burdensome. But it also argues that when authority fails to perform its appointed functions or abuses its power and deprives men of their inalienable rights, men have not only the right but the obligation to resist such abuse of authority. The Western tradition views authority not as a necessary evil, but as a positive good which can be abused and whose abuses must be resisted. The Western democrat does not readily go into the streets against his government, but neither does he exclude the possibility of doing so.

If this middle ground between Hobbes and Rousseau can be used to respond to the Hippies and the New Left in defending Western democratic forms of government, it is somewhat less effective in defending authority in the Catholic Church against attacks from Catholic enthusiasts. They argue that the Church is different from any other human organization, but they make exactly the opposite point of the old defenders of sacred authority. They assert that the Church ought to be governed not by authority but by love, precisely because it is a society of faithful followers of Christ, and that the authority in the Church ought to be the authority of service, hence different from the authority found in other human organizations. We shall consider the Church as an organization in a later chapter, but suffice it here to say that many of the defenders of an institutionless Church have not gone beyond Hobbes and Rousseau in their political thinking. While authority in the Church may very well be different from authority in any other human organization, it is not different because it is an authority of service. In modern Western society *all* authority legitimates itself in terms of the service it renders. Furthermore, it is difficult to see why authority as it is defended in the Western political tradition, and as it is emerging in its new postbureaucratic form, would be unnecessary in the Church or objectionable for the Church.

In practice its authority in certain areas is already collapsing as the Catholic population deems the Church's credibility in these areas inadequate and withdraws consensus. The laity have apparently made up their minds about birth control and a large section of the clergy have made up their minds about liturgical reform, independently of ecclesiastical authority, and are not going to be shaken from their decisions by repeated warnings from their ecclesiastical superiors. The point at issue in the present context is not whether these decisions are justified, but rather the impact that the continuing loss of credibility and corresponding withdrawal of consensus will have on the Church as an organization. A loosening of the overrigid bonds of counterreformation Catholicism is certainly in order. The standards of the papal social encyclicals, such as *Quadragesimo Anno* with its principle of subsidarity, and *Mater et Magistra* with its principles of initiative and responsibility, would have indicated that a substantial modification in the style exercised by the authority of the Church was long overdue. But to shift from a rigidly centralized exercise of authority to no authority at all is hardly an appropriate response to social change. The collapse of authority in the Church is every bit as much a failure of the Church to render witness to its own insights as is a persistent adherence to modes of authority that have long since lost their usefulness. One can go even further and assert that diehard adherence to outmoded forms of authority is precisely what has generated the collapse of credibility and the withdrawal of consensus. Ecclesiastical authority has failed to recognize the fact that in the modern world authority which does not offer leadership very quickly loses credibility. Hence, most of those who presently possess ecclesiastical authority have very little skill in moving the minds and hearts of their followers. And, if the truth be told, they don't even seem to try. Only when ecclesiastical authority is able to reclaim its function of leadership and to provide challenge and inspiration to its followers, will it begin to regain its credibility.

As we shall suggest in a later chapter, the Church ought to be in the vanguard of the social processes which are moving man toward a major evolutionary advance precisely because these forces have, to a considerable extent, been set in motion by the Christian dynamic. The quest for personal freedom and the thrust toward collegial exercise of authority certainly should have struck responsive chords in the Catholic mentality. Anyone who reads the New Testament can easily be persuaded that the frequently repeated cliché that the Church is a monarchy is utter nonsense, at least if the model of monarchy is that of the Renaissance, as it usually is in the minds of those who assert that the Church is a monarchy. The Church has leaders like any human organization, but in its earliest manifestations of leadership Jesus and Peter hardly acted like absolutist despots. Jesus treated his apostles like colleagues and called them friends, and Peter presided over a collegial consensus and did not make unilateral decisions. It would be much more accurate to say that the Church was founded not as a monarchy but as a collegium, and while the collegial governance surely did not come into human experience through the Church, it was preserved by the Church through two millennia of despotism and has recently been rediscovered, or at least reaffirmed, by Vatican Council II. Unfortunately, collegiality and its corollary, responsibility, have yet to be implemented in any effective and meaningful way in the post-Vatican II Church. Hence, even though everything in its own tradition suggests—as a matter of fact, almost demands—that the Church should be in the vanguard of the development of collegial bureaucracy (or, to use another term to describe the same thing, a neo-charismatic authority), it most assuredly is not in the vanguard, and does not seem likely to be, in the foreseeable future. Many of its bureaucrats are still defending the sacredness of their authority, forgetting that he who must defend his authority on theoretical grounds has probably already lost it or at least has lost the ability to use it effectively; such bureaucrats are not effective leaders. They lack credibility among their followers. They do not move the minds and hearts of men.

We have argued in this chapter that mankind is rapidly moving into a state of development where a consensual governance (or alternately, collegial exercise of authority) will cease to be optional for social organizations that expect to have any success in achieving their ends. It does not follow, however, that theory or research has solved all the problems involving collegiality and that the shift to this mode of authority will be easy. Collegiality presumes that the organization that is to be governed is made up of reasonably stable and mature colleagues. But stability and maturity cannot always be taken for granted, particularly since so many men still have problems with father figures. Their emotional development has been partially truncated at the Oedipal stage, and they need strong, paternalistic figures to offer them, simultaneously, protection from and release for their aggressions. Until we make notable progress to satisfy this need for a father figure to simultaneously adore and hate, collegiality is going to be a difficult art; and the more mature members of the collegium will find themselves frequently frustrated by the emotional outbursts of those who claim they want to be treated like free adults, but who, in fact, do not.

Secondly, some of the available research suggests that it is important to distinguish between policy and execution of policy. At the policy level, collegiality seems to be the most effective way to exercise authority; but at the level at which policy is executed, it seems more effective in most cases to have one man in command. Committee meetings over the purchase of stamps are, in their way, as foolish as the situation in which the head of a large organization feels the need to personally sign all the checks the organization issues. Group discussions over minor problems of policy execution are both immature and maddening. They are probably rooted in a lack of trust and confidence in the member of the collegium who has been chosen to execute a specific policy, and also the need of the less mature members of the collegium to fasten on a scapegoat for their own frustrations.

While the distinction between policy and execution may be clear enough in theory, it is frequently much less clear in practice, and one fears that it will only be through a long process of trial and error that mankind will develop a wisdom concerning the kind of work best done by committees and the kinds of work best done by one-man decisions.

Furthermore, there is also some strain between the prophetic function of leadership and its consensus-producing function. This tension is particularly obvious if one accepts the concept of prophecy found among many Protestants and some younger Catholic enthusiasts. From this viewpoint, prophecy is essentially an Old Testament phenomenon: Amos striding in from the fields and denouncing the painted women of Samaria, or Jeremiah in his cave outside Jerusalem bewailing the forthcoming destruction of the city. A prophet who does not sit in judgment is no prophet at all, and it is pretty hard to sit in judgment and at the same time obtain consent. But the Christian concept of prophecy must be modified in the light of the New Testament, where Jesus seems to have exercised the prophetic role by challenging his followers rather than by denouncing them, by asking questions rather than by predicting disaster. Such a notion of prophecy is easier to harmonize with collegial leadership, but there still remains the very difficult practical question of when the leader should challenge, and when quietly preside over, the group's elaboration of consent. We do not yet have a precise answer to such a question, though there are many leaders who instinctively know when one must challenge and when one must reassure.

In summary, we have argued in this chapter that the pursuit of the common good by groups of humans still requires authority and probably always will, not because man is bad but because he is limited. We have further contended that in a society as complex as ours, authority, if it is to be effective, must obtain the voluntary consent of its followers so that they will apply a maximum of their own personal resources to the achievement of the organizational goals. Thirdly, we have affirmed that the only effective way to obtain this consent is to treat one's colleagues in an organization not as servants but as friends. We have pointed out that the Catholic Church which, of all human organizations, ought to recognize the implications of these words, seems not to have done so in practice. Finally, we have suggested that the most critical role for authority in the contemporary world is to provide leadership—that is to say, to challenge the minds and the hearts of men (as John F. Kennedy surely did). Authority that fails to do this very quickly loses credibility and perhaps even legitimacy. The problem, then, of freedom versus authority is resolved in a fashion not unlike that of individual versus community and independence versus intimacy. It is resolved by friendship; it is resolved when a leader really calls his followers friends and not servants, and when authority and freedom blend together in the simultaneous pursuit of the individual and the common good.

Chapter 5

A WORLD TO PLAY IN

Man lives in the world. Although in his modern condition he may be able to overlook his own animality and ignore the physical setting in which he is placed, he is still rooted in the world, immersed in it, shaped by it, and dependent on it. He breathes its air, drinks its water, eats its flora and fauna, is infected by its microbes, and is ultimately buried in it. He always has been part of the world and always will be. In his early days he was profoundly convinced of his dependence on the world. Its sun scorched him in summer and its cold winds threatened to freeze him in winter. Its night was a time of fear and defensiveness, and its day, an opportunity to seek his food. His crops were threatened by its storms and its drought; he and his family and his whole community could be obliterated by its plagues.

He was profoundly ambivalent about the world; he gulped down its water when he was thirsty and saw in it a symbol of life; he also realized that floods and storms could destroy him and saw water equally as a symbol of death. Fire warmed him when he was cold and made his food more edible, but if he did not watch it carefully, fire could get out of control and consume him and his possessions. He worshiped the sun because its heat made things grow, but he also feared it because if there was too much heat it would make him wither and die. He admired the moon for its silver beauty and worshiped it too, and yet believed when a man stared at it too long he would become mad. He only realized how precious air was when he found himself momentarily cut off from it, but he also realized that slight changes in the pattern of its flow could warn the animals he was hunting and snatch from him his evening meal. The world was good and bad, gracious and destructive—a master simultaneously kind and cruel. Ambivalent about it man may have been, but ignore it he could not. Most men who have lived, including many today, have had relatively few tools with which to protect themselves from the world and almost nothing to insulate themselves against it. Small wonder, then, that men have worshiped the world, and particularly its more dramatic manifestations—the sun, the sky, rivers, fertility.

Man learned to live in the world and adjust himself to its rhythms. The first step in making peace with the world was to know it and understand it; to be at home in its forests and to probe their secrets; to walk its plains and seek their food; to listen for its sounds and know their meaning; to sense its dangers and be wary of their threats; to recognize its cycles and its moods and shape his behavior to respond to them.

But there was another step man took. Once he understood a little bit about the world, he proceeded to try to subjugate it. He captured its fire, organized its animals into herds, brought its fertility under his control, diverted its waters for the use of his crops, floated its heavy burdens on its waters, and shaped its trees and its rocks into crude wheels and used its precious stones as a medium for commerce. Slowly but surely his tools became more elaborate; the rock and the club were combined into the ax; the stones became the arrow and the knife; the wool of his herds and the yarn from some of its plants became garments and then sails, which enabled him to experiment with primitive means of navigation and venture bravely out onto its seas and lakes. Its reeds became paper, and the juice of its fruits, ink with which to write on the paper; the movement of its stars could be used to measure the passage of time, and some of its earth could be burned in the fire or converted to metals which provided him with new decorations with which to adorn himself, armor with which to protect himself, and tools for making even more useful equipment. Basic technological development increased; the compass, the clock, the steam engine, the more sophisticated refining of metal, the harnessing of electricity, the internal-combustion engine, the flying machine, the digital computer, the jet engine, the rocket.

But not only did man build better tools—he grew more

sophisticated in their use. The tent became the skyscraper; magic herbs became antibiotics; fire became the home furnace; the loincloth became the Brooks Brothers' suit or the Pucci gown (though occasionally, at least in beach wear, progress beyond the loincloth has not been particularly obvious); the cold breeze was harnessed in the air conditioner; smoke signals became intercontinental telephone communication or colored TV programs relayed live by satellite. Man therefore controls time, space, heat, cold, food, water, ground, air, health, and even his own reproductive processes.

This assertion of his control over the world has not always been a complete success. By the year 1900, one could drive from downtown Chicago to Ninety-fifth street in a horse and buggy in about thirty-five minutes. Seven decades later, courtesy of the internal-combustion engine and the Dan Ryan Expressway, one can, if it is not rush hour, make the same journey in precisely the same amount of time. If it is rush hour, one had better forget about it. The jet airplane will carry one across the Atlantic in seven hours, as opposed to the seven days of a fast steamship, and the net fatigue that results from the time change may last no longer than seven days. Electricity brings heat, light, communication and entertainment, and it can occasionally be demanded to do too much so that at 5:25 on a given evening electricity may simply go on strike and plunge the northeastern section of the United States into darkness. Air and water are at our service and we proceed to pollute them both at a prodigious rate which, if it continues, will deprive us of both our drinking water and the lining in our lungs. The metals in the ground and the forests aboveground are at our service, and we are rapidly depleting those to such an extent that they may not serve many more generations. We have medicines that work marvelous cures and other drugs that will enable us to escape from a reality we find too horrid to accept, a reality which has been made possible for many of us precisely because of these marvelous cures.[1] We are tearing down our mountains, filling up our valleys, and building steel mills on our beaches, which probably doesn't make much difference because the

[1] It is interesting to note that the majority of the readers of this book would not have lived beyond their tenth birthday even one and one-half centuries ago.

waters will shortly become unhealthy for swimmers, in any event. In the midst of our dramatic technological progress we have produced traffic jams, soaring highway-death rates, smog, slums, lung cancer, radioactivity, Napalm, bugging devices, and the hydrogen bomb. Man has indeed mastered the world, so he no longer need be greatly afraid of it. Now, however, he has ample reason to fear what he is going to do with this world which he has turned into his obedient servant.

The problem is not in technology, as some romanticists believe, but rather in man's social, organizational, and moral skills. His ability to organize his activities, and his ethical systems, have not kept pace with his technical skills. Unless he is able to recapture a sense of his own oneness with the world and his respect for its rhythms and cycles, he may find that his triumph over it is Pyrrhic, and that he has conquered the world only to place himself in a worse bondage to it.

First of all, there is the possibility of the permanent disruption of the ecological balance. Man intrudes himself recklessly and brutally into the processes of nature. He destroys one sort of animal which is a nuisance or a tasty food, only to discover that other and more disruptive animals now multiply and that the natural energy which has kept them within limits has been destroyed. He tears down trees and is shocked when the rain washes off his topsoil. He does not worry about lamprey eel destroying lake trout until that trout is no longer able to keep the alewives within limits, and they, in turn, find no food to feed upon because man's steel mills are polluting his waters. So tons of dead fish wash up on its beaches and deprive man of his recreation even if it were possible for him to swim in the lake which was rapidly growing more polluted. He dramatically lowers his own death rate only to discover that a stable birth rate and a declining death rate lead to a fantastic increase in population, an explosion which is real and ominous, despite the fact that not so many years ago the American Catholic hierarchy chose to describe it as a "so-called" population explosion.[2]

[2] Once again the Catholic Church missed a magnificent opportunity. Its historic concern for the poor and suffering should have led it to see long ago that population control was imperative for

Man thus has no regard, or has very little regard, for the cycles, the processes, and the balances of nature. Nature is there to be used and exploited. He no longer fears it as he once did, but he no longer respects it either, and he is therefore able to exploit it with a callous disinterest in what he is doing to the world around him or to the future generations who must someday live in the world. Man has mastered creation, but he has not mastered his own greed and selfishness, ambition, and insensitivity.

At the root of this disrespectful corruption of the world lies man's artificial isolation from the world—even from that part of it which he has re-created and reshaped for his own purposes. Man pollutes the world because he is alienated from it. He rejects, in fact if not in theory, his own animality, and ignores his "being in the world." The secular theologians tell us that modern man rejects mystery; since he has been able to explain and control the world, he sees no mystery in it and does not hold it in awe or reverence. In a later chapter we will consider how right the secular theologians may be, but to the extent that they are correct in their analysis, we can only lament the fact that there are no more taboos against what man does to nature—no taboos, for example, against steel companies destroying the Indiana Dunes. If modern man really thinks that all awe and reverence have been taken out of his world, then he is indeed in a sorry state, for science does not really explain sunsets or thunder or the smell of burning leaves, or the sound of a singing bird. Mystery is where man finds it—or rather, where he is willing to look for it. If he refuses to see anything in the material world that he ought to reverence or that he ought to hold in awe, he is very likely to replace thunder with the atomic bomb, sunset with smog, and the bird with the roar of the giant semitrailer.

---

the human race, but because of its narrow interpretation of the meaning of sex and reproduction, it resolutely refused for many years even to concede that there was a problem, and today it still hesitates to take vigorous leadership toward finding a solution, a solution the necessity of which is changed not one bit, in the final analysis, by the stand the Church finally takes on the morality of various means of family limitation.

There is yet another danger in man's escalating technology: the tolerance for error that sophisticated technology permits is much smaller than that of primitive technology. Thus a relatively minor mistake by a driver of an automobile is likely to produce only a remote danger to the lives of the people that are in it, but a mistake of the same physical magnitude by the pilot of a 747 could lead to the obliteration of five hundred lives. A misplaced comma in a medieval manuscript troubles no one, but a misplaced comma in a computer program can destroy a satellite worth hundreds of millions of dollars and the lives of its crew. While another log on the fire may put it out, it can be easily relit; but the failure of a circuit breaker can bring darkness to the world's largest metropolis, and it takes a long time to turn the lights back on again. Technology may make life infinitely more comfortable, but it also makes mistakes more dangerous and creates a situation in which men must live with their fellow men in great care lest, because of weariness or inner tension or worry or frustration, they accidentally make a small mistake which is gigantic in its implications.

What are the roots of the ruthlessness and the callous exploitation which presently mark man's relationship with his world? One can say, first of all, that man is too serious. He approaches life and the world with all the grim efficiency of the German tourist with his Leica, his map, his guidebook, and his implacable determination to make the most of every second of his journey. We are so serious about ourselves and our work and even about our recreation that we are necessarily serious about our use of the world—not so serious, indeed, as to respect it, but serious enough to want to get the most out of it as quickly as possible. We are also vigorously competitive, and if we do not exploit the world's goods, then we fear someone else will. If we had time to stop and think about what we are doing to our environment, we might recoil in horror. But we have no time; we are too busy; there are too many things to do, too many appointments to be kept, clients to be seen, obligations to be discharged, parties to go to. And what do we do when we have nothing else to do? We are strongly tempted to get drunk so that we can forget all the things we have to do the next day.

We are also apathetic. The pace of our lives, the seriousness with which we live, the narcotic with which we calm
our nerves—all conspire to dull our sensibilities. Many of us
feel we are caught in a trap we cannot break out of. We have
little confidence in ourselves and little hope for our lives. We
realize vaguely that we are destroying mankind's resources at
a rate which can only be called immoral, but we shrug our
shoulders and say, "So what? If there is no hope for us why
should there be hope for those who come after us?" Para-
phrasing Louis XV, we say, "After us, the worldwide smog."

As a result of our seriousness, our competitiveness, our
apathy, and our neurosis, we both de-humanize the world
and de-animalize ourselves. We deny our relationship with
the material world and the importance of the animal dimension of our own nature. In the very process of eliminating
most of the problems the world has caused for man, we
blindly create a whole set of new problems which may very
well be worse. In a paradox that future generations may find
cruel, man has been able to reduce his dependence on the
material world to a bare minimum, but in the very process of
mastering it, he has come close to destroying it and has made
himself and his descendants even more dependent on the
mechanisms of control that he has created than he was on the
material world previously. He has conquered the world and
he cannot enjoy his conquest.

It is no solution to suggest that man must return to nature.
A troop of overweight fathers and their overweight sons
tramping through a beer-can litter in the forest preserves are,
in reality, no closer to nature than when they are sitting in
their front room watching a color television set. Nor is the
fisherman sitting cold and wet in his boat on a dark and rainy
morning enjoying himself in the great outdoors, not, at least,
until he gets back to the warm fishing lodge and soothing
beverages. We cannot re-create the world of Hiawatha or
Natty Bumpo, or for that matter, the village poets of
seventeenth-century Ireland, or the folk singers of seventeenth-century England. Furthermore, it does little to dissolve our problems to wear flowers in our hair or our ears,
though it probably does increase the profits of countless
florists. Man cannot return to nature. He must, rather, learn

once again to respect it wherever he finds it, be it in a gentle fall of snow in a shopping district (before the snow becomes gray with soot, or creates an impossible traffic jam on the expressways), or in the sun rising behind skyscrapers, or even the bright lights of the Champs Elysées, Times Square, or the Ginza; for these, too, are nature's beauties as redirected by man's genius. In his respect for nature, man must then invent more sophisticated social organizations and rethink his ethical standards vis-à-vis his planet—a planet now so small and of such limited resources that the British economist Barbara Ward can speak of it as "Spaceship earth," or, in another context, insist, "The world is but a small human village around which a man can walk in a couple of hours." Man must do these things and he must do them quickly, or there won't be much left to save, and our descendants will curse us as they try to eke out an existence in a garbage dump in which a Stone Age man would have refused to live.

It is not the purpose of this chapter to suggest a detailed solution to the problem of the relationship between man and his world, but rather to offer a theoretical perspective from which man may view his world and in which he can learn to respect it once again. At the risk of being dismissed as a madman by a late puritanical age, I will contend that the world was meant to be man's playground. We have conquered it in order that we might be able to play in it. We have eliminated most of the fears the world once contained so that we can turn it into our park. Interestingly enough, the Greek word for "park" is *paradisos,* from which also comes our modern word, paradise. It was a park into which the Lord sent Adam and Eve, and as man slowly beats back the effects of the serpent's influence, he must once again come to live in a park, a worldwide paradise in which he is meant to play.

It is often affirmed that man treats material creation like a plaything. What this usually means is that man applies the "paper plate at a picnic" model to the world. He uses his plaything and then discards it carelessly, without any worry about what happens to it or the place where he has discarded it. However, this is not the way children treat either their favorite playthings or their parks. Anyone who breaks a child's toy can expect violent retaliation, and anyone who destroys a child's park had better beware of infant ire. Children protect their toys and their parks because they respect them, and if man could see the world as a place to play, he will reverence and protect it.

The Dutch scholar J. Huizinga maintains that play is the basis of culture in civilization:

> It has not been difficult to show that a certain play factor was extremely active all through the cultural process and they have produced as many of the fundamental forms of social life. The spirit of playful competition is, as a social impulse, older than culture itself and pervades all life like a veritable ferment. Ritual grew up in sacred play. Poetry was born in play and nourished on play. Music and dancing were pure play. Wisdom and philosophy found expression in words and forms derived from religious contests. The rules of warfare, the conventions of noble living were built up on play patterns. We have to concede, therefore, that civilization is, in its earliest phases, play. It does not come *from* play, like a baby catching itself from the womb. It arises *in and as* play and never leaves it.[3]

Man, then, makes progress to the extent that he is able to tear himself away from the serious activities required for staying alive to indulge in play. According to Huizinga, play is, of its very nature, free. That is to say, it is not something man has to do. It is not ordinary, so it is beyond the routine actions of life. It is unserious in that man realizes that a game does not affect the course of his life, but it is still utterly absorbing. There is no profit or gain to be obtained from play; the joy to be found in the act of playing is reward enough. It has its own boundaries of time and space, boundaries which set themselves off from the rest of the world and the rest of life, where it can proceed according to its own rules, its own conventions, and its own enthusiasms. It binds men together in close social groups, whether we be members of the Green Bay Packers or Charlie Brown's bedraggled baseball team. We are united with one another because we belong to the same team.

[3] J. Huizinga, *A Study of the Play Element in Culture* (Boston: Beacon Press, Inc., 1955).

Huizinga calls man *"homo ludens,"* indicating that man is a playing animal, indeed the only animal who is free enough of the world to be able to play in it even when he is an adult. As we have pointed out in an earlier chapter, play and friendship are inseparable. True friends are strongly impelled to play together, to celebrate their friendship and to enrich its joys. Similarly, the experience of joint play deepens and enriches the friendship.

Man is therefore an animal who, because he can control his environment and because he is able to form friendships, is capable of having fun, though modern man finds it extremely difficult to have much fun, perhaps because of the same seriousness which has driven him to ruthlessly exploit his playground. Play is closely related to the sacred, and much liturgical ceremonial can best be seen as play, as a comic dimension of the sacred.[4]

Play is at the root of human creativity because it puts aside the serious and permits the imagination to run wild and to experiment. It grants man the opportunity to give free play to the emotions, the intuition, the instincts which give him a sense of conaturality with the reality in which he finds himself, as Huizinga aptly observes:

> Play represents the intrusion of mind into matter, in the ordering of matter by mind not for any deadly serious purposes but rather for the pure sport, the pure fun of it.[5]

In this context, then, to say that one is doing something "for the fun of it" is to say that one is engaging in specific human activity and one of the most noble of human activities. Man is a permanently playing animal, an animal who is able to

---

[4] It may seem irreverent to suggest that ritual is comic, because it seems so serious. And yet of course the seriousness is an act. Man knows, at least by now, that he does not have to be serious because God demands it of him, but rather because he demands it of himself in relationship to God. But the seriousness is only skin-deep; man may have a hard time admitting it to himself, but often sacred play of liturgy strikes him as being hilarious. Witness the uncontrollable laughter that sometimes seized the clergy and seminarians in the midst of the ponderous Byzantine ceremonies of the Roman solemn high mass. The serious and the comic are often merely two sides of the same coin.

[5] Huizinga, op. cit.

have fun throughout his whole life, perhaps because he is an animal and need not lose his youth.

We are therefore suggesting that man has arrived at the crossroads where he must either become much more playful or proceed on a direct course to the garbage heap. The material world has been pretty thoroughly mastered. It will therefore become either a park or a garbage dump, and it will only become a park when we are determined to have fun in it; when we realize that it's a great big marvelous toy with which we can have a spectacularly good time so long as we resolutely forbid anyone to spoil it. Those who would destroy our world, those who would pollute our water, tear down our forests, build steel mills in our dunes, are, in the strict sense of the word, spoilsports. They have come to ruin our fun and games and we must drive them out of our playgrounds.

If we lose our park it will be difficult for us to play. Without play our lives will be seriously limited and close to unbearable because not only is play the basis of our culture and our creativity; it is also a mechanism which enables us to balance our aggressive impulses and our need for friendship. In an unserious but absorbing domain of play we can be fiercely competitive and aggressive with our friends not only without risking the friendship, but also, in fact, deepening it—at least as long as we are able to maintain a clear boundary between the world of play and the world of reality. To triumph over one's friend in a game is a great joy and to lose to a friend may be a mock humiliation, but it is also rewarding to us, at least if we are able to observe the rules of good sportsmanship. The Dallas Cowboy who has had a championship snatched out of his hands once again by the Green Bay Packers may be the loser, and yet when he shakes hands with his conqueror and as they walk off the field together, the audience applauds more enthusiastically for the vanquished than for the victor, even in Green Bay, Wisconsin.

As we remarked before, play is indispensable to friendship, and if our playground is thoroughly destroyed, friendship will become difficult, if not impossible. Since friendship is rooted in sex, the relationship between play and sex, as we observed before, is close. We play our best, or at least with our strongest attempts at style, in the presence of members of the opposite sex, and the connection between victory and play in sexual conquest is marked by a vast variety of symbols, not the least of which is the human figure on the athletic trophy. Fashion in human dress, which can clearly be understood only as a wild and somewhat bizarre game, was deeply sexual in its implications long before the miniskirt. Sexual relationship itself becomes most enjoyable when it is part of a game. And even the word "score" as a description of sexual conquest in its root meaning is not inappropriate. As a matter of fact, sex is only a game when we are not exploiting our partners, for no sportsman would dream of exploiting or abusing or degrading those who play the game with him. Friend and playmate, as the words are understood in this volume, at least, mean exactly the same thing. Human love reflects a game, and a game, in turn, is most fulfilling when it is played by people who are able to love one another.

It is interesting to note, therefore, that the beginnings of the pollution of our playground by urban industrialism was a puritan phenomenon. Those men who were too somber, serious, and strait-laced to be able to enjoy sex were also so ruthless, grim and determined that they felt no need to respect our playground. Had industrialism, perchance, been developed by more playful people who respected the world as a toy, we might have had a very different situation than that which we presently face. He who cannot enjoy sex will not enjoy the world, and he who refuses to realize that the world is a playground, that he is a playing creature, is going to be somewhat less than adequate in the marriage bed. Friendship, therefore, is only possible for us when we are able to marvel at the splendid playground the Almighty has provided for us. He has given us mountains to climb and to ski on, waters to swim in, forests to walk through, sands to lie on, flowers, sunsets, old squares in London, bustling business districts, cities by night, a cool breeze on a humid day, the taste of beef fondue, the smell of pipe tobacco and of roses, the sound of Beethoven, of jazz, and of the human voice—all as decorations for our playground. It is quite an incredible park. There is lots of fun to be had, games to be played, new decorations to be created, and wonderful friends and companions with whom to play the game. The world was designed to be a resort—a summer resort, a winter resort, a spring resort, and a fall resort.

It is important to emphasize that this view of the world is not merely bumptious, Chestertonian optimism, but a sober analysis of the nature of reality, a reality, like many other things in life, such as love, community, and leadership, that seems too good to be true. Why don't we view the creation in which we are immersed as the playground it is? At one time in our evolution we were unable to do so because we were so dependent upon it and because we had so much to fear from it. But our whole point in this chapter is that this time is over. We are no longer so dependent on the world and we need not fear it that much. We do not play in it now—we do not return to our paradise—precisely because we are too busy, too serious, too suspicious, or too sick to enjoy it.

Mircea Eliade, the noted historian of religion, points out how the paradise myth reasserted itself in the nineteenth century in the romantic version of the peaceful, pleasure-filled life of the South Sea Islands. One can understand how the dull and somber Victorians, serious about their ruthless exploitation of the world, and far too serious to have a healthy view of sex, began to create some myths in which to project their fantasies of play and of sex. And one can also understand why it had to be far, far away in the South Sea Islands where it was no threat to them. Bali Ha'i does not seem that much closer today, despite the supersonic jet, but it is good to have that island paradise far distant from us and enshrouded by mists, for then we, like the Victorians, need not face the overwhelming fact that our park is not in the South Pacific, but all around us, and is peopled by friends and playmates who are all the more rewarding because, unlike the grass-skirted inhabitants of the South Seas, they are human beings like ourselves. No indeed, it would not do at all to realize that where we are now is a paradise. If we did, we would have to become infuriated with those who are destroying our park and with those social structures that are corrupting our playmates' capacity to play and to love. We don't want to view the world as a playground, not merely because it is too good to be true, but also because of the fantastic demands it would make upon us for friendship, for love, for freedom, and for the quality that is indispensable for the first three: playfulness.

What contribution can the Catholic Church make to our understanding of play? In its own tradition there are surely rich sources of playfulness. The Church has resolutely insisted, in the face of the Manichees, that the world is good, and that through the incarnation of the Resurrection has become better. Jesus' presence at the marriage feast of Cana, and his miracle work to preserve this party from being a failure is the ultimate response to all the prohibitionists, party poopers, puritans, and prophets of gloom that have appeared upon the scene since that memorable gathering. Catholicism is not Methodism; and the great Catholic saints like Francis and St. Philip Neri and John Bosco, and near-saints like the portly Italian gentleman who convened the Second Vatican Council, resolutely refused to take themselves seriously. Hilaire Belloc's oft-quoted lines summarize the Catholic tradition:

> But Catholic men that live upon wine
> Are deep in the water, and frank, and fine;
> Wherever I travel I find it so,
> Benedicamus Domino.

Would, however, that it were so. We have kept the Manichees, the Puritans, and the Jansenists at bay, but not completely, and not without being corrupted by them. Many Catholic institutions and communities, if not indeed most of them, which presumably are bearing witness to the joy of resurrection, are as drab, dull, cold, and unplayful as the grim, dour buildings in which they are housed. We have permitted ourselves to become so obsessed with our insistence on penance that we have persuaded many of our members, at least on the semiconscious level, that pleasure is wrong and that they ought to feel guilty when they enjoy anything, be it a day off, a glass of beer, sleeping late, or the body of their spouse. We have periodically glorified poverty as though it were a virtue even more important than charity, forgetting that the masters of poverty, like Francis of Assisi, did not give up the world because it was bad, but rather gave up material possessions so that they might enjoy the world. The puritanical attitude by many of the clergy toward sex, particularly sex for the laity, is matched by an equally puritanical attitude by many of the laity toward poverty for the clergy. They are only persuaded that their priests are truly virtuous if they eat grubby food, wear run-down clothes, and drive cars that do not start on cold winter days. One remembers the Lord's comment about those Pharisees who criticized Him for attending banquets.

It must be said, therefore, as clearly as possible that poverty is not a good in itself and is not an end to be pursued; that those liberal enthusiasts who stoutly defend sex as a form of self-fulfillment are being contradictory when they decry playfulness in the world as a form of self-fulfillment. Puritanism about poverty is as un-Catholic as puritanism about celibacy. Neither celibacy nor poverty is an end in itself; it is merely a means to other ends. One can misuse sex and one can also misuse the goods of our playgrounds, but such misuse does not mean that sex is evil or that the playground is bad. What mode of sexual being a man chooses is, ultimately, a personal decision; so, too, the determination of what form his playfulness will take. Whatever personal decision is made, he who refuses to enjoy sex and to enjoy his playground cannot claim the name of Catholic.

Catholic theory must face the fact that its thinking on poverty and on man's relationship to the world in which he must play needs drastic revisions as it becomes technically possible to eliminate poverty, or at least material poverty from the world, and as it becomes increasingly obvious that self-denial has no real effect on social problems. The sophisticated child knows that whether he eats his spinach or not will have no real effect on starvation in India, and the sophisticated adult knows that whether he buys a Chevrolet or a Pontiac will have little effect on poverty in the inner city ghettos. For poverty will be eliminated, not by one man depriving himself of something, or even by tens of thousands of men depriving themselves, let us say, of dessert, or of their new cars, or their color television. Poverty will be eliminated rather from a drastic social reorganization in which the economies, the polities, and sovereignties of the nations of the world are readjusted in order that there may be rapid technological progress in underdeveloped countries. The problems of India will not be solved by sending them a larger piece of the pie, but rather by making the pie much bigger. The traditional formulations regarding poverty, then, are quite irrelevant for our contemporary problems. Indeed, one is tempted to suspect that some of the formulations need to be reversed. At one time we were led to believe that if we played less and worked more, many of the world's social problems would be resolved. However, in the frame of reference we have developed in this chapter, exactly the opposite seems to be true. If we were less serious and more playful, if we worked less arduously and played more vigorously, then the world physically and psychologically would be a far better place in which to live, and the complicated technical problems of poverty might be substantially closer to a solution.

As we noted before, the Church's tradition has been excellent. Its practice, at least in recent centuries on the matter of playfulness, has been abysmally bad. The liturgy, for example, started off as reverent play, and has through the centuries become hyperserious. Ceremonial acquired a value in itself outside its relevance as play. The current "low Church" reaction which wishes to eliminate all ceremony, vestments, and ritual from the liturgy is as puritanical as its predecessors, and the neorubricists who would impose on us casualness with the same rigidity as their predecessors imposed sobriety are, if anything, more obnoxious because they have determined that we are to be forced to be "joyful" in the forms of joy they think appropriate. On the other hand, some of the new liturgy, particularly as developed by young people (in their guitar masses in such places as somber chancery offices and music commissions permit guitar masses), has about itself authentic Christian joy. The new breed does, indeed, know how to *celebrate* mass, and it has been a long, long time since the Roman liturgy was anything but a sham celebration. Margaret Mead's comments on this subject are particularly appropriate, both because they underline the need for liturgies which make possible playful celebration and also the dangers that follow in taking play out of man's worship:

Americans, especially young Americans, are crying out for shared delight, for shared celebration of joy. This cry is expressed in many ways: by high school classes studying books about the rites of spring or puberty among primitive peoples, by lively young staffs of public parks looking for "happenings," by the counterpoint at a conference on church and society where a dancer is introduced to accentuate a scriptural reading, followed by the singing of "I am the Lord of the Dance." Why, ask those arranging a love-in or planning to perch with their guitars on the edge of a heavy marble altar, can't we have more celebrations, more fresh, invigorating, group events?[6]

She believes that the problem is a lack of imagination in "working out in a continuing and satisfying form the celebrations so earnestly and clamorously desired." What is needed in both religious and secular ceremonial is for communities to "celebrate with enough of past ritual to give shape and form to their feeling and to bind them together, and with enough that is new to make them feel alive and newly related to God, to all creation, to their fellow men, to men long since dead and to children yet to be born."

Dr. Mead further warns of two dangers inherent in ritual:

One is when the ritual is too rich and the highly elaborated symbolism too old to be appropriate to contemporary life. When this happens, one finds people who are overwhelmed, detached, alienated and apathetic. Then again, where the individual's imagination, or the imagination of a whole group, is capable of expression that is denied by the poverty of a symbolic system, one may find glossolalia —speaking in tongues, abandoning the structure of conventional speech—and states of mind that resemble schizophrenia. In fact, where the individual has no way of setting his vision, his hope or his need within any kind of boundaries, within the framework of any formal symbolic presentation, one is likely to find the most varied forms of aberrant behavior.[7]

[6] Margaret Mead, "Celebration: A Human Need," *The Catechist* (reprinted in *Overview,* March 15, 1968).
[7] Ibid.

But the joy and playfulness that ought to be in the liturgy are merely the symbols of the joy and playfulness that ought to be in the whole Christian life. My friend and colleague John Hotchkin has insisted that Christians ought to be celebrating constantly; their lives ought to be occupied by parties, feasts, banquets, and merriment, and that we ought to give ourselves over to veritable orgies of joy because of our belief in the Resurrection. We ought to attract people to our faith quite literally by the fun there is in being Christian. Unfortunately, however, we all too readily become somber and serious and pompous. We fly in the face of our own tradition because we are afraid "of wasting time," or becoming "attached." In the words of St. Teresa, "from silly devotions and sour-faced saints, deliver us, Oh Lord."

Man, therefore, must relate to the world by dominating it. But he dominates it not by running away from it, nor by running away with it. He makes the world unimportant by enjoying its importance. Only the sick and the neurotic and the prematurely aged throw away their playthings, and only the sick and the neurotic and the permanently childish are dominated by playthings. He who is overwhelmed by the world is merely the Puritan in reverse, for he takes it too seriously, just as the Puritan does, and he must gorge himself upon it. For play to be successful, we must be both detached and respectful of our game and our part. Play is both a refusal to be serious and an insistence on being earnest. Henri de Lubac once remarked that man was most fully man when the light of divinity was reflected in the face upturned in prayer, and we might add—second only to that position—man is most fully human when his face is bright with laughter in the midst of a game he thoroughly enjoys.

That the world is a park and a plaything is no longer optional. As man must be friendly, as a member of the community, with his colleagues if he is to survive the crisis caused by the rapid social and technological progress of the last three centuries, so too must he be playful. Either we must play in the world God has made for us and that we are in the process of reshaping, or we will destroy ourselves by the hyperserious mechanism we have built to dominate the world. Fortunately, man does have at hand, or shortly will have, the social organizational skills necessary to create a park and to make possible fun and games yet undreamed of, but unfortunately, we do not yet have at hand the theory or the philosophy, which is simply another way of saying that we do not have the faith or the hope. We are too serious and too cynical. We do not believe that we can remain young. We do not want to believe in Peter Pan, the Good Fairy, the Easter Bunny, or Santa Claus. For that matter, we do not want to believe in the risen Jesus of Nazareth.

Chapter 6

WORK TO BE COMMITTED TO

It may seem strange to place a chapter on work after a chapter on play, but the position of this chapter is no accident. For the first time in man's history play is more important than work, not merely because man may have more time for play than he does for work, but because work has become so sophisticated that unless man is playful he will not be very good at work. The reason for this is that the lines between work and leisure are being blurred as most work becomes more like leisure, and the old servile work of the past occupies fewer human beings.

For most of human history most men have done servile work—that is to say, work done by slaves.[1] Man kept himself alive by the sweat of his brow from dawn till dusk every day of the week, and in some societies, every week of the year. He gathered food, tended herds, hunted animals, planted, cultivated, and harvested his crops, carried water, dug in the earth, hauled burdens, and pulled oars. Most of his work was utterly mindless. Little or no intelligence was needed to understand it, and very minor skills were needed to execute it. Man was little more than a somewhat sophisticated beast of burden.

But, as man progressed, certain small groups of men began to be able to do other things which required some mental effort—artisans made tools and eventually built ships and buildings and even pyramids, or designed and supervised the construction of these projects. Still others engaged in

[1] And until the 1950s moral theology was still forbidding this kind of work on Sunday, in the somewhat archaic assumption that in the Christian world very few people did nonservile work.

commerce, attended the temples, or studied the heavens, and a few aided in the governments of cities and kingdoms. They exercised not their bodies, but their intellects and their imaginations.

It was these men, or, more exactly, their successors, whom Aristotle considered "free," for they did not do the work of slaves, but rather the work of free men. They were the ones who were to receive "liberal" training which would equip them for "leisure" activities, and in Aristotle's understanding of the word, "leisure" did not mean doing nothing, but rather engaging in liberal—that is to say, specifically human—activities: poetry, philosophy, and politics. The first category belonged to all artistic efforts; the second, all attempts to explain and to understand the world; and the third, all efforts to direct human activities. But it must be remembered that even in Aristotle's Athens, there were only a relatively limited number of "liberal" men and most were still slaves, still spending the daylight hours engaged in mindless work as human beasts of burden.

Man slowly developed tools which were labor-saving devices enabling one man to do the work of many men. Domestic animals, the wheel, the sail, were the most primitive of labor-saving devices, but also the major ones until the eighteenth century, when, beginning with the steam engine and the cotton gin, a tremendous output of labor-saving inventions occurred. Simultaneously, there also emerged a demand for much more sophisticated skills to operate the new machines. Most men still worked by the sweat of their brow, but an increasing number were required by the liberal occupations of commerce, scholarship, education, administration, and government, and even those who worked by the sweat of their brow were often confronted by minor challenges. The only ones who suffered because of the new technology were the artisans, the glass blowers, the furniture makers, the clockmakers, the silversmiths, and those other tradesmen who combined physical work and intellectual effort in the middle ground between intellectual and servile work. Machines were not nearly as skilled as the craftsmen, but they worked far more quickly.

In addition to developing new machines, man reorganized

a flow of labor so that the machines might be used most effectively, and the world was presented with mass production on the assembly line. Early phases of this reorganization of the processes of work treated the individual as though he were now not a human beast of burden, but a simple tool designed to execute a simple task. However, as the technology became more sophisticated and research on the conditions of industrial productivity became more acceptable, it was agreed in theory, if not always observed in practice, that a man worked much better if he was given a complex task rather than a simple one. The mass-production employee not only works much less, than the serf who pushed his wooden plow through the field, but he also encounters greater intellectual challenge.

However, with continual progress in labor-saving devices, the critical people in industrial society, if not yet the most numerous, were those with a very high degree of skill—the scientist, the test pilot, the entrepreneur, the corporation executive. And then in yet another phase of evolution, the critical men became those who were able to combine individual expertise with the ability to cooperate—the astronaut, the computer programmer, the various committee members at the different levels of John Kenneth Galbraith's techno structure.

Servile work diminished even in the basic industries such as mining, manufacturing, agriculture, and forestry, both because a smaller proportion of the population was engaged in such work and because the men who did such work were required to use more intelligence and less sweat. Recently in American society the so-called service industries (including the most menial and the most sophisticated kinds of work) surpassed in size the basic industries, a critical milestone in the demise of servile work. The servile tasks that remain in society are, for the most part, those for which it is as yet uneconomical to use machines; those who push a broom or a mop in a skyscraper office building at night do so because there is as yet no machine to do their work more cheaply.

There is still some servile work left in advanced society, and much other work both in the basic industries and in the so-called service industries that requires both intelligence and physical effort (in some instances not very much intelligence), but the proportion of "professionals" (men who exercise intellectual and personal skills for which they have received long training) is increasing rapidly. But the emergence of a society where there is no servile work at all and man's basic productive activity is accomplished without any physical exertion, may have to wait many years before it is realized. Nonetheless, the labor-saving devices and the reorganization of the processes of work create a situation where, for an ever increasing number of people, work is requiring intelligence, cooperation, and creativity—that is to say, men and women who are "liberal," capable of entering friendships, and possessing certain "poetic" instincts. The leisure skills are therefore critical in the work situation; and most men and women who work will do so as members of problem-solving teams.

Problem-solving, in its turn, will require playfulness, a willingness to experiment, to speculate, to take controlled risks, to "try on for size" alternative solutions, to see what the results of these solutions will be. Machines will even enable man to estimate, at least within certain limitations, what the results of the various solutions might be.

The last person in the world the creative problem-solving team needs is the somber, cautious, uncommunicative and dull puritan businessman who was the founder of the capitalist economy and its mainstay for several centuries.

Some visionaries of the future argue that most men will not work at all—that relatively few will be required to belong to the problem-solving teams, and that the efforts of most others will be replaced by computers. I have profound reservations about the predictions of the computer enthusiasts because an important distinction has to be made between what computers may be expected to do in theory and what is actually feasible for them to do in practice, or will be feasible in the foreseeable future. But even if most men are not engaged in the production of goods and services, they will be engaged in leisure activities that will require problem-solving groups as sophisticated as decision-makers in industry. The real difficulty, therefore, is not that men will not be able to engage in leisure work, or that they will not be interested in their leisure work because it is not concerned with economic production, but rather the difficulty for the future seems more likely to be a dramatic increase of the problem already with us. Leisure work is so fascinating and challenging, makes such high demands on human commitment, and provides rewards so satisfying that man is not able to limit his commitments to it and becomes so overcommitted that his effectiveness is impaired. One need only look at such typical "leisure-work" activities as law, medicine, management, and scholarship (all four increasingly involving problem-solving teams) to see how demanding and simultaneously rewarding leisure work can be.

The important distinction in contemporary society is probably not between servile work and liberal work, physical work and intellectual work, but between those kinds of jobs for which no profound commitment is required and which therefore can be left peacefully after one has put in one's forty required hours, and that kind of work which does demand commitment, and which therefore provides tremendous rewards but also very great dangers.

Why is it so easy, then, for the doctor, the lawyer, the business executive, the university scholar to be "trapped" by their work? The activities in which they engage are intrinsically interesting and challenging. The sense of accomplishment and satisfaction which their tasks provide is almost limitless. Furthermore, while the satisfactions of professional success are not as great as those of happy human relationships, they can serve as a substitute for human relationships, particularly in those personalities where human relationships have been marked by failure. Those professionals and executives most likely to throw themselves "body and soul" into their work are precisely those who lack confidence in themselves and trust in others. Intense commitment to one's professional career is also response to feelings of guilt and self-hatred. As we watch the executive or the professional work himself to death, we marvel and say, "But so much of what he does is unnecessary." It may seem so to us, but it does not to him. He is not sure of himself. He is afraid that if he does not work as hard as he does he will not be able to accomplish his tasks. He cannot permit himself to "let up" for fear that if he does his basic lack of talent and ability will be manifest. Overwork, therefore, is a response to the executive's or professional's neurotic feelings of inadequacy and incompetence.

It is also rooted in the competitiveness and the individualism of the puritan ethic. Even if cooperation and teamwork are stressed, still one is not sure that he can really trust his colleagues. If he allows himself to slip behind them, they may destroy him. It is necessary to keep ahead of them merely in self-defense.

Finally, since occupational success is the mark of the successful man, it is necessary to achieve this success in order to assert one's masculinity, a masculinity about which many American males, given the female dominance of the environment in which they are raised, are somewhat less than certain.

In the final analysis, overcommitment is counterproductive. It is less than human because it leaves no time for friendship, and it is less than creative because it does not know how to be playful, and it is less than effective because it is too neurotic to cooperate. The danger in the leisure-work areas of society is more overcommitment than undercommitment, and overcommitment in the long run is as dysfunctional as undercommitment because it makes man a slave once again and turns his job into drudgery. While the empirical evidence is not yet absolutely convincing, we can nonetheless assert with some confidence that to the extent that he has deprived himself of the capacity for friendship, playfulness, and cooperation, the overcommitted executive or professional is not an asset to his work community, but a liability. In years to come the corporate structure will realize that overcommitment is dysfunctional, and that, just as the schools must be concerned with the development of the total human personality, so must the corporate organizations in which men and women work, not necessarily because of social responsibility, but rather on the pragmatic grounds of operational efficiency.

Let us suppose, then, at least for a few utopian paragraphs, that the large corporate structures decide that, for reasons of social enlightenment and pragmatic efficiency, they will concern themselves with the development of the total personality of their executives and professionals. Let us assume it is agreed that human effectiveness degenerates without a fully human life. And also let us assume that there is a fairly plentiful supply of workers available for professional and executive jobs. Further, let us assume that training for the leisure arts is deemed essential for professional success because professional work requires the skills that leisure activity produces. Under such circumstances we would, in our Utopia, suppose that the corporate structure would do everything it could to force the promising young professional or executive into the arms of his wife and family. Just the opposite is current practice, for at the present time the ambitious young professional is required to spend long hours away from his wife and children precisely at that stage of family development where his presence is most critical and the demands on his maturity are greatest. By putting severe limitations on the amount of time the young professional can spend on a job, the corporate structure will prevent him from escaping his wife and children into the satisfaction of his career. He will be forced, then, to spend more of his waking hours caught in the ambivalence of the early-marriage situation where his passion for his wife is still very strong and also his resistance to the demands of intimacy are very strong. Thus a higher premium will be placed on his developing the skills of friendship and putting aside the barriers, the defense mechanism, and the distrust which are dysfunctional to his occupational effectiveness. The corporate structure will do this because it understands that reinforcing the marriage relationship is the best possible training experience for the executive, and that the young professional who has learned how to become a friend to his wife will be much more valuable to the job situation than the one who has attempted to escape from the terrifying demands of marriage intimacy into the much cooler satisfactions of occupational success.

There are a number of ways that corporate structures could achieve this goal. They might limit the number of days and hours the young professional can work, arguing that only a mature, trusting, and open-ended personality can be permitted the responsibilities of a full work week. It might also insist on long vacation periods with a subsidy which would enable the professional to take his wife on vacation with him, and also, at least for some vacation periods, baby-sitting service so the children need not be brought along and distract the husband and wife from one another. Further-more, the organization could make routinely available extensive counseling service both for their executives and the executives' wives. Such counseling would never be compulsory, of course, but it would also be taken as a matter of course. Many, if not most, couples would benefit greatly from the counseling. Finally, the organization could subsidize its executives in community activity and further education, provided, of course, that the education has nothing to do with direct training in career skills, but rather contributes to personal development and enrichment.

We have described in our utopian myth a situation in which the husband is the executive and professional, but it does not seem unreasonable to suppose that in years to come more and more women will be engaged in the same sort of work. We think the same sorts of requirements and facilities should be available for them as for their husbands. As a matter of fact, if the work week, at least for the young professional, were reduced to three days, it would be much easier for the young wife and mother to participate in a professional career. One might argue that if the wife worked a different three-day schedule from her husband, our goal of forcing the marriage partners to associate with one another during the early years of marriage would be frustrated. However, one need only consider how a husband would react if he found himself at home with the children and not with his wife for two or three days a week to see that this ought not to be a serious problem.

Our utopian myth is described somewhat with tongue in cheek, of course, but the point behind it is meant seriously: The professional (man or woman) who has confidence in himself, stable friendships, skills in the arts of playfulness, and a happy marriage will be able to do more in a twenty-four-hour work week than his opposite member would be able to do in a seventy-two-hour week. The myth also assumes, we think quite correctly, that marriage is the primal relationship in which goals of confidence, friendship, playfulness, are to be achieved, if they are to be achieved anywhere. Finally, the myth argues that the man who is to do liberal work must be liberal and that the Protestant Ethic must go. There is still room even in the nonservile society of the future for achievement motivation, but not much room for neurotic achievement.

We are not arguing that people should be forced to be liberal, because no one can be forced to be a free man, but rather that society, in order to sustain the general welfare, will eventually see the wisdom of creating a situation in which there are strong forces that press people toward personal freedom and friendship, and away from the easy escapes from personal responsibility and trust. Leisure work is exciting, challenging, and rewarding, for it is the extension of human control of the world, but it ought not to be permitted to turn into a competitive effort to prove one's own worth. There is every reason to suspect that even pragmatic canons of efficiency force us to view with displeasure such attempts at worth-proving.

What has the Christian Church to say about work? There is, first of all, some statistical data which suggest that the last "Protestants" (in terms of the Protestant ethic) are Irish-American Catholics, and it oftentimes seems that American Catholics have turned Calvinist not only in their attitude toward sex, but also in their attitude toward work. Quite possibly there is a connection between the two phenomena.

In some of its forms of popular piety, the Church has permitted work to become a compulsion and has even frowned on leisure as a waste of time. In years gone by, seminary training and formation of religious novitiates insisted, Calvinistically, on the necessity of keeping busy and dismissed leisure activities as a waste of time. Such a stance is hardly appropriate for an organization which was the mother of culture and the founder of holidays.

The theology of work is quite undeveloped, although the basic idea that work is an extension of God's creative and redeeming action certainly provides a solid foundation for the construction of such a theology. Perhaps the most hopeful line of development for a theology of work would be one that faces the fact that in Western society the major developing problem is not that it is too difficult or too monotonous or too degrading, but rather that it is too exciting and too challenging and can serve as a pretext for escaping other forms of human activity. Work must be seen in the context of friendship, community, faith, education, play, and celebration. It is a worthy companion of these other realities, but modern industrial capitalism has tended to pre-empt human life from such other activities, and what we *do* has become synonymous with what we *are*. As the human race moves toward greater technological sophistication and greater demand for humanized personality development, the ability to detach one's self from work will be seen as an extremely important human Christian virtue, for only one who is able to detach himself from his work would be able to make an authentic human commitment to it. He who cannot make a human commitment to it may, unintentionally, find himself making a mess of, and even destroying the complex machinery which has reduced to a minimum the necessity for man to earn his bread by the sweat of his brow.

Chapter 7

A SELF TO EDUCATE

So far we have observed that man loves, joins communities, follows leaders, and plays; but he engages in none of these activities as merely a passive responder to outside pressures, at least not if he is healthy and if his love, play, belonging, and following are to be healthy. He acts, rather, as a conscious self, as an *I*, standing distinct from others and yet interacting with them. The self which man is and which he gives to others or withholds from them is a complex blending of heredity and environment; the environmental influence on the fashioning of the self can be called education in the broadest possible sense.

There are many different perspectives from which to approach the question of the education of the self, and I find myself in this chapter in the position of wanting to begin my comments at the stage of evolution of the human personality I know best—adolescence. There are advantages and disadvantages in beginning at such a position, but chief among the advantages is that late adolescence for most human beings is their "last chance" to gain some measure of control over their selfhood and their destiny. If one determines what sort of education, again in the broadest possible meaning of the word, is most important in late adolescence, one can then extrapolate in either direction to a total picture of the meaning of human education.

A young person arrives at the teen years with a wide collection of raw materials. There is, first of all, the genetic, biological, and physiological substratum—the brain and nervous system, the digestive tract, muscular controls, physical strengths and weaknesses, the respiratory system—that he has inherited from his parents. Social science does not yet know how dependent his later behavior is on his motor, sensory, and nervous systems. So impressed is it with the power of environment, and so concerned about how the interaction patterns, particularly with mother and father in early years, shape personality, that it has been little concerned until recently with the possible link between the genetic substratum and the development of personality. It is clear, however, that the substratum is extremely important. It cannot be overlooked by anyone who recognizes the fact that man is, to begin with, an animal.

There is the personality experience of early childhood; as the child discovers that he is a self over against the rest of the world, he distinguishes slowly between his two parents and works out, in the context of the parents' interaction with each other, his own sexual identification. Next to being born, this experience of fitting into the dyadic relationships between his parents is the most important event that happens to a human being; for it shapes the broad outlines of his personality for the rest of his life. One need not be a Freudian to recognize the tremendously important influence of the early years on future personality development. Nor need one recognize this and then inevitably accept some sort of psychological determinism. There is still a great deal of plasticity in the five-year-old's personality; there is much that can still be shaped by others and much that he himself can shape as the years go on. But save for minor readjustments (and occasionally, after long psychotherapy, some relatively major ones), the broad outlines of the personality have been etched in.

At the same time he is acquiring from his parents a sense of his own distinctiveness and his sexual identity, the child is also learning the language, the values, the biases, the perspectives, the culture of his country, of his social class, of his ethnic group, and of his religion. The language itself is likely never to be modified. The child may, in time, become explicitly conscious of how his repertoire of words shapes his thoughts and actions. Values, biases, prejudices, expectations, whether they be of society, class, ethnic group, or religion, can be modified, reversed, developed, or eliminated in later life. But they are not easy to change, nor are they changed without a heavy price in effort and suffering, and for most of us most of them are not changed. We are born, for example, upper middle-class, Irish, Catholic, Democrats, with a strong orientation toward business and professional success. We may become Republicans or alternately liberal academicians. We may forget we are Irish, though our attitude toward women and toward politics may still remain distinctly Irish. It is most unlikely, however, that we will stop being Catholic or stop striving for success.

The teen-ager also possesses talents, strengths, and weaknesses that result from an almost infinite variety of possible combinations of genetic substratum, the early personality experience, and the elements of language and culture that have been stressed in his formative years. The young woman, for example, may be a gifted artist and musician, a personable organizer, and a witty conversationalist, but she also may lose things easily, be a terrible typist, and quite frightened of sex. Whether these characteristics are rooted in biology, psychology, and culture, it is virtually impossible to say, since by her teen years all three factors play a part in the formation of her developing self.

There is in most adolescents a curiosity and creativity which, in most cases, has not quite been snuffed out; curiosity and creativity are greater in some than in others, but are nonexistent in only a few. The adolescent wants to know what the world is, what life is all about, who he is, what he should believe in, what goals he ought to seek. He also wants to know what he is able to do, what his limits are, what sorts of pleasures he finds most rewarding, what others think of him, how he will handle himself in critical situations, and what are the best ways to express his thoughts, his feelings, and his beliefs.

Finally, the young person is also saddled with a whole bag of defense mechanisms, mild neuroses and self-rejections. He has not made the pilgrimage from birth to puberty without a number of psychic scars. He has known what it means to be frightened, angry, rejected, and lonely. While it may be argued that none of these experiences is necessary, and that it is possible for the young person to face the adolescent transition with confidence in himself and trust in others, it is still unfortunately true that we do not yet know enough either about our own personalities or about the rearing of children to be able to achieve such a goal. Some young people may arrive at their teens with a minimum of psychic scars and defense mechanisms and a maximum inclination to openness and trust. More young people may be capable of such early maturity today than in the past. Nonetheless, they are a very distinct minority, and most teen-agers face the traumas of adolescence already weakened by the traumas of earlier life.

It is pretty hard to grow up in American society without having feelings of inadequacy and failure. Love between the parents may be nonexistent or poor or incomplete; distrust between parents, that prime manifestation of original sin, generates a distrusting child. Further, parents in addition to producing an atmosphere of distrust which frightens the child and makes him distrusting, frequently manipulate the child for their own ends—either as a weapon against the other parent or as an outlet, positive or negative, for their own frustrations, dissatisfactions, and failures. In American society, also, competitiveness is so intense that most young people are trained for competition early in life. Love is given or withheld, depending on how successful the child is in the competitive evaluations. Comparisons begin with one's weight at birth and proceed on to the size of one's funeral, with such high points in between as one's first step, the mastery of toilet habits, marks in grammar school, social success in high school, the score of the National Merit or College Board or Graduate Record exams, the size of one's wedding, the importance of one's job, the success of one's marriage, the size of one's car, the material of one's spouse's coat, and the neighborhood in which one lives. Thus the typical middle-class American adolescent arrives at the big leap toward adulthood with a checkered record of success and failure, in most cases hardly sufficient to assure his own dignity or worth. If the adolescent is to become an adult "self," he must acquire morality, playfulness, self-respect, faith, creativity, and courage.

It is fashionable for journalistic, educational, and ecclesiastical viewers-with-alarm to decry the decline in morality or to assert happily to the contrary, that we have now entered into a "permissive society" complete with pictures of Jane Fonda on the cover of *Newsweek*. Such affirmations about moral decline almost always fall victim to the American puritan inclination to equate morality with sex and to argue that sexual behavior is much more immoral than it was at some unspecified period of "the good old days." Such heraldings of new sexual permissiveness are generally unencumbered by empirical data and correspond nicely to man's inclination to believe that the world is going to hell in the proverbial hand-basket. But I refuse to take seriously the contention that our society is somehow or other "a permissive society." Permissive, as we say at the University of Chicago, in relationship to what? More permissive than the Roman Empire at the time of Nero? More permissive than Italy of the Borgias? More permissive than the England of the Restoration of the Regency? than the France of Louis XIV? than the Parisian middle class of the nineteenth century? More permissive than Puritan New England where the practice of "bundling" was almost universal and where divines seriously debated whether sleeping with one's betrothed was really sinful? One suspects not. Chastity has never been a terribly popular virtue, and if it was honored by middle-class college students in years gone by more than it is by the college population today (and I am not persuaded that it was), the reason very likely is that the student body is not as middle class in its composition as it used to be.

But if I am profoundly skeptical about a change in sexual morality, I think the evidence for higher moral standards in other areas of behavior is so overwhelming as to be almost beyond question. Concerns about racial justice, peace, service to one's fellow men, honesty, integrity, sincerity, are, I think, far more explicit in today's highly personalist generation of college students than they were in the past. The typical heroes, be they Holden Caufield in the fifties or Ben Braddock in the sixties, are profoundly concerned about the questions of meaning, of moral evaluation, of purpose, and of responsible relationships. The problem for Ben Braddock and Holden Caufield is not that they are immoral, but rather that they cannot resolve their moral dilemmas.

The difficulty, then, is not that young people are immoral, but rather that they are almost too moral for the ethical systems which are available to them. The repertoire of moralities which American society offers to its young people has kept pace neither with the increased moral consciousness of youth nor with the increasing complexities of the moral challenges that youth must face. The traditional moralities have not yet been able to articulate systematically the proper responses of the moral man in modern America, and indeed have almost despaired of even trying to do so.

It is fashionable to argue that there is no need for a system of morality—to contend that all one must do is love. But in the words that my colleague Bruno Bettelheim has made immortal, love is not enough. One need look merely at the "love culture" of the Hippies to realize that to say that the moral imperative is really to love is simply to restate the problem. Love can easily turn into self-deception. He who claims to be loving may merely be exploiting. Furthermore, the simplistic morality of love opens the door to a privatistic withdrawal from the messy, complex problems of a larger society which does not respond to the naïve, enthusiastic love of a young person. He who says to youth, "You must love," does not tell youth what is to be done or how it is to be done, or even why it is to be done. The so-called "new morality," which frequently seems to be little more than an attempt by some divines to justify almost every kind of sexual aberration, really doesn't solve Ben Braddock's problem. Ben is well aware that he must love, but he is not sure whom to love or how to love, or how to direct his life on the basis of love.

The young person, therefore, finds himself faced with the need for constant decision-making, decision-making fraught with moral implications. Unlike young people of years gone by, today's youth are faced with a vast, almost infinite variety of choices about what to do, who to be, and how to behave. We have showered on them an abundance of riches, have given them more alternatives than their grandparents would have dreamed possible; indeed, we have given them just about everything except an explanation of reality that would provide them with norms according to which they could make their choices. Since we really don't know what they ought to do, and since our moralists and ethicians aren't sure what they ought to do either, society, in effect, says, "It's up to you, kids—you must love, then do what you will. You must evolve your own system of morality, your own vision of the meaning of man and the meaning of life. Having done this, you will achieve integrity by being honest through this moral vision that you have developed for yourself." This sounds liberal and democratic and enlightened and progressive until one stops to think of how truly absurd it is to expect that a seventeen-year-old, long on enthusiasm and generosity but terribly short on experience, sensitivity, nuance, and wisdom, will be able to evolve an ethical viewpoint that will be salutary for him and satisfactory for his fellows. Our pretense that the young are able to evolve their own morality is merely an admission of how morally bankrupt we adults are.

To make matters worse, we frequently disfigure the traditional moral systems with such an overlay of pompous bourgeois piety that the young person can only conclude that traditional ethics are invalid and indeed grotesque. I am inclined to feel that the ethical vision of the Gospels is at least a challenging one. But there aren't very many parish churches where a young person can hear that ethic preached in language that sounds any different from what he considers those vague inanities by which his parents regulate their lives. If, as I have suggested before, it is necessary for man to have systems of morality, it is also probably inevitable that these systems will have a strong tendency to become rigid, juridic, and lifeless unless they are periodically renewed by the appearance of prophets who will reinterpret them in terms of the life challenges of the day. Alas, I think the reader must agree that prophecy is a commodity which is in short supply in contemporary America. Sound and fury, yes; the noise of solemn assemblies, yes; but prophecy—there really doesn't seem to be much market for it at the present time.

I would therefore contend that the moral stress which young people experience can be traced to the fact that none of the meaning-giving institutions—family, church, or school—have been able to provide the overwhelming majority of young people with a meaningful vision of life, a system of general principles of human behavior adequate for the complex decisions that young people must make, or the increased explicit moral consciousness which they are experiencing.

My hunch is that if any prophet arises who produces a really new morality or reunifies the traditional moralities, his prophecy will have to deal with the dignity of the human person, for this is a value which young people do understand, though they find it hard in practice to concede human dignity to many of those whom they have set up as their "inkblot" enemies. The Student Left has no concern about the dignity of faculty and administrators. Peace demonstrators seem to have had little concern for the dignity of President Johnson, and Hippies are not willing to concede much dignity to upper middle-class society. But the human person is the human person, whether he be a dean, a president, or a Babbitt. A personalist ethic which does not recognize this is not worth very much; neither is an ethic of love which does not contend that one ought to love one's enemies. I am not persuaded that the traditional moral systems do not have the raw material for developing such a prophetic personalist moral system, but for whatever reason, it has yet to be done.

Does formal education have any place for the struggle to create new ethical systems? Our philosophers surely must be excused, because they are too busy agonizing over whether words mean anything and whether one can talk validly about ethics or about anything else. Our theologians must be excused, because they are too busy burying God or rejoicing over the decline of religion or marching in picket lines. The other members of the humanistic disciplines are busy trying to convert their fields from arts to science. The social scientists are counting noses and the physical scientists are building bombs. All of us, of course, are terribly busy trying to achieve tenure, and any prophet who does not have a good record of publication need not even bother applying. Administrators, of course, must pay the bills passed by the alumni and preserve law and order. All of us decry war, hatred, and other evils, but if a young person innocently asks us why, we reply with some embarrassment that we're a bit too busy to answer such a question. I once asked one of the most sensitive observers of contemporary youth, who so lamented the absence of clear meaning and morality in the youthful generation, what ideologies and moralities he would suggest. He shrugged his shoulders and replied, not unkindly, "Look, I am a third-generation agnostic. That's your problem."

As the problems in American society grow more complex, therefore, and the standards of love, friendship, community, leadership, and playfulness that we have described in the last chapter increase, there inevitably will be even higher ethical standings and more agonizing ethical dilemmas. Charity will be both more intense and more sophisticated, but barring a major breakthrough in human thought, ethical systems seem likely to lag even further behind. The situationists and the contextualists are right when they declare love as the ultimate measure of morality, and the sacred scriptures would agree. They are also right when they declare the individual conscience as the ultimate norm of moral action. Here St. Thomas Aquinas would surely agree. But neither of these statements is more than the beginning of an answer to complex moral issues, especially in our present condition of distrust and self-pity. No one is qualified to be an entirely satisfactory judge in his own case. Love grows but slowly and moral decisions cannot wait. The connection between love and moral issues, especially more complex ones, is difficult to ascertain; the accumulated wisdom of the past is not to be rejected completely out of hand. There are, therefore, two goals of moral education:

First of all, we must help the young person to break the link between conscience and superego, between the compulsive need to do something which, far from being morally obligatory, is personally harmful. Conscience is not the same as superego, but it is, rather, that part of the ego—the reality principle—that makes conscious moral judgments. It has nothing to do with the neuroses or the values and goals that we have absorbed from our parents—or at least nothing to do *necessarily* with these elements of the personality. The young housewife who feels the need to stew and worry over keeping her house spotlessly neat, even if it impedes her relationship with her husband, her affection for her children, and her own personal development, is not engaging in moral behavior, but is rather reflecting the irrational standards she has internalized from her own family. The guilt she feels when she neglects her housework and plays with her children, or enjoys a good book, or goes out with her husband, is not moral guilt. It is regrettable that during her adolescent development she did not learn to distinguish between human moral responsibility and guilt feelings generated by the unconscious.

Secondly, moral education should have as its goal the development of a sensitivity of balance, a nuance, a reserve, about moral issues. The emerging adult must be aware of how complex and ambiguous ethical reality is and how deceptive quick, easy solutions are, whether they come from a rigid, moral, theology textbook or a liberal appeal to the morality of love by a contextualist. While the ultimate judge of morality is the informed conscience, the real problem is informing the conscience, and in the information process a person cannot fall back completely on either the wisdom of ethical traditions or on the situation in which he finds himself. He must somehow balance the requirements of both. It is not easy, and it is not likely to become easier.

If one must choose between uncontrolled sexuality and inhibited sexuality as the more serious evil, in American society it is certainly still the latter. Young Americans, Christian or otherwise, are burdened with horrendous attitudes toward sex. Most young Americans have no sexual education at all in their homes. They struggle through adolescence with a curious mixture of back-alley and washroom physiology, ethereal ideas of mystical or romantic love gained from the mass media, superstition about the possibility of pleasure without pain (as enshrined in various sophisticated versions of the *Playboy* philosophy), a conviction of the "dirtiness" of sex (from the "underground" tradition), and compulsive fear (absorbed from their own parents' implicit, or sometimes explicit, attitudes toward sex). The relationship between sex and friendship and the concept that sex is both personal and relational find precious little room in such a hodgepodge, and it is small wonder that for such young people growing up sexually is a terror and marriage is painful.

A much smaller group has absorbed the clinical approach—

the accurate, technical information frequently set in the moral context of high-school hygiene courses. They are warned of the dangers of pregnancy; they have been advised not to hurt anyone, and are persuaded that sex is "just another part of life." Whistling past the graveyard in the dark, they persuade themselves that they can be serene in their approach to sexuality, ignoring the terrible power of the passion and the pain and damage it can inflict on the personality. They are equally unaware that sex without friendship is unfulfilling and can easily be destructive.

For most young people shame is a particularly powerful danger because it produces both frigidity and nymphomania (often successively in the same person), neither of which has much to do with pleasure or friendship. Shame is neurotic, as is its counterpart, exhibitionism. Modesty, on the other hand, is a virtue, but so is playfulness. Affection is essential for human growth, but it can easily be distorted into exploitation and impede human growth. Young people must learn to be both more cautious and more liberal; they must have greater reverence for their own sexuality and also learn to master their fears and their shame before sexual union begins.

Their fears are deeply rooted in questions of sexual identity: Will they be an adequate lover? Will they do and say the right things? Will the other respond? Will they make fools of themselves? Will they get all the "kicks" they ought to get? Will they be able to do it right the first time? An education which does not provide young people with both the answers to these questions and, more important, the personal security that makes it unnecessary for them to ask these questions, is an incomplete education.

Shame is more difficult to dissolve because it cannot be eliminated either by more information or by a modification of expectations. It also has a stronger hold because it is so readily confused with modesty and good taste, and because it is, in most instances, related to a lack of respect for self as a physical being. Puritanism, the underground tradition of obscenity and self-hatred, combines to persuade many, if not most, young Americans, unconsciously, that they ought to detest their bodies and particularly their body's "dirty parts."

All the bikinis in the world, no matter how much they may improve beach scenery, will not solve this problem.

The body is neither to be exploited nor given lightly, but when it is given it must be given totally and joyously, and American education has a long way to go before young people are trained to be both total and joyous about sex.

We are also only beginning to understand the nature of premarital friendship between the sexes. If society were set up deliberately to design a system of relationships between young men and young women which would most interfere with an intelligent and humane preparation for marriage, it could not come up with a better technique than our teen-age dating system in which young people are trained to exploitation and distrust, a system that puts a premium on deceiving the other as much as possible as to who you are and what you want and where you are going. Exactly how the dating system is to be reformed is not clear, though the need for young men and women to associate with one another in joint efforts outside of the dating relationship and its central location, the high school, could hardly be denied. The churches have not contributed very much beyond a morality which is essentially negative, and the foolish conviction that teen-age dances are an adequate response to the religious dimension of sexual problems of adolescence.

By now it is clear that whatever my own morose disposition may be, I am firmly committed in principle to the necessity of playfulness in the human existence. So is Professor Keniston. And he laments that the young people he knows tend to be privatists—that is to say, they seek their principal satisfactions in the world of family and close personal friendships and retreat from the public sphere of life where the major political, social, and ethical decisions are being made. In our terms, this retreat is a retreat precisely from the world in which we are supposed to play. He who runs away from the world to seek peace and tranquility with his family is far too serious to enjoy either the world or family life. My hunch is that this somber, serious retreat from both the world and from joy is based partly on the absence of any coherent system of belief in which to evaluate the world and partly on a lack of confidence about one's own value and dignity in relationship to the world. If you don't think you're worth very much, you are in no mood to play.

To quote my friend and colleague, Kenneth Keniston:

> . . . in a striving society that rewards and praises hard work, it is especially important to recall that one of the attainments of adolescence should be the development of the capacity for invigorating play. The future will bring increased opportunities for leisure, for recreation and for enjoyment. It is too easy to forget, in a society that is still emerging from the legacy of puritanism, that one of the tasks of adolescence is the development of a capacity to be childlike rather than childish, to live zestfully as well as purposefully, to be able to engage one's self fully with the world and with one's fantasies and passions, to be capable of free, buoyant, exuberant and spontaneous pleasure. In the absence of play, tomorrow's adults may be moral, virtuous and responsible, but they will also be driven, compulsive, joyless and grim.[1]

One of the remarkable things about human beings is that most of us are much better than we think we are. Indeed, we are most likely to be that which we most want to be, although we are firmly persuaded that it is quite impossible. I am constantly appalled at how widespread feelings of self-rejection are in American society. We are surrounded by beautiful women who cannot accept their beauty; by talented men who compulsively overwork because they doubt their talents; by immensely popular and respected men and women who feel unloved; and by many who are gifted with joy and laughter but afraid to let the world see it. It has often seemed to me that for upper middle-class young people, the most important single need of adolescence is that they learn to begin to love themselves. So much self-hate and distrust has been beaten into them by their parents, their relatives, and their teachers, and, if the truth be told, their clergy, that they have very little conviction of their own value and dignity. We have

[1] Kenneth Keniston, *The Tasks of Adolescence* [Draft report submitted to Task Force III (Studies of Adolescents and Youth) of the Joint Commission on the Mental Health of Children], n.d., p. 3.

argued in this volume that the giving and receiving of love, the formation of the friendship relationship, is the most important of human activities. If you are convinced that you are no good, then you have nothing worth giving. You cannot run the risk of giving yourself, because then you will be found out to be empty and worthless. Distrust that is rooted in the sense of worthlessness is extraordinarily difficult to extirpate, and our progress in the skills of psychology is only beginning to cope with it; and yet it may be the greatest single problem that American society faces.

Young people also need a faith—that is to say, a coherent series of propositions that explain to them the meaning of the world, of human life, and of themselves; a series of propositions which provides them not only with goals to strive for, but also with the vision of the good life for which they will work and against which they can evaluate the world as they now see it. In previous ages one absorbed such a faith from one's cultural environment virtually without realizing it. But just as the ethical systems have not kept pace either with man's moral consciousness or the complexity of his problems, so the philosophical and theological systems have not kept pace with man's vastly increased knowledge and scientific skills. The unfortunate, and indeed, intolerable divorce of religion and science several centuries ago and the hostility of the two have put the modern young person in an extremely difficult position. Science, despite the exaggerated claims of some scientists, or one should say some devotees of scientism, does not provide ultimate explanations, and religion, despite the absurd claims of some religionists (many of them highly placed) is not a substitute for science. But the result of this divorce is that young people today have better food, clothing, housing, recreation, and medical care than any generation of adolescents in human history, but are not provided with any coherent explanation of what life is all about. Quite the contrary, they are assured by a number of meaning-giving institutions that no such explanation is possible. If Erik Erikson, the Harvard psychiatrist, is correct in saying that you cannot have an identity without an ideology, you cannot be yourself unless you have a vision to which to be faithful, the problem of young people is very great indeed. The obligation of the meaning-giving institutions—home, school, and church—to attempt to articulate new meaning systems, or more likely, a new set of meaning systems, is imperative, but young people would be ill-advised to hold their breath until it happens.

Similarly, young people must acquire courage. They must achieve facility in risk-taking. But this is not particularly easy, because they don't trust themselves, they are afraid to give themselves to others, or to any vision that they may have. They are afraid of getting caught in a commitment from which they will be unable to withdraw. They are marvelously adept at finding excuses and escapes and are terribly eager to be disillusioned so that they can justify their own cowardice. The cool generation plays it cool, not because it is intelligent or sophisticated, but because it is frightened. It has no confidence in itself and is not at all sure what disasters might befall it if it did run a risk. The late Paul Tillich spoke frequently of the courage to be. The adolescent must acquire the courage to be himself, if he is not going to be a vague collection of unintegrated personality traits. The sort of education he receives in contemporary America does not do much toward helping him develop this courage.

It is also necessary for the adolescent to be able to be creative. By this we do not mean that he must be an artist, a writer of poetry, or a composer of songs, though more young people may be able to do these things than are brave enough to attempt them. I mean, rather, that the young person must be able to express in his own way, and according to his own style, the insights and beliefs that he has, both in speech and in writing. Some of the inarticulateness, oral and literary, of young people, is the result of bad training in the skills of expression. One is appalled, for example, at the near illiteracy of many graduate students who can hardly put a subject and predicate together correctly. But inarticulateness is often due not merely to a lack of skills. Young people who become terribly inarticulate when they are saying or writing things which they define as "really" themselves, can be quite clear and even eloquent in relaxed conversations. Inarticulateness is therefore often a mask behind which the young person can hide his fears. It takes a great deal of courage and self-respect to be able to say what one really thinks, because if one's audience rejects what one really thinks then they are rejecting the self; the self that lacks courage and confidence is quite incapable of distinguishing between disagreement and personal rejection.

While we have mentioned lack of skills in self-expression and the fear of revealing one's self in such expression as though they were two separate causes for inarticulateness, the distinction is logical and obscures the close connection between fear and incompetency that exists in the minds of young people. As we shall point out later, this is an excellent example of how education must involve both the communication of skills and the encouragement of personality development. Courses in composition which ignore the fears of self-revelation that beset many young people will be quite ineffective. Similarly, counseling that overlooks the fact that a young person may never really have learned about grammar or punctuation, will have limited success unless the young person, during the counseling experience (though not necessarily as part of it), is able to acquire some of the basic tools of speaking and writing.

To sum up what we have said about the education of the adolescent: Its goal should be the young adult who has open-ended confidence, who is convinced that he can work and learn to work better; that he can play and improve his skills in play; that he can express himself and sharpen his style of expression; that he can understand the meaning of life and improve that understanding; that he can love and make love; that he is worth loving and can become more lovable; and finally, that he can give himself to others without losing himself in the process. On the contrary, the end product of adolescent education is frequently the closed, confused, fearful cynic who knows all the answers only because he has been afraid to ask the questions, and his personality is pliable because it has no hard inner core and can therefore adjust to any situation and any set of people without ever being anything in itself. In Keniston's words:

To romanticize adolescents would overlook the existence in every adolescent of enduring childishness, underlying dependency, systematic provocativeness, and often obstinate unwillingness to accept the responsibilities of maturity. Yet we doubt that the responsibility for the foreshortening and derailing of adolescence can simply be laid at the door of adolescent ambivalence. The responsibility also lies within our families, which before and during adolescence promote anxieties, fears, rigidities and guilts that make further development difficult; within our educational system, which too rarely touches, much less strengthens or consolidates, the adolescent's capacity for rationality, ethicality, sentience, and moral passion; within our social institutions, which perpetuate injustices that deprive major groups in American society of any possibility of a constructive adolescent experience. Most often, the responsibility for the failure of adolescence lies with the vicious interaction of all of these forces, which potentiate each other most in that large minority of young Americans who are simultaneously deprived familially, educationally, and societally. Thus, although in our recommendations we will also be concerned with the facilities and services necessary to provide special help for those adolescents whose development has been clearly derailed, our primary emphasis will be on those actions, public and private, which might better guarantee for all young Americans the possibility of an adolescent experience.

Adolescence is, of all later stages in life, that which can most readily permit profound reorientations of intrapsychic and interpersonal life. A benign, responsive and confirmatory environment can enable an adolescent to undo vast damage done in earlier childhood, to heal the wounds of parental inconsistency, ignorance or neglect, and to move beyond the handicaps of his past to a responsible and satisfying maturity. Adolescence can provide those lucky enough to have one, a second chance, a chance to move away from the malignance of family pathology, social disorganization, and cultural deprivation. All too often, those who need this second chance most are precisely those who do not get it. We still know too little about exactly how the adolescent can, with a benign and supportive environment, work himself free from the scars of childhood. But we know enough to know that American society today does far too little to support the self-renewing capacities of its youth; and we insist that all Americans have the right to an adolescence.[2]

We have so far spoken of education in the broadest possible sense to include all the environmental influences which come to bear on the self as it moves from birth to maturity. There are many different institutions which participate in this educational process—family, peer group, social and ethnic class, school, church, the mass media. The fact that the word "education" is often limited to the efforts of the school indicates both that many of the other institutions are unaware of the impact they have, and that some of them would dearly like the school to do everything. But all educational institutions must participate, though in varying degrees, if the developmental process is to be successful. There is, however, very little cooperation among the various institutions; indeed, the young person often gets contradictory information from them. He must decide for himself whom to believe. For example, if he is faced with the question of how much he should study, the only consensus he will find from the various educational institutions is that they agree that success in studies is important and that study itself is competitive; both propositions, in the context of the present volume, are open to question. His family will tell him that he must get good marks, but that what he learns from his courses is not all-important in life. His teachers will insist on good marks and are likely to base the marks on the amount of information he has been able to cram into his head. His peer groups will tell him such things as, It's not what you know but who you know that matters, and, Studies are a game in which the young person can beat the system. The church will encourage him to study and get good marks, but warn him of the dangers of pride if he takes the marks seriously. Mass media will support science, scholarship, and learning, but also will make it look effortless and casual. From all these confusing messages the young person must select some kind of coherent system of viewpoints

[2] Ibid., pp. 23–24.

which will advise him how much of himself he should devote to study.

There is, therefore, an incredible disorganization and inarticulation among the various educational institutions in American society and also, one suspects, outside the psychological and counseling profession, little acceptance of the goals of adolescent education that we have described in this chapter. The child's parents want him to be successful, his teachers want him to develop cognitive skills which presumably can be measured on standardized tests such as the College Board or the Graduate Record exams. The mass media will want him to be a sophisticated consumer, though not too sophisticated. His peer groups want him to develop the ability to interaction with, or perhaps, more frequently, manipulate other members of the groups, and the church is concerned about "saving his soul." If any of these institutions are told that the goal of adolescent education ought to be a mature and positive evaluation of self, they are astonished, because this seems to have nothing to do with success or good marks or the salvation of one's soul.

I am not arguing that acquiring cognitive skills is unimportant, or that success, properly understood, is unimportant, or that relationship with transcendent powers, again properly understood, is unimportant. I am merely affirming that none of these goals can be achieved by ignoring the developmental processes the young person is going through. The mature young person, of course, will have guided his skills to meaningful relationships with transcendence and be a successful member of society. But all the cognitive skills or all the religion classes in the world will not enable him to become a mature adult unless the educational process proceeds in an atmosphere of sympathetic understanding about what is happening to his personality at the time he is in the classroom.

To focus more particularly on formal education, to which is generally assigned the task of imparting cognitive skills in our division of educational labor: It usually attempts to perform its functions without regard to what social science tells us about the development of the total personality, as though the cognitive can develop apart from the noncognitive. One university president summarized this approach when he said that there were two aspects of human education—moral and intellectual—and all the university was concerned with was the intellectual development. A curious model of man underlies such a statement—a model which the psychologists in that president's psychology department would hardly accept. It is not my intention to argue that formal education must assume the responsibility for the emotional or "moral" development of the student, because many of the influences that shape the emotional and moral dimensions of his personality are quite beyond the competency or the control of the formal educational institution. But I am arguing that formal education cannot achieve even its own basically cognitive goals unless it attempts to train young people to the realities of their personal development. If formal education is to successfully achieve its own relatively narrow and clearly defined goals, it must take into account and assume some of the responsibility for encouraging the development of the total personality. If it does not do so it may well find it is lecturing to a classroom of students who are not listening because they have other things on their mind and are unable to listen.

From this point of view, then, much that takes place in high school and college (and grammar school too, though here I am less able to offer informed comment) is counterproductive. Young people are taught in classrooms of anywhere between fifteen and five hundred students generally, because they have always been taught in classrooms and because it is assumed that a ratio of one teacher to several students is an efficient use of resources. However, there is every reason to question such an assumption. The educational needs of a given student (in both the narrow and the broad senses of the word) are such that it is dubious that effective education can be imparted to more than one person at a time. Tutoring or the apprentice relationship are, in the final analysis, the most effective and efficient means of education. Face-to-face personal teaching could be supplemented by small seminars of students and their tutor who come together as a small educational community to share their ideas in public. We have therefore arrived at the same point that we have in other chapters: Despite the complexity and the rationalization of contemporary society, the small friendship group of people who know and trust each other, is the most effective operating unit.

The suggestion that, at least in high school and college, the tutor and seminar relationships are the most effective formal educational means can readily be dismissed as utopian. But in this volume we are more concerned with the vision of possibilities for the human condition rather than with practicalities. It does seem to me, nevertheless, that my suggestion is neither utopian nor impractical, though it would require a mammoth reorganization of the educational enterprise, a reorganization that is, in fact, long overdue.

A distinction must be made between the imparting of information and acquiring of skills and the development of ideas. Information can be imparted in large groups—perhaps most efficiently by the utilization of mechanical and electronic teaching aids. To impart information in a classroom of fifty is foolish, since it can be done just as well with five hundred or a thousand. But to assimilate information into one's world view, to use it to develop one's ideas, to express one's own insight on the information, and to sharpen one's skills in working over the information, cannot be done in large groups. This fact should be overwhelmingly obvious to anyone. A mixture of educational experience in which the electronic or mechanical methods of instruction are used for imparting information and small seminars (perhaps no more than one or two a day) or tutoring relationships for the assimilation of information and the development of ideas, would probably require no more personnel than is presently engaged in higher education, although the personnel would certainly have to be better trained and more sophisticated. As in so many other areas of contemporary society, the problem is not lack of technological skills, but lack of social organization to most effectively implement these skills, and a social vision to demand stern reviews of our outmoded organizational styles.

There is no reason to believe that all young people within the same age group are capable of doing the same work. Nor that constant public evaluation of the student by the grading system accomplishes anything more than increasing the already high levels of neurotic competition. Furthermore, there is no reason to expect that young people will profit greatly from their classroom experiences unless an attempt is made to modify their family background at the same time. Effective education is education of the whole family. But despite powerful empirical evidence that this is true, we have scarcely attempted to modify our educational system to take this into account.

Finally, it is also evident that education is most effective when it relates the classroom experience to life, particularly for the adolescent with an experience in life of service to others. However, in spite of the tremendous opportunity for the sort of link between classroom and life that the volunteer movements of the 1960s have offered, there is little evidence that there is much inclination on the part of American educators to rethink the whole question of whether formal education ought to go on almost totally in a building which is separated from the rest of society. The real problem with the "progressive education" of the 1930s was that it was not really progressive enough, probably because it did not have available the sociological and psychological sophistication of the 1960s. But at least the progressive educators of a third of a century ago had the nerve to try, and there seems much less nerve today.

The gap between what we know of the needs of the self and what we do in the formal educational institution can be illustrated in a classic case from higher education. Hardly anyone involved in the study of human development would deny that a seventeen-year-old is basically a metaphysician—not a sophisticated metaphysician, and frequently a very rigid one; but he has begun to think for himself for the first time and is fascinated by "the big picture" and "the big issues." He wants to speculate about these, to play with them, to begin to fashion his world view, and to figure out his own place in such a view. A sensible educational program would view this phase of his development not as an obstacle or a burden, but as a marvelous opportunity to further simultaneously the development of the cognitive dimensions of the student's personality as well as all the rest of his personality. Therefore, it would follow that at this age learning should take place in small, informal discussion groups presided over by wise men. If there must be large classes in college, these could be best endured by seniors, who presumably have worked through some of the problems and some of the opportunities of the metaphysical awakening. However, what happens in higher education is exactly the reverse. The freshmen are herded together into large classes and handed over to the tender mercies of untrained and unproven teaching assistants, while the seniors have the advantages of the small seminars with distinguished faculty members.

Visitors from another planet trying to reconcile our practice with our psychological theories and our empirical data might be firmly persuaded that schizophrenia was epidemic in American society.

One of the most impressive examples of the absence of this schizophrenia occurred in a freshman English class in which I had the privilege of sitting for one afternoon at Immaculate Heart College in Los Angeles. The course was organized around T. S. Eliot's "The Waste Land," though the reasons were not altogether clear. When my colleagues and I arrived on the scene, the subject under discussion was the writings of Charles and Mary Lamb. The lecture was being given not by the English instructor, although he was present, but by a member of the psychology department and was devoted to the nature of the madness in the Lamb family, and particularly to the rather peculiar relationship between the Lambs and their parents. The discussion between the students and their two teachers was at first guardedly, and then quite openly, a discussion of their own relationships with their parents, a point which is of extraordinary importance to freshmen, most of whom are separated, either physically or psychologically, from their parents for the first time in their lives. To this day, I do not know whether that particular class was designed to achieve the purposes it actually did, or whether it was, rather, the instinctive reaction to the opportunities of the situation by two extremely sensitive and intelligent teachers. But planned or spontaneous, it doesn't matter. It was a classic example of how higher education can, by leaving aside absurd curricula and course requirements, blend the development of the cognitive and the non-cognitive dimensions of the human personality into a total approach to education which is far more effective, even cognitively, than are our traditional educational techniques.

I would contend, therefore, that American formal education's technology is still primitive and lags far behind our behavioral knowledge—that it is wasting a considerable amount of money on outmoded and worthless techniques, that it is justifying its efforts in language than can only be described as pompous and imperialistic, and finally, that it has pretty much failed in terms of its own goals. Despite the huge resources of time, money, and personnel that the American Republic pours into its formal educational process, we are nonetheless producing college graduates who are unable to express themselves well, do not read very much, are unable to handle themselves in foreign languages, and possess only a vague collection of unconnected information about science, mathematics, history, and literature. And I would further contend that such relative failure, however justifiable it may have been a quarter of a century ago, is no longer necessary.

But for that matter, the other educational institutions have not been particularly successful either in achieving their most important goals. The family, which presumably is charged with developing a sense of worth and a capacity for love in the young person, frequently substitutes for these goals neurotic competitiveness, while the church, in its turn, substitutes obscurantism and fear for a sense of meaning and belonging. One would be hardly prepared to contend that there are no new frontiers for American education to cross.

We have been arguing in this volume that in the world as it exists today, man's power is so great and his problems so complex that he will only survive if he is able to make major and dramatic advances in his capacity for trust, friendship, love, leadership, work, and play. We have asserted that man has arrived at the state of technology, self-understanding, and cultural vision where such a leap forward is technically and humanly possible. We have also contended that essential to the leap is man's ability to give himself in trust and friendship, and in this chapter we have focused on the process of the development of a man who is capable of such openness and trust because he has become a self. We have pointed out that, whatever the physical, cultural, and psychological experiences, and whatever the talents, strengths, and weakness with which the young person begins his adolescent experience, there is what Keniston would call "a second chance" during the adolescent years. The educational process he goes through between fourteen and twenty-one can produce, for many young people, the kind of open-ended self which is imperative for the love and trust essential to our revolutionary leap. We have also asserted that the educational institutions of our society, formal or informal, have not modified themselves in accordance with the crisis and the opportunity of the present condition, but rather are content to proceed with the traditional educational techniques, modified only by modest changes in textbook and curricular design. Only if the educational institutions of society, particularly the schools, are willing to concede that they are indeed responsible for the development of the total personality, and that their own somewhat narrower goals will not be achieved unless they integrate their educational techniques into a program that takes into account the needs of the whole person, will this revolutionary leap be possible.

No one can view American education today and be an optimist, particularly since higher education is faced with a fantastic crisis and a strain toward economic rationality that could substitute cost benefit—accounting and program budgeting (both perfectly legitimate techniques in themselves)— for the reform of educational goals and the re-evaluation of educational methods. But the pessimism must be blended also with some sort of optimism. We still have a long way to go before we understand adequately the human developmental process, but we know a lot more than we did, and knowledge, particularly knowledge with immense practical implications, has a way of breaking out of the laboratory and research report into life.

In my judgment, most of the present controversy about Catholic education is beside the point, because it does not address itself to Catholic educational problems. In the context of the developmental view of education we have advanced in this chapter, the issue ought to be not whether there should be Catholic schools, but rather, how the various agencies of Catholic education—schools, instruction classes, adult education, Sunday sermons, liturgy, family—can cooperate in an education for authentic human development. It might be thought—given Catholicism's historical emphasis on the development of the whole man, an emphasis which has been repeated in papal encyclicals and countless Sunday sermons—that Catholic education would be among the pioneers in implementing our new knowledge about developmental need in the educational experience, both formal and informal. But one need merely look at Catholic high schools and colleges to see that, however successful they have been by the standards of twenty, thirty, or forty years ago (and I am persuaded that my own research in the area has demonstrated that they have been moderately successful), they have not risen to the challenge provided by the developmental approach to education. One need only look through the goals of adolescent development described earlier in this chapter—sexuality, playfulness, moral sensitivity, self-respect, fidelity, courage, and creativity—to see that Catholic educational institutions and Catholic schools in particular have done no better than the rest of American education. That they have done no worse, one supposes, must silence most of the carping critics of the liberal Left, although some are still bent on proving that Catholic schools have done worse than public schools, despite overwhelming evidence to the contrary. But education of the whole man still seems to mean loyalty to certain devotional practices (often obtained by enforced repetition of these practices), and commitments to certain doctrinal and ethical propositions. With some few exceptions, one would look in vain for Catholic high schools and colleges that take the lead in developing integrated educational programs whose goals are moral sensitivity, healthy sexuality, playfulness, self-respect, fidelity, courage, and creativity. Discipline, order, neatness, "purity" (almost always a negative virtue), respect for authority, docility, and punctuality—are still the order of the day. Much less is heard about hope and love and joy, about the kind of behavior expected from human beings on a joyous pilgrimage to resurrection. I don't deny that there are certain Catholic educational institutions and a number of farsighted Catholic educators who push

cautious experiments in this direction. But I find it both inconceivable and intolerable that Catholicism does not stand
in the forefront of the campaign for a total developmental
approach to education.

It also seems to me that in this context alone we can in-
telligently discuss the question of whether there ought to be
Catholic schools. Given the goals or the education of the self
that I have described in this chapter and the generally ab-
ject failure of education to achieve these goals, one can argue
very strongly that Catholic schools ought to exist to show the
rest of the educational world how it ought to be done, particularly because of its own basic commitment to the integrity
of the human personality and the destiny of the human
search. Or, to put the matter more specifically, since Catholic
schools do, in fact, exist, and are likely to continue to exist in
the foreseeable future, developmental education provides the
Church with a glorious opportunity to reassume its proper
leadership role precisely in an area where it might be assumed to have the strongest commitment.

At the present time, given the crisis in religious life and
the acrimonious and usually senseless debate about Catholic
education, one hesitates to be very optimistic about Catholic
educators seeing the implications of developmental education. Eventually Catholic educators may realize that the education of the self is a sacred goal and one which is singularly
appropriate for them. I would go further and say that they
are more likely to do this than is any other major segment of
American education.

There is one warning that must be uttered, however. The
developmental approach to education which we have outlined in this chapter assumes that it is proper for educational
institutions, formal and informal, to take into account in
planning their programs and methods the developmental
needs of the children and young people with whom they
are working, and to adjust the classroom instruction so that,
being responsive to developmental needs, it may have the
greatest possible impact. There is a serious danger, however,
that education for human development can readily turn into
manipulation, especially in the hands of the semiskilled enthusiast who thinks he knows what's good for other people

and desires to impose, subtly or not so subtly, his version of good upon others. The goal of the integration of the cognitive and noncognitive development ought to be merely to create a climate in which a young person is most free to become himself, and not to force him to become a self that we have, for some preconceived reasons of our own, designed. The borderline between manipulation and climate creation is a thin one, and on the basis of its past history, as well as some of the excesses of enthusiasm for group dynamics, the Catholic Church must be particularly wary of slipping across that boundary line. Education of the self is bound to be a failure unless it is based on profound conviction of the ability of the student to fashion his own selfhood. To substitute sophisticated manipulation for unsophisticated instruction would be disastrous retrogression.

We need selves with open-ended confidence and we need them in large numbers if the vision of dramatic human progress on which this book is based is to be achieved. But as we have insisted repeatedly, the elements in the human condition are polarizing. It might be argued that the confident, open-ended self is an option and a luxury. However, given the trends of the human condition, it will not be a luxury much longer. Either such selves will emerge to live, to love, to play, to work, to lead, and to teach, or mankind will find itself on the top of the garbage heap it has made of the world.

Chapter 8

A GOD TO BELIEVE IN

God, it must be noted, has been around a long time and has been described in many ways. He usually ends up looking rather like the people who are describing Him—the fiery warrior of God of the Hebrew herdsman, the great geometrician of Aristotle, the dour gravekeeper of the Egyptians, the stern legislator of the Romans, the carnal lover of the decadent Greeks, the mighty navigator of the Polynesians, the military baron of the Middle Ages, the stern, Puritan parson of New England, the irascible old Irish monsignor of the American Catholics (or, as my friend John Denver has called Him, the Great Hangman of the Sky). All these images of God, it must be confessed, depict Him as being pretty much like those who describe Him. Man makes God in his own image and likeness, which, after all, is about all he can do. Even the God we are currently told is dead sounds much like a white Anglo-Saxon Protestant with academic tenure, and the God presented to us in the *Commonweal* symposium (a series of academic articles by prominent theologians) on the subject is much like a *Commonweal* editorial—dry, dull, quite proper and correct, and completely uninspiring (my own hunch that if God were not dead and could be killed, the dullness of the *Commonweal* symposium would have disposed of Him).

My favorite idea of God is Chesterton's notion of God as a comedian—a notion which was somewhat irreverently resurrected by the recent motion picture *Bedazzled*. Surely it can be argued that He would almost have to be a comedian to have produced such a quaint creature as man. One supposes, however, that probably the best image of God, all things considered, and one in which many human beings believed, albeit with something less than complete confidence, is God as a lover, a lover whom the Song of Songs is brave enough to describe:

> I hear my Beloved.
> See how he comes
> leaping on the mountains,
> bounding over the hills.
> My Beloved is like a gazelle,
> Like a young stag.
>
> See where he stands
> behind our wall.
> He looks in at the window,
> he peers through the lattice.   (2:8–9)

It is a bold image, and if the assumptions of this volume are correct, it is an image which is not without a future.

We are told that God is dead, which means that either modern man does not believe in Him or that we should call Him something else because modern man is put off by His name, or that the traditional God is no longer relevant to modern man's problems, or that modern man can explain the world without the need of a creator (and presumably without the need of a lover either).

The first question must be—Who is "modern man"? The vast majority of the human race, and indeed the vast majority of Americans, still believe in God, and there does not seem to be an appreciable decline in that belief in the United States. One might say in reply that modern man is really educated modern man, but in the American Republic one can find no negative correlation between educational level and belief in God. It is possible to go further. Even graduate students—even graduate students at the best colleges and universities in the country—still seem to believe in Him, and indeed still participate in religious services. It would appear, therefore, that if God indeed is dead, He is only dead for some of the senior faculty, or at least they would rather like to believe He is dead.

Atheists and secular theologians repeatedly insist that sociologists confirm the irrelevance of God and religion for modern man, but rarely if ever do they say who these sociologists are, and in fact both the sociological theorists, such as Talcott Parsons, and the empirical researchers do not believe that God and religion are irrelevant for modern Americans. It would appear that modern man who does not need God is almost as mythical as a secular city which does not need the sacred.

Two responses are generally given to this attempt of the sociologist to fall back on its theory, its empirical data, to question the alleged demise of the Deity. It is first of all said that even if modern Americans do believe in God, they're not "really" religious, and that the religion they practice is not authentic. Presumably at some undetermined point in the past, religion was authentic and no longer is. But this line of argumentation is another manifestation of the "good old days" fallacy that somehow or other in the past things were better than they are now. There is no evidence to support this, but there is a fair amount of evidence that hypocrisy, skepticism, agnosticism, unbelief, and lukewarm belief are a given part of the religious condition, and not a modern discovery. We are told that the traditional religions are irrelevant. Maybe they are. Maybe they always were.

Secondly, it is said that while Americans may believe in God, they don't believe in a "personal" God. But we must then face the question of what "personal" means. It clearly didn't mean the same thing to the fathers of the Council of Chalcedon as it does in the modern world. To the contemporary man, "person" means "someone like us," "a human being," or a "being with limitations." When modern man rejects the idea of God as a person, he is often rejecting merely the anthropomorphic fundamentalism which is the logical result of man's inevitable tendency to create God in his own image and likeness. It is contended that by calling God "the ground of being," or "the Ultimate Concern," man's faith in Him has actually been weakened because the God described is more abstract. How an abstract description weakens faith is difficult to understand. It may merely purify it of some of its fundamentalist inclinations, but abstraction is not a discovery of the modern world. The *"ipsum esse"* of Thomas Aquinas (which Paul Tillich considered as an alternative to his "ground of being"), and the "logos" of the early Church were surely abstract terms that hardly indicated a weakness of faith. Exactly what God is and how you describe Him has always been a considerable problem to man, but the fundamentalist notion of God ought not to be the benchmark of religious faith.

There are more sophisticated arguments in favor of the position that God is dead, or at least that He is irrelevant. We are told that the notion of God is not in keeping with modern scientific thought, or that modern linguistic philosophy has revealed that it is impossible for us to talk about God, or finally, that man can survive without God. It is fair, I think, to say that these are the three basic arguments used by the agnostic intellectual, though in most instances, one fears, he repeats them as dogmatically as the fundamentalist preacher quotes the Bible or the old-fashioned moralist quoted canon law.

Given the historical origins of the conflict between science and religion, one would be ill-advised to argue that the conflict is either unnecessary or nonexistent. Nevertheless, one wonders if those who are so sure that God and science are incompatible have taken a very close look at either. Theologians like Rudolph Bultman have argued that modern scientific man can't accept myths—that, for example, he who attempts to analyze the behavior of micro- or macro-matter can hardly accept the "myth" of the Resurrection. The truth, on the contrary, is that the scientist can and does accept myths. And not only that, even if he is an agnostic, he is inclined to make his own myths. As a matter of fact, he is inclined to create them in his science. Thus the "marvelous ether" of Lord Kelvin and Helmholtz was nothing but a myth conceived as a necessary support for the Newtonian concept of the cosmos as a machine, which in itself was a form of myth. Furthermore, a reading of histories of scientific thought (such as Jaki, *The Relevance of Physics*) reveals that the great scientists are men of faith. They do not necessarily believe in God or religion; but in the absence of a faith in the rationality and intelligibility of the universe, and faith even in their own pursuit of understanding of the universe, they simply cannot work. Whether he likes it or not, the scientist commits an act of faith by making assumptions that he cannot scientifically verify. Indeed, a number of historians and philosophers of science, such as Whitehead, have argued that it was only long centuries of faith (over which the Christian Church presided) in the order and rationality of the universe that made possible the breakthroughs of modern science.

Furthermore, the history of science also shows how many scientific "certainties" which no one would dream of questioning collapse in the face of new discoveries, as the traditional model of the atom collapsed before the theories of Niels Bohr or Kelvin's "marvelous ether" collapsed before the experiment of Michelson and Morley and the quantum theory of Max Planck. Furthermore, contemporary scientists admit that while they know a lot more about the world than they did even a quarter of a century ago, they also realize that there is much more yet to be known than they would have believed a quarter of a century ago. The discovery of positive electrons and blue stellar sources has merely confirmed how much must yet be learned about the expanse of space and the depths of the atom.

None of this is intended as criticism of science, whose proper role is to continue to explore the unknown and to revise its previously established ideas in the light of new discoveries. But the point is that the scientific confidence of the high school or college textbook does not correspond to the nature of current scientific research, and the notion of a conflict between science and religion based on the textbook image of science ought not to be taken too seriously. Science has yet to unlock all the mysteries of the world, and even if or when it does, the ability to describe how the universe operates does not and cannot answer the ultimate questions of how the universe came to be, or why. There surely have been many superstitious notions about the behavior of the universe which at one time were identified with religion. We know now, for example, that thunder is not a sign of God's anger, nor are earthquakes or volcanic eruptions. But knowledge of what causes thunder, earthquakes and volcanoes does not, in itself, offer insights into why the world is or how it came to be.

The scientist, or one should say, the devotee of scientism, suggests that we cannot say whether there is a God because He is not empirically verifiable. But scientists themselves are committed to many assumptions which are not verifiable, and the God that could be verified by the experimental method would hardly be a God at all. Further, the "scientist" overlooks the fact that many of his colleagues do believe in God and do engage in religious devotions; the physical scientist and the chemist are more likely to do so than the social scientist or the humanist, whose image of the nature and accomplishments of science is likely to be both oversimplified and old-fashioned compared to the models held by the men who are actually engaged in scientific effort. Historically, there has been tension between religion and science, and that tension is likely to continue. Quite possibly, however, Chesterton was not incorrect when he said the battle between science and religion was the battle between private opinions about what religion means and premature opinions about what science means. In any case, two things must be asserted:

Science does involve faith in certain assumptions which it cannot itself verify.

Science is not able, and in fact does not claim to be able, to answer the "why" question of the universe or of human life.

We are also told by the practitioners of the philosophy of language that it is impossible for man to talk about God and that therefore the God question is an irrelevant question. In some sense they are correct, of course. God talk is extremely imprecise, metaphorical, and deceptive. It is good that we be constantly aware of how inaccurate our language is for coping with the questions of the ultimate, but when contemporary philosophers say that man cannot talk about God, they are, to a considerable extent, engaging in a form of snobbery. What they mean is that man cannot talk about God with the precision of language they demand of themselves in their philosophizing. But this does not mean that man has given up, or will give up, talking about God. Man, in fact, can and does talk about God and about many of the other things which language philosophers say he shouldn't talk about, and it is most unlikely that he will cease to do so. One sometimes has the impression, when dealing with those who are obsessed with the meaning of language, that they are not eager to permit us to talk about anything beyond the difficulty of talking about anything. But it is certainly not my intention to adopt an obscurantist attitude toward language philosophy. It has an extremely important role to play in enabling us to understand ourselves and the world in which we live and the way we speak about both. But when it paralyzes us from discussing, however imperfectly, critical questions of meaning, then it may have outlived its usefulness and indeed imperiled its own position, because logically it should not even permit itself to talk about the meaning of meaning, for even its language about language is likely to be imprecise and deceptive.

Perhaps the most effective argument of the agnostics is that man can survive without God and many men, in fact, can and do survive without believing in Him. I say this argument is the most effective because it is the one that apparently causes the most trouble for nervous theists, whether they be theologians or college students. One could reply that many other men can survive nicely and be thoroughly committed to this world while they do believe in God, and that, presumably, God does not depend on the number of His worshipers. It would also be possible to analyze in somewhat greater detail the lives of agnostics to determine whether they do, in fact, survive comfortably without God, or whether they have developed God substitutes, and indeed, a whole faith of their own. Finally, and perhaps most effectively, we could describe as the young British lay theologian Brian Wicker does quite tellingly, how the humanism of the agnostic contains within it an implicit but undeniable demand for resurrection. In Wicker's words: "The Christian is but the humanist who is sure of the ground on which he stands." The humanist goal of self-fulfillment is bound eventually to be wrecked on the shoals of the problem of death. The goal of the constantly expanding human personality cannot logically cope with the idea of death. In practice, as a matter of fact, many humanists survive happily in life only by repressing as well as they can the prospect of death, and refusing to pay much attention to it when it has happened to someone who is important to them. The question of death and the Christian context of resurrection is, I think, the area for most effective dialogue between Christians and humanists, and the humanists are in no position yet to be able to assert that an ultimately satisfactory and satisfying explanation of human life can be evolved which does not ultimately offer an explanation of death.

More recently it has been argued that the whole debate about the existence of God is unfruitful. Leslie Dewart, for example, has suggested that the critical question is whether God is present, though it is not clear to me exactly what he means by that question. I would prefer to rephrase the issue so that it is expressed by the question of whether being is gracious.

By "being," I mean, in the present context, human life, the world, and our own existence. By "gracious," I mean not merely good, but beneficent—that is to say, bestowing goodness. One thinks, for example, of a "gracious" woman as one who is charming, pleasant, accepting, rewarding, one who communicates her goodness to those around her. Thus the question ought to be not so much whether there is a God, but whether life has meaning, purpose, beauty, rationality that is gracious, or whether it does not. The answer to this question is not immediately obvious. It appears often that life is not gracious and is dominated by suffering, tragedy, cruelty, insanity, irrationality, and death. On the other hand, it does contain beauty, goodness, love, fidelity, generosity, and hope. The data are mixed and of themselves do not force us to an immediate conclusion. Man can take a stand for or against the graciousness of being only by making a leap of faith—a leap that says that, in the final analysis, either the good or the evil he observes in the data is illusory. Agnosticism is simply a refusal to risk making the leap in either direction, and is nothing more than an updated version of the Manichee refusal to decide. The Manichees postulated two gods—two principles of being—one good and one evil. The agnostic won't make the leap either. For him the functional equivalent of the two principles of being is a shrug of the shoulders and the comment that he is unable to answer the question.

In practice, however, most agnostics choose one solution or the other, implicitly and unconsciously; in my experience most of them do, in some fashion or other, decide for a graciousness of being, a graciousness they are unable to explain and which they do not even wish to talk about. (As my colleague Peter Rossi once said, "Every time I try and talk about it I get a headache.") Indeed, the overwhelming majority of the human race has in the past, and still does, choose to be optimistic about the meaning of life. While such an issue cannot be settled by a majority vote, it still must be conceded that the vote of the majority is suggestive.

All men who have ever lived have had to face, one way or another, the issue of whether being is gracious, and no one has had certain evidence which forces him to one decision or the other. Faith in the purposefulness of life or the irrationality of life is no easier and no more difficult today than it has ever been. The problem is further complicated by the fact that many of those who claim to be theists—that is, claim to believe in God, and thus in the graciousness of being—are, in fact, atheists. Their attitude toward the world, toward their fellow men, and toward life itself, is characterized not by hopefulness but by negativism and despair. Furthermore, some of those who have claimed to be atheists, or at least agnostics, do, in fact, commit themselves, implicitly and semiconsciously, to some kind of conviction that life does have rationality, purpose, beauty, and goodness, though they are hard put to explain what it is and would probably resent the theists' claim that they are brothers under the skin (closer brothers, in fact, than the theist is with many of his own coreligionists, who are, whether they are willing to admit it or not, practicing atheists).

The second question that must be asked is whether the principle of the graciousness of being is a person. If, as we have said before, by "person" we mean someone rather like us, then we must cheerfully concede that this principle of rationality, purpose, goodness, and beauty in the world, is hardly a person. But do we mean that he is, in Martin Buber's words, someone who can be addressed as "Thou"? Here again we come to a question that can only be answered by a leap of faith, though it must be noted that most people are prepared to behave as though they can, in fact, address this principle of graciousness as "Thou," and more than that, as a Thou who is a lover—a lover who speaks to us most seductively:

My Beloved lifts up his voice,
he says to me,
"Come then, my love,
my lovely one, come.
For see, winter is past,
the rains are over and gone.
The flowers appear on the earth.
The season of glad songs has come,
the cooing of the turtledove is heard
in our land.
The fig tree is forming its first figs
and the blossoming vines give out their fragrance.
Come then, my love,
my lovely one, come.
My dove, hiding in the clefts of the rock,
in the coverts of the cliff,
show me your face,
let me hear your voice;
for your voice is sweet
and your face is beautiful." (Song of Songs 2:10–14)

One must also ask whether this principle of graciousness is "distant" from the world. Does he transcend it? Is he "totally other" or is he simply to be identified with the world? In some sense he must go out beyond the world because He (or It) is distinct from the nongraciousness of the world. But on the other hand, he cannot be totally distinct from the world—totally distinct from it—because the world of graciousness at least is a manifestation of that of which he is the principle, so therefore as contradictory as it may seem, we must affirm that the principle of the graciousness of being is both beyond human life and within it, though how this can be worked out in practice we must leave to philosophers and theologians.

It is not the purpose of this chapter to develop a formal apology for God or religion, but rather to summarize the issues as they exist in our time and to suggest the direction which dialogue over these issues should take. But if we are to attempt such a dialogue, we must understand that the issues are discussed in a context which is distinct from them and theoretically separable, but which historically has become closely linked with such issues. Agnosticism is not merely a theoretical position about God, but a historical result of the unfortunate style in which the discussion has proceeded for the past several centuries.

Why can agnostics implicitly, or even explicitly, accept the notion that being is gracious, and even that life may have a purpose beyond itself, and still reject the Christian notion of God and religion? There are a number of pointed answers. The God they reject is often the "God out there" of the Bishop of Woolwich, a God who is distinct from the world and doesn't really care much about what happens to it so long as He is able to snatch human souls out of it—a God, by the way, that Catholic theological tradition does not know. Secondly, they are affronted by a God that produces a world that is not to be valued for its own sake—a God that Harvey Cox rightly criticizes as imposing on men such concern for the next life that they feel no responsibilities to this life other than working out their own personal salvations while they are alive—a God and a world which Catholicism does not know in its basic theory, however it may behave in practice.

They are further offended by the obscurantism, fundamentalism, and conservatism of the churches (a church which, one suspects, God does not want to be identified with), and they are angered at religion as an excuse for attempting to obstruct human history.

Finally, the agnostics find themselves unimpressed by a God whose followers were not troubled by injustice, misery, oppression, and poverty—followers whom God has sent a number of messengers to denounce as roundly as the agnostics denounce them. In other words, what agnostics reject is often a caricature of God and a caricature of religious belief and practice—a caricature, one must confess, that comes perilously close to typifying certain kinds of religious instruction and religious activity.

One wonders if the agnostics are going to be converted by the radical or secular theologians. As Martin Marty has suggested, the agnostics seem much more impressed by a restatement of traditional religion in contemporary terms than by a description of it which implies that there is really no difference between theism and agnosticism:

> Why do my agnostic contemporaries feel compelled to read the spiritual *Markings* of an almost-mystical administrative secretary named Hammarskjöld while they can overlook the "candor" and "honesty" of bishops striving to be relevant, modern and acceptable? Why do they bypass the apologies which make Christianity so natural and so easy, in order to follow the curious *Journal of a Soul* of Pope John? Why does a Margharita Laski, as an agnostic writing in *Punch*, let us know she is curious about the Church of the ages, but not in the "radical Christianity" of accommodationist bishops?

> Could it be that a more angular, somewhat misfit kind of Church and churchman, something or some one with a treasure or secret which is not superficially and facilely appropriated and exhausted becomes both a more compelling witness and servant?[1]

The theologian who adopts the strategy that Marty criticizes may reassure himself and his colleagues on the divinity school faculties by his argument that you can be an agnostic and a Christian at the same time, but he is not likely to persuade anyone else, except perhaps a befuddled fundamentalist graduate student.[2]

[1] Martin Marty, in an article by Robert Hovda, *The Critic*, February–March, 1968.

[2] Sometimes it is argued that ours is an age without God because there is so much religious doubt. However, doubt, at least in the nontechnical sense of the word, is not a sign of religious weakness, but rather of religious ferment. Anyone familiar with the nature and extent of doubt among young people is also well aware that it often represents an attempt of the young person to achieve religious maturity—to translate the faith of his childhood

Ultimately, decisions about being, God, and the Resurrection are based on faith, and the purpose of this chapter is not to convert anyone, but rather to establish clearly several points:

The evidence for the "death of God" or its irrelevancy is meager.

One's religious commitment or religious noncommitment, such as the case may be, is based on faith. The atheist and the agnostic must leap beyond the empirical data, as does the theist, though the agnostic tries to hide the fact that he has made the leap. The arguments advanced from science, philosophy, and human experience against the existence of God merely establish that those who advance the arguments do not understand the nature of the question, since the ultimate question is not whether science can explain how the world operates, but rather whether it can explain why the world is.

This issue is complicated even more by the fact that theism has historically been identified, and not without reason, with the forces of reaction and withdrawal. It is possible to be a secularist—that is to say, someone profoundly concerned about this world—and not be an agnostic. In fact, we would be inclined to say that it is impossible to be a good Catholic unless one is a secularist in the sense we have defined the term, as the Catholic is profoundly concerned about the redemption and the resurrection of the material world.

The real problem is, in fact, the Resurrection, as Brian Wicker, almost alone among the so-called theological radicals, has pointed out. And ultimately the question is not whether there is or is not a resurrection, but whether being can be gracious without resurrection.

The question of resurrection would not have arisen if it were not for the Christian resurrection promise and the hope that it has brought into the world. Christian hope has produced a powerful historical dynamism which, unfortunately, detached from its Christian roots, is the mainstream

---

and adolescence into a system of meaning for adulthood. The crisis of faith is merely a crisis of religious growth and maturation, and if young people feel free to honestly face this crisis today, it is notable progress for the human race and for religion.

of contemporary humanism. In pre-Christian times there was a vague faith in another world, a Hades or Sheol, which in some of its catechetical manifestations has often resembled a Christian heaven. In Hades or Sheol there was not much; little life or vitality or activity. The idea that the goal of human life is some unexciting, nonhuman afterlife—an afterlife that is more "after" than "life"—is what many humanists reject in Christianity. But the Gospels know little of an ethereal, detached human soul or of an afterlife, or of a heaven detached from a sanctified world. The Gospels and the whole New Testament deal with something much more startling—Resurrection. The Lord has promised that he who eats His flesh and drinks His blood shall never die. The scandal of Christianity is not that it rejects the world, as many agnostics think, and unfortunately, as many Christians think, but rather that it proclaims that death is an illusion, that life continues after death.

Since the question has been raised, and since the hope it has generated has been kept alive for two millennia, there may be no logical alternatives other than these two: you believe in the Resurrection, and hence you believe in Jesus of Nazareth, or you believe in non-Resurrection, and you do not believe in Jesus of Nazareth. And among those who subscribe to the latter position are those who, in some sort of de-idolized folk-Catholic version of heaven, ignore the fact that resurrection in the Gospels is described precisely as a triumph over death.

In the world after Christ, then, is it possible to believe in the graciousness of being without believing in resurrection? Brian Wicker suggests that it is not, that humanism demands the resurrection:

By showing that this meeting of nature and grace has already taken place, in the life, death and resurrection of Christ, Christianity is able to offer an intelligible, even if incredible, perspective in which the humanist moral vision can be freed from its own intolerable paradox. The fact that to most people the Christian perspective is incredible is relatively unimportant. For the first thing that is demanded is a perspective which is relevant. Only if Christianity first appears to offer a concept which is meaningful, can the possibility of its being true be raised . . . the relevance of the Christian concept of death is that in it, death becomes something I enact, as a person who is in control. It is not consigning the body which I am to oblivion, but consigning it to the possibility of its own completion from beyond itself. That this completion (or "glorification") seems incredible to the humanist is due not only to limited moral vision but to his entanglement with a secularist philosophy that cannot fully support it. He cannot fully trust his own instinct. The Christian is simply a humanist who has learnt to trust the ground upon which he stands.[3]

If Wicker is right, and I am persuaded that he is, the secular and radical theologians have missed the point. In an era after Jesus Christ there cannot be hope without resurrection, particularly since the dynamic that Jesus Christ introduced into the world has created a belief in the dignity of the human person and the power of his love. One cannot conceive, in the final analysis, that man in his goodness and love perish. It is the humanist rather than the Christian who must be placed on the defensive, and Brian Wicker does just this by contending that our humanism is a fuller humanism than theirs because our humanism conquers death, as any true humanism must. If fulfillment is to be aborted by death, then man is better off without personalism. The choice, then, since the Gospel of Jesus raised the issue, is not between the vague optimism of the secular agnostics and the equally vague hereafter of the fundamentalist Christians (who seem to have forgotten the fundamentals); as long as the radical and the secularist theologians see the issues this way, they will never be taken seriously. The choice is rather between the brave despair of a Jean Paul Sartre or the bright hope of the resurrection humanist. Either choice requires faith, and neither can be proved from the empirical evidence available.

But the secularist and atheist theologians respond that the Resurrection is a myth and not a reality. One may concede,

[3] Brian Wicker, *Toward a Contemporary Christianity* (Notre Dame: University of Notre Dame Press, 1967), pp. 258–59.

perhaps, to them that some of the categories used to describe the Resurrection and the New Testament are allegorical and that some of the precise details of the description of the Lord's resurrection were not meant to be taken literally, though this is a technical matter for scriptural scholars to discuss. But as Jürgen Moltmann has decisively pointed out, the important question about a myth is what it means, and it is extremely clear what the "myth" of the Resurrection meant to the men who wrote about it and to the men who preached it. They did not take it as some vague allegory about mankind's ultimate triumph over evil; they took it rather as a statement of personal faith in their own personal destiny. As Moltmann observes, not to accept it in radically the same sense as they accepted it is to have no continuity with the central theories of Christianity.

Believing in God, therefore, at least for the Christian, is not merely an assertion of acceptance of the "Great Hangman in the Sky," or even in the graciousness of being, or that being is a Thou, indeed a Thou which transcends, in part at least, the visible world. It is also, and more specifically, the conviction that death is an illusion and that Jesus came primarily as a man of hope, a man of promise, an eschatological man, and, indeed, a personal eschaton, at that.

In the context of the present volume, this concept is important not merely as a statement of the core of the Christian faith, but also as a description of the basic dynamic which has brought first the Western world, and then the whole world, to its present critical dilemma. It is the possibility of faith and faith in possibility that has made possible the revolutions in science, technology, and knowledge, as well as the conviction of the dignity and freedom of the human person, hope in human progress, and faith in love, friendship, and community. These are all Christian notions and they have come into the world only where the Christian tradition has existed (and its brother tradition, the Jewish one); they have become temporarily, and from the Christian viewpoint, tragically separated from the Christian tradition largely through the fault of Christians themselves. From the point of view of the man of faith, the dynamic of hope which the Resurrection introduced into the world will be saved from the cataclysm of destruction and despair only by that institution which has present in its midst the personified eschaton himself.

Perhaps the greatest tragedy in the history of the last two millennia is that the Christian churches have somehow managed to place themselves in a position where they appear to be in opposition to the very dynamic of hope which they brought to the world. We have permitted the formulations of our religion, in their ordinary preaching and teaching manifestations, to cause us to miss two critical points: The Resurrection is a foundation for hope for a progressive pilgrimage, and the world is valuable not merely as a locus for redemption and resurrection, but also as destined for salvation and resurrection itself, because man—the focus of resurrection—is irrevocably part of the world. Even though we were told by St. Peter that we look forward to new heavens and new earth, we have all too frequently forgotten the implications of this statement for our own view of man in the world.

We have allowed ourselves to be backed into a corner where the humanist may accuse us of rejecting man in favor of his soul and rejecting this world in favor of some vague otherworld, when in fact we ought to be preaching, if we are true to our essential tradition, that we believe in life for the whole man (and hence are protohumanists) and in the life that this whole man brings to the whole world (and hence we are, in fact, the protosecularists). We have, further, permitted God to get caught in categories that have no meaning today, not even the meaning they had when they were first used. We have tried to reduce faith to a series of propositions concerning given doctrines which are fixed in their formulations, even though the formulations were culture-bound and less than complete in their own time and are woefully less than complete as an adequate statement of faith in our time.

This dismal performance is even more astonishing when one considers that the central doctrine of the New Testament is the Resurrection (with all its implications for value of the human body and material world), and the central ethic is charity (with its implications for friendship with our fellow men). In a world, then, where personal love, the human body, and secular values are given a high order of importance, we frequently do not respond by saying, "Of course they are, we've always said they are." On the contrary, far more frequently we act as though the central doctrine of our faith is papal infallibility, and the central ethic is either birth control or Sunday church attendance (now that Friday abstinence has been deposed). When such accusations are leveled at us, we say, "Well of course charity and resurrection are critical, but we have always assumed them, and the important things today are papal authority and sexual ethics." The only honest reply to this probably could not be printed in a book intended for general circulation. We therefore must content ourselves with the observation that resurrection and charity can never be assumed and that any time the Christian Church is not preaching these two values, in season and out, it is falling far short of its own vision.

Many theological problems remain unanswered after these socioreligious speculations. We must know more about what we can say positively of God besides: He is the source of graciousness and someone who can be addressed as God. We must try to understand more clearly how God is present in Jesus; some theologians argue that the development of the Chalcedon formulation of the incarnation (two natures, one person) is the next critical breakthrough area for theological speculation. Some Catholics are terrified by the prospect, though it seems to me that men of faith can only rejoice in the possibility of understanding more deeply the meaning of Jesus of Nazareth. We must further probe into the mystery of death and resurrection; and finally, since it is perfectly clear that doctrine does develop and evolve, and that much of our present problem results from the refusal to face the phenomenon of development, we must come to understand much better than we do now the nature of doctrinal development.

The questions, then, of the theology of Christ, death, resurrection, and doctrinal development are very likely to become much more intense in the years to come, if the assumptions of this book are correct. As human love becomes more intense and human passion more understanding and joyous, human friendship communities more rewarding, human leadership more sophisticated, the human self more trusting, and the humanized world a better place to play in, death is going to become more and more intolerable. It will become increasingly apparent to the world that the Christian resurrection dynamic has brought all these things to be, and had it not been for Christianity, we would not have begun our pilgrimage to love, friendship, community, trust, and playfulness. Men will rail against us; they will demand to know how we could have dared to raise human hopes and be unable to sustain them. They will argue that perhaps originally we did not hunger for the Absolute Lover but that you, the Christian Church, gave us this hunger. They will say that it was your dynamic of hope that has brought us to this critical condition where we will either dramatically transform ourselves or destroy ourselves. If you had left us alone this would never have happened. We would have been better off if you had never disturbed us. He who raises our hopes only to dash them to the ground is guilty of torturing us. You caused us to come this far on our pilgrimage—do you mean that now you have no idea where we are to go next? We have no choice now but to turn ourselves to friendship, community, and playfulness, but we do not know how, and you seem unwilling to teach us. It hardly needs to be noted that Christians had better be ready with answers.

For when men ask these questions of us they will be asking whether there really is a Lover who is capable of total trust, a Lover who so loved us that He gave himself completely for us, a Lover who says to us:

I awakened you under the apple tree,
there where your mother conceived you,
there where she who gave birth to you conceived you.

Set me like a seal on your heart,
Like a seal on your arm.
For love is strong as Death,
jealousy relentless as Sheol.
The flash of it is a flash of fire,
a flame of Yahweh himself.
Love no flood can quench,
no torrents drown.   (Song of Songs 8:5–7)

Chapter 9

A SACRED TO CELEBRATE

We argued in the last chapter that the Christian who understands his own tradition must be a vigorous secularist because not only does he claim, as does his humanist brother, that the material world has a value; he also claims that it's so valuable he does not intend to permit it to come to an end. He claims that he has, in fact, a message of hope that it will not come to an end because man, the most important part of the material world, is not going to die. The secular city, therefore, ought to be a city in which the Christian feels perfectly at home. But the word "secular," like most other intensely popular words, has acquired many meanings. We are told that you can only commit yourself to the secular when you reject the sacred; to the this-worldly, when you reject the other-worldly; to the mundane, when you reject the transcendental. The appropriate Catholic response ought to be, of course, that the secular is sacred and the this-worldly is merely a down payment on the next-worldly; that the mundane is destined for transcendence. But unfortunately, this answer has not been given clearly enough or vigorously enough.

Therefore, the sacred, the totally other, simultaneously fascinating and terrifying, the ecstatic, frenzied, that ultimate reality which imposes meaning and order on our own lower level of reality, is now distinctly out of fashion. And authors such as Rudolf Otto, William James, Mircea Eliade, Emile Durkheim, on whose description of the sacred we relied in the last sentence, are considered to be speaking not of man in the present, but man in the past. We use the word "sacred" so frequently and so loosely in our conversation that it is difficult to say precisely what it is. It is quite clear that some things appear to be sacred—the Roman Catholic mass, the speaking of tongues at the Pentecostal meeting, the hearth fire of the family of the Roman Republic, the rites of passage for an adolescent of a primitive tribe. We are also quite conscious that many other things are not sacred, at least for most people—turning on the ignition key in a car, opening a book, dialing for a telephone number, walking across the street. Unfortunately, there are a number of phenomena that are not so easily categorized—the funeral of John F. Kennedy (at least, once it left the Catholic Cathedral), the celebrations of Memorial Day and the Fourth of July, so astutely described by Lloyd Warner in his *Yankee City* series of books, the singing of the national anthem before an athletic contest, and the recitation of the Lord's Prayer by the Green Bay Packers after they have disposed of another hapless foe. The sacred is clearly something that leads us to behave with reverence and respect—something out of the ordinary, something apart from the mundane experiences of everyday life—though just as clearly, not everything that is extraordinary is sacred, and furthermore, what is sacred for one man need not be sacred for another, even if they share a common religious faith. Thus some Catholics would have felt that Pope Paul's visit to New York and the United Nations was a highly sacred event, while others, no less devout in their Catholicism, were not so vigorously moved by the papal visitation. Under such circumstances, we will be unable to evolve a definition of the sacred that will tell us precisely where the line between the sacred and the profane is to be drawn. We can at least listen to some of the voices that have attempted to describe sacredness so as to get a feel of what it really is. A category of thought and response so basic to human life, or at least so basic to most human lives, probably cannot be defined in any other way.

In the third lecture of his classic *Varieties of Religious Experience*, William James offers a collection of superb descriptions of man's encounters with God. In one of them he writes:

> I remember the night, and almost the very spot on the hilltop, where my soul opened out, as it were, into the Infinite, and there was a rushing together of the two worlds,

the inner and the outer. It was deep calling unto deep—the deep that my own struggle had opened up within being answered by the unfathomable deep without, reaching beyond the stars. I stood alone with Him who had made me, and all the beauty of the world, and love, and sorrow, and even temptation. I did not seek Him, but felt the perfect unison of my spirit with His. The ordinary sense of things around me faded. For the moment nothing but an ineffable joy and exaltation remained. It is impossible fully to describe the experience. It was like the effect of some great orchestra when all the separate notes have melted into one swelling harmony that leaves the listener conscious of nothing save that his soul is being wafted upwards, and almost bursting with its own emotion. The perfect stillness of the night was thrilled by a more solemn silence. The darkness held a presence that was all the more felt because it was not seen. I could not any more have doubted that He was there than that I was. Indeed, I felt myself to be, if possible, the less real of the two![1]

After reading such a paragraph, one is reminded of Duke Ellington's definition of rhythm: "If you got it you don't need a definition, and if you haven't got it no definition will help." Ecstatic experience of the sort just described doesn't happen to everybody. And even minor religious ecstasies are anything but universal. However, one can take it as pretty well established that some form of contact with the sacred, in a very much diminished fashion perhaps, has been experienced at some time by most people.

There are many phenomena that can occur in man's life which can take him outside himself, giving him the feeling of being released from the bonds of limitation, matter, and mortality and putting him in touch with the transcendent. By no means are all of them religious, though there does seem to be a tendency to equate many of them with religion—for example, the frequent use of religious terms in describing the effects of the hallucinogenic drugs. However, if not all

[1] William James, *Varieties of Religious Experience* (New York: The New American Library of World Literature, Inc., 1961), p. 67.

ecstatic experiences, major or minor, some of them are and men who have experienced the ecstasy of the sacred are quite clear that it is not the same thing as the ecstasy of art or of love, much less of alcohol—even though there are similarities in the various experiences.

Perhaps the classic description of man's reaction to that which he perceives as sacred appears in *Dasheilige* by the German philosopher and theologian Rudolf Otto. Otto says that there is, first of all, a feeling of terror in the face of the sacred, in the face of the awe-inspiring majesty (*mysterium tremendum*) and also a fear before a fascinating mystery (*mysterium fascinans*). This *mysterium tremendium fascinosan* results from man's contact with what Otto describes as a numinous and an experience of the revelation of an aspect of divine power. The numinous appears as something "wholly other" (*ganz andere*), something basically and totally different from man and before which man feels, as Abraham did before the Lord, that he is nothing but "dust and ashes."

The most careful students of the sacred, at least at the present time, are not, however, sociologists, who view it more or less in passing as they attempt to analyze human behavior in society, but rather a group of scholars who used to be called comparative religionists and are now called historians of religion. These men, of whom perhaps the most famous is Mircea Eliade, have attempted to find common patterns of religious behavior running through all, or almost all, the religious systems man has devised for himself. For Eliade the sacred is a hierophany, an experience of the nonhomogeneity of the world, a break between that which is ordinary and that which is a hierophany. There are, for example, two kinds of space—the ordinary, everyday space in which ordinary, everyday events take place, and "sacred space," that which man experiences as a manifestation of a divinity.

The sacral, according to Eliade, is experienced by religious man as the wholly other "breaking in" to ordinary experience and giving order and meaning to them just as sacred space (ground for worship or a temple or merely a tabooed area) gives meaning to ordinary space. Thus sacred times give meaning to ordinary times, and sacred rights give meaning to ordinary behavior. Eliade and his colleagues find that in most human religions there are certain key manifestations of the sacred—the sky, the sun, the moon, water, stones, earth, fertility, and trees, and on occasion, a single tree. The explanation of these nearly universal patterns is not always the same. Some writers lean to a version of Jung's collective unconsciousness; others speak of the structure of the human personality; and still others speak of "the patterns of man's reaction to existential situation." We probably do not know enough at present about cross-cultural psychology to explain, for example, why in most religions water has both the birth and death sacred symbolism, but it does, and that sacred water bringing life and death apparently enabled religious man (and still enables him) to explain the tremendous power that water exercises in human life.

As one reads through the literature of the sacred, it begins to become clear that there are two kinds of extraordinariness which seem to produce reactions that traditionally have been called religious: One is that kind of phenomenon which simultaneously imposes upon man a demand for explanation while it provides him with an explanation. The second is that sort of phenomenon which both imposes on man and provides him with a sense of being profoundly related to his fellow men. Sacredness, then, relates to man's experience of the need for meaning and the need for belonging, as well as the fulfillment of these needs. Not all meaning and all belonging, of course, excite sacred attitudes and behavior, but more precisely, those which fall into the area of the ultimate can be expected to produce in men reverence and awe for something that is outside themselves and belongs to the wholly other.

One can think of many examples of both aspects of the sacred. John F. Kennedy's funeral was a means of reaffirming faith in American society. The fertility rites of the nature religions which Eliade discusses at great length were designed as an intermediate step between the annual planting, cultivating, and harvesting of crops and the sacred realities which this process reflected. The magic words "Julie Andrews" in the movie *Bedazzled* are an explanation of the power of Mephistopheles to produce strange and wonderful effects.

Similarly, the worship owed by a Roman of the time of the Republic to his ancestors, and in fact the organization of much of the society around the principles of this worship, was an affirmation of man's unity with his family and his people. The rites of passage in primitive (and some not so primitive) religions which mark major points in the life cycle—birth, adolescence, marriage, maturity—thus reassure man at critical times in his life that he is indeed part of something larger than himself. The specific religion of American society based on such national demigods as George Washington and Abraham Lincoln, such national myths as the Civil War, such national feasts as Memorial Day, the Fourth of July, and Thanksgiving, reaffirm the basic unity of American society. Man wants to know why and with whom. The sacred represents the ultimate responses to these questions, a religion, man's reaction to such responses.

Man learns his interpretation of reality through social interaction. He is able to explain the apparently disordered phenomena around him precisely insofar as he is integrated into a culture which transmits to him as part of his socialization process a series of propositions and attitudes which enable him to interpret life. Similarly, it is the sharing of explanations and interpretations which provide the common bonds of unity and enables man to unite himself with his fellow men. Throughout most of human history religion has provided meaning and belonging simultaneously. Religious men would not have seen much point in a distinction. However, these two aspects of religion have been divorced in the modern urban industrial world, and there has been a strong tendency by those who try to analyze religion to emphasize one aspect or the other. Most recently in the United States, it seems that the social scientists, have emphasized the meaning dimension of religion, while the religious critics have emphasized the belonging dimension of American religion, a dimension which, by the way, they distinctly dislike. We will contend that only by giving serious consideration to both elements of religion are we able to understand why America has become a denominational society.

We can now address ourselves once again to the question of whether all men are religious, defining "religious" as relating in some fashion explicitly to the sacred. We can say, first of all, that most men in most societies have been more or less religious. Some anthropologists, such as Geertz, suggest that there has been too much emphasis on the "more" and not enough on the "less," and that unbelief and skepticism are by no means modern phenomena. He even goes so far as to suggest that someday a book might be called *Facing Hypocrisy and Hypocrisy in the Primitive World.*

The degree to which men are religious, one supposes among other things, is also the need created by their physiological and psychological systems for explicit affirmation of meaning and fellowship. He who, for one reason or another, does not need to affirm explicitly or consciously "the relatively modest dogma that God is not mad," and the relatively modest ethic that one's fellow man can generally be trusted, will not be religious. Whether such a superior being, modeled somewhat after the existentialist heroes of Sartre or Camus, staring bravely in the face of meaninglessness and loneliness, is superior or inferior to the religious man is a question which is beyond the scope of this volume.

Having thus elaborated on at least a working description of the sacred, we can turn to the question of secularization, which might have any one of nine different meanings:

It might mean that man no longer honors the symbols of meaning and belonging which transcend himself. This meaning can easily be rejected out of hand. Most men still do, at least in some fashion or other.

It may mean an enthusiastic concern with this world. Harvey Cox, one of the strongest defenders of this position, describes it in this fashion:

The first is that the God of the Bible does not operate only in and through religious or sacred institutions but through events we might call "secular." The liberation of the Israelites from Egyptian peonage, the conquest of the land of promise, the defeat and exile of the Jews and their deliverance from captivity are examples. Indeed, in this sense the career of Jesus is secular and has been assigned apocalyptic or sacred significance only because of the various prisms through which it has been appropriated. The Crucifixion was a secular event. It has been a truism in recent years to say that "God acts in history." Still, if God is still alive and active, the logic of this position would lead us to try to discern his activity in our present history, and this means in secular events.

The second classical doctrine that necessitates our taking this world with full seriousness is the doctrine of the Incarnation. In Christ, God discloses himself as present for man in the grime and blood, and in the parties and festivals of earth. Nor is the Incarnation to be understood merely as an isolated episode in God's life. It signifies that God is the One who is fully and irretrievably present in the life of men, that God takes our *saeculum* with life-and-death seriousness. A church which does not identify with the world, with the same thorough solidarity that God does, betrays its mission.

The third theological base of secular theology has to do with the traditional doctrine of the Holy Spirit and points more toward the interpretation of doctrines than toward the discernment of the action of God in the secular world. It suggests that our various inherited doctrines arose in the church's effort to speak to differing ages in the history of the world. Thus a proper understanding of these doctrines will be gained only as we involve ourselves in the continuation of this mission in changed circumstances. Traditional theology teaches that the Holy Spirit reveals to believers the true meaning of the Bible. But different generations of Christians have interpreted the same texts in contrasting ways. We can see that the meaning of any text or doctrine is not fixed or closed. Meaning arises as we try in the light of altered conditions to make sense of positions held in the past. To those faithfully involved in God's action in the world, what theologians once called the "Missio Dei," the Holy Spirit, reveals ever new meanings and nuances in the classical doctrines. As the famous Pastor Robinson told the Pilgrim fathers when they set sail for New England, "God has yet new truth to break forth from his Holy Word."[2]

[2] Harvey Cox, "Why Christianity Must Be Secularized," in *Should Christianity Be Secularized? A Symposium.* Reprinted from *The Great Ideas 1967* (Evanston, Illinois: Encyclopaedia Britannica, Inc., 1967), pp. 14–15.

One would not want, in the context of the present volume, to express substantial disagreement with the broad outlines of Cox's position, though many of the conclusions he draws from it might be questionable. Of course God does operate through the whole world. Yes, God is fully and irretrievably present in the life of men. Yes, the Holy Spirit does work in the world. If anyone denies these three truths, they have no claim to be Christian. Neither do these three truths have any particular claim to be theologically revolutionary, which does not diminish one bit their importance.

It may be argued that there is a decline in religion. Man is somehow or other less devout or less believing than he once was. On the face of it, such an assertion is impossible to prove because we have no adequate sophistical evidence from the past with which to compare man's present religious behavior. The only trend study of religion with which I am aware compares 1952 with 1965 and shows no major change in religious faith or behavior among American Gentiles. What man's religious behavior was like in 1852, 1752 or 1652, we must in all honesty say that we do not know with any great deal of precision. But in all likelihood, man is about as religious or irreligious as he has ever been.

By "secularization" we could mean that the world has been demythologized. That is to say, we have a far better understanding of the processes of nature than we did in the past; that we understand how thunder happens; why crops grow; how the earth moves around the sun (the condemners of Galileo to the contrary, notwithstanding); why the weather changes; why volcanoes, hurricanes, earthquakes, tidal waves, and other such natural disasters occur. But such an assertion, while unquestionably true, is neither new nor particularly relevant to man's religious condition. It merely means that man is less superstitious. But it does not mean that he has approached any nearer to ultimate answers which will not require a leap of faith.

Secularization may mean that the direct influence of religion on society has declined. Such an assertion is certainly true, though again it does not represent something that has happened in the 1950s or the 1960s. On the other hand, such sociologists as Talcott Parsons and Robert Bellah are prepared to contend that the indirect influence of religion on society, through the function of shaping man's ultimate belief system, is as powerful as it ever was. Parsons goes on to suggest that many of the so-called secular institutions of society have internalized, to a considerable extent, the ethical values of Christianity, and are therefore implicitly influenced by religion. However, conclude Parsons and Bellah, the striking difference between contemporary religion and religion of the past is not that its influence is now indirect rather than direct, but rather that religious decisions are made not so much by the total community but by the voluntary behavior of free individuals, and that therefore religious influence is necessarily not through the Church as an organization formerly in other organizations, but through individuals who belong simultaneously to the Church and to other social groups. It is worth noting, however, that in American society organized religion still has a considerable influence on national life. While it is not yet possible to say with any precision to what extent efforts of the churches on the racial issue have promoted changing attitudes among white Americans, it is nonetheless true that one study shows that the strongest single predictor of change in religious attitude within a given year is whether one's minister or priest has preached a sermon on race.

Secularization may mean that people are not authentically religious, but as we have suggested in the last chapter, most human beings probably never have been authentically religious.

It may mean that some people can do without the sacred or a transcendent, but as we observed in a previous chapter, most people, including most well-educated people, cannot.

Secularization may simply mean that young people are more inclined to have religious doubts. We may concede this and simply note that what it probably indicates is that young people are now free to make their religious doubts and troubles explicit.

Secularization may mean, as Harvey Cox has argued in *The Secular City*, that nonrational ties are less important in the city than they would have been in the past. That they are less important, one may concede, but that they are unimportant seems almost ludicrous to someone who lives in a conglomerative ethnic coalition like Chicago, Detroit, or New York.

We may conclude, therefore, that the statements of secularization which are true are not new, and those which are new do not seem to be true. And yet the concept of secularization has vast appeal, both because it revolts against the irrelevancies of some manifestations of religious behavior, particularly as they are manifested in a local parish, and because it stresses the importance of activity in this world and indeed is quite optimistic about the outcome of such activity. But some reservations are in order:

If one must choose between optimism and pessimism, then optimism is surely better, though frequently the optimism of the secularist seems mindless. Secondly, stress on the importance of activity in this world is not a recent discovery. It can be found both in the classical Calvinist ethic, to say nothing of the whole incarnational tradition of Catholicism. Thirdly, it seems to be taken as axiomatic by many of the secularists that you cannot give values to the secular unless you reject the sacred. Such an axiom may be true in some religious traditions, but it is hardly true of Christianity, for the dynamic of the resurrection promise has made possible the worldly concern of the Western world and provided the Christian with a way of breaking down the barrier between the sacred and the secular.

Apparently most primitive tribes see the sacred everywhere. Animism, the name for the religion which sees the sacred lurking behind every possible object, even a stick or a stone, is considered to be a very primitive religion because it is not yet able to draw the line between the sacred and the profane. But it is not without its own form of beauty. Colin Turnbull in his book *Forest People* describes how the pygmies think of their musical instrument, the molimo, as a means for communicating with the sacred:

He (Moke) went on to tell that the Pygmies call out their molimo whenever things seem to be going wrong. "It may be that the hunting is bad," he said, "or that someone is ill, or, as now, that someone has died. These are not good things, and we like things to be good. So we call out the molimo and it makes them good, as they should be."

"The forest is a father and mother to us," he said, "and like a father or mother it gives us everything we need—food, clothing, shelter, warmth . . . and affection. Normally everything goes well, because the forest is good to its children, but when things go wrong there must be a reason."

"Normally everything goes well in our world. But at night when we are sleeping, sometimes things go wrong, because we are not awake to stop them from going wrong. Army ants invade the camp; leopards may come in and steal a hunting dog or even a child. If we were awake these things would not happen. So when something big goes wrong, like illness or bad hunting or death, it must be because the forest is sleeping and not looking after its children. So what do we do? We wake it up. We wake it up by singing to it, and we do this because we want it to awaken happy. Then everything will be well and good again. So when our world is going well then also we sing to the forest because we want it to share our happiness."[3]

But as man grew more sophisticated, some activities were defined as sacred and others as not sacred, and the sacred activities were placed under a taboo so that the sacred and the profane might not mix with each other and disturb the order of the world. In still further stages of development, sacred activities and places became rituals and temples involved in the re-enactment of sacred activity and in manifestations of sacred power. In the view of some defenders of secularization, the domain of the sacred has been pushed back until now it operates and occupies only a very small part of society and will soon even be pushed out of this last bailiwick, although as others, such as Talcott Parsons, have suggested, and as we have noted, the sacred merely operates in a more indirect fashion, now that the distinction between the secular and the sacred has reached the ultimate in precision.

However, in the Catholic view the evolution has now come full circle. In Karl Rahner's words: "All is grace." Creation

[3] Colin M. Turnbull, *The Forest People* (New York: Doubleday & Co., The Natural History Library Edition, 1962), pp. 89–90.

and redemption are the same. Mankind's pilgrimage toward fulfillment and the church's pilgrimage toward the resurrection are in some fashion the same pilgrimage. Distinction between the secular and the sacred is therefore irrelevant, and everything is simultaneously secular and sacred. In such a context the world has new value because God became present through the incarnation in Jesus, present in and for the world. Indeed, some human actions are explicitly sacred, but not because they are to be separated from the rest of the world; rather in order that they may symbolize that the rest of the world is, in fact, sacred; is, in fact, destined for resurrection.

Liturgy, then, or worship, is man's contact with the sacred —contact which is sometimes expressed in sacrifices and sacrificial banquets by which he has attempted to establish a commonality with the sacred; other times in ritual dances which are re-enactments of sacred events; and yet other times in rites of passage where the members of a community move from one state of life to another and are the recipients in that act of movement of elements of the sacred tradition they did not previously understand. Worship is man's way of proclaiming publicly his union with other men, with the natural processes, and with the ultimate graciousness of the world. Worship is sacred play, a celebration of man's unity with the past, of his unity with his spouse and sexual intercourse, of his unity with the community and friendship, of his unity with the world in playfulness, and of his unity with God and faith. If liturgy is celebration of unity, and if we can look forward confidently to the future state of man where there will be much more unity, then it seems reasonable to expect that there will be more celebration and hence more worship.

Man is a liturgy-building animal. One need only look at the "sacred" traditions and rituals the American public has built up around its presidency in the brief history of the nation to see that the human urge to sacralize what it finds important is powerful.

Man would therefore have a sacred to worship, to reverence, even if there were not a transcendental. He would pray to God even if there were no God to pray to, for he who does not pray is estranged, cut off, alienated. Man cannot survive as man unless there is a sacred in his life. No one has stated this intriguing theory better than Everett Hughes:

> Those who have the cure of souls—pastors and psychiatrists —can tell better than I what burdens break and what sicknesses ravage the souls of those who, in the name of self-reliance, emancipation or progress, try to act as if there were no cycle of youth, maturity, old age and death; no rhythms of inner peace and conflict, of guilt and freedom from guilt, of grief and of the healing of its wound.[4]

> How ghastly can be the smile of a suffering man who is pretending that all is well; how pathetic the stiff but tottering stance of a man who, because he does not know how to share his troubles with others through the historic liturgies, is about to break under them. How pathetic, also, the man who, in his time of trouble, expresses the ultimate of that individualism in which we have all been reared, the insistence that his troubles are so private and so unique that no social salve can soothe them.[5]

The modern secular man, therefore, who does not pray and eschews ritual, is as alienated as one can be. He is cut off from the processes of the world, he is cut off from ceremonial union with his fellows, and he is, in all likelihood, cut off from himself. If man feels union he wishes to celebrate, but if he does not want to celebrate his union or if he has no union to celebrate, he's in a bad way.

There are few more incredible failures of the Catholic Church than its inability to realize the potential of liturgy. It is the master liturgy builder of the Western world. It co-opted much of the ritual of the nature religions, and indeed did a far better job at salvaging the best of the nature rituals than did any other world religion. It was far more imaginative in integrating the creative arts into its ritual than any religion has been. It has devised a convincing theoretical explanation of the link between man's two forms of worship—ritual and contemplation—and institutionalized this theory in the mo-

[4] Everett Hughes, *Men and Their Work* (Chicago: University of Chicago Press, 1959), p. 17.
[5] Ibid., p. 18.

nastic system. It was able to bring into its worship the developing popular arts and simultaneously to spin off new art forms from its liturgy (both modern drama and modern opera have their roots in medieval worship). The Roman Church's liturgical accomplishments were therefore truly extraordinary.

But one would not have believed it to look at the Roman liturgy in 1960. It was recited in an audible monotone in a foreign language to a bored, silent congregation assembled out of stolid loyalty but with little comprehension of what was going on. New art forms had long since been rejected, and even the slightest modification was considered to be a violation of canon law. What had once been the most exciting, flexible, and dynamic form of worship the world had ever known had degenerated into an atrophied Byzantine court ritual executed mechanically and routinely with no relevance for human needs or world problems. Damasus, Gregory the Seventh, the builders of the thirteenth-century cathedrals, and Thomas of Celano, the author of the *Dies Irae,* would have rubbed their eyes in disbelief.

But with Vatican Council II there came an explosive revolution which caught even the tiny band of enthusiastic liturgists off guard and which must, at least thus far, be judged something less than a success, for the liturgical revolution of the 1960s was poorly planned and poorly executed. Further, the scholarship was not developed well enough to be able to give coherence to the change. In many places the shifts were grudging and reluctant, at least in part because they were not understood, and in some places the changes were indeed strongly resisted. Practically no thought was given to the pedagogy which should have accompanied the liturgical revolution, and some serious mistakes were made. For example, however desirable the presence of lay readers and commentators may be in theory, in practice it must be admitted that laymen in the sanctuary are often inarticulate and inaudible, and their presence is a serious obstacle to people's understanding and prayer.

But despite the mistakes and the incomplete success of the liturgical revolution, it has nonetheless been overwhelmingly popular, as a few scientific studies of the Catholic population's reaction have demonstrated. Young Catholics in partic-

ular are enthusiastic about a ritual they can now use to celebrate their friendship and their community, their play and
their work. The change in campus liturgy in Catholic schools
and in Newman Clubs in the last two years has been dramatic,
and one suspects that no one will take away from these young
people this new liturgy which means so much to them.

But as the Roman Church rediscovers its tradition as master
builder of liturgies, it is faced with some serious and apparently abiding difficulties. Doctrinaire "secularists" like Daniel
Callahan say that liturgy has failed because it has not yet
turned out authentically dedicated Christians, an argument
reinforced by some of the absurd claims made by liturgical
enthusiasts in the past. Liturgy surely cannot, by itself, create
community, much less create religious dedication. It is designed, rather, to celebrate community and dedication, and by
the act of celebrating, reinforce. But the liturgical enthusiasts
are now in the peculiar position of having to defend themselves from the attacks of those like Callahan who took the
pre-Vatican II claims seriously.

Second, and more seriously, ecclesiastical leadership has
apparently made another one of its classic blunders in failing
to read the signs of the times—interpreting the noisy protests
of a tiny minority of the population who are opposed to
liturgical change. Leadership, nationally and internationally,
has determined that the change has happened too rapidly—
that the time has come to bring liturgical renewal to an abrupt
halt. This loss of nerve, based perhaps on some leaders'
projections into the general population of their own insecurity
in the face of liturgical change, is a prototype of what has
happened to much of the initial enthusiasm generated by the
Council. The leadership grew frightened at how fast things
were changing, panicked over the thought of losing control,
tried to slam on the brakes, and then in a marvelous display
of hypotheses, did, in fact, lose control. A more sophisticated
and secure leadership would have tried to direct the course of
the liturgical revolution rather than trying to stop it.

Thirdly, largely because of the failure of the leadership
to read the signs of the times, there has emerged a liturgical
underground which believes that every man is capable of
being his own liturgist.

As a result, leadership in the liturgical revolution has rapidly passed from ecclesiastical authority into the hands of a lunatic fringe that is historically uninformed, doctrinally naïve, and frequently lacking in good taste. As we have observed before, many of the young clergy take liturgical rules no more seriously than the young laity take birth-control rules. The degeneration, chaos and anarchy of the liturgical revolution can only be described as a tragedy, because at the very time when it was possible to make a major breakthrough in responding to man's need for worship and celebration, the Roman Church has reacted by either arguing about home mass and guitar music (as though these were important issues), or pretending that it was a really decisive and important innovation to make up your own canon, to say mass in shirtsleeves, or even to consecrate hotdog buns.

To make matters worse, in the midst of the leadership vacuum, several new varieties of pseudo liturgy have emerged. I have no objection at all to either psychotherapy or group discussion, and no unanswerable objections to Cursillo or to sensitivity-training sessions. But they are not ritual, they are not a substitute for contemplation, and they are not worship. While, for example, the group homily may sometimes be inspiring, at other times be tedious, exhibitionistic, and dull. The marriage of some of the manifestations of groupism with ritual as a substitute for both contemplation and worship are often an escape from self into talk, an escape to which some people are easily addicted, since it provides marvelous outlets for aggression, exhibitionism and bad taste. But even if discussion can be integrated into worship, and I am surely prepared to concede that it can, there is still need for ceremony which brings man into relationship with the sacred together with his fellows. And there is also a need of contemplation in which man by himself seeks out that silence which is essential in almost every kind of human activity that is worth anything, in every sort of human relationship that has meaning. Contemplation and ritual are essential to worship, the former as preparation for the latter, the latter as a continuation and reinforcement of the former. In contemplation, man turns in on himself in order that he might turn out once again, as he must do in any relationship that has any meaning. Worship makes it possible for man to contemplate, and contemplation makes it possible for man to worship. Group discussion may provide the raw material for both activities, but it is no substitute for them.

Finally, there is the "low Church" liturgy which denies the value of the ceremonial and devotes itself to a cult of spontaneity, informality, and casualness, symbolized most completely by the young priest reciting a canon he makes up as he goes along, while saying mass in a sport shirt. Worship in the front room of a house or in a dining room can be a profoundly moving experience the first time, the second time, and perhaps even the third time, but if one loses one's sense of reverence and transcendence in the process, then in the not too distant future the home liturgy becomes as meaningless as was the old Byzantine-style solemn mass to most Catholics. The current "low Church" tendency is an understandable reaction to the stagnation of the past, but when one is dealing with the sacred, too much familiarity breeds contempt. The sacred is, after all, our link with the Other, and the awe and fascination when encountering the Other are psychologically necessary and appropriate. Paradoxically, liturgy must be joyous and relaxed and at the same time reverent and respectful. That these characteristics need not exclude one another is evidenced by most of the Catholic liturgical tradition. Unfortunately, the exclusion of joy and relaxation in the last several centuries, and the emphasis on reverence and respect have now produced a counterreaction which threatens, especially given the lack of leadership, to produce a liturgy equally meaningless for the human condition, because man can celebrate effectively only when reverence is mixed in with his celebration.

From the perspective of this volume a number of principles might be established setting directions for the development of man's worship of the sacred:

Worship is practiced by a *community*. Worship is necessarily interpersonal behavior, at least in its ritual and ceremonial manifestations. But in the new world we are postulating in this volume, the basic pattern of interpersonal behavior will be of friendship and love; therefore the worshiping community must be a community of friendship and love. Impersonal aggregations of isolated individuals may be considered a community by extending the meaning of the term, but liturgy does not by itself create friendship communities. It reinforces existing ones and perhaps transforms them. It celebrates the creation of new communities which are brought together to begin new tasks, and it may also unite groups of communities into a community of communities (which is the shape of parish liturgy in the future if the traditional large parishes are to continue). Worship must be thought of, therefore, as a joyous celebration of friendship. Further, if the friendship between God and His worshipers is compared with the marriage union, as it frequently is in both the Old and New Testaments, then it is safe to say that the worshiping community is, in fact, celebrating the marriage feast.

Worship must be secular. That is to say, it must respect the valuableness of the world, take its inspiration from the world, both natural and man-made, respect and integrate the natural processes, and also the cultural processes that man has created, and adapt for its own purposes the best of man's artistic endeavors. Catholic worship affirms that the secular is sacred, and that the sacred is secular, that the Resurrection has obliterated the division between the sacred and the profane. Therefore, it cannot cut itself off from the ongoing development of the world.

Worship must be sacred—that is, it must link man to the ultimates of meaning and belonging, to the graciousness of being, to that ultimate in seductiveness which most completely demands that man come out of himself. It must touch upon man's ecstatic tendencies. It must be extraordinary so that it can symbolize even the ordinary as extraordinary. Worship must be reverent and dignified. It must realize that when it touches upon the ultimates in meaning and belonging, it touches upon something that man has always considered to be both awesome and fascinating, yet simultaneously intimate and familiar.

Worship must be personalist; it must be both preceded and followed by contemplation, and must involve the whole man, body and soul, in the web of interaction networks in which he is immersed. It must both respect his independence and dignity as a person and also inspire him to joyously give himself to the rest of the worshiping community with the full knowledge that this will enhance his personhood.

Worship must be joyous and hopeful. It must have about it the atmosphere of the wedding banquet. It must bear witness to the dynamic of the resurrection promise. It must not be slow or stodgy or repetitious or dull. It must have a rhythm of movement which both catches the accelerating pace of man's pilgrimage and also reinvigorates the pilgrims for their continued journey.

Worship must be free—free particularly from the multitude of rules, regulations, compulsions, provocations, and the rigid application of these by the neorubricists. While there is some need, of course, for general norms and guidelines, man's worship cannot become rigidly stylized so that one format is forced to fit every possible situation. Rather, it must be flexible and malleable so that it can fit into a multitudinous variety of situations and still remain itself.

Worship must be creative. The arts, particularly the popular arts, must be brought into service once again. While there ought to be some fear that the new arts may introduce temporary irreverence in the liturgy, there ought to be a much greater fear that worship will stagnate if it is cut off from the vitality and energy of man's artistic endeavors. One might remark, incidentally, that the guitar, while a perfectly useful and even noble instrument, is not the only instrument that people can play and that folk music is not the only music that they can sing.

Worship, then, is a celebration—a celebration of unity and union. Man affirms in it his unity with the world, with his friends, with his God, and with himself. But celebration is more than merely a reflection on the past—more even than anticipation of the future. It is a positive strengthening of the relationship so that the future may be better. Thus a husband and wife when celebrating their wedding anniversary not only rejoice over the happiness already theirs, but if it is a marriage relationship of friendship, they pledge themselves to even greater efforts to deepen that friendship in the years to come. Their union on the marriage bed after the celebration party is over is particularly pleasurable not merely because it recalls past delights, but also because it promises and anticipates even greater delights to come as their love grows deeper and richer. The same thing can be said about every other sort of authentic celebration of union —it is both a recollection and a promise. Therefore the celebration that is worship not only reflects the union which already exists between man and his fellows, his world, and his God, the fellows he loves, the world he plays in, and the God he believes in—it also furthers and deepens that union. Liturgy is not merely man's promise that he intends to move forward to new heights of friendship and love; it actually causes some of this promised movement. Celebration is not optional, and the same world that will demand of us that we show it how to love will also demand of us that we show it how to celebrate love, for without celebration love cannot continue and grow.

We are moving into a new liturgical era, and the question is whether it will be the sort of liturgy that the Nazis celebrated at Nuremberg or the liturgy the Chinese use in their deification of Mao in Peking, or the grave, dignified, civil liturgy that surrounds the President of the United States, or the dynamic liturgy of the freedom songs of the civil-rights movement, or perhaps even, please God, the offbeat joy of the liturgy of Immaculate Heart College's "Mary's Day." Mankind is seeking liturgy with which to celebrate his unities. The kind of liturgy he chooses will, in part, shape the future of the unities he is forming. One wonders how long we must wait before the most experienced practitioner of liturgy in the world is able to see the signs of the times.

Chapter 10

A CHURCH TO ORGANIZE

It has never been difficult to make a telling case against the Catholic Church. What is surprising about many of the recent books written against the Church by former priests is that the criticisms are so mild. In other eras other critics who, incidentally, did not find it necessary to leave the priesthood had much harsher things to say, but perhaps they did not sell as many books as some of the contemporary critics.

The criticism leveled at the Catholic Church in this volume is focused on the fact that the Church has, in the last several centuries, consistently missed almost every major opportunity that has been offered to it. It has not taught falsehoods, nor even ignored the truth, but rather, has chosen to respond to the challenge of the times by stressing elements of its own tradition that were irrelevant to the challenge and minimizing precisely those elements within its tradition which would have been most effective as a response. This habitual retreat from opportunity came to an end at the Second Vatican Council, but even the opportunity and the challenge that the Council itself has provided are still being resisted strongly by powerful elements within the Church, and much of the initiative the Council made possible has been lost, though probably not irrevocably.

The faults, then, of the Church leaders, and of the Church followers, too, have been many:

We did not follow our basic scriptural insights on sex, and responded to the personalist revolution in sex with stern, negative prohibitions and little else.

We lost sight of our own communitarian nature and became rigidly juridic at the very time the rest of mankind began to understand those notions of community which the Church had brought to the world.

We became more authoritarian and less responsive to grassroots pressures at the very time when collegiality, democracy, of which we have been the custodian for a thousand years or more, became widespread in human government.

We forgot the importance of resurrection as a ground for humanism and secularity at the very time that science, art, technology, and culture, under the influence of the resurrection of the dynamic of hope, made astonishing advances.

We became sour, suspicious, and distrustful when the hope and the possibility of joy which we brought to the world began to spread over the earth.

We permitted ourselves to be caught in fundamentalist notions of God and doctrine precisely at those times when we were supposed to be fighting rigid Protestant fundamentalism, and we became closed in our approach to other religions precisely at that time when dialogue became widespread.

When modern psychology discovered that man was a total person and not a collection of disparate instincts and impulses, we forgot our own teaching about the unity of the human person. Instead, we became confused by absurd exaggerations of the body-soul dualism. We should have been able to embrace Sigmund Freud, but instead we suppress monasteries which engage in psychoanalysis.

When outrage against social injustice grew fierce, we forgot our own outrage over injustices of the past, an outrage we inherited from our Jewish predecessors, and rather, permitted ourselves to be viewed throughout much of Europe as the allies of repressive, conservative, and reactionary governments. We should have been able to give at least a partial welcome to Karl Marx's social criticism, but instead we forgot the implications even of our own social encyclicals.

When theories of evolution began to develop we forgot our own vision of mankind on pilgrimage, and the Church as a people seeking the fulfillment of a promise, and insisted on trying to be even more fundamental than the fundamentalist Protestants. We should have been able to welcome Charles Darwin. Instead we silenced Teilhard de Chardin and many other great scholars, too. Even in the 1950s we were able to assert defensively that "evolution is not yet proved."

When mankind began to take literally the Church's teaching about the dignity and freedom of the human person, and to defend human rights more strongly, we developed a rather nasty juridical system in which most basic human rights were violated. Anonymous denunciations, secret trials, no right to confront accusers, no right of appeal, no right to one's own counsel, no separation of prosecution, judge, jury, and executioner—all these are to be found in the Church, which was the first human organization to insist on the dignity and equality of all men.

When man was seeking liturgy to celebrate the new unity he was discovering, we allowed our own liturgy to grow sterile and stagnant and unrealistic. And even now we are timid about pushing liturgical renewal to an ultimate conclusion.

When Pope John and the Second Vatican Council offered us a golden opportunity to make a dramatic impact on the modern world, we allowed most of the enthusiasm and good will, inside and outside the Church, to be frittered away in nervous hand-wringing and warnings about extremism.

When man desperately needed a message of hope and joy, we forgot that we were the original bearers of Good News, and contented ourselves with a repetition of denunciations of materialism, atheism, secularism, paganism, liberalism, and any other ism we could find available.

It is a sad picture and a powerful indictment—more powerful, in my judgment, than that of Charles Davis or James Kavanaugh, but less strong, perhaps, than that of Jerome, Francis, Bernard, or even St. Paul in speaking to the Church of Corinth. But is such an indictment a reason to leave the Church or to despair of it? I should think it would be only for those who have no sense of Scripture or history. The parables of the Kingdom, the description of the Church as Israel, the warning that the bride would be without spot only when the bridegroom returns—all these should be more than ample evidence that, while the Lord did promise His Church survival, He certainly did not promise it perfection, much less intelligent administration. Further, if we but look at the history of the last two millennia, we will be saddened, but not surprised, by failures of the Church in its relationship to the modern world. In fact, it must frankly be asserted, despite all the lost opportunities, that the Church is not nearly as bad as it was many times in the past; that our mistakes today result more frequently from mediocrity and stupidity, while in the past, in addition to these vices, we were also plagued with corruption, immorality, simony, political ambition, nepotism, and a host of other ugly things which can be observed only very rarely at present.

The Lord did not promise perfection, but only survival and painful growth, and the growth has certainly been painful. But despite the incredible array of lost opportunities, we are still forced to say, with Peter, "Lord, to whom shall we go?" Our faith is not based on the performance of the Church, and if any Christians' faith had been based on the performance of the men who run the Church, it is dubious that we would ever have got out of Jerusalem. If anything, our faith is more likely to be based on the Church's constant regenerative powers, its ability to bounce back after the failures and mistakes of its leadership—an ability which reveals, at least for the man of faith, the presence of the risen Lord and the Holy Spirit among us, refusing to let human weakness interfere with the pilgrimage.

While we have faith in the Church, we also realize that it is an organization of human beings. If the relationships among these human beings are to be better tools for the work of the Lord and the Holy Spirit than they have been in the past, we must examine the human element in the Church to discover what has gone wrong.

First of all, it must be said that there has unquestionably been a failure of leadership in the last three centuries. The Papacy has not been in the forefront of human progress as it was for over fifteen hundred years. On the contrary, it has been seen by many men outside the Church as one of the prime obstacles to mankind's progress. It is not the fact of the Papacy that has created this problem, but rather the way the Papacy has operated—perhaps has been forced to operate. Nor does the problem have anything to do with the virtue of the

men who have occupied the Papacy, since as far as personal
sanctity goes, there is no question that the Popes of the last
two hundred years represent the most impressive line of holy
men since the very beginning of the Church. But even these
holy men have not been able to break out of the prison that
history and social structure have imposed upon them. The
greatest of all the Popes of the last three centuries, John
XXIII, repeatedly told his friends that he was in "sack."
Only when the sack is broken will the Pope be able to be that
which he ought to be—the most influential and charismatic
leader in the world.

Many components went into the making of the sack, but
unquestionably the power of the Papacy was one of the most
important. However necessary and useful the power may
have been at one time, in recent centuries, particularly with
the rise of nationalism, it became a burden. The question
of the papal states, then the so-called Roman question of
papal independence, and more recently the critical importance of Italian elections in determining papal policy, have
necessitated a focus on local or national concerns when its
leadership and its mission ought to have been broadly international. Closely related to the question of the power of
the Papacy has been the long line of Italian pontiffs. This is
not to say that Italians make poor Popes; on the contrary, both
because of their experience and temperament, they were
perhaps better than any other Europeans as ecclesiastical
leaders, but one half a millennium of leadership from one
country is bound to give a church which claims to be catholic
and universal a provincial appearance, and even a provincial
viewpoint. It is no exaggeration to say that from the point of
view of the modern world, as well as, in all honesty, from
the point of view of many Catholics, the Church will not enter
into the modern world, will not become catholic or universal
in its impact until the Papacy becomes non-Italian.

Partly as a result of this provincialism, the international
structure of the Church has been weakened. There has not
been enough decentralization or enough sensitivity to the
grassroots problems and difficulties. The communication
flow upward has been consistently blocked, and many papal
decisions and appointments must necessarily have been based

upon very inadequate information. Nor has communication downward been appreciably more effective, at least in part because *stylus curiae* of so many papal statements makes them virtually unintelligible to the ordinary Catholic. It is odd that the Church's international structure is weak, because the Church was, for all practical purposes, the only international organization from the time of the Roman Empire to the League of Nations. It developed a great facility in coping with international problems, but unfortunately this facility has slowly atrophied in the last several centuries, and the new international agencies which have grown up in the last four decades would not have thought of looking to the Church for hints on how mankind might become international.

Such a failure is doubly strange because the Church has always tended to reflect in its internal structure the most sophisticated kind of organizational style that was to be found in the world outside. Sometimes, in fact, it shaped the organizational styles of the world outside. Unfortunately, it is the tragedy of the Church at the present time that it became frozen in the Renaissance style of absolute power because the Tridentine strategy of resistance to the Reformation has only recently begun to be unfrozen. Hence we were unable to keep pace not only with the growth of the new internationalism, but also with the general democratization of the use of authority which took place in the world of the industrial revolution.

Democratic styles emerged in the Western world partly for ideological reasons, but mostly because they were perceived as effective ways to deal with the complex needs for skill and information created by the industrial revolution. One might go so far as to say that even had there not been a democratic ideology to justify the political revolutions of the seventeenth, eighteenth, and nineteenth centuries, the need for skill and information in the modern world would have driven men to establish social systems very much like modern democracies. The basic trouble with the Church as an organization is that it does not have the skills and information necessary for administrative decision-making in the modern world precisely because it is not democratic enough in its styles of leadership. Leadership is virtuous, but it is not charismatic. It is kindly, but it is not confident. It would like to have consensus, but is timid in the face of a dissent which is a necessary prelude to consensus. It would like to dream dreams, but is threatened by the language with which other men dream dreams. It would like to have splendid visions, but is afraid to allow itself to be imaginative. It wants now to dialogue with the modern world, but it is not sure that it can trust its own membership to keep their faith in such dialogue. This has been the story of the leadership in the Church, national and international, for most of the last three centuries, not, let us repeat, because the leaders have been evil men, but rather because the social system of the Church has lost its flexibility, its ability to roll with the punch, to change with the times, to adjust to new problems and challenges. Even now leadership seems to be losing control of the renewal begun by Vatican Council II, which would suggest that the change from the old styles of leadership to the new, instead of being peaceful, may well be a difficult and painful transition.

The man of faith is profoundly troubled by these comments on the failure of leadership in the Church to be able to seize the opportunities that have slipped away, and the failure of the Church to be sufficiently malleable in its structure to enable the leadership to see the opportunities. He is profoundly troubled, not in his faith, which, as we have said before, is quite independent of the performance of leadership or the excellence of structures; but rather, he is profoundly troubled because the pilgrimage has been so badly slowed and the good news so badly obscured. He is confident that the work begun in the Second Vatican Council will be successful in the long run (though "long" seems to be longer now than it seemed at the end of the Council). He believes that the Holy Spirit is at work in the world, as perhaps never before, and will not permit us to resist Him, as He blows whither He will. Nonetheless, we who must participate in the renewal of the Church need a perspective from which we can systematically think about its organizational problems.

One perspective which might be useful (and let it be established that I am not holding that this is the *only* perspective) is to view the Church as a people—that is to say, as a society—as an aggregation of people and of groups of people, a community of communities, if one wishes. To put the matter somewhat more systematically, the Church is a complicated system of interacting patterns and relationships among individuals and collections of individuals. It is, in other words, a system of interacting patterns not unlike those found in any large human organization. It may differ from these organizations in its origin and its goals, but the patterns of relationships tend to be very similar.

We Catholics would argue that our society is the bearer of the dynamic of the resurrection promise and a continuation of the incarnation, the intrusion of the transcendental into the secular and the vanguard of man's pilgrimage toward fulfillment. We would further contend that the optimism, secularity, and humanism of the modern world are rooted in this dynamic, even though some of the dynamic of hope has been separated from its original custodian because of historical tragedy. We would further argue that through its faith in the risen Lord present within it, the Church is in an excellent position to play a critical role in mankind's future progress and in the future growth of both secularity and humanism.

Now if this be true, if the Church is not only a society but the leader of society, the vanguard of society, it is reasonable to expect that it would exercise its leadership precisely by its ability to establish a pattern of relationships within itself which will demonstrate to other societies how man is able to cope with his contemporary problems. Society is based on relationships. The Church as society will lead precisely insofar as the quality of its relationship is such that man cannot resist imitating it. Therefore, I would argue that the Church's leadership role lies precisely in its ability to display friendship, community, leadership, playfulness, self-fulfillment, commitment, and celebration more effectively and more richly than these relationship patterns can be found in other human societies. Or to put the matter more simply, people must be able to say of us once again, "See how they love one another."

Until the Church as a society becomes once again the leader in human relationships, it will not be a light to the nations. Whatever other ways available to it in the past to play this role, none is left to it now save excelling in the quality of the love that is to be observed in its members' relationships with one another. That there is a long way to go, no one in his right mind would deny. We have argued in this book, for example, that the relationship between man and woman is the primal relationship of love which all other relationships must strive to imitate if they are to be worthy the name of friendship. One need merely consider the relationship between men and women of the Church to see that the practice of this primal relationship among Catholics has not yet become exactly what one would call a light to the nations. Women of the religious are second-class citizens; are expected to be docile, passive, in the face of the exercise of all male authority. All too many celibate clergymen are awkward, threatened, and at the same time dominating in their relationships with women parishioners, or indeed, with any women.[1] Even marriage itself in the Church, despite the immense riches on the scriptural resources, of its dignity, is only now beginning to emerge from a situation where it was viewed as a second-class vocation available to ordinary people as an alternative to fornication. The actual marriage relationship between Catholic husbands and wives is still frequently blighted by the folk Catholicism (only recently explicitly rejected by the official Church) that equated successful marriage with fertility.

However, in the remainder of this chapter I want to view the Church not so much as a system of personal or communal relationships, but rather precisely insofar as it is a society, a large and complex human organization, which is what it surely is, certain theological enthusiasts to the contrary, notwithstanding. I will contend against these enthusiasts that as a large aggregation the Church is a light to the nations, not by abolishing organization or administration, but rather by being the model for how a society should work in the most efficient, effective, and humane way, not merely despite its size, but because of it.

[1] As one friend of mine said, "Talking to a priest is like going to your first eighth-grade boy-girl party."

As we have noted before, this is an extremely important question in the modern world as more and more issues are settled at the society level, or at the level of large corporate bodies which are, in fact, societies in miniature. We have suggested earlier in the book that these larger groups can function effectively only when the organized structure of the society does everything in its power to facilitate the relationships of love and friendship among its members. Therefore, the mission of the Church, insofar as it is a society, is to take the lead once again in demonstrating not merely how love and effectiveness are compatible at the societal level, but also how they are indispensable to one another.

As we have frequently stated, there is a long way to go, but on the other hand, we do have certain advantages. We can avoid some of the mistakes that secular organizations have made in the past, such as, for example, a task dividing to its simplest component parts and assigning a single component to each person. Such an approach to the assembly line actually is inefficient and ineffective, because production is superior both in quantity and in quality if we use our human resources for something more than just one simple task. Whether the Church will, in fact, avoid the mistake of dehumanizing persons and their relationships remains to be seen. We may not be able to leap from traditional authority to the neocharismatic authority described in an earlier chapter, but if we do not make such a leap it is simply because we are unwilling to learn from the mistakes of other societies and societal organizations.

It is not my intention in this chapter to repeat in detail suggestions I have made elsewhere about the practical reorganizations needed in the Church and in its social structure. But I do want to emphasize what was not nearly so clear to me, at least not explicitly, when I made these suggestions: The purpose of structural reorganization is to facilitate loving relationships among the members, relationships that will be so powerful and so appealing that other societies will imitate us.

But without describing plans for structural forms in detail, it is still necessary in the context of this volume to describe the concerns that are necessary for the Church as a society, if it is to achieve this structural reform. Where our treasure is, there also will our heart be, and unless these concerns represent our treasures, we are not likely to be able either to see our structural reform in perspective or to realize its full importance.

The Church must be concerned about the flow of communication upward and downward, because we cannot love that which we do not know, and we cannot know someone unless we are able to understand what he is saying. Without communication there is no love. Communication in a complicated society is extremely difficult. There is much happy talk in the contemporary Church, at least in the United States, about communications, though not much sophistication about it and not much willingness to spend money for research on the subject, and not even much inclination to display the minimum virtues necessary for communication—a willingness to listen carefully to what the other is saying. One does not need to search very far to find grandiose plans for facilitating communication within the Church, plans which are generally thought up in some quiet, a priori ivory tower and are expected to be imposed without any prior research or experimentation. It is likely to be some time before we realize that communication is not improved by master plans, but only by slow and careful experimentation with existing processes.

The Church must be concerned about the maximum protection of the human rights of its membership. Its appeals processes must be more careful; its respect for due process more serious, and its abhorrence of delayed justice more intense than in any other human society. We must be willing to lean over backwards to avoid even the appearance of the violation of human rights, and in this matter above all others, the Church must be like Caesar's wife.

We must be concerned about the facilitation of friendship groups within our society and strive to create the best possible climate for trust and confidence in the activities within our organization. We must have the profound conviction that the problems of a large organization can be solved only if there is friendship and love in the face-to-face groups which constitute the organizations' grass roots.

The Church must be concerned about having the broadest possible participation in decision-making and about building effectively operating consultative structures at all levels. Unilateral, a priori, and hasty decisions are not to be tolerated save in the gravest crisis. The Church's concern about participation in decision-making may or may not flow from its theology of the nature of authority, but it is surely based on the practical realization that in the modern world the only kind of authority that will be effective will be authority that operates with broad participation in decision-making.

The Church must be concerned about building within its structures mechanisms for self-criticism, self-examination, and self-study to avoid the iron law of oligarchy—to keep means from becoming ends. Internal research, study by outside organizations, free press and free universities are all absolutely essential, if for no other reason than to prevent the Church from again becoming stodgy and stagnant, thus inhibiting the growth of love among its members.

The Church must be concerned about maintaining a maximum openness to growth and development. Presumably it will no longer be afraid, no longer suspicious, no longer distrustful, and therefore it will be willing to look at long-range goods more than at short-range problems, and far from discouraging experimentation and innovation, will absolutely insist upon them as the only means to guarantee growth and development.

The Church will become concerned about popular participation in the selection of leaders wherever it is feasible, and perhaps even about imposing clear limitations on length of service, not, once again, necessarily for reasons of theory, but simply for practical reasons. Unless this is done, it will be extremely difficult for the Church to prevent its arteries from hardening again and from growing both unresponsive to the needs and the problems of its membership and unable to move with agility in response to these problems.

In line with the principles Pope John set down in his encyclical letter *Mater et Magistra*, the Church will be concerned that within its society limitations of human freedom will be kept to an absolute minimum and that there will be maximum encouragement for individual leadership and responsibility. We recognize that laws and regulations are not a good in themselves but are only a means to an end, and that we impose regulations not to create virtue but only to protect rights and facilitate the pursuit of the general welfare. We may not want to trust people with issues of responsibility (despite Pope John's insistence that we must), but we must face the harsh fact that in the modern world we don't have much choice.

The Church ought to be concerned about ways of maintaining the highest possible service orientation in its leadership; the leadership group must not consider itself as a caste separate and distinct over against the rest of the people, but rather, it must be in fact, as well as in vague and hyperbolic theory, at the disposal of those whom it serves. It exists to help them. They do not exist to be its pawns or tools. The image of the Lord washing the feet of His apostles at the Last Supper ought to be honored in practice and not merely in pious sermons.

The Church should be concerned about the professionalization of its leaders, of those holding critical positions. "Professionalization" is used here to mean adherence to high standards of performance and competency. If someone in a leadership position in the Church does not measure up to these standards, he must be removed. However, someone ought not to be entrusted with such a position unless he has demonstrated previously that he is competent to fill it. It is the role of the leader in the Church to facilitate relationships of friendship and love among followers; hence, his role is of extraordinary importance. If he is good at it, then his good influence is almost limitless, and if he is "bad," his bad influence is almost incalculable.

The Church must be concerned about promoting both diversity and harmony among the various groups which constitute it as a society. About this final point I wish to comment in somewhat greater length.

The human race comes to us in variously packaged formats. Some of us are white, some of us are black, some of us are yellow, some of us are brown, and many, many of us are a mixture. Some of us have long hair, some short hair, some straight hair, some kinky hair. Some of us have tall, thin bodies; others have short, squat bodies. Some of us have slant eyes and some of us have straight eyes. Some of us have blue eyes, some brown, and some gray. Some of us have big noses, others have small noses, others have hook noses, and yet others have slanted noses. Some of us cover ourselves with clothes and others wear very little. Still others wear a vast variety of different forms of dress and undress to respond to situations. Some of us speak elegant languages, and some of us speak harsh and guttural languages. Some of us tend to be efficient workers, and others of us like to sit and stare at the mist rising from the peat bog.

While this diversity is alarming at first glance, it is also, if we stop to think about it, delightful, for with only one skin color or one kind of bodily perfection, or one kind of cooking skill, or one approach to poetry or music, the world might be a dull place. Indeed, we may look forward hopefully to the day when a block of houses inhabited by men whose skin is all one color is thought to be intolerably dull; if we have enough money, we will choose to live in neighborhoods where there are a vast variety of shades of human skin, shapes of human noses, and styles of human hair.

But if the variety of human packaging is delightful, it is also threatening, and most men have not been able to get beyond the threat imposed by diversity. Those who are different from us are not to be trusted, for they not only *look* different —they *are* different. They have different values, they are culturally and biologically inferior, their morals are no good, they are lazy, shiftless, and will destroy us if they get the chance. Therefore we destroy them first, or at least keep them under oppression. Ethnicity, the grouping of men in diverse groups based on inheritance, physical appearance, and culture, ought to be seen as a marvelous phenomenon which offers the world a richness of cultural and biological diversity. In fact, however, it has all too frequently been a means by which man has institutionalized his own personal fears, suspicion and distrust. So we have the Malays fighting the Chinese, the Indians quarreling with the Pakistani, the

Jews and the Arabs at each others' throats, the Ibos and the Hausas trying to destroy each other, the Zulus and the Africaner plotting each others' destruction, the Indians and the half-breeds in Latin America eying each other suspiciously, the English and the French preparing to renew their old quarrels when the first opportunity arises (if the English are able to prevent the Welsh and the Scotch from renewing *their* quarrels with Mother England first), the Northern Irish and the Southern Irish peering grimly across their boundary line planning the day when the battle of the Boyne is renewed. The English-Canadians and the French-Canadians, not content with cheering on their cousins across the Atlantic, are quarreling more fiercely with each other; the Kerner Commission reports that the United States could easily become an apartheid society as blacks and whites alike continue to pay for the sins of the slave trade; within the European Church the ancient conflict between Germans and Italians continues, with some of the partisans of the latter suggesting that the changes of Vatican Council II were merely the result of the Rhine River conquering the Tiber. And finally, in American Catholicism itself, we can only hope that the ecumenical movement will be able to heal the conflict between Irish Catholics and Polish Catholics, probably long after it reunites the Catholics and the Lutherans.

It is hardly necessary to say that all these ancient hatreds are absurd. It is equally unnecessary to say that they are dangerous, and that the real threat to the modern world is not a confrontation between capitalism and socialism because men, at least most men, are not likely to want to die for philosophies, much less for economic systems. But the battles between East and West, North and South, yellow and white, Slav and Latin, Russian and Pole, Vietnamese and Chinese, Saxon and Celt, are precisely those things for which men have always been ready to die, and still seem quite ready to die. If there is a major truism of international politics that should have been reinforced by the quarter century since the end of the Second World War, it is that nationalism is stronger than socialism and democracy. The capitalist world and the communist world find themselves torn apart by the nationalistic and ethnic rivalries within their supersystems.

In the face of this dangerous and destructive disunity the Christian Church responds that we are neither male nor female, Jew nor Gentile, Greek nor Roman, but are one in Christ Jesus, and the world is inclined to laugh at us—if it listens at all—because it knows better. You cannot trust your fellow man, particularly when he is a different color or speaks differently, or lives somewhere else. The Church as a society, therefore, should be profoundly concerned about how it can tolerate within itself, and indeed even encourage, a rich diversity of customs and values and modes of expression, and still facilitate love and trust among the subgroups and subsocieties which constitute it. Decentralization combined with the formation of new international institutions, such as an authentically internationalized curia and especially the international Synod of Bishops, are absolutely indispensable organizational means for the Church to be able to show that it is authentically international and that it can have, simultaneously, unity and diversity; that it can be at the same time the most diversified and the most unified society in the world. The Second Vatican Council, for all its hesitancies and mistakes, for all its initial unwieldiness, was able to develop into a fairly effective international assembly, although the Synod of Bishops seems to be moving somewhat more hesitantly in the same direction. Synod and Councils are not merely institutions for governing the Church. They are also, and perhaps more importantly, witness to the Church. They use the vast diversity that exists among men to encourage love rather than discourage it, to eliminate hatred rather than enforce it.

These concerns which I am demanding of the Church as a society are going to impose a severe burden on Church leadership and make severe demands on Church followers. The society which results from the persistence of these concerns is likely to be more, not less, organized, but also much *better* organized. We do have certain advantages, for our society is not organized to make money or war or to govern troubled countries, or even to instruct recalcitrant adolescents, but to spread the good news, to promote friendship and love, to facilitate charitable services, to convene communities, to celebrate man's unities. There is, if we are open and honest, much less for us to fight about and even much less fear to over-come than there would be in other human societies. That we have not progressed further in the direction of a loving society is perhaps evidence that we are still among the early Christians.

I should like to emphasize that it seems to me that an approach to the renewal of the Church ought to begin from a theoretical perspective similar to the one described in this chapter, and ought to have generalized goals and concerns not completely diverse from those listed above. What is required is that we rethink the role of organization in any society, and understand that organization is not an end in itself, but a means of promoting the welfare—that is to say, the quality of relationships in this society. The important point is the quality of our relationships. All too frequently, however, those who think and write about reform in the Church are more inclined to focus on specific aspects of structural reform and specific institutions that they wish to see eliminated—generally the institutions that rub them the wrong way. We are told, therefore, that we must sell our buildings, or that we must have a married clergy, or that we must abolish the monsignorate, or dispense with purple robes. I am inclined to think that most of these are nonissues. Buildings, celibacy, even the monsignorates and purple robes are not, in themselves, a threat to the quality of relationships. On the contrary, they become problems precisely because relationships are poor. I am willing to concede that the monsignorate is probably an anachronism, and that purple robes, while they may be pretty in processions, may not be appropriate in modern society. I would also be prepared to say that some of our buildings ought to be sold, though probably we ought to build other buildings in different places, and I certainly cannot object to a married clergy since the Church already has a married clergy in many of its rites. But I will insist that none of these changes will solve anything by themselves unless the basic pattern of human relationships is changed and the basic structures which shape these patterns are dramatically revised along the lines indicated in the preceding paragraphs. Refusal to see the issue in these terms and insistence on focusing on specific practical controversies are dangerous and self-destructive.

As we have said before in this chapter, our failure has not been, for the most part, a failure of good will, nor even of intelligence, much less of basic theory, though God knows we've managed to overlook much of our basic theory. Our failure has been a failure of organization brought about by strategic decisions made long ago amidst the historical and social contexts which have since dramatically changed. Structural problems can be serious, but fortunately, they are much less serious than are problems of good will, intelligence, or basic theory, because there is no substitute for intelligence or sound theory, and there are all kinds of substitutes for organizational structures.

As we have suggested before in this volume, mankind is entering an era when big corporate bodies must be humanized if we are not all to become the functional equipment of IBM cards, and if the organizations are not going to eventually fall of their own dead, nonhuman weight. Furthermore, the knowledge, or at least the beginning of the knowledge we must have to humanize the corporate bodies, is at hand. Both because of its ideology and its goals, the Catholic Church ought to be the ideal model of the organized society where love and operational effectiveness mutually reinforce one another. Admittedly, we have a heritage of several centuries' duration to put aside, but no one can deny that Catholicism has demonstrated great flexibility in the past, and the Second Vatican Council has demonstrated that flexibility is still present. If the Catholic Church really believes it is the vanguard of the human pilgrimage, it must organize itself so that it acts like a vanguard—smooth, efficient, open-ended, flexible, orderly but informal, concerned about the welfare of the individual members, skeptical but happy, professional but with the common touch. It might even take a good look at the Israeli Army to see what a vanguard ought to be like. This, it must be admitted, would surely be an interesting turn of history.

Will the Church once again organize itself into a vanguard? Will the quality of the societal relations within it shine forth as a light to the nations? If one merely looks at the available empirical evidence, one is forced to be dubious, but the man of faith has more evidence than just the empirical, and he finds it not at all unreasonable to expect confidently that the Church is about to become once again an impressive city set on the mountaintop.

Chapter 11

A PRIEST TO TURN TO

Just as man has created many different varieties of gods, so he has called upon the services of many different sorts of religious functionaries. There is the reformer who appears out of the mists and demands a return to pristine simplicity and sanctity; the prophet who strides in vigorously from the fields and announces judgment and destruction on the faithless people; the seer who is wrapped in visions of the transcendent reality and reports back to his followers the nature of this reality; the magician who negotiates with the powers of good and evil and acts as a presumably honest broker between his followers and the benign and malign forces of the universe; the diviner who can read the omens, be they in the stars or the clouds or the entrails of animals; the saint who by the holiness and purity of his life shows man how he ought to live; the priest who offers sacrifices to appease the anger of the divinity and presides over the sacred meals; and the wise man, the man of learning, the man who understands reality, who can explain it to his followers. In most human societies these roles tend to be distinct. The prophet may be a reformer; the seer may also be a diviner or a magician; the saint may be a wise man. But rarely is the reformer expected to be a magician, or the prophet a wise man, or the magician a saint.

However, in Christianity, particularly in its Catholic branch, the religious functionary is called upon to assume almost all of these roles—to be a priest, to be wise, to be holy, to see things as they are, to provide reassurance, hope, and vision, to sit in judgment on evil, and to warn that the Church must always be reformed. It ought not to be a dull task, but visitors from another planet would be astonished to read in Joseph Fichter's *America's Forgotten Priest* that over one half the Catholic priests in the United States do not find their work challenging.

Because the religious functionary is concerned with such transcendental values as holiness, prophecy, vision, and reform, it does not mean that he has been socially useless, for it was the priestly caste of the ancient agricultural villages who, in their efforts to understand more deeply the mysteries of the rites they were celebrating, began the forward march of civilization. The priest as wise man and as scholar has been the leader in the development of human knowledge from Mesopotamia to the Renaissance. The words "cleric" and "clerk" come from the same root and until very recently meant the same thing. It is no exaggeration to say that until very recently, civilization was the work of the "leisure" priestly class. Yet even this role of the wise man must be seen as part of the broader role of the religious functionary to be "God's man," for he was assumed to have special access to the divinity, whether by his own personal powers or by community approbation or by his profound understanding of the mysterious wisdom of what makes the world work. He was the man one "turned to" for guidance, help, prayer, vision, reassurance, blessing, wisdom, sympathy, ritual, and perhaps even love. The religious functionary was supposed to "care" about you. The view of the priest as "God's man" whom you "turned to" for "care" or "love," is almost a universal of human existence, and exists today wherever there are clergy. Therefore, the question of the "role of the priest," at least from the viewpoint of the behavioral sciences, seems to be settled. The priest is the man who has the most "affective" or "expressive" role in society, and with the decline of belief in magic and divination, the least "instrumental." The priest is primarily a "useless" man, a man who is expected not so much to *do* as to *be*, "a poet of the word of God" whose poetry by itself may accomplish nothing, but whose vision and love, which flow more from what he is than from anything he does, profoundly affect all around him.

Nevertheless, there continues to be considerable agitation about "the role of the priest," and one must strive to understand the reasons for such agitation. First of all, there is justified dissatisfaction with the way the outmoded structures of the Church permit a priest to exercise his role. Fichter's finding that half the priests in the country are not challenged by their work would also suggest that half the priests in the country are disappointed and frustrated, because if one has dedicated one's life enthusiastically to the service of others and then finds that one cannot, in fact, engage in such service, one is bound to be frustrated. No more serious judgment can be leveled against a contemporary church than that it has wasted such immense talent and enthusiasm in well-trained and strongly motivated personnel.

There is, secondly, in the present era of uncertainty, a great deal of uncertainty about what the priest ought to be doing, an uncertainty that some forms of the religious personality find hard to accept. If old structures are outmoded they must be torn down and replaced by ready-made new ones. If celibacy is the question, one must have a wife. If the religious life as it presently exists needs to be changed, then let us destroy it. If authority needs on occasion to be questioned, then let us abolish it. The rigid personality must jump from one set of certainties to another, from white to black, and then perhaps back to white again, never pausing in the ambiguous borderland of gray. Rigid personalities were re cruited in the priestly life, and whatever rigidity existed in others was reinforced. In stable and stagnant conditions, rigidity is an asset, but in dynamic and ambiguous situations, rigidity is a liability, and the Catholic Church has many such liabilities today.

Yet other priests are convinced that the priesthood must be defined vis-à-vis the laity, and one can only have a clear notion of what a layman is by defining what a priest is not. Still others are caught in an identity crisis. They are not sure what they ought to be or whether what they are doing is "relevant," or whether they are doing anything, or what kind of training they ought to have, or whether they are professional, or whether they have a role or a function, or whether they ought not to be "like everyone else."

Most of these questions cannot be answered from the viewpoint of theology. The universally valid theoretical answers which many clergy, particularly younger ones, seek to the questions in the previous paragraph are not to be had, because revelation tells us very little about what priests *ought* to be doing. It would therefore seem more appropriate to ask what priests *have* been doing and what they *are* doing, and what the people of God *want* them to do.[1]

The response of the historians and the social scientists to this question are astonishing and, to many, disconcerting. Priests have done all kinds of things, indeed just about everything, and they have found arguments justifying what they have done as *priestly*. Until the thirteenth century a priest was expected to support himself by his own work in the fields or in an artisan's shop or the monastery library. It was argued that such work was priestly because it sanctified the work and because it enabled priests to exercise their ministry toward those with whom they had worked. Priests have therefore been artists and architects, farmers and craftsmen, teachers and governors and military leaders, geneticists and astronomers, demographers and mathematicians, philosophers and sociologists, generals and prime ministers, and even fishermen, carpenters, and pen makers. Some have preached, some have gone to the poor, others to the rich; some to the Christians, others to the non-Christians. Some of them have been learned, others have had little learning. Some have worked with large numbers, others with very small groups. Some have been deeply involved in the politics, culture, and problems of their times, and others have been completely detached; some have been doctors, others lawyers, others explorers. Some have built cathedrals and others have built nothing. Some have wandered the length and breadth of the world while others have never departed from their village. Some have lived in communities, others alone in the desert. And all of them have said Mass. The Mass seems to be about the only common action we can find, and therefore, in all probability, the central one.

[1] Unless you assume that the Holy Spirit works only through theologians. Thus, one would-be Catholic prophet rejects the notion that priests can learn what they ought to be doing in their ministry by dialoging with their role opposites—that is to say—their people.

In the face of this vast variety of priestly activity, the neo-simplicists of our time would have us believe that there is only one priestly function, one kind of priestly work, that everyone else is a hyphenated priest, and that those priestly activities which are nonliturgical or "non-community-building" functions are not "priestly." This is to argue that the past was completely wrong, that countless thousands who thought their work priestly were wrong, that the Church, in endorsing their work as priestly, was wrong, and probably that the Holy Spirit, in inspiring the history of the priesthood, was wrong. Apparently only the youthful amateur theologians and enthusiasts of today are right. But one is forced to remark that this is a rather un-Catholic view, especially in an expanding world and in an expanding Church. If the Church is to be an open-ended institution, and the whole human development is the open end itself, then most assuredly the priesthood ought to be an open-ended role.

The priest's role, therefore, is to be what the role of the religious functionary has always been—to be God's man—to be the one others can "turn to" for care and love. He presides in love over the celebration of man's unity, and in his life promotes and facilitates the growth of that unity. In an open-ended Church, there will be, as there always has been, a vast variety of ways in which priests exercise their "leadership" role: the leadership of celebration, proclamation, and continuation of love. It is inconceivable it would be otherwise.

"What, then," we are asked, "happens to the layman?" Hopefully, as the Church moves forward in the next phase of its pilgrimage, we will be able to dispense with this tiresome argument. You really don't define a layman's role by opposing it to the cleric's (as, indeed, in the modern world we should have learned that one approaches reality not by trying to establish disjunctions but, rather, conjunctions). It is only a historical accident that we have come to view the role of the priest as something to be described over against the role of the layman. This description is invalid, as are many other false dichotomies, such as matter-soul, body-spirit, intellect-love, sacred-secular, which man is beginning to realize are not apt categories for describing the world in which he lives. We are asked if the layman can't represent the Church just as well as the priest in the kind of work the priest is doing. But in fact the question is absurd, narrow, and contentious. The priest and layman both represent the Church, though in different modalities. Both modalities are good, both are necessary, and neither ought to be considered "superior" to each other. Both ought to be considered, rather, as complementing one another. However, if the question is still pushed, if one is forced to answer it, the answer has to be a blunt "no." The priest sociologist, to cite a very personal example, represents the Church at a secular research center in a way that a layman cannot. And the reasons are obvious, no matter what a priori theories one might hold. He who says the layman and the priest represent the Church in exactly the same way will have considerable difficulty in persuading those to whom the Church is supposed to be represented, for their senses and their reasons tell them differently. The priest is viewed by his people as God's man in a special way, and he will be so viewed even by those who are not his people. No amount of simple-minded enthusiasm is going to change the nature of that social reality.

Just as the Church is plagued by nonissues such as whether it ought to have buildings or schools or hospitals or monsignorial robes, so the priesthood seems to be obsessed by equally unimportant nonissues such as what kind of clothes the priest should wear or whether he might be married or what kind of living quarters he ought to have. In the developing Church, one presumes, there will be much more freedom to choose in these matters than there is now. Further, one presumes that after a while, good taste and common sense will prevail and priests will realize that a tie and/or a wife don't make them any more manly, any more men of God, any more effective as leaders or as lovers of their people, than do a Roman collar and a single bed.

It is presumably true, in the open-ended church of the future, that we will be spared the pathetic happiness of the priest who has donned lay garb for the first time in his ministry, feeling that since he is just like everyone else now, he can really be effective in his work. What is pathetic is not the lay garb itself, which in some circumstances might be appropriate, but the utterly absurd notion that clothes can make or unmake a man.

Finally, we shall also come to realize that even if celibacy is optional, anyone who thinks he can serve others with as much time and freedom and intensity when he has a wife and family as he can if he was celibate, knows little about either marriage or priesthood.

One of the pains of the present transition is that we have displayed a marvelously immature genius for discovering the relatively unimportant while missing the important: The structural inhibitions on freedom and maturity and responsibility which prevent priests from being the kind of "God's men" whom people can "turn to."

I still remember with considerable embarrassment my early years in the ministry, and what embarrasses me is not my social awkwardness and inexperience when I left the seminary, for these are relatively minor problems. I am embarrassed, rather, by my total lack of awareness of what my priesthood was all about. From my Irish ancestors I have inherited tremendous, if neurotic, energy and strong achievement needs. From these same ancestors, along with my Catholic training, I also seem to have picked up a strong superego which makes me feel responsible and take on responsibility, and from some forgotten Irish forebear I have also acquired the gambler's impulse to try something new. Coop up someone with this kind of energy and drive for twelve years in a seminary and expose him to certain ideas about the mission of the Church in the twentieth century, then set him down in a well-educated parish where the most obvious kinds of social and religious pathology are absent, and you are going to have a veritable whirlwind of organizational activity, which, alas, is all too easily confused with zeal, even by the poor victims of such activity. So we will have CFM, YCS, and YCW, Legion of Mary, discussion groups, libraries and basketball teams, participating liturgy and teen-age dances, college summer programs, social-action projects, bridge clubs and bake sales, plays and concerts, and the Good Lord only knows how many other frantic adventures.

In the midst of this, of course, one easily comes to believe that the priest's role is primarily to organize, to provide ideas and to ride herd on those who are to implement the ideas. If the priest is energetic enough and the people are cooperative and intelligent enough, the result may be deceptively impressive and the priest may never learn that, while all these things are good and praiseworthy, and perhaps even necessary, they are not what is most important for him to do. As a matter of fact, he may be so busy being useful or relevant that he will forget that his real job is to be useless and irrelevant.

But if the priest is fortunate enough to stay around the same section of the beach for long enough, he will discover that most, if not all, these projects come to naught, and that the whirlwind of activity, at least by itself, may give temporary satisfaction, but it accomplishes relatively little either for the priest or for his people. He is even more fortunate if he finds himself forced into a relationship with his people that is somewhat outside the established structure of parochial busyness and makes the astonishing discovery that while people may enjoy the activity, what they want from their priest is not that he be a dynamic fomenter of activity, but someone they can "turn to," someone to love them. He may have been persuaded in the seminary that ideas and principles and goals are important, and that personality and relationships and affection are not only unimportant, but dangerous. But if he is fortunate he will learn during his priestly life that his real vocation is to love his people in the same powerful and intensely human way that Jesus loved His disciples ("Behold I do not call you servants, I call you friends")—that Jesus who permitted the sinner the incredible intimacy of drying His feet with her hair, and the obstreperous teen-ager, John, the temerity to lean his head upon His shoulder.

The priest is therefore a man to turn to, but to turn to for what? In the context of this book, we would say that he is a man to turn to to find playfulness, a man from whom we can learn by word and deed that the world is a playground, and that we are meant to be joyous and happy and playful. One wonders, therefore, why so many priestly lives seem to be without joy or playfulness.

He is also a man whom we can turn to for concern over the community, because he is a man of the community. He presides over its consensus in charity, and has given himself both to the celebration and the extension of that charity. Let us make no mistake about it, we can turn to this man for concern over the community and expect his concern to be more effective if he is a celibate.

We must be able to turn to the priest as a man from whom we can learn to respect our selfhood, because he respects it. The priest is therefore necessarily a counselor, and hopefully a counselor with some training, even though he may not be a professional therapist. For if fear and distrust are the prime results of original sin, and the priest is a man who wages relentless warfare against fear and distrust, then he must be a man with some skill in helping others commit themselves to the painful and arduous struggle against their own self-rejection, suspicion, fearfulness, and despair. We spoke in an early chapter about the "seductiveness" of friendship, that quality which enables a friend to bring out that which is best in the partner of his friendship by breaking through the barriers behind which the other timidly hides what is best in him. The priest must be particularly skilled in this kind of seductiveness, for he must encourage his people to be most fully themselves and to have the courage and fidelity they need to love those who are most intimate with them. While the priest must always beware of manipulation in trying to force others to do good, he must simultaneously always be conscious of his role as the one who creates a climate and an atmosphere of trust in which people are free to express what is best in themselves.

The priest must be a man to whom we can turn for hope—hope in the future that will be better than the present, and hope in the present which builds toward a better future. The priest is a man of hope because he possesses an abundance of hope in himself and because he can communicate this hopefulness to those who turn to him. He is a visionary of the better world to come, and in his own way, creator of that world by his involvement in the world that is.

The priest is a man we turn to for celebration because he is one who sees the links between the sacred and the profane, or rather, because he is the man who perceives most clearly that the profane is suffused, transformed, redeemed, and res-

urrected by the sacred. We turn to him when the time has
come to celebrate the new unities we discover, whether it be
the unity of marriage or the unity of birth or the unity of a
community or the unity of forgiveness or the unity of maturation, or even the unity of death, he it is who convenes our
celebrations and leads us in them. As a matter of fact, his own
specialty as "God's man" and also "the people's man" makes
him a symbol of these unities, and his life, hopefully, a celebration of them.

Most of all, the priest is a man we turn to for love, because
love is above all else what people seek when they "turn to"
him. He is a "friend" in the sense that we have used the word
—a man whom they can trust and who will trust them. He has
the most affective role in human society because he, even
more than the psychiatrist, is "a professional lover."

I was once preparing a document for submission to a committee of bishops on Catholic education and, I fear, somewhat mischievously, I included a phrase which suggested
that Catholic schools ought to be more effective educationally
because, given the Church's principles, there ought to be
more love in the atmosphere of the schools and the teachers
ought to be better lovers. I was warned that the bishops would
surely cut out the phrase because they would feel uneasy at
the thought that Catholic teachers might be lovers. I must
say that, even without the warning, I was not surprised
when the word vanished from the text.

Again, a friend and I were once sitting in the Center House
of a mission community in a country in the Far East, and a
bishop from that community (I wouldn't dream of telling you
what country he was from, except to say that he talked with
a rich brogue) was engaging in a very witty discussion of the
American hierarchy. He came to the name of the Bishop of
Rochester. "Well, now," he said, "the man's a fine orator; I
must give him credit for that—a very powerful orator indeed.
But do you know, Fathers, sometimes I am disturbed by his
choice of language. He uses words that are inappropriate for
a bishop to be using altogether."

"Inappropriate words, my Lord?" I asked, I fear somewhat
impatiently. "Inappropriate, indeed, Father," he replied. "He
uses the word 'love' too much altogether. Everything is love

love, love. Now, Father, that's not the kind of language a bishop should be usin' because, after all, that word is primarily *matrimonial* in its meaning."

In some sense, of course, the good bishop was right, for as we have suggested earlier in this volume, the love of a man and a woman for each other is the prototype and the model of all human friendship. But if bishops are to be forbidden the use of the word, then judgment against St. Paul, and indeed the Lord Himself, seems to be rather strong. The Lord's injunction that all men will know us by the love we have for one another must clearly have been inappropriate advice "altogether."

I am not inclined to dismiss these stories as merely mildly humorous. We are not afraid of the word "love" because we have misunderstood its meaning and linked it with sexual passion. We are more likely afraid of it precisely because of the passion and intensity it implies. Presumably, however, the Lord chose to use it precisely because He demanded intensity in the relationship of His followers, one to another —that same kind of intensity He demonstrated in His affection for them. Instead of speaking of love, we have tried to substitute for it the word "charity," from which we have tried, generally successfully, to drain not only all passionate intensity, but also all implication of personal and human contact. The Latin word *carus* is translated into French as *cher*, and into English as *dear*, but we can conveniently forget it and maintain our strong conviction that the love which is supposed to exist among Christians, particularly between priest and people, is some kind of devitalized, angelicized, dehumanized, and etherealized equivalent of tossing a quarter into a beggar's basket. No wonder people are not attracted by it or attracted to a life which is supposed to be given over to it. For charity without care, love without intensity, friendship without involvement, concern without commitment, and compassion without passion, are, at least for creatures less than angels, not only contradictions in terms, but repellent hypocrisies.

The result of trying to live according to these contradictions shows that when one behaves as though love is a word that is inappropriate "altogether," one very easily becomes a crusty, stale, cynical bachelor from whom all humanity has been drained and who faces the world not as something more than a man, but something less.

The priest is not going to be relevant, therefore, by marching on picket lines or by pouring blood on draft files, or being an expert teeny-bopper, or by marrying, or by drinking beer, praiseworthy as these activities may be. He is going to be relevant in a real sense when he stops worrying about relevance and starts worrying about *being*—that is to say, being a man to whom others can turn, a man who, whatever else he may do in society (and he may do very much) is still expected, more than anyone else, to transcend his doing and to *be* for others. He is a man to whom others can turn, not because of what he is able to do, but because of what he is—a friend to love them, one who generates an atmosphere of warmth and trust in which they are able to love in return.

I often find myself wishing I had realized this when I was a younger priest, because for all the sophistication, wit, and polish of the people of the parish I was in, there was much loneliness, fear, and insecurity, particularly among the young with whom I was supposed to be working, which is to say, of course, in my present terminology, whom I was supposed to be loving. The people needed from their priest vision, motivation, and organization, but what they needed even more was reassurance, hope, affection, and love. They needed someone to tell them that they were, indeed, valuable, that they were worth something, that they could be loved and were loved. I managed, apparently, to do this for some of them, despite myself, but things could have been so very much different had I only known.

The mission, then, of the man to whom people can turn may be demanding, frightening, wearying, threatening, but one cannot imagine how it could be unchallenging, and the fact that it is, indeed, unchallenging for half the priests in the country strongly suggests that the priesthood is caught in intolerable structures, both of training and work, which prevent priests from being the truly "useless" men of the community, men of love, men of hope, that they ought to be. The Church, in an effort to reassume its proper role in human society, must give the highest priority to reforms which will not only enable priests to be lovers once again, but will even enable them not to be anxious about the use of the word, much less think that it is inappropriate "altogether."

Some of the prophets of doom (despite Pope John, they are still very much with us) herald the end of the priesthood either through revolutionary structural and doctrinal change or simply from the drying up of vocation. One is permitted to be skeptical of such gloom, because most of the developments we are projecting in this book depend upon priesthood. If we believe that the world can now, for the first time, learn to solve its major problems of friendship, community, leadership, work, playfulness, organization, secularity, and celebration, and if we further believe that the world will finally learn to solve these problems from observing the quality of relationships in the Church, and if we also believe that the critical relationship in the Church is the one involving the man of God to whom we turn for love and hope and joy, then it becomes clear how important is the priesthood and how crucial are the relationships between priests and people. We will also, incidentally, become aware that we still have a considerable distance to go before we come to the Point Omega.

To be the man of God to whom others turn, to be the man whose relationships are the most important in the world, to be the one who is held ex officio to display models of friendship for others to imitate, may be terrifying, but it is hardly dull. And if men turn away from the possibility of assuming such a role, it is not because there are not risk-takers in the human race—there still are—but because stupidity and apathy and inertia and stubbornness and immaturity have allowed the role to become obscured, dehumanized, and buried within the walls of the rectory. But the man of faith and hope is quite confident that the walls are going to come tumbling down.

Chapter 12

A FUTURE TO HOPE IN

As we catch our breath in the midst of the dizzying pace of the changes we see all around us and try momentarily to pause and read the signs of the times, we find ourselves caught in a conflict between pessimism and optimism. Never before have things looked so good for man, and, simultaneously, never before have they looked so bad. Unless we allow ourselves to be swept along by the rush of events, we must find a perspective, a frame of reference, into which we can fit our experience. We must determine whether we should be pessimistic or optimistic.

There are more than enough reasons for pessimism. There has been a proliferation of nuclear weapons and the means to deliver them. Perhaps more than a quarter of a million nuclear weapons are stored away in various places in the world, and there are other even more sophisticated forms of chemical and bacteriological warfare available to anyone brave enough to run the risk of using them. We have had peace of a sort for a quarter of a century, although there was the indecisive war in Korea and the ambiguous and corrosive war in Vietnam, and many other brush-fire and limited wars. But the peace is an anxious peace, a balance of terror, with the possibility of almost instantaneous destruction always lurking around the corner.

Ethnic and racial conflicts persist, and if anything, have grown more violent; in the United States they threaten to quite literally tear apart our society. The credibility of leadership is declining, and we do not know when our leaders are telling us the truth or if, in fact, they ever tell us the truth. We are faced with a nightmare of population explosion creating misery and economic havoc in many places of the world, and threatening the whole world in the next century.

We observe the rationalization, the computerization, the bureaucratization of society, and watch giantism become more rampant and corporate irresponsibility more uncontrolled.

We see the depletion of the natural resources of the world and the slow conversion of our playground into a garbage heap, and we marvel at the irresponsibility of the new nations and the dull, unimaginativeness of the old. All in all, it is not a bright picture.

On the other hand, the optimists have a case too. Psychology has made great progress in understanding and coping with human fear and distrust, and is moving in the direction of making major breakthroughs against the psychic evils which are much worse than any of the physical evils science has thus far been able to eliminate or control. Sociology has made progress also, though perhaps less, in understanding the problems of human community and organization and the means to cope with them. We have developed a personalist philosophy and even a personalist culture which stress the human person, his fulfillment, and his relationships with his fellows as the central concern of existence. And we are in the process of developing a theology which reaffirms the value of the person and his relationships in the world in which he is immersed.

Advances in transportation and communication have created the raw material for world consensus. Technological progress makes feasible for the first time the elimination of most poverty and misery. It is possible to create a liberal-leisure society for the whole world and to eliminate many, if not most, human diseases. Leisure for artistic creation and enjoyment has been broadened, and moral consciousness and generosity seem to be stronger among the best of our young people than they have ever been before. Our new understanding of the marriage union and child-rearing gives us hope of greater sexual fulfillment and greater personality development in the future. Indeed open to us is a vision of sexual pleasure so overwhelming as to be almost unbelievable and personality maturity so powerful as to be almost irresistible. Finally, we look around us and see that, despite all the conflict and hatred in the world, the timid beginnings of world organization, begun with the League of Nations, have slowly, inch by inch, moved ahead. A world political community, a community based on consensus and perhaps even on trust, is slowly beginning to be formed, though one wonders if it will be formed in time.

How can these opposing trends be balanced? For the first time, man can recapture paradise. He can create his own park to play in, or he can create hell, or he can end the whole evolutionary experiment which is *Homo sapiens*. The options are narrowing; within the next century it may be one or the other—paradise or hell.

The system does not contain any answers within itself. Depending on one's disposition, one can say that man usually makes a mess of things or that man usually manages to survive. Depending upon one's philosophy or faith or endocrine system, or the state of one's stomach, one responds either optimistically or pessimistically. But how does the Christian reply? Jürgen Moltmann, one of the most exciting of the contemporary theologians of hope, describes how the Christian must respond:

Man's hopes and longings and desires, once awakened by specific promises, stretch further than any fulfilment that can be conceived or experienced. However limited the promises may be, once we have caught in them a whiff of the future, we remain restless and urgent, seeking and searching beyond all experiences of fulfilment, and the latter leave us an aftertaste of sadness. The "not yet" of expectation surpasses every fulfilment that is already taking place now. Hence every reality in which a fulfilment is already taking place now, becomes the confirmation, exposition and liberation of a greater hope. If we could use this as a help towards understanding the "expanding and broadening history of promise," if we ask the reason for the abiding overplus of promise as compared with history, then we must again abandon every abstract schema of promise and fulfilment. We must then have recourse to the theological interpretation of this process: the reason for the overplus of promise and for the fact that it constantly overspills history lies in the inexhaustibility of the God of promise, who never exhausts himself in any historic reality but comes "to rest" only in a reality that wholly corresponds to him.[1]

For the Christian, then, there isn't much choice. He may be neither optimistic nor pessimistic, but he must be hopeful. Indeed, he must be increasingly hopeful. Hope is not a conviction based on the data that everything is going to be all right, but rather faith and a promise that transcends the evidence, good or bad. Nor is it merely the possibility of a personal spiritual salvation, though personal happiness is certainly involved. For we cannot, in the world of incarnation and resurrection, distinguish between a salvation in the next world and a salvation *of* this world. In Moltmann's words:

> The Christian Church has not to serve mankind in order that this world may remain what it is, or may be preserved in the state in which it is, but in order that it may transform itself and become what it is promised to be. For this reason "Church for the world" can mean nothing else but "Church for the kingdom of God" and the renewing of the world. This means in practice that Christianity takes up mankind—or to put it concretely, the Church takes up the society with which it lives—into its own horizon of expectation of the eschatological fulfilment of justice, life, humanity and sociability, and communicates in its own decisions in history its openness and readiness for this future and its elasticity towards it.[2]

Therefore man's pilgrimage, in which the Church is deeply involved, is no mere pilgrimage from some small beginning toward an indefinite and undescribed end, much less toward an explosive destruction, but a specific pilgrimage toward a promised goal. We are an exodus Church. We have come forth, but we are going somewhere, and the human race is an exodus: people moving from one land to another. And as

[1] Jürgen Moltmann, *The Theology of Hope* (New York and Evanston: Harper & Row), pp. 105–6.
[2] Moltmann, op. cit., pp. 327–28.

we look at the present stage of our mutual exodus, we will understand that we must be deeply involved in it if only because we perceive that the dynamic of our own resurrection promise is undeniably responsible for bringing man to the position where he is, for having forced him into a situation of rapidly narrowing options.

According to Moltmann:

> This world is not the heaven of self-realization, as it was said to be in Idealism. This world is not the hell of self-estrangement, as it is said to be in romanticist and existentialist writing. The world is not yet finished, but is understood as engaged in a history. It is therefore the world of possibilities, the world in which we can serve the future, promised truth and righteousness and peace. This is an age of diaspora, of sowing in hope, of self-surrender and sacrifice, for it is an age which stands within the horizon of a new future. Thus self-expenditure in this world, day-to-day love in hope, becomes possible and becomes human within that horizon of expectation which transcends this world. The glory of self-realization and the misery of self-estrangement alike arise from hopelessness in a world of lost horizons. To disclose to it the horizon of the future of the crucified Christ is the task of the Christian Church.[3]

The Church cannot, therefore, permit itself the luxury of either pessimism or optimism, the luxury of being completely possessed by the present state of the exodus or standing apart from it, for the Church is in the vanguard position with one foot in the camp where we are and one foot out on the desert, as we begin to move forward. It must therefore take upon itself the vanguard responsibilities:

It must stir up and probe. It must refuse to let complacency and satisfaction or fear and timidity cause man to close off his options. We must see the vision of the promise more clearly than others and proclaim this vision to our fellows. The Church, according to Moltmann:

> . . . will therefore endeavour to lead our modern institutions away from their own immanent tendency toward

[3] Ibid., p. 338.

stabilization, will make them uncertain, historify them and open them to that elasticity which is demanded by openness towards the future for which it hopes. In practical opposition to things as they are, and in creative reshaping of them, Christian hope calls them in question and thus serves the things that are to come. With its face towards the expected new situation, it leaves the existing situation behind and seeks for opportunities of bringing history into ever better correspondence to the promised future.[4]

By the example of its own relationships, as friendship, as community, and as society, the Church will show to the world the kinds of love which will be completely fulfilled in the promise, and even now are a preparation for it, for as Moltmann points out, *promissio* means *missio:*

Its language is the language of promises. It understands history as the reality instituted by promise. In the light of the present promise and hope, the as yet unrealized future of the promise stands in contradiction to given reality. The historic character of reality is experienced in this contradiction, in the front line between the present and the promised future. History in all its ultimate possibilities and dangers is revealed in the event of promise constituted by the resurrection and cross of Christ.[5]

By our excitement about the possibilities of the promise and our confidence in its certainty, we must radiate hope to those who need it, and all men need it. Our life, our celebration in liturgy, our priesthood emanating confidence and love, and our laity loving each other and their fellow men with ever more intense passion, are a sign that pessimism and optimism are irrelevant and despair is folly.

We will inspire men to reverence for the world in which they live and the history in which they are taking part, because the world is a place and history the process for the fulfillment of the resurrection promise.

God is not somewhere in the Beyond, but he is coming and as the coming One he is present. He promises a new

[4] Ibid., p. 330.
[5] Ibid., pp. 224–25.

world of all-embracing life, of righteousness and truth, and with this promise he constantly calls this world in question —not because to the eye of hope it is as nothing, but because to the eye of hope it is not yet what it has the prospect of being. When the world and the human nature bound up with it are called in question in this way, then they become "historic," for they are staked upon, and submitted to the crisis of, the promised future. Where the new begins, the old becomes manifest. Where the new is promised, the old becomes transient and surpassable. Where the new is hoped for and expected, the old can be left behind. Thus "history" arises in the light of its end, in the things which happen because of, and become perceptible through, the promise that lights up the way ahead. Eschatology does not disappear in the quicksands of history, but it keeps history moving by its criticism and hope; it is itself something like a sort of quicksand of history from afar.[6]

The Church, then, stirs men out of their complacency, instructs them by the power of its love, inspires them with its hope, and reassures them by its respect for the world and for history—or, at least, this is the mission of the Church, a mission rooted in promise, a mission which, in the final analysis, must be irresistible.

It is terribly difficult to see how there is any other source for hope besides one founded in faith and manifested in love. The rational approach of the secular humanist simply cannot cope with the evil in the world and the possibility for greater evil, and so the rational optimist is forced to neurotic repression if he is serious. The alternatives are, in reality, as we have said before, either existentialist despair or Christian hope, and the latter must commend itself with the thought that having brought us to our present possibilities for paradise or hell, it might conceivably be able to bring us through the dangers inherent in such possibilities. But for the Church the basic problem is not to persuade the humanists that they are unsure of the ground on which they stand (and it is pretty shaky ground), nor the existentialist that they are the monu-

[6] Ibid., pp. 164–65.

mental party-poopers of all history, but rather to persuade ourselves that we have reason to hope, and thus time to love. If we search for an explanation of why many of us see no reason to hope and have no time to love, the answer must be, because we do not yet have the courage to believe.

So we find ourselves stuck with the poor, battered, inefficient, stumbling Catholic Church, unquestionably the leader of Christianity, even if it does not want to be. It does not look like a very promising vessel to carry such faith, hope, and love, particularly as it now seems bent upon wasting the possibilities of Vatican Council II—for which God forgive it. Yet neither did Peter's fishing boat look like much to carry the promise. The Roman Church is, in truth, not much, but it is all we have. It is, for all its weakness and incompleteness, our single best hope—the bride still quite blemished, but eagerly awaiting the return of the bridegroom.

If it is the vessel of promise—and a man of faith believes it is—it will have to become once again the light of the nations, and pretty soon, at that, because the way things look now, the nations will need a lot of light in the immediate future.

The final speculation of this highly speculative volume is that if our faith in the promise is correct (which unquestionably it is), and if we read the signs of the times correctly (which we may not), then Christianity will make immense progress in the years to come and immense progress in mankind, of which Christianity is the vanguard, and immense progress in the Catholic Church, which is, whether it likes it or not, the center of Christianity. The promise will not be frustrated even by a lover who, because of ineptitude and misunderstanding, has tried his best to be faithless. The Lord does not repent of the promises He has made even if those to whom He has made the promise do their best to forget its implications.

Hope does not mean that the promise will be fulfilled without trouble and suffering, for resurrection only follows crucifixion, and presumably most of us who are alive are not going to live to see more than the beginning of the major evolutionary breakthrough this volume postulates. But this does not matter greatly, because we can see it even now through the vision of faith; also, we know that somehow or other, because of the resurrection promise, we will be around at some point in the game to collect the rewards for our efforts. "Eyes have not seen nor ears heard nor has it entered into the heart of man the things which God has prepared for those who love Him."

For our hope is not merely in the future yet to come but also in the future as dimly and inchoatively present now, as man becomes more conscious of himself and more clearly aware of the splendor of his possibilities, and realizes that these possibilities exist, if only minutely, in the present moment. Our faith is not merely in the Omega to come, but also in the Omega here in our midst.

OTHER IMAGE BOOKS

OTHER IMAGE BOOKS

OTHER IMAGE BOOKS

OTHER IMAGE BOOKS

Keeping Watch

Viking

KEEPING WATCH

A History of
American Time

Michael O'Malley

VIKING
Published by the Penguin Group
Viking Penguin, a division of Penguin Books USA Inc.,
375 Hudson Street, New York, New York 10014, U.S.A.
Penguin Books Ltd, 27 Wrights Lane, London W8 5TZ, England
Penguin Books Australia Ltd, Ringwood, Victoria, Australia
Penguin Books Canada Ltd, 2801 John Street,
Markham, Ontario, Canada L3R 1B4
Penguin Books (N.Z.) Ltd, 182–190 Wairau Road,
Auckland 10, New Zealand

Penguin Books Ltd, Registered Offices:
Harmondsworth, Middlesex, England

First published in 1990 by Viking Penguin,
a division of Penguin Books USA Inc.

1 3 5 7 9 10 8 6 4 2

LIBRARY OF CONGRESS CATALOGING IN PUBLICATION DATA
O'Malley, Michael.
Keeping watch : a history of American time / Michael O'Malley.
p.   cm.
ISBN 0–670–82934–X
1. Time—Systems and standards—United States—History.
I. Title.
QB223.O43   1990
389'.17'0973 — dc20   89–40681

Printed in the United States of America
Set in Cochin
Designed by Michael Ian Kaye

To Kimberly,
and to my family

Preface

I wasted time, and now doth time waste me;
For now hath time made me his numb'ring clock.
                                    —*Richard II*

America, *Time* magazine announced in April 1989, is "running itself ragged." "These are the days of the time famine," the cover story insisted; everywhere you look you find Americans desperately trying to do more with less. Bosses demand longer and longer hours. Combining work and child rearing makes parents frantic, unable to keep up, and meanwhile the jet stream of new information rushes past, ever faster. Time-saving devices never seem to save us any time—computers, cellular phones, and fax machines make international business go round the clock. We live in a global community, *Time* pointed out, knit together by instantaneous communication and standard time. An architect complains that his staff managed to reach him while he sat on the beach at Anguilla, supposedly on vacation. "There are times," he says, "when our lives are clearly leading us." The "time famine" strikes both rich and poor—who has never glanced resentfully at the clock, racing a deadline, and not wondered how the machine became so powerful? According to *Time*, the average American now enjoys 37 percent less leisure than in 1973. Why this shortage of time?[1]

To explain our problem, we have to sort out the difference between what we think about work and how we understand *time*. Life in America has always been plagued by one peculiar fact: work nearly always expands to fill the time available. Time-saving devices and strategies for more efficiency only raise our expectations about what we can get done. Save time in one job, and some other task appears to fill that time up. Buy a microwave oven, and the time you gain heating up dinner goes to chores, or classes, or work brought home. We resent this tendency, but in fact most Americans believe strongly in work, and have a deep suspicion of loafers.

Eighty years ago Max Weber called this the "Protestant Ethic," the belief that idleness is sin and that work, pure and simple work, is virtuous for its own sake. Weber's classic analysis rooted modern society's obsession with saving time in the Calvinist sense of anxiety about salvation. But belief in the virtue of work precedes the Puritans. Benedictine monks of the thirteenth century believed that "work is prayer," and that wasting time offended God. They set up elaborate and rigorous schedules designed to thwart the lazy and spur the productive to greater effort. The first mechanical clocks, in fact, were simply automatic bell ringers designed to rouse pious monks from bed and keep them on schedule. Why, in what most people would probably like to imagine as a simpler, more leisurely era, did they have to work so hard?[2]

The answer lies in what they believed about time. In the Judeo-Christian heritage, time has always belonged to God. According to Genesis, God began time by dividing light from dark and setting the heavens moving. And since Adam and Eve's eviction from Eden, God's ownership has demanded hard labor—time on earth must be spent working, to earn our daily bread. If you believe God intended you to work, then it follows that the harder you work, the more you please God. Time in this sense is like a loan from God: men and women have an obligation to use it wisely, to "improve the time," as the Puritans put it. Of course not all Protestants work hard; nor are all hardworking people Protestants.[3] The impulse to work hard is related to the understanding of time, but it's not the same thing.

This is not a study of the pressure to work harder, or a study of how hard people actually worked, but a study of how American ideas about time and its authority changed. It focuses on how we built the web of interconnected, standardized clock time that structures our lives and labor, and how it altered the way we think about ourselves and our society. In the nineteenth century, time changed from a phenomenon rooted in nature and God to an arbitrary, abstract quantity based in machines, in clocks. The development of standard time zones, the mass production of watches and clocks, the invention of instantaneous, synchronized time transmissions and factory punch clocks; all these established new patterns for self-discipline, social order, and the organization of knowledge.[4]

Standard time amounted to a reconstruction of authority—the authority Americans used to govern themselves both in private and public life, at work and in play. By supplanting nature and God with clocks and watches, standard time replaced religious guidelines for dividing up the day, or "natural law," with secular authorities based on efficiency and convenience. Standard clock time, and the mass production of mechanical timekeepers, forced people to reconsider the meaning of machines and mechanical invention—what happened to old notions of individuality, of the individual's place in the scheme of things, when machines became the pattern for social organization instead of nature? Standardized time changed the way Americans thought about themselves and their world.

Not all people experienced these changes in the same way,

because different ethnic and cultural groups approached them with different ideas about time and work. But everyone had to confront them at some point, just as no one living in the United States today, rich or poor, rural or urban, can avoid running up against this framework of standardized clock time. Working, waiting in line, going to a movie, watching TV: all of these demand that we pay attention to the clock, and to an international network built on uniform timekeeping. The history of American time shows how we came to grant the clock such an enormous influence on our lives.[5]

Chapter One describes a small crisis in antebellum American culture, as a sense of time rooted in nature and religion confronted mechanically based sources of time that offered new models for social organization. Chapter Two follows the evolution of a partial answer, regional standard times based on astronomy. These regional standard times helped rationalize interstate commerce and trade. The introduction of national standard time zones by the railroads is the subject of Chapter Three, along with the lasting and virulent hostility they provoked. Chapter Four discusses the mass production and marketing of clocks, watches, and factory punchclocks, exploring the strange interdependence that developed between timekeeping machines and their owners. Standard time established new ways of ordering knowledge, new models for self-discipline. Taylorism, discussed in Chapter Four, provides the transition to the next chapter, which speculates about the connections between time and progressive politics by examining motion picture narrative. The final chapter relates the introduction and repeal of daylight saving during World War I, using the debate to guess at Americans' attitudes toward the framework of standard time created over the preceding fifty years. It ends with the struggle over time, nature, and evolution at the Scopes Trial.

Finishing this book demanded a great deal of ruthlessness,

because a subject as vast as "time" constantly threatens to sprawl out of control. Along the way, friends and fellow scholars suggested many fascinating and potentially rewarding areas of research which I ultimately had to ignore. The book is poorer for it, and the fault is mine. My thanks to the many people, too many to mention all by name, who made working on this project so intriguing. Lawrence W. Levine, Mary Ryan, and Michael P. Rogin, members of my dissertation committee at the University of California, Berkeley, offered a model of generosity and provocative, challenging scholarship. I hope that Professor Levine's commitment to fairness, sympathy, and freedom from clichés echoes in these pages. The graduate students at Berkeley, especially Mark Meigs and Jeff Lena, made it an exciting, friendly intellectual environment, and gave me a chance to play the low post. My thanks also to Anne Hyde, Mary Odem, Lucy Salyer, Nina Silber, and Brian Wiener.

The dissertation that preceded this book was written with the benefit of a Smithsonian Institution Predoctoral Fellowship, 1987–88. The staff, and fellows, of the National Museum of American History made things easier than I had any right to expect, especially Peter Liebhold, Bonnie Lilienfeld, Steven Lubar, Charles McGovern, Jim Roan, and Kay Youngflesh. I owe a very great deal to Carlene Stephens, curator of the Section of Mechanisms at the museum, for her extraordinary generosity in sharing her work, her thoughts, and her time. She exceeds that remarkable Institution's commitment to the diffusion of knowledge, and this project could not have been accomplished as quickly or as well without her help.

A Mellon Postdoctoral Fellowship from New York University, 1988–89, provided time for revisions, while Thomas Bender helped make my stay at NYU both pleasant and productive. Scott Grimaldi let me watch him edit a movie, and Alice Fahs offered useful comments on Chapter Five. Special thanks to Walter Benn Michaels for his perceptive criticisms of a late draft, and to Dan Frank for his skillful editing.

My greatest thanks go to Kimberly Latta, for her critical insights, patience and love.

Contents

Contents

V

Therbligs and Hieroglyphs · 200

VI

The Golf Stick and the Hoe · 256

Keeping Watch

I

Time, Nature,

and the Good Citizen

In 1826, New Haven's town fathers paid Eli Terry, Connecticut's most celebrated clockmaker, two hundred dollars to install a clock in the town hall. They wanted a proud symbol of their commitment to order, regular habits, and the virtue of conserving time, and at first the clock served them well. But soon they noticed a growing disagreement with their other source of public time, the Yale College clock. Gradually Terry's clock fell farther and farther behind its rival—five, ten, then fifteen minutes. Perhaps it only needed adjusting. Then it slowly began catching up, raising hopes that it might settle down into steady work as it matured. But instead with each passing day it moved ahead of Yale's timepiece. Finally, almost fifteen minutes faster, Terry's perverse clock began sinking back into its old slothful habits, only to once again start gaining on the faithful college clock, week by week. Had Terry saddled the city fathers with an incompetent timekeeper, or some reckless whimsy?

It seemed unlikely—Terry's reputation for Yankee cleverness

and resolute sobriety had made him famous well beyond Connecticut. Yet there stood the finished clock, proud in its lofty place on the town hall and just as proud in its seemingly bald-faced error. But was Terry's clock wrong at all? Perhaps Yale's clock, faithful for many years, had begun showing its age and running erratically. What if Terry's clock revealed the truth, and Yale's timekeeper only now confessed old habits of duplicity? Then who could say what time it really was?

A letter in the New Haven *Columbian Weekly Register* admitted that the two clocks had become "a subject of much observation and enquiry." But the writer insisted that their disagreement, which "might seem to proceed from negligence," in fact came from two completely different ways of arriving at a definition of time. Yale's clock, designed by the late and well-respected Simeon Jocelyn, followed the sun. Terry's clock offered *mean time,* an average of the sun's daily variation.[1] The letter set off a flurry of heated correspondence, and indeed the difference seems as confusing now as it did then, because Terry's clock posed a difficult but particularly timely question—not what time is it, but what is time?

A bustling market town like New Haven demanded solid answers to both questions. Yale's President Timothy Dwight boasted proudly of New Haven's particular "industry and economy." Busy citizens leavened their business acumen with the college's theological tradition and growing scientific prestige—in 1826, Yale planned on soon establishing one of the first permanent astronomical observatories in America. Native industry, fed by the freshening stream of learning and banked by Protestant religious piety, made his fellows the equal of any Americans in "intelligence, refinement, morals and religion," Dwight happily concluded. He reflected with pleasure on the town's "peace and good order," its freedom from crime and strife, and anticipated a prosperous, peaceful, and well-governed future for his city.

But he also lamented the rapid growth of a class of *"laborers,"* generally "either shiftless, diseased, or vicious," who lacked the sense of order and time-discipline Dwight found so laudable. Their presence cast a darkening cloud over New Haven's industrial future. Dwight's praise of his fellow citizens linked the wise use of time to industrious self-discipline and orderly progress. Yet his sharp criticism of the laboring class, with its apparent lack of industry and indifference to the future, hinted at alternative visions of time and its use, of conflicts to come over both the nature of time and its role in ordering civic affairs.[2] A few years after Dwight's remarks, Eli Terry's clock gave those conflicts substance.

Understanding New Haven's problem requires a brief explanation of the principles of timekeeping. Without really thinking about it, Terry's customers measured time in two different ways. Their simplest measure depended on the sun. When Sol reached the highest point in his passage across the sky, any sundial or even a simple post stuck in the ground read "noon." Anyone could see that, or read the hours on a sundial. But the earth both circles the sun elliptically *and* tilts on its axis. More observant Yankees noticed that the sun's apparent position in the sky varied during the year—noon passed at different points, sometimes higher in the sky, sometimes lower. Astronomers call this annoying habit the sun's *declination.* The variation made no difference if the sun was the only measure of time. When the sundial showed "noon," it was noon—God created the sun to give light and measure time, after all, at the very Genesis of Time itself, and so noon was noon when the sun said so.[3] For obvious reasons, this was called *apparent time.*

But once clocks entered the scene, things got more complicated. Ordinary clockwork cannot follow the sun's irregular movement. Instead, most clocks tell only *mean time,* a convenient average of the sun's apparent variation. Any ordinary, mean time clock set to solar noon on a given day soon begins to drift away from the sun. At its extremes, an ordinary clock read up to sixteen minutes fast or fifteen minutes slow of the sundial four times a year.* Clockmakers had known about the difference between clock and sun time for centuries. They even had a name for it — "the equation of time" — and had devised a few special mechanisms that reproduced the sun's movement. But a clock that showed this "declination" demanded special skills to make and maintain, and cost a lot of money. The vast majority of ordinary clocks told mean time alone, as they always had and still do. When clock and sun varied, most people assumed the clock was wrong, and simply reset it to agree with time by the sun.

Yet the difference between clock and sun was exactly what New Haven confronted, because unbeknownst to most of the town, Jocelyn's Yale College clock had "an apparatus attached to it, invented by himself, which produces a daily variation from [mean time] exactly equal to the variation of the sun."[4] The late Jocelyn's clock, lo and behold, was an *apparent time* clock. It reinforced the astronomy lessons at the college by demonstrating the solar principles of timekeeping, and kept Yale running with the sun. But now it rested in awkward intimacy with an ordinary, mean time clock, with which it would agree only four times a year.

This two-timing arrangement upset New Haven clock watchers. The two clocks questioned the nature of time itself: was it celestial movements or the mechanical timepiece? Signing himself "True Time," one reader of New Haven's *Connecticut Journal* attacked Terry's mechanism. "To have a clock in a town to tell the public what the time is *not* is certainly a novel scheme," he declared sarcastically. "It is said that the clock gives *mean* time," he continued. "But why mean time? Mean time is not true time, nor is true time mean time. A public clock, which tells the truth four

---

* Today, standard time zones and daylight saving have shifted things around, and computing standard clock time from most sundials now requires a whole set of compensating tables.

times only in a year, is something very much like a public nuisance," he concluded.[5] "True Time" demanded to know why the sun—the source of "true" time—had been abandoned for a capricious approximation. Seemingly unaware that almost all clocks could only show mean time, "True Time" echoed a common ambiguity and confusion about time's relationship to clocks.

Clocks were still relatively rare in 1826. Most people, if they owned a clock at all, kept one of Terry's fifteen-dollar "pillar and scroll" shelf models on their mantle. Terry had begun experimenting with interchangeable parts around 1800. By 1826, he had worked out the problems of mass production and was growing wealthy and famous by making and selling ordinary mean time clocks to farmers for miles around. Attractive and affordable, Terry's wooden clocks were not particularly accurate—two or three minutes' variation in a week was optimistic at best. There were also tower clocks, typically situated, like New Haven's, in a church or town hall. These were more accurate, but not by that much; and not always conveniently located, either. The wealthy owned watches, but these also tended to vary, and different timepieces rarely agreed. "Twenty gentlemen in company," almanac maker Nathaniel Low had claimed in 1786, "will hardly be able, by the help of their thirty-guinea watches, to guess within two hours of the true time of night . . . whilst the poor peasant, who never saw a watch, will tell the time to a fraction by the rising and setting of the moon," Low boasted, "which he learns from his almanack."[6] Forty years later clocks were a little more common, but for rural people especially the only reliable indicator of time remained the heavens—the moon and sun's hours of rising and setting as published in the almanac, or the sun's passage shown on a sundial.

"True Time's" letter makes sense, then, if understood by light of the solar timepiece. But it inspired several replies. One "J" explained the difference between mean and apparent time and pointed out "True Time's" mistaken belief that ordinary clocks told apparent time. He insisted that "the public must decide on the comparative utility of these clocks." While suggesting that Jocelyn's apparent time clock might help the faculty at Yale, who conducted their classes by daylight and were concerned to teach astronomy, "J" conceded that most people would simply check their timepieces against a sundial or noon mark occasionally, as they always had. Rather than posing a challenge to New Haven's good order, he explained, the two clockfaces merely demonstrated the scientific principles of timekeeping.

A second, anonymous reply to "True Time," unconcerned by astronomical niceties, insisted that "all the business of our life— our meals—our labors—our hours of rest—everything requires that the day should be divided into equal and uniform portions." It mattered not what standard prevailed, the writer insisted pragmatically, so long as all agreed to use it. Most ordinary clocks and watches could show only mean time—"surely," he reasoned, "the public at large ought not to have all their operations deranged, or their timepieces injured, by attempts to follow the variations of apparent time."[7] But "True Time," even more incensed, dashed off a second letter for the next week's edition.

"Astronomers," he retorted, "have always calculated almanacs, not for *mean* but for *apparent* [solar] time." A clock like Terry's waged "constant war" with the almanac, in fact rendering the almanac nearly useless. "The rising and setting of the sun, of the moon, of the stars . . . and most other celestial appearances are given in every ephemeris in apparent time," he continued, and "all these times are deranged by a clock regulated like the town clock of New Haven." Terry's clock, rumbled "True Time," constituted "an evil of no small magnitude."[8]

The controversy continued over the following months. One correspondent sarcastically wondered if progress might someday enable men to "regulate the sun by the clock." Until that day, he insisted, "we had better be content to go the old way," and, following the college, "regulate our clocks by the sun." He charged that "the citizens of New Haven have been taxed to pay for a clock which gives us false notions of time. Have they not been imposed upon?" If Terry's clock "cannot be so regulated as to keep true time," then "the sooner it is silenced the better. We believe this to be the opinion of MANY," went the conclusion.[9]

In Terry's defense, a reply lamented that "MANY's" remarks had "given uneasiness" to "that worthy artist." It offered the startling claim that Terry's clock "is so constructed as to keep either *mean* or *apparent* time, and also the difference between them." The citizens of New Haven could choose either way of keeping time, "for the clock will do as bid by them." As a young man, Terry had in fact patented an apparent time clock in 1797—the second patent ever issued by the United States. The clock had special gearing and two minute hands of different colors, one for mean and one for apparent time. It had never made him a dime, and so perhaps an inventor's pride had led him to revive the clock for New Haven. At any rate, Terry's champion concluded that when the facts about the new clock "are well known, I trust they will be satisfactory not only to 'many' but to ALL."[10]

But what time would they choose? A final letter, from "A Citizen of the United States," offered a carefully worded description of the difference between apparent and mean time. Although "Citizen" pointed out that in European cities especially, mean time had proven a great convenience, he admitted that New Haven might choose either system. The town's decision remains a mystery, as the correspondence stops here. If Terry's clock could indeed show apparent time, then most likely New Haven kept its public clocks in line with the sun. The clocks could then be regulated by an almanac, or by astronomical observation.[11]

The whole affair might strike the modern reader as silly, but in 1826 there was more to this little incident than the time of day—"True Time" and his opponents debated the nature and source of time itself. The clocks had juxtaposed several concurrent ways of thinking about time. By pitting clock time, a man-made approximation, against the "true" standard of time as revealed in the heavens, and throwing business affairs into disorder, the two clocks dramatized a profound philosophical difference over what time was, who could control it, and how it might be used.

Conflicts like this undoubtedly occurred all over America in the 1820s, because the antebellum decades witnessed a small crisis in the authority of time. As clocks became more and more common, and more and more popular as tools for social organization, Americans began asking these questions more often. Was time a natural phenomenon, rooted in religion and the agricultural traditions of centuries? Or was time an object of rational inquiry, subject to mastery by inquisitive scientists? Or was time simply a convenience, an arbitrary number useful for doing business?

Historians have documented a transition in antebellum America, as an older system of public and private relations, characterized variously as "paternalism" or "republicanism," gave way to new organizations of authority and power. Industrialization and immigration shifted accustomed class relations; new technologies of communication and transportation disrupted market patterns and local economies. The same social and economic pressures that led to religious revivals, to utopian communities, to temperance movements, to reformations in the system of prisons, asylums, and schools, brought with them reorganizations in the systems of time governing labor and public life.[12]

In America at the dawn of the industrial revolution, nature gave evidence of time's passage. The sun's transit, the moon's phases, the passing seasons—all these indicated time and offered a model for using it wisely. In a very real sense, "nature" and "time" meant the same thing. Even the earliest settlers knew about clocks and watches. But they understood mechanical timepieces as mere representations or symbols of time, not as the embodiment of time itself. Where individuals and communities had clocks or watches, they set them to the local sun—each city, town, village, and farm kept its own local time. As the natural world revealed it, time offered Americans lessons in hard work, diligence, thrift, cooperation, rationality, and moral virtue. In almanacs, schoolbooks, and in the patterns of farm work itself, natural phenomena reinforced God's authority and men and women's duty to labor hard and use time, following nature's model, in God's service. But the industrial revolution challenged these assumptions. By the 1830s, a sense of time rooted in nature confronted a seemingly arbitrary time based in commerce, revealing itself in machine movements and the linear progress of invention.

In an agrarian society making the transition to industry, time-keepers posed a difficult and even threatening dilemma. Clocks were first invented to *tell* time, to give a more reliable indication, on cloudy days or at night, of the passage of a quantity belonging to God. The very first mechanical clocks, not surprisingly, simply rang bells to signal the pious monk's hours for prayer. But in the act of telling time the clock tended to become the thing it represented—clocks became not imitations or transcripts of time, but time itself. There was nothing particularly new about clocks governing human movements. In Europe clock bells had been organizing town and village life for generations, and the constant tension between "natural" and "mechanical" time they fostered mirrored the conflict of secular and religious authority.[13] But the mass production of clocks—that was new. So too was the factory system, and the rapid communication and travel it both demanded and encouraged. Nature offered one model for social organization, but as the industrial revolution progressed—bringing with it thousands of Terry's Yankee clocks—the time-telling machine began imposing its own imperatives on life and work.

―――

How did you tell time before the clock? The first and most obvious answer was the sun. Even on cloudy days the sun's passage marked the lapse of time, and on clear days the shadows it cast translated into hours on a sundial or a noon mark inscribed on a wall. In a world less concerned with precise timekeeping, the shadows of trees, rocks, or buildings served the same purpose. Hourglasses measured periods of duration and often timed the minister's sermon, the parishioners perhaps groaning inwardly as the more zealous preachers announced that they would "take another glass." A few tower clocks stood in eighteenth-century America, and the wealthier colonists owned clocks of varying quality, but for people away from major towns the sun, moon, and stars provided the only consistent standard.[14]

On the farm, labor provided its own measures of time. Cows demanded milking twice a day, other animals had to be fed, watered, or sheared; planting, pruning, harvesting—each month, each day brought a round of specific tasks conducted "in their season." Anthropologists, who call this system "task orientation," often view the "natural" time of preindustrial societies as more relaxed, more humane, more respectful of individual autonomy. But for American farm families at least, it is simply wrong to automatically view "task orientation," both in the home and out, as uniformly somehow freer or more leisurely. Farm and house work, spurred by Protestant theology and biblical warnings against idle hands, demanded constant effort. Simply because no mechanical clocks oversaw their activities does not mean that Americans ignored time's passage; in fact, time often presented itself in terms of a sacred duty. Esther Burr, daughter of Puritan divine Jonathan Edwards, frequently complained about the daily grind of her domestic labors. "But I must submit," she wrote in her journal, "my time is not my own but God's."[15]

Two beliefs inform Burr's lament: one about the origin of time, meaning its belonging to God, and the other about the ways time should be used, in her case meaning pious submission to a wearying routine. That she believed time could be possessed is significant in itself; that she believed God's possession of time required her to work hard in obedience to His paternal authority is even more so. We usually understand time in terms of how we use it—the organization of life, the distribution of work and leisure. But this approach obscures the abstract idea of time we use to make our decisions. "Time" must have an origin; it must be considered to have come from somewhere. These origins give time its authority, determining how it should be used. Max Weber's classic analysis suggested that time's origination in God led Calvinists especially to reorganize work and life, as Esther Burr did, around the new imperatives of the Protestant Ethic. Burr needed to "redeem the time," to give evidence of her respect for God's gift—time—by scrupulously saving and using it with piety and care.

What is there of freedom in her obligation to work ceaselessly at turning God's time to profit? What is relaxed about farm and house work's constant round of labor and repair? Where is leisure in a religious creed demanding scrupulous self-improvement even in "leisure" time? Obviously Burr represents an extreme. Lazy people co-exist with busy people in any society, and for every example of industry an example of sloth sits idly by in the shade, laughing. The point here is not to document the amount of work done by any given set of people in a given hour, but rather to explore time's authority—where it comes from, how it is understood, and from this how it can be used to order life. There is a difference between preindustrial time and the understanding of time that replaced it. But the sheer amount of work accomplished measures the difference poorly at best. Often what may look like fundamental differences in attitudes about time in fact have more to do with the kind of work undertaken or the industriousness of the individual.[16]

The difference between Esther Burr's sense of time and our own lies in the symbols and abstractions we use to represent time in public and private life. She found the authority for using her time in God, and saw time revealed in nature; we might find the authority for our decisions about using time in a notion of "efficiency," under the spur of the clock. No precise point of transition from "traditional" to "modern" understandings of time can be fixed; different conceptions of time often co-exist simultaneously in the same society. But understanding the transition between the two requires exploring the idea of time — and the role of the clock — in daily life.

Western European cultures have traditionally understood time both as a circle — a series of repeated natural events like sunrise and sunset or the passing seasons — and as an arrow, shot by God at the dawn of time and stopping only God knows where. Linear and cyclical time have always co-existed, and still co-exist, in our thinking, just as any given society may contain different and even contradictory ideas about time. We depict time, for example, as both a dial, with its endlessly repeated sequence of twelve hours, and as years, totaling an ever higher number toward an uncertain future. Linear time may mean technological and industrial "progress" into that future; it may also recall the inevitability of death and decay. Cyclical time often accompanies the idea of balance in nature, but it just as often recalls the repetitive, clocklike movements of machinery. Our time, in a sense, is like a hoop rolling down a road. In different phases of history and culture we emphasize different aspects of time's duality.[17]

Colonial and antebellum Americans paid remarkably strict and close attention to time's passage and the obligations it imposed. Almanacs were by far the most popular books in the colonies and remained so well after the revolution. American almanacs emphasized the cyclical quality of time, by offering a yearly review of seasonal tasks. But they also served as guides for understanding, interpreting, and managing time correctly as it rolled along toward God's eternity. The second book published in America was an almanac, at Cambridge in 1638 or 1639, and the Cambridge press dominated the field for its first thirty-five years. Products of Puritan Harvard, these early "Philomath" or astronomical almanacs concentrated on explaining the phenomena of the heavens in terms of God's providence, willfully overlooking any contradiction between science and religion that might suggest itself. Typically they combined the two, supplying the times of the holy Sabbath and helping clarify the mysteries of God as revealed in the heavens and the natural world.[18]

Almanac maker Samuel Atkins, traveling through Maryland in 1686, declared that the people "scarcely knew how the time passed, nor that they hardly knew the day of rest, or the Lord's Day, when it was, for want of . . . an Almanack." Without a guide to time reckoning Marylanders simply could not organize their days properly, he claimed. "On the other side," Atkins continued, "having met with Ingenious persons, that have been lovers of the Mathematical Arts, some of which have wanted an Ephemeris to make some Practice thereon," he decided to offer his own almanac "to these my Country men."[19] Atkins's solar and lunar timetables merged Christian piety, science, and the practice of farming. As a guide to holy days his almanacs enabled people to orient themselves within God's time and respect sacred law—to observe the "correct" times for work and worship—while his precise measurement of the heavens' movements satisfied and encouraged scientific fascination with God's creation.

After about 1680, almanacs began to reflect less concern with theological orthodoxy and more with worldly affairs. These newer almanacs increasingly blended Copernican science with the flavors of deism, as the following poem from "Abraham Weatherwise's" 1759 Almanac demonstrates:

On A Watch

> Could but our Tempers move like this Machine,
> Not urged by Passion, nor delay'd by Spleen;
> But true to Nature's regulating pow'r,
> By virtuous Acts distinguish'd every Hour;
> Then Health and Joy would follow as they ought,
> The Laws of Motion, and the Laws of Thought:
> Sweet Health, to pass the Laws of Moments o'er,
> And everlasting Joy, when Time shall be no more.

"Weatherwise" borrowed from an Enlightenment tradition which used the watch as analogue to God's creation. The movements of the heavens indicated time, as did the watch; they operated according to fixed and discernible principles, like the watch, and the poem suggests that we model our behavior after these movements. The regularity of the physical world as it marks time should be our pattern, and since we can discover laws within its motions, it follows that there must be laws governing our "Tempers"—"Laws of Motion" as well as "Laws of Thought." The well-tempered farm, like the well-tempered society, imitated the regular and clocklike movements of nature, the source and measure of time.[20]

But the clock, in this passage, never represents the *source* of

time. Rather, it serves only as an embodiment of human understanding—of our ability to comprehend nature and natural laws,
and through them the passage of time. The watch is "true to
nature's regulating power": nature, not the mechanical device, is
the model for the organization of society, and time, in this typical
instance, is a by-product of nature. Nature's regular and predictable movements provide clues to the mind of God and thus to the
proper management of time as God intended it. Almanacs charted
these natural movements—which were understood by readers as
Time itself—and helped interpret them.

Although colonial almanacs included much more, solar and
lunar timetables, together called the *ephemeris*, were their main
attraction. The ephemeris usually offered the precise hours and
minutes of the sun's rising, the moon's southing, high and low
tides, eclipses, and the movements of the major stars. Typically
they devoted one page to each month, and combined the times
and dates of celestial appearances with astrological symbols for
interpreting them, weather forecasts, historical information, and
miscellaneous advice to farmers.

The celestial rationalism evident in the poem quoted above
blended easily with what we would call superstition. Eighteenth-
century almanacs usually included a drawing, called the "anatomy"
or "the man of signs," of the human body marked by the signs of
the Zodiac. Each zodiacal symbol controlled or affected a specific
part of the body. By consulting the anatomy, one could learn the
best time for bleeding a diseased arm or leg, or conceiving a child.
Even more commonly, the stars offered advice on farming—when
to plant, wean animals, mend fences, and so on. Cotton Mather,
for example, believed that timber cut in the waning moon of August would never suffer from worms. Like occultism and folk
astrology, the practice of reading the stars for advice on farming
continued well into the twentieth century.[21]

The almanac offered a guide to the stars, helping users understand and manage their lives by situating them in time. Within its pages astrology and astronomy, theology and husbandry, medicine and science combined to schedule work. Readers went to the almanac's timetables for help in managing these different categories of knowledge—on the one hand to discover what time it was at that moment, and on the other to discover the most appropriate time for doing some task. The connection of time to nature, and thus to God, that almanacs reinforced points to an American obsession with time, its measurement, and its proper use.

The most successful almanacs made time management their explicit focus, and of these Robert Bailey Thomas's *Old Farmer's Almanac,* by the early nineteenth century, had become the model for imitators all over the country. Thomas added practical and homely advice to the ephemeris while downplaying astrology and homeopathy somewhat. His "Farmer's Calender" specialized in cautionary messages—for the first week of October 1800 the calendar urged: "Winter apples should now be gathered up, as the frost hurts them much . . . harvest your Indian corn without delay—the birds and squirrels I am confident will."[22] Thomas reminded dilatory readers that each task had its season, and its season was short. But much of the material Thomas printed, like the pages reproduced in part below, now seems nearly indecipherable—such common familiarity with the sun and sky has largely passed away.

Tables like these suggested that a prosperous, orderly, and well-tempered life could be gained by following nature, by running life according to the clock in the sky. They make little distinction between different kinds of events—Bonaparte's death in 1821 (bottom panel, line six) has the same significance as the quadrature of the Sun and the planet Uranus. Though dropping the "man of signs," this most successful of almanacs continued charting the heavens' effects on the human body—column nine of the

MAY, fifth Month.   1830

Blossoms scattered o'er the trees—
Odours wafted in the breeze
Is the bliss of every day,
Towards the last of blooming May.

M.M	D.W	Courts, Aspects, Holydays, Weather, &c. &c	FARMER'S CALENDAR.
1	7	St. Phil. & St. Ja. ☽ ☾ ♆	Farmers should be as busy as Bees.
2	C	3d Sun. past Ea. *Fine*	See now, while the flowers are in
3	2	Mid *weather.*	blooming, the inhabitants of the hive
4	3	[Gen. El. R. I. & Con.	are all in motion! The laborers take
5	4	St. Jn. Ev. ♃ Sta. ☽ Apo.	wing and go abroad in search of hon-
6	5	tide. [Bonap. d. '21. ag. 52.	ey and wax. Honey is a limpid juice
7	6	*The weather*	found in the blossoms. Wax is made
8	7	*continues* ☽ ☉ �8	by the bees from the dust contained
9	C	4th Sun. past Ea. *fine.*	within the blossoms. These different
10	2	*More* [Con.	materials being brought to the hive,
11	3	S. J. C. Len. & Ply. C.C.	the laborers in waiting take the wax,
12	4	*unsettled for some*	and form of it those little six-sided
13	5	Jup. sou. 4h. mor. *days.*	cells, which serve as storehouses for
14	6	*High winds.*	the honey, or nests for the young. The
15	7	Spica so. 9h. 45m.	honey is partly distributed for present
16	C	5th Sun. past E. ♀ G. El.	food to the inhabitants, and the re-
17	2	C. P. Edg Quite *Rain.*	mainder laid up for winter. The
18	3	[D. Dav '80 ☌ ☽ ♀	queen bee now begins to deposit her
19	4	St. Duns. C. C. Edg. ☽ per.	eggs, about 50 each day, in the empty
20	5	Ascen. H. Thur. △ ♀ ♄	cells. The egg, being soon hatched
21	6	high *More*	into a little grub, increases the em-
22	7	tides. *showers.*	ployment of the laborers, whose care
23	C	Sun. past Ascen.	it is to feed it with purest honey.
24	2	C. P. Nant. *Cooler.*	When it is full grown, its cell is seal-
25	3	*Fine settled*	ed up with wax. Its form then alters,
26	4	Gen. El. Boston. *weather.*	and in a few days it breaks its prison,
27	5	Jup. sou. 3h. mor.	being changed into a perfect bee, quits
28	6	Low *Signs of*	the hive, and, joining in the general
29	7	tides. *rain*	employment, goes in search of honey
30	C	Whit-Sun. *Very warm.*	for the public store. Let man take
31	2		a lesson from this little economizer.

" Be cheerful, social, friendly, kind,
Such as may improve the mind ;
Where health and temperance may join,
And Virtue own the soft design."

Pages from Robert Bailey Thomas, The Farmer's Almanac,
May 1830 (Boston, 1829). *Thomas began calling it* The Old
Farmer's Almanac *in 1832, to distinguish
himself from imitators.*

ASTRONOMICAL CALCULATIONS.

Dys.	d.	m.	Dys.	d.	m.	Dvs.	d.	m.	Dys.	d.	m.	Dys.	d.	m.
1	15 N	0	7	16	45	13	18	20	19	19	43	25	20	55
2	15	18	8	17	1	14	18	34	20	19	56	26	21	5
3	15	36	9	17	18	15	18	49	21	20	8	27	21	16
4	15	54	10	17	34	16	19	3	22	20	20	28	21	26
5	16	11	11	17	49	17	19	17	23	20	32	29	21	35
6	16	18	12	18	4	18	19	30	24	20	44	30	21	44

● Full Moon, 7th day, 7h. 18m. evening.
☾ Last Quarter, 15th day, 11h. 34m. morning.
○ New Moon, 22d day, 2h. 29m. morning.
☽ First Quarter, 29th day, 6h. 4m. morning.

D. M.	W. D.	☉ r.	☉ s.	L. D. h.	L. D. m.	D.inc. h.	D.inc. m.	☉ F. A.	● F. sea. h.	● F. sea. m.	☾'s place.	● r. & s.	● ☾ h.	☾ sou. m.
1	Satur.	5	3	7	13	54	5	0	3	9	7	6 heart	2	7	7	56
2	SUN.	5	2	7	13	56	5	2	3	10	7	52 belly	2	49	8	40
3	Mond.	5	1	7	13	58	5	4	3	11	8	37 belly	3	10	9	23
4	Tuesd.	4	59	8	14	2	5	8	3	12	9	20 reins	3	88	10	5
5	Wedn.	4	58	8	14	4	5	10	3	13	10	3 reins	4	6	10	47
6	Thurs.	4	57	8	14	6	5	12	4	14	10	49 secrets	4	56	11	31
7	Friday	4	56	8	14	8	5	14	4 ●	0	11	34 secrets	● rises	morn.	
8	Satur.	4	55	8	14	10	5	16	4	16	morn.		secrets	7	52	0	15
9	SUN.	4	54	8	14	12	5	13	4	17	0	20 thighs	8	46	1	2
10	Mond.	4	53	8	14	14	5	20	4	18	1	5 thighs	9	40	1	49
11	Tuesd.	4	51	8	14	18	5	24	4	19	1	53 knees	10	30	2	39
12	Wedn.	4	50	8	14	20	5	26	4	20	2	41 knees	11	17	3	29
13	Thurs.	4	49	8	14	22	5	28	4	21	3	31 knees	morn.		4	21
14	Friday	4	48	8	14	24	5	30	4	22	4	21 legs	0	1	5	13
15	Satur.	4	47	8	14	26	5	32	4	23	5	12 legs	0	40	6	4
16	SUN.	4	46	8	14	28	5	34	4	24	6	6 feet	1	17	6	56
17	Mond.	4	45	8	14	30	5	36	4	25	7	0 feet	1	53	7	48
18	Tuesd.	4	44	8	14	32	5	38	4	26	7	55 head	2	28	8	41
19	Wedn.	4	43	8	14	34	5	40	4	27	8	50 head	3	3	9	35
20	Thurs.	4	42	8	14	36	5	42	4	28	9	46 neck	3	41	10	30
21	Friday	4	42	8	14	36	5	42	4	29	10	45 neck	4	22	11	27
22	Satur.	4	41	8	14	38	5	44	4 ○	11	42 arms	☽ sets.	eve.	26	
23	SUN.	4	40	8	14	40	5	46	4	1	ev	39 arms	8	49	1	25
24	Mond.	4	39	8	14	42	5	48	4	2	1	36 breast	9	49	2	24
25	Tuesd.	4	38	8	14	44	5	50	3	3	2	30 breast	10	42	3	20
26	Wedn.	4	37	8	14	46	5	52	3	4	3	22 heart	11	28	4	14
27	Thurs.	4	37	8	14	46	5	52	3	5	4	10 heart	morn.		5	4
28	Friday	4	36	8	14	48	5	54	3	6	4	56 heart	0	8	5	51
29	Satur.	4	35	8	14	50	5	56	3	7	5	41 belly	0	40	6	36
30	SUN.	4	34	8	14	52	5	58	3	8	6	26 belly	1	12	7	20
31	Mond.	4	34	8	14	52	5	58	3	9	7	10 reins	1	41	8	2

"Astronomical Calculations," for example, indicates the moon's effect on heart, belly, reins (ribs), and "secrets," respectively. These astrological remnants reinforced the idea of men's and women's connection to cosmological mechanism, suggesting that just as in a watch each part affects the other, so we too are affected equally by the parts of the physical world.

And by connecting seasonal labor to celestial motion, the almanacs made it possible to regulate work and find the best way to do it — if the signs were read correctly, or nature's example was understood properly. But again, this "natural" time should not be mistaken for a more leisurely approach to work. "System, Mr. Hasty, system," the almanac warned in 1832. "Your plans for the whole season should be well laid out and adjusted, in doing which, you should take some account of foul weather as well as fair."[23] *The Old Farmer's Almanac* supplied the system, using nature as its regulating authority. The quotation above ended by reminding the farmer that time is money, and that "system" — organizing time by natural signs — helped enormously in straining the most value from hired help.

American almanacs, by the 1830s, reflect a transition in thinking about the ends of work; natural examples begin emphasizing work for money rather than work for work's own sake. Samuel Atkins's pious and scientific fascination with the stars merged with the profit motive in the almanacs of these years. But though *The Old Farmer's Almanac* of the 1830s reflected a close connection to market economies — it included tables of interest, mileage between principal cities, and the hours of county, state, and federal courts — it insisted on nature as the pattern for success in life and the guide to time usage. The "Farmer's Calender" reinforced the point by comparing the farm family to a hive of busy bees — while the flowers bloom, the inhabitants of the farm-hive, "the laborers," are up in motion. While the sun, moon, and stars marked time, the prosperous farm family looked to nature for living models of diligence, thrift, and hard work.

"Pretty bee, will you come and play with me?" asked "the Idle Boy" in an early *McGuffey's Reader.* But the serious-minded bee replied, "No, I must not be idle, I must go and gather honey." Rebuffed, the idle boy asked a dog, a bird, and a horse in turn, but each was righteously busy. "What, is nobody idle?" the boy asked in a moment of revelation. "Then little boys must not be idle." So he "made haste, and went to school, and learned his lesson very well."[24]

Like almanacs, nineteenth-century schoolbooks linked time to nature and farm work. But they nagged even more about the morality of working hard—"the industry of the ant and the bee and the fecklessness of the grasshopper are ever present."[25] Primers and readers emphasized the sin of wasting time, hinting at disasters waiting in ambush for all those who stopped to smell the roses. "Little girl," one *McGuffey's Reader* warned, "never be a moment too late. It will soon end in trouble or crime."[26]

What sort of crime was idleness? "Time," wrote educator Lyman Cobb in 1843, "we ought to consider as a sort of sacred trust committed to us by God; of which we are now the depositories, and are to render an account at the last." Cobb offered a variation on the old Puritan phrase "improve the time." Time was a loan from God, an investment made in men and women, and God expected some return, some increase in spiritual (or worldly) profit. Such a gift could neither be wasted nor taken lightly; it required the same regular ordering seen in God's example, nature. "Where no plan is laid," Cobb continued, "where the disposal of time is surrendered merely to the chance of incidents, all things lie huddled together in one chaos, which admits neither distribution nor review." Idleness, and failure to adopt nature's model, profaned God's intentions and opened the door to chaos.

Cobb's little homily suggested that "system," or the organization of time, on the one hand ensured God's favor and, on the other, made the individual's time both usable and useful to society—subject to "distribution and review." "The orderly arrangement of time," Cobb continued, "is like a ray of light, which darts itself through all affairs."[27] Temporal discipline, Cobb implied, is the road along which knowledge travels, and his essay suggested that organized time served as the die that stamped good citizens out of formless material. The ubiquitous textbook example of the bee and the ant, both social insects, reinforced this message of organization and control. Rigorous organization of individual time made for an organized and rational society. And as an organizing principle, time rooted in orderly nature illuminated the dark corners of society and put the loafing minions of "chaos" to useful work.

The idea of organized time as an illuminating principle recurred frequently when time was related to nature, and especially the sun. "Behold the sun in his splendor moving over you by day; and the moon at night," suggested one 1810 reader. "Contemplate a steady and powerful Hand, bringing round spring and summer, autumn and winter, in regular course." The sun and moon gave evidence of God in action, and illuminated God's plan for men and women. "Can you believe," the lesson asked, "that you were brought hither for no purpose, but to immerse yourselves in gross and brutal, or at best, in trifling pleasures?"[28] The march of time, revealed by blazing sunlight in the glory of nature, encouraged imitation by God's foot soldiers on earth.

In its emphasis on system and relentless hard work this rhetoric may now remind us less of a grand march than a lockstep—it sounds a bit like "scientific management," the late nineteenth-century credo that treated workers like parts in a clock/machine. But in these lessons, time came from nature, not clocks. Time's authority demanded systematic work, but the authority submitted to, the steady and powerful hand, belonged to God. The use of time remained tied to local, natural imperatives. Cyclical nature embodied time, not clocks, and nature recalled the power of tradition and the moral virtue of a productive, well-ordered society of farmers. One reader, as late as 1857, still explained the "division of time" in terms of the seasons and their labor rather than as hours, minutes, or seconds. "In September, October, and November the produce of the fields is gathered. The farmer cuts his grain. . . . It is put in the barn and threshed." The lesson ended by pointing out that it is now more than 1850 years since He [Christ] came on earth."[29] One thousand eight hundred and fifty years in the unfolding of God's design, ticked off in the circle of passing seasons — time, God, nature, moral virtue, and economic prosperity were inextricably linked.

Schoolbooks ignored the lilies of the field, never known for their industry, in favor of the tireless bee or ant's example of diligence and frugal, orderly social organization. "Nature [was] never neutral" in children's texts.[30] In its relentless glorification of hard work, the "natural time" these readers and almanacs set forth hardly seems leisurely. The lessons alone, of course, fail to tell us how hard antebellum Americans actually worked or would work. Most reflect the religious and class biases of the New Englanders who wrote them. Schoolbook homilies on the busy bee may have amounted to little more than a nagging buzz in the ears on "Saint Monday," the artisan's traditional leisurely day of recovery from weekend revels. But schoolbooks and almanacs do tell us about how differently time was once understood.

The crucial issue, again, is time's perceived source. Time belonged to God — and God demanded hard work — but time revealed itself in nature, which showed in turn how it should be used. "Time is measured by clocks and watches, dials and glasses," Noah Webster admitted. But "the light of the sun makes the day, and the shade of the earth makes the night . . . the day time is for labor, the night for sleep and repose." "Children," he added for good measure, "should go to bed early."[31] Natural cycles still modeled the child's habits in this passage. But Webster's description hints at a crucial transition to come—a transition from time rooted in nature to time originating in the clock itself. To explore this transition, we need first to examine the ambiguous place of clocks in antebellum American culture.

Settlers brought clocks with them to the colonies as far back as 1638. Boston had a town clock, and a man assigned to tend it, in 1668, and clockmakers plied their trade in Philadelphia in the 1680s. There were probably clockmakers in every colony by 1700. Advertisements for tower clocks appeared in Boston's first newspaper, and tower clocks themselves in Connecticut in 1727.[32] These earliest tower and house clocks were relatively crude affairs, technologically primitive by the standards of the Old World. But though no substantial domestic watch industry appeared before the Civil War, American clock production soon rivaled Europe and England in quantity at least. It would be interesting to know who wanted these early clocks, how they were paid for, and who owned them, but very little research on the subject exists. The best estimates to date suggest that by 1700, roughly one white adult in fifty kept a clock, and one in thirty-two a watch, and that among this minority merchants, professionals, innkeepers, and shopkeepers predominated. Artisans were twice as likely as farmers to have the means of telling time, and on an average "almost half of the men who lived in major cities had a timepiece of some kind."[33]

In the city a different kind of time prevailed. Since the Middle Ages and probably earlier, city life had made special demands on people's time.[34] The hours of markets needed attending to, artisans and merchants needed to assemble at a given time, courts and government offices had their schedules of operation; plays and festivals had to begin at a certain time. On the surface, this busy round looks like the city life of today. But the eighteenth and early nineteenth centuries paid considerably less attention to punctuality and saving time than ourselves. Some evidence, for example, suggests that colonial businessmen worked at a far more leisurely tempo than today's. The starting times for plays, public festivals, or political meetings remained loosely defined—and loosely observed, by our standards—until the late nineteenth century. And antebellum workers cheerfully ignored the more structured hours of clock time whenever they could get away with it.[35]

But life in cities and larger towns did make unique demands on people. It involved them in each other's lives and work, requiring agreement about when to meet. And since work and leisure in the city often continued year round, rain or shine, only mechanical timekeepers allowed business as usual on cloudy days, or at night. In most communities a town clock, the sort of prominent tower clock New Haven's city fathers had envisioned for their town, filled the bill. In New England, town clocks usually appeared first on churches, paid for by public subscription. Such clocks, placed on the steeple, connected clock time to God while tying social organization to religious authority—founded solidly on the Bible and the Church, these clocks stood above the dirty business of industry and commerce. Later, as town clocks appeared on public buildings other than churches, they symbolized order and the impartial regulation of daily life.

Despite their use as public timekeepers and their technological sophistication, these sort of town clocks rarely acquired the negative connotations attached to other equally complex machines, like the railroad or cotton loom. They conveyed a time sanctified by religion and tradition and thus "natural." As late as the 1840s the town clock's summons to Sunday service remained a set piece in pastoral writing, recalling the orderly, Godly life of the rural past. A good example appeared in Hawthorne's 1844 *American Notebooks*, when the retiring author described a locomotive's rude desecration of the woods. Before the locomotive arrived to disturb his reverie, Hawthorne listed a variety of the soft and pleasant sounds he heard in the woods, including the striking of the village clock. The ringing village clock, in fact a bravura technological achievement and a symbol of social regulation, is passed over as part of the pastoral scene that precedes the train's arrival—akin to the natural sounds of farm labor and totally unlike the hellish locomotive. More than simple timekeepers, in this pastoral guise mechanical clocks represented the principles of natural law and their applicability to a virtuous, orderly local government.[36]

An age that often compared God to a watchmaker and the universe to a clock, like "Abraham Weatherwise" in his almanac, regarded clockmakers as much more than artisans, and attached far more than local importance to their work. The trade required a great deal of mathematics and astronomy, and the best American clockmakers claimed equality with philosophers and scientists. David Rittenhouse, the foremost example, rivaled Franklin as a leading thinker among his peers. Besides establishing the first astronomical observatory in America, Rittenhouse also produced elaborate, extraordinarily well-crafted clocks depicting the movements of the moon, stars, and planets along with hours, minutes, and seconds. His crowning mechanical achievement was an *orrery*, or clockwork model of the solar system, made for the University of Pennsylvania. The orrery inspired Jefferson to claim that Rittenhouse "has not indeed made a world, but by imitation approached nearer its Maker than any man who has lived from the creation to this day."[37] The orrery emphasized, like almanacs and schoolbooks, time's cyclical aspect, and the orderly beauty of nature's movements.

Rittenhouse created a machine that imitated and displayed natural law; his clock revealed not just the time of day but time's

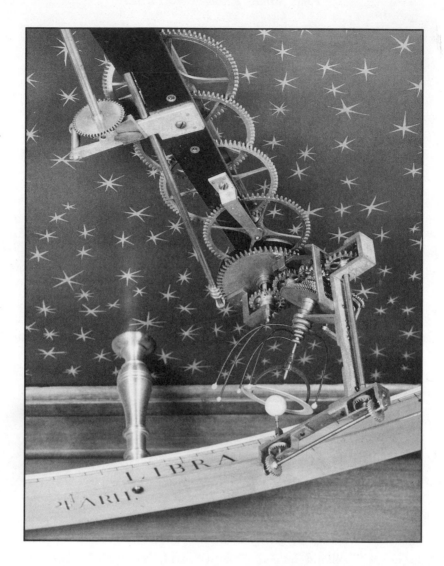

The Saturn arm of David Rittenhouse's orrery, 1767–71.
One of two very similar orreries built by Rittenhouse, now in the
Van Pelt Library of the University of Pennsylvania. The orrery
dramatizes the era's connection of mechanisms to the
"clocklike" workings of natural law. (National Museum of
American History, Smithsonian Institution.)

celestial cycle itself, as well as it could be understood. Inspired in part by the model of a clockwork universe, American political thinkers interpreted these celestial movements as a pattern for government. Federalist political theorists often compared the Constitution to a clock/machine, "a machine that would go of itself," like the deist's perfect watch. Like the seasons, or the mechanical forces that governed planetary movement, the Constitution was supposed by some to be "timeless," a permanent restraint on democracy's inevitable and universally assumed tendency to decline into tyranny over linear time. With its system of "checks and balances" on the mechanical forces of human nature, "the Federal Constitution was . . . a pendulum clock in perfect balance." As a rational machine based on scientific principles, the Constitution "governed" natural political forces like the safety devices on a steam engine.[38] Just as the village clock preserved the orderly virtue of the pastoral village, so the clockwork model promised to order politics and preserve stability.

But two potential interpretations of the clock/machine vie for supremacy in this understanding of the Constitution. One locates political authority in imitation of natural law, while the other implies supplanting natural law with human ingenuity—as Rittenhouse's machine makes him literally godlike, so too the achievement of the convention brings the delegates, as creators themselves, closer to God. Thus the Constitution represents not just stability but *perfectibility,* the virtue of progress and enlightened reform. The two interpretations echo the tension between cyclical and linear time, between stasis and progress. The Constitution could be seen as a regulating machine, maintaining regularity and stability. But it might also be seen as a sort of throttle on the speed of progress. If government, like Rittenhouse's orrery, could be brought ever closer to perfection, then there need be no end to human tinkering with government, society, and technology—no end to "progress."

The tension inherent in these two interpretations, and the idea of time that informed them, reappeared in the conflict between Jefferson and Hamilton and their respective political camps. On the farm, Jefferson passionately maintained, life followed nature and the seasonal cycle. Natural law governed farming, assuring its virtue. A society of Jefferson's "yeoman farmers," almanacs in hand, was a "naturally" virtuous society. Associating industry with corruption and dependence, Jefferson hoped, not without skepticism, that the agrarian republic might preserve itself intact by expanding geographically across western space, rather than through time in the ore-car of industrial progress. It is true that Jefferson, an inventor himself, admitted no objection to home manufactures and local, cottage industry. Such small-scale manifestations of technological cleverness stayed within the framework of cyclical time and natural imperatives. But he feared the centralizing tendencies of large-scale manufacturing and the inevitable formation of a laboring class to support it — England's Manchester slums haunted his dreams. Jefferson's generation interpreted the "fall" of classical Greece and Rome as the collapse of agrarian democratic virtue. For Jefferson, progress through time presaged American democracy's senility and eventual death.[39]

But where Jefferson saw possibilities for decline, Hamilton dreamed of progress. Democracies may have collapsed repeatedly in the past, but the Enlightenment hinted at the eventual perfection of philosophy and technology — in a climate of political stability, America's future held fantastic promises of industrial progress and wealth. Hamilton hoped to follow the path of time's arrow and set the new states on course into an industrial future. Jefferson's system "sustained a vision of social and economic development across space, whereas the other system [Hamilton's] supported an alternative vision of development through time."[40]

Supporters of Hamilton's program of manufactures, as Leo Marx has pointed out, were forced to drape their arguments in pastoral sheep's clothing; Tench Coxe, for example, used Ritten-house's orrery to promote machine power and industry. Coxe "enlisted the immense prestige of Newtonian mechanics in support of his economic program" while directing society forward into industrial development. He tried to claim that textile machinery, like the orrery, embodied natural laws. In this sense the very perfection of Rittenhouse's orrery, like the natural laws embodied in the Constitution, could lay fears about the corrupting power of machinery to rest. Having discovered the principles of rational government and learned how to reproduce them, society was free to advance into the Hamiltonian future of industrial improvements.[41]

The career of John Fitch, inventor of the steamboat, offers another example of the tension between cyclical and linear time and the ambiguity inherent in the clockwork metaphor. Fitch, a Connecticut Yankee, began his career as a clockmaker's apprentice. The craft gained him familiarity with metals, tools, and the techniques of working them, as well as insight into the harmonious movements and principles of Newtonian mechanics. But his pious, Puritan master's disregard for profit, pleasure, and advancement, his insistence on limiting both mechanical innovation and business opportunity, left Fitch frustrated. Rejecting both theological orthodoxy and the clockmaker's trade, Fitch embraced a flabby deism as he turned his attention toward the steam engine. The steam engine satisfied his mechanical predilections while deist philosophy, assuring the rationality of his actions and his machines, allowed him to vault the restricting theology of his forebears and set his course into the linear time of the industrial future.[42] Fitch's famous invention mirrored changing ideas about time and clocks: it converted the cyclical, clocklike motion of the steam engine's parts into linear progress through the water and through time. Only by rethinking his understandings of cyclical and linear time—and turning his clockmaker's skills to more innovative ends — could Fitch free himself from tradition and liberate his mechanical creativity.

Mass-produced, affordable clocks and watches exacerbated the tension between industrial, linear time, and the cyclical time of nature. When tied to nature, as in Rittenhouse's orrery and the pastoral village clock, clocks represented cyclical time. They recalled the governing mechanisms God had established and God's children discovered in natural law. A clock regulated by the almanac, as "True Time" recommended, humbly imitated God's time. On the other hand, mechanical clocks kept working when the shy or modest sun draped himself in clouds. Their value in organizing city life and labor suggested that mechanical creations had improved on nature's timepiece.

The progress of industry and commerce itself depended on clocks and clock time. If a mechanic, out of earshot of the town clock, needed to leave home for work by noon, owning a clock made his task easier on a cloudy or rainy day. If men worked under him, the good fortune of owning a watch gave him power, since he could now call the hours of work and rest if no other clock stood nearby. The watch itself, in the latter instance, becomes the authority for time, and its owner derives power from ownership. Life in the cities and market towns demanded manmade, mechanical sources of time, sources of time that could be possessed and controlled.

If the almanacs and schoolbooks quoted previously established time's connection to nature, these city clocks threatened to overturn nature and substitute human authority for God's. Recalling the incident in New Haven that began this chapter, we can see why "True Time" was so agitated. As machines, clocks could stand for either cyclical or linear time. On the one hand, clock metaphors helped make the universe both comprehensible and reassuring while offering a model for the justly organized society—in its pastoral guise the clock illustrated cyclical time and the ideals of Jeffersonian republicanism. On the other hand, clocks also represented human cleverness, commercial improvement, and progress—the Hamiltonian vision of an industrial future. "True Time" called Terry's clock "an evil of no small magnitude" because by exploring the nature of time it echoed lasting debates over the foundations of political and moral authority. Was society to be regulated by nature and God, or by the clock, with its associations of industry and the ideal of progress?

Industrial progress demanded clocks, and ironically the first application of interchangeable parts to manufacturing came at Eli Terry's Connecticut clock factory. Terry had served a traditional apprenticeship and then run a small shop making tall case clocks for several years. But in 1806 he began producing clocks on a larger scale, converting an old textile mill to a clock factory and using a small water wheel to turn gear-cutting engines. By 1822, after a series of production and design innovations, Terry had perfected his most lasting and lucrative product, the "pillar and scroll" shelf clock made almost entirely of wood. Its relatively small size made it easy for peddlers to carry while its simple, attractive design made it easy to sell and its familiar materials easy to repair. The clock "completely revolutionized the whole business," and set the standard for an industry.[43]

Most clockmakers had waited for a customer's order, then laboriously crafted a clock by hand. Terry assumed the market already existed—he either guessed that demand for clocks was increasing or assumed aggressive sales would move more clocks, or perhaps both. The "pillar and scroll" clock quickly became associated with the archetypal fast-talking Yankee peddler, the glib salesman of wooden nutmegs.[44] Terry's great success initiated a long period of intense competition, innovation, and "progress" in the design and marketing of clocks. Though he filed a barrage

Eli Terry "pillar and scroll" clock, ca. 1820. This particular clock is somewhat unusual in having the escapement and pendulum rod in front of the dial plate rather than hidden behind. (National Museum of American History, Smithsonian Institution.)

of patents, Terry's clock was widely copied. Clockmaking boomed in Connecticut, and in 1836, the peak year, more than 80,000 Terry-styled clocks sold for ten dollars or less.[45]

Terry's clocks, and later, the cheaper brass clocks Chauncey Jerome and others sold for as little as $1.50, brought mechanical timekeeping within the easy reach of mechanics, farmers, artisans, and laborers for the first time. They sold extremely well in every state. One traveler claimed in the 1840s that "in Kentucky, in Illinois, in Missouri, and here in every dell in Arkansas," and even "in cabins where there was not a chair to sit on, there was sure to be a Connecticut clock."[46] By 1835 Yankee clocks were so popular in the South that a number of states, hoping to promote manufactures at home, raised the clock peddler's license fees to discourage their sale. Chauncey Jerome's firm responded by shipping disassembled clocks to Richmond, Virginia, and Hamburg,

South Carolina. Assembled on southern soil, Jerome's popular clocks satisfied the demand for local manufactures.[47]

Associating clocks as we do with punctuality and industrial labor, we tend to assume such popularity reflects the spread of commercial markets and industrial capitalism—the linear time of industry. But a closer look at the clocks suggests that such an interpretation is too simple. Their design, for example, tended toward the austere, mimicking traditional furniture designs and eschewing the whimsical, consumerist frivolity that would characterize clock styles after the Civil War. One of Jerome's most popular designs, the "Gothic" shelf clock, looked remarkably like a New England church. Simple and even grave in appearance, Terry's clocks called attention to the seriousness of time.

Most Terry clocks included a small painting, called a "tablet," beneath the face. The tablets often depicted a mill or factory, and indeed the clocks were used to regulate manufacturing.[48] But they more typically depicted farm life, the rural village or conventional landscape, firmly connecting time to nature and the pastoral. The pendulum, clearly visible through the opening in the tablet, recalled the pulse of time in nature's cycle and the balanced mechanism of the natural world as it operated in daily life. Such a clock advertised its owner's piety and respect for God's time.

While the ticking clock may have been connected to cyclical nature in Terry's designs, a substantial body of American folklore linked clocks with mortality and the linear brevity of life. Their striking, coming unexpectedly, was said to denote death. A mysterious ticking, heard where no clock stood, was commonly referred to as the "wall clock" or "death watch." Recalling "the ticking of an old-fashioned clock, reckoning time towards eternity," this superstition appears as a portent of death in the folklore of at least thirteen states.[49] A suddenly silent clock indicated death or at least very bad luck. "A clock stops when someone dies . . . when there is a death in the family. . . . If a clock suddenly stops, it's a sure sign of death."[50] The clock, in these examples, embodies God's time—a silent clock showed that death had brought someone's time to a halt.

Altering the time, or allowing a clock to run down, was therefore dangerous: "never turn a clock counterclockwise . . . a run-down clock is a sure sign of death." Other proverbs held that broken clocks should be buried or stored well out of sight, and that one should "never keep a clock that does not run . . . it is bad luck to keep a clock that is not running."[51] The uneasiness stemmed from the fact that though they measured God's time, clocks were also easily susceptible to human control. Adjustable at the owner's whim, they threatened to present an alternative source for time, a secular time made and controlled by men and women. Time's measurement, and its authority, were not to be trivialized—keeping a broken clock suggested an indifference to God and God's time, much as gambling flouted God's control over earthly events.

The repeated appearance of a belief that "it's bad luck to have two clocks running in the same room . . . two clocks running in the same house" further attests to this anxiety. "Never leave two clocks ticking in the same room at the same time, very bad luck," one folklorist's informant claimed. "My Grandmother would not do that for anything, for she said it was a sure sign of death."[52] No two clocks can be made to keep the same time, so having two clocks in the same room, like having two public clocks in the same town, called the authority of both into doubt. Worse, it called the nature of time itself into question.

Mechanical timekeepers, when they appeared in schoolbooks, poetry, and popular literature, usually recalled time on this grand scale—clocks were not portrayed as machines for telling the time of day, but as mechanical embodiments of mortality, symbols of eternity and the brevity of life. The old-fashioned tall case or "Grandfather" clock most often filled this role, creaking its doleful message of regret in countless poems. Longfellow's "The Old Clock on the Stairs," included frequently in children's texts, is typical of the genre:

> Somewhat back from the village street
> Stands the old fashioned County seat.
> Across its ancient porticoe
> Tall poplar-trees their shadows throw;
> And from its station in the hall
> An ancient timepiece says to all—
>   Forever—Never!
>   Never—Forever!
>
> Half-way up the stairs it stands,
> And points and beckons with its hands
> From its case of massive oak
> Like a monk, who under his cloak,
> Crosses himself, and sighs, alas!
> With sorrowful voice to all who pass—
>   Forever—Never!
>   Never—Forever!

Longfellow connected the clock to the New England past he helped create, to the preindustrial rural ideal—the same pastoral vision that appeared on the tablets of Terry's clocks. He also tied it to religion and unknowable mysteries, hence the reference to the monk. But time's face turns grim:

> In that mansion used to be
> Free-hearted Hospitality;
> His great fires up the chimney roared;
> The stranger feasted at his board;
> But, like the skeleton at the feast;

That warning timepiece never ceased —
Forever — Never!
Never — Forever!

Longfellow mined this vein for several more verses, his mood growing ever darker till relieved at last by the final lines, which as usual in these poems is resolved by hinting at reunion in eternity.[53]

The somber Grandfather clock spread its pall of gloom on every happy occasion, inflicting itself again and again in children's textbooks. *McGuffey's Third Reader* described how "in the old, old hall the old clock stands, / And round and round move the steady hands." As a little girl stood before it, trying to decipher its meaning, *McGuffey* supplied it: "Tick, tock, tick! Time passes away."[54] When clocks were absent time itself, in the abstract or personified as gray-bearded Father Time, filled the same role. "What is Time?" inquired a poem in one *Reader*. "I asked a dying sinner, ere the tide of life had left his veins: 'Time,' he replied; 'I've lost it! Ah, the treasure!' and he died."[55] Typically baleful if not particularly eloquent, this sinner's last words, or at least his sentiments, might characterize a whole generation's thinking about time. Such gloomy musings filled children's schoolbooks and popular magazines. Why were they so popular?

The idea of time as both a devouring entity and a scarce, precious commodity dated back at least as far as the Renaissance. But these poems also typified the characteristic morbid sentimentality of antebellum culture, the overwrought yearning and nostalgia for better days that Mark Twain later satirized in *Huckleberry Finn's* Emmeline Grangerford — the "Shall I Never See Thee More Alas" school.[56] Exaggerated sentimentality offered a counter to the harsher realities of Jacksonian commerce, and these poems reminded their readers that worldly accomplishments were fleeting. They also tended to reinforce filiopiety — *Grandfather* clocks,

Father Time—the poems connected authority to older male figures, whose experience and memory of better and presumably more virtuous days made their judgments on modern times all the more wise.

But in these poems the paternal clock, paradoxically, also tolls its own death knell. The genre's popularity reflects the decline of traditional paternal authority that characterized the 1830s and 1840s. As the factory system overtook more traditional methods of craft production, it dissolved the paternal relationship between the boss or owner and his employees. Under factory production, instead of working for someone they knew personally, even intimately, employees toiled for a distant stranger whose authority worked its way down a chain of managers and foremen. In these poems, older paternal authority is dead or dying. And the sense of time associated with that authority—old-fashioned clocks, pastoralism, and the cycle of life—threatens to give way before a new order. Death, and happiness under the ultimate paternal authority of God, is the consolation the poems offer for paternalism's decline.[57] With the decline of patriarchal authority came a change in the idea of time and clocks that went with it.

In terms of clock imagery, Longfellow's poem makes an interesting comparison with a common children's lesson, "The Discontented Pendulum." Early one morning, went the tale, an old farm clock suddenly stopped moving. Fed up with mindlessly swinging back and forth in the dark and jealous of the dial's better working conditions, the pendulum had quit. Alarmed, "Mistress Dial" reminded the pendulum that his work, though dreary in the aggregate, amounted to no great effort at each swing, and that all the other parts had their work to do as well, even if theirs did seem more pleasant. Chagrined, the pendulum went back to work. "As if with one consent, the wheels began to turn, the hands began to move," the clock struck, and the farmer got up. The moral of this story was obvious: keep your nose to the grindstone and know your place in the social machinery. Notice that the clock, not the sun or the industrious chirping birds, wakes the farmer up.[58]

The dual role of clocks and time in American culture reveals itself in a comparison of the clocks in the two stories. In Longfellow's poem, the clock insists on the inevitability of decline and mourns the passing of the old order. In the second example, the busy, bustling "Mistress Dial" regulates the new. In Longfellow's poem and the genre it represents, clocks symbolized the natural, cyclical time of the disappearing past. They reminded their readers, through the imagery of the clock, that death was the ultimate, inescapable judgment on human folly. In "The Discontented Pendulum," the clock served as the model for social organization, not because it mimicked nature, or symbolized some gloomy abstraction, but because it reproduced social hierarchies working together harmoniously—the story described the clocklike movements of industry as a positive virtue.

In the story, clocks, not nature or patriarchal authority, regulate life and labor. It was in this sense that Henry Clay enthused: "who has not been delighted with the clock-work movements of a large cotton factory?"[59] Clay's comment, and the story of the disgruntled pendulum, point out the clock's growing role, its increased authority, in ordering daily life and work.

In the 1830s clock time was entering the work place through the factory system. In the first years of factory work textile mills, for example, operated only in sunlight. True, most mills listed precise hours of opening and closing. We have examples of these schedules, and in their typographical finality they make it seem to the modern observer as if the worker's days were strictly counted out in numbers on the clockface. But in fact those hours of work depended on fluctuations in consumer demand and, most notably, available sunlight. Factory schedules invariably changed with the passing seasons, since artificial light was both expensive and dangerous. "The period of labor is not uniform; in some cases from sun to sun," one workman claimed. "It is most common to work as long as they can see."[60] The connection between hours of work and the sun suggested that early factory labor mirrored the cyclical time of farm work to some extent. In many instances, that may have been the case—mill timetables may only present us with an ideal, as fluctuations in available daylight and demand for goods affected the hours of labor.[61]

But as clocks grew more common, artificial light became more practical, and regional trade networks regularized, factories began adopting more rigid hours. The gradual imposition of clock time through the factory system constituted one of the central conflicts of industrialization. Workers struggled hard to preserve some control over the pace and hours of their labor, instead of conceding their schedule to clocks, and the process of resistance and accommodation to factory time has been well documented.[62] But these men and women's objections to the conditions and extent of work—meaning the number of hours demanded, time allotted for meals, work conditions, and so on—should not be automatically mistaken for opposition to regulation by the clock. Resistance to factory time itself is different from the quest for shorter hours, and resistance to clock authority is different from objections to work schedules themselves. There are many examples of workers resisting the boss's demands. Examples of workers debating the nature of time itself are less common, but no less interesting.

With the proliferation of factories and the consolidation of the factory system, clock time became increasingly common in daily labor. *Defining* that time—especially defining time as factory bells—gave owners an edge over their employees. Factory bells could be made to ring at will, and their sounding might easily be delayed to wring an extra half hour's work out of employees who had no reliable way of measuring time themselves. As accustomed paternal relations between labor and management deteriorated, workers began feeling the lack of a reliable standard of time.

In 1832 the New England Association of Farmers, Mechanics and other Workingmen reported with outrage that in Hope Factory, Rhode Island, the time for shutting the factory gates at night was "eight o'clock, by the *factory time,* which is from twenty to twenty-five minutes *behind* the true time," and that in Nashua and Dunstable, New Hampshire, "the *factory time* [was] twenty-five minutes *behind* the *true solar* time." At the Arkwright and Harris Mills in Coventry, Rhode Island, the report continued, "labor ceases at eight o'clock at night, *factory* time." In Pawtucket, the situation was found to be similar, "with the exception that, within a few weeks, public opinion has had the effect to reduce the *factory time* to the *true solar* standard."[63] Obviously, the mill owners were cheating, hiding behind impressive-looking clocks while they tampered with time for their own advantage. Investing the authority of time in clocks gave them an edge, while their workers insisted on connecting time to the impartial sun.

Controlling and defining time translated directly into economic and political power. Workers in Pottsville, Pennsylvania, a mining town, discovered another way clocks might cheat them in an 1843 election dispute. Officially the Pottsville polls closed at seven, but numerous witnesses saw civic-minded voters exercising the franchise till at least eight-twenty. Or so it seemed — "it is well known," claimed the Pottsville *Miner's Journal,* "that we have no exact or certain standard of time in this borough; it is notorious," insisted the editor, that watches and clocks in Pottsville varied by differences "frequently being as much as one hour." An election inspector, using a chronometer regulated in Philadelphia not three days earlier, insisted that the polls had closed at seven. But Philadelphia's time was not Pottsville's, and the losing side mounted a drive to declare the election invalid.[64]

The hearings that followed revealed the multiple sources of time the town used, and the confusion — and political opportunism — that resulted. Several local witnesses deferred to "Heywood and Snyder's Foundry bell" as their source of time. The bell's prominence made it a common point of reference, but at least one local resident admitted that he routinely set his watch "fifteen minutes slower than that bell" because "I was under the impression that the bell was too fast." One watchless voter testified, "I went down to Geisse [a local jeweler] . . . and at his clock it was twenty minutes past eight." "Henry Geisse's clock," he added, "is always ten or fifteen minutes slower than the [foundry] bell." A watchmaker concurred: Heywood and Snyder's bell was "one quarter of an hour faster" than the sundial he used to regulate his shop. The bartender at the local hotel reported yet another time, about 9:00 p.m., on their "best regulated clock," while Nathaniel Mills insisted that "by my clock the election closed at a quarter after seven."[65] Who owned the most reliable watch? Whose clock told the correct time? In Pottsville, with no agreed-upon standard, it was impossible to tell.

These men objected to being victimized by an arbitrary standard of time—a time derived from clocks they couldn't verify or control. Since watches were still too expensive for most people, the sun offered an indisputable standard honored by tradition and religious authority, free from the owner's influence. In 1832, the *Pawtucket Chronicle* had praised a plan to put a tower clock in the Congregational Church, since "all are aware of the vexatious confusion occasioned by the difference of time in the ringing of the factory bells . . . which can only be remedied by creating a clock that will always give *the time of day*." The clock, paid for by subscription and blessed by location in the church, was to provide an impartial standard based on local sun time, and keep the mill owners from cheating.[66] Tying a clockwork regulator, like the Pawtucket clock, to the rational, impartial, and objective traditions of celestial mechanics—having it show sun time—made it seem benevolent and impartial rather than harmful or oppressive.

And indeed as artifacts, viewed independently of who controlled them, clocks and watches offered a stunning example of human genius and skill. "What a miracle of art," Edward Everett exclaimed to the Massachusetts Charitable Mechanics Association in 1837, "that a man can teach a few wheels, and a piece of elastic steel, to out-calculate himself; to give him a rational answer to one of the most important questions that a being traveling toward eternity can ask!" "What a miracle," Everett repeated, "that a man can put within this little machine a spirit that measures the flight of time with greater accuracy than the unassisted intellect of the profoundest philosophy." Addressing the Massachusetts mechanics on the usefulness of mechanical arts, Everett praised the watch's capacity to serve as a model for rationality and the organization of the mechanic's time. "By means of a watch," Everett enthused, "punctuality in all his duties—which in its perfection, is one of the incommunicable attributes of Deity—is brought within the reach of man."[67] Everett made the watch holy. He reconnected timekeeping machines to heavenly mechanical principles and the rationally ordered society.

Everett's platitudinous address to the Mechanics Association posited a pettifogging deity who listed flawless, clocklike punctuality first among his virtues. It reflected a social need for docile, well-disciplined employees, but it also reflected the further spread of clock time into everyday life. Thanks to cheap, mass-produced timekeepers, the clock time that confronted labor in the work place found its complement in clock-based regulation of the private sphere and the household labor as well.

Home advice manuals of the 1830s focused on systematizing the household economy. Lydia Maria Child's *The American Frugal Housewife* (1835) reminded its readers on page one that "Time is Money," and urged them to "gather up all the fragments of *time* as well as materials."[68] William Alcott's popular handbook *The Young Housekeeper* (1838) began its advice on "having a plan" by recalling the clockwork universe. "Order is heaven's first law," Alcott wrote, "and should be the first law of that which properly managed would, of all places below the sun, most nearly resemble heaven."[69] Alcott recapitulated the clichés of celestial mechanics, but his home resembled heaven because its members, in following heaven's law, had internalized the clock's authority, not natural examples.

Alcott offered detailed advice on waking at regular times. "There is no difficulty in waking at a desired hour of the morning, when one has a strong motive for it," he wrote, but in such cases one sleeps uneasily. Alcott suggested that "there should be some ingenious contrivance, to awaken the housekeeper at first—perhaps an alarm clock . . . till the habit is effectively formed; after which, she will find little difficulty in awakening." Alcott offered the clock as a model of regularity, order, and self-government, and suggested that the machine be fully incorporated into the unconscious. Having internalized clock time, the virtuously punctual could rest easy.[70]

The result, he believed, would secure regular and precise habits at home and in public life. "The hour for breakfast," he asserted, "should also be assigned, and when thus fixed, should not be delayed except on special occasions." It was better in all respects, he continued, "to sit down a few minutes before the time, than even one minute or one half minute later;—better for the body, better for the mind, and better for the whole character." Let these moments be fixed, Alcott continued, "and except in emergencies, as in the arrival of a friend or the occurrence of an accident, let [them] seldom if ever be departed from."[71] Alcott's devotion to punctuality and regularity was so fierce, so religious, that a friend's arrival caused a household emergency.

These domestic management guides point to the continuing evolution of new, clock-based systems of social order. Lydia Maria Child's admonition to "gather up all the fragments of *time* as well as materials" hardly differs from Esther Burr's submission to God in labor, or the almanac's promptings to save time. But Alcott's handy alarm clock allowed a woman to organize the entire household on a machine-inspired model of regularity—the clock governs both the home and the woman who oversees it. Recalling "Mistress Dial" of "The Discontented Pendulum," Alcott's women readers could use the clock to systematize the small hierarchical machinery of the home, in turn preparing their families for regulation in the larger machinery of the public work place. These advice manuals represent, like the factory bells, the growing power of clocks and clock time.

But conflicting beliefs about time's source—natural or mechanical—and its character—cyclical or linear—continued to haunt American culture and politics. The writers of the American Renaissance in particular greatly feared a social time transformed permanently by industry. "For a great many years past," wrote Hawthorne in 1838, "there has been a wood-cut on the cover of the Farmer's Almanac, pretending to be a portrait of Father Time." Hawthorne referred to the traditional depiction of Time as a quasi-deity, a winged figure with an hourglass and scythe. These days, Hawthorne continued, Father Time "has exchanged his hourglass for a gold patent lever watch, which he carries in his vest pocket; and as for his scythe, he has either thrown it aside altogether, or converted its handle into a cane." Hawthorne made Time a prosperous and respectable figure, a man about town strolling the avenues in the latest clothes. If Time's transformation mirrored the farmer's conversion to city life, it also suggested the changed understanding of time. Father Time still cuts down the living in Hawthorne's story, but in 1838 he moves to the bustling pace of city life, with a watch to guide him.[72] Hawthorne offered an ironic commentary on the clock's ascendence in everyday affairs.

Hawthorne's "The Artist of the Beautiful" opens with the artist, Owen Warland, laboring unhappily as a town clockmaker. Endowed with a genius for intricate mechanism, Warland hates the unimaginative work of clockmaking and labors to create beautiful, living "spiritualized mechanisms." "If a family clock was entrusted to him for repair," Hawthorne mused, "one of those tall, ancient clocks that have grown nearly allied to human nature, by measuring out the lifetime of many generations," Warland would install some mechanical whimsy of his own design—hands that spun rapidly about, figures that danced to chimes that rang too many times. "Several freaks of this kind," Hawthorne continued, "quite destroyed [his] credit with that steady and matter of fact class of people who hold that time is not to be trifled with, whether considered as the medium of advancement and prosperity in this world, or preparation for the next."

In the passage above, from 1844, Hawthorne pointed out two contemporary interpretations of the meaning of time and made Warland, the rebellious artist, violate both by taking neither seriously. Warland's spirit, however, is too delicate for sustained rebellion. Repeatedly crushed by the cold-hearted sneering of his former master in the clockmaking trade, a sagacious Yankee interested only in practicality and production, Warland for a time keeps regular hours and even succeeds in repairing and regulating the town clock. "The town in general thanked Owen for the punctuality of dinner time," but Warland's refined creative ambitions return to haunt him. He stops keeping regular hours, he "wastes the daylight" in walks and begins working feverishly at night. He triumphs in the end, making peace with himself and realizing the Enlightenment dream of living mechanisms, but only after completely throwing off the compulsion to regular hours, practical work, and clock time, and freeing himself finally from the need to "progress" in invention. In the end, the real achievement is not Warland's mechanical invention or his concession to social regularity but his own spiritual self-realization.[73]

In "The Devil in the Belfry" (1839), another attack on clock time, Edgar Allan Poe described a small Dutch town, "Vondervotteimittis," literally patterned after a clock. As the story begins, a tall clock tower stands in the center of a valley, and around it "extends a continuous row of sixty little houses. . . . Every house has a small garden before it, with a circular path, a sundial, and twenty-four cabbages." The town looks like a clock, and the clock holds the authority for the organization of both time and space. According to the story, all the inhabitants of the town and even their animals wear watches; they all "wonder what time it is" all the time. At noon every day all action stops as the worthy burghers count along with the strokes of the bell. But one day their orderly lives are disrupted when a small figure appears on the horizon, in the form of a fiddler dressed in black and having "not the remotest idea in the world of such a thing as keeping time." The fiddler ascends to the belfry, begins playing madly, and this time at noon the clock strikes thirteen times, plunging both the towns-people and their machines into chaos.[74]

Poe satirized the authority of clocks, linking them to middle-class complacency and obsession with order. In Vondervotteim-ittis, political authority, the ordering authority for the town, stems from the master clock. Its satellite clocks in each house, like their owners, are enslaved to it.[75] Poe pursued the connection between political authority and time more subtly in "The Pit and the Pendulum," written in 1843. Here Time's traditional scythe is transformed into a giant clock pendulum with a razor edge. The benign pendulum of Terry's clocks becomes for the narrator, bound to a table in the center of the pit, an instrument of torture in the hands of an invisible political enemy. The time remaining to the victim is tied directly to the swings of the clock pendulum, and not to Time in the abstract.[76]

Poe and Hawthorne, as Romantics, loathed the oppressive power of clock time, its mechanical regulation of life and thought. They expressed resentment and even rage at a familiar bind; unable to support themselves in a trade, writing, that demanded flexibility, freedom, and time for contemplation, they located the source of their oppression in clocks and their unceasing regularity. Both reacted specifically to industrial society and its new controlling device, the mechanical timekeeper. Recognizing time located in mechanical sources as an expression of political, economic, and social power, they interpreted their society's beliefs about time as moral issues involving personal freedom.

Objections to clock time in industry and self-government transcended Hawthorne and Poe's narrow literary circle. The Sabbatarian movement of the 1840s also connected time usage to morality, and recognized tyranny in the ticking clock. The question of how to observe the Sabbath was a major bone of contention for American Protestants throughout the nineteenth century. Mormonism and Seventh-Day Adventism both emerged from Sabbatarian debates over time and how it should be defined. Sabbatarian reformers saw factory work as unpleasant and often exploitive, yet necessary and potentially good. They objected to its apparent Godlessness, and wanted some way of restoring Christian belief to the humming mills. Sabbatarian activists agitated for the suspension of all labor and commerce, by law, on the Sabbath. Sundays, they felt, should properly be spent at home, in thanks to God and quiet meditation on the state of one's soul. Such Sunday laws would bring God back to the industrial week.

"Those who demanded strict Sabbath observance," according to one historian of American religion, "insisted that the principle of a day's rest in seven was planted in the very order of nature and in the original constitution of humanity." Recalling the almanac and the virtue of natural law, the Sabbatarians posited a natural, internal "moral clock" in need of rewinding every seven days.[77] "The Lord's day," wrote one Sabbatarian, "is not merely the day of religious duty and rest, but the restoring, the awakening day—the day of recovery and reformation." Like other Sabbatarians, he imagined a "higher" sense of time that God had built into the machinery of the soul. "If the Sabbath be desecrated," he continued, man's "whole spiritual prosperity and existence are endangered."[78]

Not just spiritual prosperity but financial prosperity as well suffered, for the two were linked. Sabbatarians recognized clock time's ascendency in public life and labor—they knew the factory system was here to stay. But they hoped, by setting Sundays aside from industrial hue and cry, to prevent industrial time from completely overcoming the "natural time" of the soul. Sunday laws, they claimed, would help employers by rejuvenating tired workers and ministering to their moral health, and help laborers by mandating at least one day's rest per week. Keeping the trains from running on Sunday, Sabbatarians hoped, would bring the working classes back into the wholesome sphere of home and church on the holy day, restoring some semblance of God's time to the weekly work schedule. Ironically, William Alcott's example, quoted previously, suggested that home now offered little relief.[79]

But what the Sabbatarians saw as a way to ease the laborer's burden, and regulate his or her moral health, their more extreme opponents rejected as an accommodation with industrial time. Most opponents of Sabbath laws argued that the strict Sabbath observances violated the separation of Church and State, threatened individual liberty, or "paganised" Christianity by imitating Jewish customs. More radical Anti-Sabbatarians loathed Sunday legislation as a dangerous and misleading endorsement of industrial time and the evils it caused.

Convening to protest Sabbath laws in 1848, a group of men and women including William Lloyd Garrison, Francis Jackson, Bronson Alcott, Theodore Parker, and Lucretia Mott attacked

Sabbath legislation as a false friend of the laborer and a tool of oppressive power. Garrison exhorted the working classes to "claim more and take more rest . . . strike at the exercise of that power . . . which is eating up your hard-won substance, and keeping you in shameful vassalage." Do this, he continued, "and you shall redeem all days from servile toil, and enjoy a perpetual Sabbath." Garrison urged industrial laborers to resist the employer's division and control of their time.[80]

Even more explicitly, the Anti-Sabbatarians objected to imposing clock time on Christian practice. One delegate claimed, "Our Sabbatarian friends have a queer way of setting the right and the wrong of actions." According to them, "if you want to know whether it is right to walk out, and take the air on Boston Common, look at the clock! If the finger points to a particular hour, it is very sinful; if it points to another hour, it is perfectly right! If you want to know whether it is right to read a newspaper, or write a letter, to post a letter, or to carry a letter, ask, not whether the act is right or wrong, but ask, what time of day it is, and what day of the week it is! Consult the calender and the clock."[81] Directly attacking clock time and its new role in society, the speaker deplored the clock's place as the arbiter of personal morality and the governor of civil affairs. In his view the once private, unbounded world of ethics and religious feeling now lay exposed, like the narrator in "The Pit and the Pendulum," subject to mechanical regulators unrestrained by religious authority or natural law.

The Sabbath debate revealed the degree to which changing conceptions of time and its source were working to rearrange time in both the public and private spheres. It focused on that new but scarce industrial phenomenon, leisure time—how was it to be spent? Sabbatarians, who accommodated themselves to industry, wanted to shut down industry's most visible symbol, the railroad, every Sunday, to take brief refuge from clock time in the peaceful, "natural" world of the home. Their opponents, who hated industrial excesses and linked them to slavery, hoped by controlling industry to smash the clock and return society, and social time, to its natural origins.

One of the most coherent and sophisticated attempts to comprehend and define social time came from the daughter of a Sabbatarian activist, Catherine Beecher. Regularity and loathing for wasted time formed the core of her 1841 best-seller, *A Treatise on Domestic Economy*. Like Esther Burr, quoted at the beginning of this chapter, Beecher saw work as a duty to God. Her chapter "On Economy of Time and Expenses" reminded her readers, "Christianity teaches that for all the time afforded us, we must give account to God; and that we have no right to waste a single hour." Though she recognized recreation as necessary to health and insisted that play receive its just allotment of time, she urged that women not squander their time in trivial pursuits. Temporal virtue required unstinting watchfulness and discipline, and play remained useful only to the extent that it promoted useful work: "A woman is under obligations to so arrange the hours and pursuits of her family, as to promote systematic and habitual industry; and if, by late breakfasts, irregular hours for meals, and other hinderances of this kind, she interferes with, or refrains from promoting regular industry in others, she is accountable to God for all the waste of time consequent on her negligence."[82] Superficially, Beecher's admonitions resembled the promptings in household manuals like Alcott's and Child's. But Beecher specifically rejected clock time in favor of a virtuous temporal rigor drawn from the Bible.

Women's example for organizing their days, she concluded in a long discourse on the *"right apportionment"* of time, must be the demands in time and property God asked of the ancient Hebrews. "In making this apportionment [of time]," she continued, "we are bound by the same rules as relate to the use of property."

Beecher's connection of time to property acknowledged time's role in labor and commerce, but also recalled women's position in society; Beecher implied that time was women's only real property, since material property typically belonged to men. She wrote to improve the sad state of society as she saw it. Women, as examples of kindly diligence and temporal thrift, were to quietly promote the moral organization of society using the same model of time she suggested for the home.[83]

Beecher emphasized hard work and saving time. But she rooted her conception of time in nature, rather than in clocks — "it thus appears," she wrote on the length of the work day, "that the laws of our political condition, the laws of the natural world, and the constitution of our bodies, alike demand that we rise with the light of day . . . and retire when this light is withdrawn." Beecher revived the cyclical aspect of "natural" time, but she relocated it squarely in the home, not the public work place. In her interpretation of nature's pattern for time usage, women's subservience to man, God, and natural rhythms became a weapon for the ethical reform of society through efficient, diligent, morally justified work in the production of good citizens. The home would serve as the virtuous, rationally ordered nest in which fledgling members of industrial society would learn the right principles for organizing their time.[84]

The immense popularity of Beecher's manual attests to both the applicability of her ideas and the growing division between private and public time. Beecher attempted to reestablish time's authority through religion and natural law, and thereby to make order out of the new ideas of time that prevailed outside the home and now knocked insistently on home's front door. Like "Mistress Dial" of "The Discontented Pendulum," she sought authority to regulate society, but she hoped her elaborate theological justification for time usage would transcend the secular self-interest that characterized other definitions of time, and put time on a less arbitrary basis. She used her emphasis on work to empower women—in the home, women controlled the pace of their labors and decided what tasks to do. In setting the terms of their labor they answered to God, not to factory schedules and clock bells.

Beecher consciously limited her ideas to the home, retreating from the challenges industrial time posed, or rather meeting them only halfway. Her biblically justified time made sense for many women and men, and helped establish a split between home time and public time that persisted long after her book went out of print. Beecher made home the place of "natural" time, morally virtuous hard work, and religious feeling, in opposition to the uniform, standardized public clocks, based on astronomical observation and telegraphed time signals, that were emerging as an alternative for regulating public time even as she wrote.[85]

Seeking, like Beecher, a reliable, uniform, justifiable, and objective standard of time, the 1851 timetable of the Lowell mills specified exactly when the yard gates opened and closed, the times for meals, and exactly how long work began after each bell: "WORK COMMENCES, at Ten minutes after last morning bell, and at Ten minutes after bell which 'rings in' from meals." "In all cases," it continued, "the *first* stroke of the bell is considered as marking the time." The timetable also specified "the Standard time being that of the meridian of Lowell, as shown by the regulator clock of JOSEPH RAYNES, 43 Central Street," so no confusion could result. The Lowell mills allied themselves with astronomy and science to invest their factory bells with an unimpeachable authority.

Based on the meridian of Lowell and the sun, Raynes's clock minimized the possibility of cheating and ensured that in Lowell, noon by the sun and noon by the clock would seem nearly the same. Adopted as the standard of the mills, the clock lent an aura of impartiality and natural law to the work schedule. Earlier, the Lowell owners had relied on paternal supervision to ensure the

TIME TABLE OF THE LOWELL MILLS,

To take effect on and after Oct. 21st, 1851.

The Standard time being that of the meridian of Lowell, as shown by the regulator clock of JOSEPH RAYNES, 43 Central Street

	From 1st to 10th inclusive.				From 11th to 20th inclusive.				From 21st to last day of month.			
	1st Bell	2d Bell	3d Bell	Eve. Bell	1st Bell	2d Bell	3d Bell	Eve. Bell	1st Bell	2d Bell	3d Bell	Eve. Bell
January,	5.00	6.00	6.50	*7.30	5.00	6 00	6.50	*7.30	5.00	6.00	6.50	*7.30
February,	4.30	5.30	6.40	*7.30	4.30	5.30	6.25	*7.30	4.30	5.30	6.15	*7.30
March,	5.40	6.00		*7.30	5.20	5.40		*7.30	5.05	5.25		6.35
April,	4.45	5.05		6.45	4.30	4.50		6.55	4.30	4.50		7.00
May,	4 30	4.50		7·00	4.30	4.50		7.00	4.30	4.50		7 00
June,	"	"		"	"	"		"	"	"		"
July,	"	"		"	"	"		"	"	"		"
August,	"	"		"	"	"		"	"	"		"
September,	4.40	5.00		6.45	4.50	5.10		6.30	5.00	5.20		*7.30
October,	5.10	5.30		*7.30	5.20	5.40		*7.30	5.35	5.55		*7.30
November,	4.30	5.30	6.10	*7.30	4.30	5.30	6.20	*7.30	5.00	6.00	6.35	*7.30
December,	5.00	6.00	6.45	*7.30	5.00	6.00	6.50	*7.30	5.00	6·00	6.50	*7.30

* Excepting on Saturdays from Sept. 21st to March 20th inclusive, when it is rung at 20 minutes after sunset.

YARD GATES,

Will be opened at ringing of last morning bell, of meal bells, and of evening bells; and kept open Ten minutes.

MILL GATES.

Commence hoisting Mill Gates, Two minutes before commencing work.

WORK COMMENCES,

At Ten minutes after last morning bell, and at Ten minutes after bell which "rings in" from Meals.

BREAKFAST BELLS.

During March "Ring out"........at....7.30 a. m........"Ring in" at 8:05 a. m.
April 1st to Sept. 20th inclusive.....at....7 00 " " .... " " at 7.35 " "
Sept. 21st to Oct. 31st inclusive.....at....7.30 " " .... " " at 8.05 " "
Remainder of year work commences after Breakfast.

DINNER BELLS.

"Ring out".......... ....12.30 p. m........"Ring in".... 1.05 p. m.

In all cases, the *first* stroke of the bell is considered as marking the time.

1851 timetable of the Lowell Mills. Notice that the hours of operation vary not just with the seasons, but with the days of each month, presumably to follow available sunlight.
(Reproduced courtesy of the Baker Library, Harvard Business School.)

morality of the work that went on there—"The supervisor's mind," it was claimed, "regulates all, his character inspires all; his plans . . . control all."[86] Supervision of the workers' home lives combined with a pastoral setting and the ostensibly temporary nature of the work to "republicanize" the factory town.

But native New England women fled Lowell's exploitative conditions in the 1840s, and Irish immigrants began taking their places at the machines, immigrants with less love for the hard lessons of *McGuffey's Readers*.[87] For the mill owners, astronomically regulated time shored up the Protestant Ethic with "natural law" while putting unruly immigrants on a more fixed schedule. Even better, the new standard time linked the mills and their owners to national scientific movements, especially astronomy, that by the 1850s were being increasingly associated with the economic, moral, and physical progress of the nation.

By synthesizing science, commerce, and mechanical time-keeping, the mill owners "moralized" their regulation of labor time, putting it on a reputedly objective and scientific basis; in this new scheme Raynes's clock, regulated astronomically and hence rational, replaced the human supervisor as the authority governing work. Over the next three decades, astronomy emerged as the regulating principle and source of public time, partially resolving, as Catherine Beecher had for the home, the confusions over time that plagued industrializing America. Rapid communications by telegraph, faster travel by railroad, stage, and steamboat, interstate and interregional commerce all demanded a uniform standard of time. By 1860 astronomical time, telegraphed time signals, and regional standard time had risen to fill the void. In the process, these innovations established new authorities for time, and new models for self-government and social regulation.

II

Celestial Railroad Time

I f the years before 1850 saw a growing confusion over time and its source, the next thirty years saw at least a partial solution in the rise of astronomy and astronomically based telegraph time signals from observatories. Astronomical time recapitulated the laws of nature. Legitimized by science, it offered a seemingly impartial and rational standard for regulating commerce and industry. But astronomical time was also closely tied to geographical and commercial expansion, industrial patronage, and personal and corporate gain. The scientists who advanced observatory time signals vied for professional reputation and financial reward. Their work changed the nature of public time, turning a quasi-sacred abstraction into a commodity, a useful tool of industry capable of being owned and sold.

Since David Rittenhouse and well before, Americans had been fascinated with the heavens and tried to interpret their meaning, even applying Newtonian mechanics to political theory. Fittingly, the first public reading of the Declaration of Independence came from the platform of a temporary observatory Rittenhouse had built in the State House yard, to observe the transit of Venus. But astronomy, when linked with timekeeping devices, offered more than a glimpse at the mechanism of the physical world or a model for political organization.

Applied to navigation, astronomical observations facilitated shipping by determining the longitude of prominent shore points and ships at sea. Used in surveying, astronomy helped divide the vast space of the new continent into accurately mapped parcels, rationalizing interstate trade and aiding westward expansion. And applied to industry, as at Lowell, astronomical time eventually became the guiding principle behind uniform, standardized clock time and the operations of the railroads.[1]

Nearly all astronomical measurement requires precise timekeeping, especially determining longitude. Charles Mason and Jeremiah Dixon, the English surveyors sent over in 1763 to settle the boundary dispute between Pennsylvania and Maryland, packed an English astronomical regulator along with them on their muddy colonial mission. They built a temporary field observatory, mounting the precious clock on a log sunk into the ground to minimize vibration. With some preliminary assistance from David Rittenhouse, the intrepid pair then conducted measurements of colonial longitude by comparing local time to Greenwich time as kept by the clock. The legal boundary they established settled questions of political jurisdiction between the two colonies, facilitating further settlement and trade.[2]

The conquest of western space was intimately linked to accurate measurement of space in time. While President, Jefferson oversaw the establishment of the United States Coast Survey in 1807. The Survey sent its minions, with chronometers, to the

loneliest, most forbidding places on the continent. They charted
the nation's coasts, harbors, and land formations to fix the location
of prominent shore points and keep American ships from unexpected encounters with *terra firma*. The Survey also conducted
longitudinal studies of points inland for the benefit of mapmakers, explorers, and the settlers who followed. Following custom, the Survey reckoned longitude from established Greenwich
meridians.[3]

Toward 1812, as tensions between the United States and
England mounted, patriotic Americans began calling for an American National Observatory, reckoning longitude and time from
the meridian of Washington. The Observatory, as "an appendage,
if not an attribute, of sovereignty," would lessen "dependence" on
England and Greenwich while assuring the reliability of American
navigational and geographical standards.[4] Though the War of 1812
passed without such an institution, proponents of American distinction in science continued to lobby for a National Observatory—most prominently President John Quincy Adams in his first
address to Congress in 1825.

Adams called European observatories "lighthouses in the
sky," illuminating man's passage through this world. His phrase
connected astronomy to navigation, while his conclusion tied
knowledge of the land to national self-knowledge. Without an
American Observatory, he claimed, "the earth revolves in perpetual darkness to our unsearching eyes" and we navigate our
destiny—not to mention our oceans and muddy frontiers—
blindly.[5] Though his address resulted in little action, it anticipated
a rising interest in astronomy as a symbol of rational, orderly
exploration of the physical world.

Exploiting the new continent's economic potential required
accurate information about land formations, resources, wa-
tersheds, and indigenous plants and animals. But before settlers
or speculators could take advantage of America's earthly bounty,

they needed to establish a philosophical or legal order that would prevent the pursuit of happiness from degenerating into chaos. As they moved west, American mapmakers laid out unclaimed land not according to natural features like hills or rivers, but in vast, perfectly square "sections" of 640 acres. These "Cartesian" grids would help ensure a homogeneous, democratic social space for American expansion. The vagueness of laws regarding the settlement and ownership of land had spurred western expansion by giving opportunists room to maneuver. Precision surveying, dependent in part on accurate timekeepers and a standard time of reference, helped resolve legal disputes over title and possession by providing a firm basis, as in the Mason-Dixon Line, for dividing up property.[6] To its most enthusiastic partisans, astronomical time promised to regulate the whole process of exploration, settlement, and industrialization by organizing society on rational principles.

As the conflict between clock time and "natural" time outlined in Chapter One intensified, American passion for scientific astronomy surged. Practices like reading the almanac to puzzle out the meaning of heavenly movements, a common American habit for generations, increasingly came under attack from nascent scientific elites, who deplored its superstitious overtones. Interest in the stars encouraged the foundation of formal, permanent observatories and schools of astronomy. A National Observatory was finally established in 1834, and in that decade Harvard, Yale, the University of North Carolina, and a great many other universities and towns established observatories of their own. Enthusiasm for astronomy grew markedly over the next decades.[7]

In 1843 Adams, now a congressman, marked the founding of the Cincinnati Observatory with an oration explaining astronomy's importance to the new nation. Adams began by recalling the glory of America and its unique political system, which required a rational, enlightened electorate to work properly. He then retraced the history of scientific knowledge and human advancement through a learned review of astronomy and its progress. Claiming an interest in the heavens as a universal human attribute, Adams noted the parallel development of astronomy and astrology with disdain. "We must remember," he asserted, "that of the genuine and the spurious science, of the chaste matron and the painted harlot; the parentage is one and the same." Adams attacked astrology for being, like the harlot, undisciplined and available to anyone. He spurned the common *Farmer's Almanac* and its tables in favor of a "chaste" scientific discipline requiring years of patient courting to master.[8]

Astronomy surpassed all other sciences because "it is from the skies, that the inhabitant of the earth is provided with a measure of time, without which, the mind of man would be unconscious of its own succession of ideas." Without appreciating time, derived from the heavens, man would be "unable to trace the connection between effects and their causes, and incapable of the exercise of reason." Since American government required the exercise of reason from its citizens, and astronomy recapitulated the laws of right reason, Adams reasoned that there was no science "that so urgently needs the protecting, patronizing and encouraging hand of power" as astronomy.[9]

By linking an attack on astrology to his program for publicly supported observatories, Adams aimed to remove control of time from the individual's sundial and almanac, and place it under the "patronizing power" of educated men and the government. In 1843 individual definitions of time, or unregulated time, subverted the order of public life in the same way that "harlots" disordered paternal authority and the home. Longfellow's "The Old Clock on the Stairs" and poems like it had connected time to clocks and clocks to traditional paternal authority, even while mourning that authority's decline. Adams made time female, acknowledging both the decline of the paternal authority embodied in poems like Longfellow's and the popularity of domestic manuals like Catherine

Beecher's. But by pointing out the need to protect time's virtue, Adams empowered a new kind of temporal authority based on scientific education. He took pains to establish the stars as the ultimate timekeepers, but insisted on the need for trained (male) observers to interpret them. Scientific observation of the heavens, and astronomical time, would regulate industrial culture in place of traditional paternal authority.[10]

What made scientific public time such an urgent need? Part of the answer lies in the confusion over time cited in Chapter One. But the new relationships between time and space developed by American commercial expansion probably played a larger role. Travel in the early nation was arduous and slow. In 1790 it took five full days for news to travel from Philadelphia to New York, and fifteen days for the same tired news to reach Boston.[11] But the surveying techniques that made American wilderness accessible furthered interstate commerce by helping in the design of roads and canals. Canals, by linking distant regions, promoted national cohesiveness — Robert Fulton, engineer and canal builder, concluded in 1807 that "when the United States shall be bound together by canals," with their corresponding market relations, "it will be no more possible to split them . . . than it is now possible for the government of England to divide and form into seven kingdoms."[12] Road building surged as well; by one estimate, the number of postal routes increased over eighty times between 1804 and 1834. By 1817 Philadelphia newspapers made the trip to Boston in under ten days, half the time of 1790, and by 1840 they traveled the same route in less than five. A journey from New York to Cincinnati that took three weeks in 1800 took just a little over seven days by 1830.[13]

But close and rapid connection brought problems as well; it demanded an unprecedented degree of organization across ever-increasing geographical space, and the market economy, wherever it spread, profoundly altered social relations. No technological innovation reflected both the promise and the problems of interregional commerce better than the railroad.

Early railroad builders all grappled with a basic functional dilemma. Should railroads be built for speed, simple transport from point A to point B as quickly as possible? Or was the iron track better suited to meandering along between each little market town? Although expected to regularize commerce and run on schedule, early railroads often disappointed their backers. Between confusion about their purpose and frequent mechanical failures, the first railroads were hardly paragons of regularity — the postmaster general concluded in 1835 that the railroads "cannot be relied upon with that degree of certainty, which is all important in the transmission of the mail."[14] In the beginning the quality of railroad service, clattering along at ten miles an hour, mattered less than the fact that it ran at all.

But the railroad's failure to reach the ideal detracted little from its revolutionary impact. Between 1840 and 1860 total American railroad mileage increased more than ten times, while average speeds doubled.[15] Its tracks carved up the land, its smoke and noise filled the air; its speed and range extended the businessman's realm of action. The ambivalent cultural response to the problem of the railroads has been well documented, and needs no detailed review here. But one good example of a different understanding of the new machine — and how unsettling to the experience of time it could be — appears in Hawthorne's 1843 story, "The Celestial Railroad."

In Hawthorne's nightmare revision of Bunyan's *Pilgrim's Progress*, the railroad compresses the "natural" moral journey through time established in Bunyan's classic, the patient and brave endurance of life's inevitable troubles and temptations. The moral shortcuts offered by Mr. Smooth-it-away, Director of the Celestial Railroad, completely overturn the traditional relations between good and evil — Apollyon, Christian's old enemy in Bunyan's tale, now drives the iron horse to heaven, racing past the few humble, old-fashioned pilgrims who still walk the traditional slow path to salvation. Mr. Smooth-it-away's cars dash easily through tribulations that sorely tested Pilgrim's faith, allowing Hawthorne to reduce Bunyan's lengthy allegory to a few pages. Although the dreaming narrator, a passenger on the celestial line, fears for his soul at points, he takes comfort in the dazzling efficiency of technology; the holy parchments that guided Christian are now pasteboard tickets, "much more convenient and useful along the road," and the Valley of the Shadow of Death now blazes with gas lamps. But the railroad's promises turn out to be empty as its vaunted speed, out of control, resolves finally into a headlong rush toward an industrial hell. Two humble pilgrims, who insisted on making the journey on foot, enter joyfully into heaven just as the trusting narrator is swept onto a sinister, smoking steam-ferry and certain damnation.[16]

Hawthorne condemned not just the railroad, but industrial society and the factory system as well. The moral landscape of Hawthorne's story, leveled to build the railway roadbed, offers few reliable signposts. Christian's encounters through life's slow journey—their homely familiarity, their inevitability—collapse before a whole new set of mechanical temptations to faith, the most tempting of all being the convenience of speed. Hawthorne's railroad of 1843 stands for pure reckless speed, rather than punctuality or scheduling, which imply speed under control. The world of the story is a world of revolutionary and dangerous industrial forces running unchecked, not power systematically and willfully imposed.

Published in the same year as "The Celestial Railroad," Adams's Cincinnati speech addressed similar fears. Hoping to check the locomotive rush of invention and regulate it with reason, Adams promoted a new temporal authority for daily life, an authority that used astronomical time as its mapping and regulating principle. Edward Everett, the Massachusetts senator and sometime editor of the *North American Review,* gave a similar address dedicating Albany's Dudley Observatory in 1856. Everett, one of the most popular orators of his day, defended the high cost of stargazing as Adams did. In an age of ever more common and rapid railroad travel, Everett reminded his audience, clocks regulated to local time were useless. When carried east or west they "will keep home time alone, like the fond traveler who leaves his heart behind him."[17] In the thirteen years between the two speeches American railroads had experienced continued growth. But as Everett's comment pointed out, when individual railroads grew and expanded their areas of operation they ran into more and more difficulties with the lack of standardized time.

Running north to south caused relatively little trouble, since the differences in time between individual towns of the same approximate longitude was slight. Moving east to west, on the other hand, highlighted differences of meridian and thus of time. A traveler on a westbound train, setting his watch at departure, might find after less than half an hour's travel that his watch and the local time no longer agreed.[18] To make matters worse, individual railroad and steamship lines each ran by their own standards of time — usually the time of the city the line originated in. When two lines met, or shared a track, or terminated at a steamship landing, it threw differences in timekeeping into high relief. Could a railroad passenger arriving in Pittsburgh at 1:30 p.m. New York local time catch a connecting train leaving Pittsburgh at 1:30 p.m. Pittsburgh time? Confusing at the least, the situation was partially resolved by the appearance, in the late 1840s, of monthly traveler's guides, bound collections of railroad and steamship schedules.[19] But these schedules raised more troubling questions. What time prevailed when two or more standards conflicted? Did the railroad and steamship set the time, or did the local sun?

Such confusion, like the conflicts over time's authority discussed in Chapter One, demanded uniform standards of time usable by all. Like Adams, Everett insisted on a basis in astronomy. "Our artificial timekeepers," he noted, "are but a transcript, so to say, of the celestial motions, and would be of no value without the means of regulating them by observation." Everett stressed how completely, by 1856, "the daily business of life is affected and controlled by the heavenly bodies. It is they and not our main-springs, expansion balances, and our compensation pendulums, which give us our time."[20] Like Adams, Everett advanced celestial mechanics as an ordering principle. And like Adams, Everett favored taking control of time out of the individual's hands and placing it in the care of scientists and learned men. But Everett's speech, with its references to clock time, reflected the continuing spread of Eli Terry's cheap clocks. And his example of traveler's time recalled both the unprecedented growth of American railroads and the troubling profusion of authorities for time.

Everett's awareness of time, astronomy, and railroad travel came from personal experience—he had served as president of Harvard around the time that William Cranch Bond, astronomer and clockmaker of Boston, established the first regional time standards for the New England railroads. Hoping to improve punctuality and safety while ending the confusion over time, in the 1840s a number of railroads issued detailed regulations specifying the time to be used on their lines. The New England roads turned to William C. Bond for their standard.

Bond, a highly successful maker of fine marine chronometers, had assumed charge of the skeletal Harvard Observatory in 1839. There he soon managed to acquire one of the largest telescopes in the world. He also took part in longitude measurements for the United States Coast Survey, where he used a marvelous new invention, the telegraph. American astronomers working, like Bond, for the Coast Survey, had recognized early on that they could use the telegraph to send time signals between their observatories. The time signal made it possible to determine the longitude of one point relative to another—the longitude of Cambridge, Massachusetts, for example, relative to Washington—with far more accuracy than before. From his experience with the Survey Bond invented the drum chronograph, a new, telegraphic method of recording time in the "American Method" of astronomical observations that netted him a medal at London's 1851 Crystal Palace Exhibition.[21]

Railroads, canals, roads, and steamships increased the speed of travel and the flow of goods between regions. The telegraph, perhaps the most marvelous invention of all, bound that network of transportation and trade together. Thanks to the telegraph, news of business transactions and market prices now traveled with lightning speed; so too events in distant places gained a new and pressing relevance for those waiting at the end of the wire. Oliver Wendell Holmes found in the telegraph a "network of iron nerves which flash sensation and volition backward and forward to and from towns and provinces as if they were organs and limbs of a single living body."[22] But telegraphic connection highlighted differences in time even more dramatically. What time was it in Boston when banks closed in Philadelphia? Astronomers like William Bond and his son George began using telegraphed time signals to augment the synchronicity Holmes applauded, and to organize some of the temporal chaos by establishing uniform regional public times in place of local variation.

Bond's eminence as an astronomer, clockmaker, and telegraphic innovator led the New England Association of Railroad Superintendents, meeting in Boston in hopes of consolidating their running times, to recommend in 1849 that "all the railroad companies in New England [adopt] a time two minutes after the true time of Boston as given by William Bond & Son, No. 26 Congress St., Boston." Just why they chose a time two minutes after Boston time remains a mystery. But the Superintendents' determination to formalize timekeeping seems unmistakable. They further recommended that "all station clocks, conductor's watches, and all time tables and trains should be regulated accordingly" to the Bonds' clock. By 1851, railroad officials received daily time signals,

William C. Bond's apparatus for "The American Method"
of determining longitude. Bond's work stood at the intersection of
commercial expansion, rational government, and national identity.
He won a prize for his inventions at the 1851 London Crystal
Palace Exhibition. (National Museum of American
History, Smithsonian Institution.)

by telegraph, from the Bond shop and later the Harvard College Observatory itself. The relationship between the Bonds, the university, and the railroads in effect established the first regional time zone in the United States.[23]

The railroads fulfilled Adams's vision of American commercial life ordered by scientific principles. They drew their time from the Harvard Observatory, standardizing their operations and coordinating their movements through a uniform standard of time. But in the process they attacked the rational appreciation of the heavens Adams treasured. Everett had pointed out that clocks carried east or west soon lost all meaning. It was to synchronize clocks that the railroads adopted the Bonds' standard. By tying their time to the standard *clocks*, the railroads—the preeminent "machine in the garden"—in effect severed the connection between time and nature. Their resolution made the railroad's clock the source of time.

"I watch the passage of the morning cars," wrote Thoreau in *Walden*, "with the same feeling that I do the rising of the sun, which is hardly more regular." As Leo Marx notes, Thoreau understood the railroad through the master metaphor of the clock; in his case, the railroad clock that increasingly ordered life. The clock, the railroad, and their effects on time pervade *Walden* as they did Concord.[24] "The startings and arrivals of the cars," Thoreau claimed, "are now the epochs of the village day. They come and go with such regularity and precision, and their whistles can be heard so far, that the farmers set their clocks by them, and thus one well-conducted institution regulates a whole country." Writing in Concord in the early 1850s, Thoreau described the results of the Bonds' cooperation with the New England railroads.

Thoreau's railroad, unlike Hawthorne's, controlled and regulated its speed and thereby regulated society. "Have not men improved somewhat in punctuality since the railroad was invented?" he continued. "Do they not talk and think faster in the depot than they did in the stage office? There is something electrifying in the atmosphere of the former place."[25] It was the railroad that worked this change in the way people understood and used time. Thoreau often wrote about time in terms of natural law and the conventions of pastoralism — earlier in *Walden* he describes hearing the nearby village tower clocks, "a sweet, and, as it were, natural melody, worth importing into the wilderness." The clocks merge with the pastoral scene, and even the whippoorwills follow this natural time. "They would begin to sing," he slyly observed, "almost with the precision of a clock" each evening at seven-thirty.[26] Thoreau acknowledged the railroad's spiritual origins in Rittenhouse's orrery and Newtonian mechanics — he described "the engine with its train of cars moving off with *planetary* motion" (my italics). But later in the same sentence he corrected himself. The railroad, he observed, followed the course into the future like an arrow — "or, rather, like a comet."

Thoreau went on to compare the trains to bolts shot from some archer's bow — the railroad, he was claiming, embodied the cyclical movements of nature where nature was regarded as a mechanism. A railroad engine's gears and wheels moved in predictable and regular cycles, like the Newtonian universe. But the train of cars had broken the cycle of seasonal time and headed off into the future; it moved, like an arrow, with frightening energy and speed toward an uncertain and potentially disastrous future. He ended by grimly concluding, "we have constructed a fate, an *Atropos*, that never turns aside. (Let that be the name of your engine.)"[27]

Thoreau's famous description sums up the changing American experience of time: an increase in punctuality, surely, but more subtly a shift in the nature and source of time itself, with corresponding changes in work and life. His deliberate and sly comparisons between the railroad, nature, and the regularity of men and the heavens reflected the new public face time began assuming in the 1850s. Astronomical time tied the railroads to natural law and rationalized their operations. But its use in daily life, on the railroads or in the Lowell mills, invested more and more power in what Everett had called a mere "transcript" of heavenly motions—the clock.

The following running regulations, issued by the Camden and Amboy Railroad in 1853, dramatize the effects of the new thinking about time and timekeepers. "Each Conductor, Engine Driver, Switch Tender and Bridge Tender," the rules began, "will be supplied with a good watch by the company." Previously the company had been mostly indifferent about whether or not its employees carried watches. Now they even specified the source of time for each watch, and how it would be secured: "the CON-DUCTOR will call for and receive two Watches at the office, preceding each departure—compare them with the Standard Clock, and be sure they agree before leaving the room." The conductor was then to hand one watch to the engine driver, receive it back again at the end of the route, and finally return both watches to the office. Along the way, regulations instructed the conductor to "compare his time with the Clocks at the Stations he stops at, and notify the Agents of any discrepancy."[28]

The regulations make perfect sense. How could a railroad be run without such precision? But by using precise and accurate time as a justification, regulations like these construct an elaborate hierarchy and daily ritual for conferring power, in which authority comes through carrying or reproducing the master clock. The workers' jobs are controlled by the clock, and they in turn spread the authority of the master clock to points along the line. Schoolbooks earlier connected moral virtue to the wise use of time as seen in nature's example. Under these rules wisdom resides in the regulating clock, and virtue lies in the good worker's obedience to it.[29]

━━━━

The public debate over time's source and its meaning might help explain the peculiar analogy Herman Melville chose for *Pierre,* in his pivotal chapter on moral authority, "The Journey and the Pamphlet." The pamphlet in question, "Chronometricals and Horologicals," by "Plotinius Plinlimmon," compares God's moral precepts to Greenwich time, the navigator's standard, and Christ to a fine chronometer, regulated, like a ship's clock, to Greenwich time. Men and women on earth, in Plinlimmon's analogy, correspond to ordinary watches, each regulated to the more precise standard occasionally but inclined to run fast or slow and drift from Greenwich. Individual consciences, like individual watches, vary from the heavenly standard of morality as watches drift away from Greenwich time.

Moreover, Plinlimmon maintains, the Greenwich standard itself, like Christian morality, stops making sense in other countries, other cultures—keeping English time in China denies the "rightness," the native logic, of China's own standards of time and of personal conduct. "In an artificial world like ours," Plinlimmon claims, "the soul of man is further removed from God and the Heavenly Truth, than the chronometer carried to China, is from Greenwich." For Plinlimmon, "As China watches are right as to China, so too the Greenwich chronometers must be wrong as to China," and so "no single earthly moral position may predominate over another."[30] Trying to keep to celestial standards of conduct in a world so distant from God mirrors the foolishness of keeping Greenwich time in China, and so Plinlimmon advocates an intellectually lame "virtuous expediency," a compromise between God's standards and local realities.

Melville's experiences as a sailor obviously familiarized him with Greenwich time, and the "Chronometricals and Horologicals" conceit seems like a somewhat playful reflection of his years before the mast. But treating the chapter this way ignores the social context he drew on when he chose such a peculiar analogy. On one level, Melville's chapter discussed morality, but at a second level, Melville questioned time's role in daily life. By comparing morality to standard time, the chapter reiterated the connection between metaphors for time, social regulation, and personal conduct. Writing in 1851, Melville satirized redefinitions of time like those engineered by the New England railroads and William Bond.

Even more, Melville probed the connection between time and political authority. The metaphor relates standards of time to personal conduct and morality—just as we use Greenwich time to navigate our way through the stormy seas (and to rationalize land divisions), so we need a reliable standard to use in dividing our time during life's moral squalls. A trip to London in 1849–50 must have acquainted Melville with the recent introduction of Greenwich time as the standard for all of England. Only one year before, most British railroads had set their clocks to Greenwich, in defiance of local time and tradition. The controversial move brought a host of objections, still lingering during Melville's visit. Some condemned "railway-time aggression," others complained that placing Greenwich time over the local standard was "usurping the power of the Allmighty."[31] The authority for time, be it Greenwich Observatory, the railroad, or God, informed the principles, moral, economic, or otherwise, that governed daily life.

Greenwich time symbolized England's maritime dominance— when American sailors consulted their almanacs for information about celestial movements or tides, they made their calculations against the English time. As Melville worked on *Pierre*, patriotic stargazers were lobbying Congress for an *American* prime meridian based on Washington instead of Greenwich. After much agitation from 1846 to 1851, Congress authorized the publication of an American nautical almanac to be reckoned from some spot on American soil.[32] The *American Ephemeris and Nautical Almanac* would help establish the scientific credibility of the United States and formalize an *American* standard of time for commerce and surveying. Though its supporters claimed the American Prime Meridian contributed to the national glory, the plan provoked "great excitement" and widespread hostility from businessmen and shipping interests, who objected to the change from established practice.[33]

Melville's richly ambiguous satire pointed out the political and ethical coercion inherent in standardized, government regulated time in a society, like America in the 1850s, that linked strict attention to time with moral virtue. If a man "seek to regulate his daily conduct" by Christ's chronometrical soul, according to Plinlimmon, "he will but array all men's earthly timekeepers [souls] against him, and thereby work himself woe and death."[34] The way people used time was central to the way society judged them. Deviation from the standards of public time, like deviation from established morality, marked the dissenter as a danger. Through Plinlimmon, Melville satirized the idea of standard public time based on machines.

Plinlimmon's "virtuous expediency" paralleled the system of astronomically regulated, telegraphed time signals recommended by Adams and Everett and adopted by the New England railroads. Virtuous because regulated astronomically, the railroads' time was expedient in that it ignored the "truth" of local time solely to expedite commerce.[35] But while Plinlimmon espoused flexibility, within limits, in moral and temporal affairs, the railroads rewrote the terms of his argument; the railroads were becoming the chronometrical standard *and* managing to impose uniformity. Made specious by changing times, Plinlimmon's philosophy answered nothing. As Thoreau suggested and the Camden and Amboy running regulations pointed out, the railroads' "virtuous expediency" in timekeeping imposed a new, clock-derived logic on the ordering of human affairs.[36]

As Melville published *Pierre* yet another writer addressed the standardization of time, linking it to the health and progress of the nation. "The railroad system of the United States," railway editor Henry Poor claimed, "is destined to be one of the most potent physical instruments in the onward course of the nation. Any improvement that will give to this mighty engine of modern civilization increased safety, efficiency, and order, should be promptly adopted." Time was the key innovation in his opinion, for the railroad demanded close attention to time from its employees — "it is necessary that they should regulate all their movements in time."

A single clock, linked to others, would oversee both worker and trains' movements. "The magnetic telegraph," Poor continued, resorting to organic metaphors that linked man and machine, "the nerve to this vast muscle," would serve to synchronize all clocks. "And before many years," he concluded, "the beats of the great regulating clock in the heart of New York will pulsate with the vibrations of its pendulum on the clock escapements from Halifax to New Orleans."[37]

Poor's vision, of unified national time regulating industry, commerce, and the individual, was premature. National standard time was more than sixty years away, and the railroads deferred any unified action until 1883. But the growth of the railroad and telegraph network — and the public's increased participation in its benefits — dramatized the lack of a nationally uniform, easily distributed time. For example, in 1869, as the transcontinental railroad neared completion at Promontory, Utah, its backers began planning a national celebration of their achievement. They prepared a special sledgehammer, connected by wire to a nearby telegraph transmitter. Swung by the soft-handed Leland Stanford, the sledgehammer would electrically signal its contact with the last "Golden Spike," and the railroad's completion, to an anxiously waiting nation. Transmitting the exact moment of completion by telegraph, they reasoned, would join the entire country, urban and rural, great and small, in celebration of the iron link between east and west, while dramatizing the new interconnectedness technology promoted. It would be perhaps the first experience of true simultaneity in American history.

Fate, and Stanford's unfamiliarity with sledgehammers, intervened: he missed the spike completely. The wired sledge, striking wood, transmitted only a dull thud. A more experienced official drove the last spike home with a regular sledge as a telegrapher cabled "done" to waiting stations east and west. But even then confusion reigned: what time was the spike actually driven? So many places with so many watches, and no official standard of time—at Promontory the telegraph clicked around 12:45 p.m., in Virginia City at 12:30; San Francisco had "precisely" either 11:46 or 11:44:37, depending on which paper one read, while in Washington, 2:47 seemed approximately right.[38] Railroad and telegraph officials could imagine a simultaneous, synchronized "media event" taking place across the continent and the world. But the nation lacked both the mechanical and intellectual precedents necessary to accomplish it. Telegraph transmitting equipment was still too crude, the Babel of local times too chaotic.

In the years between 1850 and 1880, following William Bond's example, other American observatories began building standard time services: the Dudley Observatory in Albany, New York, in 1856, the Cincinnati Observatory in 1860, the Naval Observatory in 1865, and Chicago's Dearborn Observatory sometime before 1871. Each standardized and regulated, to some degree, the time of the immediate area and in most cases the railroads nearby.[39] Samuel P. Langley's career in Allegheny, Pennsylvania, dramatizes the observatories' effect on public time after the Civil War.

In Pittsburgh, a series of lectures on the celestial science in 1859 had lead a group of prominent Pittsburgh citizens, including railroad magnate William Thaw, to form the Allegheny Telescope Association in hopes of bringing astronomy to Pittsburgh. Although it acquired an excellent telescope and a serviceable building, the Association failed as popular enthusiasm for astronomy ebbed. When the original astronomer quit in disgust, the growing industrial town was left with a practically useless instrument. After ceding their creation to the Western University of Pennsylvania, the struggling Observatory's trustees began searching for a new director to reorganize its operations.

Langley, the future Secretary of the Smithsonian Institution, came highly recommended from Harvard College Observatory, where he had served as an assistant. Hired in 1867, he spent his first months improving Allegheny's spartan facilities, soon managing to ally himself with both William Thaw and the Coast Survey. He persuaded Western Union to connect the Observatory with the city, entering into a series of observations designed to precisely fix its longitude. The Observatory was then to be used by the Coast Survey to determine the location of other inland cities.[40] Most of the money for this work initially came from Thaw, himself an amateur astronomer. Only Thaw's flowing cash and social influence kept the Observatory afloat.

The struggle for funds plagued scientists everywhere, but American citizens disdained supposedly "impractical" research with special vigor. An ambitious man, Langley recognized that he would never make a name for himself in the combative world of American science if he spent all his time scrounging for dollars or performing tedious longitude calculations for the Coast Survey.

He needed to set his new Observatory on a financially secure basis, independent of public and private largess. It would not be easy. What need had Pittsburgh, a booming industrial city with relatively few cultural pretensions, for a telescope and a professional stargazer?

Langley's clever innovation lay in his decision to *sell* observatory time signals, by telegraphic transmissions, to Pittsburgh's industries. Drawing on his experiences with William Bond, Langley first selected a reliable system for telegraphic time distribution developed in England. In 1869, he issued a pamphlet proposing that Allegheny supply standard time to the mighty Pennsylvania Railroad. Thaw's business association with A. J. Cassatt, president of the Pennsylvania, got the proposal a more than fair hearing. In early 1871 Cassatt issued orders making Allegheny Observatory time the standard for the Pennsylvania Railroad. Langley converted Allegheny meridian time to the longitude of Philadelphia, and sent it to the railroad in return for $1,000 a year.[41]

Time for sale:
Samuel Langley, probably
in the years he was working on
time transmission at Allegheny.
(National Museum of
American History,
Smithsonian Institution.)

Langley also convinced a number of local jewelers to buy time signals at $500 per annum—a practice that jewelers in most other cities eventually adopted. In nineteenth-century America, jewelers were the primary suppliers of high-quality watches and clocks. Seeing a prominent clock labeled "standard time" in the shop window suggested that this jeweler carried accurate goods. It also tended to make the jeweler's store a source of accurate time for passers-by. William Bond had presented visitors to his watch and clock shop with elaborate clocks that proudly showed "Bond's Standard Time." Langley must have made the practice especially attractive to Pittsburgh jewelers.

He also began explaining the idea to the people of Pittsburgh. A series of articles in local newspapers laid out his views on this "startling and novel" proposition.[42] Langley reminded readers that "from the Atlantic to the Mississippi, every city and town is keeping a time of its own." He proposed to "do away with the present vexatious changes of time" in railway travel by overturning the "custom" maintaining local times. Such times, he claimed, were "founded in no natural necessity" and merely a legacy of the past. Langley recalled the difference between mean and sun time. "The time kept by our clocks and watches," he insisted correctly, "is a much more artificial thing than is generally supposed. . . . *No natural phenomenon designates the hour of noon.*" Local noon was a "fiction" by the clock. And since "there is no natural necessity for repeating this fiction . . . there is consequently no reason why Philadelphia and Pittsburgh clocks should not be set to agree with each other." Langley moved to replace natural phenomena with scientific and commercial rationality.

Recognizing the railroad as the key to Pittsburgh's industrial economy, Langley also recognized its role as titular public time-keeper. But he needed to persuade the railroads, and the public, that his standard time offered more than the haphazard system then in use. John Quincy Adams had connected the stars to rationality and virtue, but in his advocacy of Allegheny Observatory time Langley promoted accuracy and precision above all. His clock, he claimed, having been "rendered practically perfect by the hourly comparison with the heavenly bodies . . . will be kept within a second of absolute truth" every year.[43] "Absolute truth," in this case, meant truth as to the meridian of Allegheny; the system's accuracy and universal applicability assured its value to society, its "moral truth," as well.

Langley's novel idea made time a commodity. Local time, as a "fiction," paled besides Allegheny's new and improved version — Langley called it "a relic of antiquity" like local coinage or local weights and measures, which "the progress of centralization, and the interchange of commerce and travel" outmoded. Traditional local time expressed a relation between the individual and the place he or she lived; time of day depended on where you were at a particular instant. Its authority rested entirely on inherited tradition and customs of the past. It became "fictional" when two or more times disagreed, when two possible "presents" confronted each other. Standardized time, on the other hand, expressed a relation between the individual and an entire region — it acknowledged the links between places forged in commercial expansion. Railroad men like Cassatt and Thaw traveled — they administered business empires covering vast stretches of territory, each part dependent to a considerable extent on movements along another. Scientific hourly signals established a more comprehensive "present" equally useful in all places.

By emphasizing the service's scientific accuracy, Langley offered Cassatt and Thaw a rational aid to the problems of controlling such a vast empire. It aided further commercial and geographic expansion. Allegheny Observatory time eliminated the paradox that worried Melville's Plinlimmon; Langley's service derived its authority from his accuracy and its "nonfiction" from its supposedly universal applicability. Standard observatory time made it possible for a centralized railroad organization to oversee and synchronize its many moving parts, human and otherwise. It became the standard of conduct for railroad employees.

Like standard money, this new time also lent itself to circulation. Easily transmitted by telegraph, it could be bought and used by anyone whose line of work demanded it. In Philadelphia Henry Bentley, an enterprising businessman, connected his Philadelphia Local Telegraph Company to the clock the Pennsylvania Railroad used to receive Langley's time signals. He then offered Langley's astronomical time to other local businesses as "Philadelphia Standard Time." Through his central office Bentley provided a synchronized "telegraphic exchange." Subscribers could conduct transactions, send or receive news, and keep abreast of commodities prices by wire.[44] Langley compared standard time to standardized denominations of currency—an apt comparison, since telegraphed standard time facilitated the same exchange of goods and information that money encouraged. Standard time, like standard money, was a universal solvent dissolving the glue of local tradition and custom.

Langley's innovation made economic and scientific sense, and other observatories quickly adopted their own versions of the Allegheny system. Over the next ten years, Langley and his fellow astronomers began organizing, promoting, and selling first time services and later national standard time obtained from observatories. Each assumed that the superior accuracy and convenience of their services doomed "free" local time to extinction.[45]

Others, not surprisingly, held more tightly to local time. Earlier in 1869 Charles F. Dowd, an amateur scientist and principal of Temple Grove Ladies' Seminary in Saratoga Springs, New York, had begun advancing the first plan for uniform national time, one involving four standard time zones remarkably similar to those in use today. His scheme asked all railroad lines to adopt the meridian time of Washington, D.C., and the Naval Observatory. This "railroad time" would be distinct from local time, with the difference to be posted at each station. The energetic Dowd calculated a set of "plus or minus indexes" for virtually every train station in the country—roughly 8,000 separate calculations—and mailed off the resulting large pamphlet to managers of the leading roads.[46]

Dowd correctly recognized two distinct kinds of time, one rooted in nature and tied to place, the other springing from telegraphy and rapid travel between distinct places, and little affected by natural imperatives. He kept them separate. Emphasizing the autonomy of small towns, Dowd's plan invested the authority for time and timekeeping in tradition and local custom rather than in scientific measurement.

Although his plan received favorable notices from a number of railroad managers, no action resulted. The rapacious train lines of the 1870s warred more often than they cooperated, and the scope of Dowd's plan required more united action than normal. Posting "plus and minus indexes" posed an expensive and troublesome solution to a relatively minor problem.[47] More importantly, his emphasis on retaining local times jarred with both regional time systems like Allegheny's *and* the railroad's apparent tendency to regulate the public time. Dowd continued to lobby railroad managers over the next ten years, but as an outsider in both the railroad and scientific communities he remained a marginal figure.[48]

By the mid-1870s, most railroads operated within a specific region, and like the Pennsylvania Railroad used a standard of time derived from a nearby observatory or city. In effect, they had developed a system of regional standard times. Smaller lines adopted the time of their larger neighbors, and the relatively few frequent travelers probably either stayed within one region during each day's travel or else knew enough about time differences to adjust for them.[49]

ADIRONDACK RAILWAY.
STATIONS.

0Saratoga[-13]
0Greenfield[-13]
0King's[-13]
0South Corinth[-13]
0Jessup's Landing[-13]
0Hadley[-13]
0Stony Creek[-13]
0Thurman[-13]
0The Glen[-13]
0Johnsburg[-12]
0North Creek[-12]
0Fourteenth[-12]

ALABAMA AND CHATTANOOGA RAILWAY.
STATIONS.

1Chattanooga[-27]
1Wauhatchie[-27]
1Morganville[-27]
1Trenton[-26]
1Dademont[-26]
1Rising Fawn[-26]
1Cloverdale[-26]
1Eureka Coal Mines[-26]
1Valley Head[-25]
1Hollomen's[-25]
1Brandon's[-25]
1Portersville[-25]
1Collinsville[-25]
1Greenwood[-25]

ALBANY AND SUSQUEHANNA RAILROAD.
STATIONS.

0Albany[-13]
0Adamsville[-13]
0Slingerland[-13]
0New Scotland[-12]
0Guilderland[-12]
0Knowersville[-12]
0Duanesburg[-12]
0Quaker Street[-11]
0Esperance[-11]
0Schoharie Junction[-11]
0Schoharie[-11]
0Middleburg[-11]
0Howe's Cave[-10]
0Cobleskill[-10]
0Sharon Springs[-10]
0Cherry Valley[-9]

Albany and Susquehanna Railroad.
(Continued.)
STATIONS.

0Richmondville[-10]
0Carryville[-9]
0East Worcester[-9]
0Worcester[-9]
0Schenevus[-9]
0Chaseville[-8]
0Maryland[-8]
0Colliers[-8]
0Cooperstown[-8]
0Emmons[-8]
0Oneonta[-8]
0Otego[-7]
0Wells Bridge[-7]
0Unadilla[-7]
0Sidney[-6]
0Bainbridge[-6]
0Afton[-6]
0Harpersville[-6]
0Tunnel[-5]
0Osborn Hollow[-5]
0Port Crane[-5]
0Binghamton[-4]

ALEXANDRIA, LOUDOUN AND HAMPSHIRE RAILWAY.
STATIONS.

0Alexandria[0]
0Carlinville[+1]
0Falls Church[+1]
0Vienna[+1]
0Hunter's Mill[+1]
0Thornton[+1]
0Herndon[+2]
0Guilford[+2]
0Farmwell[+2]
0Belmont[+2]
0Leesburg[+2]
0Clark's Gap[+2]
0Hamilton[+2]

ALLEGHANY VALLEY RAILWAY.
STATIONS.

0Pittsburg[+12]
0Lawrenceville[+12]
0Sharpsburg[+11]
0Brilliant[+11]
0Ireland's[+11]
0Armstrong[+11]
0Verner[+11]

Page one of Charles Dowd's system of "plus and minus indexes."
The number to the left of each station indicates its zone
(numbered 0–3); the number to the right, the local difference,
in minutes, from the zone standard. Dowd had this "railway time
gazeteer," including indexes for over 8,000 stations on every railway
in the country, published at his own expense and sent to railroad
managers. (Charles F. Dowd, *System of National Time and
Railway Time Gazetteer* [Albany, N.Y., 1870].)

At train stations, two clocks often told the difference between local and railroad time. Dowd claimed that Buffalo's station included three separate clocks, one for each line using the station plus Buffalo city time. He estimated over eighty distinct railroad times confronting the traveling public in 1870.[50] Though confusing, the situation hardly constituted a crisis, especially if the primacy of local time, sanctified by tradition and the evidence of nature, was assumed. Conductors could call out time differences as they arose, and most cities and towns simply adopted the most convenient local source—usually the time of a jewelry store or factory, as at Lowell; often the railroad time if not too different from the local sun.

The conflicts over the nature of time evident twenty years earlier relaxed in the early 1870s, probably thanks to the kind of local and regional standardization already described at the Lowell mills and at Harvard, Allegheny, and elsewhere. Outside of commercial life, away from telegraphs and train stations, local time ruled the day. Taking national standard time for granted, we can hardly appreciate today how new the idea appeared as late as 1880. Abandoning local times in daily life seemed unthinkable to many—as the Superintendent of the Naval Observatory rhapsodized: "the sun regulates all life upon the earth . . . by local time [man] must live, move, and have his being."[51] Though cumbersome and awkward-seeming to us, if the haphazard system bothered anyone other than a few railroad men and scientists they left little record of their dismay.[52] The potential advantages of standard time, on the other hand, readily impressed anyone stopping to think about it, and between 1870 and 1880 the number of standards used on the railroads decreased by about thirty, thanks to consolidation and cooperation between roads.[53]

Standard time was more than just convenient; it offered a new model for regulating work and public life. The Pennsylvania Railroad's business with Langley certainly did the Observatory a favor—a thousand dollars meant little to the railroad but a great deal to Langley. But what probably intrigued Cassatt most was Allegheny's ready facilities for easy and largely *automatic* telegraphic transmission of a standard time. Langley's system used a small lever just touching one of the toothed wheels of a clock. When struck lightly by the teeth of the gear wheel as the clock ticked, the lever pivoted, regularly making and breaking contact with a telegraph receiving terminal. A subscriber to the time service, Langley wrote, hears what "sounds like a clock ticking somewhere in the room . . . it *is* a clock ticking," he continued, "but the clock is many hundreds of miles away."[54] Allegheny time extended the regulating authority of a single central clock—and by extension, of A. J. Cassatt—over hundreds of miles.

Shortly after securing Cassatt's business, Langley and Thaw began lobbying J. D. Layng, manager of the western divisions of the Pennsylvania, asking an additional thousand dollars a year for time service on the western roads. The Observatory, Thaw enthused, was "a perfect machine for determining that standard time, and communicating it to all needful points."[55] Later that year the two enthusiasts talked Pittsburgh into dropping another thousand dollars per annum to receive Allegheny time on its new City Hall clock.[56] To justify the substantial expense and draw more customers, Langley explained the benefits of his service in a number of letters, addresses, and newspaper and magazine articles.[57]

The most extensive example, in *Harper's Monthly*, made a fetish of accurate observation to sell Observatory time to the general public. Langley described his transit instrument, mounted on massive stone piers "carried down to bedrock" to preserve it from even the slightest vibration. The position of the transit marked the meridian, and tiny cross hairs, made from the "cocoon of the little wood-spider (common cobweb is too coarse)" mapped the regular passage of certain "clock stars" across the instrument's field of view. These stars gave the best indication of the earth's rotation and thus of time. The problem lay in measuring them accurately. Langley described the numerous and pesky sources of possible error facing the astronomer—the stone piers shrank and expanded in heat or cold, shifting the transit to the right or left; the tap of a finger set the transit vibrating hysterically. The axles of the transit, "though turned with a diamond," remained uneven, for "mathematical perfection is not attainable."

Finally, the human observer inevitably introduced a whole new set of errors. Individual reaction time varied from day to day and person to person. Even the delay between the time a star was perceived to have passed the cross hairs and the instant the observer's hand struck a telegraph key, regulating the time service sending clock, counted significantly. "Yet this time must be measured," Langley wrote, "for though we cannot get rid of the faults of the mechanism employed, whether it be of stone or brass, or that of nerves and brain, we can [correct] for their effects, and so finally evolve truth from what appears to be a maze of error."

Langley used machine metaphors to make the observer and the Observatory part of one mechanism. He made "nerves and brain" analogous to "brass and stone." By calling attention to sources of error Langley only increased the reader's admiration for the Observatory's precision and the system of knowledge that kept error in check. Like Adams's defense of astronomy, Langley's time service offered scientific accuracy in place of individual judgment or local custom. But Langley went further than Adams. Adams had looked to the stars as the inspiration for rationality, but Langley sought to make the regulating influence of heavens automatic and unconscious—to bind daily life to mechanical, automatic accuracy.

He described "the immense movement of freight and passenger traffic" roving across the continent. "During the day the rush of passing cars is incessant," he continued, "and when night comes on, the noise of panting engines, which pass the window with a crescent shriek, makes it seem as if our broken sleep had been passed in the vicinity of interminable rushing trains." Hawthorne's "Celestial Railroad" journey, thirty years earlier, took place in a nightmare. Langley's shrieking trains similarly disturbed the nation's sleep, the more so given the vast scale of continental railroad enterprise. Trains entered into everyone's daily life whether they knew it or not, Langley implied, and their effects might not always be wholesome. Scientific *observation* offered a solution to the problems they caused.

"The amount and intricacy of this movement grow on us the more we study it," he mused, and "an eye which could survey the whole at once" would see "two endless processions of trains separated from each other by but a few minutes distance." Langley's imagery, repeated in a number of his other articles, made railroad operations into a kind of national unconscious, a constant circulation taking place even in dreams, vaguely disturbing and fraught with potential danger. The movement of trains defied visual comprehension or the most vigilant human surveillance. Only one thing preserved the system from chaos—"*Time* exactly obtained and kept is the regulator of this complex system of moving parts, which, in theory at least, should resemble one great piece of clockwork." "To make things 'move like clockwork' is not merely a figure of speech," Langley concluded, "here where our lives depend on the accuracy of a conductor's watch."[58]

In his 1856 speech Edward Everett had likened the telescope "to a wondrous Cyclopean eye, endowed with superhuman power, by which the astronomer extends his view to the further heavens."[59] Langley's clockwork metaphor turned the telescope on society. The astronomer extended his view into daily life, using the "superhuman power" of the standard clock and telegraphic signal to regulate social and commercial time. Langley replaced human frailty and propensity for error with automatic, consistent, mechanical observation. His clockwork metaphor replaced Adams's rational electorate with dependent wheels turning in a complex social mechanism.[60]

"The perfect disciplinary apparatus," Michel Foucault remarked in his study of social discipline and criminality, "would make it possible for a single gaze to see everything constantly."[61] Everett and Langley described such an apparatus, an apparatus of standardized time that would oversee and regulate social movements of all kinds. The standard observatory clock transmitted the time, and lesser clocks relayed it to cities, towns, factories, and homes. Standard time offered a framework for social reorganization along new principles, principles of fixed, regular, and automatic control. "Accuracy" bound the framework together and assured its virtue, just as in medieval theology regular schedules of prayer had assured the prayer's piety. Langley posed a new system of social organization and regulating authority propped up by automatic accuracy. The more accurate and precise time signals seemed, the more legitimate their authority over daily life became. Automatically, unconsciously, standard public time offered a new pattern for ordering everyday life and labor.

By 1878, the date of the *Harper's* article, other observatories had begun promoting time services of their own. Harvard's Observatory, for example, started selling time signals in 1871, following Langley's example. A year later the director reported the service losing money, and "its discontinuance seriously considered." But accurate time, the Observatory claimed, was now essential to railroads and their patrons, factories, jewelers, watchmakers, and cities and towns generally. Instead of canceling the service, the Observatory began "active measures . . . to secure a wider knowledge of our time signals, by circulars, letters, and personal interviews."[62]

One such circular issued in 1877, "for distribution among those interested in a common standard of public time throughout New England," stressed again and in considerable detail the accuracy of Observatory time signals and their ease of transmission across vast distances. The circular introduced the Observatory's growing interest and work on behalf of national standard time. Though making no great claims for the advantages of such a time, the circular must have made an impression, since in 1878 the Observatory cooperated with the Signal Service Bureau to place a time ball on the Equitable Life Assurance Company's headquarters. The time ball brought uniformity to Boston's public time.[63]

Now largely forgotten, time balls once played a significant part in the daily life of American cities. We live surrounded by accurate, synchronized time. Computers, office clocks, telephones, radios, televisions, all announce the time. Even the cheapest quartz watch keeps a more regular rate than the earth's rotation, and so we have no special need for assuring the accuracy of any particular timekeepers—there are more than enough to go around, and the framework for standard time is well established. But in the nineteenth century accurate time was a far more precarious quantity. Watches tended to vary, and even the best public clocks drifted away from each other. Time balls provided a free public display of time that checked the accuracy of city clocks and watches. Typically placed on a pole atop some tall tower or readily visible building, the large metal globes usually rose and fell once daily at noon, signaling the time. Ships at anchor regulated their chronometers from a ball visible in port. Watched from an office window, the noon ball called the hungry to lunch. Pedestrians throughout American cities paused a few minutes before twelve, faces turned to the tower, to check their watches. (The time ball survives today to inaugurate New Year's Day from Times Square.)

Harvard's time ball theoretically only standardized Boston time. But the Observatory's actions reflected both increasing interest in national time standards and newly emergent, competing commercial efforts to define public time. As the idea of selling standard time grew more common, competition among time-sellers increased.

In 1877, the Western Union Company had installed a time ball on the tower of its New York headquarters. The New York ball dropped once daily at *local* noon, on a signal received from the Naval Observatory in Washington. The system preserved the time of the New York City meridian, while establishing Western Union's time ball as the most accurate standard of New York time. The telegraph company's particularly cozy relationship with the Naval Observatory had started in 1865. This relationship, redolent of scientific accuracy and objectivity, strengthened perceptions of the telegraph company as a public-spirited, benevolent, and useful institution. Western Union gained the right to distribute free time signals to its offices in return for allowing the Observatory limited access to telegraph wires when official business demanded it.[64] By 1877 the telegraph giant was selling those same time signals— obtained free from the government—to private citizens. Circulars sent to the residents of cities of over 20,000 people began what later became a virtual monopoly on commercial signaling of time. The service placed "controlled clocks" in the "house, office or manufactory" of subscribers, charging between $75 and $375 per year for daily signals. Western Union's time ball bore public witness to the company's concern for accuracy, and had the happy effect of establishing Western Union as *the* standard of time in New York City. By heightening public awareness of time in gen-

The Western Union time "ball," placed atop the company's building at Broadway and Dey streets in 1877, and the mechanism used to hoist the ball to the top of the mast and then drop it automatically at noon on a signal from the Naval Observatory in Washington. (From Scientific American, 39, n.s. [Nov. 30, 1878], p. 335. National Museum of American History, Smithsonian Institution.)

eral, the company created an interest in its service and advertised itself as the solution in one stroke.[65]

The Naval Observatory helped promote the system as well. Naval astronomer E. S. Holden, in *Popular Science Monthly*, explained the new service and time ball in detail and praised Western Union's "public spirited" measure "for the benefit of the citizens and the shipping of New York City."[66] Samuel Langley, on the other hand, found the measure an outrage and a threat to the lucrative systems he and other astronomers had been building. The Naval Observatory, he complained to an ally at Harvard, "had not waited for a popular demand but had sent out canvassers so to speak to get business." True, Langley also advertised heavily. But he found the Naval Observatory's public spirit "more mercantile than scientific."[67]

Both time signal systems reiterate the growing public awareness of time and the emergence of time as a commodity, a good to be sold outright or "laid on like gas or water," as Langley put it.[68] Once time seemed nearly indistinguishable from nature and God. Now, thanks to controlling clocks and telegraph lines, the heavens themselves were laid open and mined for profit—time became secularized, a thing identifiable, quantifiable, packageable, and saleable. Formalized in electrical signals, observatory time promised to bring the rationality of science to whatever task lay at hand. Patrons bought the authority and prestige of scientific time through telegraph wires, and applied it where needed to regulate daily life.[69]

Standardized time grew from a regional innovation to a national reform in the 1870s, and "time" became not a matter of local imperatives and individual interpretation, but the subject of bureaucratic wrangling, commercial competition, and scientific backstabbing. The protracted and complex dispute between the Signal Service and the Naval Observatory offers perhaps the best example of the struggle to define public time.

The Army's Signal Service Bureau had long used the telegraph to link regional observatories. Cleveland Abbe, director of the Cincinnati Observatory and father of the Signal Bureau's national weather service, began taking advantage of this network to compile weather bulletins in 1869. Abbe received reports from other observatories and telegraph-equipped weather stations giving conditions at each place. Coordinating the reports through the Signal Service, he translated them into maps with the now familiar "isobars" depicting warm or cold fronts.[70] To Abbe's annoyance, each station, except those kept by astronomers, gave the time of its report by the local standard. Phrases like "railroad time," "local time," or "city time," in the absence of a single standard, offered only ambiguity and confusion. Having pursued standard public time for Cincinnati,[71] Abbe's work with the weather service lead him naturally to the idea of a national standard.

As chair of the American Metrological Society's Committee on Standard Time, in 1875 Abbe began working with other scientists, including Langley and Edward Pickering of Harvard, on a zone system of time based on Greenwich meridians. The Metrological Society, founded in 1873, was a federation of scientists, educators, and other professionals, including F. A. P. Barnard of Columbia, interested in the reform of time and other units of measure and value. It played a crucial role in the adoption of national standard time.[72]

The astronomers also began comparing the meridian times they telegraphed to the Signal Service in Washington. Inevitably, small errors plagued each observatory on occasion. To minimize this variation, they planned to establish a mean standard from the average error at each observatory, unified with the Greenwich time used by much of the international scientific community. Under this "clearinghouse plan," coordinated by the Signal Service, each observatory would be informed of its error from the mean. Local times could be calculated from the clearinghouse standard.[73]

For someone engaged in diverse national meteorological observations, like Abbe, such a time was far more useful if the general
public adopted it — otherwise local time standards still clouded the
temporal skies. Useful to scientists because calculated from Greenwich, the clearinghouse system's greater accuracy and *international*
applicability, according to advocates, made it ideally suited to
regulating public time as well. Hoping to make regional time standards a national issue, Abbe's committee began promoting the idea
to railroad officials and the federal government in the late 1870s.[74]

The Signal Service, as a first step, had cooperated with Harvard to establish the Boston time ball. It now planned, in 1881,
to place a second ball, on the Equitable Insurance Building in
New York. But this second time ball would be dropped by the
nearest Greenwich meridian, setting up two times for New York
City and calling the authority of the Western Union ball into
question. The Signal Service hoped, with the help of a $25,000
annual appropriation, to do the same in other cities and eventually
standardize American time according to the more accurate and
scientifically useful Greenwich signals. Those interested in ob-
taining the signals were directed to their friendly local observatory
and its telegraph time system.[75]

Western Union offered mean local time to its New York
customers. The company's time ball kept *New York* noon, calculated
from Washington Naval Observatory time. Their circular included
a table listing the difference between noon by the Naval Observatory signal and local noon at the meridian of prominent points
in cities the service was aimed at. The chart shows the informality
of American timekeeping practices — no definitive authority rings
the time in any of the cities listed. Instead, there are only prominent
public clocks or civic buildings which serve as symbols of the city
and its "local time." The service left the question of local time up
to the customer; he or she might keep the "controlled clock" on
local time or adopt the Washington standard. The Signal Bureau's

TABLE showing the mean time at various places in the United States when it is noon (12h. 0m. 0s.) at Washington, and the annual charges made by the Western Union Telegraph Company for transmitting the Washington Noon Signal to the main office of the Company in such places.

City.	State.	Point to which the Longitude is referred.	Mean time when it is noon at Washington.		Authority	For a Daily Signal.	For a Weekly Signal.
			H.	S.			
Atlanta.........	Ga.	City Hall or Court House.........................	11 30	38 61	C. S.	$225	$37 50
Albany.........	N. Y.	Dudley Observatory, Dome....................	12 13	12.34	C. S.	150	25 00
Allegheny City.	Pa.	Allegheny Observatory, Dome...............	11 48	9.16	C. S.	150	25 00
Bridgeport.....	Ct.	Spire, Middle Bridgeport (1834).............	12 15	26.42	C. S.	150	25 00
Bangor.........	Me.	C. S. Astro'l Station on Thomas Hill, near corner Union and James streets..................	12 33	4.17	C. S.	225	37 50
Baltimore......	Md.	Washington Monument.........................	12 1	44.13	C. S.	75	12 50
Boston.... ..	Mass.	State House.....................................	12 23	56.74	C. S.	150	25 00
Brooklyn........	N. Y.	City Hall......................................	12 12	14.28	C. S.	75	12 50
Buffalo...,.....	"	Van Duzee's Observatory......................	11 52	43.81	*	150	25 00
Chicago........	Ill.	City Hall or Court House......................	11 17	40.20	*	300	50 00
Covington......	Ky..	....			....	225	37 50
Cambridge.....	Mass.	Harvard College Observatory, centre of Dome........	12 23	41.11	C. S.	150	25 00
Charleston......	"	Bunker Hill Monument.........................	12 23	57.44	C. S.	150	25 00
Chelsea........	"	Neptune House Flagstaff.......................	12 24	17.03	C. S.	150	25 00
Camden.........	N. J.	Church Spire...................................	12 7	42.69	C. S.	75	12 50
Cincinnati......	O.	Mitchel's Old Observatory (1848)............	11 30	13.05	C. S.	150	25 00
Cleveland.......	"	Marine Hospital, Dome........................	11 41	26.39	C. S.	150	25 00
Columbus......	"	Dome of Capitol................................	11 36	13.13	C. S.	150	25 00
Charleston......	S. C.	St. Michael's Church............................	11 48	28.84	C. S.	150	25 00
Davenport......	Iowa.	Court House....................................	11 5	53.5	A. A.	300	50 00
Dubuque......	"	Centre of the City (1859)....................	11 5	32 4	A. A.	300	50 00
Detroit........	Mich	U. S. Lake Survey, New Observatory.	11 35	59.88	*	225	37 50
Dayton.........	O.	....	11 31	28.—	A. A.	225	37 50

Excerpt from a table describing Western Union's time service. Under "authority," "C.S." means "Coast Survey," "A.A." means "American Almanac." Note the exaggerated accuracy of the mean times, and the remarkably high cost of the signals. (From Proceedings of the American Metrological Society, II [Dec. 1878–Dec. 1879], p. 35.)

New York time ball, on the other hand, would have put Gotham on the nearest Greenwich meridian, approximately four minutes behind New York local time.

Word of the Signal Bureau plan filtered into the press. Abbe himself accused the Naval Observatory of sloppy timekeeping, an *astronomical* sin, in the New York papers, and his comments cast the reliability of the New York time ball into doubt. Angry denunciations of "meddling" by the Naval Observatory followed.[76] To head off the Signal Service program, the Observatory in 1882 sponsored a bill placing time balls, controlled by Washington, on customshouses in the major port cities at taxpayer expense.[77] The bill, Langley sadly assumed, "means the end of our local time services" and thus the Signal Service clearinghouse plan.[78] The bill failed, to Langley's relief. But the clearinghouse idea, never fully established, also collapsed in 1884, when "some evil-minded person" convinced the Secretary of the Navy to suspend Signal Service Bureau timekeeping operations.[79] The "evil-minded person" probably had something to do with Western Union. A falling out in 1874 had put the Signal Service and the telegraph company on bad terms — the Bureau maintaining its right to round the clock transmission of official dispatches, Western Union resisting the Bureau's claims as an attempt to nationalize the telegraph industry.[80] More importantly, if the Signal Bureau succeeded in establishing standard time based on its own measurements, Western Union lost its increasingly lucrative near monopoly on government-derived time signals.

Western Union's house organ, the *Journal of the Telegraph*, ran editorials in 1882 denouncing the idea of standard time for the general public. Although several years earlier the magazine had waxed enthusiastic about the company's New York time ball, now the *Journal* proclaimed standard time contrary to the laws of nature and a tyrannical imposition by "so-called men of science." It ignored local times, they charged, and instead imposed "English time" (Greenwich) on America.[81] With government unwilling to act, no resolution seemed likely. But the terms of the entire disagreement were altered a year later when the railroads intervened, as Chapter Three will show.

The inter-agency squabbling made little impression on the public before 1880. Most probably realized, as the city fathers of Pittsburgh had when considering Langley's hefty bills for time service, that "the consideration of *unity* comes even before that of *accuracy*, and it is not hard to see that if every clock and watch in the community were agreed in being wrong by exactly the same amount, little public inconvenience would result."[82] But the controversy allowed the scientists and businessmen involved to market the idea of standard time to the public.

Advocates of observatory time, again, stressed accuracy, mechanical precision and universal applicability in place of tradition, religious piety, and nature's local example. They found attention to time "strikingly indicative of the character of a people in the scale of civilization." "The increasing requirements of a complex civilization," one astronomer concluded, "demand more and more attention to the keeping of accurate standard time."[83] Astronomers linked standard observatory time to the linear progress of American industry, pointing out that only synchronized, accurate time could regulate business.

Time balls and observatory time signals, advanced as a public-spirited commercial boon, helped make their case. Commenting on Western Union's New York time ball, the *New York Tribune* freely admitted the advantages of standardized time, and praised the improvement in punctuality such innovations encouraged. But the paper cautioned that using Washington time for the entire nation, as Western Union proposed, "would require almost a revolution of ordinary ideas." To preserve local times the editors suggested equipping clocks with two sets of hands, one showing Washington time, the other local time.[84]

The Signal Service astronomers had heard suggestions like that before, and wanted no part of them or of local time. Leonard Waldo, director of the time service at Harvard and later at Yale, claimed in the *North American Review* that "the people have been dictated to by their jewelers regarding their standard of time." "A little reflection shows," he continued, that only a very questionable advantage arose from maintaining a local time "simply because the jewelers of the city insist on a time which shall appeal to the local time of their customers."[85]

Waldo proposed instead having the people dictated to by scientists. "The furnishing of correct time," he intoned, "is educational in its nature, for it inculcates in the masses a certain precision in doing the daily work of life which conduces, perhaps, to a sounder morality."[86] In a report to the railroad commissioners of Connecticut, Waldo referred to the "many thousands of persons" engaged in factories. "Any service which will train these persons into habits of accuracy and punctuality," he claimed, "which will affect all employers and all employees with the same strict impartiality, so far as wages for time employed is concerned, will be a great benefit to the State." Waldo proposed standard time as arbiter and schoolmaster, as the regulating authority for disorganized workers.[87]

By 1880, Waldo had become the most prominent spokesman for national standard time and the Signal Service clearinghouse plan. But his pieties about improving the masses and benefiting the state barely concealed his own profit making. Shortly after leaving Harvard for Yale, Waldo founded a Horological Bureau at Yale's Winchester Observatory. The Bureau was to "encourage the higher development of the horological industries" and promote the idea of standard time by testing and rating watches. Circulars sent to railroads, watchmakers, and jewelers lauded the Bureau's special temperature-controlled vaults and scientific equipment, encouraging corporate clients to send their watches to Yale, with a fee, for examination.[88]

As director of the Horological Bureau, Waldo began lobbying both the local railroads and the railroad commissioners of the state of Connecticut. In March 1881 the state legislature, following Waldo's persuasive recommendations to the railroad commissioners, adopted the time of New York City, signaled from Yale's Observatory, as the legal standard of public time in Connecticut. Their action marked the first example of legislation on public time at the state level, and in intent legally abolished local time.[89]

A year later Waldo formed the Standard Time Company, a joint stock enterprise organized, like Western Union's time service, to provide accurate telegraphed time signals to home and office.

The Standard Time Company enjoyed an exclusive contract with Yale Observatory, sharing its staff and facilities, and offered to spread the bounty of science to all those willing to pay.[90] The phrase "time is money," for Waldo, was now thrice true. He made money as director of the Observatory time service, as manager of the Horological Bureau, and as secretary of the Standard Time Company. The contract with Connecticut made standard observatory time law, increased public attention to accurate time, and brought Waldo business.

Even more than Langley, Waldo made a commodity of time, harvesting, packaging, and selling it to the state and its citizens. Like most advocates of standard time, Waldo based his appeal largely on the ideal of commercial circulation—observatory time facilitated the free movement of goods, services, and information necessary to a modern economy. Connecticut, Waldo reminded businessmen, was essentially a manufacturing center, with "many thousands of persons engaged in her factories upon whose precision and economy of time the success of the State in her struggle for trade must ultimately depend." Observatory time signals, thanks to the prestige attached to their great accuracy, reformed the timekeeping habits of these "persons."

Harvard and Yale's time services, Waldo boasted to the railroad commissioners, "fostered a certain emulation among the employees as to the accuracy and timekeeping qualities of their watches." They acquire a "personal pride in being authorities on the subject of correct time."[91] That is, they internalized the new time and made it part of themselves. Even better, the Connecticut legislature's adoption of New York City time synchronized the state's economy with both the commercial giant to the south, and "that broad expanse of territory between Buffalo and Rhode Island."[92] Within that broad expanse, people and goods supposedly "moved like clockwork," as Langley had put it, synchronized to and improved by the beats of Yale's Observatory clock.

Forty years of wrangling over the nature of time in an industrial society had moved American understanding away from nature and toward the machine. Time had been a quantity invented by God and expressed in nature. Factory schedules, like farmers' almanacs, merely expressed a particular division of an abstract, universal quantity—they described how people were to act within the daily passage of time, according to the demands of the task at hand. They affected not the *sense* of time as much as its *use.*

Observatory time, on the other hand, was something new; a utility, like gas or water, a tool for improving the "morality" of laborers, facilitating the movements of trade, and synchronizing the economies of different regions. It reconstituted the authorities that governed daily life. Technology's "annihilation of space," in the era's ubiquitous phrase, put men and women in distant places in new relations with each other, demanding new understandings of time sensible to commercial operations.[93] Waldo believed, like Langley, that "the railroads ought to be the most useful means in securing uniformity." As the most visible and powerful symbol of both the circulation of goods and money and the necessity for accuracy, railroads were "the great educators and monitors of the people in teaching and keeping exact time."[94]

The railroad's power ultimately did Waldo no good. After 1883, when the railroads adopted a uniform time of their own, Connecticut canceled its contract with the Observatory.[95] The Horological Bureau and the Standard Time Company both folded after the railroads endorsed Naval Observatory time and Western Union's time service.[96] Waldo himself resigned from Yale under a cloud after an inquiry into his fiscal relations with the Observatory.[97] But the railroads largely succeeded where scientists like Waldo failed, establishing the zone system we use today across most of the continent. Railroad time reorganized public time to suit the needs of commerce. In the process it exposed both a deep-seated ambivalence about this new public time and a wide range of objections to its implications.

III

The Day of Two Noons

American astronomers, drawing on technological innovations like the telegraph, had created a new understanding of time by 1880. The observatories made time a product. They captured an apparently natural phenomenon, distilled what they understood to be its essence — order — and then offered this essence for sale in tidy, attractive packages. Observatories profited financially by selling time, but even more, each hoped to see standard astronomical observatory time replace the confused and by now obsolete system of local times inherited from the past.

But no scientist or scientific society commanded enough leverage to force the idea of standard time on a largely unimpressed public. Time, after all, remained a fairly hazy idea for most people, fraught with vaguely unsettling religious implications and perhaps better left alone. In America in 1880, relatively few people traveled often enough to suffer from the lack of a standard time. Certainly large corporations, especially those doing business by telegraph, felt the lack of a standard time keenly. But for most people, es-

pecially outside of cities, "time" and "place" seemed nearly synonymous. In "Up the Cooly," one of Hamlin Garland's short
stories on rural life in the Midwest, the protagonist's farmer
brother describes how an oppressive mortgage "ate us up in just
four years by the almanac." The years passed in poor harvests
and almanac pages, not in calendars or clocks. The protagonist's
mother, asking about her actor son's life in New York, simply
cannot understand "how one could live in New Jersey and do
business daily in New York."[1] Away from the world of telegraphs
and railroad trains, there was just no reason to care. Only the
railroads, the ultimate symbol of commercial expansion, progress,
and the conquest of space, had the motive and the power to reform
public timekeeping.

In 1883 an association of railroad managers adopted a system
of standard time zones basically the same as that we use today.
Without benefit of federal law or public demand they managed to
rearrange the nation's system of public timekeeping at a stroke,
an administrative and public relations coup of impressive propor-
tions. Following the progress of the railroad's innovation reveals
some of the implications of the new time. The times before and
after November 18, 1883, "the day of two noons," point not to
uniformity, but to lingering divisions over time and its meaning.
But the measure's practicality in day-to-day railroad operations
lent railroad officials an unquestioning belief in its value for ordinary citizens, while the vast economic and political power of the
railroad industry assured them of the measure's success.

American railroads traditionally confronted time mostly as a
problem of scheduling. Summer's burden of extra passenger
traffic, for example, demanded more trains and revised timetables
each vacation season. As the railroad network grew, adjoining
roads saw a need to coordinate passenger connections and through
traffic. By 1872, a large group of railway superintendents had
formed a permanent Time-Table Convention, subsequently known

as the General and Southern Railway Time Conventions, the American Railway Association, and finally the modern Association of American Railroads. Besides issues of scheduling and running times, the Convention addressed uniform signal systems, coupling devices, and protocols in handling through freight.[2]

Thanks to such cooperation the railroads had evolved a haphazard but practical system of regional times. Most kept a single time across an entire line, usually the time of the largest city they served. Time changes occurred either at breaks between divisions of a large company, or where two different company's lines met. For example, in 1874 the Pennsylvania Railroad bought its time signals from Samuel Langley's Allegheny Observatory. In the East the line used Philadelphia time, but west of Pittsburgh, the breaking point between the eastern and western divisions of the company, trains ran on Columbus, Ohio, time. Smaller lines usually followed the larger, and one line's rescheduling meant headaches for another.

According to its first secretary, William F. Allen, the General Time Convention's semi-annual meetings were intended to "promote harmony by permitting an interchange of views between the superintendents and managers of the various interests." As the only professional organization of railway managers, the group would allow a "more intimate acquaintanceship" between the superintendents of feuding roads, and help smooth over disagreements. But fierce competition between lines, augmented by the Panic of '73 and subsequent railroad rate wars, soured the harmony and kept the meetings rather sporadic. As late as 1882 Allen had to write its president asking if the Convention still existed.[3]

Allen, born in 1846, was a lifelong employee of the railroads who began his career as a surveyor and engineer on the Camden and Amboy line. Rising to the post of resident engineer, Allen helped lay out the company's new track, gaining in the process a thorough familiarity with the day-to-day business of planning and

William F. Allen, "inventor" of standard time. (National Museum of American History, Smithsonian Institution.)

running a road. Allen envisioned railway management, as he put it later in his life, as "a great and wonderful piece of mechanism, strong yet flexible, capable of rapid and powerful exertion, but exceedingly sensitive." In 1872 he joined the staff of the *Official Guide of the Railways and Steam Navigation Lines in the United States and Canada*, becoming the publication's editor a year later.[4]

As its ponderous title implies, the *Guide* (later retitled and hereafter referred to as the *Traveler's Official Guide*), was largely a collection of transportation timetables and schedules. Before standard time, travelers used guides like Allen's to help puzzle out the profusion of times then in use. Allen's *Traveler's Official Guide*, which also listed railway personnel and their offices, served as the "officially recognized standard of reference in the transaction of business between railroad companies," and under Allen eventually replaced the numerous "unofficial" guides it competed against. Allen's work with the *Traveler's Official Guide* — the official catalogue of railway timetables — led naturally to his appointment as secretary of the newly reorganized General Time Convention/Southern Railway Time Convention in 1875.[5]

The Conventions had been hearing about standard time from a number of sources, described in Chapter Two. Besides Langley's contract with the Pennsylvania and his promotional campaigning, Charles Dowd had persisted in bending the railroad ear with his "plus and minus indexes." Dowd got favorable reports from the Convention after addressing it in 1873, and even saw one of his proposals reprinted in the *Traveler's Official Guide* before Allen joined it. But though most railroad men readily admitted the utility of standard time as an idea, few believed it practical. "Circulars on the subject," Allen claimed, "found their way promptly into the pigeon hole or the wastebasket." Competition remained a more interesting diversion, especially since local times seemed firmly fixed by tradition and custom. As one railroad engineer put it, local time was "clearly beyond the power of the greatest power in the land [the railroads] to alter."[6]

But while the railroads sidestepped the subject of multiple times, American scientists and engineers began tunneling into it. Between 1872 and 1882 a number of scientific and professional societies and concerned individuals wrestled with the problem of uniform public time. Often sharing membership and information, most had generally settled on some system of time zones by 1880, following the lead of Cleveland Abbe and the American Metrological Society.[7] But each proposal left the boundaries of the zones largely unsettled, and resisted tampering with the local sun. While nearly all wanted to do away with local time, no individual or group could imagine changing the traditions of centuries.

The director of the Naval Observatory, for example, strongly opposed any tampering with the local sun's authority. He suggested that while Washington, D.C., time could be adopted nationwide for railroads and shipping, custom would demand putting two sets of hands on watches, to tell local and railroad time apart in ordinary life. The American Society of Civil Engineers, led by the Canadian engineer Sandford Fleming, had published a lengthy proposal for world standard time in 1882. The report favored adopting twenty-four world time zones while suggesting some changes in the nomenclature of the hours.[8] Most of the Society's members liked the idea of standard time but feared the change from local custom.

As Brigadier General Montgomery Meigs put it, "if you derange the habits of a people too much they will have none of it." "We travel greatly," Meigs admitted, "but more millions stay at home than go abroad. The housewife keeps the time for the hours of meals and retiring," the general felt; "we men and boys only follow."[9] Meigs associated local time with the home, that familiar, ostensibly tradition-bound bulwark of social order and virtue. In his view, time was a part of the web of inherited customs women spun to give men a sense of place, an anchorage in the rough seas of commercial life.

Echoing Meigs in part, the United States Senate concluded that "it would appear to be as difficult to alter by edict the ideas and habits of the people in regard to local time as it would be to introduce among them novel systems of weights, measures, volumes and money."[10] Meigs linked time with tradition and the cyclical measures of life at home. The Senate report, on the other hand, associated time with mediums of commercial circulation — units of measure and value which, properly reformed, facilitated commerce and industrial expansion while breaking down traditions of particularity and isolation.

Astronomers Samuel Langley and Leonard Waldo had used similar arguments to attack local time. Both viewed local time as an impediment to progress and a hindrance to commercial circulation. By 1880 they had joined, with Edward Pickering of Harvard, the American Association for the Advancement of Science's Committee on Standard Time. The AAAS Committee, like most scientific groups, rejected the idea of one single time for the United States. Such a time "rudely disturbed" the "historical and deeply seated prejudices" regarding local time. Instead, the Committee recommended four time zones, each based on the meridian of a large commercial city. The eastern zone would use New York time, the central, St. Louis time, and so on. The AAAS feared that times based on Greenwich meridians, which as scientists they preferred, would make no sense to the average citizen. Basing time on the nearest large city would unify commercial regions while following the tendencies business exchange and commercial circulation established on its own.[11]

A fourth group, the rather self-importantly named Association for the Reform and Codification of the Laws of Nations, pointed out that "one of the earliest needs of an intelligent being . . . is a means of measuring the lapse of time." Chaired, like the American Metrological Society, by President Barnard of Columbia, the Association claimed that the need for accurate time grew more urgent as civilization advanced. Mechanical clocks marked a high state of civilization, but "social duties and pleasures imply the concurrence of numbers," and an advanced society demanded "a common standard, to which every individual timepiece shall be made to conform."[12]

But ensuring that conformity seemed unlikely. Cleveland Abbe, dubbed "Mr. Isobars" for his work with the weather service, had enrolled William F. Allen in the American Metrological Society in 1879, hoping the railroads could make common cause with astronomers in reforming public timekeeping habits. "Abolish local times," Abbe wrote to Allen enthusiastically, "is the watchword." Allen published, early in 1881, the American Metrological Society's proposals for time reform, and saw to it that the General Time Convention of October 1881 heard reports from Abbe, Barnard, General William B. Hazen of the Signal Service, and the

AAAS. But the reports were largely ignored, and simply referred to Allen for further study.[13]

Even with Allen's help the railroads seemed unlikely to bestir themselves on behalf of uniformity. Most roads had worked out a practical system of regional standards, and as long as profits continued, further cooperation among lines remained unlikely. No one thought the system perfect, but it worked well enough in practice. The last decade had seen a natural decrease in the number of times used, as lines combined or consolidated their positions— from seventy-odd in 1872 to fifty-three in 1882. It seemed reasonable to assume the process would continue, albeit slowly. Complicating matters further, another rate war broke out in 1881 and suspended the Convention. "You represent," Abbe told Allen, both "the desirability" of standard time and "the hopelessness of the situation."[14]

But the situation was not quite as hopeless as Abbe imagined. Western Union's time service attracted publicity, as did Langley's articles. Constant lobbying by astronomers paid off. Thanks to Leonard Waldo's exertions, for example, Connecticut had adopted a uniform legal standard of time in 1882. The measure included no provisions for enforcement, and several railroads ignored it altogether, but it set a precedent for government action on the subject. Almost simultaneously, the Naval Observatory advanced its previously described bill establishing time balls at customs houses and in port cities. The bill and the ensuing public debate, along with Connecticut's legislation, brought standard time into the daily papers.[15]

Growing worldwide interest in uniform time offered another source of encouragement. Other industrializing nations were experiencing the same time problems America did—confusion about timetables, imprecision in the expiration of contracts, lack of synchronization in international scientific work. Increased telegraphic traffic, both national and international, only made the problem worse. In France, "Paris time" competed with railway clocks, which kept "l'heure de la gare," five minutes behind Paris, and local city clocks showing "l'heure de la ville," whatever that might be. German railroads kept to one of five different regional times, while rail travelers kept track of local time by adjusting their watches according to posts set in the ground next to the tracks. Each post alerted the punctual to a ten-minute change in local time. Count Von Moltke of Prussia pointed out that "we have in Germany five different units of time . . . which, since we have become an empire, it is proper should be done away with." Von Moltke warned the German Parliament that confusion over time could greatly impede coordinated military operations.[16]

As in America, most of the impetus for international standardized time came at first from the scientific community. The First International Geophysical Congress, held in Antwerp in 1871, had passed a resolution urging the adoption of Greenwich meridian as the common zero for determining longitude, and the second IGC four years later renewed the resolution.[17] But scientific well-wishing hardly seemed enough to overcome ancient (and modern) political disputes between nations.

Sandford Fleming, chief civil engineer of the Canadian Pacific Railway, had begun pondering the issue of standard time after missing a train connection on a visit to Ireland. Fleming started corresponding with British and American scientific societies in 1876, advancing his plan to divide the world into twenty-four one-hour time zones. But only two years later he was denied a chance to address the British Association for the Advancement of Science on the grounds that his ideas were "too utopian." Many scientists hesitated to shape public policy. George Airy, England's Astronomer Royal, did concede that the question of standard time should be "extensively ventilated by the memorialists." Still, he doubted that the scientific community could dictate public practice.[18]

Fleming began exchanging ideas with Cleveland Abbe in the

spring of 1880, and together their efforts increased discussion of the subject among scientists, mapmakers, and mathematicians. Most recognized the utility of a standard time system, but many wondered why Greenwich should serve as its basis. The Third International Geophysical Congress, meeting in Venice in 1881, heard several new suggestions. Why not use the Great Pyramid of Egypt to mark the prime meridian, asked Scotland's Astronomer Royal? It occupied a central place in Western antiquity, and its shape certainly helped one visualize the idea of an invisible meridian line passing overhead. An Italian astronomer advanced Jerusalem as a likely choice, one with good symbolic potential, while a Swiss astronomer suggested the Bering Strait.

Not all members of the scientific community favored international cooperation. Simon Newcomb, superintendent of the American *Nautical Almanac*, endorsed a standardized time for America. But he met the idea of worldwide standards with hostility. Americans, he declared, "don't care for other nations; we can't help them, they can't help us." Newcomb saw "no more need for considering Europe in the matter than for considering the inhabitants of Mars." But American progress toward standard time, led by Cleveland Abbe, must have encouraged the international scientific community, for in October 1883 the Seventh International Geophysical Congress managed to firmly and decisively recommend the adoption of Greenwich as prime meridian and standard of international time.[19]

Encouraged by international scientific debate, the American Metrological Society had combined with the American Geographical Society a year earlier, to petition Congress with "the names of several thousand signers." The petitioners asked Congress to authorize President Arthur to call an international conference establishing a common longitude and time. The measure was adopted that August, and preliminary inquiries regarding an International Meridian Conference went out in October 1882. The conference would bring together not scientists but diplomats, and take the first steps toward making standard time international law.[20]

The International Meridian Conference would finally meet in October 1884. In what is now Washington's Old Executive Office Building, forty-one delegates from twenty-five countries assembled to hear arguments in favor of standard time and a prime meridian. Greenwich formed the crux of discussion—why should England's Observatory precede all others? Negotiations broke down briefly when the French delegation refused to accept Greenwich over Paris. After some days, the French offered a compromise: they would accept the distasteful Greenwich when the United States and England adopted the metric system, pride of France. But lobbying by delegates from the United States, Canada, and Great Britain, especially Sandford Fleming, carried the day. The International Meridian Conference formally endorsed Greenwich on October 13, with 22 ayes, 1 nay (San Domingo), France and Brazil abstaining in protest.

The conference could only offer its recommendations, not make law, and most countries acted slowly if at all. Germany took up Von Moltke's advice and adopted Greenwich in 1893. France simply chose Paris time as its national standard, and refused to accept Greenwich time until 1911. Even then the proud French fell back on the transparent ruse of defining their standard as "Paris Mean Time, retarded by nine minutes twenty-one seconds"—Greenwich time in all but name. As late as 1905 Portugal, Holland, Greece, Turkey, Russia, Ireland, and most of South America still shunned Greenwich.

Continued uncertainty about time intensified the diplomatic crisis that began World War I. The volume and pace of telegraphic communication outraced diplomats' ability to keep up, and confusion about the precise hour messages were sent only made things worse. But once fighting began, coordinated standard timetables and synchronized watches kept the whole machinery of violence running as smoothly as possible. The war probably did more than any action of scientist or politician to fix world standard time by law, although Holland rejected it until 1940, and the Ayatollah Khomeini deplored its presence in Islam in the 1980s.[21]

Even though in 1882 the International Meridian Conference was little more than a warm invitation from President Arthur, for the American railroads the movement toward world standard time meant trouble. Common practice, as has been described, fixed railroad time changes at the meeting of individual roads or at the eastern and western division of a single company. The resulting jagged, uneven borders made little sense from a scientific point of view, but for the railroads they had the virtue of practicality. Federally established time zones, on the other hand, might divide at inconvenient places, forcing railroad lines to overturn schedules, running regulations, and established custom generally. At least two railroads in Connecticut, for example, found that state's law obnoxious enough to partly ignore, and simply continued to run on Boston time.[22] Early in 1881 Allen published an open letter to his peers in the *Traveler's Official Guide*, requesting suggestions on standardizing time. He received a number of replies, some of which he published a year later, in April 1882, for the benefit of interested railway men.[23] The replies, combined with the legislations cited above, brought Allen to "certain conclusions" which he stated "in informal conversation" at the fall meeting of the General Time Convention in 1882.

Allen's unspecified "conclusions" awakened "a decided interest" at the Convention, where government regulation of the railroads had always given off a bad odor. The delegates asked him to formulate a standard time proposal of his own, and present it at their next meeting.[24] Allen began studying the problem from his position with the *Traveler's Official Guide*. He recognized the utility of using four American time zones, the system most scientists had favored. A zone system deviated the least from local time and its customary association with the position of the sun. What nagged at Allen was the problem of boundaries between zones.

Most time reformers had drawn the boundaries with scientific precision. Cleveland Abbe's American Metrological Society plan, the one most familiar to Allen, suggested four zones exactly fifteen degrees of longitude—one hour—apart. It ignored both state boundaries and the regional time divisions already established in daily railroad practice. Such a plan made scientific sense, but what was science to a trundling freight car? Allen saw no problems with using Greenwich meridians as the zone standards. Practicality ruled the minds of railroaders, and they felt no sentimental or patriotic attachment to the time of one particular city or country. What they wanted most was a plan that altered existing division breaks, and the accustomed day-to-day operations of the roads, as little as possible.

Drawing largely on the existing divisions between lines, Allen proposed a four-zone scheme fitted entirely to the needs of the railways, and presented it privately to a number of managers of the largest roads.[25] With their support arranged in advance, Allen unveiled his plan at the General and Southern Railway Time Conventions in April 1883. He showed delegates a railroad map of the United States with each of the more than fifty standards of time drawn in a different color. The map vividly depicted what Allen called "Hard Scrabble Time," the seemingly chaotic profusion of local standards.

He then revealed a second map displaying the four zones he proposed, the railroads within each zone all drawn in one color. On the second map zone *standards* corresponded to Greenwich meridians, but zone *boundaries* corresponded to existing breaks— part of the eastern and central zones, for example, met at Pittsburgh, where the Pennsylvania road's two divisions already joined and had switched from Philadelphia to Columbus time since 1874.

Under Allen's plan, few railroads would have to change their schedules or their running times. Most would change only clocks and watches, since the breaks between lines remained largely the same.[26]

"Contrasting the two maps," Allen asked the Convention,

OUTLINE MAP

WITH DIALS SHOWING

Standard Railway Time

PROPOSED BY W. F. ALLEN,

(Secretary Railway Conventions and Editor Travelers'
Official Guide.)

ENDORSED BY GENERAL AND SOUTHERN TIME CONVENTIONS,
APRIL 11 AND 18, 1883,

ADOPTED BY THE CONVENTIONS OF
OCTOBER 11 AND 17, 1883.

AND ORDERED TO TAKE EFFECT ON
NOVEMBER 18, 1883.

DARD TIME	75TH. MERIDIAN
,,	90TH. ,,
,,	105TH. ,,
,,	120TH. ,,

COPYRIGHTED 1883 BY W. F. ALLEN.

William Allen's map of proposed standard time zones in 1883. The map shows how the zones broke at points convenient to the railroad. (National Museum of American History, Smithsonian Institution.)

"which appears more desirable?" The first map, "as variegated as Joseph's coat of many colors," or the second, "with its solid masses of uniform tints?" Joseph's story, of course, told of interfamily jealousy and murder. The old map represented, in Allen's language, "the barbarism of the past" and the pitfalls of divisive competition. The new map represented "the enlightenment which we hope for in the future." Allen's plan received nearly unanimous approval. It deviated as little as possible from established practice, kept most time changes to half an hour or less, and minimized the adjustments railroads had to make while unifying their running times.

Even more importantly, in presenting his plan Allen insisted that local times, once the railroads had made up their minds, were simply irrelevant—in fact, railroad time would practically abolish

A clearer view of the zone borders as established by the railroads in 1883. (From *Scientific American*, 17–18 [March 15, 1884], p. 6834. National Museum of American History, Smithsonian Institution.)

them. "What is local time?" Allen asked. "Merely a mean arrived at by calculation and adopted for convenience. For all ordinary business transactions one standard is as good as another so long as all agree to use it." Allen claimed that "railroad trains are the great educators and monitors of the people in teaching and maintaining exact time." The people would take their time from the railroads, no matter what other authorities might deign to intervene, no matter what local traditions prevailed.

"With the standards that cities or governments may adopt,"

Allen continued, "we should have nothing to do." He recalled Connecticut's standard time law and its inconvenience; similar actions, he warned, "may be naturally expected if we do not act for ourselves." Allen voiced all the arrogance of Gilded Age industry when he told the Convention, "we should settle this question ourselves, and not entrust it to the infinite wisdom of the several State legislatures." State legislatures might have their own priorities, scientists their pretty theories. But, Allen insisted, "If we agree that the system here proposed is the one best adapted for practical use on our railway lines, whether it be the best for scientific purposes or not, whether it conforms to the whims of 'the ruling classes' who run our legislatures or not, it is clearly a duty we owe to the great interests intrusted to our charge."[27]

With the Convention's blessing, Allen began sending circulars to the managers of every road, describing the plan and asking whether or not they would accept it. The circulars came back favorably in all but a few cases. Final approval of the plan and the announcement of the date for changing times were scheduled for the Convention's October meeting.[28]

Beneath the brag, Allen and the railroads were worried about state or federal legislation—the "whims," as he put it, of the "ruling classes who run our legislatures." Allen confided to the president of the Michigan Central that he "fear[ed] that nothing short of Congressional action is likely to bring about any uniformity" of time, and that "Congressional action on this subject is to be deprecated." "There is little likelihood of any law being adopted in Washington," Allen continued, "that would be as universally acceptable to the Railway Companies as this movement has proved to be."[29] Government regulation of railroads, with its ominous possibilities for reduced profits, was always a problem. Charged with implementing the change to national standard time, Allen enlisted the most impressive authorities he could find, short of the federal government, on the railroads' behalf.

By basing his zones on the 75th, 90th, 105th, and 120th Greenwich meridians, Allen had already ensured the theoretical endorsement of those scientists pursuing world standard time. Shortly after gaining the Convention's approval Allen wrote to the Connecticut Railroad Commissioners, who had only a year before formulated a legal standard of their own. That state's adoption of New York City time, he declared, was a stumbling block in the way of the new plan—"would it not be possible to have a joint resolution passed . . . endorsing the seventy-fifth meridian line (four minutes slower than New York City time)?" The pliant Commissioners returned their hearty personal approval of the new standard, and the change in law, to the state legislature.[30]

In Boston, however, the 75th meridian differed from local time by sixteen minutes, a fairly substantial change. A number of New England lines agreed to adopt the new time only if the Cambridge Observatory time ball fell by the same standard. Allen replied assuring them that even if the Observatory refused, which was unlikely, the public followed the railroads, not the observatories.[31] But he wanted to make certain. The sort of standard public time Allen campaigned for depended heavily on the imprimatur of scientific authority. Samuel Langley, after all, had sold his time signals on the basis of their irrefutable accuracy, and the Harvard Observatory's endorsement would dispel any taint of intellectual expediency.

Allen wrote to Pickering of Harvard detailing the plan and asking his cooperation. To his alarm, he found Pickering out of the country and an assistant, J. Raynor Edmands, in charge. Edmands expected that Pickering would approve the change, but lacked the authority to approve it himself. Having crawled out on a limb with the railroad managers in private, Allen now needed to avoid a "potentially embarrassing" public failure by selling the eastern standard to the citizens and officials of Boston. If Boston rejected the new time, the whole plan collapsed. Fortunately for

Allen, assistant Edmands burned with enthusiasm for the new time. Loaded down with Allen's maps and the Observatory's prestige, Edmands traveled New England over the next few weeks, addressing the boards of aldermen in Boston and other cities generally. Cleveland Abbe pitched in by writing to President Eliot of Harvard, to assuage Eliot's doubts and present his weighty endorsement to Boston's citizens.[32]

Between Allen's assurances and the scientists' apparent enthusiasms, most New England lines agreed to go ahead and adopt the new standards early, on October 7, 1883, the date of a previously arranged fall schedule change. As it happened, Pickering returned to the country via New York that same day. Edmands met him on the docks, secured his approval, and immediately sent the good news to Allen. Sanctioned by the Observatory, the New England test case proved a limited but encouraging success. Edmands, now joined by Pickering, continued lobbying for public acceptance of the new system. No opposition here, he cabled Allen on a trip to Portland, Maine; "only a lot of cautious men who needed to have doubts satisfied."[33]

But more than a few New Englanders needed their doubts satisfied as word of the railroads' plans spread. "Let us keep our own noon," the prestigious *Boston Evening Transcript* demanded. Referring to Allen's zone boundaries, the editors called the railroads' plan unscientific, since "beginning with a scientific fact, a departure for the convenience of the railroads is made wherever it is deemed wise." Allen's assertion that the railroads controlled public time, moreover, constituted "an impertinence, which is quite of a piece with the familiar claim set up for the railroads that they are the creators of civilization." But in this matter, the railroads *were* the creators of civilization, a new kind of civilization based on standard timekeeping. A letter from "Local Time" urged the *Transcript*'s editors to "expose yet more thoroughly the needlessness and evil of the scheme, and give voice to the general opposition." "Is there no way," "Local Time" plaintively asked, "to prevent the hasty adoption of the scheme by the Fire Commissioners?"[34]

In many cities firehouses supplemented the time ball system, tripping bells or sirens at noon to signal the hour. Boston's firemen had received their time signals from the Cambridge Observatory for many years, and the fire commissioners, after meeting with Pickering and Edmands, had recently come out in favor of the change. As "Local Time" wrote, the Common Council's Committee on Standard Time had added its assent. Rejecting the new railroad standards, the Committee argued, would isolate Boston from the economic life of the rest of the country. Most of Boston's newspapers liked the idea of standard time. The measure awaited only the Council's approval to become law.[35]

But the new standards, the *Boston Daily Advertiser* retorted, "will cause confusion of the worst sort." And "all the confusion and hazard of the change is to be risked, for what?" the paper asked. "Merely to accommodate a handful of people who go between places where there is ten or fifteen minutes difference in local time."[36] The paper had a point—relatively few people traveled that far very often. Little or no popular demand for standard time existed; the change served the railroads above all. Why should Boston have to accommodate the railroads, instead of the reverse? Let them print schedules with local and railroad time, both newspapers declared.

The *Evening Transcript*, and especially the *Advertiser*, spoke for the Boston Brahmin, for the old money that predated Gilded Age industry and industrial time. Standard time struck the editors as yet another modern vulgarity, yet another mark of the relentless industrial stamping mill that crushed out regional distinction and exclusivity. Draped in the raiment of science, the measure in fact represented a cynical disregard for astronomical realities. Boston's time was Boston's particularly, rooted in the history and culture that made Boston different from its southern cousins. Why surrender time to corporate interests? It was in this sense that Reverend William B. White, pastor of the prominent Berkeley Street Congregational Church, rose up and denounced standard time as an immoral fraud, a lie and a "piece of monopolistic work adverse to the workingman's interest."[37]

The fire commissioners, on the other hand, represented new Boston—a rising generation of immigrants, businessmen, and capitalists with few ties to Boston's past and little stake in maintaining its separation. Fire Commissioner Fitzgerald and Alderman O'Brien readily embraced the new time's undeniable practicality and commercial expediency, its tendency to synchronize the economies and markets of eastern cities. The *Daily Advertiser* tried rather feebly to fight fire with fire, claiming that standard time would increase expenditures on gas and electric light.[38] But their opposition cast no new light on the measure's obvious advantages, and seemed out of step with the general tendencies of the city and the age.

"The city, the railroads and the Cambridge Observatory," Edmands cabled Allen, "only await the affirmative action of the Convention before fixing the date for changing all public time in Boston." Read at the fall meeting of the General Time Convention, Edmands's telegram brought a hearty outburst of spontaneous applause from the normally staid managers. On that same day Allen heard word from Leonard Waldo of Yale that his Observatory would also agree to telegraph the new standards to its customers in Connecticut.

Shortly before the Convention Allen had written to the Naval Observatory as well, hoping to gain its cooperation.[39] The Naval Observatory functioned as the quasi-official source of local time in New York, thanks to Western Union's time ball and time service. John Rodgers, Superintendent in 1882, had publicly expressed his objection to abolishing local times on several occasions and in no uncertain terms. Fortunately for Allen, Rodgers was no longer in charge by the fall of 1883. While the new director, Admiral R. W. Schufeldt, pointed out that "we think a single standard would be better, from a scientific point of view," he assured Allen of the Observatory's hearty cooperation. Schufeldt even detailed a junior officer to the Convention to explain how the Observatory's system worked.

This left several ticklish points. The Naval Observatory, a government institution, had agreed to telegraph the new railroad time without legal sanction. No law prevented it from doing this, but then no federal law of any kind had ever been passed regarding standard time. Lieutenant Moore of the Observatory reminded the delegates of the recent bill to provide time balls on customs-houses at Naval Observatory signal. He assured them, incorrectly as it turned out, that the bill was likely to pass in the next session. If it passed, whatever time the Naval Observatory signaled became the national standard.

Whether it passed or not, the railroads planned to present the government with a fait accompli. Once railroads had adopted the new time, they assumed, the railroad's importance to commerce would combine with the measure's universal superiority and practicality to make the new standards indispensable to the public. With the most obvious obstacles to public support now removed, the Convention set the day and hour for the change: twelve o'clock noon on Sunday, November 18, 1883.[40]

As the day drew near Allen began worrying about the Naval Observatory's partner, Western Union. The telegraph company had initiated a time service, described in Chapter Two, based on Naval Observatory signals, and had dropped a time ball daily at New York local noon since 1877. The company sold *local* time. "You are probably aware," Allen wrote the president of the New York Central, "that the Western Union time ball is connected by wire with the workshops of all the principal watchmakers of this city." If Western Union changed its time, Allen admitted, the watchmakers, and thus the watches, of the entire city would follow.[41]

Allen informed General Eckert of Western Union that "your assurance in this matter will materially aid in securing the adoption of the plan." Contemplating a standoff between two of the most powerful industries in the country, Allen cautioned Eckert, "I think that you will find it both practical and desirable to acquiesce in the suggestion."[42] But in private meetings with Eckert and his assistant, General Superintendent Bates, Allen obtained only luke-warm assurance of cooperation from both.

To kindle their enthusiasm, he wrote to Charles Pugh of the Pennsylvania Railroad. "I will arrange to have some little pressure brought to bear upon Messrs. Eckert and Bates," Pugh returned. "Rest assured that all enterprises of this character will promptly adopt the standard after it has been thoroughly established by the railroad companies." Encouraged by Pugh's intervention, telegrapher Bates's regard for standard time soon warmed enough to invite Allen and his family into the company's operating room on November 18, where they could watch the ball drop at the new time.[43]

With help from James Hamblet, supervisor of Western Union's time service, Allen converted Mayor Edson of New York to the new standards on October 19. Allen and Hamblet wrote to several other city departments, but as in Boston the final success of the plan rested on the work of astronomers. J. K. Rees of Columbia, another member of the American Metrological Society, approached the board of aldermen, who resolved to change New York's time with the railroads on November 18. A number of interviews and addresses by Rees and F. A. P. Barnard helped persuade the public, while New York newspapers added their nearly unanimous approval. Allen had managed to remove the most important formal obstacles to the new plan.[44]

Sunday, November 18, the "day of two noons," came and went with hardly a hitch. Each railroad line issued detailed orders on making the change, many of which Allen preserved. The Baltimore and Ohio Railroad, for example, ran its trains on Columbus time, twenty-eight minutes faster than the new central zone standard. At precisely 12:28 p.m., "all Conductors, Engineers and others concerned," orders read, "must be on hand at a telegraph station" to receive the new standard and set their watches back twenty-eight minutes. Those not near a telegraph station simply followed train conductors as they set their watches back. Trainmen on the road set their watches back, then proceeded cautiously to the first station to verify the time.[45]

In most cities people gathered at jewelry stores and near public clocks, waiting expectantly to see what happened. After all, the *New York World* pointed out, "the number of people who understand what this innovation is" was fairly small.[46] Crowds of several hundred began forming in front of New York's Western Union building as early as 11:30 a.m., to await the time ball's drop. In Boston a similar crowd of about two hundred waited with "a sort of scared look on their upturned faces."[47] Several papers claimed that immigrants especially had trouble understanding what went on. The *New York Times* described two stock Irishmen, supposedly watching in puzzlement as the clock stopped, waited, then started again. "Begorra," remarked one in newspaper Irish, "Divil a change at all, at all I can see." The pair walked away in disgust.[48]

A surprising degree of uneasiness attended the transition to the new time, even among those who approved it. Americans could find no precedent for such large-scale tampering with clocks, and the fetish of accuracy that buoyed up the new standards heightened anxiety about the change. In Chicago the stationmaster hovered over his chronometer with a powerful magnifying glass, while anxious railroad employees gathered round. "All looked unusually solemn, and their faces showed that something of an extraordinary nature was about to happen." After the appointed hour came and went, "everybody departed with a sigh of relief." Other newspapers reported a similar sense of relief when the change finally happened.[49]

Standard time posed a new authority for time, a new definition of its source. Newspapers frequently compared the railroad's innovation to Joshua's miracle at Jericho, and though they meant it in a spirit of fun the comparison made sense—in each case the authority for time bent to the will of social forces. *The Washington Post* called the new system of timekeeping "scarcely second to the reformation of the calendar by Julius Caesar, and later by Pope Gregory XIII." The *Post* was right in pointing out that standard time represented the triumph of new priorities for social organization. But it felt obliged, tongue in cheek, to reassure

Circular issued by the Yale College Observatory alerting employees and time service subscribers to the time change. (Courtesy of William F. Allen papers, Manuscript Division, New York Public Library.)

LOUISVILLE & NASHVILLE RAILROAD CO.

OFFICE OF THE GENERAL SUPERINTENDENT OF TRANSPORTATION

Louisville, November 9, 1883.

CIRCULAR No 80.

Important Notice--Change of Standard Time.

TO TAKE EFFECT ON SUNDAY, NOVEMBER 18, AT 10 O'CLOCK A. M.

8897

On Sunday, November the 18th, at 10 o'clock a. m., the standard time of all Divisions of this Road will be changed from the present standard, Louisville time, to the new standard ninetieth meridian or central time, which will be eighteen minutes slower than the present standard time.

The system to be adopted in changing **Regulators, Clocks,** and **Watches** will be as follows :

On Saturday, November the 17th, at the usual hour for sending time—namely, 10 o'clock a. m —all Clocks and the Watches of all Employes must be set to the exact present standard time. On Sunday, November the 18th, all Telegraph Offices must be open, and all Operators on hand for duty not later than 9 o'clock a. m., and remain on duty until relieved by the Chief Dispatcher of the Division.

All Work Engines and Crews, Road Masters, Supervisors, Section Foremen, and all other Employes who are required to have the correct standard time, must report at their nearest Telegraph Station not later than 9:30 a. m., on Sunday, November the 18th, and remain at the Telegraph Office until the new standard time is received, and their Watches are set to the correct new standard time.

On Sunday, November the 18th, the present standard time will be sent over the wires as usual, at 10 o'clock a. m., and as far as possible Dispatchers must have regular trains at Telegraph Stations at that hour.

At Precisely 10 o'clock a. m., by the present standard time, all **Trains and Engines,** including Switch Engines, must come to a STAND STILL FOR EIGHTEEN MINUTES, wherever they may be, until 10:18 a. m. by the present standard time, and at precisely 10:18 a. m., by the present standard time, all Clocks, and the Watches of all employes must be turned back from 10:18 to exactly 10 o'clock, which will be the new standard time, and the new standard time will then be given from Louisville over all Divisions of the road.

Bulletin alerting employees of the Louisville and Nashville Railroad to the change to standard time on November 18, 1883. This particular line required all trains in motion on that Sunday morning to STAND STILL FOR EIGHTEEN MINUTES. (Courtesy of William F. Allen Papers, Manuscript Division, New York Public Library.)

those "who may imagine that this shaking up of time standards may endanger the stability of the universe" that the sun, moon, and stars would continue to move as they always had.[50]

Most newspaper reporters were unable to pin down just what the change in time meant, and their humorous musings on the subject betrayed their confusion. The *Indianapolis Sentinel*, for example, asked puckishly if on November 18, a man slipping on a banana peel would have sixteen minutes more time to fall before hitting the ground, and if in that time he might secure a mattress to cushion the impact. The *New York Times* included a poem asking "Presidents! Train starters valorous / Astronomers also of all degrees . . . makers of Time Tables rigorous / dispatchers quick as the darting bees" to "Give us the minutes you've snatch'd away!"[51]

Though most cities adopted the new time readily and with little trouble, in Chicago confusion reigned for a few days—city officials as well as a major commuter line and one of the streetcar systems refused to make the change. Allen had done no lobbying in Chicago and failed to secure the Dearborn Observatory's assent. Those holding time service contracts with Dearborn, including the city government and most major jewelers, were reluctant to adopt a time other than that they had paid for. But as other cities and the Observatory adopted the measure, Chicago fell into line. The clock showing "New York Time" came down from the wall at Union Station, and a sign declaring "Philadelphia Time" over a second clock disappeared beneath the legend "Standard Time."[52]

A few wily businessmen incorporated the new time into their advertisements. "Standard time," a Maine druggist reminded customers, "gives us sixteen minutes more in which to do our shopping." A major New York jewelry firm asked Allen for copies of his new map, to sell while promoting themselves as "Keepers of

City Time." An Atlanta jeweler followed a picture of a smoking locomotive with an offer to put a second set of "gold railroad time" hands on any watch. And a St. Louis clothier blared "T-I-M-E! We think the change from local to standard time a most excellent and practical scheme—the future great don't lose any time by it either." Then the tag line: "as the time of year has arrived when warmer attire must be provided. . . ."[53]

Newspaper and magazine editors especially liked the new time. The *Atlanta Constitution* commented on "the utter contempt into which the sun and the moon have fallen. Formerly the rising and setting of the sun was the standard of time in all localities, and in the country the almanac and the sun together enabled many a farmer to do without his watch or clock."[54] Under standard time, the editor pointed out, the sun rose twenty-two minutes ahead of the almanac's prediction. While confessing some misgivings, the paper called the new system of time "the blue line standard on which Atlanta will progress into the future."[55]

The Atlanta paper recalled the pervasive tension between cyclical and linear time. If the almanac and the sun in concert represented cyclical time, then standard time, as the writer pointed out, seemed to emphasize the linear side of western thinking about time—the "blue line standard" of "progress into the future." The phrase repeats the transition from Rittenhouse's orrery to Allen's railroad locomotives. An orrery was a machine that reproduced celestial mechanics—it depicted the movements of the planets, and cyclical time. Like the orrery, clockwork wheels reproduced cyclical time. But clocks also recalled inexorable linear progress into the future. A steam locomotive, with its cyclical, clocklike mechanism of gears, recalled the orrery's complex of parts. But a locomotive *moved*; geographically across space, and forward into the industrial future—a locomotive orrery, a moving clock. Standard time governed this progress. As the accuracy, the precision, of a locomotive's parts regulated and ensured the safety of its progress, standard time regulated, ordered, and ensured the safety of American society's industrial future.

A Nebraska editor, punning unintentionally, called standard time "a striking event" in "our progressive civilization." Its invention counted as "signal proof" that the railroads "are the most potent factors of that civilization." Allen had needed to do little or no campaigning for standard time in the West. In many cases the railroad was probably so important that its example went unquestioned, and in less populous states, settled comparatively recently by whites, there may have been no long-established patterns of life to upset. The Nebraska editor praised the railroad's new time for giving structure to progress. Early American political theorists had looked at the clock and seen a model for rational government. Partisans of standard time looked at the railroad's innovation and saw an intellectual/mechanical device for social regulation. "In a quarter of a century," the Nebraska railroad partisan hymned, "they have made the people of the country homogeneous, breaking through the peculiarities and provincialisms which marked separate and unmingling sections." Standard time, a virtual "revolution," apparently completed the process of homogenization the railroads began.[56]

Accustomed as they were to gathering accurate information from distant places, newspaper editors praised standard time's imposition of uniformity. "Had there been stretched across the continent yesterday a line of clocks," the *New York Times* wrote, "there would have been a continuous ringing from the east to the west." "Half a million clocks," a Pittsburgh daily enthused, "were disturbed at the same instant." "Railroad time everybody's time," declared a headline in St. Louis, while even the cranky *Boston Daily Advertiser* praised the fact that "all laborers who wait until the clock strikes seven a.m. before they strike in with the pick and shovel, will strike together" under standard time.[57]

While mistakenly crediting Charles F. Dowd for the change,[58] *Harper's Weekly* concurred—after standard time, "all the clocks on the continent struck together." Formerly, in respect to time, "the whole country was a pathless wilderness." The poor traveler's watch "was to him but a delusion; clocks in stations star[ed] each other in the face defiant of harmony," striking like "incoherent cowbells in a wild wood." Now, thanks to standard time, "the minute hands of all were in harmony with each other."[59] Like the newspapers, *Harper's* celebrated the apparent fulfillment of Samuel Langley's vision, an industrial society made to "move like clock-work." The widespread and genuine success of standard time gave the impression of a unified, synchronized, and rational society approaching the future in an orderly fashion.

"The system adopted by you," Allen boasted more or less accurately to his fellow railroaders at the next Convention, "now governs the daily and hourly actions of at least fifty million people." Strengthening Allen's case, the International Meridian Conference, meeting in Washington in 1884, voted to recommend a system of Greenwich meridian zones for the world. Despite France's gallant resistance to time based on an English standard, World Standard Time began making slow headway in the international scientific community almost immediately.[60]

Standard time altered relations between individuals and society. In 1883 William Graham Sumner, America's leading social Darwinist, had described the transition from a society based on local traditions of status to a society based on contract. "In the Middle Ages," Sumner wrote, "men were united by custom and prescription into associations, ranks, guilds, and communities of various kinds." These ties were lifelong, and thus "society was dependent, throughout all its details, on status, and the tie, or bond, was sentimental." In modern America, however, "more than anywhere else, the social structure is based on contract." Contract relations are "rational . . . based on sufficient reason, not on custom or prescription." Standard time was fundamental to relations of contract, which required uniform, unvarying units of time. And like contractual relations it was based on nothing more than convenience. Under standard time, men and women governed themselves not by some "sentimental" moral criteria drawn from nature, but by business expediency.[61]

Allen's triumph, and his claim of standard time "governing" daily life, bore out his belief in the power of the railroads—commerce, in effect, now made up its own rules regarding what time was and how it should be understood. Even the venerable *Old Farmer's Almanac* acknowledged the railroad's influence—and changing times—by offering translation tables to help farmers figure the new time against local meridians. In a final insult to solar authority, Philadelphia's park commissioners debated whether or not to adjust the city's sundials into harmony with the new time.[62]

But Allen's innovation, for all his effusive rhetoric, never enjoyed quite the popularity he claimed. Though he omitted much of it in his accounts, from the beginning there was opposition—decidedly in the minority, but vigorous and lasting opposition nevertheless. The problems arose most often, not surprisingly, in places where standard and local time differed more than a few minutes. Residents of these places experienced not just a few minutes' change on the face of a watch, but a dramatic variation in sunlight—in some cases more than half the effect we gain today from daylight saving. Such a difference highlighted the arbitrary nature of the new time, and brought objections on the grounds of legality, hostility to the railroads, regional pride, and religious truth. Boston provided an early example.

Many Bostonians, as described above, were already some-

Cover of William Allen's Travelers' Official Guide *for December 1883.*
(National Museum of American History,
Smithsonian Institution.)

what hostile to the new standards. Shortly before standard time one Horace Clapp, a debtor, had been ordered to appear before Edward Jenkins, Commissioner of Insolvency, between nine and ten in the morning of November 19. Debtor Clapp appeared that day at what he thought was 9:45 eastern time, only to find that Commissioner Jenkins was running the court on the old time — it was 10:01, and Clapp was in default. Clapp sued Jenkins, and the case wound up before Massachusetts Supreme Court Justice Oliver Wendell Holmes. After several weeks' deliberation Holmes proved true to legal pragmatism. Though no law specifying the legal standard then existed, Holmes ruled that standard time, by its general adoption, was the time in effect when Clapp appeared.[63]

Holmes's decision, backing the authority of an innovation as yet unsanctified by law, strengthened Allen's case, since the legality of standard time troubled many. A number of communities in Maine were sharply divided over the same issue, most prominently the small city of Bangor. When Bangor's City Council voted to adopt the new standards, the mayor vetoed their resolution. He found the change of time involved, almost twenty-five minutes, needless and confusing. "Philadelphia time," as Mayor Cummings called it, seemed senseless in Maine. Any innovation "that disarranges the customs of a people handed down from time immemorial," Cummings concluded, "should at least have the sanction of State legislature."[64]

The mayor's stand drew jeers from around the nation. Advocates of standard time, especially railroad journals, scorned poor "Mayor Dogberry" (Shakespeare's fool in *Much Ado About Nothing*) as an old-fashioned, foolish, and shortsighted impediment to progress. He stands, the *Boston Journal* mocked, like "Leonidas at Thermopylae," alone against the railroad monopoly and the "centralizing tendency of the age."[65] By elaborately spoofing the mayor's rather reasonable objections, and identifying him as typical or representative of objections to the new time, partisans of

Allen's innovation made their opponents seem like cranks, hicks, and relics of the past. Since most major cities had adopted the new time, *Railway Age* asked, "why should any other places, big or little, be allowed to retain the obsolete fashion? Local time must go."[66]

Voters in Bangor felt otherwise. A referendum on standard time in March 1884 disclosed that better than three fourths of the city opposed the railroad innovation, especially among the working class. Opposition grew statewide — despite the public scorn heaped upon Bangor, the Augusta, Maine, *Journal* reported in 1884 that "the cities of this state, one after another, are returning to local time." Anxious to quell any opposition to the new standards, Allen worked privately to swing Maine into line. He wrote letters to the New York papers denying the collapse of standard time in Maine, while privately urging railroad officials and the editor of the *Maine Farmer* to promote the reform more aggressively. With their help Allen shepherded a standard time bill through the state legislature in 1887, despite the continued reluctance of citizens in Bangor and a number of other cities.[67]

Though Allen downplayed it, in fact the range of opposition to standard time was remarkably wide, and confined neither to rural people or small towns. In Washington, Attorney General Benjamin Brewster issued an order forbidding government offices to adopt standard time until Congress authorized it. Like Mayor Cummings, Brewster also became a figure of fun — a common apocryphal story had him rushing to catch a train, only to stand chagrined at the platform as it pulled away by the new time. Congress adopted eastern time for the District of Columbia in March 1884, thus answering Brewster's objections. But the federal legislature largely avoided the issue of national standards.[68]

"Today the 75th meridian is standard, because the railroad kings have so ordered it," declared one congressman, hoping to establish a legal standard. "Tomorrow the railroads may make it the 76th, or the 80th." Why not have a time standard determined by the people? he asked. One of his statesmanlike opponents demanded instead that Congress legalize the new railroad time, since "it is never too late," as he put it, "for the Representatives of the people to catch up with the business interests of the country." Posed as an issue of the railroad's power, the bill died in Committee, and Congress left the matter undecided until 1918. Time seemed like a difficult subject to legislate, especially if the railroads rushed in where politicians feared to tread.[69]

In the absence of federal law, many cities attacked the new time. The *Louisville Courier-Journal* called it "a compulsory lie," "a monstrous fraud" and "a swindle." Can you tell me, a letter asked the editors, "if anyone has the authority and right to change the city time without the consent of the people, and what benefit Louisville can derive from it?" The editors responded that no such authority ruled, and no benefit seemed likely from what was "only a disguised step towards centralization . . . a stab in the dark at our cherished State's rights. After they get all our watches and clocks ticking together," the editors asked in reflexive alarm, "will there not be a further move to merge the zone states into districts or provinces?"

The 90th Greenwich meridian set Louisville back almost eighteen minutes. Why, the paper asked, "should we concede to John Bull's dull Greenwich the position of time dictator? Now what is Greenwich to us? A dingy London suburb." In June 1884 Louisville dropped standard time, and though it would be readopted by the city over the next years, as late as 1905 the Supreme Court of Kentucky could point out that "sun time" was still in use among the bankers of Louisville. According to the Court the word "noon" had no legal meaning in Kentucky except as its usage in a given community described — railroad time could not be considered the legal standard.[70]

Without legal guidelines, cities on the new time zone borders, like Pittsburgh and Wheeling, West Virginia, were just "betwixt and between," as the *Wheeling Daily Register* put it. Wheeling wavered between the eastern or central zone; one moved the clocks ahead twenty-three minutes, the other back thirty-seven. The city waited four years before adopting eastern time. Pittsburgh rejected standard time until 1887. "All the people have to say on it," a Pennsylvania railroad superintendent wrote to Allen, "is that they have always used local time and that it would confuse them to change." "God Almighty," one Pittsburgher exclaimed, "fixed the time for this section just as much as he did for Philadelphia or New York."[71]

In Georgia, bisected by Allen's eastern and central zones, the change proved even more confusing. Augusta, on the border of two zones, opted at first for eastern time, while Savannah and the rest of Georgia were put on central. Assigned by Allen only to accommodate existing railroad division breaks, the partition sat poorly with many Georgians, and both cities soon dropped standard time.[72] Although for a time Augusta moved into the central zone, the problems returned when Augusta and Savannah adopted eastern time in 1888. Even then opposition lingered. "The only people that want standard time are the railroad people," declared a Savannah alderman. "The city doesn't want it, the laboring people don't want it . . . nine tenths of the population of the city are opposed to it." "And the ladies," the courtly alderman added, "why, they have always been opposed to it."[73]

Georgia's hostility to standard time was more cogently phrased by its Supreme Court, ruling in 1889 on whether standard or local time prevailed in the expiration of contracts. "To allow the railroads to fix the standard of time," the Court proclaimed, "would allow them at pleasure to violate or defeat the law." "The standard of time fixed by persons in a certain line of business," the decision continued, "cannot be substituted at will . . . for the statutes of the state, as well as the general law and usage of the country." The Georgia Court clearly saw standard time as a measure limited only to the railroads and having no binding authority.[74]

The railroad's presumption of authority angered and puzzled the Indianapolis *Sentinel*. Labeling standard time "a revolution . . . anarchy, chaos," the *Sentinel* sarcastically added, "we presume the sun, moon and stars will make an attempt to ignore the orders of the railway convention, but they will have to give in at last." People would have to marry by railroad time, eat, work, be born, and die by railroad time. The Indianapolis editors resented railroad time's—and the clock's—displacement of the sun. We compare the city clock with our almanacs, a second Hoosier complained, only to find that "the city clock is a moving falsehood." Which authority prevailed? Could someone really be born by railroad time?[75]

In Charleston, South Carolina, "A Planter" claimed that "country people, not having access to the general press, have failed to see the essential points." "By whose authority," he asked in perplexity, "was the variation [in time] made?" The Natchez, Mississippi, *Daily Democrat* simply if rather confusedly declared, "we fail to see the necessity for the new sidereal time business. The old way of time has answered the purpose for several centuries past, and we think it is about as good a system as can be inaugurated."[76]

No state objected to railroad time as strenuously as Ohio. The *Cincinnati Commercial Gazette* especially objected to adjusting clocks back twenty-two minutes. "The proposition that we should put ourselves out of the way nearly half an hour from the facts so as to harmonize with an imaginary line drawn through Pittsburgh," railed one of a series of editorials, "is simply preposterous . . . let the people of Cincinnati stick to the truth as it is written by the sun, moon and stars." The *Commercial Gazette* thought it "a great stupidity" to assume that people would "accommodate themselves to the railroad convenience." Up to 1890, it published railway timetables under the proud heading *"This is Cincinnati Time. Twenty-two minutes faster than railroad time."*[77]

While other Cincinnati papers favored the new standards, a number of Ohio cities shared the *Commercial Gazette*'s hostility. A Dayton City councilman failed to see "why Dayton should keep railroad time—they don't even recognize the city, nor confirm their time to suit Dayton's, no more should Dayton change to suit them." The *Columbus Dispatch* reported that after the change, "jewelers were flooded today with the watches of customers left [to have] a third hand put on." One jeweler received more than sixty. Columbians saw little reason to give up local time. After briefly embracing the central zone, the City Council officially abandoned it a week later. Asked if his city would adopt the new time, Toledo's mayor replied, "I do not see why we should. The difference is so great that . . . it would result in no little inconvenience." Akron's *Daily Beacon* warned of confusion "if some of these illogical enthusiasts" of standard time "are not muzzled."[78]

Opposition reached a height of some kind in 1889, when Bellaire, Ohio's, Board of Education attempted to set the schoolhouse clock ahead to eastern time. City Council, objecting to the change, had the entire board arrested. Proud of Bellaire's action and deploring any attempt to legislate a state-wide standard time, the county newspaper declared, "if any members of the Legislature are anxious to set their watches at what they call 'Central Standard Time' they should forthwith do so; but when some crank among them proposes to enact that time into law—to correct and regulate the sun . . . he is carrying the joke a little too far."[79]

But a local court upheld the Board of Education's right to regulate its schoolhouse clock, leaving Bellaire with three times: the "true time" of the sun, "Philadelphia [eastern] time" on the schoolhouse, and "St. Louis" [central] time at the railroad station. Bellaire's rather silly dilemma recapitulated the widespread and diverse popular hostility to standard time in Ohio. Neither an isolated rural phenomenon nor a pet project of cranks, Ohio's hostility denied the railroad's claims of temporal hegemony. Back in 1884 Allen had written to railroad managers asking for lists of those communities rejecting standard time. In Ohio the list included Cleveland, Columbus, Springfield, Dayton, Cincinnati and neighboring Muncie, Indiana, each a substantial city and important manufacturing center.[80]

Standing midway between two meridians, Ohio saw no advantage to adopting any other region's time. A letter to the *Commercial Gazette* suggested that if zone times must be adopted, a separate "Ohio zone" halfway between eastern and central time would better serve the public. Detroit expressed the same reluctance, and despite statewide adoption of central time in 1885, Detroit changed standards repeatedly well into the twentieth century. The difference between railroad and local time, wrote young Henry Ford, then amusing himself by fixing watches in his native Dearborn, Michigan, "bothered me a good deal." Ford designed a watch with two dials, keeping local time separate from the railroad's. The region's hostility to standard time led Charles Dowd to work up a plan calling for a similar "intermediate zone" between central and eastern time.[81]

Partially consoled by the fact that in Ohio "the traveling public, at least, will have to eat, drink and sleep by standard time," Allen welcomed an offer of assistance from Professor T. C. Mendenhall of the Coast and Geodetic Survey. Arming himself with copies of Allen's maps, Mendenhall addressed the Ohio Society of Civil Engineers in 1890. The Engineers in turn sponsored the final passage, after several failures, of a bill making central time the legal standard of Ohio in 1893.[82]

Ohio's hostility testifies to the lingering belief in an older conception of time — time linked to nature, to the sun, to a specific place and to that place alone. Accepting standard time as pure commonsense, we might judge their objections silly, backward, and provincial. But in fact most of the communities cited above held no grudge against commerce, no hostility to modern science and learning, no objection to the railroad as a clever device for moving people and goods. What each found puzzling, saddening, or infuriating was the assumption that time was arbitrary, changeable, susceptible to the whims of the railroads or defined by mere commercial expediency. Surely the world ran by higher priorities than railroad scheduling.

The Texas Circuit Court insisted in 1895, for example, that "the only standard recognized by the Courts is the meridian of the sun, and any arbitrary standard set up by persons in business will not be recognized." In even stronger terms, the Iowa Supreme Court declared in 1899: "we are not quite ready to concede that, for the mere convenience of these companies, nature's timepiece may be arbitrarily superseded." "The apparent daily revolution of the celestial body," the Court pointed out, "has from the remotest antiquity been employed as a measure of time." Local time, it insisted, "cannot be lightly set aside on the mere pretext that certain lines of business so demand."[83]

Between 1883 and 1915 standard time came to trial before the Supreme Courts of various states at least fifteen times. The Supreme Courts of Nebraska (1890) and Kentucky (1905), and the United States Court of Appeals (1907), all ruled that although standard time had been adopted in many places, local time still ruled the day unless the law said otherwise.[84] Standard time was also tried in Minnesota (1898), North Dakota (1905), Utah (1911), New York and California (1917). Though upheld in each case, the willingness to test standard time points to public awareness of alternatives, or outright hostility, to the system of time we now take for granted.[85]

These dissenters, to be sure, were decidedly in the minority—most communities and states adopted standard time readily and even enthusiastically, if the newspapers are to be believed. As an innovation, standard time added the weight of scientific endorsement and the power of the railroads to its eminent practicality and usefulness. In some cities, the reform passed almost unnoticed, or was treated in the matter-of-fact way befitting what almost seemed like "common sense." Standard time advanced with all the weight and momentum of industrial progress, and its opponents were clearly out of step with prevailing opinion in most published sources.

But neither should their objections be lightly dismissed. They objected not only to standard time itself, but to the new ideas about time and time usage it represented. Many raised questions of political, cultural, and religious authority that would find echoes in years to come. What principles, they asked, should govern our society? Most of the states which saw standard time brought to trial, for example—Georgia, Texas, Kentucky, Nebraska, Minnesota, North Dakota, California—were hotbeds of rural radicalism and Populist support. Iowa, whose Supreme Court ringingly denounced railroad time, gave birth to General James B. Weaver, while another standard time case originated in Iron Gate, Virginia, home of several Farmer's Alliance cooperatives and a strong Populist community.[86]

An analysis of Populist rhetoric, offered here only as the briefest suggestion, suggests that they rejected the kind of linear, "industrial" time implicit in the new standards. "All nations of history," declared the *National Economist* in 1889, "have had a rise, a period of brilliant prosperity, a decadence and a fall." Depicting history as a series of rises and declines obviously involves a cyclical understanding of time, and in the series on world history quoted, the Populist newspaper laid the blame for decline on neglecting agriculture.[87] "When Rome," another Populist rhetorician added, "suffered her noble citizens to 'crush out' the cultivators . . . her power began to wane." Similarly, "retrogression in American agriculture means national decay and inevitable ruin."[88]

Populist writings insisted on nature as the source of time and natural imperatives as guides to using it. "Land," lectured agrarian firebrand W. Scott Morgan, "is the gift of God." Morgan quoted the Bible to make a point about nature's model for time usage. "In the sweat of thy face shalt thou eat thy bread. This decree was uttered 6,000 years ago," he concluded. "It is as immutable as time itself." Farmers must cooperate, Morgan urged, and seek their model for cooperation "in the mechanisms of heaven, and in the animal, vegetable, and mineral kingdoms." Even the name of one of the earliest radical farmer's organizations—"the Wheel"— suggests cyclical time, with agriculture and natural law, rather than geared mechanisms, acting as a sort of social governor on the many wheels of industry.[89]

Recalling the almanacs and schoolbooks cited in Chapter One, these Populist writers objected not so much to machinery— or clocks, or industry, or the railroads—as to the ideas and as- sumptions about time and progress that governed them. None mentioned standard time explicitly, but each source framed its conceptions of history and good government in the circularity of "natural" time. The phrases they used to describe men's and wom- en's relation to nature would echo again thirty years later in strong rural opposition to daylight saving.

If these cases suggest rural hostility to standard time and the culture that made it, the regulations cited below, drawn up by the General Time Convention in the wake of its success, hint at the new time's implications for industrial workers. These new guidelines called for "all conductors, engineers, train hands, road foremen," etc., to provide themselves with timepieces. Each was to take his watch to a jeweler or watchmaker, who would record the watch's serial number and issue a certificate of accuracy, to be renewed every three months. "All train men," the regulations continued, "should compare their time with standard clocks . . . regulate their watches therebye and register their names, and the time at which they register, in a book provided for that purpose," before every trip.⁹⁰

These regulations, of course, seem eminently logical and practical. The point here is not just that railroads needed accurate time, but rather that in the wake of standard time such close attention to timekeeping was now common sense—standard clock time had become the regulating and organizing principle for industrial labor, and "common sense" about time now meant following an elaborate set of practices that reinforced the clock's authority. The virtue of ever greater "accuracy" was the path this time discipline traveled.

Compare these regulations, for example, with the Camden and Amboy's 1853 regulations cited in Chapter Two. Both emphasize the watch as timekeeper, and establish a set of routines for assuring its accuracy. And, not surprisingly, by 1884 the whole procedure has become more ritualized, more formal, and more elaborate. In 1853 workers had used company watches, and returned them at the end of the day. Now each employee was to provide himself with a watch and register his name daily next to the watch's serial number, to prove he had checked in with the standard clock. The daily registry testified to the accuracy of both worker and watch, while the standard clock served as the authority both man and machine were measured against.

The worker's regularity in signing the book, and in regulating his timepiece, defines the performance of his duty and thus his worth to the company. His accuracy, regularity, and dependability—certified by the registry—mirrors the watch's accuracy, regularity, and dependability as shown on the jeweler's certificate. But both exist in a subsidiary relation to their ultimate model, the standard clock. Standard time eliminated the kind of public—and private—conflicts that resulted when each man could make a legitimate claim for the authority of his own time. But it did so by merging men and women and their time-telling machines.

The *Indianapolis Journal,* for example, claimed that "there is something remarkable about the fascination which watches exert over their owners." Published two days before the establishment of standard time along with a favorable description of Allen's plan, the article insisted that "a man who prides himself on his watch identifies himself with it . . . the watch becomes a part of himself." The *Journal's* article, a discussion of time and timekeepers by a local professor, described the situation that standard time, and the railroad regulations, were supposed to prevent.

Among men who pride themselves on owning good time-pieces, the professor continued, "the infallibility of their watches is the firmest article of faith." But no watch keeps perfect time, and "meanwhile every man in his own breast doubts his watch. He gives an intellectual assent to the doctrine that his watch is infallible, but in the silence of the night he confesses to himself that perhaps it needs regulating." Spoofing the conventions of inner guilt and the nagging conscience, the article recalled Melville's *Pierre* and its intriguing connection of time with moral authority. Standard time solved the dilemma both Melville and the professor posed, by establishing an ultimate standard all were measured against.[91]

The article, and the regulations, testified to the questions of moral and political authority implied in railroad standard time— the exchange of local and individual autonomy for regulation by distant, even faceless (or rather, clock-faced) authority. Allen's innovation resolved public and private doubts about time and conduct by establishing a seemingly universal, arbitrary, and con-sensual standard. Standard time reaffirmed the priorities—com-merce, trade, unity, the free exchange of goods and information above all—that now largely regulated the daily life of an industrial society.

Not all found that regulation comforting. On November 18, 1883, the day that standard time was implemented, the *Cincinnati*

Commercial Gazette ran a descriptive piece on that new phenomenon of industrial capitalism, the commuter. On any given day, the reporter found, the same pattern of "types" and classes among these "railroad regulars" repeated itself hourly at the local station. So regular were their movements that "the longer a man is a commuter, the more he grows to be a living time table—a model of cast-iron punctuality." The *Commercial Gazette* called the commuter's timetable "a hideous specter" that "sleeping or waking" haunted its victim. "It is upon his back," the article concluded, "and can not be shaken off."[92]

Though not writing about standard time per se, the reporter expressed some of the uneasiness the new understanding of time, and the newly developing relationship between men and women and their watches, provoked. Again, comments like these were strictly in the minority. But even those who celebrated standard time viewed its effects in ways we might find slightly uncomfortable. "Going down Broadway yesterday, I saw a man who stepped with odd precision," went an 1883 account in a New York paper, and "I called my companion's attention to this singularity." "He is running himself on an imaginary time-table," came the reply; "that is William F. Allen, the author of the new time system. He is an expert in Railway time-tables, and what you see in his gait and movements is a mannerism gained from his business."

Allen liked the account so much that he included it in his papers.[93] The description recalls the career of one of Allen's contemporaries, Frederick W. Taylor. In 1883 Taylor was measuring his stride to find a more efficient gait, and just beginning to apply the stopwatch to his fellow employees at Midvale Steel. The material cited here hints at some of the implications of standard time. Over the next twenty years the meaning of the new time the railroads fostered would reveal itself most clearly in the rise of scientific management and the growth of the American watch industry.

Keep a Watch on

Everybody

Trying to express the meaning of standard public time in 1883, the *New York Herald* reflected on its pervasive tendency to infiltrate ordinary life. Standard time, the *Herald* concluded, "goes beyond the public pursuits of men and enters into their private lives as part of themselves." The *Herald*'s comment implied that the railroad's innovation was more than a simple public convenience—that the change in the understanding of time marked, in fact, a reformation in the internal, private understanding of the self. Once individuals experienced time as a relationship between God and nature. Henceforth, under the railroad standards, men and women would measure themselves in relation to a publicly defined time based on synchronized clocks. The *Herald* knew standard time was an important change, but lacked words enough to explain why.[1]

A more pointed commentary came twelve years later from James O'Connell, president of the International Association of Machinists. Asked at a trade union meeting why labor might not form a trust like Standard Oil, O'Connell recalled the story of the Pennsylvania Irishman, who when told that his train left at eight o'clock "standard time," remarked irascibly, "Well, that settles it." "Settles what?" queried the train's conductor. "Why, the whole of it," replied the stock Irishman. "They'll be gittin' the wind next, they've got the time now." O'Connell's joke dramatized the exercise of power inherent in controlling and defining time. Standard time marked, as the *Herald* had realized, a major shift in the understanding and authority of time in everyday life. It turned time from an abstract quantity into a commodity, and more specifically—at least in the eyes of O'Connell's Irishman—turned time into a tool of corporate power. If Standard Oil could own time, then time itself became the laborer's antagonist.[2]

This is not to claim, again, that standard time *itself* caused any major change in people's lives. On the contrary, the new time zones usually amounted to just a small adjustment of watches and clocks. Most people met the innovation with praise and simply reset their watches, quickly forgetting all about railroad standard time, what it was and where it came from. In many cases, the railroads' 1883 innovation only formalized a regional trend. But standard time, in fact the whole concept of standardizing time, epitomized new ideas about time's nature, ideas that in turn contributed to a major reorganization of work, leisure, and the individual's relation to society. Standard time rebuilt the framework of time in everyday life, as the ideas about time that had inspired it left the railroad station and began moving into the work place and home.

Railroad time zones were only one manifestation of a whole range of new experiences of time. Electric lights altered the patterns of work and rest. Telephone lines brought the distant near and made conversation instantaneous. Clock and watch manufacturers doubled, tripled, even quadrupled their output, surrounding the time-conscious with a staggering variety of mechanical timekeepers in every size and shape imaginable. Each of these factors combined to create, in the decades after 1880, a generally heightened sense of punctuality and urgency about time and clocks, a new and widespread formality in the experience of time in everyday work and life. But just as some Americans had consciously resisted standard time, so many Americans continued to resist the clock's authority over time in their daily lives.

Americans experienced one aspect of this reformation of time consciousness in a new emphasis on strict punctuality in work, in private life and at public events, theaters and concerts. Historian Lawrence Levine has recently documented the "bifurcation" of American culture in the nineteenth century, the conscious creation of a split between "highbrow" and "lowbrow" forms of art and entertainment. According to Levine the loose, relaxed, socially mixed quality of public events in antebellum America began to clash with a more circumspect, formal model of decorum advanced by the new arbiters of elite culture. As rules about public behavior changed, previously relaxed customs about starting times and times of arrival gave way to highly structured and closely enforced rules against lateness. "Unpunctuality," a Boston newspaper claimed in an 1884 example, "shows a relaxed morality in the musical community." Indifference to time stigmatized the latecomer as a moral leper and a social inferior.[3]

Ideally, this temporal self-discipline—the "standard time" of the work place—should have carried over into recreation, but too many people seemed to be ignoring it. "It is very singular," scolded a magazine article of 1892, "that in a country where railroads, with their inflexible time schedules, are such an important and universal feature of life, the habit of punctuality should not be more generally diffused." This editorial proposed using railroad standard time, so useful in organizing labor and business, as the model for ordering leisure. But while praising the ideals of clock time the editorial also remarked on a lingering resistance, in 1892, to the clock's authority in leisure hours. "Few people are habitually late to a train, to business, or to dinner, but many seem to consider it of little consequence," the author lamented, "to be from ten to thirty minutes behind time for every concert, lecture and theater." The same rigid schedules that the author found in work, business, and the home still lacked binding authority over public recreations.[4]

The latter decades of the nineteenth century saw, as this editorial reflects, both continued resistance to clock time and a constant process of negotiation and redefinition of time's role and meaning in daily life. In commercial life, the hegemony of standard time seemed fairly clear. For example, by the 1880s traditional schoolbook homilies on the evils of idle time were being fortified with strictures against tardiness of any kind. *McGuffey's Readers* from the antebellum decades had always stressed conserving time, but later revisions began emphasizing the urgent necessity of punctuality in meeting debts and following orders. "A railroad train was rushing along at almost lightning speed," one 1881 fifth-grade lesson began. "The conductor was late . . . but he hoped to pass the curve safely . . . in an instant there was a collision: a shriek, a shock, and fifty souls were in eternity, and all because an engineer was behind time." A commercial firm failed, the lesson continued, because its agent had been late in remitting payment, and an innocent man died because the watch of a messenger, who bore pardon, was five minutes late. "Napoleon died a prisoner at St. Helena," a final grand example claimed, "because one of his Marshals was behind time." "It is continually so in life," went the conclusion. "The best laid plans, the most important affairs, the fortunes of individuals, honor, happiness, life itself are daily sacrificed because somebody is 'behind time.' "[5]

If only Napoleon's marshals could have owned a set of *McGuffey's Readers*! *McGuffey's* lesson embodies many of the new ideas about time typical of the late nineteenth century, in particular the *interconnectedness* of events. Time is expressed not in nature and seasonal tasks, but in terms of legal, industrial, and political obligations, conditions whose binding authority comes not from God, but from the interdependencies of a commercial economy. Standard railroad time, like the new emphasis on punctuality in schoolbooks and in public life, grew out of these new conditions, out of the same need to order and control financial events and human movements across space and time. It offered a uniform gauge for regularizing market relations, and *McGuffey*'s lesson reiterated the importance of keeping to the standard.

But resistance to clock authority continued—a third-grade *McGuffey's Reader* of the same year, for example, persisted in locating time in nature and the sun. One often reprinted story, "The Clock and the Sundial," related the humiliation of a boasting steeple clock, who had laughed at the humble and primitive sundial in the church yard below. The clock praised itself for telling time on cloudy days, and at night, but fell into embarrassed silence when the sun "broke forth from behind a cloud, and showed, by the sundial, that the clock was half an hour behind the right time." The moral cautioned against boastfulness, but the dial's triumph named the sun as the ultimate timekeeping authority. While daily life and business seemed to demand ever more attention to clocks and watches, tradition—and nostalgia—insisted on the wisdom and virtue of nature's example.[6]

"The chopping up of time into rigid periods," writer and editor Charles Dudley Warner wrote early in 1884, shortly after the invention of standard time, "is an invasion of individual freedom, and makes no allowances for differences in temperament and feeling." Warner was speaking about the difference between man-made and "natural" time, between relations of "sentiment" and relations of contract. He linked periodized, man-made time to creditors and their economic power—"they watch the manner of these artificial periods with interest," he punned, "in order to send in their bills and extort their profits." Warner mourned the apparent decline of "natural," precommercial time. The debtor, he claimed, "hates this artificial and vexatious arrangement of time" and "would like [time] to flow on unbroken like a river, peacefully, without dams, and without the constant apprehension of checks to his serenity."

Against the practical human divisions of clock and calendar Warner advanced natural metaphors for time, nostalgically yearning for an earlier period when life seemed freer. But he admitted that "in giving [time] a name and a certain space of duration we have made it an entity, and we cannot escape from the thralldom of this arbitrary succession." Warner's musings pointed out, like O'Connell's joke, that customary divisions of time also served as methods of control that privileged one economic class over another. Warner's time is not an indescribable "something" one exists in, a relationship between the individual and the natural world, but rather an assigned standard value, a number, that the less fortunate struggle frantically to keep even with. His comments, like the lessons from *McGuffey*, depict the constant tension between modern, arbitrary standard clock time and its preindustrial counterpart.[7]

In a similar vein, George M. Beard's pioneering 1881 study of *American Nervousness* partly blamed "clocks and watches" and the "necessity of punctuality" for the American middle class's generally strained nerves. For Beard, "clocks and watches" and the "necessity of punctuality" were nearly synonymous—they reinforced and mirrored each other. The very perfection of timekeeping instruments, he claimed, "compel[s] us to be on time, and excite[s] the habit of looking to see the exact moment." "A nervous man cannot take out his watch and look at it," he argued, "without affecting his pulse." Beard's watches and clocks "excited," "compelled," and increased the pulse—they laid claims on both body and spirit. Beard depicted a fierce and rigid social time discipline that demanded unhealthily intimate relations between people and their time-telling machines. If he shared Warner's distaste for the tyranny of standard public time, Beard perceptively located the problem in the peculiar—and fascinating—relationship between the watch and its owner.[8]

Americans in the Gilded Age bought watches and clocks in huge numbers, in a vast range of designs, and for many different purposes. Between 1870 and the first decades of the twentieth century, the design of American clocks and watches, and the advertising and publicity they generated, consistently reiterated a few basic themes.[9]

Mechanical timekeepers stood for getting control—gaining power over the confusing and potentially hostile world of schedules, appointments, and standard time, or gaining power over unruly employees. But they also encouraged a strange merger of personal authority, of identity, between timekeeping machines and their owners. Clock time, machine time, savored unmistakably of discipline, surveillance, and control in both the design of the objects themselves and the discourse surrounding them. Yet the same objects that symbolized industrial and social discipline also empowered its victims. Standardized time marked no advance or decline in the extent of freedom or individuality. Instead, it represented a reconstruction of governing authority—both self-government and the organization of work and public life. What did it mean when ordinary people, engaged in the usual compromises required to earn a living, adopted machines as their models?

As the basis of time moved further away from nature and closer to the mechanical timekeeper, standardized clock time became a tool of education and industry, a sort of uniform that all laborers in the commercial army were required to put on at childhood and wear through life. And if standard time established the new battle dress of industrial competition, then the pocketwatch and regulating clock, mass-produced in unprecedented numbers after 1880, became its shield and insignia. But not everyone understood or used these weapons in the same way. Rural Americans insisted on tying time—and clocks—to nature. On the job, cheap pocketwatches offered an alternative to the boss's factory clock. And in the home especially, clocks became friendly expressions of individuality rather than grim sentries of industry.

Two themes predominated as standardized clock time spread: on the one hand, outright resistance to clock time, or the desire to control it, and on the other a peculiar concern with internalizing clock authority and finding one's niche in the new framework of standardized time. The two themes co-existed uneasily, reproducing a general uneasiness about time in society as a whole. One theme, followed in the industrial work place, led to time clocks, to Taylorism, and the ultimate establishment of machines as authorities for time and models for labor. The other led toward continued hostility to standardized time and factory discipline, to the idealization of leisure time, and to the bifurcation of public and private time in the home. Both themes revolved around the form of the mechanical timekeeper.

A number of innovations in timekeeping and time transmissions helped reinforce the authority of mechanical timekeepers after 1880. William Bond, and later Samuel Langley, had pioneered in transmitting commercial time signals, as Chapter Two related. Following Langley's profitable example, Leonard Waldo and the Western Union Company, among others, had established competing time systems of their own by 1883. Each offered a fixed authority for time—after 1883 the widely adopted railroad standard zones—and each claimed to lessen the confusions and anxiety allegedly stemming from idiosyncratic local times. But the proliferation of watches, time clocks, synchronized program clock systems, and time services over the next decades suggests instead that standardized time and time transmission only made people more anxious about time's passage.

Companies like Waldo's promoted synchronized clock systems. They linked "slave" or "controlled" clocks with a single, more accurate "master clock" located many miles away. An 1882 example, the "electrically controlled system" of P. H. Dudley, used signals from a local observatory to "control any number of clocks within telegraphic communication." When the Naval Observatory agreed in 1883 to telegraph standard railway time, it greatly increased the prestige of standard zones while creating the impression that its signals were the "official" standard of time for the nation.[10] Only Western Union offered subscribers the chance to receive standard time signals direct from the Naval Observatory. By 1893 they dominated the field through a partner corporation, the Self-Winding Clock Company.

"The Western Union Telegraph Company," promised the application for time service, "will furnish to its subscribers, once each working day, as correct Time Signals as it can obtain from the United States Naval Observatory Standard Time at Washington, D.C.," along with one or more clocks designed to receive the signals. "Said clocks," went the contract, "are the property of the Self-Winding Clock Company of New York, and are constructed and used under its patents." The relationship between the two companies was rather obscure, but the impressive effect of the partnership between the Naval Observatory and Western Union was not.[11] Regulated by electricity and far more accurate than daily life required, the company's clocks embodied time itself rather than merely depicting it.

The Self-Winding Clock Company's advertisements empha-

Tower and Pavilion of the Self-Winding Clock Company at the World's Columbian Exposition, 1893. The regulating clock, located in the pavilion, sent out signals governing the tower and the other clocks in the building. (From *Scientific American*, July 29, 1893. National Museum of American History, Smithsonian Institution.)

sized the Naval Observatory connection and the completely automatic nature of their service. Thanks to an electric motor, the aptly named clocks wound themselves, and in offices, factories, and homes were guaranteed to run for over one year without attention. At the World's Columbian Exposition of 1893 the company built an ornate, 150-foot clock tower demonstrating its wares, and boasted of regulating over two hundred smaller clocks from its central pavilion. A pamphlet accompanying the exhibit asked, "what is standard time?" The answer, written for the company by the naval officer in charge, was that standard time was the railroad meridian zones as measured by the Naval Observatory and registered on Self-Winding Clocks.[12]

"Standard time," in this sense, meant not "the railroad time zones" but rather Time itself. The establishment of a standard clock time, ticking away independently of local conditions, made standard clocks, rather than nature, the source of time—time becomes what the clock shows, instead of some abstract quantity the clock merely serves to represent. And as time became what the clock showed, the clock became the model for using time. The

Self-Winding Clock Company, and its imitators, largely perfected the time transmission networks envisioned by Langley and others, making standard time service cheap, automatic, and accessible. There was no denying the virtue and even necessity of accurate standard time in this age, wrote *Scientific American* of the Columbian Fair exhibit. But previously, "only the most prosperous jewelers" could afford time signals. Western Union's service, the magazine enthused, "places standard time within the reach of everybody."[13]

But what would everybody do with standard time once they had it? Would they become automated "self-winders," like the clocks themselves? Previous systems of time transmission had suffered from a number of technological shortcomings. Electrical contact points, for example, frequently corroded or simply wore out. As manufacturers solved these and other problems a wide variety of related electrical clock systems entered the marketplace. Although not all sold Naval Observatory standard time — Western Union enjoyed a monopoly in this respect — each offered to run all the clocks in any office, factory, or school on a uniform standard. And each company also took great pains to associate

Time itself with their clocks. Like the Self-Winding Clock Company's, these systems did more than place standard time within the reach of everybody; they placed everybody within the reach of standard time.

The Electric Signal Clock Company's 1891 catalogue, for example, lauded the virtues of synchronized program clocks—basically clock/timers set to ring bells or trigger machines at certain intervals. Clock-bound bell ringers like these still administer the daily schedule in high schools everywhere, and most of us probably take them as one of the "givens" of modern life. But in 1891 their novelty demanded explanation. "If there is one virtue that should be cultivated more than any other by him who would succeed in life," the catalogue preached, "it is punctuality: if there is one error to be avoided, it is being behind time." The company argued that its best model, appropriately named the Autocrat, "gives military precision, and teaches practicality, promptness and precision" wherever adopted. A school, office, or factory installing this system, the pamphlet went on, "is not at the caprice of a forgetful bell ringer, nor anyone's watch, as the office clock is now the standard time for the plant." In other words, human authority is replaced by the clock—or rather, human authority merges with the clock's.

The Autocrat, the brochure claimed, did more than simply standardize time; it extended the supervisor's disciplinary reach beyond his office and throughout the building. It "revolutionizes the stragglers and behind-time people," went the explanation, since "there is no appeal from these signals—they are the voice of the principal speaking through the standard clock in his office." Thanks to the Autocrat, the principal's authority fused with the clock's. And according to the pamphlet's idealized description, the automatic pattern of master clock/controlled clock—the kind of regularity and precision that the Autocrat exemplified—would reproduce itself in employer/employee relations.

"It [the clock] will call 'time,' " the brochure proclaimed, "on the teacher who rides hobbies in public school work, who devotes fifty minutes to teaching Geography and ten minutes to Arithmetic."[14] The clock imposed mental discipline and regularity on teachers who lacked such discipline and whose enthusiasm threatened to run wild. A competitor, the Blodgett Signal Clock Company, claimed that "order, promptness and regularity are cardinal principles to impress on the minds of young people," and that "no better illustration of these principles than this clock can be secured in a school."[15] These program clocks exemplified and reproduced the supervisor's ideals of punctuality and discipline.

Thanks to synchronized clocks, "school officials, superintendents and principals will have the satisfaction of knowing that whether they are in the school building or absent from it . . . their schools are running on exact time," one brochure claimed.[16] The program clock in effect allowed the supervisor to be in two places at once. A testimonial letter from the principal of a Massachusetts high school affirmed that "no assistant in the school is superior to [the Blodgett clock] in promptness and faithfulness . . . I have no hesitation," the letter continued, "in recommending them to any school officer who is searching for a valuable (I might almost say indispensable) assistant in the school."[17]

A strange identification between the clock and its users permeates these phrases. The principal or supervisor's function seems in large part a mechanical one—imposing strict time discipline on recalcitrant employees and students. But these clocks not only imitated the supervisor's internal virtues, his discipline, his punctuality; they augmented them. The clock's mechanisms, like a sort of mirror that improved what it reflected, taught lessons in self-discipline, self-regulation, and self-improvement. "By its promptness and precision," went the claim, the Autocrat "has an invigorating effect on all about the school."

Why the word "invigorating"? Was the clock invigorating

because it took over certain tedious and mechanical tasks, loosing the creative impulse? Or did it invigorate in the same way that fear of the boss's wrath, and unemployment, invigorates? In theory, the Autocrat freed school personnel from the necessity of disciplining themselves about time — "it will save the teachers nervous force," went the argument, since "it prevents the necessity of watching the clock and teaching at the same time."[18] But installing a program clock would only make employees and students truly "self-winding," screwed to a tighter, more controlled level of tension about keeping to schedule. The very perfection of these clocks, as George Beard had suggested, only increased anxiety. By locating time in mechanisms, they made time discipline automatic and external — they made machines rather than people the keepers of time. But that very use, in schools and factories, made machine precision, and machine discipline, the prototype and model employees were forced to emulate in their daily work. The machine patterns human behavior.

Consider, for example, this illustration from the 1908 Self-Winding Clock Company catalogue. What did the prospective client see when he looked at this ad? Each room, except for those lower rooms reserved for management, is identical, transparent. Each room is empty of people, which implies that no matter who uses the room, no matter what they bring to the building, they will have an identical experience inside. Any group of people walking into this building would assume the pattern of discipline and regularity sent out by the master clock. Management too — despite the fireplaces, the books, the swivel chairs — the boss runs by the clock as well, even if he does have the power to set its automated alarms. The public building becomes a machine for instilling the clock's virtues.[19]

If synchronized clock systems like the Autocrat offered a pattern for the relations between employer and employee, between principal, staff, and students, then the invention of factory punch

An example of master and slave, synchronized and programmed clock systems from the 1908 Catalogue of the Self-Winding Clock Company. (National Museum of American History, Smithsonian Institution.)

clocks—synchronized electric clocks with time-stamping mechanisms added—carried the tendency even further. Devices for recording laborers' time date back at least as far as Josiah Wedgwood's early factories, and the English inventor Charles Babbage designed a mechanical punch clock in 1844. The National Museum of American History has a mid-nineteenth-century weaver's lamp, a small, clear glass oil lamp marked with hourly gradations running from 8:00 a.m. to 6:00 p.m. As an inscription on the base proclaimed, the lamp provided "time and light" to laborers using it.[20]

But before the 1880s most factories simply stationed a man or woman at the entrance gate and logged a handwritten record of employees' names as they entered and left. The simple system worked reasonably well, but human timekeepers introduced a number of problems. They were slow—in larger firms anxious employees waited in line, losing wages, while the timekeeper ran down the list. They were inaccurate and subject to tampering— a timekeeper might forge the record to protect a tardy friend or penalize a punctual enemy. And the timekeeper's authority might easily be challenged by an employee whose watch showed a different time.

The first American patents on time-recording clocks followed shortly on the heels of standard time, from Willard Bundy, a New York jeweler, and Alexander Dey, a Scottish physician and mathematician. In about 1885, Bundy observed the clumsy methods then in use in local factories. Typically, each man or woman received a brass check with a number on it. On entry, he or she presented the check to a timekeeper, who then wrote the employee's number and the time in a log book. Bundy instead assigned each worker a brass key. Inserted in a special clock of Bundy's design, the key triggered a stamp that printed the number and time on a tape. Alexander Dey's system was basically similar, but his clock presented each employee with a large dial with numbers on it. The employee swung a pointer around to his or her number, then pushed a small rod, which printed time and number on a prepared sheet. Both men received patents in 1889 and went into business shortly after.[21]

Bundy boasted that under his system, "each employee is his own timekeeper," and that "favoritism and collusion are impossible." The clock's "infallible printed record" tended toward "encouraging promptness" while preserving the "order and discipline so necessary to the conduct of every well-regulated establishment." Bundy promised that his system benefited employees by protecting them from cheating, adding for the employer's benefit that the printed record of time surrendered itself only to those holding the special key that opened the clock.[22] By 1894 the first time card stamping system had appeared, and by 1907 nearly all the leading manufacturers in the industry had been bought up by the International Time Recording Company, later to be known as IBM.

The International Time Recording Company hit its stride in the second decade of the twentieth century. Its clocks, advertisements declared, allowed employers to record, organize, and control their own and their employees' use of time. "Evanescence," a 1916 catalogue proclaimed, "should be the watch word of every employer of labor." The company defined evanescence as "the state of being liable to vanish and escape possession," and its catalogue warned that "the avenues of 'escape' for valuable time are many." To those employers working against time's slippery escape the company stressed the accuracy, impartiality, and prestige of the printed record. "Should the fifty-hour week become a law," cautioned the company's New England sales manager in 1913, "you will doubtless require a more careful accounting of your labor costs than heretofore." With profit margins growing ever tighter, "minutes will count—a penciled record is not impressive, not sufficiently accurate." The company's clocks, on the other hand, would "save money, enforce discipline and add to the productive time." Even further, "the time recorder induces punctuality," a brochure proclaimed, "by impressing the value of time on each individual."[23]

In other words the company's clocks not only aided cost keeping, they improved the temporal morality of the plant as well. "There is nothing so fatal to the discipline of a plant nor so disastrous to its smooth and profitable working," went another pamphlet, "as to have a body of men irregular in appearance, who come late and go out at odd times." In a large factory the employees became faceless and indistinguishable—a typically double-edged aspect of industrialization. If the tardy colluded with human time-keepers, they might be able to escape between the cracks and go undetected. The time recorder helped management "to weed out these undesirables."[24]

One 1911 advertisement showed a line of thirteen men and women laborers approaching the time clock. Arrows reaching out from the clock pointed to four figures drawn in solid black. "Un-profitable employees," went the text, *"mean* to be on time . . . but experience shows that it is the same old story again and again with the tardy ones." Since "the habitual late-comers and early-leavers do not work so well" as the punctual, with the clock "you can sift out the efficient employees from the inefficient." You might never know which employees were inclined to be late and thus to work badly, the text implied, unless the clock revealed the internal flaw—the failure to internalize clock discipline—in each person's character.[25]

The mechanical timekeeper, again, forms the model or pattern for labor, the authority for conduct. The time clock pointed its bony hands at any employee who managed, thanks to collusion or sheer anonymity in numbers, to conceal his or her deviation from the standard. As another pamphlet boldly declared, an International Time Recording Company clock formed "the connecting link between employer and employee" where sheer size had severed it. The clock replaced the personal relations that regulated paternalistic factory management with electromechanical links.[26]

By 1910 that Holy Grail of factory management, efficiency, began appearing more frequently in company publications. A time system, clients learned, "affords an index to efficiency," unerringly flagging "efficiency failures" and "enabling the management to judge whether men and machinery are measuring up to the proper

Points out your Unprofitable Employes

Most employes *mean* to be on time.

If they come late one morning they *intend* being on time the next; but experience shows that it is the same old story over and over again with the tardy ones.

The *only way* to make employes appreciate the value of lost time is *to let them pay for it themselves*. With an

INTERNATIONAL TIME RECORDING SYSTEM

you can stop losses through late coming and early leaving—and you can do even more:

You can sift out the efficient employes from the inefficient, because late-coming and early-leaving are twin-brothers to inefficiency; the habitual late-comers and early-leavers do not work so well as those who come at the appointed hour and work until quitting time.

International Time Recording Systems are fairest to the employe because they make him his own time-keeper. He is protected against any injustice in figuring time. His record is always accessible for verification when he calls for it.

International Systems are preferred over all others at the ratio of nine to one—that is, 90% of all the time recorders now manufactured in this country are Internationals.

Tell us what your present time-keeping system is—we'll suggest a better one with International Time Recorders. Ask for literature. Our corps of time-keeping experts is at your service.

The two-colored ink ribbon device, by which the records of late arrivals are automatically printed in a different colored ink, has been held by the United States Court to be covered by our patents and therefore can only be furnished by this company.

The International Card Time Recorder   The International Dial Recorder
Punctuals in Blue—Lates and Irregulars in Red   Punctuals in Green—Lates and Irregulars in Red

INTERNATIONAL TIME RECORDING COMPANY
of New York

LONDON OFFICE	Lock Box 970	BERLIN OFFICE
International Time Recording Co.	**Endicott, N. Y.**	International Time Recording Co., m. b. H.
151 City Road, London, E. C., England		135-136 Alexandrinenstr, Berlin, S. W., Germany

Advertisement, from a magazine of factory management, for the International Time Recording Company (later IBM), 1911.

standards of efficiency." The Progressive era felt a near obsession with the subject of efficiency. As one historian of the period has written, "efficient and good came closer to meaning the same thing in these years than in any other period in American history."[27] "Efficiency" meant self-mastery, conservation of time, and the elimination of wasteful activities, but in its progressive crusade armor it described social activism and missionary zeal as well as energy, modernity, cleverness. And in the history of American industry no single figure better embodies both the fetish of efficiency and its relation to time, timekeepers, and their authority than Frederick W. Taylor.

The "father of scientific management" sought efficiency above all — maximum yield with least possible waste. He claimed to have found the key to eliminating human obduracy and laziness, the peculiar and troublesome quirks or corruptions that always resulted wherever men and women worked for others. Adopted by the public at large after the turn of the century, thanks in part to Taylor's ready self-promotion, the word "efficiency" concentrated the familiar American tight-fisted conservation of time into a social rallying cry, a call to arms for the well-meaning and the educated.[28] Scientific management, or "efficiency engineering," as the systems of Taylor and his peers came to be known, became a pet reform among crusading Progressives — a veritable "efficiency craze." Based supposedly in scientific principles, it seemed to many capable of rationalizing a vast array of social evils by eliminating all sorts of generalized "inefficiency."

Scientific management also sought to rearrange the relations between individuals and society. In an efficient world, each person would work to his or her full potential, instead of according to some slipshod amalgam of tradition, chance, and misguided personal preference. Forget following your father's trade; forget cooking dinner as your mother did. Instead of struggling along gamely at a job that didn't really suit, you the efficient employee would have been scientifically evaluated and put to a task perfectly fitted to your unique physical and mental attributes. If that meant rote work on an assembly line, so be it — "efficiency engineering," undertaken by trained experts, would rearrange the priorities that governed life and labor. In its most benign guise scientific management promised a utopia where all individuals worked at their individual best. A frankly machinelike process, it directed itself at perfecting each individual's functioning within the larger system. Scientific management reached its zenith under Louis Brandeis's aegis in the Eastern Rate Case, and perhaps reached its nadir a few years later in 1915, when reaction against Taylor's work at the Watertown, Massachusetts Arsenal resulted in a prohibition of stopwatch time study in government contracts.[29]

Taylor came from a well-to-do and genteel Philadelphia family. He inherited an active and productive temperament from his Quaker mother, heiress to the sort of tireless, unstinting industry Max Weber identified in Benjamin Franklin. According to Taylor's laudatory official biography, "work, and drill, and discipline" characterized life in her house. A fairly peculiar boy, plagued by nightmares and revolted by disorder, Taylor would transfer his mother's organizational energies to the realm of machine production. At age eighteen he began working at the nearby Midvale Steel Company, owned by family friends, as an apprentice pattern maker and later a machinist.[30] At Midvale Steel his obsession with rationalizing ordinary habits and motions focused on the problem of time.

Historians often approach Taylor as if he represented some sharp and peculiarly "modern" break with preindustrial thinking about the organization of labor time. But in fact American history offers numerous antecedents to Taylor's rationalizing thrust. Catherine Beecher's 1841 *Treatise on Domestic Economy*, for example, equaled or excelled any of Taylor's writings in its emphasis on the moral necessity of squeezing the utmost value from the time at hand. And Beecher's model kitchen certainly anticipated Taylor's concern with minimizing needless motions and unproductive distractions. Like Beecher, Taylor worked in a familiar vocabulary, drawn from schoolbooks and children's stories, that most middle-class Protestants memorized and recited as the catechism of success. There was nothing new about his determination to extract the maximum yield from a given effort; in this Taylor simply chose one particularly vivid color from the palette of American thought. Taylor became a true innovator only when he approached the standardized time of factory production with his stopwatch, and attached the gospel of efficiency to the idea of standard time.[31]

Taylor maintained that on most jobs only a blend of custom, inherited experience, and calculated resistance to working harder determined a worker's rate per piece. By analyzing the motions that went into any given task with a stopwatch, Taylor tried to find the minimum time in which the work might be done—to find an unvarying, uniform, and supremely efficient "standard time" for any job. Using stopwatches, Taylor timed the component movements of the job or set of jobs making up an industrial process. He separated "waste" motions—like scratching the head, hitching up the pants, or talking—from the movements he judged productive, and by combining these productive motions established the correct and scientific "standard time" for each worker's task.

Applying the same techniques to the factory as a whole, he reorganized the flow of information and materials, regulating all under the authority of a central planning office. Take, for example, the manufacture of machine parts. Taylor would begin by observing work processes—say, perhaps, unloading raw ore from freight cars. Did the workers make any "extra" motions? Did they stoop when they didn't have to? Were they using the right tools, at the proper speeds? Which were the actually *productive* motions, and which were simply bad habits?

After establishing a minimum time for each stage of the process from shoveling coal for fuel, to molding, to casting, to finish work on a lathe, Taylor and his disciples linked the component jobs together in a routing procedure regulated by a master clock in a central planning office. At the start and finish of each step in the production process, workers went to a secondary "slave" clock which stamped a card. The cards then went to the central planning office, where the "time clerk" checked them against the official standard. The planning office would ensure that each part of the process took precisely the correct time—fifteen minutes exactly for molding, ten for rough machining, and so on, till the piece had passed through the factory and was finished.[32]

Though the stopwatch, then and now, tends to symbolize Taylor and his work, in fact most of the supposedly "scientific" principles behind stopwatch study amounted to little more than guesswork, as angry laborers managed to point out. The genuine effectiveness of the Taylor system, in any factory or plant, depended at its core on a total managerial reorganization using synchronized master and slave clocks like those described above. Stopwatches might be used to determine the standard rate for the various jobs that went into making a part, but only the factorywide management system, directed by time clock from the planning office, ensured the efficiency and harmony of the whole operation.

Taylor was primarily a "system builder." His most lasting innovation was not stopwatch study but the reorganization of plant management. Though Taylor rarely mentioned it, the importance of time-recording systems to his entire process is unmistakable. By 1900 time-recording systems were undoubtedly simply taken for granted, and emphasizing their importance would have diminished Taylor's pretensions to innovation. But they were nevertheless essential to the process. In one of his first actions at the Watertown Arsenal, Taylor's assistant, Carl Barth, installed a new system of specialized time cards, time-stamping machines, and secondary clocks regulated electrically by a master clock in the planning room. In the ideal factory, Taylor insisted, each worker became "one of a train of gear wheels" regulated, like the plant itself, by the standard clock in the planning office and its "slave clocks" throughout the plant.[33]

Taylor's system evolved from the intellectual and technical innovations—like synchronized program clocks—that accompanied standard time zones. Taylor first conceived of time study either in 1881 or 1883–84, depending on either the definition of time study or Taylor's varied accounts.[34] The point is not the specific date but the fact that Taylor began his experiments precisely as the movement for national standard time peaked. Like the astronomers and scientists who advocated standard time, like William Allen and the railroad managers, or Bundy and Dey, inventors of the punch clock, Taylor hoped to crystallize "time" in mechanical timekeepers whose authority resisted dispute.

"Evanescence," the International Time Recording Company had suggested, should be the watchword in any modern business. Railroad standard zones ideally regularized time's flow, helping eliminate the local variations that had made time such a troublesome, "evanescent" industrial commodity. Using the standard time fixed in regulating master clocks, Taylor took that now uniform commodity and broke it into pieces. Taylor's stopwatch studies pinned evanescent time down for deliberate and close scrutiny.

It was the stopwatch, not the standard time clock, that came to stand for Taylorism and galvanize its enemies, and rightly so. Taylor's ideas came under close public scrutiny when his attempt to reorganize the government's Watertown, Massachusetts, Arsenal, which manufactured gun carriages and other weapon systems, ended in a strike and a congressional hearing. As historian

Daniel Rodgers pointed out, even a quick perusal of the testimony in the Watertown Arsenal hearings dramatizes the workers' intense hostility to stopwatch study. "I don't object to their finding out how long [a job] takes," testified machinist Orrin Cheney, "but I do object to their standing over me with a stop watch as if I was a race horse or an automobile." Another testified that he "did not believe in putting the stop watch on any man." Machinists and molders at Watertown repeatedly objected to having a man "stand over them with a stop watch."[35]

In the hands of a hostile observer, the stopwatch dramatized the worst aspects of mechanization in the factory. Even Watertown's most militant strikers assented with the principle of timing labor to determine a proper rate, and nearly all declared their allegiance to an honestly determined day's work. They were well accustomed to punching time clocks, and voiced no objection to them. Indeed, master and slave clocks with auxiliary time stamps had been installed at Watertown well before Taylor's arrival, with no complaint. What they resented most was the stopwatch's tendency to lend the phantasm of scientific impartiality to yet another form of sweated labor.[36]

Taylor knew the anger a stopwatch might provoke. He even acknowledged the "occasional" utility of hiding the stopwatch in the hollowed-out body of an ordinary book while timing went on.[37] The Watertown molders knew more than they cared to about stopwatch time study and were already grumbling about its use in other shops at the Arsenal. When the molders learned that one of Taylor's assistants planned on timing their work the next day, they secretly timed Taylor's timer with an ordinary pocketwatch. Taylor's man, using his stopwatch to time only the *productive* motions while ignoring "waste" motions, arrived at an ideal time of twenty-four minutes. Perkins, the molder, used an ordinary watch to time the entire job from start to finish. Making no attempt to separate "productive" from "unproductive" motions, he arrived at a total time of fifty minutes. The discrepancy in times outraged the molders: they struck the next day.[38] The resulting massive congressional inquiry into the utility of scientific management is their gift to history.

Both sides of the dispute rested their arguments on the watch's evidence. Taylor's man, the molders pointed out, lacked even the slightest experience with the molder's craft—he based his judgments of productive time on apparently arbitrary and mysterious criteria. The molders, on the other hand, derived their figure from the ordinary, common-sense time or duration of everyday experience. A man started at nine and finished at nine-fifty— what could be more straightforward? "Do you think you could get a practical record of how long it takes to do a piece of work," a Watertown machinist was asked, "without having a stopwatch?" "Yes," Olaf Nelson replied; "I think my watch will do, the one I carry in my pocket is close enough for all practical purposes." Nelson's ordinary watch measured the immutable flow of Time. But the stopwatch fractured Time to suit the boss's agenda. Under scientific management, as the molders' union representative put it, "the stopwatch is equivalent to a whip."[39] As a whip cut the air and the skin to discipline labor, Taylor's stopwatch cut and sliced Time itself to impose the machine logic of scientific management on human movements. With the stopwatch Taylor's assistant literally took time into his own hands, and wrenched it around and reordered it to fit Taylor's vision of time efficiently used.

Perkins's pocketwatch galvanized the opposition by giving the molders an alternative authority for time. The watch made them see Taylor's system, with considerable accuracy, as an elaborate deception. They acted to protect their control over the terms and pace of their labor, to preserve their authority as experts and masters of their craft. But they waged their battle over time and its definition. Whole time was their time, stopwatch time the re-structured time of machine-derived logic and the imperatives of efficiency. At the Arsenal, the pocketwatch became their best weapon.

At Watertown Arsenal the pocketwatch empowered the workers—it allowed them to counter Taylor in a rough semblance of his own language. But as E. P. Thompson pointed out in his exploration of time in industrializing England, their resistance also constituted an accommodation, a concession to the terms of the new factory system. Industrial capitalism triumphed, Thompson concluded, when workers accepted the clocklike regularity of the factory work day and began working to shorten it—when they "accepted the categories of their employers and learned to fight back within them."[40] In resisting Taylor's stopwatch, the Watertown strikers only affirmed the factory system and clock time.

There is no doubting either the triumph of the "second factory system" or the importance of Taylorite notions to its success. Nor is there much room for doubting that workers at all levels were drawn both willingly and unwillingly into its embrace. The Watertown Arsenal strike and the hearings it sparked brought the philosophy of the new factory system before the public for the first time. Taylor's ideas merited investigation because, as Congress correctly realized, the "management revolution" intimated a larger social and cultural reorganization of time and life patterned on clock efficiency. When schoolmasters installed synchronized clock systems, they reorganized education on machine models. When the acolytes of high culture demanded greater punctuality from their audiences, they sought to manage the audience's time more efficiently. To some, the emphasis on conserving time even seemed to be corroding the contemplative values of high culture itself. Henry Cabot Lodge, for example, deplored the quest for efficiency and greater speed for its pervasive effects on culture. "It has deteriorated style, it has deteriorated literature, it has deteriorated art," he complained on the House floor. "It is deteriorating manufacture."[41]

———

Late nineteenth-century Americans, like the Watertown strikers, witnessed a reformation in public time—a greater emphasis on accuracy, on punctuality; a greater level of anxiety about watching the clock. And along with this reformation came a veritable explosion of suddenly affordable timekeepers. Mass-produced in an enormous variety of sizes, colors, shapes, and grades, the promotion and design of these watches and clocks adds depth, nuance, and even contrast to Thompson's portrait of militant defeat. In their variety and diversity these mechanical timekeepers reflect vast differences in the understanding and apprehension of time. And in their popularity, their sheer abundance, clocks and watches, the roles they played and the literature they generated, contained one of the central problems of industrialization—what effect would mechanical inventions have on their inventors?

A Yankee mechanic and watchmaker, Aaron Dennison, founded the first American watch factory in 1850. Known early on by shaky finances and a succession of names, Dennison's Waltham Watch Company flourished during the Civil War. Waltham's remarkably inexpensive "William Ellery" model brought watches within the common soldier's reach for the first time, albeit at some sacrifice. Dubbed "the soldier's watch," the Ellery accounted for nearly half the company's sales by 1865.[42] Inspired by Waltham, a number of new companies entered the field, improving manufacturing techniques and driving down prices in the process. By 1876, American mass-production innovations allowed Waltham and Elgin, the two largest companies, to produce over 200,000 watches a year. The combination of high quality and low price

that Americans attained threw the Swiss, then the world leaders
in watchmaking, into despair. In 1876 a Waltham watch might
cost three times less than a Swiss watch of comparable grade,
while the quality of Waltham's workmanship, one Swiss reported,
was simply "incredible." "One would not find one such watch,"
a representative of the Swiss industry declared, "among fifty thousand of our manufacture." Prices declined as the century progressed. By the 1880s reasonably good American watches sold for
as little as three to five dollars, and in 1898 the Ingersoll Company
offered its popular dollar watch, dubbed "the watch that made
the dollar famous."[43]

As David Landes points out, American watchmakers led the
field not only in manufacturing but in advertising and promotion
as well. "The outpouring of timepieces," Landes writes, "was accompanied by a comparable flood of publicity." As early as 1859,
Waltham boasted with typical hyperbole that its watches rivaled
the sun's accuracy. The Elgin Company went Waltham one better—its official trademark showed Father Time in silhouette, abandoning his hourglass and rushing off with a new Elgin watch. In
Elgin's drawing Father Time looked like the venerable figure on
The Old Farmer's Almanac, but he raised a small cloud of dust as
he bustled about on his busy errands.[44]

The demand for watches mirrored the changes in public time
and timekeeping. Elgin's Father Time, like America, was making
progress, innovating, and speeding up the pace of his labor, and
American watches announced their owner's membership in the
fraternity of success and progress. In Horatio Alger stories, for
example, the hero nearly always gets a watch upon his entry into
the middle class. In Alger's stories, "the new watch marks the
hero's attainment of a most elevated status, and is a symbol of his
punctuality and respect for time . . . Alger makes much of the
scene in which his hero receives from his patron a gold pocket
watch, suitably engraved."[45] Alger's watches grant a degree of

power to their owners—in *Struggling Upward, Or Luke Larkin's Luck,* Luke's watch is like the lance, shield, and armor conferred on some medieval knight. It expresses his identity as a good servant of industry while helping him do his job.

Henry Ford, tinkering with his neighbor's watches in 1883, claimed later to have realized that a watch might be manufactured for as little as thirty cents. But he never followed up on that insight, assuming that "watches were not universal necessities, and therefore people generally would not buy them." As he freely admitted later, Ford was badly wrong. In an age of increased attention to time, watches helped their owners cope, like Alger's heroes or the Watertown strikers, with appointments and schedules. Americans were so anxious to own watches that poor but watch-hungry citizens formed "watch clubs," to which each member contributed a certain amount per week. At the end of a week the members drew straws, the winner using their collective funds to buy a prized timekeeper.[46]

Then even more than now, owning a watch made everyday tasks easier, since consistently accurate public clocks were still hard to find. Accuracy, not surprisingly, was the single most consistent theme in watch advertising. But the expanding watch market drew on more than the simple need to tell time. A watch made a definite statement about its owner's relation to society as a whole. In *Struggling Upward,* Alger reiterated the hierarchy of watch ownership: gold was better than silver, silver better than gold plate, gold plate better than base metal. Different grades of watch ideally marked a boy's progress through life. The watch in this case served as more than a simple timekeeper—it established the owner's identity, symbolized his or her social status.

Echoing the relationship between the school supervisor and the supervising clock, the most striking theme in watch advertising stressed the close and peculiar identification of the watch with its owner. American watch manufacturers early on directed a vast arsenal of psychological appeals toward this curious relationship between the two. The Waterbury Watch Company especially loosed a flood of pamphlets and booklets aimed at children, offering insipid adaptations of nursery rhymes and songs—"Little Miss Muffet, sat on a tuffet, winding her watch so merry," bleated one.[47] "Children," asked another, "did you ever see a Waterbury watch? In many respects it is like you." How, you might reasonably ask, is a child like a watch? "Its face is always bright and shining," answered Waterbury, and "its hands are never idle, except when run down, which is like going to sleep."[48]

The simple identification of biological mechanisms with machines was an old idea, dating back hundreds of years and still common in the 1880s. One 1887 ad for patent medicine, for example, compared "the human system" to "a kind of machine. If one part goes seriously out of order the whole goes wrong."[49] What Waterbury suggested was something more; its watches taught their owners lessons in social and personal regularity. "It is a good idea to wind [the watch] often," the ad cited above continued, "just as it is a good plan to wash your hands often." A Waterbury "teaches a useful lesson, by always being regular and trustworthy. It is never late, like some children are at school. It helps children to be punctual and prompt."[50]

The identification between the watch and its owner was more than just some advertising firm's clever idea. It repeated itself in the mechanical peculiarities and design of the watches themselves. Telling time with a nineteenth-century pocketwatch is a very different experience than simply glancing at your wrist. Nineteenth-century watches have a certain weight and size, a substantial heft. A heavy gold watch registered its value, and its owner's success in life, conspicuously, like a big belly or an extravagant meal. In its size and mass and in the showy gestures involved in taking it from the pocket, opening the case, and announcing the time, the watch pronounced its owner's status. And like gold or silver coin, a gold or silver watch transcended the fluctuations of an unstable economy by freezing transitory economic value into solid form. Tucked into the bulging vest of newspaper-cartoon capitalists, the gold watch helped symbolize the Gilded Age plutocrat. Ironically, like most watch owners, that plutocrat was literally chained, a kind of slave, to his watch. Yet ornaments worn on the watch chain — lodge emblems, cigar cutters, small golden tokens of achievement — testified to the owner's progress through life, and connected his progress to punctuality and respect for time.

But most commonly watches recalled the present, and the modern individual's need to synchronize him- or herself with the passage of public time. The mechanical design of watches in particular mirrored this association. Pocketwatches were originally wound with small keys. For example, the Phi Beta Kappa key, symbol of academic achievement, was originally modeled after a watch key. American companies pioneered in the mass production of stem winders, wound instead by a knob at the top of the watch. Their innovation entered the vernacular as a synonym for the new, the progressive, and the clever. The phrase, "He's a real stem-winder," described a young man on the rise. It also implied, like the watch itself which required no key, that the young man came out of the box prepared for industrial employment and ready for anyone's use. The stem winder reflected standardization of jobs and of employee behavior.[51]

Even more suggestive is the peculiar fact that spring-driven watches, if wound at precisely the same time every day, become more accurate. "The winding of a watch is a matter requiring special attention," one instructive text proclaimed in 1883. "Some special hour should be selected for it." "The man, woman, boy or girl who will not take the trouble to wind a watch regularly," the author concluded, "is an undeserving and unreliable person who cannot be depended upon, and is not worthy of the cheapest watch in existence." Winding the watch at the same time every day minimized variations in the mainspring's force and thus in rate. Books and articles on timekeeping mentioned this point frequently, most notably the United States Bureau of Standards, which by 1910 had become the sine qua non of things accurate. In 1914 the Bureau suggested that if a watch owner passed some source of standard time every day on his way to work, he should wind his watch by that clock at precisely the same time every day. Standard time regulates the man, and the man's regularity regulates the watch, which in turn regulates the man again.[52]

"A watch seems almost a part of a man," one 1887 advertisement claimed. "It is next to a living creature in its steady work and usefulness." Pocketwatches were probably the only example of a clearly industrial machine carried close to the body. Watches, one journalist claimed, were "the things most alive and human in the entire range of [man's] handiwork."[53] Waterbury published a monthly magazine extolling its products to jewelers and retailers. One 1888 illustration, titled "Evolution," depicted a short, round man who bought a watch "that so pleased him that he could not stop looking at it, and from constant attention he underwent the following series of changes." Six drawings followed; in each the man came to resemble the pocketwatch more and more—his head becoming the stem and knob that wound the watch, his body growing rounder. Finally the "Evolution" ended when the little man literally became the object of his fascination—a Waterbury "series E." stem winder.[54]

The implications of this advertisement seem more than a little unsettling—Waterbury's version of "Evolution" leads toward an inevitable fusion of man and machine. In fact for more tradition-minded Americans, this was precisely the problem with Darwin's theory. Understood through the "social Darwinism" of Herbert Spencer and William Graham Sumner, evolution seemed like a cold, heartless, mechanical process, a relentless industrial competition that crushed human values beneath it. As we will see in

1888 illustration from The Waterbury, *an advertising almanac published from about 1887 to 1895.*

the later chapters, efficient machines became analogous to the "survival of the fittest" in human society. Would men and women have to become like machines—amoral, running with mechanical regularity—in order to survive industrial society?

In antebellum America, time had been resolutely linked to social discipline and control. Politicians warned against idle hands, ministers urged their parishioners to "redeem the time," schoolbook homilies reminded children of the busy bee and industrious ant. But the crucial difference between the earlier period and the Gilded Age lay in the source of time. When time came from nature, men and women were part of that relationship—they lived *in* nature and *in* time, since the two were the same. Contemplating nature meant, in great part, contemplating the vast span of time nature encompassed, and men and women's place in it. In Waterbury's advertisement, contemplating the watch led to the same sort of merger. But in the late nineteenth century, merging identity with the watch seemed to mean absorption into the public system of industrial time discipline.

The ideal of a disciplined and regulated industrial work force, which runs throughout these advertisements, is simply inescapable. The cover of a similar pamphlet, published by Waterbury in 1887, depicted a board fence, plastered over with handbills bearing the names of several famous anarchists and some of their associated themes. "WORKINGMEN ATTENTION," the pamphlet declared. "In these times it is necessary to KEEP A WATCH on everybody." "Your time is at hand," it continued. "Eternal vigilance should be your watch-word. Keep a watch on everybody. On the statesmen. On the capitalists. On the clergy. On the Police. On yourselves." The pamphlet used the materials at hand in 1887—standardized public time, clock-time discipline in the factory, fear of hidden and overt class resentments—to make a joke out of the connection between mechanical *watches* and political, industrial, and social surveillance and control.

The illustration on the last page showed a solitary working-man, walking the city at night, being accosted from behind by a uniformed policeman with a lamp in hand. Behind them stands the same collage of anarchists' posters and slogans that made up the cover. The officer claps his hand on the workman's shoulder, but the man exclaims, "No need to keep a watch on me, Mr. Cop, for I already have the best watch in the world—THE WATERBURY."[55] The pamphlet blurred the distinction between owning a watch, watching, and being watched. There is no need to observe the watch owner, it asserted, because in buying the timekeeper he has announced his membership in the class that needs no watching—that group which is already safely under

Front cover, back cover, and last page of a pamphlet ad for the Waterbury Watch Company issued in 1887. (National Museum of American History, Smithsonian Institution.)

surveillance and control because it accepts the mechanical time-keeper's authority.

Some advertisements, like that cited above, betray considerable uneasiness about the close relations between machines and the self. One of Elgin's 1875 advertisements depicted two boys and their teacher in an old-fashioned schoolhouse. The first boy, captioned "Waiting to be adjusted," stands by as the second, labeled "Adjusted to position," receives an apparently well-deserved caning.[56] The phrase "Adjusted to position" described a watch that had been certified to run accurately in up to seven positions—upside down, face down, on various edges. True, this was obviously a joke. But all jokes must have some correspondence with everyday life. Elgin's joke, like the Waterbury pamphlet, equated the watch's role as a "regulating" device with punishing authority.

These ads promoted the internalization of machine time, advancing watches as models for behavior, a sort of mechanical prosthetic conscience. It might be suggested that identifying consumers with the products they buy is an old advertising trick, and indeed represents nothing either new or startling. But in 1890 the identification between consumer and goods was a new idea—watch advertising may even have pioneered in this approach. More importantly, there is something different about watches, because of their close connection to the idea of time.

Louis Mumford once claimed that "the clock, not the steam engine, is the key machine of the modern industrial age." Mumford referred to both clock technology's contribution to machine design, and the role of the clock in regulating factories and timing labor.[57] To Mumford's claim could be added the mechanical timekeeper's role as an expressly *political* device, as a model for both self-government and the regulation of social groups. Where natural examples had once provided both the evidence of time's passage and a guide for its use, now in the environment of American industry, machines modeled behavior and their presence assured order and self-government. In the wake of standard time, and the rise of synchronized time clock systems, watches became little personal primers, little examples of the nature of good conduct and the social mechanisms that enforced it. To "keep a watch" on employees, and separate deceptive, unreliable workers from more regular ones, employers began relying on punch clocks shortly after the invention of standard time. To attest to their membership in the reliable class, American consumers wore their vest-pocket watches close to the heart.

It might be a mistake to claim too much for these advertisements—the fact that one makes a joke of surveillance indicates that surveillance, perhaps, was less threatening than a gloomy historian might be tempted to make it. "Keeping a watch on everybody," after all, was what led the Watertown Arsenal's molders to their successful strike. In many cases watches were posed as a means of *gaining* control rather than *being* controlled. Watch manufacturers offered their wares as the only way of coping with industrial time's imperatives. "When you have no watch," Waterbury claimed, "then time becomes aggressive and the moments gain the upper hand." Waterbury's products helped stave off such deplorable lapses in "your frantic daily struggles with time." One 1889 Waterbury promotion, for example, showed a woman and her son asleep and dreaming in different rooms. The boy dreams of "a watch as good as Papa's," the mother of "a lady's watch that will really keep time."[58] The illustration connected time and watches to power, especially adult male power. Owning a watch, the ad implied, made both woman and child more like a man, more like those in power.

Early in 1888 Waterbury revised the familiar tale, quoted from *McGuffey's Readers* early in this chapter, of the clock and the sundial. In Waterbury's version the boastful clock and the modest dial still show different times, but now neither prevails. Rewritten, Waterbury's moral advised: "Carry a Waterbury watch, which is

never wrong, and be independent of either dial or town clock."
The advertisement promised to give the Waterbury owner autonomy and personal authority over the time. In a busy world, Elgin
warned in 1909, "time may be gained by the miracles of rail and
wire, only to be lost by the inaccuracy of a watch." Hand in hand
with modern time savers—"the limited, the telegraph and the
telephone"—went the modern timekeeper, the Elgin watch. An
Elgin synchronized its owner with the confusing, interrelated
world of rapid communication and travel.[59]

The demand for watches brought prices steadily downward
after the Civil War. By the 1880s, cheaper pocketwatches were
regularly given away with suits of clothing, or awarded for selling
magazine subscriptions. Newspapers abounded with such pro-
motions. An 1883 issue of the *Cleveland Gazette*, for example, offered
"this handsome stem-winding Waterbury watch and fifty dollars
cash!" to "anyone who will sell fifty copies of The Life and Times
of Frederick Douglass."[60] But the most intensive sales of watches
took place in the mail-order catalogues that sprang up in the 1880s.
Sears, Roebuck began in 1886, when Richard Sears, an enterprising railroad station agent in rural Minnesota, wound up with
an unwanted shipment of pocketwatches. Sears sold the watches,
at slightly above cost, to other agents along the line, who in turn
sold them locally for significantly less than a jeweler's markup.
He soon began turning this profitable trick on a regular basis, and
later that year quit the railroad to form the R. W. Sears Watch
Company. Within a year he was writing advertising copy for the
burgeoning business.[61]

Like his main competitor, Montgomery Ward and Company,
Sears aimed mostly at the rural market. Ward's identified itself
as "the original Grange supply house," while Sears claimed to
democratize watch ownership. "The boys, the girls, the rich, and
the poor," Sears promised, "can all carry watches at the prices
we ask." Both emphasized their opposition to the middleman and

the parasitic trusts that leached extra profit from the isolated farmer. In one of its several incarnations, Sears advertised frequently in the Populist's weekly *National Economist.*[62] In 1897 Sears prefaced thirty-nine pages of catalogue watch ads with a warning about the local jeweler. "Step into his store at any time of year," the catalogue jeered, "and you will find him gossiping with a neighbor merchant, reading the newspaper, or both he and his clerks are cleaning up and polishing some of the old shop-worn goods . . . trying to make them look like new."[63] Sears depicted the merchant as an idler and a fraud. Producing nothing, he tries to put a shiny face on his own sloth. Even more significantly, Sears attacked the merchant's temporal world—"Step into his store," went the warning, "at any time of year"—the jeweler's trade was unaffected by the seasonal cycles of natural time.

The sheer abundance of watches in mail-order catalogues argues for the importance of time telling among rural Americans. And indeed this should come as no surprise, given the near obsession with time measurement routinely displayed in that most stereotypically rural document, *The Farmer's Almanac.* But the fact that farmers wanted watches does not necessarily indicate an endorsement of industrial time. Chapter Three discussed rural opposition to standard time, and hinted at the connection between the cyclical time of nature and Populist rhetoric about the moral virtue of agriculture. The design and marketing of these watches suggests continued rural hostility and resistance to standard time and the understanding of time it represented.

Early on, Sears realized the importance of showing the merchandise, and copious illustrations marked his catalogues. His 1889 catalogue, eighty pages long, devoted seventy-three pages to men's and women's watches and watch chains. In Sears's day most better pocketwatches were sold as "movements" alone—the basic mechanical works with a dial and hands. After choosing a movement, buyers then picked out a case from a wide variety of sizes, materials, and styles. The vast array of case styles parading across the catalogue pages of Sears and Montgomery Ward overwhelmingly connected time to rural life. Of the 228 cases illustrated in both catalogues in 1895 and 1897, the majority depicted some rustic bucolic scene—a rural village, a country church, a farmhouse; a horse, a hunting dog, flowers and leaves, or a pair of birds on a fence. Only six depicted an even vaguely urban or industrial scene, and all six were of locomotives. True, the engravings often had a "machined" appearance, and combined leaves and flowers with "engine turned" patterns. But the preference for familiar rural archetypes and symbols is unmistakable.[64]

The most popular style by far, the "hunting case," had a hinged cover over the dial, engraved on both front and back. To look at the time, the owner had to take out the watch, turn it face up, and open the cover. At first glance he or she saw a reassuring symbol of rural values, a representation of country life. The owner might use the watch to cook a meal, or to catch a train, but no matter what time the dial showed, the engraving on the case amounted to a ritual identification of time with nature. These case designs linked commercial or industrial time, in the form of the watch, to its natural origins. They reflected a basic ambivalence about time's new origins in machines.

Lavish decoration also made these watches like jewelry, like ornaments rather than essentially utilitarian machines. Why, after all, would a farmer living away from markets or towns even need a watch? These watches were less timekeepers than declarations of self. They linked their owners not to the specific work they did—there are no depictions of haying, for example—but to an idealized vision of the world they lived in. For women this was especially true. Women's watches had always tended to be smaller and more highly ornamented, more decorative than functional. Montgomery Ward sold the "Lady Grange" model, for example, with "a beautiful solid gold Victoria chain, and a handsome oak case, silver trimmed, with lock and key." More jewelry than time-keeper, watches like this made clock time into a luxury, a bauble adorning the successful farm wife.[65] "Lady Grange" may have been at least partly identified by her ownership of the watch, but the watch signifies her status more than her work—such a watch probably went along to social occasions or shopping trips rather than timing supper in the kitchen. It symbolized not work, but status enough for leisure.

Ward's advertisement—and indeed the rise of mail-order consumer goods in general—brings us to the subject of time in the home, and the difference, if any, between men's and women's experience of time. In many ways men's and women's understanding and interpretation of time seems nearly identical. Historians of American women have noticed the overwhelming concern with time saving and efficiency that runs throughout the historical literature of domestic feminism, especially the importance of spatial reorganization in housework. Women involved in American utopian and communitarian movements, like the Shakers or the Oneida collective, systematically rearranged domestic work spaces to make household labor both easier and more productive. Catherine Beecher's immensely popular books on domestic economy elevated this spatial rationalization and temporal efficiency to a creed. Like the communitarian feminists who preceded her, and like her advice-giving peers, Beecher shared the general American preoccupation with saving time. Throughout her career she reiterated the fundamental morality of tireless labor at home. "We have no right," she insisted, "to waste a single hour."[66] In this sense, the strong emphasis on saving and conserving time, women's experience of time at home probably differed little if at all from men's.

Almost without exception, nineteenth- and twentieth-century manuals of home management and housekeeping rang with disdain for idleness and waste. Open a book of advice for housekeepers from any period of American history and it will forthrightly advise you to develop a system, organize your labors, and make better and more efficient use of your time. It would be foolish to argue that these books' promptings describe the reality of time usage in the home. Most women probably balanced such exhortations against the fatigue and boredom of housework and took their rest where they could find it.

But recent histories of housework and the extent of women's labor at home have concluded that such rest was hard to come by.[67] Some have suggested that technological innovations for the home—refrigerators, iron stoves, vacuum cleaners, for example—rarely decreased women's work. Instead, such devices often either concentrated previously shared "work processes" into less work for some but "more work for mother," or raised the level of expectations and thus the work required to meet them.

Take, for example, the vacuum cleaner. After the new machine, the job of cleaning rugs, once limited to beating the carpet outside once or twice a year with help from other family members, became a weekly and even daily task done by women alone. Where a broom might once have sufficed, or husband and children helped to move furniture, roll up the rugs, and carry them outside, now the housewife vacuumed alone, and more often, to keep her rugs up to the new standard of cleanliness.[68] The significant fact is not the amount of work a given woman may have done, but rather that, under the prevailing middle-class ideology of time usage, *work expanded to fill the time available.* Ever higher standards and expectations demanded investing ever more time in pursuing the ideal, so that the vacuum cleaner's boasted savings in time seems suspect at best.

While acknowledging the sheer mass of the work involved in housekeeping, most historians of the subject have seen the home, with some justification, as free from the sort of clock timing that came to rule industrial labor. Indeed, the most articulate and influential spokesperson of "woman's sphere"—Catherine Beecher—worked hard to ground her provisos about time usage in Protestant theology and natural law rather than in clock chimes or market imperatives. She never added clocks to her home designs, insisting instead that the natural hours of the sun should govern time and life. In the ideology of "separate spheres" that Beecher helped to formulate, the home posed as a refuge from the hectoring press of industrial competition and clock time. Housework is even more resistant than factory labor to the timing, regularity, and repetition scientific managers loved.[69]

But the clocks that increasingly governed the industrial work place began moving further into the home as the century progressed. Even Beecher, in 1869, admitted that "a clock is a very important article in the kitchen." "Clocks are so cheap now," one domestic encyclopedia advised in 1873, "that their usefulness and companionableness should secure them a place in every room in the house." "The kitchen must have a clock," another concluded, "for on it a great deal of the comfort, and some of the good temper, of the family will depend."[70] Illustrations for the Kitchen Garden Association, a national organization dedicated to teaching the principles of housework to four- and five-year-olds, showed children laboring busily under the clock in 1883.[71] Near the turn of the century, recipe books began listing precise cooking times for various foods, in minutes, instead of estimating the time or judging doneness by color or texture. As one home economist put it in 1908, not just any clock but "a clock that is an accurate time-keeper" seemed "a necessity in the kitchen."[72]

By the 1890s the impulse to rationalize labor, save time, and conserve effort had coalesced into a formal educational curriculum, home economics. The house of home economics, built on efficiency, modernity, and scientific observation, threw its doors open to Taylorite principles, and by 1910 the first time studies of household tasks had begun. Christine Frederick, and later Lillian Gilbreth, among others, made their livelihood dispensing ostensibly scientific counsel to the overworked and "ignorant" mother. Frederick, Gilbreth, and their colleagues attempted, with mixed success, to make the home a place of industrial efficiency. As one scientific home manager pointed out in 1917, the modern husband's life "is systematized." "He arranges his time so that he arrives at his office or place of work at a stated hour, faithfully performs the allotted task . . . and at a stated time, returns to his home when his day is done." What would happen, the writer asked hypothetically, "if this standard of daily habit were not required of everyone connected with it?" Home life, she concluded, must follow the same regular, clock-disciplined pattern.[73]

If the ideal twentieth-century home reproduced the clocklike regularity of the factory and the commercial world, then was there no difference between public and private time? Certainly the imperative to save time recurs consistently throughout the written sources on housework. But the home sheltered other ideas besides work for work's sake. Beecher's ideal domestic refuge was moral both in its temporal organization and in its *furnishings;* her model housewife labored joyfully to create a wholesome home environment, not just a well-run kitchen. But industrialization made whole realms of mass-produced goods—clothing and textiles, fancy furniture, chromolithographs, phonographs, pianos, kitchen appliances—available to the middle class for the first time. If these products had little effect on the amount of time devoted to housework, they most certainly affected both the ways that time was spent and the experience and meaning of private time itself.

The spate of household consumer goods made the home a place of self-expression for middle-class families, and especially for women. Domestic advice manuals of the late nineteenth century groaned with advice to women on managing the new abundance: what to buy, where to put it, how to arrange it, how to cultivate your own taste and culture while evaluating others. Mrs.

Henry Ward Beecher (Eunice White Bullard), wife of the famous minister and sister-in-law of Catherine Beecher, published her own household guides in 1873 and 1883. Just as her husband, Henry Ward Beecher, adulterated the strength of his forebears' work ethic in his writings and sermons,[74] so Mrs. Beecher joined her sister-in-law Catherine's industry to the special problems of consumption and taste. "Money," she advised women, "can always buy a housekeeper," or the consumer goods to fill a house. "*Love* only can secure a *home-maker* . . . unite the housekeeper and homemaker—let them be one and indivisible," she urged, "and that union will provide a refuge from all outside trouble."[75] Mrs. Beecher urged that industrial commodities for the home be invested with that most "female" of qualities, love. In the abundant material culture of industrial capitalism, women's nurturing role increasingly combined with a newfound calling as tastemaker. The physical surroundings came to reflect the woman's temperament and character—as one wealthy arbiter of taste, Elsie De Wolf, declared years later, "it is the personality of the mistress that the house expresses."[76]

For women, the traditional emphasis on conserving time in the home, familiar from generations of domestic guidebooks, blended into the new ideas of "efficiency" as embodied in home economics curricula. At the same time efficiency, in the consumer marketplace, became a manifestation of the modern "personality," of the trendy modern individual's search for uniqueness. If clocks in the home paired efficiency, on the one hand, with scientific regulation, they also linked "efficiency" to a sense of modernity, novelty, and individualism—to the up-to-date personality.[77]

Paradoxically, in the home the energy unleashed by the doctrine of efficiency forced middle-class women into creating an illusion of leisure. In the ideology of separate spheres, the home stood as a place of rest for men and nurture for children. The clutter of detail in the Victorian house was supposed to embody

cultivated taste and deliberation, gentility and ease, moral uplift
and peace. A man coming home from a long day would find its
aesthetic effect a soothing balm to his wounded nerves. But maintaining this illusion took time; it took energy, effort, and organization. Creating and bolstering the illusion of leisure brought
women both more work and a fiercer commitment to the principles
of machine efficiency that governed factories and schools. After
about 1880 one of the foundations of the appearance of leisure,
ironically, was the clock.

In the context of the cult of taste and refinement, clocks in
the home became yet another mode of personal expression, an
aspect of personality in consumption. "It is no longer possible,
even to people of only faintly aesthetic tastes," wrote De Wolf in
1913, "to buy . . . a clock merely that it should tell time." De
Wolf, who admitted to keeping a clock in every room, devoted
five pages to selecting the proper clocks in her book.[78] Clocks
designed for home use reflected the trend toward personal expression through furnishings. Factory time clocks, even at the height
of Victorian ornamental excess, remained remarkably frank and
straightforward in appearance. Though ornamented, the decorations never detracted from the clock's timekeeping function. A
simple rectangular design, severe and imposing, marked most factory or school clocks, reinforcing the seriousness of their role as
regulators. There was, to put it mildly, little room for whimsy in
the industrial work place. But in the home, whimsy ran amuck—
clocks seemed to fasten themselves like barnacles to the most
unlikely places.

The marketplace for clocks offered a bewildering variety of
odd or even bizarre styles: clocks in painted swells of porcelain
sea foam, or perched on the shoulders of bronze Cupids; clocks
in the shape of brushes, sleighs, baseballs, apples, or doghouses.
In the trade catalogues of the late nineteenth and early twentieth
century, cast figures of the Bard of Avon or Voltaire leaned

thoughtfully on elaborately scrolled clock/cushions, and clocks placed improbably in the trunks of plaster trees supported little girls on swings. The riot of detail and adornment in so many designs often rendered the clock itself almost invisible—clockfaces in the center of hanging platters struggled pathetically for light amidst a gaudy profusion of scrolls and flourishes. Over nine hundred such clocks, for example, vied for attention in the Ansonia Clock Company's 1904–05 catalogue.[79]

These clocks, like the mail-order watches described above, made time into an expression of self or an ornament to the private realm. If the world outside answered to synchronized regulating clocks, standard public time, and train schedules, then time in the home, private time, posed as its opposite. Standard time, by 1900, was de facto law in most urban places—unauthorized by statute but honored almost unthinkingly in practice. It set a fixed and dependable standard for the conduct of business and industry. In public life and in the factory, for most men and women, clocks and watches epitomized the need to fit oneself into the orderly and regular system of this standardized time. But at home, time-keepers recalled artistic taste, individual expression, "personality," and even playfulness, just like any other home furnishing. And for rural Americans, at least as their taste is revealed by Sears catalogues, timekeepers paid homage to the idealized natural world. The point is not that clock and watch decoration differed from common decorative motifs, but rather that it did not—clocks and watches became ornamental expressions of individuality rather than grim tools of industry. One would no longer think of buying a clock simply to tell time, Elsie De Wolf insisted in 1913, any more than one would "buy chairs merely to sit on." In the home, clocks epitomized a whole range of alternatives to the necessarily restrictive time of public life.[80]

Although watches were traditionally associated with regulation in public life and work, the connection between timekeeping machines and individual personality began infusing watch advertising as well, co-existing with the earlier themes of control and regulation. "A watch," one typical 1916 advertisement insisted, "is a part of you, like your eyes and hands. It moves and throbs with you, goes with you everywhere, lives as you live—as long as you live." The identification of watches with their owners, familiar from the nineteenth century, continued here. But even after death, the advertisement continued, when the heirloom watch passes to your children, "you live again in their lives." In this theme the watch both embodied and transmitted its owner's beliefs, values, and achievements. "A man and his Elgin," the text enthused. "What pride of possession, what comradeship the words express!" As "comrade," the Elgin began acquiring a personality of its own while embodying or carrying on that of its owner.[81]

Watches continued to be offered as empowering devices, though now in more dramatic terms. In one curious Hamilton offering, a huge, vaporous hand reached out to clutch an anxious-looking, well-dressed man. "Too Late!" the caption warned. "There are certain types of men who haven't much respect for time . . . men of little character, idlers and dreamers, rather pride themselves on their contempt for Time. Sooner or later, that ghostly, implacable hand reaches out and turns them back." "When you come to think of it," claimed the text, "there's something awe-inspiring in having in your vest pocket a mechanism so delicate, so fine, so perfect, that it actually knows and measures Time—the power above the stars!"[82] Hamilton's advertisement, however preposterously, implied that good watches helped their owners to actually control Time. It also pointed, more reasonably, to a Hamilton's capacity to distinguish its owner from other personalities—especially idlers and dreamers. Hamilton sold the watch as a way to get some logic, order, and apparent control over temporal chaos while declaring your personal feelings about the seriousness of time.

In this ad, the watch enacts a paradox: it simultaneously makes its owner both more and less an "individual," both more unique and less so. The watch is a possession that singles the owner out as special, and the watch is also a possession that assures that the owner can't be singled out. Standard time established a uniform framework for conducting public life, using timekeeping machines as a model. Earlier watch and clock advertising, following the framework of standard time, had stressed a close identification, a merger, between time-telling machines and their owners. This merger cost the watch owner—like the little man who turned into his watch—a kind of individuality. But it also provided a margin of safety and a sense of belonging for the worker who "needed no watching because he already owned a watch." Watch and clock advertising from the early twentieth century stressed the watch's power to secure the owner's place in the framework of standard public time, and thus his or her virtue. But it also invested this place in the machinery of standard time with the trappings of individuality and distinction.[83]

In the process of identifying and empowering their owners, watches soon began either to confer personality or to acquire specific personalities of their own. "Out from the lee of the dreadnaught darts the destroyer; gaunt, fearless—all a-quiver with pulsing speed," an Elgin ad breathlessly narrated. "On board these eager hounds of the sea, guiding their every move, invariable under storm, stress or shock, you will find . . ." not venerable sea captain nor brave first mate but "an Elgin watch" at the helm, controlling course and speed. Elgin took the regulating function of ordinary watches and dressed it up in the sailor's rugged wool coat. It promised that Elgin watches would make their owners captains of their fate rather than mere cargo.[84]

"Is your watch a gay deceiver?" asked one 1916 advertisement for Hamilton watches. "Are you part of that inaccurate watch market?" In the illustration, a bespectacled solid citizen looks at

Hamilton Watch Company ad, 1916.

his watch. The watch's face bears human features, and it smiles and winks at its owner, as if tempting him to a night of roistering or a moral debauch. "The only market for such watches," the conclusion argued decisively, is with those "lacking in orderliness of mind." The personality of such watches played games with time—in the illustration the minute hand wavers back and forth, making the time uncertain. Hamilton's ad linked inaccurate watches to sensual tempters, men and women of bad character, while a Hamilton's accuracy and sobriety distinguished its morally upright owner from "the thousands of Americans who year after year carry a deceptive, unreliable watch."[85]

The personification of timepieces reached its absurd height in advertisements for the "Big Ben" alarm clock. There was nothing at all special about the clock itself, which was simply a good, reliable alarm. But in a major campaign begun in 1910, Westclox, the manufacturer, distinguished itself from competitors by giving the clock itself personality. "Be at your desk when the bunch flies in—begin your day with a flying start," exhorted a typical example, brisk with the rhetoric of business enthusiasm. "It's sure to get around to the old man's ears—'Five minutes early, sometimes ten, it raises salaries' says Big Ben." Big Ben, the ad went on, "is a punctual, handsome and long lived sleepmeter. He tells you just how late it's safe for you to sleep. He tells you just when you ought to start down town."[86]

Any alarm clock might tell you that, but Big Ben possessed that magic twentieth-century ingredient, personality. Nineteenth-century watches shored up or reinforced a shaky character, but the Big Ben alarm clock was a character unto itself—it worked equally well regardless of its owner's burden of laziness or sloth. Big Ben even had a son, Baby Ben, "a bright-faced little chap who tells really truly time and will wake you promptly at any time you say." Baby Ben was designed not for children, as you might expect, but for adults—Ben Jr. was a traveling alarm clock, and

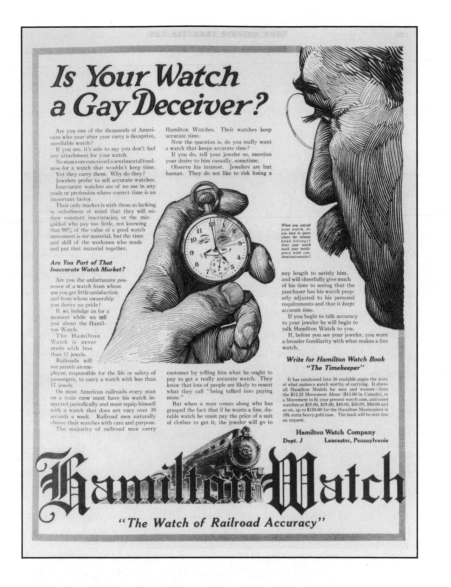

Hamilton watch ad, 1916. Here the watch is clearly developing a character or personality of its own — bad watches tempt to indiscretion, good watches keep their owners running with "railroad accuracy."

his childish prattle seemed appropriate speech for an infant timekeeper.[87]

In Westclox's ads the product, the timekeeper, literally assumed a life external to the person using it. If the old relationship between the timekeeper and its owner was that of a mirror, Big Ben and his tiny spawn acquired efficient, cheerful, independent personalities of their own. Through sheer force of personality they persuaded rather than compelled, like good, efficient salesmen. Waking up to Big Ben was like being awakened by a friend, a useful friend with a brisk, efficient, modern personality.

These last examples extend the tension between individuals and machines apparent in earlier ads. On the one hand, by making watches and clocks servants of human personality, an expression of self, they empower their owners and grant them a certain freedom. With a Big Ben alarm or Hamilton watch, *you* didn't *have* to be punctual—the timekeepers assumed the burden of punctuality for you. But on the other hand, by granting watches a separate, external identity, making them, literally, sentient beings with character and personality, these ads strengthened the mechanical timekeeper's autonomy and power. In a sense, they give the machine life. In the ads cited earlier, the watch and its owner merged. Their relation of mutual dependence and shared characteristics—regularity, punctuality—encouraged a fusion of identity. But in these last few examples the watch and its owner split away from each other—the watch and clock become separate from their owner and more independent.

The progression described here, from clocks that merge with their owners to clocks that express their owners' individuality, and finally to clocks having personalities of their own, parallels the evolving role of time in daily life. In the 1880s, the date of the earliest ads, accurate, standardized public time was still a highly uncertain quality. Standard time zones had just been introduced, and were strongly resisted in many areas. These early ads suggest an urgent need to integrate oneself into a system of public order whose most obvious symbol was the watch. Other examples, like the illustrations in the Sears catalogue, suggest a pointed hostility to clock time and its implications. These last examples reflect the partial hegemony of standardized public time, and the simultaneous development of a private, personal time unhedged by schedules, timetables, and machines. In sum, these ads suggest that Americans granted the authority for time to mechanical clocks, gaining in return a limited range of genuine psychic freedom. In the next decade, the tension between gaining control over time and surrendering control to time would repeat itself in that most uniquely modern art form, the motion picture.

V

Therbligs and Hieroglyphs

Standard time helped establish new ways of organizing life. Telegraphed time signals, automated signaling systems, synchronized "master and slave" clocks—all these offered new templates for governing work, leisure, and education. These new systems were linked with the problems of self-discipline and social surveillance in an industrial society—in essence, with defining the self in relation to others. While supposedly decreasing anxiety and confusion over time, by making time measurement automatic, standardized time and the innovations it inspired only increased the pressure to fit in with the new framework of clock-based organization. None of these changes went unopposed. Workers resisted Taylor's dismemberment of time; farmers resolutely identified their timepieces with rural life; women turned utilitarian timekeepers into aspects of self-expression. Americans engaged in an ongoing and contentious dialogue about time and its meaning.

From the last decades of the nineteenth century to the first decades of the twentieth, the fascinating history of the American movie offers one example of how this dialogue might be resolved. Motion pictures, following the pattern established by standardized time, offered new models for organizing not just work and life but thought. By World War I, movie makers had learned that by manipulating time on screen they could manipulate the imagination. And the structure of this "movie time" duplicated the themes, concerns, and methods of Progressive politics. The history of movies dramatizes standardized time's profound effects on American culture, politics, and thought.

Peering back into the origins of the motion picture, historians usually turn up the eccentric figure of the English-born photographer/artist Eadweard Muybridge. In the 1870s Muybridge was making photographic records of California for the U.S. Coast Survey, where he met Leland Stanford, the railroad baron and sometime horse fancier. Stanford had just bought a fast thoroughbred, Occident, and he wanted an answer to an old artist's question: When a horse gallops, do all four hooves ever leave the ground at the same time? They seem to, but horses weigh a lot, and they looked silly painted floating in midair. Stanford had supposedly bet a friend that all four feet did leave the ground, and he hired Muybridge to settle the question.

The photographer placed a series of cameras a few feet apart in a row. As Occident galloped down the line, a trip wire triggered each camera in sequence. When he developed the sequence later, Muybridge saw that Stanford had won his bet. In several pictures the weighty horse floated serenely and convincingly in midair, all four hooves off the ground. With Stanford's funds, Muybridge began a series of similar experiments on animals and people. In

1881 he published the results, *The Attitudes of Animals in Motion*, as a tool for artists who struggled with the representation of movement.

Muybridge's novel technique fixed the horse's gallop in fragments of time, images no artist had ever seen before. The unprecedented pictures, each a frozen instant, allowed a careful analysis of the individual components of motion—movements too fast for the eye to follow, like a horse's flashing hooves, could be subject to careful, objective scrutiny. Within a few years he had developed the "zoopraxiscope," a machine for projecting a series of his photographs in rapid sequence. Muybridge's zoopraxiscope, the forerunner of the motion picture projector, reconstituted the dry photographic elements of a horse's gallop in the quicksilver of light. Now a celebrity, Muybridge traveled first to Paris, where he observed the closely related work of physiologist Etienne Jules Marey, and then to Philadelphia, where he began new studies of human figures with the painter Thomas Eakins in 1883.[1]

In 1883, Philadelphian Frederick Taylor was pondering the relation between time and efficiency, trying to find a "standard time" for any job. Autumn of 1883 saw much discussion of time in the city's newspapers. The railroad standard time zones, a new and novel proposition, promised to link individuals and regions under a single, unified clock time. It would eliminate the multiplicity of customs, traditions, and improvisations that governed time. The goal of standardization linked Muybridge and Taylor as well. Taylor began his time study techniques at Philadelphia's Midvale Steel just as Muybridge began his Philadelphia experiments, and it seems very likely Taylor must have known about Muybridge's work. After all, the two men shared certain approaches to the problems of their respective disciplines. Just as Taylor sought a "scientific basis" for quantifying and regulating labor and human movements, so Muybridge hoped, with Eakins, to find a "scientific basis" for objectively analyzing objects and movements in time and space.

Standardized public time offered Taylor, Eakins, and Muybridge an intellectual precedent that suited each's exacting bent. It fixed and objectified time—a traditionally illusory quality—into a reliable, quantifiable, unvarying form. Like time in Taylor's stopwatch studies, motion and light might now be frozen, analyzed, and reassembled in Muybridge's photographs, then subjected to rational analysis in discrete, controlled instants. Taylor and his disciples used watches and clocks as a means of breaking down specific jobs into their component parts, then reassembling them in a more productive order. With Muybridge's photographs, a worker's motions might be taken apart for study; so also an athlete's stride might be analyzed piece by piece. The worker might learn a more "efficient" way of working, the athlete gain a better appreciation of his or her technique, and the artist a finer sense of the qualities of movement.

In terms of their use of time the two fields—art and factory management—pursued similar agendas. Muybridge and Taylor never collaborated in any way. But in the urban America of 1883 they shared a cultural, social, and intellectual milieu that was remaking time. It had taken decades to relocate time from nature to mechanical clocks, and decades more to develop a technology that made clock time practical and useful for governing everyday life on a busy continent. And now Muybridge and Taylor were attacking the standard time of everyday events, dissecting it, finding ways to make it more useful.

Muybridge's work, like Taylor's, represented a new consciousness of time—on one hand of time's diminished stature, its arbitrariness, and on the other of its susceptibility to human control. In this sense, Muybridge's photographs and Taylor's practice of scientific management welled from the same source. Art historians have charted the connection between Muybridge and the evolution of cultural "modernism," especially the Cubists' destruction of space and form. Similarly, the connection between Muybridge's work and the development of motion pictures has also been well established. Historians have paid far less attention to the extraordinary connections between standardized time, scientific management, and the later evolution of motion pictures.[2]

Between 1890 and 1920, American movie makers evolved a new form for presenting ideas. They learned to cut up and recombine time after movie cameras recorded it, to impose narrative structure on the "real" time of ordinary or staged events. Analytical control over "real" time created a new medium of communication with extraordinary power—even created, perhaps, a new way of thinking about communication and politics.

From the beginning, motion pictures and the ideal of efficiency kept close company. The American movie industry began with Thomas Edison's 1891 Kinetoscope, a simple box equipped with viewing slot, lamp, shutter, and a short loop of film moving along rollers. Edison saw his invention as an educational tool and an aid to business, a way to demonstrate machinery or sell products. In a competing device, the "Mutascope," viewers watched a sequential series of cards, arranged somewhat like a modern Rolodex file, flip past the viewing window and give the illusion of motion. The Mutascope's backers also imagined their apparatus as a way of showing machine operations to factory owners and employees. But as aids to efficiency, both devices failed.[3]

More imaginative entrepreneurs instead set up "Kinetoscope parlors," urban storefronts offering long rows of the clattering movie machines to a working-class, largely immigrant audience. Most popular in the mid-1890s, Kinetoscope films typically presented brief, documentary snippets of ordinary events—trains coming and going, street traffic, notable incidents of local news or sporting events. Other loops of film offered short vignettes with a mildly salacious or anti-authoritarian cast—kissing, exotic dancing, skirts blown up by wind. Edison began producing films as soon as their entertainment value became apparent. Most of his early output consisted of excerpts from vaudeville and novelty acts. Largely unburdened by plot, Kinetoscope films depended chiefly on novelty and the appeal of the taboo. Like the modern-day "peep show," which they resembled closely in form if not content, Kinetoscope parlors suffered from a mildly unsavory reputation among the genteel. By the late 1890s, their popularity had begun to decline.[4]

After effective film projectors appeared around 1896, the movies revived. For a time motion pictures appeared between acts in vaudeville houses. But by 1900, movies began running independently, in more or less formal theaters or simply in curtained-off sections of larger rooms. These "nickelodeons" gained movies a larger working-class audience. For a nickel, customers saw a program of very short films run continuously. Over half these early nickelodeon shorts came from Catholic Europe, and few showed any special regard for the "Gospel of Success" and the moral values of the native Protestant middle class—"more often themes ridiculed Victorian values." Early American film entrepreneurs also showed a strain of native, small-town morality— deeply suspicious of new wealth, industrial capitalism, and urban excess. But their productions tended toward documentary footage of current events, satires on familiar public figures, or short, simple stories, often laced with slapstick attacks on authority.[5]

Except in cases of documentary, these films usually mimicked the vaudeville audiences' point of view both visually and thematically. They simply presented a filmed record of what the audience saw live, through a single, fixed camera. Within a few years, however, movie entrepreneurs learned to play a few tricks with the camera and projector, speeding up or slowing down the action or reversing the film, producing novel effects that only made the films more appealing to what remained a largely working-class crowd.[6]

The movies' growing popularity, coupled with their vaguely shady character, soon drew the gimlet eye of the middle class. After about 1905, when the phenomenon grew too popular to ignore, middle-class magazines and newspapers "discovered" the motion picture. They began describing the phenomenon regularly, trying to puzzle out its unique and vivid effects. What was going on in those dark rooms? Intrigued and concerned, *The Nation* went into picture houses for the first time, and came out calling the movies "the first democratic art," reverberating "with the very ideas of the crowd in the streets."[7] What made movies so appealing?

Movies cost very little, and they presented no language barriers to their immigrant audience. Both factors undoubtedly helped draw the crowds. But as early as 1908, observers had pointed to the motion picture's power to compress and expand everyday time. Following the lead of the French magician–film maker Georges Méliès, early directors learned how to speed up, slow down, reverse, double-expose, and otherwise manipulate camera and film to produce apparently magical effects. Projectionists too felt free to crank the films at whatever speed they wished, or reverse direction, when the audience got a little bored. In the movies, marveled *The Independent,* "the building of a skyscraper within a few minutes is a feat easily accomplished." "Time exposure pictures" of a local theater under demolition made it possible "to throw on screen a perfect reproduction of the work. The theater could be demolished within five minutes, and by reversing the films rebuilt within the same period."[8]

Pondering the temporal distortions the movies introduced,

Harper's Weekly called the motion picture houses of 1907 "get-thrills-quick theaters." In the "cops and robbers" genre, claimed an account of "nickel madness," "the speed with which pursuer and pursued run is marvelous . . . a hunted man travels the first hundred yards in less than six seconds," while "a stout officer covers the distance in eight." The earliest films violated the expected, common-sense time span and course of ordinary events with startling effect. Movies altered both the speed and the *direction* of ordinary occurrences — apples fell up, people walked backward, flowers grew from nothing in seconds, shattered rubble leaped up and formed itself into buildings. In the movies, one fan hymned, "all miracles are possible, even that most dramatic of miracles, the reversal of the course of life."[9]

The flexibility of motion picture time paralleled film's spatial plasticity. Even in "documentary" films, which shunned the temporal sensationalism of Méliès-type productions, the ordinary boundaries of time and space shattered. In 1909, the *Survey* glowingly described how film brought disparate places and times into immediate and vivid contact. "On an island 2,000 miles out in the Pacific Ocean" the commentary began, "the exiled lepers of Molokai gather daily before the flickering wonders of a screen that shows them the world of life and freedom. Seated in the luxurious saloon of an ocean liner, a group of travelers study the life-like pictures of the places for which they are bound," while "in Iceland, excited Eskimos applaud the heroism of a cowboy who rescues a captive maiden from the redskins." Movies made far-off places familiar. "I enjoy these shows," one patron confessed, "for they continually introduce me to new places and new people. If I ever go to Berlin or Paris I will know what the places look like."[10]

Movies denied the apparent concreteness and stability, the common-sense fixity, of ordinary time and space in daily life. "We have had many . . . inventions to overcome us in recent years," wrote a critic of the cinema: "the telegraph, the telephone, the wireless, the bicycle, the automobile." Each of these inventions helped overcome the limits of space and time, "but none," he concluded, "is more miraculous in essence or has spread over the world so instantaneously as the moving pictures." Movies disturbed the ordinary, standard time of everyday experience. The phenomenon drove this critic to rhetorical heights of exaggeration; since the movies, he insisted, "events have been taught to record themselves, so that Time seems to merge into Eternity. Yesterday is abolished!"[11]

His frustrated charge reflected the peculiar way temporal certainties appeared to dissolve in the projector's light. The first objection, that "events have been taught to record themselves," referred to both the extraordinary realism of the movies and the mechanical nature of movie making. The novel vividness of movie images gave them the aura of truth. Any movie camera set up, turned on, and left running recorded the events before it with apparently objective, unvarnished realism. Even more, the events were largely self-evident—no one needed to describe them, to say what was happening, when and why. Without such a filter of journalistic interpretation, the events simply "recorded themselves." In Kinetoscope parlors, working-class customers had watched nearly plot-free depictions of ordinary scenes—"spectators were quite content with views of factory employees going to and coming from their work, the arrival and departure of railway trains, the passing of street parades, and similar scenes."[12] Simply "events" presenting themselves, these early films eliminated the interpretive distance normally imposed between events and a mass audience; no cultural or political authority explained the events' meaning. The stay-at-home movie fan quoted above could see what Berlin looked like without anyone telling him what he was supposed to be seeing.

The odd claim that "Time seems to merge into Eternity" referred in part to the novel special effects the movies introduced, like the speeded-up policeman or the building that reassembled itself. Such effects rent the fabric of ordinary time, making illogical or impossible events seem real and vivid. Time, space, ordinary physical reality gleefully disintegrated in the hands of a master illusionist like Méliès, whose films reached a wide American audience. *The Clockmaker's Dream,* a typical Méliès short of 1903, began with an old clockmaker falling asleep in his chair. As he slept, the three ornate clocks in his shop turned into fashionably dressed women. When a giant pendulum appeared, the women used it to form a human clock as their formal dress grew more casual. Finally the shop dissolved into a pastoral tableau and the women's clothes into loose, diaphanous robes. Inspired by their beauty, the clockmaker stood to kiss one of the women, who promptly dissolved back into a clock at his touch. The clockmaker woke to find all as it had been. Méliès played sly games with the fixity and seriousness of clocks, and clock time, in everyday life.[13]

Time also seemed to "merge into Eternity" through the missing narrative voice—the interpreter who could say with certainty what the events were, when they happened, and what they meant. An early slapstick comedy, for example, might depict a little boy kicking a policeman from behind several times. Audiences neither expected nor received any information about why the boy kicked the cop, or about what bad results came of kicking cops. Humor, and interest, came simply from the boy's impudence and the officer's frustrated reactions. While it would be wrong to claim such a film had no ideological content, or even no narrative structure, its primary appeal is a simple delight at seeing authority flaunted. With no plot and little story, these short films largely ignored temporal sequence—the normal links between past, present, and future that the middle class at least depended on to make judgments.[14]

Lacking such a logical sequence in time, middle-class critics charged, movies denied history, denied morality, denied even the possibility of rational thought. The motion picture, *Harper's Weekly* complained, "makes no demand whatever on its audiences, requiring neither punctuality—for it has no beginning—nor patience—for it has no end—nor attention—for it has no sequence."[15] Historic time, meaning the relationship between what has been and what will result from it, seemed to disappear; hence the claim that in the movies, "Yesterday is abolished!"

Film historians once regarded the first decades of the twentieth century as a fairly sterile period. An emphasis on simply grinding out novel footage supposedly reduced the movies to formulaic, uninspiring banalities, with "none of the intellectual excitement and creative ferment which we might expect to find at the birth of an art form." This approach wrongly judges early films only in relation to what followed. More recently, film historians have reevaluated the aesthetic and political content of these first efforts.[16] In later years Dada and Surrealist artists would find in Méliès and the early silent film makers an inspirational model for absurdist attacks on bourgeois "reality." Though they certainly lacked the complexity and highly developed narrative structure of later productions, in the sense of the "timelessness" they fostered, the first generation of silent films marked a profound challenge to middle-class values about time and time usage.

"Timelessness" on the movie screen fostered a sense of "timelessness" in the real world of the theater seats. When motion pictures moved into theaters, they kept their working-class patrons and subject matter drawn from public life in urban industry. The films' brevity and unstructured narrative helped make filmgoing a social experience very much like the convivial world of vaudeville and burlesque—many of the earliest films were again simply records of notable vaudeville acts. With no dialogue to miss, silent movie audiences talked, sang, and laughed along with gusto. "Certain movie houses," commented the *Survey* in 1909, "have become genuine social centers where neighborhood groups may be found any day of the week; where the 'regulars' stroll up and down the aisles between acts and visit friends." While suspending the common-sense time of ordinary events, the working-class movie theater also ignored middle-class norms for behavior in leisure time.[17]

Simple plots contributed to an easygoing, informal attitude about time and time usage. The concept of the feature film, a longer "main attraction" surrounded by lesser entertainments, was yet to come. Early movie audiences dropped in on and left the short films at their convenience, without fear of detention by a long, slow-moving directorial opus. "Stay as Long as You Like," one Massachusetts theater reassured patrons in 1906. In the audience and on screen, ordinary time dissolved. Movie theaters at once disdained the clock-scheduled time of work life, the temporal sequence of narrative, and the inexorable flow of Time itself. In 1912 the Mutual Company, a major film producer, plastered New York with billboards and posters bearing its proud slogan: "Mutual Movies Make Time Fly."[18] Time flew on the screen, where ordinary time melted away, and in the audience, where moviegoers came and went as they pleased.

In terms of time, the closest modern analogue to the early movie houses might be the pornographic movie theater. Pornographic movies rarely depict complex plots, and they run continuously, in near-total indifference to structured time. People come and go as they like. The comparison stigmatizes the early movies unfairly, but at the same time it approaches the way in which the early silent films threatened middle-class values, especially concerning time and its productive use. The early movies offered an alternative to the public, standard time of efficiency and factory production—their temporal plasticity both denied and undermined the version of standard time and clock discipline constructed by industrialization over the preceding thirty years.

It was precisely this difference between time at the movies

and the mechanistic, regular standard time of everyday life that gave movies their special appeal, claimed *Scientific American* in 1915. An article on "Motion Picture Magic" began by describing how "many a railroad man learns to dispense with an alarm clock. If his call is for four thirty in the morning, he will wake with a start at four o'clock." The reference to railroad men and alarm clocks established the mechanical character of the modern "time sense." "Plenty of people," the writer went on, "railroad men in the lead—can tell the hour to within a few minutes any time of day without reference to a watch." These men had internalized clock time, and it now structured their lives automatically.

Yet certain things, the article went on, could disrupt this routinized work clock—unusual events, emergencies, or mind-altering drugs like opium or hasheesh. Such things stimulated and sensitized the awareness of time, which life's ordinary routine dulled. "Opium and hasheesh fiends live days, weeks and months of experience," the article claimed, "in a few hours." But while drugs liberated the "time sense," unfortunately "such drugs affect the body in the exact opposite from the way they trick the brain." Drugs freed the mind but paralyzed the body. The motion picture, on the other hand, "does for us what no other thing can do save a drug . . . it takes normal intervals of time and expands them one, two or a thousand fold, or compresses them by the same ratio." Enchanted by movie time, "we leave the theater with wonder in our hearts and admiration on our lips." The article praised films' ability to liberate the mind from its routinized time sense, to break down the standard time of everyday life and restore "the magic of our childhood," lost, presumably, when we joined the work force.[19]

By drawing the distinction between harmful drugs and healthful movies, *Scientific American* hoped to point out that movies soothed clock-tired minds and aided productivity. If the movies refreshed tired laborers by suspending ordinary time, perhaps that only made them all the more energetic for the next day's work. True, the comparison of movies to drugs betrays some uneasiness about the cinema's effect. But the assurance that movies left the body unharmed makes the movies seem benign, therapeutic; a "safe" form of leisure.

Extending the movies' tentative relationship to industrial productivity, cinema partisans frequently promoted movies as the natural alternative to the saloon. Saloons gave the workingman some much-needed recreation, but at what terrible cost! Soaked in gin, the drunken laborer lost all sense of time and responsibility. But the motion picture, *Scientific American* claimed, offered the same mental recreation without the physically damaging, family-sundering effects of demon rum and the immoral pub.

But the very "timelessness" of the whole movie experience subverted the middle-class version of time and ordinary reality. Middle-class ideology imposed an apparently logical temporal order on life: work hard, don't waste time, be patient, punctual, obedient, and prompt, and you will succeed in due time. Or, conversely, waste time; be lazy, impulsive, and disrespectful of authority, and you will fail. This may be true, or it may not, but early cinema registered a simple and maddening indifference to this temporal structure. As *Harper's Weekly* suggested earlier, an audience of largely working-class immigrants fascinated by time-less movies, unimpressed by the virtue of punctuality, unhampered by sequence, and indifferent to patience, outraged native middle-class values.

Middle-class critics looked at movie audiences and saw instead of a vibrant neighborhood crowd a somnolent, unthinking mass, hypnotized by the flashing light. "Rarely does such an audience betray animation, scarcely ever awareness . . . its dull eyes unresponsively meeting the shadowy grimaces on the flickering film," worried *Harper's*. Theater critic Walter Eaton charged that "motion picture audiences sit hour after hour without smiling, without weeping, without applauding. They sit in solemn silence in a dim dark room." Like *Scientific American,* these critics also saw movie time as druglike, trance-inducing, but without the positive therapeutic effects. *Harper's* especially viewed the movies of 1913 as a drain on both the minds of its audience and the productive resources of the nation. "You wonder how it can be possible, in an alleged busy world . . . to assemble daily, for long blank periods, so many people who have nothing to do and who are obviously not worrying about it."[20]

Just three years earlier, *Harper's Weekly* had described movie audiences' boisterousness and loud interaction with the screen. What accounted for the difference? It might have been only a reflection of the writer's hostility to the movies—he may have seen only what he wanted to see. But audience behavior may in fact have changed drastically by then, thanks to the rapid rise of the narrative "feature" film, and its connection to time discipline and social efficiency.

The noisy debates about moviegoing that filled magazines after 1910 dwelt almost obsessively on productivity and social efficiency—what good, if any, did movies do? In that timeless movie sleep, progressive reformers worried, what dreams did come? Were movies simply a harmless waste of time? Or did their unique temporal and spatial plasticity lend immorality a special allure? What happened when the lights went out and ordinary time was suspended? Did tired workers get some much-needed relief from strain, or simply mire themselves deeper in bovine thoughtlessness? The cinema's growing general audience only increased reformer's concerns. What messages were the movies conveying?

The answer, it seemed, was that the fluidity of time and space in silent films wore away at the temporal foundations of morality.

The early photoplays appeared to lack even the barest skeleton of plot, and their notorious indifference to moralizing conclusions denied "normal" standards of cause and effect—laziness, bad behavior, or gross criminality often went unpunished on screen. Middle-class reformers began working early on to introduce some sense of cause and effect, some temporal rigor, to the silent shorts. Outright censorship offered the most direct form of control over the silent evil.

Movie censors paid special attention to making celluloid crimes connect to their (bad) outcomes. The National Board of Censorship, organized in 1908 to oversee film content, proclaimed that since in real life, as everyone knew, "punishment naturally and fatally follows crime," so it must in the movie house. If the Board had its way, the hypothetical cop-kicker in the imaginary short film described before would now be caught, and hauled tearful and repentant before the local magistrate. By connecting movie crimes to the consequences reformers thought they should have—by showing, literally, that "crime (or laziness, or disrespect) doesn't pay"—movie censors hoped to impose their own version of narrative moral logic on movie time.[21]

Evolutions in cinema style made their task easier. By the second decade of American movie making, the simple novelty of seeing ordinary scenes, or the same scenes at different speeds, had largely worn off. Jaded audiences soon demanded more than simple depictions or manipulations of the ordinary, or rehashes of familiar plots, while reformers began insisting on causative moral sequence. Film makers began finding ways to tell more complex stories. To do this, they had to find new modes for representing narrative.

Edwin S. Porter's 1903 *Life of an American Fireman*, often described as the first American attempt at "story" film, depicted the rescue of a woman and child from a burning building. To modern eyes, Porter's intriguing film handled time and narrative awkwardly. It began with firemen hearing an alarm, assembling quickly, and then racing off and arriving at a burning building. The scene then dissolved to the interior of the building and the mother's room. Mother and daughter pace frantically in thickening smoke, finally fainting onto the bed. A fireman then appears by knocking down the door. After breaking out the window and calling for a ladder, he carries first mother and then child out the window and down, off camera, to safety. Finally the view dissolves to the exterior of the building, and audiences this time saw the whole sequence—the fireman entering the building, calling out the window for the ladder, then carrying first mother and then child down the ladder—again from outside the building.[22]

Looking at Porter's film today is startling; it approaches narrative in ways that hardly make sense to us. Film historians call Porter's narrative technique "temporal overlap." Instead of cross-cutting rapidly between simultaneous scenes, as a modern director would—juxtaposing, for example, the woman in the burning building, the firemen rushing off, smoke pouring from the building's windows, the rescue from inside and out—Porter kept the various scenes of action separate from each other. The key sequences maintained their integrity, their "real" temporal continuity, and the audience viewed them through a single, mostly unmoving camera. Porter in effect had to show the rescue twice, once from each perspective. Film makers had not yet learned how to compose what we take for granted—a focused, omniscient narrative that could combine separate points of view easily. Porter's immensely popular film represented a different way of seeing the world.[23]

Making "modern" films—movies that tell stories in the ways we expect—required new ways of organizing and representing reality *and time*. Porter used "temporal overlap" to show events that occurred simultaneously in different places. He kept them separate, each on its own "local time." A modern director would instead show simultaneity by cutting rapidly between the two scenes of action, ignoring each scene's "local time." In a modern film the "standard time" of the narrative, like the standard time zones that overcame local differences, joins the separate spaces of real experience together. As standard time zones linked distant communities under one time, film makers began learning to knit distinct realms of action together in the fabric of narrative time.

A 1908 film by D. W. Griffith, *The Fatal Hour*, played on this theme. The improbable story concerned a young woman captured, bound, and set before a pistol rigged to a clock. When the clock's hands reach noon, the pistol will fire and kill the woman unless her rescuers arrive in time. Griffith cut back and forth between the woman, the clock, and the rescue party, uniting separate realms of action in one standard time—that shown on the clock-face. Or so it seemed: in fact Griffith accelerated time to increase the feeling of suspense, simply moving the clock's hands forward between shots. An early, limited example of modern editing, the movie used control over time in the film-making process to rein-force the idea of a "standard time" governing and uniting simul-taneous events. Control over time, through narrative, valorizes the clock's power.[24]

By 1910, thanks to innovators like Griffith, pressure from middle-class reformers, and the reorganization of film production, many of the narrative techniques we take for granted—cross-cutting, multiple camera angles, close-ups—had come into limited general use. "The motion picture," one admirer realized seven years after Porter's film, "has it in its power to show us what is going on simultaneously in two different places, inside and outside a house for example, or in two adjoining rooms."[25] Film makers quickly learned that compressing or expanding the time of events allowed them to put more complicated plots on celluloid. The new sophistication in handling movie time encouraged the rise, after about 1912, of "feature films"—multiple-reel productions up to several hours long, often with stories lifted from the canon of literature.

Adapting novels and classic stage plays for the silver screen "legitimized" the motion picture; as one magazine put it, after 1912, "college professors didn't have to apologize for going to the 'movies.' "[26] Theater owners turned increasingly to such films, which drew a middle-class audience willing to pay extra for longer, more "serious" productions. The rise of feature films changed both narrative style and the nature of moviegoing. "Features" typically presented far more complicated plots, with dramatic shifts in time, place, and point of view. Missing the beginning of a feature film condemned the tardy viewer to befuddlement. The more complicated stories demanded close attention, discouraging latecomers from leaning over their neighbors for a summary. Using literary plots "uplifted" motion picture content, making middle-class behavioral norms seem more appropriate. As notions of punctuality and decorum adopted from the "legitimate" theater crashed the gates of movie houses, the whole experience became less sociable, more sedate, and more structured in time. If the working-class moviegoer of 1910 came and went at will, chatting with neighbors, his or her middle-class cousin made sure to be on time for the feature film of 1915, and waited silently for the start, clucking at others for their lack of decorum.

As time and space on the screen became more fluid, more flexible, more amenable to directorial control, time in the motion picture theater grew more fixed, more regular, and more defined. In the era of the short one-reelers, motion picture theaters, if they advertised at all, usually listed only their hours of operation— "films shown continuously, noon to 11." By 1915, major "features" were being listed like theatrical productions, with specific starting times.[27] Feature films introduced a paradox central to the experience of the motion pictures: they subjected leisure time to the same standards of punctuality and decorum that ruled work. By putting their audiences on a stricter, less variable schedule, these films imposed punctuality and clock time in the process of freeing the imagination from it. In the hands of a skilled director, cinematic time—the temporal structure of the images on the screen—obliterated the ordinary, inflexible, rigid clock time of everyday experience, substituting the giddy freedom of shifting scene for the clock's unvarying tick. But to experience that freedom, audiences had to show up on time.

Juxtaposing the two experiences of time defused some of the movies' subversive aspect. Showing feature films at scheduled times was like turning a chaotic, lush woodland into a formal park; it replaced apparent disorder with thematic, formal organization, and created a structure or form capable of bearing more complex ideological messages. The experience of movie time, like the experience of nature in the park, became both more intense, more freeing, and at the same time more discrete, safer, further separated from public life and ordinary reality. Feature films concentrated recreation.

And their ability to hold an immigrant audience, to fix their attention on the screen while distilling complicated plots silently, offered reformers special advantages. "The very people who most need instruction," claimed an article on how motion pictures might "Make Good Citizens," "are the ones who patronize the cheap theaters." "This immense audience is more easily reached through the motion picture than by any other medium," argued the Progressive journal *American City,* and the impression movies make "is often deeper than those of editorials or sermons." Reformers quickly realized that moviegoers, especially after the rise of the feature film, were literally a captive audience—simultaneously passive, receptive, and contained. One movie censor reminded his readers of the restless, energetic young people who filled modern cities. Before the movies, he claimed, "thousands of them were on the streets in small groups, searching for friendship, excitement, and mates. Many of the social and moral barriers are let down." But thanks to the cinema, "these young people, nightly, now find their way to the 'movie,' and are at least held under the spell of something more impersonal than each other."[28] Under the spell of movie time, audiences learned the value of punctuality and public decorum. Even the "greenest" immigrant would soon learn to arrive promptly at eight for a promising new "feature," and sit quietly in appreciation.

Feature films separated time more clearly into past, present, and future. They embedded an action in its context, making it easier to trace the chain of events from a given deed to its inevitable results. The multiple lines of action woven into a bad decision could all be portrayed, and each thread followed in time and space as the fabric of crime unraveled. Reformers consistently maintained that only a morally uplifting finale safeguarded public welfare. The National Board of Censorship issued a detailed set of guidelines for movie makers in 1914, again reiterating its particular vision of cause and effect. In all pictures in which "questionable scenes" occur, the guidelines demanded "that the main argument and effect of the picture shall be for good. To this end the censor should see to it that the evil characters in the picture come to harm as a direct result of their evildoing." Regarding drug use, crime, scanty clothing, smoking by women, irreligious speculation, drinking, and drunkenness as social evils, the Board insisted that movies must depict, and depict convincingly, the process of decline that each began.[29] A bad ending to bad business restored the middle-class version of cause and effect in time.

Guidelines like these make cinematic time an instrument of political power—establishing a chain of causation leading from crime to punishment, from drug use to addiction, from scanty clothing to prostitution, makes movie time a disciplinary tool. It imposes a specific temporal structure disguised as real life. Take, for example, the idea that work leads to success. Movies built around this theme would show the process whereby hard work is recognized and rewarded as time passes. An alternative narrative might depict hard work leading to growing exhaustion and finally physical and mental breakdown. In both narratives, a particular idea of work bridges time, spanning the gap between point A—the time when work began—and point B—work's end result. Both tie time's passage to a larger message—on the one hand that work is bad, on the other that work is good. Either alternative subverts someone's idea of the truth, but each one attaches its ideas to and depends on a narrative structure. A more truly subversive film, like the early shorts that working-class audiences watched, almost ignores narrative altogether. Such a film simply depicts work, without an "arrow of time" pointing toward any outcome. By providing movies with the arrows of time necessary to forming political opinions, narrative films restocked the reformer's quiver.

But claiming that narrative served only one point of view would gravely distort the history of American film. The evolution of narrative was neither as smooth nor as uniformly useful for do-gooders as this abbreviated chronology suggests. For one thing, many filmgoers resisted the feature film's dominance into the twenties. As late as 1917, one producer insisted that "the movie fan must be able to drop into a show at any time and get a complete piece. He must not feel that he has to appear at 7 p.m. and stick it out until 9 p.m. to get something. He must be able to drop into two or three shows of an evening and get a complete story at each." Movie theaters were still offering "continuous showings" into the 1920s.[30] And of course even the most articulate, carefully structured film might fall helplessly before its audience's creative interpretation. Simply by dramatizing crime and the exotic, movies made criminals and exoticism glamorous and attractive. But film historians recognize that by 1915 a standard narrative vocabulary had developed, a "classical Hollywood style" that would characterize American film at least until the advent of the talkies.[31]

The rise of feature films suggests both how changing ideas of time derived from industry worked their way into popular entertainment and leisure, and how these new ideas of time served different ideological and class agendas. The short films of the early period, their brevity and lack of plot, made time discipline irrelevant. Narrative movies broke time up and then reassembled it, so it could bear the weight of political persuasion. They embodied complete control over time, yet by putting their audiences on a more fixed schedule, narrative films reintegrated movies into the framework of standard time. In reforming time, narrative films became the entering wedge of Progressive reform—even dreary subjects like hygiene and cleanliness could be dressed up in a romantic plot with general appeal. The story of a young wife, torn from her husband in the prime of life by drinking tainted milk, united the before with what followed it, and theoretically dramatized the need to clean up conditions at the local dairy farm.[32] Film narrative lent even the most mundane political agendas new vigor.

Superficially, movie narrative may seem no different from narrative in novels or plays. Shakespeare's mastery of time, after all, is often cited as one of the hallmarks of his work, and novelists compress and expand time routinely. There are definite similarities. But on a mechanical level, books can never shift from one scene of action to another as fluidly as movies. Imagine a chase scene. No writer could alternate between pursued and pursuer as quickly as a film does; the results on paper would be jumbled and hard to follow.

Even more, cinematic narrative marked a departure in the understanding of time and its relation to reality. A writer cuts up imaginary time in retelling a story that exists only in the imagination. Even if the story a playwright tells actually happened, those events have passed, and the form the author discovers them in bears only a symbolic relationship to the actual duration of the events when they occurred. Two thousand words may express virtually any span of time. But 2,000 frames of film at normal speed equals just over one minute of lived experience—literally, feet per second. To make a narrative, the movie editor cuts up segments of real time on film—mechanically, physically—and then reassembles these segments with a new duration.

With their mechanical control over time, the movies represented a new kind of temporal logic, which by reordering the standard time of everyday life seemed to some even capable of reordering ordinary thought. "These motion pictures are more degrading than the dime novel," insisted *Good Housekeeping*, "because they represent real flesh and blood forms, and impart their lesson directly from the senses. The dime novel cannot lead the boy farther than his limited imagination will allow him to go, but the motion pictures . . . give him first hand experience."[33] Though by our standards these jerky, flickering, silent images hardly seem realistic, early audiences marveled at their realism—when celluloid trains rushed headlong toward the screen, audiences shrank back in fear. *Lippincott's* called the movies "a panorama which is true to life in every detail, because it is reproduced from that wonderful artificial eye, the camera lens. So we know we are seeing actual occurrences—at least, we think we are—and they are so realistic we may laugh or cry or watch the screen with every thought centered on it, as we would read an absorbing novel."[34]

The analogy of film to book acknowledges the growing narrative similarity between the two forms. But at the same time it also points to significant differences. The film is read like a book; it absorbs in the same way, carving up time and space to construct its narrative. But the film exists outside the mind, outside the imagination of the person watching. The viewer is excited, and accepts an illusion of reality, because what he sees in his head when he reads is now projected on the screen—the temporal and spatial freedom of imagination reproduced in two dimensions. Narrative films seemed to make the imagination, with all its boundless command of time, external, vivid, and real.[35] And what's more, movies allowed hundreds of people to share the experience simultaneously.

And this is where feature films represented a new way of visualizing reality—they made the power of imagination, its control over time and space, real at a mass level. Porter's *Life of an American Fireman,* with its technique of "temporal overlap," maintained the integrity of different points of view—the rescue shown first from inside a room and then from outside. The two spaces of action never intermingled in time. Feature films in the "classical style" broke down this integrity and subsumed different points of view in the narrative line. Instead of watching as separate slices of reality presented themselves in turn, audiences were "swept away by an imaginary time flow"—literally by time flowing like the imagination—that combined different realms of action, different actual realities, in one story.[36] The story becomes *their* story, more real than the separate incidents and spaces that make it up, because it incorporates them, breaks down the boundaries in space and time between them. Movies represented a new way of thinking about narrative in time. In this, they seem to have echoed the central agenda of the Progressive era—the desire to create consensus, a unified public opinion and culture, from the diversity of American society.

This last point may seem far-fetched. It would certainly be wrong to say that movies created Progressive politics, or that progressivism invented movie narrative. But it would be equally wrong to ignore the relationship between the two, and the fact that the relationship grew out of new understandings of time. Standard time involved new ways of organizing knowledge, new ways of conceiving the relations between individuals and society. And in the Progressive era, the clearest expression of time's new meaning was the model of efficiency and the machine. Following the relation between movies, social efficiency, and politics through America's entry into World War I will help clarify the way new understandings of time shaped American culture.

———

In their control of time, movies seemed to offer the potential for a sort of mass psychotherapy. The German-born Harvard psychologist Hugo Münsterberg, impressed by the fluidity of the feature film, emphasized the transcendent quality of cinematic time in his widely excerpted book *The Photoplay: A Psychological Study.* Münsterberg reiterated the difference between cinema time and the standard time of everyday life. He concluded in 1916 that the photoplay worked "by overcoming the forms of the outer world, mainly space, time and causality, and by adjusting events to the form of the inner world"—the world of the imagination. At the movies, he wrote, "the massive outer world has lost its weight; it has been freed from space, time and causality, and it has been clothed in the forms of our own consciousness."[37] If standard time forced an artificial, clock-based time structure on the mind, Münsterberg posed movie time as a more natural alternative, an imitation of the pure freedom of thought and dreams.

But again, paradoxically, the apparent freedom of motion picture time lent itself to a vision of control. Münsterberg came to the movies through his work on scientific management, particularly the relationship of attention and fatigue to efficiency. He advocated scientific career choice based on testing psychological factors like attention span, reaction time, and memory. A fan of the cinema well before 1916, he had recently contributed a series of picture puzzles designed to test "attention, memory, constructive imagination, capacity for making quick estimates, etc." to the Paramount company's screen magazine, *Paramount Pictograph*. His interest in movies paralleled his interest in social and industrial efficiency. In the right hands, he thought, movies might become a therapeutic tool, recharging the imagination by reproducing the workings of the mind on screen, with a commonality that books never approached.

For reformers like Münsterberg, the final difference between movies and books—and this is a crucial point—came in the fact that the movies united the audience in a common imaginative experience, so that all felt the same thing, all "imagined" the events on screen in the same way. At the end of a film, *Lippincott's* concluded, "we may feel so enthusiastic that we unconsciously applaud along with all the others."[38] The audience undergoes a kind of spontaneous union, welded together by film's representation of the form of the imagination just as the film's narrative line welds together distinct, separate realities. Though movies seemed to reproduce the freedom of individual imagination, they also seemed to make everyone imagine things in the same way. Münsterberg envisioned movies as a new art form capable of revolutionizing the aesthetic tastes of millions while promoting psychic and social well-being—that is, of changing the way people think.[39]

To those who feared the movies as a narcotizing waste of time, Münsterberg pointed out that if nothing else the movies invigorated, because "happenings which would fill an hour on the stage can hardly fill more than twenty minutes on the screen," and "this heightens the feelings of vitality in the spectator."[40] An age that made efficiency a secular religion not surprisingly interpreted movies through the quest for efficiency and speed. "Modernism calls for abbreviated action," insisted one magazine, and "in photoplays the plot is unfolded in the least possible time . . . if a stage play requires three hours, in the photoplay it is pictorially told in one hour, and just as effectively." "Have the movies changed us?" asked *Scientific American* in 1917. Indeed they had—corrupted by the movies' brevity and speed, the magazine claimed, the public now "wishes other things to be treated in the same manner."[41] Theatergoers and readers in general, insisted a dramatist, now wanted "Quick Action." "They want to see drama in speed-record time. They want comedy and tragedy that is rapid-fire." The dramatist of the future, she concluded breathlessly, "must tip his pen with radium—and it must leap!"[42]

Carving up and compressing narrative time gave movie makers an aesthetic of streamlined speed. Prospective screenwriters were urged to hone their scripts to the minimum, and focus on compacting the time of events to keep the plot moving. "Any scenes which threaten to be unduly long," suggested a professional script writer, "should be broken up by 'flashing back' to some other scene," or by occasional close-ups which refocused audience attention. *Colliers* reminded hopeful screenwriters to concentrate on action and avoid "wasting words." In a motion picture, proclaimed one movie expert, "everything must be condensed to the irreducible minimum without forfeiting coherency," because for a movie producer, "one factor is all important—time. A producer," he continued, "will spend five minutes in the effort to condense by five seconds the action necessary for a certain situation." *Moving Picture World* urged the would-be scenario writers of 1911 "to cut out every act that does not have a direct bearing on the development of the plot." Only those scenes most productive of an intended effect should remain.[43]

With the rise of feature films, motion pictures returned to their origins in the quest for efficiency, in the parallels between Muybridge and Frederick Taylor. Thirty years earlier Taylor's disciples, armed with stopwatches, had first cut and pasted time according to "scientific" principles. Motion picture scenario writers applied Taylor's now-familiar emphasis on cutting out extraneous, unneeded, "waste" motions to celluloid. Taylor timed a space of labor, separated "productive" from "unproductive" motions, then reassembled the productive motions alone into a standard time for any job. Narrative films mirrored Taylor's understanding of time. They carved up the ordinary, standard time and duration of everyday events and then re-formed it according to the director's particular agenda. Taylor cut out wasted motions and recombined productive ones. In the movies, as in Taylorism, "wasted" footage wound up cut out, while only those most "productive" shots survived. The two techniques, time study by stopwatch and movie editing in frames per second, are directly analogous—each lays out time for dissection and reassembly.

While the director, editor, or censor's cutting and pasting mimicked the time study man's, the organization of production on the movie lot soon came to resemble Taylor's idealized factory. At first, early movie makers had paid little attention to costs, to saving props and materials, to following scripts or dividing labor. Production centered on the director and his team—cameraman, set designer, lighting expert, etc.—all of whom collaborated extensively. Directors and their crews improvised gleefully as inspiration struck them. Divisions of labor blurred in the quest for footage, while without a fixed script directors often wasted time, money, materials, and effort on building sets or shooting scenes only to scissor them out later. But by 1916, when the rise of feature films had raised both the level of movie sophistication and the intensity of competition within the business, major producers like Thomas Ince had streamlined not just the cinematic time of narrative films but the studio time and effort required to make them.

"System and efficiency," insisted the *Saturday Evening Post* in 1916, "have found their way into the manufacture of motion pictures."[44] Major producers, most notably Ince, began working to bring the techniques of scientific management onto studio lots. Early directors proceeded from a simple outline or plot sketch and modified it as they went along. They kept few if any records of specific costs incurred or delays involved in filming any particular scenes. At his Edendale, California, studios Ince substituted a detailed "continuity" script with specific instructions for all employees involved, from director to set designer to carpenter. The scripts described each shot in relation to those preceding and following it, and Ince personally reviewed each script under production, insisting that subordinates adhere to it without alterations.

The innovation was so useful that within a few years Ince retired from directing altogether and settled into the role of "Director-General." Continuity scripts allowed Ince, from this position, to simultaneously control direction (editing and shot choice), oversee and schedule the construction and design of materials in advance, and review future costs. Each script also served as a written record of the film as it moved through the studio on its way to release. In this sense the continuity script echoed Taylor's system of punched time cards, which monitored a given part's movement through the factory. The Director-General's office recalled the routing and planning office Taylor established to oversee production. And like Taylor's machinists, told what to do, how to do it, and how much time to take by an expert, studio employees lost control over the organization and pace of their work to a distant central authority.[45]

While streamlining production and centralizing authority, continuity scripts also helped maintain temporal and causal consistency in movie narrative. As films gained complexity it became harder and harder to unify action from scene to scene, especially without a formal script. Few directors could remember clearly, after a few days' delay, where one shot left off and another began. It would jar even the most unsophisticated audience if, for example, a character entering a room from the right wearing a hat exited the same door from the left, hatless, a few shots later. Continuity scripts let the production manager, and later a continuity specialist, spot such potential inconsistencies in advance, and reorganize camera placement, scenery, and action accordingly. The continuity script made it easier to "tame" and "unify" the spatial and temporal flexibility feature films introduced.[46]

For the audience, the experience of motion pictures as fast, concentrated entertainment related movies to the efficient, productive use of leisure time. Reformers seemed especially sensitive to the relationship between time and efficiency in the movies. The heightened drama that resulted from tight, concise editing lent moral preachments, and the uplifting conclusion, a special force. "While I was studying at Hull House," went a letter to the *Survey*, "I saw in their theater a moving picture of the life of Moses. The dial of time turned back," he asserted, and "it was all there, vivid, true to the Bible story and reverent in tone." Cinema time concentrated and intensified the tale's meaning, so that "even today the motion picture which ran its course in fifteen minutes is more vivid than the story which I have read and taught from childhood."[47] Compressed into fifteen minutes and augmented by the apparent realism of the screen, Moses' story, and the values it embodied, gained new vigor and impact.

Educators were especially anxious to exploit film's potential contributions to efficiency. Münsterberg's comparison of movies to mental processes echoed in the rhetoric of progressive educators, who hoped film might teach lessons faster, more lastingly and more efficiently. In 1913, the *Survey* conducted a symposium on the motion picture in education, inviting prominent educators and reformers to comment on Thomas Edison's elaborate plans for a series of educational films. "Much has been done in the way of scientific management in the field of bodily toil," remarked the editor. "Perhaps Mr. Edison thinks of himself as an efficiency engineer reaching into the mental process—for, of course, time saving and mental efficiency are the very essence of his dreams." In a qualified endorsement of the project, John Dewey of Columbia admitted that certainly in many subjects, "much more information . . . will be given more efficiently, more understandingly, quickly and vividly" by moving pictures. "Two or three performances may easily make an impression more indelible and more intelligent than weeks of reading."[48]

But the most intriguing union of Taylorism, motion pictures, and education came at the hands of efficiency experts Frank and Lillian Gilbreth. Seeking industrial efficiency and an ill-defined "One Best Way" for doing any job, the Gilbreths aimed movie cameras at nearly any human undertaking in hopes of "analyzing an activity into its smallest possible elements, and from the result synthesizing a method of performing the activity that shall be more efficient"—the word "efficient," they added, "being used in its highest sense."[49] By using the motion picture camera to make "micromotion studies" of workers in action, the Gilbreths connected Taylor's principles of time study with the movies' command over time and space. Commenting on a Gilbreth project in Rhode Island, *Current Opinion* suggested that "the foreman of the future will no doubt have to modify his vocabulary, if he is to keep abreast of the times. 'Get a movie on you' will take the place of 'get a move on you.' "[50]

Born in 1868, Frank Gilbreth was working as a bricklayer's apprentice when he first saw the light of motion study. After each skilled bricklayer showed young Frank a different way to lay bricks, he turned the understandable confusion that resulted into the consuming passion of his life—what was the one best way to do this work? In the copy of Taylor's paper on "Shop Management" he came across sometime after 1903, Gilbreth recognized greatness, and when he finally met Taylor in 1907 he venerated the very spot of their meeting to the end of his days.

Gilbreth met and married Lillian Moller, the other great influence on his life, shortly after she finished her M.A. thesis, on Ben Jonson, at Berkeley. His love for efficiency quickly kindled

in her, and when Lillian entered the Ph.D. program she switched
from literature to psychology at Frank's urging. Her dissertation,
eventually completed and published in 1914 as *The Psychology of
Management*, attempted to harmonize the principles of psychology
with those of scientific management. She drew heavily on the work
of several prominent psychiatrists, including Hugo Münsterberg,
whose earlier study *American Problems* had suggested a link between
the two fields. Together she and Frank produced twelve children
and at least as many articles and addresses. Gilbreth was obsessed
with efficient production in every sphere. Twelve children, he
contended, would pose no strain on a scientifically managed household (especially a household he frequently left on business). The
best-selling book and movie *Cheaper by the Dozen*, written by Frank
Jr. and his sister Ernestine, depicted their genuinely affectionate
family in detail.[51]

Encouraged by his wife, Gilbreth accelerated his motion
study work after meeting Taylor. The two collaborated on a *Primer
of Scientific Management*, and Gilbreth even helped found the Taylor
Society, dedicated to commemorating and spreading its name-
sake's influence. But by 1910 Gilbreth was growing dissatisfied
with obvious inaccuracies in Taylor's stopwatch studies, especially
the perplexing problem of "the human element." Stopwatch methods seemed too arbitrary, plagued particularly by errors stemming
from the observer's reaction time. Stopwatch study left no visible
record other than the observer's description, and besides, it routinely irritated or enraged most of the workers who encountered it.

A habitual moviegoer, Gilbreth broke with Taylor when he
replaced Taylor's stopwatch with a movie camera. While viewing
some films of his earlier concrete work, Gilbreth realized that
movies offered a more objective record of labor and the results of
innovation. The pictures themselves could be examined minutely,
frame by frame, isolating the components of any set of motions

and screening out waste without reliance on memory or snap judgment. Placing a clock within the camera frame, he reasoned further, would give an indisputable record of elapsed time. Even better, films of Gilbreth's innovations gave prospective clients an apparently indisputable record of his method's practicality. Bursting with pride, he described his "micromotion study" approach to Taylor in 1912. But the prima donna of scientific management seemed unimpressed by the implied challenge to his stopwatch.[52]

At Lillian's urging, the disillusioned Gilbreths went into business as scientific management consultants specializing in motion study. To bolster their claims to precision, the couple continually elaborated their movie apparatus. Like Muybridge they placed subjects against a cross-sectioned grid background, to measure the distance their motions traveled. They developed special clocks and watches (emblazoned GILBRETH in bold capitals), designed to show smaller divisions of time—supposedly "up to the millionth of an hour." Finally they attached small blinking lights to their subjects' hands, then photographed them so that the lights left a continuous record of the hand's passage. Called "chronocycle-graphs" by the Gilbreths, these light paths were then reproduced in wire as life-sized, three-dimensional "motion models." Workers in training were to run their hands along these wires and thus learn the proper motion paths. A clock or system of regular beeps kept them moving at the right speed.[53]

The Gilbreth films gave control over time, and dramatized the process of learning. "We not only see ourselves as others see us," they wrote, "but we can go much further and see ourselves *as no one has ever seen us* . . . element by element," instant by instant, frame by frame.[54] In itself this differed little from Muybridge's work, but micromotion films offered a new dimension—they allowed employers "to observe the worker performing the work at practically any speed that we may desire to see him use." Time in a Gilbreth film, like time in the movie theater, could be slowed

A Gilbreth "chronocyclegraph." The dramatist of the future,
Harper's Weekly *had insisted in 1914, "must tip his pen with*
radium — and it must leap!" Gilbreth almost literally made that pre-
diction a reality. (National Museum of American
History, Smithsonian Institution.)

down and speeded up at will. The Gilbreths made the comparison
between their studies and commercial films explicit; "those of you
who have made a study of motion picture films," they continued,
"and who have analyzed trick films, where people move far above,
or below, the normal speed of real life, will at once realize the
possibilities in motion analysis that lie here."[55]

The Gilbreths claimed these possibilities were educational — that viewing fast actions at slower speeds made them more comprehensible, while viewing ordinary motions speeded up either made wrong motions ludicrous or planted the ideal of faster work in the viewer's head. In fact, by controlling projection speed, they finalized the comparison of workers with machines that Taylor had begun. The Gilbreths' fundamental goal — the concept they sold to their clients — was stripping workers of their autonomy and subjecting them to machine logic. Watching a Gilbreth subject go through precisely the same motion, over and over again, at any speed the projectionist desired, reduced the subject to a mechanism with a throttle.

The image seems grotesque, and indeed Charlie Chaplin, most notably, would later use some of the same cinematic techniques in *Modern Times* to spoof scientific management with deeply ironic comic effect. And here lies the irony: both examples reflect time's new susceptibility to control. Though we might find Chaplin's use of the technique far more palatable, Chaplin and the Gilbreths both did the same things — cut, pasted, reassembled, retarded, and accelerated fragments of time on celluloid. Their intention differed, but their approach to time was the same.

The Gilbreths edited workers' motion rather than motion picture film; they typically filmed someone at work, revised his or her movements after studying the film, then refilmed that person going through the new, scientifically correct motions. But by breaking down movement their experiments distilled time and motion into discrete units, like the individual shots comprising a film. Just as narrative films reassembled separate pieces of duration, the Gilbreths synthesized the elements of any motion in a new narrative of work. All tasks, the Gilbreths concluded finally, consisted of no more than sixteen fundamental, standard elements. They dubbed each of these sixteen elements a "Therblig"[56] ("Gilbreth" spelled backward, almost).

Frank and Lillian Gilbreth's "Therbligs." The symbols could theoretically be written as hieroglyphic sentences, to describe any job as a sequence of standardized actions. "Avoidable delay" is a sleeping worker, "unavoidable delay" a broken worker, "plan" a man scratching his head.

⬭	SEARCH	◡	INSPECT
⬭	FIND	⬯	PRE-POSITION
→	SELECT	⌒	RELEASE LOAD
∩	GRASP	⌣	TRANSPORT EMPTY
⌣	TRANSPORT LOADED		REST FOR OVERCOMING FATIGUE
9	POSITION		UNAVOIDABLE DELAY
#	ASSEMBLE		AVOIDABLE DELAY
U	USE		PLAN
⫶⫶	DISASSEMBLE		

The ridiculous term parodies itself; but the silliness of much of the Gilbreths' work nevertheless fails to obscure their importance. It seems only fair to note that the Gilbreths, even more than Taylor (and like Chaplin), claimed to have the laborer's best interests in mind. The vision of workers helplessly repeating the same motions obscures the real value of some of their projects, particularly the attempts to adapt office machines and procedures for the handicapped. In the context of the era's cult of efficiency, the Gilbreths seemed to be pursuing scientific management's logical course, and though Frank was more than a bit of a faker, their work was taken seriously indeed. Frank and Lillian's central goal—promoting efficiency and the standardization of time, work, and experience—harmonized with many of the basic tenets of the Progressive era.

The Gilbreths viewed "the transference of experience" as their most important goal, and projecting motion pictures of workers in action seemed the most accurate means of reproducing and teaching right and wrong ways to work. Once the "best way" had been established, motion pictures made it possible to reproduce that experience infinitely, to create a standard, universal language of efficiency. By 1918 they approached all tasks as strings of Therbligs, winnowed, organized, and reordered, like the shots in a film, to fit a specific task.

Therbligs broke down the processes of work. If a given job—shoveling, for example—traditionally consisted of eight Therbligs, after the Gilbreths finished studying the task and cutting out unproductive motions, only four might remain. The "first couple of efficiency" hoped to create a standard language of movement for the "transference of experience." They assigned each Therblig both a special color and a symbol. Once time was provided as a line of numbers, ideally any task might be represented on graph paper as a cycle of these symbols. Any motions could be translated into a permanent record of their Therblig components, reconstituted with the aid of movies and wire models, and then reproduced infinitely.

Here again, the Gilbreths nibbled at the edges of one of the central questions of their age. Given the extraordinary vividness of motion pictures, and the control over time and narrative they offered, might not political messages be assembled in the same way, and reproduced infinitely as well? If you could make a universally applicable narrative of the best way to work, could you also construct universally effective moral and political narratives—narratives of the best way to think? As the United States flirted with entry into the European war, the question of the movies' role in political propaganda would become more pressing. Could movies create a standard language of political ideology that could be reproduced exactly, and without limits?

Motion picture studies led the Gilbreths to view all motions as standard, discrete instants in time, each with its own representative symbols. These symbols could be recombined, like the shots in a narrative film, in more productive orders. Similarly, the poet and movie fan Vachel Lindsay speculated on the "hieroglyphic" nature of movies in his 1915 book *The Art of the Moving Picture*. Lindsay compared silent film shots to Egyptian picture writing. Just as, in Egypt, the hieroglyphic of a bowl could stand for a whole range of ideas and associations, so in the movies a

single shot conveyed a wealth of meaning. Lindsay inserted hieroglyphic characters in his text to make the point. "In the Egyptian
row is the picture of a throne," he wrote in one example. When
you see a throne flashed on the movie screen, he continued, "you
know instantly you are dealing with royalty or its implications."
Lindsay viewed movies as a potentially unique and profound art
form, but complained that too few directors really fulfilled this
potential. "It would profit any photoplay man," Lindsay insisted,
"to study to think like the Egyptians, the great picture writing
people." He advised any aspiring scenario writer to cut a set of
hieroglyphic characters from cardboard, and "construct the outlines of his scenarios by placing these little pictures in rows."[57]
The exercise would teach film makers to think in terms of pictures
rather than words.

Lindsay's "hieroglyphics" differ from Therbligs in important
ways. Lindsay's symbols collapse distinctions, while Therbligs
were intended to break apparently unified things apart—one is
analytical, the other synthetic. Their similarities come in the approach to time and narrative. Like the Gilbreths, Lindsay envisioned motion picture shots as a chain of interchangeable, movable
parts. The Gilbreths reorganized work into a movie narrative of
efficiency; Lindsay hoped to combine the visual "words" of silent
film language—the individual shots—into narrative sentences of
greater power, greater ideological "efficiency."

All three tied movies to the same goal: efficient production.
As a poet, Lindsay hoped to see more compelling, effective melodrama produced on screen, "Whitmanesque scenarios," which
could "show the entire American population its face in the mirror
screen." Similarly, the Gilbreths claimed that through their movies
"the observed and observer become one," and that watching a
Gilbreth film created a fascination with one's movements and a
compelling desire to make them more efficient. Lindsay, a Populist
by sympathy, hoped that movies would "bring the nobler side of

the equality ideal to the people who are so crassly equal," and create a higher form of democracy. In his theories the movie crowd becomes, like the Gilbreths' subjects, fascinated with its own movements, producing greater self-awareness and a commitment to self-improvement.[58]

Lindsay and Gilbreth both echoed the common perception that motion pictures represented a new language, a new way of communicating across class and geographic boundaries. "The cinematograph is doing for the drama," claimed *The Independent* in 1910, "what the printing press did for literature, bringing another form of art into the daily life of the people."[59] A nation of immigrants looked with special affection on a medium requiring no words, a "universal language" communicated by visual symbols. Symbols seemed free from the ambiguities attached to words. "If a class of a hundred students learn an oral lesson a hundred mental pictures are formed," went an article in *Scientific American*. "If, however, the lesson is taught by motion pictures the hundred mental impressions are all alike." "Shall we be challenged," wrote one critic in *The Bookman*, "when we assert that [the motion picture] is the language of democracy which reaches all strata of the population and welds them together?" "Can it not be made," he continued, "to bring all degrees of people into a coordinated organism, working in harmony for the greater things of the world?"[60] As a new way of organizing and conveying information, based on new standards of control over time, motion picture imagery promised to unify and standardize perceptions.

Lindsay envisioned "hieroglyphic" movies tied to a mass art that united and improved its audience. "In a photoplay by a master," he wrote, "when the American flag is shown, the thirteen stripes are columns of history and the stars are headlines."[61] For Lindsay, the image literally spoke volumes. At its best, he hoped, the photoplay's universally comprehensible imagery might bridge the barriers of language and class, producing a nation of more passionate, better-educated citizens. Lindsay's widely quoted book suggested that once reconstituted in the movies, the multiplicities and fragments of a nation's life might be reproduced infinitely, with greater impact and unlimited appeal. The entire process depended on control over time, and on narrative structures based on the ability to reorder and manipulate the "real" time of experience.

Lindsay drew his inspiration largely from the work of one man—the master film maker D. W. Griffith, whose wildly popular film *Birth of a Nation* was setting attendance records as Lindsay published. Griffith's epic of 1915 marked a high point in the evolution of cinematic time. Griffith understood more clearly than any of his peers that the fundamental unit of film "was not the scene but the shot." He doubled and even tripled the number of individual shots that had made up the average movie. He used cross-cutting, flashbacks, and close-ups with virtuoso flare, dynamizing movie time with unparalleled facility and vivid conviction. Griffith's innovations completed the transition from short, story-less movies to full-length feature films. His achievement marked the maturity of what film historians have since termed the "classical Hollywood cinema." After Griffith, complex and ambiguous stories could be rendered briefly, vividly, and effectively, thanks to the director's dramatic new control over movie time.[62]

Birth of a Nation also dramatized, as Lindsay understood, the enormous persuasive power of narrative film. *Birth,* based on Thomas Dixon's virulently racist best-seller *The Clansman,* posed the Ku Klux Klan as the heroes of Reconstruction, riding bravely to rescue beleaguered whites from a corrupt and repressive black regime. Knit together by its racist vision, the film fragmented both real and historic time to promote Anglo-Saxon unity. In its famous climax, the sheerest invention on Griffith's part, a galvanized Klan rode en masse to rescue the protagonists, recapturing the South and restoring white unity. Griffith used rapid cross-cutting to build suspense and increase sympathy for the beleaguered whites. As the camera switched back and forth, in close-up and distance, from the two groups of menacing blacks to the rescuing Klan, audiences could not help but *feel* Griffith's belief in the justice of his cause.[63]

The movie encapsulated narrative film's power to create political consensus by manipulating time. It overcame differences in space and point of view—between North and South, between menacing Negroes and noble whites—by subsuming them in a narrative line which unified white society by marginalizing blacks. In Griffith's view, the "birth" of the *real* American nation came only when northern and southern white men reached a consensus on the subject of racial purity. The movie built this consensus by intercutting separate social spaces through narrative. *Birth*'s narrative unity and its vision of political unity both depended on control over time and space.

Although the film evoked widespread protests from civil rights organizations, including the NAACP, audiences flocked to see it in record numbers—*Birth of a Nation* remained the most popular movie in American history till *Gone With the Wind*. Critics lauded its ability to reforge a coherent, gripping political message from pieces of cinematic time. Vachel Lindsay deplored the film's racism, but praised it for fulfilling his vision of the cinema as a unifying force. Inspired by *Birth*'s fantasy of political consensus, he anticipated the jingoist excesses of World War I when he predicted that "in the future mob-movements of anger and joy will go through fanatical and provincial whirlwinds into great national movements of anger and joy."[64]

Birth of a Nation made fantasy seem real. A St. Louis critic claimed that the film was "soaked with great moral ideas" that Griffith and his cast had felt in their hearts. While lesser movies only mimicked emotions beyond their experience, for *Birth*'s cast, "America, the Civil war, the agony of the South and the romantic idealism of the Ku Klux Klan; all these were real." "Where anything was not real," the critic added in a telling sentence, "the producers and actors were convinced that it was. The spirit of a crusade was behind it all." The movie externalized fevered racist imaginings. In the photoplay of the future, went his overheated conclusion, "the playing must be done by people who have themselves been gripped by great themes and have an impelling need to spread by contagion their own overmastering feelings."[65]

The power of Griffith's film came from the juxtaposition of apparent realism—the documentary quality of film—with the extraordinary emotional and imaginative power that arose from the manipulation of time. *Birth*'s impassioned urgency overrode the facts of history as its celluloid Klan overrode "Black rule"; the film's narrative coherence granted it the aura of truth because it combined different scenes that looked so real. President Woodrow Wilson himself, after a private screening arranged by Griffith, reportedly termed the film "history written with lightning." Lightning flashed and lit up the dark for a single moment, but Griffith had frozen a string of lightning instants on film, then reordered them into a narrative time that flowed toward a vivid political conclusion. "My only regret," Wilson mused of the film, "is that it is all so terribly true."[66]

Combining diverse points of view was what seemed to make movies true for Wilson. In January 1916 he made a short speech to the Motion Picture Board of Trade which hinted at the similarities between movie narrative and political consensus. Wilson, who had only recently seen Griffith's film, began by confessing, "I have sometimes been very much chagrined at seeing myself in a motion picture." The screen's distortions, its jerkiness, the "apparently automatic nature of my motion," he claimed, missed the reservoir of thought, compassion, and emotion that lay beneath the stiff screen facade. But he then described how he had recently discovered the truth about the "Mexican situation" despite the fact that each of his many informants lied to him somewhat. "I think," he told the movie men, "the psychological explanation will interest you."

Wilson explained how he pieced together a coherent narrative of events in Mexico by assembling small parts of each account he received—that is, he recombined segments of each separate narrative into a narrative of his own, "the truth" of the situation. Given that Wilson addressed the Board shortly after seeing Griffith's brilliantly edited film, his description suggests a parallel between the President's construction of political reality and the director's cutting and reassembling of scenes and shots. In speculating that the Board might find the "psychological explanation" interesting, Wilson alluded to narrative film's ability to reconstruct a convincing version of the truth from fragments of temporal continuity.[67]

Compare Wilson's speech to D. W. Griffith's explanation of how movies alone could give a true picture of war. Griffith pointed out that no single individual could possibly comprehend the scope of a conflict like World War I—not even the general in command "can see a tithe of it." As he spoke, Griffith was engaged in filming his own war picture, *Hearts of the World*, which like *Birth* used a romantic plot to fuse the fragments of cinematic time into a coherent narrative. Only a movie could unite the disparate aspects of the war into a coherent reality, Griffith felt, for "the camera possesses a thousand eyes and reaches out in every direction, so that it can catch the grand panorama in one instant and in the next it can disclose a minute detail of the most illuminative and atmospheric close-up." The quotation described the construction of movie time, how Griffith took the various viewpoints each shot gave and reassembled them into a "grand panorama," a narrative that he hoped would depict the glory of the crusade for democracy.[68]

Both Wilson and Griffith describe a process of ordering

reality—combining separate points of view into a unified narrative. Like many native-born Protestants of the period, both men worried about American diversity; Griffith wanted America "reborn" in white supremacy, while Wilson feared the presence of immigrants who clung to their native heritage. Irish-Americans, German-Americans, Italian-Americans, Chinese-Americans, "any man who carries a hyphen about with him," Wilson once said, "carries a dagger that he is ready to plunge into the vitals of the republic." As President, Wilson imagined himself embodying an American consensus that united these disparate groups into one will. "I am speaking with the voice of the American people," he insisted; "I express the spirit and purpose of the American people."[69]

As America's entry into World War I began to seem inevitable, the problem of diversity grew more pressing. Wilson knew that most Americans could see little reason to sacrifice their lives and their time in someone else's cause. Why should Irish, Chinese, or German Americans care about England or France? But he also saw America's participation as essential; how, then, to create favorable opinion for war? Wilson, who genuinely hated the idea of war, came to see the war as a crusade for democracy, a mission of moral uplift that would solve the problem of diversity by bringing people—Americans first, then the world—together.

The process of constructing movie narrative is in this sense analogous to the process of building support for the war. Americans would sacrifice their separate opinions in a narrative of growing patriotic enthusiasm—the "story" of the war as a crusade—just as in a narrative film separate realms of experience were edited together by the story. Wilson's approach to political consensus and the construction of movie narrative share a similar organization of time. It would be foolish to claim that Wilson was directly inspired by movies, or that movies somehow either caused the war or caused Wilson to think as he did. But in terms of time and narrative, the congruence between the two forms of communication—political consensus building and movie editing—is startling.

The point is that new ways of understanding and organizing time permeated American culture at every level, from work to politics to entertainment. They offered politicians, film makers, and factory managers alternative models for ordering reality. Over the next five years, as the United States drew closer to war, industrial production and the production of political opinions merged in the cinematic propaganda inspired by World War I.

Commercial movie producers, by 1915 mostly settled in Hollywood, had at first stayed largely neutral on the question of the war, following the mainstream of political opinion as represented by President Wilson. In 1916 Thomas Ince had even produced a pacifist film, *Civilization*, that may have helped Wilson's reelection.[70] By 1916, however, pacifist films like Ince's were rapidly losing ground to "preparedness" pictures which promoted war from behind a thin veil of neutrality. Newsreel footage of the fighting had excited public interest, and propaganda films released by Germany, France, and England had provoked near riots on several occasions. Sensing money, American film producers used the theme of preparedness to present our boys in fictional conflict without blatantly choosing sides.

As products of the industry's maturity, the by now largely standardized narrative techniques of the "classical style," such films encouraged hawkish sentiment, and started anti-German feeling to boiling over. Ironically, anti-Germanism claimed one of its first victims in Hugo Münsterberg. As a prominent spokesman for the German cause, Münsterberg spoke frequently against both the war and American intervention. He found himself increasingly ostracized by his colleagues and vilified in the press as anti-German feeling grew. The strain of public hostility was too much for him: he died of a heart attack in 1916, brought on, according to his daughter, by the pressure of public hostility to Germany.[71] Münsterberg fell victim, in part through the cleverly structured preparedness films, to the phenomenon that fascinated him.

Although Wilson generally condemned anti-German excess and distanced himself from most prewar efforts, he did endorse two quasi-fictional preparedness films, *Uncle Sam Awake* and *The Eagle's Wings*.[72] But when the United States finally entered the war in April 1917, Wilson helped the motion picture industry elbow its way to the front of the parade. Government and the movie industry enthusiastically collaborated in a series of war bond drives, and over the next two years Hollywood ground out a long series of patriotic titles, including *The Kaiser, The Beast of Berlin, The Claws of the Hun,* and *The Prussian Cur.* The latter's climax, lifted from Griffith, featured the Ku Klux Klan riding to crush German spies.[73] The enemy had changed, from rampaging blacks to the bestial Hun. But Griffith's temporal structure—the unifying climax and last-minute rescue—applied equally well to either enemy. Chopping up real time and giving it narrative unity helped unify the audience's feelings about the enemy.

These films proved enormously popular, and certainly helped build sentiment against Germany. From Wilson's point of view, however, they flirted with a dangerous sensationalism. Hating Germany was all well and good, but a progressive war for world freedom had to be tied to uplifting moral values, to a positive vision of change. The narrative speed and trajectory of these films headed not toward moral uplift, but toward unproductive and possibly dangerous hate.[74]

To help build consensus in favor of the war, and direct the manipulation of public opinion more closely, Wilson established "America's first propaganda ministry," the Committee on Public Information (CPI). Under the directorship of muckraking journalist George Creel, the Committee joined censorship of the press and private citizens with an intensive campaign for public opinion.

This "is the war of the American people," Creel insisted, "only they all don't know it yet."[75] To tell them, Creel turned to what he called "the three great agencies of appeal in the fight for public opinion: The Written Word, the Spoken Word, and the Motion Picture."[76]

Creel, a Colorado journalist before his appointment to the CPI, had worked as an extra on some of "Broncho Billy" Anderson's Western films, films which in later years he occasionally screened for his friends and the White House staff. Creel had even written a few short scripts for Anderson at twenty-five dollars each.[77] Besides a love of motion pictures he brought the CPI a familiarity with the power of short, catchy phrases and slogans. Under Creel, the CPI sent forth its famous corps of speechifying "Four-Minute Men" (up three minutes from the Revolutionary War), who condensed war propaganda into punchy, rousing talks exhausting less than 240 seconds of the audience's precious time. CPI guidelines advised them that "there is no time for a single wasted word." The four-minute men worked mostly in movie theaters, usually either preceding a feature film or afflicting the intermission. Cooperation with Creel's fast-talking boosters helped the motion picture industry stave off classification as a "nonessential industry" later in the war, and kept movies in the forefront of CPI operations.[78]

Wilson hoped that the Committee on Public Information could oversee and channel the film industry's patriotic enthusiasm, and at first movie makers cooperated. A specially formed committee of film industry leaders, including D. W. Griffith, pronounced itself ready and willing to work closely with the CPI.[79] But hopes that private industry would bear the burden of patriotic film production faltered in late 1917 over problems in censorship and the distribution of war footage. So, under the leadership of George Creel, Uncle Sam himself went into movie making through the CPI's Division of Films.

At first the CPI merely censored and distributed the copious footage supplied by the Army's Signal Service cameramen. The Signal Service, to document the war effort, had been cranking out as much footage as its limited staff, budget, and equipment allowed, all of which passed to the CPI for review. Unfortunately for Creel, the war resisted cinematography. Heavy, bulky cameras slowed the photographers down, and what few battles the army allowed them to film usually took place at dawn, when low light made decent pictures impossible. Most of the footage consisted of largely static scenes shot behind the lines, especially pictures of industrial and weapons production. But the public craved war news, any war news, and so when he began making feature films Creel attempted to turn this disadvantage to his favor.

The CPI's Division of Films tried to follow Griffith's editorial path, creating unity out of fragments both on celluloid and in American society. "What we had to have," Creel later reminisced with typically cascading ballyhoo, "was no mere surface unity, but a passionate belief . . . that would weld the people of the United States into one white hot mass instinct with fraternity, devotion, courage, and deathless determination."[80] As Griffith carved up and reassembled space and time to promote a coherent vision of war, the Division of Films made a number of multiple-reel "features" by combining Signal Service footage, splicing together shots of vastly different activities to create the impression of a simultaneous, unified commitment to the war in all its phases.

As an official government agency, the CPI felt compelled to restrict itself largely to "real," documentary footage of the war. But from a cinematic point of view the footage was mostly dull. To liven up the drearier scenes and inject narrative momentum, the CPI borrowed some techniques from the commercial cinema. CPI officials enlisted ad man Bruce Barton—"a master," as the Committee put it, "of the short phrase"—to write catchy titles that would help unify and enliven scenes of shoemaking or training camp drill.[81] With Creel's blessing, New York theater magnate Samuel Rothapfel spliced in scenes from other films, used several projectors to simulate filmic dissolves, and reordered CPI short films to present them in the most effective sequence.[82]

Such modifications introduced a greater sense of unity and narrative continuity. With their diverse and wide-ranging scenes of the Allied war effort, CPI publicists claimed, films like *Pershing's Crusaders* and *America's Answer* showed "how every man, woman and child is helping Uncle Sam."[83] In his address at the premier of *America's Answer*, Creel attacked dissenters and pleaded, "let 110,000,000 people stand as one" in determination to win. "America's answer," he insisted, "cannot be made by any single class or by any single endeavor."[84] To spur industrial production for the war, CPI films adopted techniques from commercial movie making. With these editorial strategies, the CPI tried to present an image of unity out of disjointed footage, and increase the very factory production and unity it depicted.

But in comparison to Hollywood efforts, these CPI films suffered gravely from the lack of a coherent narrative structure and unified editorial control over time. Though an energetic campaign of arm twisting guaranteed CPI films a reasonably enthusiastic audience, at least one otherwise favorable review asked, "why not have woven a little heart interest story through the genuine scenes of the front?"[85] Next to their commercial competition, surviving CPI efforts seem disjointed and dull. Throughout the war, Hollywood issued a steady stream of anti-German films using the standard cinematic vocabulary of the "classic style." "These film dramas," the British *Fortnightly Review* recalled later, "had the qualities we have been accustomed to expect in the work of the great American combinations . . . the scenarios were constructed according to the recognized rules, with 'heart interest' and 'punch' and all the rest of it."[86] But "the Signal Service films and CPI productions," as movie historian Terry Ramsaye remembered them, "resembled a history of the war about as much as a scrapbook resembles a historical novel."[87] In other words, they had succeeded in freezing and breaking up time—like a scrapbook—but not in establishing the narrative continuity and momentum necessary to engaging the viewer.

The CPI tried, with mixed success, to exploit the temporal vocabulary of commercial film. Without continuity scripts and centralized directorial authority, the CPI films failed to knit their temporal components into a coherent whole—they lacked "punch." Without plotting, without a consistent narrative thread, they lacked the "heart interest" that skilled directors used to bind the elements of a story together. They remained, as Ramsaye observed, a scrapbook patchwork, never taking on the illusion of reality. To overcome the problem and make CPI productions more like their Hollywood counterparts, toward the end of its brief career the CPI's Division of Films began writing its own scripts through a scenario department, then offering the scripts with approved footage to commercial producers. "The idea," the CPI wrote to James Hoff of *Moving Picture World*, was "adapting to the screen the idea that is back of the Four Minute Men," a brief, condensed, coherent message of patriotism.[88] Before many scripts were completed, however, the armistice finished both the scenario department and the CPI. When the Committee disbanded hastily in 1919, most records of the department's work were destroyed. But in its brief career the CPI had grasped an essential fact: that restructuring time on the screen translated directly into political power.

A more detailed record of time's new role in political persuasion came from the even briefer military career of efficiency expert Frank Gilbreth. When war broke in 1917, Gilbreth offered his services to the government. "If you do not know how to use me," he wrote Washington, "I will tell you." The Army assigned the freshly coined Major Gilbreth to Fort Sill, Oklahoma, and the

production of training films. Gilbreth set to work at once repli-
cating his laboratory environment. He suggested putting cross-
sectioned grid backgrounds in each film, and insisted that "we
have *at least* one clock in every film . . . if there is any unused
background or foreground or space anywhere in the picture."
Gilbreth wanted clocks in every shot to drive home the need for
efficiency and conservation of time. "This is the era of waste
elimination," he wrote to a fellow officer. "Time must be 'spread
out on the table and examined' before it is thrown away."[89] Film
editors spread time, in the form of movie footage, on the editing
table to be examined; Gilbreth tried to use motion pictures to
examine soldiers' chores the same way.

Gilbreth focused in part on speeding up ordinary military
duties by dissecting the time they usually took. He used "Therbligs" to show soldiers how to break down and reassemble their
weapons in less time, or how to aim and fire more productively.
He proposed making micromotion studies to find the most efficient
motions for a bayonet thrust.

But he also concerned himself with questions of duty and
obedience; how to march more efficiently, how to salute faster
and more uniformly. Prospective captions for one of his films
defined discipline as "the instant and willing obedience to orders."
Micromotion dissections of time, a subsequent Gilbreth caption
pointed out, showed that "the average man can come to attention
in 75/100 of a second. Watch this man and see that he comes to
attention in 60/100 of a second. Can you best it?" Fast-saluting
soldiers were more efficient in their obedience.[90]

Dissecting soldiers' motions formed a substantial part of his
work, but Gilbreth also used the special capabilities of movies to
make more obedient, loyal, and willing crusaders for democracy.
He borrowed from psychology in an attempt to make his films
more involving—"we need a psychologist here," he wrote his wife,
"to put 'interest' in these films," and "make the audience partic-

Still photograph of a soldier under study for one of Frank Gilbreth's training films. (National Museum of American History, Smithsonian Institution.)

ipate." Better training films, he assured his superiors, would require "a humorist, a jingle writer, and a scenario writer."[91] He adopted cinematic techniques that made his pictures more persuasive and more gripping, including progressions from distant shots to close-ups that he thought built curiosity. Gilbreth suggested using captions that forced soldiers to respond. "It was his suggestion," a colleague later wrote, "that we commence each reel with what he termed 'hate pictures' showing the atrocities of our opponents." "It was his thought," the officer continued, "to make each headline short and peppy" and "insert a great many human interest scenes" to "hold the attention of the soldier." "It was his thought to use slow motion pictures" and "insert a great many close-ups in each reel."[92] Gilbreth tried, by restructuring the temporal flow of information on film, to enter the minds of soldiers and bring back the prize of loyal obedience. Like Creel, he sought a more "efficient" means of persuasion, and tried to translate control over movie time into control over thought. But serious illness, and a subsequent discharge, cut short his military career after a few months, and Gilbreth never made most of the films he planned.[93]

Gilbreth's army career encapsulates the government's attempts at movie production—brief and halting, yet potentially of enormous importance. Private industry produced far more effective war films, or at least far more popular ones. The examples of Gilbreth and Creel really prove nothing about the success or failure of government propaganda. Nor are they even the best example of the era's obsession with conserving time—the four-minute men are probably a much better one. What they do suggest, however, is how Americans' new understanding of time offered new modes for representing reality.

Standardized public time established a universal medium for ordering communication in business, a standard located in clocks. Standard zone time, transmittable by electricity to subsidiary clocks, turned synchronized clocks into models for social organization and factory production. Men like Taylor and Muybridge began carving up that standard time, subjecting it to rational scrutiny. Taylor cut out non-essential movements to boost industrial efficiency, and Muybridge turned continuous motions into instants, seconds, frames of time, to increase the artist's knowledge of movement. But with movies, experiments on time entered the realm of the mind, and the ways information about the world was conveyed and received. Creel, Taylor, Lindsay, Münsterberg, Griffith, the Gilbreths; each sought a universal medium for ordering ideology.

Historians have characterized the middle-class political culture of the early twentieth century as a response to diversity, an attempt to rebuild an imagined consensus ravaged by industrial culture and immigration. Movies began as a largely immigrant phenomenon—their silence transcended the barriers of language. "Motion pictures," one critic suggested in a 1918 article on "Motion Pictures and Democracy," "might have saved the situation when the Tower of Babel was built." But now, during the war, he continued, the motion picture "is helping to mobilize the various points of view of the allied countries and marshal them into a single front."[94]

When Edwin Porter experimented with movie narrative, he resisted working time with too heavy a hand. "In the early days," recalled an article on war films, "only the pictorial values of motion pictures were grasped." Later, "its power of narration was discovered and made use of," and "its fact uses became apparent," till "finally argument and persuasion came within its scope." Now, in wartime, films of American unity and commitment to the war "are sent over to disprove German claims and set America in the true light . . . such pictured facts cannot be ignored."[95] Movies took the diversity and heterogeneity of American opinion and appeared to weld it, as Creel insisted, into "a white hot mass" united by the projector's light. "Influencing and binding all men," one movie fan asked at the height of World War I, "who shall say what levels of common thought and achievement shall be attained through the medium of the motion pictures?"[96]

If standard time offered a way to reorganize society on the clock's model, then movies offered a way to reorganize mental processes on a model of efficiency and control over time, a model of continuity and unity streamlined out of fragments. It was, like

Taylor's vision of clockwork factories, a machine model. "If Uncle Sam can teach, write history, plan strategies, argue, persuade and convince by means of motion pictures," went an editorial in *Current Opinion*, then why not create "a cinema university . . . reducing the length of college courses from four years to six months; cinema newspapers to be glanced at in handy assembly halls," and finally, "picture libraries, where they flash facts instead of handing out a book."[97] In the quest for speed, efficiency, and unity, what "facts" would be flashed? The facts themselves are interchangeable, but the underlying structure, the fragmented time recombined into narrative, is still with us today. Do movies mimic our imagination? Or have we come to think in movie time?

VI

The Golf Stick
and the Hoe

"Modern life," the pioneering sociologist Thorstein Veblen observed in 1916, "goes by clockwork." Standard railway time and clockwork machinery had replaced "the mechanism of the heavenly bodies," Veblen declared, and now "the discipline of the timepiece" paralleled "the discipline exercised by machine process at large in daily life." Veblen summarized the clock's emergence as the ruling principle of public life, and described the unconscious clock dependency industrialization required.

Industrial nations, Veblen concluded, developed a dual sense of time: one sense of time public and overtly clock-based; the other private and ostensibly "natural," but in fact every bit as bound to the clock. We now use mechanical clockwork as the pattern for governing ourselves, Veblen lamented, and in what he thought a futile attempt to escape "the machine-like process of living," more and more often we resort to "vacations," and the false promise of a "return to nature." Though they masqueraded as a different experience of time, vacations, Veblen felt, only strengthened the clock's control.[1]

When Veblen wrote his gloomy commentary, the word "vacation" had only recently acquired its modern meaning. Noah Webster's 1828 *American Dictionary of the English Language* defined the word primarily as "the act of making void," secondarily as "the intermission of judicial proceedings" or "the regular studies" of a college or school. Webster did include "the intermission of a stated employment" among his definitions, but this hardly corresponded to our modern sense of an institutionalized break from work itself. The word began acquiring its current meaning, "a period of relaxation from one's customary occupation," with the rise of industrial employments in the late nineteenth century. The *Oxford English Dictionary* describes "vacation," in our sense of "a holiday," as "chiefly U.S." and dates its appearance to around 1878—its emergence corresponds, more or less, with the rise of fixed hours of work and standardized public time.[2] The modern idea of the "vacation" makes sense only in a society with a sharply divided understanding of time, a society which pits clock-based public time against a more natural, pastoral alternative.

This divided sense of time characterized the revolution in leisure that accompanied the new century. Preindustrial societies enjoyed less of a distinction between "work" and "rest." Far more than they do today, the two varieties of experience, "labor" and "life," meant nearly the same thing—they intermingled constantly in the course of living. A wise and diligent farmer, finishing one task, went straight to work on another, and even at rest, the farmer remained a farmer; there was relatively little sense of "time off" from *being* an agriculturalist. But industrial labor, along with wage work and clock-time discipline in the factory, brought a heightened sense of distinction between work time and leisure. Actual time off, by our standards, often seems to have been pitiably brief in the late nineteenth century, especially for the poor. Still, industrial labor gave the growing class of wage earners a new kind of "free" time. Time off after the whistle blew at the end of the day could be spent as one wished—to the eternal chagrin of middle-class reformers, appalled at the spectacle of unstructured idleness.

Along with the increase in leisure came new activities for "free" time—movies, phonograph records, travel by train and later by car, a virtual explosion of consumer goods. A few critics, like Veblen, worried that these things all revolved around machines and mechanization. Machines for leisure, or leisure products made by machines—in embracing machine culture, did people themselves become machinelike? But by the 1890s, the fruits of industrialization had grown too tempting for even the most self-disciplined to resist. As the middle class found itself with more free time, more money to spend, and more places and things to spend it on, some of the old taboos against enjoyment in leisure time began collapsing. As they discovered leisure, "respectable" citizens threw off much of their inherited suspicion of pleasurable indulgence. By the late nineteenth century, to a far greater extent than before, conspicuous self-gratification had become the credo of the successful and the envy of the urban middle class.

But these new leisure pursuits mixed pleasure with peril. Old constraints against idleness lingered, and the middle class's discovery of indulgence raised unsettling questions—did the new emphasis on self-gratification herald the collapse of social order and personal discipline? How could society justify uses of time that seemed to produce nothing but empty pleasure? As the middle and upper classes adopted forms of leisure once confined to those beneath them in the social scale, they tended to "moralize" leisure pursuits and shape them into more comfortable forms. Most commonly, leisure time was tied to production. Industrial work enervated people, tired them out and left them pale and listless. Workers of all kinds who enjoyed themselves after work would revive, the argument went, and return to work the next day refreshed. As the history of motion picture narrative shows, techniques borrowed from industry served to make films seem like a socially efficient and productive form of leisure.

But besides the specter of Veblen's mechanized work force, this argument raised other problems. Could mechanized leisure ever truly offer human "re-creation"? And how could one judge a society that lived for transitory pleasures, instead of productive work? Did such a society really use time wisely?[3] These contradictory impulses — the desire for play and the feelings of uneasiness or guilt play engendered — revealed themselves most clearly in national debate over daylight saving.

Daylight saving first became a national issue in 1916. It was implemented briefly during World War I, then rejected by Congress after a fierce debate in 1919. While the debate over daylight saving reflected ambivalent feelings about leisure, it also gave evidence of a deeper unease about industrialization and machine time. Like "vacation" in its modern meaning, daylight saving only made sense in a society ruled by the clock. Its proponents argued that like a vacation, it would restore people to closer contact with nature and preindustrial rhythms. But opponents of daylight saving shared Thorstein Veblen's perception that it only reinforced the authority of clocks and machine time. To farmers, whose work still ran by nature's calendar, daylight saving simply made no sense — if you want more daylight for recreation after work, American farmers retorted scornfully, then why not simply rouse yourself from bed earlier?

The question looks deceptively simple and even a little foolish. But in fact it gets at the heart of changes in the understanding of time and their impact on American society. Why not, for example, simply declare that after April 30 of every year, all the employees in your foundry or office should report to work an hour earlier, at seven instead of eight? Then they could leave an hour earlier, at four instead of five, and get home in time for gardening and sandlot baseball. Seventy years before, American manufacturers had done just that—mills varied their hours with the seasons, to follow the sun. Railroad and steamship lines adopted new schedules each summer, following the seasonal patterns of employment and recreation. This earlier approach certainly seems easier and much more rational, on its surface, than convincing a whole nation to perform the strangely illogical, self-deluding task of simultaneously adjusting its clocks just before bedtime.

But by 1915, insisting that your employees report an hour earlier than the rest of the city subjected everyone involved to undue hardship. Suppose the streetcar lines only started running after seven—how would the employees get to work? Suppose their children's schooling commenced at eight—who would get the little tykes ready and see them off? And suppose your job demanded close attention to the stock and commodities markets—in that case, your competitors savored an extra hour of profitable trading while you nervously shagged fly balls. In a complex, interconnected economy that demanded agreement as to time, simply changing the clocks seemed the easiest, least painful way to simultaneously change the habits of millions.

The two alternatives—changing schedules and hours of operation, or simply changing the clocks—stem from two different approaches to social organization, and two vastly different conceptions of time. The first approach, changing schedules alone, says in effect, "time is nature, and natural imperatives govern our use of time." The second alternative, altering the clocks, insists, "time is what the clock says it is, and we can change the clock to suit ourselves." In the first, "6:00 a.m." is defined by the sun's position, in the second by the clock's hands. If the goal is simply more light after work, then either approach secures it. Certainly we can imagine a society that shifts its customs with the seasons—Americans traveling in Italy, for example, have traditionally been puzzled and frustrated by that country's custom of taking August off, and only modern air conditioning allows us to forget the old necessity of altering work patterns in the hot summer months. We don't make these sorts of seasonal adjustments today, because we have machines that help us ignore nature and run our affairs with mechanical regularity. By 1915, most Americans had already become so clockbound that daylight saving seemed the only way to change their habits.

Standard time, obviously, had already posed the same questions about time and nature, and its rapid acceptance in many quarters had also already answered them—for most people, time was simply what the clock showed, and for them, daylight saving made sense. But this is too simple. For one thing, large segments of the population, as congressional investigators were soon to discover, simply ignored standard time altogether. And again, in many places standard time had marked only a small, indeed imperceptible change from the local time of the sun. Years of custom made the standard clock time seem a "given"—by 1915, even those who bothered to wonder how standard time came about probably didn't know the answer. They looked to the clock for time, simply assuming a connection between the clock and the sun. The real point is that daylight saving posed these questions about time and society anew, and in far more dramatic terms.

If daylight saving epitomized the clock's dominance of everyday affairs, it also reflected a new sense of control over time, a perception that human time might be adjusted to suit not just business needs, but pleasure and convenience. As Chapter One described, an earlier age saw time as a sacred quality, not to be tampered with at mortal whim; indeed, one could no more tamper with time itself than one could alter the sun's passage across the sky. Clocks imitated God's time, and tampering with them trivialized God's will. But industrialization captured time and located it firmly in mechanical timepieces. Nearly one hundred years later, the rapid rise of daylight saving reiterates the fact that for many

Americans, in the cities especially, time had been desacralized, reduced from an object of awe to a servant of the desire for recreation.

Yet at the same time, the widespread opposition daylight saving provoked points to a stubborn refusal to abandon the older relationship between time, nature, and the organization of life. Although today it looks like commonsense, the idea of altering clocks to suit some human whim made daylight saving seem both unnatural and almost monstrous to its many opponents. The fight over daylight saving dramatized some of the essential conflicts of the period—tradition versus modernity, fundamentalism versus science, farming versus industry, the austerity of the Protestant Ethic versus leisure and consumerism—debates which had at their center conflicting beliefs about time's nature and its use. As an Illinois representative put it in 1919, at the height of the daylight saving debate, "this is a contest between the golf stick and the hoe."[4]

His phrase contained the symbols of two very different ways of life, one rooted in clock-governed work and leisure time, the other in religion and local farm traditions. By the end of World War I the country seemed poised for a sharp break with tradition. The 1920 census startled Americans by revealing that for the first time in the nation's history, more people lived in cities than on farms. True, the census bureau counted villages with as few as 2,000 residents as "urban" areas. But there was no mistaking the prevailing trend toward urban life, and toward the abstract, changeable, clock-based time that governed it. More and more, Americans defined themselves against arbitrary social con-structs—like standardized clock time, or notions of "efficiency"—instead of the natural world. The intense counterattack on "mo-dernity" that characterized the twenties aimed at rejecting these secular abstractions and returning society to some basis in natural moral law.

In the twenties, the word "modernity" encapsulated a whole range of the changes wrought by industrialization. It included not only new approaches to scientific inquiry and social reform, but also new attitudes about leisure, sexuality, new styles of dress, new kinds of work and entertainment. As the debate over daylight saving suggested, "modernity" and revisions in the idea of time went hand in hand. But the temporal challenge of modernity transcended daylight saving. "Modernity" revised many Americans' most fundamental religious assumptions—about the earth's age, and the origins of men and women; about the great flood—modernity challenged the very legitimacy of the Bible itself. At the 1925 Scopes Trial in Dayton, Tennessee, tradition and modernity fought one of their most celebrated battles, as Americans asked themselves which priorities should govern life—the priorities of the clock, the machine, and an interconnected economy, or the priorities of nature and the Bible. This chapter ends with a reminder, through the Scopes Trial, that attitudes about time are fundamental to our thinking about ourselves, our society, and the terms we use to organize our lives.

When the railroads adopted standard time in 1883, most of the country followed with little complaint. Or so the railroads told it; in fact, as we have seen, resistance to standard time continued well into the twentieth century. A surprising number of communities simply refused to abandon local time, or switched back and forth from one time to another, trying to find a satisfactory standard. In Cleveland, Ohio, for example, many businesses and even whole neighborhoods ignored standard time in favor of the local sun, well into the twentieth century. The *Cleveland Plain Dealer* reported in 1914 that "sun time is used in many Cleveland factories and many homes," especially in "the West Side and the Newburg section."[5] These neighborhoods kept to the sun, apparently with no adverse effects, while the rest of the city used central time intermittently.

Standard time enjoyed as little success in Detroit as in Cleveland. Michigan adopted standard time early on, but Detroit had wavered continually since 1883, and as late as 1900 the issue of central standard versus sun time still rankled. The city had used local sun time till November 20, when the common council tried proclaiming central time the legal standard. A week later they reversed themselves under public pressure, but by 1907 Detroit had returned, temporarily, to central time. Newspaper cartoonists lampooned the city's confusion. "It would not be surprising," a neighboring editor scoffed, "if the old village returns to its first love, horse cars, before spring."[6] Why the conflict over time in the two cities?

Their problems stemmed largely from standard time's effects on daylight. Central time synchronized Detroit and Cleveland with the railroads, with Lake Erie shipping, and with Chicago markets. But it put both cities approximately half an hour behind local sun time. The ninetieth meridian of longitude, which provided the standard of time for the central zone, passed almost directly through Memphis, Tennessee, well to the west. Using the central zone in effect put Cleveland and Detroit on Memphis local time. By central time, Cleveland sunrises and sunsets thus occurred roughly half an hour earlier than they would have by the local time. Since the advantages of central time—synchronization with Chicago and the railroads—only slightly outweighed the disadvantages of early darkness, most Clevelanders kept central time with no particular enthusiasm, or simply ignored it and followed the sun.

Eastern time, on the other hand, adjusted Cleveland's clocks to the seventy-fifth meridian, approximately Philadelphia local time, and put Cleveland on the same standard as the major eastern financial markets. Even better, eastern time slowed the sun. On eastern time, the sun arrived fashionably late in the morning and lingered pleasantly into the evening. Like Cleveland, Detroit stood almost exactly midway between the eastern and central zones, and so again choosing either zone made a perceptible difference in the hours of daylight. On eastern time, the Detroit sun rose much later—at seven o'clock in the morning, eastern time, Detroit's children straggled off to school in darkness, but had more time to play outdoors in the evening. On central time, the sun rose much earlier—Detroit's children awoke in full daylight at seven o'clock central time, but darkness cut their playtime short.

"We are creatures of the clock," reasoned Detroit's More Daylight Club in 1907; "our habits are governed by it to an even larger degree than we suspect." The founders of the More Daylight Club, Dr. George Renaud and C. M. Hayes, saw that no matter what zone Detroit chose, the clock, not the sun, governed life— schoolchildren woke up when the clock said seven, not when sunlight kissed their rosy cheeks. "We get up in the morning, we go to bed at night, we go to work and quit, and we eat, when the clock says to," they asserted. Since Detroiters answered to the clock and not the sun, casting Detroit into the "fast time" of the eastern zone would give later sunsets, and more light for recreation and play, to workers on regular hours. Why not exploit this allegiance to the clock, instead of suffering thoughtlessly under its heel? With partisan enthusiasm, the More Daylight Club began trying to move Detroit into the eastern time zone.[7]

Detroit's More Daylight Club promoted an early version of that familiar illusion, daylight saving. We all know how daylight saving works today—Spring ahead, Fall back, one hour twice a year—and the advantages and disadvantages it brings. But few people realize that daylight saving has a history, and that its history is inextricably bound up with evolving ideas about time. The idea dates back at least as far as Benjamin Franklin, who twice proposed tongue-in-cheek antecedents of daylight saving for London and Paris.[8] Franklin's sarcastic proposal evoked amusement, not action. But by the time the More Daylight Club came across it, the idea of shifting the hours of work had begun to take hold.

Detroit's early risers drew on the singular obsession of William Willett, a prosperous English builder. Like many fans of daylight saving, Willett loved golf, and regretted the early sunsets that robbed Englishmen of healthful exercise outdoors. As a businessman, he resented wasting fuel to light the darkness. In 1907 he wrote a pamphlet, "The Waste of Daylight," which proposed setting all British clocks ahead two hours each summer. His plan provoked ridicule at first, but gradually gained supporters after Willett sent his pamphlet to members of Parliament, businessmen, "Physical Culture Organizations," and foreign governments, including the U.S. Congress. In Detroit and Cleveland, Willett's idea strengthened the movement toward eastern time. The More Daylight Club's constant agitation brought Detroit to a vote on the issue by 1911, and enthusiasm for the plan spread southward. Cleveland adopted eastern time on May 1, 1914, and a year later Detroit, following a similar protracted battle, set its clocks to "fast time."[9]

In both cities, newspapers endorsed the measure's contributions to leisure time. The Cleveland Athletic Club celebrated the time change with a special party for five to six hundred guests. Two professional dancers from New York "demonstrated the hesitation waltz, Argentine tango and Maxixe with variations and introduced a new one to Cleveland called the Parisian one-step," while two local couples "gave an appreciated version of the cakewalk brought up to date." In both Cleveland and Detroit, commercial firms rushed to exploit the new time: Cleveland papers included a full-page ad headed: "Eastern Time Adopted by these Progressive Concerns." It offered the timely sales pitches of thirty-three different firms, all grouped, however loosely, around the time change. "More time for pleasure," one local store blared, "with the Connersville system of vacuum cleaning." "No matter what time you adopt," suggested a newly opened amusement center, "spend a part of it this summer at LUNA PARK."[10] The advertisements and the Athletic Club's celebration both related the change in daylight to the pursuit of pleasure in leisure time.

But newspapers also hastened to connect daylight saving to productive work and structured leisure. The front page of the *Cleveland Plain Dealer* showed a harried man rushing along behind a lawn mower, over the caption: "One More Hour of Daylight." The picture recalled family life and the responsibilities of an orderly, well-kept home, not nightlife and dancing. One local factory owner proposed dramatizing the benefits of the extra hour of light by staging an exhibition baseball game between the city's amateur and professional players. The Chamber of Commerce lauded the move's contribution to outdoor recreation, and listed "more efficient work in industrial plants" prominently among its supposed benefits.[11]

In 1916, England, France, Holland, and Germany all adopted the "fast time" of daylight saving as a way to promote efficiency and conserve fuel for the war. Impressed by Europe's example, and the measure's success in Cleveland and Detroit, American partisans of more daylight began agitating Congress for a national daylight saving law. Such a law, they argued, would greatly aid productivity, by saving fuel and by giving tired industrial workers an extra hour of health-giving recreation outdoors. Even better, daylight saving would reverse the ongoing trend toward keeping late hours, and return society to harmony with the sun. American politicians began studying the value of turning the nation's clocks ahead.

The Senate Committee on Interstate Commerce met in 1916 to consider "a thorough investigation of all questions involved in the standardization of time in the United States and its territorial possessions." The Committee recognized the fact that without a national legal standard, cities, towns, counties, states, or regions might all adopt any time they chose—as in fact they had done and were still doing—and that such a situation hardly furthered efficient commerce. And the wartime adoption of daylight saving by the European belligerents made the measure's supposed contributions to efficiency particularly intriguing. Certainly the United States deferred to no nation in its commitment to maximum efficiency. The Committee decided to proceed with an investigation into daylight saving.[12]

While Congress pondered, the daylight saving issue dawned in the popular press. There, however, the quest for more daylight met with suspicion. Almost universally, early comment on daylight saving depicted the measure as an ill-disguised attempt to make early risers out of late sleepers. Even its opponents had to admit, as one engineering magazine put it, "that the early morning hours are hours of exceptional efficiency." Germany had adopted daylight saving, after all, and Germany "sets the pace in many lines of efficiency." But most articles depicted the measure as the pet project of moralizing insomniacs. "Stated plainly," declared the *Literary Digest* of daylight saving, "this amounts to a plan for making people get up earlier by telling them it is later than it really is." Most writers resented daylight saving as some sort of fakery, a sugar coating on the bitter pill of morning. The *Saturday Evening Post* called it "a harmless piece of buncombe," but asked sarcastically "why not 'save summer' by having June begin at the end of February?"[13]

The measure's association with industrious living and efficiency made it look like another in an ancient series of nagging imprecations against lying late in bed, a tyrannical imposition by joyless reformers. "The Kaiser has declared that noon shall be called one o'clock," went an article on "fiat time" in *The Independent;* but "we question whether setting the alarm clock of a nation one hour too fast will make people get up earlier in the long run. If they really wanted to get up earlier they could do it now, most of them, without any legislation." "The early morning hours," they suggested, "are highly spoken of by poets who nevertheless are apt, like the rest of us, to spend them in bed." "What special good is going to be accomplished?" asked the *Engineering Record*. "The hours of labor will be neither lengthened nor shortened," and "the actual savings in artificial light," despite claims to the contrary, "is rather illusory."[14]

Daylight saving at first met largely with skepticism and suspicion. The *New York Times* resented the supposition that clocks ruled life, and that tyrannical timekeepers alone could snatch the reluctant sleeper from Morpheus' grasp. "Are we slaves of the clock?" asked an editorial. "Would you get up if your alarm clock told you to, even if there were no sunshine through the bathroom window? Would you go to bed an hour earlier just because your watch said it was the proper thing to do? Does the world move by the clock or by the sun?"[15] The *Times* asked the central question—how far away from nature had society moved? Was American society based on nature or the machine?

One of the more peculiar aspects of the debate on daylight saving centered on the apparent (and apparently welcome) decline of early rising. Changes in American technology, after all, had helped alter not just the idea of time but the schedule of life and leisure itself—electric lights, for one example, brought light and laughter to nighttime hours formerly too dark for all but sleeping. "The fact of the matter," declared *The Independent*, "is that people prefer darkness to daylight for their hours of recreation, and whenever they get money and leisure enough they shift their working day to later hours."[16] So much modern leisure seemed to take place under artificial light—would Broadway lose its thrill by daylight?

Industrial societies stayed up later to consume the fruits of their achievements—"in all civilized countries," insisted *Scientific American*, "there is a tendency to keep later instead of earlier hours, and the daylight saving plan appears to be a somewhat violent plan to combat the instinct, whatever it is, that underlies this tendency." "The real question," continued a second editorial, "is whether it is desirable for the bulk of the population to keep earlier hours."[17] Industrialization may have imposed rigid schedules on work, but it also offered free time after hours, and a dazzling spectrum of new leisure time diversions. Questioning the worth of nighttime pleasure seemed to challenge the redeeming virtues of industrial progress.

By this light, daylight saving looked like a reactionary attempt to beat back change. "It has yet to be proved," declared an editorial in the *Times*, "that a return to the hours kept by hens and savages confers any ponderable benefits."[18] These early critics interpreted daylight saving as an attack on modernity. They resented it as an attempt to regulate life by some health reformer's clock, a thin excuse for wresting more "efficiency" from the vast majority who chose to sleep late. The idea appeared not as a way to use more daylight in the evening, but as a poor ruse to get people out of bed earlier, made all the more offensive by its implicit assumption that people were simply foolish dupes of their bedside alarms. Over a century before, Benjamin Franklin had issued his famous and tiresome maxim "Early to bed and early to rise, makes a man healthy, wealthy and wise." Much of the early reaction to daylight saving suggested that Franklin's descendents still resented the advice.

But by early 1916 a powerful coalition of businessmen and politicians had begun to embrace the idea of changing the hours. The *Times* reported support for advancing the clock among "influential members of the Stock Exchange" who hoped to restore customary relations with the London financial market altered when England passed its new "Summer Time" law. Our present timekeeping customs, Commissioner of Immigration Frederic C. Howe pointed out to New Yorkers in another example, "are a hold-over from when we were more or less an agricultural country." The really modern thing to do was change the clocks — Howe cited the example of Cleveland and Detroit, and suggested that Gothamites could use the extra daylight to "play tennis, go to the country, or to Coney Island."[19]

Manhattan's borough president, the alliterative Marcus M. Marks, formed a committee, including representatives of government, business, and labor, to study the question for New York. By 1917 he had organized the National Daylight Saving Association, a lobbying group including delegates from state and local governments, chambers of commerce and trade organizations, prominent businessmen, and labor organizations. After six months of extensive lobbying in New York and Washington, the National Daylight Saving Association held its first meeting in New York City on January 30, 1917. Over one thousand eager National Daylight Saving Conventioneers converged on the city for two days, "wearing lapel buttons bearing a picture of Uncle Sam turning the clock forward one hour." Speakers on the virtues of more daylight included John Tener, president of the National Baseball League, who spoke on "why fans favor the movement," and the president of the National Lawn Tennis Association.[20]

More significantly, by January 1917 the United States was being drawn ever closer to the European conflict, and in April of that year the country declared war. An obsession before the war, efficiency acquired near-religious status once the war began. Representative Borland of Missouri introduced a bill to begin national daylight saving shortly after the declaration of war. The bill died quickly, but it helped rally nationwide support for the idea. To promote the measure's practicality, the National Daylight Saving Convention printed up and issued mailing cards for concerned voters. Each three-by-five card featured a picture of Uncle Sam with a rifle over his shoulder and a garden hoe in his hand, turning back the hands of a large pocketwatch. The pocketwatch had legs and a face, and wore a doughboy's hat. It exclaimed: "Turn the clock ahead ONE HOUR Uncle. No longer working day for anybody but all in daylight—and you GAIN ONE HOUR for National Efficiency." On the reverse, the cards read: "If I have more Daylight I can work longer for my country. We need every hour of light."[21] In hitching daylight saving to the war effort, its partisans had found their most effective strategy.

While the National Daylight Saving Convention bombarded congressmen with these cards, the Boston Chamber of Commerce, led by department store magnate A. Lincoln Filene, printed up and circulated its own pamphlet on the advantages of daylight saving, "An Hour of Light for an Hour of Night." The pamphlet, which emphasized the need for increased efficiency in war, went to Congress and to commercial organizations in other cities.[22] As a leading member of the U.S. Chamber of Commerce, Filene led that organization's endorsement of daylight saving as well, and won its position substantial publicity. In May 1917, Filene, Marks, and a varied assortment of daylight saving partisans traveled to Washington at the request of the Senate Subcommittee on Interstate Commerce.

The Subcommittee had met to consider S. 1854, "A Bill to Save Daylight and Provide Standard Time for the United States," introduced by Senator William Calder of New York the month before. Marks, opening testimony in favor of the measure, began by emphasizing its potential contributions to wartime production. "The purpose that brings us here at this time," Marks solemnly intoned, "is President Wilson's message that the food supply needs increase." A month earlier Wilson had listed increased food production among the Allies' most pressing problems. Under daylight saving, Marks claimed, "the stimulation of gardening is tremen-

Mailing card from the campaign for daylight saving during World War I. (National Archives.)

dous"—patriotic Americans, spades in hand, would fall out into their backyards and begin digging at once.

Marks even carried a brief letter from President Wilson endorsing "any movement which has the objects of the daylight saving movement."[23] The Subcommittee did hear some testimony in opposition to the bill, from a representative of the railroads who expected the time change to decrease safety on certain lines. But impressed by the potential to increase efficiency, its members recommended that the bill be passed, if amended to take effect on January 1, 1918. When the Subcommittee reported its findings on May 25, 1917, it stressed the innovation's usefulness in time of war, and the relatively minor inconveniences that would result.[24]

Fertilized by congressional and presidential endorsement, Marks's energetic campaign began bearing motley if abundant fruit among the general public. "We have been slaves of the clock," Marks exclaimed; "it is time now to make the clock yield to our needs." In New York, Mrs. Vincent Astor pronounced her approval of the measure, followed shortly by the National Civil Service Reform League and a Dr. Eugene Lyman Fisk of the "Life Extension Institute, 25 W. 45th St." *Automobile*, the magazine of motoring, published a series of favorable comments on a measure that offered more sunlight for motor jaunts in the country after work. The magazine's enthusiasm was tempered, however, by reports that in England, daylight saving had actually *increased* fuel consumption by over-eager evening motorists.[25]

On the more serious side, the move for more daylight gained the support of Samuel Gompers and the AFL. "We urge the inauguration of a daylight saving project," Gompers wrote, "for the conservation of time and opportunity for greater leisure and open air exercise." And the Pennsylvania Senate reflected the anxieties of war when it resolved that since "enemy governments have passed laws advancing the time one hour during the long summer days for the purpose of conserving their resources," so too should Pennsylvania and the nation.[26]

Over the next nine months, the National Daylight Saving Convention issued a series of posters emphasizing the measure's contribution to food production and wartime efficiency generally. Each depicted both Uncle Sam and the doughboy watch that Marks's organization had used in its earlier congressional mailing campaign. "Saving Daylight!" blared one, a poster of Uncle Sam and the doughboy timepiece marching off with hoes and rifles over their shoulders. "Mobilize an extra hour of daylight and help win the war!" In another, Uncle Sam stretched sleepily in his bed while the tireless doughboy clock pointed out his window, where "Germany" and "Austria" forged swords and tilled the soil of "Middle Europe." "Uncle Sam," the caption read, "your enemies have been up and are at work on the extra hour of daylight— when will *you* wake up?" The posters all stressed the importance of staying even with the enemy, and sacrificing at home to win the war.[27]

The idea of the soldier as a watch might seem vaguely discomfiting—it makes the soldier into a machine who tells Uncle Sam what to do. The timekeeper offers a model for patriotic, diligent, early-rising service in the first truly mechanized war— Uncle Sam literally follows the watch. The war required unanimity; as Chapter Five discussed, Wilson oversaw an unprecedented barrage of propaganda and publicity for the war effort, aimed at repressing dissent and uniting Americans in enthusiasm for the fight. Part of daylight saving's appeal lay in its mechanical universality—it affected everyone, regardless of race, ethnicity, or gender, and united them temporally in a measure of sacrifice for the war. But paradoxically, it also seemed to free people from work-place mechanization, and restore a measure of contact with natural time. By the summer of 1917, daylight saving lobbyists had changed opinion on daylight saving in popular magazines from largely skeptical to almost universally enthusiastic.

Encouraged by growing support for the measure's popularity and apparent contributions to efficiency, in January 1918 the House of Representatives entered into debate on Senate 1854, Calder's bill "to save daylight and provide a standard time."[28] Over a dozen speakers in favor of the bill reiterated the by now familiar points: the measure's success in Europe, its boons to efficiency, health, and recreation, and especially to home gardening. A broad coalition of manufacturers, businessmen, and recreational associations supported the idea, its proponents reminded. Form letters, sponsored perhaps by Marks and his organization, demanded the passage of the Calder bill. "What is holding up the daylight saving bill?" asked one. "One million tons of coal might have been saved if Congress had passed this bill a year ago . . . and yet it is allowed to remain dormant."[29] Herbert Hoover, head of the recently formed United States Food Administration, pronounced himself "only too pleased" to endorse a measure so conducive to home gardening.[30] Such testimonials made a persuasive case for saving daylight in time of war.

A few congressmen found these arguments unconvincing at best, and ludicrous at worst. Representative Otis Wingo of Arkansas especially distinguished himself with sarcastic humor in the folksy southern tradition. Apparently serious, Wingo cited a recent article proposing "that Congress provide for a winter thermometer and fix the freezing point at 45° Fahrenheit." Placed in American homes, Wingo continued, the thermometers would read thirteen degrees higher than the actual temperature, and so "they could look at the thermometers and be fooled, and in that way save fuel next winter." The idea seems ridiculous, but it operates on precisely the same principle as daylight saving—the assumption that people obey their measuring instruments unthinkingly. Most of the men who advocated daylight saving, Wingo scoffed, were trying to dupe themselves and their constituents out of lazy habits; they "have not seen the sun rise in twenty years, and they will not see it if you pass this bill." We have more important things to do in this time of war, he insisted disgustedly; but "while our boys are fighting in the trenches we are here like a lot of schoolboys 'tinkering' with the clocks."[31]

Kentucky's Robert Thomas condemned those "modern Joshuas" who sought to alter the planet's course "by any legislative legerdemain or so-called daylight saving device." "This bill," he declared, "was sired by an uplift magazine and will be damned by a majority of the people."[32] The barb struck home — no single magazine had "sired" daylight saving, but the measure was part and parcel of the era's determined emphasis on "efficiency and uplift" through rational legislation. Both men felt uneasy about a measure that depended on rote obedience to mechanical timekeepers, a measure so clearly and unequivocally designed with the industrial wage earner, not the farmer, in mind. But their objections paled before the barrage of testimonials and endorsements loosed by the proponents of daylight saving.

After a lengthy debate, the bill passed the House by a vote of 253 to 40. The Senate added its approval the next day, officially declaring that clocks be moved ahead one hour at 2:00 a.m. on May 31, 1918. The change elated its supporters in New York. Members of the National Daylight Saving Committee gathered at the Aldine Club to watch the clocks change, but otherwise the move excited little controversy and came and went smoothly. "It was as a war measure that Joshua commanded the sun to stand still," recalled the *Times*. If there had been clocks in those days, continued the article, "Joshua might have put the clocks forward an hour or two in order to save that much daylight for the battle." On April 1, the newspaper reported, uncounted thousands of New Yorkers used the extra daylight for baseball, golf, tennis, and thrill-seeking at Coney Island. Little over a month later the newspaper praised the innovation's contributions to social well-being, and asserted confidently that "the idea of abandoning it, ever, in peace or war, never enters any mind."[33]

National magazines registered the same confident approval, with glowing encomiums on the virtues of evening sun. Here, it seemed, was a progressive measure that actually worked. It increased national efficiency, claimed *Current Opinion,* and in addition let working women walk home by daylight; it gave parents a new hour outside with their children, and cut electric and gas bills in half. As the bill's term neared expiration in late October, the *Survey* praised its apparently universal virtues. "Not only recreation in the recognized sense," wrote a Chicago correspondent, "but a general feeling of freedom of life, of neighborliness, of time to visit with the home folks . . . and invite one's soul through the convenient exercise of leisure have been promoted by daylight saving."[34]

As this letter shows, though the measure promoted efficiency it also provided genuine relief from the nagging press of ordinary time, and restored tired citizens to natural pleasures. Daylight saving has made us, the *Literary Digest* concluded, "a healthier, wealthier, wiser land." The measure was not evidence of a mechanized, machine-enslaved society, but rather evidence of control over machines. We have not merely deceived ourselves, the magazine added, but instead as the *Boston Transcript* put it, have "simply demonstrated our moral superiority to our mechanical arrangements."[35] The *Transcript's* observation touched the heart of the matter—daylight saving took the "mechanical arrangements" that governed ordinary affairs and turned them to more pleasant uses. Supporters of daylight saving used "efficiency" to put their bill through Congress, and depicted a civilian army of fervent war gardeners, patriotically weeding the tomatoes after work. But in descriptions of the measure's benefits the themes of "efficiency" and home gardening largely fell away, replaced instead by glowing accounts of the soothing, relaxing effects of late evening sunshine.

In the grim, urgent, workday world, the enemy time ever threatened to vanish; harried laborers in all fields of work seemed to chase endlessly after ever smaller fragments of time. But not only did daylight saving extend sunlight; it also seemed to unite a whole society in renewed appreciation of nature, leisure, and healthful recreation. A letter to the *Survey* imagined "a well-nigh universal ground-swell of feeling on the part of people of all sorts" in favor of daylight saving. "The daylight saving scheme has represented the annexation, as if from out of nowhere, of a new strip of life," continued the letter.[36] If clocks enforced simultaneity, unanimity, and unflagging obedience, here was an example of clock time creating a shared, apparently unanimous experience of wholesome, neighborly, renewing leisure.

Still, the idea of everyone experiencing the same relaxation at the same time every day gave credence to Veblen's charge about the mechanization of leisure. And the appearance of unanimity over daylight saving proved deceptive. Besides instituting daylight saving, the Calder bill also legalized the railroad standard time zones invented in 1883, and empowered the Interstate Commerce Commission to investigate the borders between the zones and alter them as it saw fit. The Commission's investigation disclosed a surprising diversity in America's timekeeping habits. State statutes legally governed the time in many instances, yet the Commission found those statutes widely ignored in places where railroads used a different time. Complicating matters further, in some of these places local communities used a still different time from the railroads. The Commission stressed that "it appears clearly from the record that there is need for a closer connection between the sun and the clock than has obtained in many parts of the country," and that moving the clock too far from the apparent time of the sun seemed both highly impractical and unlikely to succeed. Using these principles as its guide, the Commission systematically readjusted the zones, taking care to preserve the natural relationship to the sun and place the zone borders in sparsely populated areas as often as possible.[37] By respecting local timekeeping practices, and deviating as little as possible from established practice, the Commission managed to rule on standard time without awakening much opposition.

The same could not be said for daylight saving when the issue came before Congress again in 1919. In that troubled year, so scarred by violence and social change, the apparent consensus about daylight saving's virtues collapsed. After the armistice in November 1918, daylight saving lost the justification of wartime emergency. American farmers, who had kept largely silent on the idea during the war, began expressing their disapproval in no uncertain terms shortly after the new year. Farmers, it seemed, claimed that the new time forced them to rise in darkness and begin their chores too early. The cows refused to give milk, and the heavy morning dew made work in the fields impossible. "The farmer," the *Digest* summarized, "objects to doing his early chores in the dark merely that his city brother, who is sound asleep at the time, may enjoy a daylight motor ride in the evening."[38] As attempts to renew the daylight saving bill began, letters from disgruntled farm organizations began pouring into Washington. A typical petition, from the citizens of New Britain, Connecticut, echoed the claim that daylight saving inconvenienced the farmer, and added that "the time should be set by Nature, that is, by the sun, which is the best timepiece in the world."[39]

"The farmers," warned the *Times*, "are bombarding Congress with demands" for the repeal of daylight saving. "Write or wire immediately to [your congressman]," urged the New York Merchant's Association; "and urge your friends to also wire against the proposed repeal." "When we were informed," began an editorial in *Scientific American*, of a bill "aimed to kill the Daylight

Saving Act, we experienced a distinct shock." The bill had seemed so universally beneficial, and "we had always looked upon the farmer as one who delighted in early hours and who would love to have the rest of the world routed out of bed with the sun." To city dwellers, the farmer's hostility seemed inexplicable—did not daylight saving return society to closer harmony with nature, while saving fuel? Marcus Marks could only imagine that in fact the farmer had little to do with it; "although the sentiment against daylight saving seems to have come from farmers," Marks suggested, "it is really fostered by the large gas companies, which would benefit from repeal of the law."[40]

When Congress convened in June to discuss the repeal of daylight saving, the farmer's hostility occupied hour after hour of debate through the summer. Just why were farmers so upset? The congressional debate revealed the growing gap between rural and urban cultures, between patterns of life rooted in clock time and wage labor, and ways of living modeled on nature's example. It also anticipated the backlash against modernity that would later result in the Scopes Trial. Some farmers experienced genuine economic hardship as a result of daylight saving, and many more suffered serious inconvenience. But others resented having the arbitrary strictures of machine time imposed on their lives.

The two sides attacked each other in symbolic terms: urbanites, rural citizens claimed, lived off the farmer's ceaseless labor, yet had crust enough to demand more leisure time for their unproductive play. The urbanite lived in the thrall of the diabolical machine, while the farmer enjoyed the moral virtue of harmony with nature. Or, conversely, the farmer wallowed in ignorance and superstition, and trembled lest altering the clocks bring down the wrath of the almighty, while the city dweller tolerated and even welcomed modernity, innovation, and change. The farmer rhapsodized over nature, but selfishly allowed mere habits of tradition to deprive the toiling factory masses of the same sunshine and fresh air he praised so fulsomely. The debate over daylight saving in 1919 helped draw the boundaries between tradition and modernity, the conflict between inherited beliefs and scientific inquiry, that would characterize American intellectual life for decades to come.

The most common source of the farmer's complaint, the one most easily lampooned, was the morning dew. Under daylight saving, farmers protested, the dew evaporated an hour later than it had before, delaying the onset of field work and slowing the harvest. The farmer's hired help arrived at seven o'clock in the morning, as usual. But on daylight saving time seven by the clock meant 6:00 a.m. by the sun—the morning dew still lay heavily on the fields, and now the farmer had to figure out what to do with a whole crew of hired hands, standing idly, on the payroll, waiting for the dew to dry. We accepted this foolish arrangement during the war, rural voters wrote to Washington; now let us have a return to peacetime conditions.[41]

Urban congressmen found this objection preposterous—why not simply have the hired hands report an hour later than they did before daylight saving? If they began at eight, the dew would be gone, and if they then quit their eight-hour day at six instead of five the farmer lost no time. Many interpreted the farmer's apparent unwillingness to make this easy adjustment as pure stubbornness. Fiorello LaGuardia, then a representative from New York, called these arguments mere "camouflage." "Let us be frank about it," LaGuardia taunted his rural colleagues. "You are trying to repeal this law at the request of the employers of farm help, of the absent landlords . . . you are trying to get another hour of work out of [the laborer] at the end of the day." If farmers are so anxious to repeal all war measures, LaGuardia countered, "I ask how many of these gentlemen are ready to repeal war-time prohibition?"[42]

In fact, the situation was more complicated than LaGuardia

understood. The farmer might try changing the hours his help worked, but it seemed they adamantly refused to quit at the new time. For one thing, quitting at six instead of five deprived the farm laborer of the very benefits daylight saving was supposed to confer. Instead of gaining an hour of evening sunshine, the laborer lost it. Moreover, claimed an Indiana congressman, "the farm hand of today is rapidly assimilating the hours of labor in the industries, and, in rapidly increasing number, he quits with the blowing of the whistle in nearby towns."[43] When that customary quitting time came around, the hired help dropped their tools and raced off to meet their friends for baseball, movies, dancing, and the other activities of modern leisure. The problem came not from the farmer's hostility to innovation, or any superstitious dread of the dew, but from two opposed understandings of time. In the farm towns, clocks governed life and brought people together on schedule, but on the farm itself natural conditions refused to bend to the clock's rule.

City dwellers derived much hilarity from a second objection, that the dairy farmer's cows resolutely ignored the clock and refused to give milk by the new time. But here again two differing systems of time clashed, to the farmer's detriment. Suppose a dairy farmer traditionally milked his cows at five in the morning, and got his milk to the depot to be taken off for processing and sale by seven. Under daylight saving, he now milked the cows at six by the clock, too late in the morning to catch the milk train before it pulled away at seven o'clock. If he rose an hour earlier, he lost that much milk, if the cows gave milk at all. And of course he had been rising to his chores before dawn's light at four; now had to rise at 3:00 a.m., stumble around in the dark, and sell less milk, all so city dwellers could play at gardening after dinner. Citing his constituents' complete hostility to the measure, a Missouri congressman called daylight saving "the most mischievous and pestiferous experiment this country ever undertook."[44]

Farmers had enough trouble keeping their children "down on the farm" as it was, and daylight saving made farm life both less pleasant and more isolated than it had been. It deprived farm families of the modern pleasures and conveniences that were only just reaching rural America, for the farm family "is put out of joint with the situation in [the] local market town."[45] Nearby movies, lectures, meetings, dances, and other cultural and social events were over before farmers and their families could get to town. Farm wives rose with their husbands and worked in darkness, while their children either neglected vital chores or lost time in school.[46]

To make matters worse, some of America's most productive farm regions experienced far more drastic changes in daylight than the cities. The boundaries between standard time zones had been set to fall in rural areas as much as possible. A farm located at the extreme edge of a zone—like much of rural Ohio, for example—was already half an hour or more ahead of the "real" time of the sun, unless it ignored standard time. Daylight saving put some places nearly two hours ahead of the solar time; in some Ohio communities, the clocks showed "noon" at what had been one forty-five or even two in the afternoon by the sun. Such cases only compounded the problems already described.[47] These disadvantages combined to present farmers and their families with a considerable hardship, or at the very least with substantial and genuine reasons for wanting the bill repealed. But the relatively small economic and social hardship daylight saving engendered fails to explain its opponent's vivid rhetoric.

In their arguments against the bill, rural congressmen blamed it for the manifest ills of the age. It embodied the trend away from real production and toward idle consumption: the bill "is a pet of the professional class, the semileisure class, the man of the golf club and the amateur gardener, the sojourner at the suburban summer resort," charged a Minnesota representative, "who can all close their desks an hour earlier and hie them to an extra hour of play."[48] As a thoroughly non-productive, silly game played on the coiffed and manicured surface of perfectly good land, golf symbolized the utter decadence that underlay the daylight saving movement. The enemies of daylight saving scorned golf, again and again, as the wasteful indulgence of a parasitical class. By their honest sweat the farmers wrested the world's sustenance and ease from stubborn ground; instead of asking more sacrifice from the farmer, or laughing at his ignorance, rural politicians claimed, "you should rise up in your refinement and call him blessed."[49]

One of daylight saving's most outspoken opponents, Representative Edward King of Illinois, extended the attack on "refinement" to include progressivism generally. King saw daylight saving as the impractical child of the professional reformer and the university dreamer. During the war, King insisted, the farmer supported all sorts of boneheaded "scientific" measures for " 'economy,' 'efficiency,' 'coordination' " in good faith, even to the outrage of commonsense. But now King lambasted "the impractical, the Utopians, the theorists, political astrologers, medicine men, and advance agents of the millennium" who, he insisted, constituted daylight saving's main support. A year earlier one of King's colleagues had laid daylight saving's invention to "an uplift magazine"; now King charged its continuance to "that intangible professorial influence which we all recognize as occupying a sort of dictatorial attitude during the war and whose decrees we have so often observed and felt." Desirous of "applying the pedagogical whip to the backs of what they deemed the unruly and uneducated people," "the Professariate" have forgotten in "their theoretical air navigation both God and nature."[50]

Doubtless much of the sentiment against daylight saving reflected a general weariness with the pretensions of the "Professariate," and with Wilsonian Progressive crusading in particular. Wilson twice vetoed the repeal of daylight saving after the appropriate majorities of both houses had approved it, in pronouncements thick with Progressive pieties. His first veto message lauded the "competent men" whose "careful study of industrial conditions" had led to the bill's formulation, and his second stressed the "immediate and pressing need" for "increased and increasing production." The bill "ministers to economy and efficiency," Wilson suggested, but his congressional opponents would have none of it.[51] "Now that the whole world has been made safe for democracy," remarked a member from Illinois sarcastically, "perhaps it is appropriate that the President should insist that every day in this country be made safe for the joy rider and for the patron of the golf links and tennis courts."[52] Members of Congress frequently suggested that perhaps the President should spend more time at home, listening to the people, and less time in Europe saving the world.

But beneath all these objections there lurked a fundamental resistance to the clock's authority, and to the mechanization of society. The "Professariate," Congressman King had charged, have forgotten in their theories both God and nature. Again and again, rural Americans and their representatives pledged their allegiance to natural time, God's order, and "nature's timepiece," the sun. Senator Oscar Underwood of Alabama spoke for many when he insisted that "time has been fixed for ages by the movement of the sun." Now that the war is over, he asked, "let us stand by the custom that generation after generation has adopted." Daylight saving interferes, added an Iowan, "with the natural order of things as regulated by the rising and setting of the sun." Come out to Iowa, Congressman Burton Sweet invited his urban colleagues, "and really live as you should live," not in violation of "the mandates and decrees of the Eternal God." Representative Ezekiel Candler of Mississippi delivered perhaps the most stirring peroration on behalf of the sun when he angrily insisted that "the rising of the sun and the going down thereof fixes the time." "God's time is true," Candler rang out; "man made time is false." "Let us repeal this law and have the clocks proclaim God's time and tell the truth," he thundered to his colleagues' applause. "Truth is always best. It is mighty and should always prevail."[53]

Their urban opponents found these claims patently ridiculous. Since 1883, they pointed out, Americans had been using four standard time zones based only loosely on the sun's position, with no ill effects, no celestial wrath. But these countercharges missed the point. For one thing, congressional investigation had only recently disclosed that where people found the standard clock time too far removed from the sun, they simply ignored it; and indeed as Chapter Three discussed, their decision to ignore standard time had the backing of law in many states. But more importantly, rural congressmen argued not for perfect fidelity with the sun, but rather for a life regulated by natural principles, in which clocks served as useful approximations of the time rather than time itself. When daylight saving threw their lives out of synch with nearby towns, they interpreted the move as slavery to clocks and industrial clock time.

Declarations of principle like Congressman Candler's brought only scorn from the partisans of daylight saving, for whom such phrases sang of a thick-minded, foolish obstinance. By couching their arguments in religious terms, farmers made it easy for their opponents to tar them with the brush of ignorance, backwardness, and reaction. One typical letter to Congress, for example, charged agitation against daylight saving to "a few mossbacks, hayseeds and night riders" making a bigger noise than their number warranted.[54] In an illustration in the *Literary Digest*, a bearded farmer shook his fist at a departing automobile, which in its speeding haste had knocked the cans of milk he carried out of his wagon. At the wheel of the car, Father Time left a cloud of dust as he stepped on the gas. "UPSETTING EFFECT OF FATHER TIME'S NEW BURST OF SPEED," read the caption. A Philadelphia editor attacked the "obstinate pigs and cows who dictated to Congress" on daylight saving.[55] These jibes fed the desire to seem modern and "up to date." But in assigning the movement for repeal to what they imagined an ignorant, hidebound minority, daylight saving's partisans ignored the class and social biases built into the daylight saving scheme.

Though its supporters claimed universal benefits for the measure, in fact daylight saving best served certain limited segments of society—middle-class, urban wage earners in the Northeast especially. It penalized groups more dependent on natural rhythms—farmers, obviously, but also housewives, children, and less skilled workers in low-status jobs—as well as people living near the boundaries of time zones. During the debate over daylight saving most of the attention focused on the farmers, whose legendary conservatism supposedly explained their resistance to modern, rational innovations. But the measure might never have been repealed had only farmers opposed it. The fatal blow to daylight saving came at the hands of industrial workers, and particularly the American Federation of Labor.

For certain groups of workers, daylight saving only worked an inconvenience and depressed the spirits. For example, workers unable to afford a house within easy commuting distance of their job, then as now, had to rise that much earlier than their more fortunate co-workers. Most of the year they rose in darkness; only in summer did they have light to dress by.[56] Daylight saving deprived them of that morning sun. Representative King of Illinois pointed especially to the coal miners of his state, who had voted, along with the Illinois State Labor Federation, for the repeal of daylight saving. The situation in Illinois was made doubly unpleasant by the state's location in the far eastern section of the central time zone. Here were men engaged in difficult, arduous work, vital to the nation, in nearly constant darkness. Should they be deprived of morning sun just so city dwellers could play golf?[57]

Starting early often meant finishing early, and one of the few benefits of such jobs had been the extra daylight after work. But with the new time, the blessing became a curse as the extra daylight, and the noises of summer recreation, often intruded far into the hours for sleep. In parts of the Midwest especially, the sun that once set at nine o'clock now set at ten-thirty or even later, making it all the more difficult for parents to get children to bed, and to get to sleep themselves. A second problem, one we are inclined to take for granted in the air-conditioned present, stemmed from the resulting heat. Before daylight saving, workers made their way home in the waning heat of day, and enjoyed the cool evening hours sitting on the porch or sleeping; but under the new time an extra hour of hot sunlight made working conditions, and the evening, all the more unpleasant. "These are trifles, you will say," wrote "a workingwoman" to *The New York Times*. "Yes, but trifling things like flies and mosquitoes are a nuisance. Why continue?" During the war we were all glad to make small sacrifices, but now we workers too want an end to daylight saving— "it is not all the farmers, as you seem to think," she added.[58]

Labor leaders like Samuel Gompers pronounced themselves all in favor of daylight saving, and their testimony had helped pass the bill in the first place. But at the AFL's June 1919 convention, the delegates soundly defeated a measure protesting the repeal of daylight saving. Prominent speakers against the resolution included John L. Lewis of the United Mine Workers, whose members resented having to rise as early as three-thirty in the morning, sun time, and trudge to work in gloomy darkness. The Convention's actions gave credence to the farmer's charge that daylight saving in fact favored mostly idlers and the wealthy classes. There is no way of judging the actual extent of workers' opposition to daylight saving time. But the AFL's rejection of the bill, coupled with other scattered letters and resolutions by lesser labor organizations, hints very strongly of opposition to daylight saving among the least skilled, least organized, and least represented members of the working class.[59]

These objections to the measure point not to any great harm worked by daylight saving, but rather to the inequity, in 1919, of trying to regulate all social affairs by one clock time. There seems little doubt that daylight saving worked a positive good for most, if not all, factory and office workers in the cities. But benefits for one segment of society equaled losses for another, and the enormous differences in patterns of living between different groups, across so vast an expanse of land as the United States, made the clock-changing law impractical at best. Over twenty-eight bills for the repeal of daylight saving were introduced in the summer of 1919. Two surviving bills reached President Wilson's desk, only to be vetoed each time. Congress finally overrode Wilson's second veto on August 21, 1919, ending national daylight saving until the next world war.

Almost immediately, Marks and the United States Chamber of Commerce began lobbying for "daylight saving by local ordinance." The original Daylight Saving Act of 1918 had legalized standard time zones and empowered the Interstate Commerce Commission to establish the time regulating interstate commerce. The repeal movement focused only on national daylight saving, and nothing in the law seemed to prevent cities, states, and local communities from adopting any time they wished, as they had before the war.[60] Massachusetts adopted a statewide daylight saving law in 1925, prompting the Massachusetts State Grange to bring suit against the measure. The case reached the United States Supreme Court, and Justice Oliver Wendell Holmes, a year later. Over forty years before, as a Massachusetts Supreme Court Justice, Holmes had offered the nation's first ruling in favor of standard time. Now Holmes ruled that individual cities and towns could legally adopt daylight saving if the difference from standard time amounted to no more than one hour. Thereafter, most major cities and some states adopted daylight saving in the summer months, simply ignoring the hour difference between the time their environs and the railroads used.[61]

Which brings us to an intriguing question: Who stood to gain, or lose, the most by saving daylight? The measure's recreational benefits seem the most obvious today, and indeed they figured prominently in every account of the law's virtues. Many of those businesses involved in recreation, like baseball leagues, for example, stood to gain dramatically from extended daylight. Shortly before the passage of the Calder bill in 1918, President Ban Johnson of the American Baseball League spoke enthusiastically of plans to begin ball games an hour later under the new time. Previously (before artificial lights), games started at three-thirty, leaving many office workers no time to get to the ballpark. Under the new time, sunsets came a hour later. Beginning games at four-thirty gave fans more time to get to their seats, raising attendance and profits. Here seemed a perfect example of the charms of saving daylight, especially for the wallets of baseball leagues and team owners.[62]

But the plan to change hours collapsed under pressure from Washington. "Slackers," declared Charles Lathrop Pack of the War Garden Commission — "Slackers of the worst type is the brand placed upon baseball team owners or managers who plan to move down the scheduled times of starting games." President Wilson, Pack recalled, had named food production for the war effort a top priority, and to waste the increased daylight at the ballpark "violated the spirit of the law." Changing the starting times "will take thousands of hours of time from gardens," and the daylight saving law, Pack preached, "was not intended to give extra hours of recreation." "I hope," he added, "this is not the attitude of those in control of the greatest of national games." In the climate of war, such appeals touched a weak spot in the nation's psyche. That same day President Tener of the National League responded contritely that no, "he had not heard of any contemplated changes in the time of games."[63]

For Pack and the War Garden Commission, thousands of baseball fans flinging down the sports page and heading out to buy garden tools sounded like money. Despite its official-sounding name, the War Garden Commission was in fact a lobbying organization for the makers of garden products—tools, seeds, fertilizers, canning and preserving equipment, including jars, cans, and rubber ring seals—who stood to gain dramatically from any increase in wartime gardening. Pack issued pamphlets and newspaper advertisements insisting that "the preservation of vegetables and fruits . . . is a patriotic duty and a national war time need." Accompanying the message of conservation came a list of manufacturers of garden products. Masking itself as a government agency, Pack's organization used daylight saving to raise sales, and used patriotism to head off the competition.[64] In this case, one recreational business—baseball—lost out to another—the makers of gardening and canning equipment.

By 1919, the United States had developed substantial and important industries based on leisure time. Chambers of commerce and boards of trade were daylight saving's most enthusiastic supporters by far, and though it has proven difficult to establish any direct link between the organizations that supported daylight saving and increased profits, much evidence suggests a connection. For example, A. Lincoln Filene, one of daylight saving's strongest supporters, owned Boston's largest department store chain. Women customers especially may have been more comfortable shopping under the new time, because, as the New York State Republican Women's Association put it, the "law safeguards the young woman returning from her business before darkness has fallen."[65] If women felt safer walking home in the light, then daylight saving gave them an hour more time for shopping in Filene's stores.

Daylight saving particularly threatened motion picture companies, and especially theater owners, who saw attendance fall drastically on pleasant summer evenings. A scrap of silent film title in this writer's possession, from approximately 1915–16, declares: "If California adopts daylight saving, she will tell the world she hasn't enough sunshine. Say NO to daylight saving."[66] California toyed with adopting statewide daylight saving in 1916. The piece of film was apparently part of a counterattack co-sponsored by the movie industry and real estate developers, who promoted California as the land of warm, boundless sunshine and oranges. Later, in 1930, Fox West Coast Theaters of Los Angeles led a second fight against daylight saving for California, which its spokesman claimed brought "unlimited possibilities for evil" to the movie industry. Fox pledged $50,000 to stopping such a measure.[67]

More recently another lobbying organization, the Daylight Saving Time Coalition, managed to move back the starting date of daylight saving, from the last Sunday in April to the first. James Benfield of that organization works on behalf of the makers of sporting equipment, charcoal briquets, insect repellants, and other accouterments and necessities of leisure time, including Seven-Eleven stores, which do more business by daylight, and candy companies, who maintain that daylight saving on Halloween night keeps small children out longer and increases candy sales.[68] For years, Benfield complained, politicians from certain states — Idaho, for example — had refused to see the benefits of daylight saving. When he discovered that fast-food franchises do more business under daylight saving — "up to eight hundred dollars per unit per day" — he called the leading franchises to ask where they got their raw supplies. Told that Idaho supplied McDonald's with the bulk of its potatoes, Benfield relayed the story to that state's representatives in Congress, who promptly reversed themselves and henceforth went along with daylight saving like a burger with fries.[69]

Changing the clocks by law, then as now, inevitably favored certain groups at the expense of others.

Daylight saving most benefited those segments of society that were strictly governed by clocks and clock time. It gave them extra daylight for recreation in a period that saw a virtual explosion in recreation and leisure time pursuits. The same objective—more daylight after work—could have been more easily, or at least more fairly, achieved by the simple expedient of rising earlier, or changing work schedules. But as one editor suggested, "so completely have we become slaves of the clock that when we think it desirable to get up an hour earlier we could not think of any better way than to pass laws setting the clocks an hour ahead of time."[70]

The apparent unity daylight saving encouraged was one of its most attractive points: it gave the impression of a society united in relaxation and cooperative leisure, united in rejecting, to some extent, the very principles of efficiency, industriousness, and temporal thrift that had given the clock such power in the first place. "100,000,000 people changed by an hour their time of getting up in the evening and going to bed at night—and of everything they do between," marveled the *Times*; "when one remembers the number of activities, great and small, that were affected . . . the disproportion between the means employed and the results accomplished is nothing less than astounding," a "revolution without one tremor."[71] The word "revolution" was an interesting choice. Daylight saving readjusted the predominant governing mechanism of urban society—the clock—to suit that society's new desire for greater leisure. It represented a kind of triumph over time, a revolution both in the sense of control over time that it fostered, and in its pure celebration of pleasure and fun over workday dreariness.

But daylight saving contained a paradox, in that it used the key tool of a mechanized society—the clock—to create a sense of freedom from mechanization and clock time. The great thing about daylight saving, according to the *Times*, was that everyone apparently experienced the same feeling of freedom and relaxation at the same time. Daylight saving mechanized leisure in the pursuit of freedom from mechanization.

The resistance to daylight saving, and the law's eventual repeal after two presidential vetoes, points to stubborn and lingering hostility to clock authority, to a refusal to abandon natural models for organizing life's work. Rural Americans used clock time to symbolize a wide range of changes brought about by industrialization—factory labor and mechanization, the political and economic dominance of the city, the growth of nightlife and leisure, a perceived decline in the work ethic, the "scientific" reformation of society by academic experts. If we might fault them for willful ignorance, we might also applaud their acute choice of symbols. In daylight saving, they found an unparalleled example of the falsity, the self-delusion, the distance from natural imperatives they perceived in a society regulated by mechanical timekeepers.

The daylight saving debate offers only one example of how "modernity" changed time. It seemed in a small way to make men and women godlike—as Joshua commanded the sun to stand still, so the modern nation stopped its clocks to suit its needs. But American technology had always inspired wonder at how the United States, like a child imitating its parents, seemed to constantly encroach on the Almighty's prerogatives. "God said, 'let there be light,' and there was light," reminded Senator Orville Platt of Connecticut in an 1891 speech on "Invention and Advancement." Think, he continued, of the electric light. "You will feel it scarcely irreverent to exclaim 'And man said, 'let there be light,' and there was light."[72]

But did human emulation of God drag God down to earth?

Did advancement lead only to arrogance and immorality? In a 1919 essay on "the psychology of daylight saving," an Iowa professor pointed out that with the electric light, "there has come about a displacement between the daylight day, and the human day," so that we rise well after daylight and stay up long into darkness. This displacement of the "natural" times of work and rest is now "going on faster than ever," he wrote. "Every year it seems a little harder to go to bed or to get up at the old accustomed time. Automobiles, unlike the horse, travel as well by night as by day and keep increasingly late hours. College and high school students study later at night or engage in social activities . . . more and more industries continue through the night." "Without doubt the number of people who sleep to noon is constantly increasing," he warned his readers, and "darkness is a cover for every evil thing." How far shall we go? he asked. "Will day and night finally be wholly transposed?"[73] In so many ways, "modernity" upset the traditional relationship between time and the natural world.

Modern science called old authorities for time into question. After 1920, for example, astronomers began using clocks accurate enough to detect variations in the earth's rotation. These modern clocks regularly revealed the passage of the days, once the sine qua non of steadiness and sober reliability, as little better than an uncertain and capricious wobble. Even worse, since the war newspaper editors and scientific magazines had kept up a steady babble about time's relationship to the speed of light and the observer's point of view, a whole new physics of time.[74] Each development questioned the authorities for time.

Modernity altered not just the authority, but the *experience* of time as well. In *Middletown* (1929), the pioneering sociological study of the American Midwest, Robert and Helen Lynd recorded the automobile's effects on life in Muncie, Indiana. Owning a car expanded the owner's spatial and temporal universe. But it also destroyed old customs and altered family relations. Instead of staying home, or socializing with neighbors, friends, and family, auto-mad Americans dashed off to distant pleasures. The Lynds described the automobile "blasting its way through such accustomed and unquestioned dicta as 'Rain or shine, I never miss a Sunday morning at church;' 'A high school boy does not need much spending money'; 'I don't need exercise, walking to the office keeps me fit'; 'I wouldn't think of moving out of town and being so far from my friends'; 'Parents ought to know where their children are.' " They observed a Sunday School class. "Can you think of any temptations that we have today that Jesus didn't have?" asked the teacher. One boy blurted out "Speed!"[75] Not just speed in automobiles, but speed in daily life—fast music, fast dancing, fast living, late hours. Modernity shattered notions of time and space, and disrupted traditional relations between the individual and society.

In the 1920s, opposition to modernity took many forms, including Prohibition and movie censorship, which both involved attempts to control leisure time. But no single attack on modernity attracted as much attention as the fundamentalist movement and its crusade against evolution. Historians often treat American fundamentalism as a reactionary movement of the disaffected, a dangerous trend born in ignorance. Educated urban elites have always found fundamentalism—and its substantial popularity—threatening. H. L. Mencken unfortunately set the tone for much subsequent academic discussion: "Heave an egg out a Pullman window," Mencken sneered in 1926, "and you will hit a fundamentalist anywhere in the United States today." According to historians, fundamentalists suffered from "status anxiety"; they perceived themselves losing power and reacted irrationally, denying scientific progress and imagining vast modernist conspiracies in "the paranoid style."[76] Doubtless fundamentalism offers plenty of ammunition for such attacks. But American fundamentalism also addressed a widespread and genuine sense of unease about modernity and modern time, an unease that deserves to be taken seriously.

The fundamentalist movement had its roots in Millenarianism, or the belief in and study of Christ's return. Millenarians scrutinized biblical chronology to chart the present status of God's prophecy—they used the Bible as a record of time to predict the future. In contrast to the buoyant confidence and optimism typical of the antebellum years, most American Millenarians looked around them and saw evidence of immorality and approaching collapse. The extraordinary popularity of Millenarian thinking—Mormons, Seventh-Day Adventists, and Sabbatarian crusaders all drew from Millenarian ideas—constituted a popular critique of secular industrial culture.[77]

Nineteenth-century American Protestant thinkers had also drawn heavily on a Scottish intellectual tradition, "Common Sense Realism." "Common Sense" philosophy insisted that the evidence of the senses was reliable, and that ordinary people could be trusted to know and grasp the truth. It depended on an interrelation between science, the Bible, and the natural world. "If God is the Creator of the Universe," insisted a Yale theologian in 1852, then "the study of the creation [must] be interlinked at every point with the study of the Creator, and thus become, to the devout mind, the study of theology." When *McGuffey's Readers* encouraged students to study nature for models of Christian good behavior, they reflected common-sense realism.[78]

But when modern science studied the world, it reached conclusions that disputed the Bible account of creation. Geology, for example, turned up evidence of the earth's vast, almost incomprehensible age, and fossil records of animals and plants that the Bible never mentioned. Most American theologians managed to reconcile modern science with Christianity by abandoning their belief in the literal truth of Bible accounts. As the challenges of modernism continued, however, more conservative "fundamentalist" theologians began emphasizing the Bible's "inneracy," or literal truth. When science contradicted the Bible, fundamentalists presumed, it had moved away from religious truth and the evident "common sense" gained from observing the world in everyday life.[79]

By the twentieth century this emphasis on the literal truth of the Bible had become a crusade. One Georgia legislator recalled common-sense philosophy when he directed his constituents to "read the Bible. It teaches you how to act. Read the hymn book. It contains the finest poetry ever written. Read the almanac. It shows you how to figure out what the weather will be. There isn't another book that is necessary for anyone to read."[80] His statement linked nature to the Bible in terms of practical daily affairs, recalling schoolbook lessons then close to a century old. The Bible and the almanac—together the two books spelled out the nature of time and the terms for scheduling life.

In the twentieth century, "fundamentalism" came to serve as a linguistic umbrella sheltering a wide range of anxieties and fears about the direction of American society. American cultural "fundamentalists" worried particularly that new ways of experiencing time threatened the foundations of morality—late hours, necking in movie theaters, Sunday drives instead of churchgoing. And the most pressing temporal challenge to tradition came from the theory of evolution. Much of the fundamentalist opposition to evolution is familiar—it seemed to degrade human beings, to bring men and women down to the level of apes. But Darwin's theory also subverted traditional notions about time in profound and crucial ways.

Evolution upset the "temporality" of Genesis. Claiming that higher animals had evolved from lower did more than just deny God's act of creation. It denied Genesis' structuring of time—the creation week from the first day through the seventh. If organisms evolved over long ages of years, instead of appearing at once on successive days, then the seven-day cycle of creation made no sense. And it was those seven days that gave Judeo-Christian religious practice its temporal structure. The "clock-like rhythm of the weekly Sabbath" was deeply rooted in American culture, and Sabbath observance helped sanctify the week's labors and keep the family on an even moral keel. Take away the creation week, and one day was just like another; you removed all justification for Sabbath observance, and desecularized the framework, the schedule, that organized daily life. The weekly ritual became arbitrary, empty motion devoid of any meaning other than social convenience.[81]

Darwin's theory depended on the earth's great age: evolution could only have occurred over millions of years. Starting in the eighteenth century, geologists had found irrefutable proof of "deep time"—proof that the earth's history stretched back almost beyond comprehension. Evolution linked the "deep time" of geology to a narrative of human development.[82] And once again Darwin's history of man threatened the temporality of events in the Bible.

In Genesis, God established "the day" as the measure of time. The creation story linked the present to the very beginning in a series of recognizable, familiar increments. The Bible gives a historical record, the narrative account of humanity's progress. If the single day was taken as a stable unit of measure, then the Bible could serve as an accurate record of *all* time. Seventeenth-century European scholars, including Isaac Newton, had made strenuous efforts to calculate the earth's age from Scripture. In 1658, Bishop James Ussher of Ireland used the record of generations to make his famous estimation: the earth was created on October 23, 4004 B.C. American Protestant Bibles almost routinely offered the bishop's dates as footnotes or supplementary material.

For ordinary readers, Ussher's chronology connected biblical events to the fundamental unit of "natural" time—the day—and gave Bible stories a tangible connection to the present. A "day" in 1920 was just like a day Jesus lived in Jerusalem, Moses passed in the desert, and Adam saw at creation. To study nature was to study creation; to work six days and rest on Sunday was to relive, in a small way, the cycle of Genesis. The passage of days, one after another, from past to present to future offered confirmation of God's prophecy unfolding. But Darwin's alternative chronology stood Ussher on his head. It severed the connection between nature, human history, and the Bible, knocking one more brick from the foundation of biblical authority.

Evolution robbed time's passage of its meaning, or rather, it substituted new meanings for old. Nineteenth-century "social Darwinists" like Herbert Spencer related Darwin's theories to social class on a crude model of "survival of the fittest." In this view the rich got rich because they were more fit than the poor, while the poor, conversely, suffered because of inferior genes. Most such misreadings of evolution hinged on enthusiasm for progress. It only took a bit of intellectual carpentry, for example, to make evolution dovetail with notions of efficiency and industrial advancement. If Darwin's laws of evolution produced better and better organisms, then the progress of invention must be evolving ever better and more efficient mechanisms, better and more efficient ruling classes. In this view, the process of getting rich "measures the amount of efficient management that has come into the world and the waste that has been eliminated." Late nineteenth-century Americans, especially those who had benefited most from industrialization, hailed Spencer as a genius, the prophet of a new order.[83]

But Spencerian evolution could also seem cruel, immoral, even anti-democratic. Instead of hailing "the people" as the backbone of the republic, as common-sense philosophy had, it branded ordinary, plain people evolutionary losers by their very lack of worldly success. These were, of course, misinterpretations: natural selection never produces "better" organisms, only different specializations for different environments. But much of scientific management's appeal stemmed from seeing evolution as a mechanical process of constant improvement, and relating that vision to society. In simplistic interpretations of Darwin's theory, "time" meant "the machine-like progress of efficiency," not the revelation of God's will.

Linking evolution to technological and social progress made it a hard theory to argue against, as long as progress seemed benign and steady. World War I, however, shattered confidence in progress and the benevolence of social evolution, for instead of vindicating dreams of a more enlightened future it presented a world of nightmarish, mechanized death. American fundamentalists saw the war not only demonstrating the failures of modernity but also vindicating their hostility to Darwin, because the war denied that the secular time of evolution led to a better world.[84]

By the 1920s, evolution had emerged as the fundamentalists' best target in the fight against modernity. Linked to modern science in a general way, evolution supported most of the false gods that corroded morality and tradition. Southern legislatures especially began introducing measures designed to ban or restrict its teaching. These laws offered fundamentalists both an effective symbolic action against modernism and national media attention. The most dramatic confrontation between fundamentalism and the modernist impulse occurred in 1925, on a hot July day in Dayton, Tennessee, when Clarence Darrow brought William Jennings Bryan to the stand in the notorious Scopes "monkey trial." At the Scopes Trial, fundamentalism and modernity clashed over the issue of time.

Tennessee had passed a "monkey bill" earlier in that year, prohibiting the teaching of evolution in state schools. Scopes, a Dayton high school teacher, freely admitted that he had violated the statute and agreed with the American Civil Liberties Union to make his a test case. When word spread that Clarence Darrow would appear in Scopes's defense, and William Jennings Bryan assist for the prosecution, the trial quickly turned into a national obsession. The two men symbolized the opposing forces of tradition and change.

William Jennings Bryan burst on the American scene at the 1896 Democratic Convention, where the young Nebraskan had electrified his party with his famous "cross of gold" speech. The speech's impassioned defense of the poor and downtrodden over the wealthy and privileged earned Bryan a reputation for oratory, and when the Populist Party endorsed him in 1896, it cemented his association with rural discontent and hostility to industrial capitalist excesses. Three losses in the race for President failed to tarnish his reputation as the people's champion, and throughout his career he remained true to his nickname, "the great commoner." Bryan never really believed in a strictly literal interpretation of the Bible, as the Scopes Trial would reveal to his detriment. But this profoundly religious man shared both the fundamentalists' unease about the direction of American culture and their hostility to modern science. "It is better to trust in the Rock of Ages than to know the ages of rocks," he often said; "it is better for one to know that he is close to the heavenly Father than to know how far the stars in the heavens are apart." By 1925 he had emerged as America's most prominent critic of modernism.[85]

His opponent at Dayton, Clarence Darrow, also grew up in farm country, in rural Ohio. But there the resemblance largely stopped. Darrow's father, something of a village eccentric, taught him to doubt and question accepted wisdom almost as a reflex. He became a lawyer, he said, mostly because he wanted to avoid working for a living. A religious agnostic, Darrow made his name defending unpopular causes, especially those that offended the religious sensibilities he grew up challenging. He defended Eugene Debs in the Pullman strike, Big Bill Haywood and the IWW, Chicago murderers Leopold and Loeb, as well as Hinky Dink Kenna, the Chicago political boss. In his commitment to free speech and cosmopolitan inquiry he at least equaled Bryan's passion for the average man, and like Bryan he fancied himself the underdog's champion. But where Bryan clung to the values of his rural past, Darrow saw those values as shackles to cast off. By the time of the Scopes Trial, he was America's most famous — and notorious — trial lawyer, spokesman for marginal causes, and darling of the H. L. Mencken/*American Mercury* set.[86]

Even Mencken left his accustomed haunts for the Scopes Trial, drawn by the prospect of a clash between Darrow and Bryan. He was not alone; the humble courthouse in Dayton, Tennessee, drew journalists from around the country, including technicians struggling with motion picture and radio equipment. A national audience awaited the outcome of the "monkey trial," and Dayton quickly took on the atmosphere of a circus. For weeks the surrounding hills echoed with the sounds of Holy Rollers, while in town, a motley group of itinerant preachers, hot dog and soda vendors, trained chimps, would-be prophets of the apocalypse, and cranks of all sorts vied for media attention. "The thing is truly fabulous," Mencken crowed. "I have stored up enough material to last me twenty years."[87]

Once the trial got under way, Scopes's lawyers bridled under the rule of Judge John T. Raulston, favorite son of Gizzards Cove, Tennessee. Raulston, stopping frequently to pose for cameramen, barely bothered to hide his empathy for Bryan, rural America, and the fundamentalist cause. He may have even set his watch by local sun time.[88] A banner emblazoned "Read Your Bible" hung over his courthouse door, and he began the trial by quoting Genesis, his voice carried by loudspeaker to the crowds gathered on the lawn outside. The first days of the trial saw considerable wrangling over whether or not the judge would allow scientific testimony. When Raulston ruled it inadmissible, it seemed to leave the defense without a case. But then Darrow called Bryan to the witness stand. By this time, driven by the stifling heat, the court had removed itself to the courthouse lawn, where a large crowd listened intently.

Again and again, relentlessly and even cruelly, Darrow challenged Bryan's belief in the literal truth of the Bible. Most of his questions concerned time and time measurement. Darrow asked Bryan if he really believed that Joshua had made the sun stand still. Didn't the earth in fact revolve around the sun? Bryan dodged that question, but Darrow quickly began asking about the date of the great flood—2348 B.C., by Bishop Ussher's calculation. How did Ussher arrive at his figure? Darrow handed Bryan a Bible giving Ussher's dates for major events at the top of each page. "How old is the world?" Darrow asked again; "how long ago was the great flood?" Someone produced a pencil and paper, and the two of them, absurdly, began doing addition and subtraction.

Ironically, the two men were engaged in an old American exercise. Nineteenth-century schoolbooks routinely used the Bible for arithmetic lessons—we know a day is 24 hours, and a year 365 days, primers reminded, so careful calculation should give us "the interval from the Creation to the birth of Christ," or tell us "how many seconds have passed since the creation of the world."[89] Both Bryan and Darrow had probably tackled these or very similar questions in childhood, as part of their math exercises. In their youth everyday experience—literally *every day* experience—combined with mathematics to confirm the Bible's truth.

But modern standardized time and science undid that relationship. Darrow quoted from geologists who estimated the earth to be hundreds of millions of years old, and cited proof of ancient civilizations far in advance of Ussher's dates. When at one point in the trial Bishop Ussher was quoted placing creation, with lunatic precision, at "9 a.m., on October 23, 4004 B.C.," some audience wag had shouted out, "eastern standard time!"[90] The point, of course, was that deprived of its religious origins, "time" seemed to have lost its definition and become arbitrary, meaningless.

Or rather, that time had gained a new meaning, more suitable to industrial society. Where the Bible defined time as the solar day, industrial society defined time as whatever it pleased, so long as all agreed to use it.

So when Darrow asked Bryan, "Do you really think the earth was made in six days?" he knew the charge the answer carried. Did the evidence of the senses, the natural world, offer a valid model for comprehending time and organizing society? Or was time simply an arbitrary construct, variable at will? Bryan's answer reportedly shocked his supporters in the audience: "Not six days of twenty-four hours," he replied. "Doesn't the Bible say so?" Darrow continued. "No sir," retorted Bryan. The response brought gasps from the crowd, and a cry of "What does he want to say that for?"[91] Darrow pressed Bryan further, till he confessed that the "days" of creation might have been periods of indefinite length. Bryan had never wholly believed in the Bible's literal truth. But he had appointed himself the defender of fundamentalism, and his dismayed supporters counted the admission a victory for the other side. If you questioned the day as a measure of time, then you questioned the natural world's use as the pattern for living—questioned, in other words, the ways people organized their time, their lives, and the things they chose to believe.

Bryan and Darrow's confrontation has passed into national folklore; the play *Inherit the Wind*, later made into a movie starring Spencer Tracy as Darrow and Fredric March as Bryan, depicted Bryan as a foolish, windy, and defeated old man, and interpreted his loss as a triumph of learning and intellectual freedom over bigoted repression.[92] Darrow did make Bryan look very bad—he proved himself poorly educated, evasive, and unable to respond to fairly standard questions. The trial came to symbolize a conflict between urban and rural America, between "enlightenment" of the H. L. Mencken variety and what Menckenites thereafter permanently labeled "ignorance."

But fundamentalists, rather than being simply "ignorant" or anti-intellectual, in fact stood fast by an older conception of science and the world. They judged "the standards of a later scientific revolution"—Einstein's, Darwin's—"by the standards of the first—the revolution of Bacon and Newton."[93] The critics of daylight saving understood time in the same terms—the terms of Newton's mechanistic universe. Like Bryan, they took the rationality, the perfection of natural movements as an article of faith, and saw nature's timekeepers as harmony with those principles.

Bryan died shortly after the trial. But before he died, he wrote a lengthy response to Darrow and the evolutionists. Though he clearly misunderstood most of Darwin's theory, he left some eloquent statements of why evolution struck him as a profoundly immoral doctrine. Evolution, he claimed, "discourages those who labor for the improvement of man's condition." Instead of giving them a tangible, meaningful connection with the past, "it chills their enthusiasm by substituting eons for years. It obscures all beginnings in the mists of endless ages." Evolution, in other words, severed the link between time and God established in the Bible. It replaced the unfolding of God's will from day to day with a purely mechanical, "cold and heartless process, beginning with time and ending in eternity." Like a machine, evolution operated on imperatives of efficiency, according to an arbitrary framework of time, indifferent to human needs.[94]

Bryan joined his hostility to evolution with an attack on modern science and industrial machinery. "Science . . . can perfect machinery," he charged, "but it adds no moral restraints to protect society from the misuse of the machine. It can also build gigantic intellectual ships, but it constructs no moral rudders for the control of storm-tossed human vessels." Bryan perceived the theory of evolution as an intellectual by-product of industry and industrial time. It replaced the natural cycles of the Bible, unfolding with a purpose toward the resolution of God's will, with a hostile, mechanistic process, a savage competition occurring over a mindless span of empty ages.

Bryan tied evolution specifically to the modern machinery of warfare—submarines, airplanes—through which "science has proven itself an evil genius." We read almost every day, he noted, of newer and more terrible weapons of destruction, and industrial evolution seems to carry us toward disaster.[95] His point is still relevant today—who never wonders if the dangers of technological progress don't outweigh the benefits? Evolution, of course, is not responsible for nuclear proliferation or global pollution. Like Bryan, American fundamentalists responded not to Darwin's writings per se, but to the context they confronted them in—scientific management, factory labor, the decline of American farm culture. Bryan and the fundamentalists linked belief in evolution to a society governed by mechanical principles, by unmoral machines and heartless standards of efficiency. By what authority, they asked, do we govern progress? By what authorities do we find the meaning of our time?

Epilogue

I n the one hundred years between Eli Terry's Connecticut
clock and the Scopes Trial, Americans evolved a new sense
of time based on machines. In 1825, time had come from nature
and God; women and men lived *in* time, just as they lived in nature
and the world, and nature served as the example for organizing
time. But industrial progress demanded a uniform medium of
exchange, a way of rationalizing and ordering interstate commerce
and communication. By 1925, most people got their time from
clocks and watches. Arbitrary, uniform, easily distributable, this
new time kept industry and commerce running smoothly, but it
drove a wedge between men and women and the natural world,
forcing them to divide their lives between "work time" and
"leisure."

Standardized, machine-based time also established new priorities for organizing society, new models for patterning daily life.
Clock and watch advertising insisted on a merger of identity between timepieces and their owners, in which clocks served as the

standards for personal conduct and good industrial citizens could be measured by the extent of their fidelity to their timekeepers. Standardized, arbitrary, divisible time made it possible to restructure the patterns of everyday life and thought—streamlining work routines, editing sequences of real time on film into narratives. The notion of "efficiency"—the final justification industrial society could offer for the changes it brought about—could not have insinuated itself into virtually every walk of life without standardized time. By 1915, and the debate over daylight saving, even leisure and play had to pass the test of efficiency in standard time.

But as Bryan and Darrow's clash at Dayton makes clear, not all Americans accepted the authority of standardized time. A substantial number of citizens—perhaps even a majority in 1925—insisted that time, and the priorities for governing and organizing life and thought, should come from nature. At Dayton, the culture of machines and efficiency ran up against stubborn, entrenched convictions about time and natural law. These were two world views, two simply irreconcilable ways of ordering and making sense of reality.

Are they reconciled today? The answer is not quite clear. Certainly nearly everyone accepts standard time, mandated firmly by law since 1966.[1] But two states—Arizona and Indiana—still refuse to adopt daylight saving, and Congress still gets letters from citizens who regard changing the clock twice a year as an abomination. Even if the issue has been largely settled in the United States, it remains a powerful force in international politics. Some religions—Orthodox Judaism, for example, and Islam—demand observances based on nature and not mechanical time. Muslims must pray at sunrise, noon, and sunset, not at clock hours; and when Ayatollah Khomeini seized power in Iran, he attacked standard time zones as a Western evil and a threat to the virtue of the Islamic nation.

American culture gives more subtle evidence of mixed feelings about time. Americans buy digital watches, which emphasize a linear time—the numbers tick irrevocably toward the future without showing, as an old-fashioned watch dial does, where they were in the past, a few minutes ago. But Americans also love to buy whimsical, silly fashion watches, like the Swiss-made Swatch, which comes in a profusion of constantly changing styles. One recent Swatch model had a black face, no numbers, and black hands—practically unreadable. But you can't make jokes about something your audience doesn't understand, and the popularity of Swatches and their imitators only confirms the pervasiveness of standard time. On TV, through international computer and phone links, at work and rest, we live surrounded by the network of standardized timekeeping. The old devices, time balls or street clocks, have largely disappeared, or else become charming relics buried in museums.

Yet behavioral scientists have discovered patterns of sleep, of alertness, of fertility that run independently of clocks. The human body itself is a clock, with its own internal tickings and hourly indications, and it responds to cues from the natural world. It demands that we respect our internal natural cycles, the circadian rhythms that govern biology. Of course, the same behavioral scientists are hard at work figuring out ways to overcome this internal time. Experiments aimed at fooling the body into overcoming jet lag by controlled exposure to light recently received national press coverage. This line of work only perpetuates the increasing merger between clocks and watches and their ostensible human masters.[2]

It is possible to imagine an industrial society governed by priorities drawn from natural cycles and biological time. Suppose, for example, that American business practices were restructured to allow men and women to fully share work and child rearing. Truly flexible work hours could make it easier to share babysitting—a child's father staying home till three, then working till eleven, for example, while the mother worked during the day. Computers, fax machines, and telephones could make office work at home a realistic possibility. This might not be a better society, or a more pleasant one, but it would be a society that based its decisions about time use on "natural," biological imperatives, not the schedules of the clock.

The history of American time shows that like other values we tend to take as eternal certainties, time is for the most part a plastic, changeable notion, a social creation. Our ideas about what time is have changed over history, and will keep changing as we confront the mixed legacies of industrialization. It seems very likely, for example, that as global concern for the environment grows, we will have to develop renewed respect for the rhythms and cycles of natural time. Will we move away from clocks and watches and back toward nature's example? Only time will tell.

Notes

Abbreviations

ACR *Appendix to the Congressional Record*

AHR *American Historical Review*

AP Papers of William F. Allen, Manuscript Division, New York Public Library

BAC Business Americana Collection, Archives Center, Smithsonian Institution National Museum of American History, Washington, D.C.

CP Papers of George Creel, Manuscript Division, Library of Congress, Washington, D.C.

CPI Records of the Committee on Public Information, 1917–1919, National Archives, Washington, D.C.

CR *The Congressional Record*

DEI Files of the Section of Mechanisms of the Division of Engineering and Industry, Smithsonian Institution National Museum of American History, Washington, D.C.

DP Papers of Charles F. Dowd, Manuscript Division, Boston Public Library

GP Set of microfilm reels, "Frank B. Gilbreth, Selected Papers, ca. 1910–1924," from the Gilbreth Library, Purdue University Libraries, Lafayette, Indiana

LP Papers of Samuel P. Langley, Smithsonian Institution Archives Center, Arts and Industries Building, Washington, D.C.

NA National Archives, Washington, D.C.

Preface

1. *Time*, vol. 133, no. 17 (April 24, 1989), pp. 58–67.

2. On time and clocks in medieval Europe, see David Landes, *Revolution in Time: Clocks and the Making of the Modern World* (Cambridge, MA, 1983); Jacques Le Goff, *Time, Work and Culture in the Middle Ages* (Chicago, 1980), pp. 29–34; Carlo Cippolla, *Clocks and Culture, 1300–1700* (New York, 1977); Lynn White, *Medieval Religion and Technology* (Berkeley, CA, 1978) and *Medieval Technology and Social Change* (New York, 1962). Otto Mayr, *Authority, Liberty and Automatic Machinery in Early Modern Europe* (Baltimore, 1986), discusses the relationship between time, clocks, politics, and machine design in England and Europe.

3. Max Weber, *The Protestant Ethic and the Spirit of Capitalism* (New York, 1976). Anthony Giddens's introduction to this edition offers a review of the various critiques of Weber's thesis. See also Le Goff, *Time, Work and Culture in the Middle Ages*, pp. 29–34, for an example of changing time sense among Catholic merchants, and Edmund Morgan, *American Slavery, American Freedom* (New York, 1975), chs. 3–6, and "The Labor Problem at Jamestown, 1607–1608," in *American Historical Review*, LXXVI (June 1971), pp. 595–611, for examples of "unethical" Protestants.

4. See Michael O'Malley, "The Idea of Time in American Culture" (Ph.D. diss., Berkeley, 1988), introduction. On time and politics, see John G. Gunnell, *Political Philosophy and Time: Plato and the Origins of Political Vision* (reprinted ed. Chicago, 1987); J. G. A. Pocock, *Politics, Language and Time: Essays on Political Thought and History* (New York, 1971); and Hannah Arendt, "Tradition and the Modern Age" and "The Concept of History: Ancient and Modern," in *Between Past and Future* (reprint ed. New York, 1985). On time and literature, see Paul Ricoeur, *Time and Narrative*, vols. I–III (Chicago, 1988), esp. vol III, pp. 3–22; Samuel L. Macey, *Clocks and the Cosmos: Time*

in Western Life and Thought (Hamden, CT, 1980); and Georges Poulet, *Studies in Human Time* (Baltimore, 1956). Useful sociological studies include Michael Young, *The Metronomic Society: Natural Rhythms and Human Timetables* (Cambridge, MA, 1988); Pitirim A. Sorokin and Robert K. Merton, "Social Time: A Methodological and Functional Analysis," in *American Journal of Sociology*, XLII (March 1937), pp. 615–629; Eviatar Zerubavel, *The Seven Day Circle: History and the Meaning of the Week* (New York, 1985) and *Hidden Rhythms: Schedules and Calendars in Social Life* (Berkeley, CA, 1985). On science and time, see Richard Morris, *Time's Arrows: Scientific Attitudes Toward Time* (New York, 1985); J. T. Fraser, *Time, the Familiar Stranger* (Amherst, MA, 1987), pp. 222–288; and Fraser, ed., *The Voices of Time: A Cooperative Survey of Man's Views About Time as Expressed by the Sciences and the Humanities* (Amherst, MA, 1981).

5. Historians are currently debating about the "new social history," which brought the lives of women and ethnic and cultural minorities into the historical mainstream for the first time. Some defend this as healthy cultural pluralism, enriching our knowledge of the past, while others attack it for supposedly fragmenting the practice of history and making it unintelligible. See *American Historical Review*, 94 (June 1989). Understanding and even sympathizing with the desire for consensus, I wish to declare myself unequivocally on the side of the "new" history. This book discusses nearly universal changes, but it doesn't claim that all experienced them in the same way. It traces abstract, standardized public time back to what I believe to be its American origins, but makes no claims that the ideas and beliefs that led to standard time were universally held. At best, this book might help future studies use attitudes about time to explore the complexity and diversity of American culture.

I

Time, Nature, and the Good Citizen

1. New Haven *Columbian Weekly Register*, Oct. 21, 1826, p. 3. Same anonymous letter reprinted in *Connecticut Herald*, Oct. 24, 1826, p. 3.

2. Timothy Dwight, *Travels in New England and New York, 1821–1822* (reprint ed. Cambridge, MA, 1969), vol. 1, pp. 139, 141.

3. Genesis 1:5, 14: "Let there be lights in the firmament of the heavens . . . and let them be for signs, and for seasons, and for the days and years."

4. *Columbian Weekly Register*, Oct. 21, 1826, p. 3.

5. *Connecticut Journal*, Nov. 14, 1826.

6. Quoted in Milton Drake, *Almanacs of the United States*, 2 vols. (New York, 1962), vol. 1, p. ix. For Eli Terry, see Chauncey Jerome, *History of the American Clock Business for the Past Sixty Years and Life of Chauncey Jerome* (New Haven, 1860), pp. 5–17; Penrose R. Hoopes, *Connecticut Clockmakers of the Eighteenth Century* (New York, 1930), p. 113; Carl Dreppard, *American Clocks and Clockmakers* (New York, 1947), ch. VI; and Chris Bailey, *Two Hundred Years of American Clocks and Watches* (Englewood Cliffs, NJ, 1975).

7. *Connecticut Journal*, Dec. 5, 1826.

8. Ibid., Dec. 12, 1826.

9. Ibid., Feb. 6, 1827, p. 2.

10. Ibid., Mar. 6, 1827, p. 2. On Terry, see Hoopes, *Connecticut Clockmakers*, p. 113.

11. *Connecticut Journal*, Mar. 27, 1827. Other New Haven papers are silent on the matter as well. After 1830, perhaps influenced by the controversy, Terry began pasting equation tables inside his ordinary mean time clocks, so that buyers could make their own adjustments as they saw fit.

12. Relevant works in the vast literature include Mary P. Ryan, *Cradle of the Middle Class: The Family in Oneida County, New York, 1790–1865* (New York, 1984); Michael Rogin, *Subversive Genealogy: The Politics and Art of Herman Melville* (Berkeley, CA, 1983); David Rothman, *The Discovery of the Asylum* (Boston, 1971); Paul Johnson, *A Shopkeepers Millennium* (New York, 1978); Jonathan Prude, *The Coming of Industrial Order* (Cambridge, 1983); Sean Wilentz, *Chants Democratic* (New York, 1984); and Alan Dawley, *Class and Community* (Cambridge, MA, 1982).

13. On the early history of clocks and timekeeping, see Carlo Cipolla, *Clocks and Culture, 1300–1700* (New York, 1977), pt. 1, and David

Landes's remarkable *Revolution in Time: Clocks and the Making of the Modern World* (Cambridge, MA, 1983), pts. 1 and 2.

14. Hoopes, *Connecticut Clockmakers,* gives some description of early American timekeeping, as does Dreppard, *American Clocks and Clockmakers,* and Bailey, *Two Hundred Years of American Clocks.*

15. Quoted in Laurel Thatcher Ulrich, *Good Wives: Image and Reality in the Lives of Women in Northern New England, 1650–1750* (New York, 1983), p. 78. For a more detailed critique of "task orientation" and its uses in history, see Michael O'Malley, "The Idea of Time in American Culture" (Ph.D. diss., Berkeley, 1988), pp. 5–12. Most studies of time in preindustrial cultures mistake the absence of clocks for indifference to time, and fail to see the coercive or compelling social and cultural forces that govern work. See Peter Rigby, "History and Time," in *Persistent Pastoralists: Nomadic Societies in Transition* (London, 1985), pp. 67–91. The most famous use of "task orientation" is probably E. P. Thompson's influential "Time, Work-Discipline, and Industrial Capitalism," in *Past and Present,* 38 (December 1967), pp. 56–97. Thompson errs by not paying enough attention to the strictures that governed time use before the factory system, and by assuming that all preindustrial societies experience the transition from "task orientation" to industrial time in the same way. See especially Thomas Smith, "Peasant Time and Factory Time in Japan," *Past and Present,* 111 (May 1986), pp. 165–197.

16. T. H. Breen's discussion of Washington the farmer in *Tobacco Culture* (Princeton, NJ, 1985), p. 55. See also Breen, *Puritans and Adventurers* (New York, 1980), pp. 164–196. On the applicability of the Protestant Ethic, see Edmund Morgan, *American Slavery, American Freedom* (New York, 1975), chs. 3–6, and "The Labor Problem at Jamestown, 1607–1608" in *American Historical Review,* LXXVI (June 1971), pp. 595–611.

17. A clear and typically concise description of the duality of Western time appears in Stephen Jay Gould, *Time's Arrow, Time's Cycle: Myth and Metaphor in the Discovery of Geological Time* (New York, 1986), pp. 10–16. Thomas Cole's four-painting sequence *The Voyage of Life* represents the coexistence of cyclical and linear time as it was com-

monly understood in antebellum America. See Barbara Novak's discussion of the paintings in *Nature and Culture: American Landscape Painting, 1825–1875* (New York, 1980), pp. 109–110.

18. On American almanacs, see Herbert Leventhal, *In the Shadow of the Enlightenment: Occultism and Renaissance Science in Eighteenth Century America* (New York, 1976), and David D. Hall, *Worlds of Wonder, Days of Judgment: Popular Religious Belief in Early New England* (New York, 1989), pp. 58–61. See also Marion B. Stowell, *Early American Almanacs: The Colonial Weekday Bible* (New York, 1977); George L. Kittredge, *The Old Farmer and His Almanac* (Boston, 1904); Robb Sagendorph, *America and Her Almanacs: Wit, Wisdom, and Weather, 1639–1970* (Boston, 1970); and Robert T. Sidwell, "The Colonial American Almanacs: A Study in Non-Institutional Education" (Ph.D. diss., Rutgers, 1965). See also Jon Butler, "Magic, Astrology, and the Early American Religious Heritage," in *AHR*, 84 (April 1979), pp. 329–330.

19. Quoted in Stowell, *Early American Almanacs*, p. xiv.

20. Ibid., p. 180. On the role of science and Newtonian mechanics, see Brook Hindle, *The Pursuit of Science in Revolutionary America* (Chapel Hill, NC, 1956); Thomas S. Kuhn, *The Copernican Revolution* (New York, 1959); and Herbert M. Morais, *Deism in Eighteenth Century America* (New York, 1960).

21. Mather described in Leventhal, *Shadow of the Enlightenment*, p. 41. The drawing helped in treating farm animals as well. It divided the body into twelve regions—heart, belly, reins [ribs], secrets [genitals], thighs, knees, legs, feet, head, neck, arms, and breast. While the "anatomy" was often attacked as foolish superstition, it was just as often defended. Some claimed that an almanac without the "man of signs" was practically unsalable. See Butler, "Magic, Astrology and the Early American Religious Heritage," pp. 330–332. Modern collections of folklore and superstition, as Leventhal noted, abound with similar interpretations of natural portents.

22. Kittredge, *The Old Farmer and His Almanac*, p. 81.

23. *Old Farmer's Almanac*, April 1832.

24. William Holmes McGuffey, *The Eclectic Second Reader* (Cincinnati, 1836), pp. 16–17.

25. Ruth Miller Elson, *Guardians of Tradition: American Schoolbooks of the Nineteenth Century* (Lincoln, NE, 1964), p. 19.

26. *McGuffey's Third Reader* (Cincinnati & New York, 1879) pp. 56–57. This particular lesson appears in an 1879 *Reader* and not in an 1853 edition. It may have appeared in an earlier edition I could not locate, although having read a great number of antebellum schoolbooks I regard it as typical of the earlier period.

27. Lyman Cobb, *Cobb's Sequel to the Juvenile Readers* (New York, 1834), p. 16.

28. Lindley Murray, *Sequel to the English Reader* (4th ed., Philadelphia, 1810).

29. John E. Lovell, *Lovell's Progressive Readers* (New Haven, 1857), no. 3, pp. 28–30.

30. Elson, *Guardians of Tradition*, p. 19.

31. Noah Webster, *The American Spelling Book* (New Haven, CT, 1831), p. 57.

32. Information on clocks and clockmakers is dominated by the work of collectors. See below and Dreppard, *American Clocks and Clockmakers*, pp. 29–38, ch. 11; Hoopes, *Connecticut Clockmakers*; and Bailey, *Two Hundred Years of American Clocks*.

33. Brook Hindle and Stephen Lubar, *Engines of Change: The American Industrial Revolution* (Washington, D.C., 1986), p. 220.

34. On the time of city life in early modern Europe, see Jacques Le Goff, *Time, Work and Culture in the Middle Ages* (Chicago, 1980), pt. 1; Carlo Cipolla, *Clocks and Culture, 1300–1700* (New York, 1977), pt. 1; and David Landes, *Revolution in Time* (Cambridge, MA, 1983), pts. 1 and 2.

35. Arthur H. Cole, "The Tempo of Mercantile Life in Colonial America," *Business History Review*, 33 (Autumn 1959), pp. 277–299. On theater and public festival, see Lawrence Levine, *Highbrow/Lowbrow. The Emergence of Cultural Hierarchy in America* (New York, 1988). On labor, see Herbert Gutman, *Work, Culture and Society in Industrializing America* (New York, 1966), ch. 1.

36. Hawthorne's musings have of course been admirably described in Leo Marx, *The Machine in the Garden: Technology and the Pastoral Ideal in America* (New York, 1964). For other examples of the village

clock's connection to virtue and natural harmony, see Hawthorne, "Sundays at Home" and "Sights from a Steeple," in *Tales and Sketches*, Roy Harvey Pearce, ed. (New York, 1982). On early public clocks, see Hoopes, *Connecticut Clockmakers*, pp. 37–41.

37. Query VI of Jefferson's *Notes on the State of Virginia*, quoted in George H. Eckhardt, *Pennsylvania Clocks and Clockmakers* (New York, 1955), p. 35.

38. Quote comparing the Constitution to a clock from Michael F. Lienesch, "The Concept of Time in American Political Thought" (Ph.D. diss., UC Berkeley, 1977), p. 303. On the Constitution, see Michael Kammen, *A Machine That Would Go of Itself* (New York, 1986), and Marx, *The Machine in the Garden*, p. 165. For the connection of time and the clock to European political theory and science, see Otto Mayr, *Authority, Liberty, and Automatic Machinery in Early Modern Europe* (Baltimore, 1986).

39. Jefferson clearly believed in progress, but he just as clearly expected an inevitable decadence. The emphasis on Rome envisions historical cycles on a grand scale, and indeed he and many of his peers interpreted history as a record of rise, decline, and fall. He never believed that America's decline could be permanently avoided; he only hoped to postpone it. See Drew McCoy, *The Elusive Republic: Political Economy in Jeffersonian America* (New York, 1980), esp. ch. 5; Lienesch, "Concept of Time in American Political Thought"; and Major L. Wilson, "The Concept of Time and the Political Dialogue in the United States," in *American Quarterly*, XIX (1967), pp. 619–644. Wilson follows the tension between cyclical and linear time into the Jacksonian period.

40. McCoy, *The Elusive Republic*, p. 136.

41. Quote from Marx, *Machine in the Garden*, p. 161.

42. Henry F. May, *The Enlightenment in America* (New York, 1978), p. 24.

43. See Jerome, *History of the American Clock Business*, p. 16.

44. B. A. Botkin, *A Treasury of American Folklore* (New York, 1947), says that "the yarns about Yankee clock peddlers are legion" (p. 29). For an example, see Thomas Chandler Haliburton, *The Clockmaker* (New York, 1871), and John Cawelti's description of Haliburton's

and other characters in *Apostles of the Self-Made Man* (Chicago, 1965), pp. 69–70.

45. The only scholarly study of Terry's career is John Joseph Murphy's article, "Entrepreneurship in the Establishment of the American Clock Industry," *Journal of Economic History*, XXVI (June 1966), pp. 169–186, and his Ph.D. dissertation, "The Establishment of the American Clock Industry" (New Haven, 1961).

46. George Featherstonhaugh, quoted in Richard D. Brown, "Modernization and the Modern Personality," in *Journal of Interdisciplinary History*, 2 (1972–73), p. 220.

47. Jerome, *History of the American Clock Business*, p. 23.

48. An example appears in Alan Dawley, *Class and Community: The Industrial Revolution in Lynn* (Cambridge, MA, 1982). The illustration on p. 43 depicts a shoemaker's "ten footer" with a typical forerunner of Terry's "pillar and scroll" design.

49. Newman Ivey White, ed., *The Frank Brown Collection of North Carolina Folklore* (Durham, NC, 1961), no. 5049; Wayland Hand, et. al., eds., *Popular Beliefs and Superstitions: A Compendium of American Folklore* (Boston, 1981), nos. 27350–27352; Harry M. Hyatt, ed., *Folklore from Adams County, Illinois* (Chicago, 1960), nos. 513–514.

50. White, *Frank Brown Collection*, nos. 5052–5055; Hand, *Popular Beliefs and Superstitions*, nos. 27326–27329, 27337; Hyatt, *Adams County Folklore*, nos. 286–287; Anthon S. Cannon, *Popular Beliefs and Superstitions from Utah* (Salt Lake City, 1984), pp. 291–292; William I. Koch, *Folklore from Kansas* (Lawrence, KA, 1980), no. 1842.

51. Hyatt, *Adams County*, no. 11425; White, *Frank Brown Collection*, no. 3053.

52. Hand, *Popular Beliefs*, nos. 17353–17356; White, *Frank Brown Collection*, no. 3056; Hyatt, *Adams County*, nos. 14950, 11433; Cannon, *Popular Beliefs and Superstitions from Utah*, no. 6468.

53. Henry Wadsworth Longfellow, *Evangeline and Selected Tales and Poems*, Horace Gregory, ed. (New York, 1964), pp. 42–43.

54. *McGuffey's Third Reader*, pp. 137–138. See also "The Old House Clock" in *McGuffey's Fifth Reader*, pp. 232–233; "The Kitchen Clock" in *McGuffey's Second Reader*, pp. 78–81.

55. Jesse Olney, *The National Preceptor* (New York, 1839), p. 221.

56. Mark Twain, *The Adventures of Huckleberry Finn* (1884) in Guy Cardwell, ed., *Mississippi Writings* (New York, 1982), pp. 724–727.

57. Thanks to Michael Rogin for help with this material. On sentimental culture, see Anne Douglas, *The Feminization of American Culture* (New York, 1977), esp. pp. 17–139, 241–272; Karen Halttunen, *Confidence Men and Painted Women: A Study of Middle-Class Culture in America, 1830–1870* (New Haven, 1982). On the decline of paternalism, see Mary P. Ryan, *Cradle of the Middle Class: The Family in Oneida County, New York, 1790–1865* (New York, 1984), chs. 4 and 5; David Rothman, *The Discovery of the Asylum* (Boston, 1971); and Paul Johnson, *A Shopkeepers Millennium* (New York, 1978).

58. John Pierpont, *American First Class Book* (Boston, 1831), pp. 314–316. See also *McGuffey's Fifth Reader*, pp. 114–116. Like a lot of material in readers, the story came from England. The two stories reverse our common understanding of women's relationship to nature. In the former, men stand for preindustrial patriarchal authority and the cyclical, natural inevitability of birth, youth, aging, and death. In the latter, women, as "Mistress Dial," represent the regulating industrial machine and the virtues required for progress. See discussion of Catherine Beecher below.

59. Herbert Gutman, *Work, Culture and Society in Industrializing America* (New York, 1966), p. 26.

60. Anthony F. C. Wallace, *Rockdale: The Growth of an American Village in the Early Industrial Revolution* (New York, 1980), pp. 328, 179. I am not sure if or how cotton mills were lighted after dark, except that Lowell was lighted by arc lamps in the 1830s. The hours listed in mill timetables are deceptive — it is now difficult for us to guess how much daylight was left, for example, in Pawtucket, RI, at 7:30 p.m. in July, thanks to time zones and daylight saving time.

61. Gutman, *Work, Culture and Society*, p. 27. Gutman points out that collective protest at Lowell began only after a "rationalization" in the 1840s, when stricter time schedules appeared.

62. E. P. Thompson, "Time, Work-Discipline, and Industrial Capitalism," in *Past and Present*, 38 (December 1967), pp. 56–97. Among the many historical studies building on Thompson's anaylsis are Herbert Gutman's enormously influential *Work, Culture and Society* *in Industrializing America* (New York, 1966), ch. 1; Jonathan Prude, *The Coming of Industrial Order* (Cambridge, MA, 1983), pp. 15–17, 36–37, 130–131; and Alan Dawley, *Class and Community* (Cambridge, MA, 1982).

63. "Report of the Committee on Education of the New England Association of Farmers, Mechanics and Other Workingmen," printed in *The Free Enquirer*, June 1832, and reprinted in Gary Kulik, ed., *The New England Mill Village* (Cambridge, MA, 1982), pp. 495–496. See also Kulik, "Pawtucket Village and the Strike of 1824: The Origins of Class Conflict in Rhode Island," in *Radical History Review*, 7 (Spring 1978), p. 28.

64. Pottsville, Pennsylvania, *Miner's Journal and Pottsville Daily Advertiser*, Oct. 21, 1843, p. 2; Dec. 16, 1843, p. 2.

65. "Witnesses in the Contested Election of Jeremiah Reed," Dec. 8, 1843, in Christopher Loeser Papers, Schuylkull County Historical Society, Pottsville, PA, v. 24, pp. 73–74. I am greatly indebted to Grace Palladino of the Samuel Gompers Papers for sharing this information with me, and to John Joy of the Schuylkill County Historical Society for confirming the dates.

66. Kulik, ed., *The New England Mill Village*, pp. 265–266.

67. Edward Everett, *An Address Delivered Before the Massachusetts Charitable Mechanics Association, 20th September 1837, On the Occasion of Their First Exhibition and Fair* (Boston, 1837), p. 18. Thanks to Carlene Stephens for bringing the address to my attention.

68. Lydia Maria Child, *The American Frugal Housewife* (Boston, 1835), p. 1.

69. William Alcott, *The Young Housekeeper* (Boston, 1838), p. 61.

70. Ibid., p. 63.

71. Ibid., pp. 64–65.

72. Nathaniel Hawthorne, "Time's Portraiture," in *Tales and Sketches*, Roy Harvey Pearce, ed. (New York, 1982), p. 587. The Elgin Watch Co., after the Civil War, adopted as its symbol Father Time discarding his hourglass for a pocketwatch, as in Hawthorne's story.

73. "The Artist of the Beautiful," in *Tales and Sketches*, Pearce, ed., pp. 910, 914.

74. Edgar Allan Poe, *Poetry and Tales*, Patrick F. Quinn, ed. (New York, 1984), pp. 298–306. Poe satirized the navigator's confusion over time standards in "Three Sundays in a Week" (1841).

75. It was during these years that it first became possible to electrically synchronize one clock, later called the "master" clock, with another, less accurate "slave" clock. See Chapter Two.

76. Poe, *Poetry and Tales*, pp. 491–505. In "The Pit," the enemy is the Inquisition, the fusion of Church and State power run amok. It suggests Poe's hostility to the secularization of time, or perhaps the perversion of Time, an abstract, religious quality, by secular power. Poe used the motif of the clock more than once. "A Predicament," part 2 of the 1838 parody "How to Write a Blackwood Article," describes a woman decapitated by the razor-sharp hands of an enormous tower clock. In "The Colloquy of Monos and Una," 1841, Poe insisted on a higher concept of time and chronology, perceptible only to the soul and perverted by crude mechanical timekeepers.

77. Robert T. Handy, *A Christian America: Protestant Hopes and Historical Realities* (New York, 1985), p. 45. See also George Marsden, *Fundamentalism and American Culture* (New York, 1980), p. 13.

78. Daniel Wilson, *The Divine Authority and Perpetual Obligation of the Lord's Day Asserted in Seven Sermons* (New York, 1831), p. 173. See also John Holmes Agnew, *A Manual of the Christian Sabbath* (Philadelphia, 1834); John S. Stone, *Lectures on the Institution of the Sabbath* (New York, 1844); J. B. Waterbury, *A Book for the Sabbath* (New York, 1840); and Silas M. Andrews, *The Sabbath at Home* (Philadelphia, 1836).

79. Handy, *A Christian America*, p. 232, n. 58: "Sabbatarians usually argued that without Sabbath rest prosperity would fail." An example of hostility to the railroads, in the form of a petition to the Massachusetts legislature asking for a ban on Sunday travel, appears in *Proceedings of the Anti-Sabbath Convention* (Boston, 1848; reprint ed. (New York, 1971), pp. 116–117.

80. *Proceedings of the Anti-Sabbath Convention*, pp. 39–40.

81. Ibid., pp. 113–114.

82. Catherine Beecher, *A Treatise on Domestic Economy* (1841), (New York, 1970), pp. 170–175.

83. On Beecher's background and motives, see Katherine Kish Sklar, *Catherine Beecher: A Study in American Domesticity* (New Haven, 1973).

84. Beecher, *Treatise on Domestic Economy*, p. 109. A diligent search disclosed only one sentence in any edition mentioning clocks.

85. This is not to claim Beecher originated the split between home time and work time, only that she was its most articulate spokesperson.

86. Henry A. Miles, *Lowell As It Was, and As it Is* (Boston, 1845), pp. 65–66, quoted in John F. Kasson, *Civilizing the Machine: Technology and Republican Values in America, 1776–1900* (New York, 1976), pp. 75–76. Kasson points out the supervisor's strategic location between the dormitories and the mills. The clock tower, on the other hand, overlooked all, and the association with the city of Lowell made factory time and city time the same.

87. Kasson, *Civilizing the Machine*, pp. 103–106.

II
Celestial Railroad Time

1. Determining longitude involves comparing local time, measured astronomically, with the time at another location. Comparing the two times gives the two points' distance apart. At first highly accurate, portable clocks or chronometers were used, but the telegraph made them less necessary. On the relationship between longitude, navigation and timekeeping, see Derek Howse, *Greenwich Time and the Discovery of the Longitude* (Oxford, 1980).

2. On Mason and Dixon, see Brook Hindle, *The Pursuit of Science in Revolutionary America* (Chapel Hill, NC, 1956), pp. 166–167. On Lewis and Clark, see William H. Goetzmann, *New Lands, New Men: America and the Second Great Age of Discovery* (New York, 1986), pp. 110–115, and John C. Greene, *American Science in the Age of Jefferson* (Ames, IA, 1984), pp. 196–197. Not all surveying demanded clocks, but the most accurate measurements did.

3. Greenwich Observatory was closely associated with accurate time and navigation, having originally been established to aid English navigators. As early as 1714, Parliament had offered a prize for a

clock capable of keeping accurate Greenwich time at sea. See Howse, *Greenwich Time.*

4. J. E. Nourse, "Memoir of the Founding and Progress of the United States Naval Observatory," in I. Bernard Cohen, ed., *Aspects of Astronomy in America in the Nineteenth Century* (New York, 1980), p. 6. On the Coast Survey, see Robert V. Bruce, *The Launching of Modern American Science* (New York, 1987), pp. 171–186; the *Annual Reports* of the Superintendent of the Coast Survey, 1846–51; and Willis Milham, "Early American Observatories," in Cohen, ed., *Aspects of Astronomy,* pp. 8–10.

5. Nourse, "Memoir of the Founding," in Cohen, ed., *Aspects of Astronomy,* p. 10.

6. Ordinary surveyors did not carry chronometers. But mapping a territory requires some stable reference point from which to refer subsequent measurements. The Coast Survey's work offered such reference points for routine, less precise surveying. On disputes over title and western expansion, see Michael Rogin, *Fathers and Children: Andrew Jackson and the Subjugation of the American Indian* (New York, 1976), ch. 3. On the rationalization of mapping and land use and its relation to culture, see Philip Fischer, "Democratic Social Space: Whitman, Melville and the Promise of American Transparency," in *Representations,* 24 (Fall 1988), pp. 60–101; and John Stillgoe, *Common Landscape in America* (New York, 1977).

7. One historian of science even compared the enthusiasm for astronomy with the twentieth century's passion for Lindbergh. G. Edward Pendray, "How the Telescope Came to America," in Cohen, ed., *Aspects of Astronomy,* pp. 210–212, and Bruce, *Launching of Modern American Science,* passim.

8. John Quincy Adams, *An Oration Delivered Before the Cincinnati Astronomical Society on the Occasion of Laying the Cornerstone of an Astronomical Observatory* (Cincinnati, 1843), pp. 12–18, quote at p. 39.

9. Ibid., p. 68.

10. Adams's metaphor also recalls once again "Mistress Dial" of the children's story "The Discontented Pendulum," and suggests that time is a female principle organizing domestic production, especially the production of good democratic citizens. See Chapter One.

11. Allan R. Pred, *Urban Growth and the Circulation of Information: The United States System of Cities, 1790–1840* (Cambridge, MA, 1973), p. 37.

12. Quoted in Hugo Arthur Meier, "The Technological Concept in American Social History" (Ph.D. diss., Wisconsin, 1951), p. 85.

13. Pred, *Urban Growth and the Circulation of Information,* pp. 45, 53, 176–177.

14. Quoted in Carlene Stephens, " 'The Most Reliable Time': William Bond, the New England Railroads, and Time Awareness in 19th Century America," in *Technology and Culture,* 30 (January 1989), p. 5. Stephens points out that the postal service was far more interested in punctuality—and more punctual—than the early railroads. Thanks also to Coleen Dunlavy of the University of Wisconsin at Madison and Steven Lubar of the National Museum of American History for information on early railroads.

15. Allan R. Pred, *Urban Growth and City-Systems in the United States, 1840–1860* (Cambridge, MA, 1980), p. 149.

16. Nathaniel Hawthorne, *Tales and Sketches,* Roy Harvey Pearce, ed. (New York, 1982), pp. 808–824. The short story form, compacting Bunyan's lengthy book into a few pages, sharpens Hawthorne's pointed critique of industrial society. The railroad and its quickening pace have even changed the terms of communication—the railroad travels Bunyan's narrative landscape in fraction of the time.

17. Edward Everett, "The Uses of Astronomy," in Cohen, ed., *Aspects of Astronomy,* p. 19.

18. Since the railroad was significantly faster than the apparent course of the sun, and every fifteen degrees of longitude equals one hour of time, rapid east-to-west travel made regional time differences more glaring. See Elias Loomis, *The Recent Progress of Astronomy,* 3d. ed. (New York, 1856), p. 288.

19. For example, see *Appleton's Railroad and Steam Companion,* first published in 1848, and *Dinsmore's Railroad and Steam Navigation Guide,* 1853–1863.

20. Everett, "Uses of Astronomy," p. 19. See also Loomis, *Recent Progress of Astronomy,* pp. 287–292.

21. Stephens, " 'The Most Reliable Time,' " pp. 1–24.

22. Quoted in Michael P. Rogin, *Subversive Genealogy: The Politics and Art of Herman Melville,* (Berkeley, CA, 1985), p. 138.

23. Stephens, " 'The Most Reliable Time,' " p. 7. There are several conflicting contemporary accounts of exactly what time the railroads adopted. The best history of the Bonds' work is Stephens's article and her monograph in preparation on William Bond and Son. See also Bessie Zaban Jones and Lyle Gifford Boyd, *The Harvard College Observatory* (Cambridge, MA, 1971), ch. 2.

24. Leo Marx, *The Machine in the Garden* (New York, 1964), p. 248. Marx explores Thoreau's sophisticated and ambivalent feelings about the railroad in ch. 5, pt. 2, pointing out that Thoreau's feelings were by no means all negative. Background on time and the clock in the writing of the American Renaissance appears in Samuel Macey, *Clocks and the Cosmos: Time in Western Life and Thought* (Hamden, CT, 1980), and in Georges Poulet, *Studies in Human Time* (Baltimore, 1956), pp. 323–349.

25. Brooks Atkinson, ed., *Walden and Other Writings of Henry David Thoreau* (New York, 1950), pp. 106 and 107.

26. Ibid., pp. 111 and 112.

27. Ibid., pp. 105, 107, respectively.

28. *Running Regulations of the Camden and Amboy Railroad,* 1853, on exhibit at the National Museum of American History, Washington, D.C., and reprinted in John H. White Jr., *The John Bull* (Washington, D.C., 1981), p. 133.

29. Such rules also obviously heighten the difference between work time and leisure time—work time means carrying a watch and watching (in both senses of the word) the clock.

30. Herman Melville, *Pierre, or The Ambiguities,* Harrison Hayford, ed. (New York, 1984), pp. 247–252. Melville may also have been related to J. Melville Gillis, in charge of the National Observatory in the 1840s.

31. Howse, *Greenwich Time,* pp. 49–53. See also Nigel Thrift, "Owner's Time and Own Time: The Making of a Capitalist Time Consciousness, 1300–1880," in *Space and Time in Geography,* Allan Pred, ed. (Lund, 1981), pp. 56–84.

32. Nautical almanacs charted the appearances and movements of stars and planets, listing the times of their appearance. The English *Nautical Almanac*, used a reference guide to the heavens by sailors, astronomers, and surveyors since the early nineteenth century, listed its calculations in Greenwich time.

33. William Bond, then engaged in determining the location of Cambridge, Massachusetts, relative to Greenwich, personally collected signatures on a petition demanding the retention of Greenwich time. Though Congress eventually settled on a compromise, an *American Almanac* including calculations in both Greenwich and Washington, D.C., time, the American Prime Meridian was never widely adopted. See Charles Henry Davis, *Remarks Upon the Establishment of an American Prime Meridian* (Cambridge, 1849); Stephens, " 'The Most Reliable Time' "; Craig Waff, "Charles Henry Davis, the Foundation of the American Nautical Almanac, and the Establishment of an American Prime Meridian," in *Vistas in Astronomy*, 28 (1985), pp. 61–66; and *The Congressional Globe*, June 16, 1846, pp. 961–963; May 2, 1850, pp. 891–892. A number of maps were produced showing the meridian of Washington and the Observatory. Several remain in the Library of Congress.

34. Melville, *Pierre*, p. 249.

35. The railroads accepted Bond's standard in lieu of the proposed American Prime Meridian described above. The time was calculated on a Greenwich meridian crossing the middle of Massachusetts Bay and reflected the railroads' solid opposition to the Washington standard. See Stephens, " 'The Most Reliable Time.' "

36. For a fuller explanation of the passage's importance for the novel, see Michael Rogin, *Subversive Genealogy: The Politics and Art of Herman Melville* (Berkeley, CA, 1983), pp. 177–178. "Bartleby the Scrivener" echoes the theme of time and moral coercion. The lawyer's two original copyists are difficult but not unmanageable, because each is tied to "natural" time. Melville took great pains to establish that each one's personality changed at "twelve o'clock, meridian," or noon by the sun. Bartleby, on the other hand, has no past, no future, no natural appetites, and no schedule — he is nearly "timeless," unregulated and ungovernable. Bartleby's refusal to keep regular hours,

to accept standard customs about the organization of time and self-government, thrusts the bourgeois narrator into an unresolvable moral quandary. In "The Bell Tower," one of the "Piazza Tales" written after the failure of *Pierre*, Melville's protagonist, a driven, monomaniacal artist, constructs a mechanical timekeeper in the shape of a man. The whole town gathers to hear the clock strike, but the clock/man kills the artist in the act of striking, making the artist—and, by implication, Melville—the victim of mechanical time and the regular universe he constructs.

37. "Railroad Time," in *American Railway Journal*, 25 (Aug. 21, 1852), pp. 529–530, 530.

38. J. N. Bowman, "Driving the Last Spike at Promontory, 1869," in *Utah Historical Quarterly*, 37 (Winter 1969), pp. 89–90. Thanks to Anne Hyde for suggesting the ceremony at Promontory.

39. *Proceedings of the American Metrological Society*, II (New York, 1880), p. 18; *Annual Report of the Astronomer, Dudley Observatory* (Albany, NY, 1878), p. 14; *Annual Report of the Director, Cincinnati Observatory* (Cincinnati, 1869), pp. 35–36; Gustavus A. Weber, *The Naval Observatory: Its History, Activities and Organization* (Baltimore, 1926), p. 34; *Annual Report of the Board of Directors of the Chicago Astronomical Society* (Chicago, 1881), p. 1.

40. Donald Leroy Obendorf, "Samuel P. Langley: Solar Scientist, 1867–1891" (Ph.D. diss., Berkeley, 1969), pp. 1–11. Langley was requested to participate in weather surveys, but felt unable to oblige so early in his tenure.

41. Pennsylvania Railroad Company, *General Order No. 4*, Jan. 26, 1871, in microfilm copies of the Langley Papers at the Smithsonian Institution Archives (hereafter referred to as LP, Reel 2, sec. 2). Thanks to the Coast Survey, which had fixed the precise longitude of major cities, Langley could cable Philadelphia time to the eastern divisions of the Pennsylvania, and later Columbus, Ohio, time to the western division.

42. Obendorf, "Samuel P. Langley," pp. 10–12, Langley to the Allegheny Observatory Committee, May 1872 (LP, R. 1, s. 2).

43. *The Pittsburgh Commercial*, Feb. 12, 1870.

44. Carlene E. Stephens, "The Impact of the Telegraph on Public Time in the United States, 1844–1893," in *Technology and Society*, 8 (March 1989), p. 6.

45. Langley to Allegheny Observatory Committee, May 1872 (LP, R. 1, s. 1), p. 5. A provocative discussion of time, space, and money appears in geographer David Harvey's *Consciousness and the Urban Experience: Studies in the History and Theory of Capitalist Expansion* (Baltimore, 1985), ch. 1.

46. Charles F. Dowd, *System of National Time and Railway Time Gazetteer* (Albany, NY, 1870). Dowd's first plan, proposed in 1869, called for Washington time alone as the standard. The idea of zones occurred to him a year later. Dowd's inspiration, or the sources of his ideas, remain obscure. His personal papers, at the Boston Public Library, consist of little more than published accounts of his work. See Charles North Dowd, *Charles F. Dowd and Standard Time* (New York, 1930).

47. Dowd, *A Paper Read Before the American Metrological Society, Dec. 27, 1883* (Saratoga Springs, NY, 1883). The railroad managers who reviewed the plan pronounced it eminently workable but unnecessary. Most customers, they claimed, traveled only short distances and kept time changes in mind. See *Railroad Gazette*, May 24, 1873, p. 206.

48. Dowd wrote Cassatt in October 1870, briefly explaining his plan and enclosing a testimonial from other railroad managers. See Dowd to Cassatt, Oct. 20, 1870 (LP, R. 1, s. 4). Cassatt wrote Thaw that "if the thing is to be done, as of course it will be in one shape or another, we would prefer to have our Pennsylvania Institution have the credit of it, and I therefore thought it better to put Mr. Dowd off with an evasive answer." See Cassatt to Thaw, Oct. 24, 1870 (LP, R. 2, s. 2). Langley also wrote to Edward Pickering of Harvard University warning him that unless astronomers came up with plans of their own, Dowd's might prevail. Dowd eventually abandoned local time, but by then others, better connected, were pursuing the question, and his natural desire to be paid for his efforts made him unwelcome. Thanks to an energetic promotional campaign on his own behalf, however, when standard time was adopted in 1883,

Dowd received credit for its invention from many sources, including *Harper's Weekly,)* 27 (Dec. 29, 1883), p. 843. A mildly hostile and confusing public debate ensued over standard time's origins. See also Charles North Dowd, *Charles F. Dowd,* and William F. Allen, *Short History of Standard Time and Its Adoption in North America* (New York, 1903).

49. Evidence for this comes from a multitude of sources. Besides the example of Bond and Langley, see *Annual Report of the Astronomer, Dudley Observatory* (Albany, NY, 1878), p. 14; *Report of the Director of Harvard College Observatory,* Nov. 14, 1878, pp. 9–10; Obendorf, "Samuel Langley," pp. 14–15; and William F. Allen, *History of the Adoption of Standard Time. Read Before the American Metrological Society, on December 27, 1883* (New York, 1884), pp. 14–15. The best evidence comes from the papers of William F. Allen at the New York Public Library (see Chapter Three). As editor of the *Traveler's Official Guide,* Allen sent circulars to the managers of every American railroad in 1882, asking what standard of time they used. From the responses he drew up a map showing the fifty-three railroad times he found in use in 1882. The responses and the map clearly show the railroads organized into regional time zones. Allen's map is in the archives of the Division of Engineering and Industry of the National Museum of American History. See also Ian R. Bartky, "The Adoption of Standard Time," in *Technology and Culture,* 30 (January 1989), pp. 25–56, and "The Invention of Standard Time," in *Railroad History,* 148 (Spring 1983), pp. 18–20.

50. Dowd, *Paper Read Before the American Metrological Society,* pp. 4–5.

51. John Rodgers to William F. Allen, Feb. 20, 1882, in William F. Allen Papers, Manuscript Division, New York Public Library (hereafter referred to as AP), v. I, p. 10.

52. Several extremely rare examples of agitation for uniform time appeared in the *Railroad Gazette* in 1870. See April 2, p. 6; April 9, p. 29; April 16, p. 31; May 7, p. 1; and May 31, p. 181. The editors commented favorably on the resumption of public time signals from Dearborn Observatory, and also excerpted one of Langley's descriptions of his service (April 9).

53. Compare Dowd, *Paper Read Before the American Metrological Society,* pp. 4–5, with Allen, *History of the Adoption of Standard Time,* pp. 14–

15. Allen claimed that the number had been reduced to fifty-three by 1882.

54. Langley, "The Electric Time Service," in *Harper's New Monthly Magazine*, LVI (April 1878,) pp. 665–671, quote at p. 666. The *Harper's* article provides a fuller explanation. Specifications for the system are in LP. Despite Langley's talk about accuracy, the system never worked all that well.

55. Thaw to Allegheny Observatory Committee, May 15, 1872, quoted in Obendorf, "Samuel Langley," p. 15; Langley to Cassatt, Feb. 20, 1872 (LP, R. 1, s. 1). Obendorf misread Layng's name, understandably given his very poor handwriting, as "Layny."

56. Pittsburgh, Commission on the City Hall, *The City Hall* (Pittsburgh, 1874), pp. 41, 36; Obendorf, "Samuel Langley," pp. 20–23.

57. See below and Langley, *Report of the Director of the Allegheny Observatory* (Pittsburgh, 1873); *Railroad Gazette*, April 9, 1870, p. 29; *Scientific American* (Jan. 13, 1872), p. 34; *American Journal of Science and Arts* (November 1872), pp. 377–386; *Telegraph Engineer's Journal*, 1 (1872–73), pp. 433–441; *The American Exchange and Review*, XXIV (January 1874), pp. 271–276; and the numerous letters from Langley to the Observatory Committee in LP.

58. Langley, "The Electric Time Service," in *Harper's New Monthly Magazine*, LVI (April 1878), pp. 665–671; quotes at pp. 669, 670, 671, 665. The article was adapted from several previous ones.

59. Everett, "The Uses of Astronomy," in Cohen, ed., *Aspects of Astronomy*, p. 17.

60. Langley's imagery is also William Alcott's recommendation of an alarm clock for the restless sleeper (see Chapter One) writ large.

61. Michel Foucault, *Discipline and Punish: The Birth of the Prison* (New York, 1979), pp. 173, 173–175.

62. *Annual Report of the Director of Harvard College Observatory* (Boston, 1877), pp. 9–10; *Annals of the Astronomical Observatory of Harvard College*, III (Boston, 1877), pp. 11–12.

63. Leonard Waldo, *Standard Public Time* (Cambridge, 1877), p. 1; *Report of the Director of Harvard College Observatory* (Boston, 1878), p. 8; Edward C. Pickering, "Time Service of Harvard College Observ-

atory," in *Popular Science Monthly,* 19 (Feb. 12, 1892), p. 88. In 1878 the time ball dropped on Boston local time, although plans to drop it on Greenwich time were afoot.

64. Gustavus A. Weber, *The Naval Observatory: Its History, Activities and Organization* (Baltimore, 1926), p. 34. The terms of the arrangement remain obscure, as does much of the next sixty years' profitable cooperation between the two institutions. Western Union's archives are now in the Archives Center of the National Museum of American History. There is almost nothing on the time service besides a collection of early twentieth-century newspaper clippings.

65. *New York Tribune,* Feb. 3, 1877, p. 6; Mar. 15, 1877, p. 4; *New York Times,* Sept. 8, 1877, p. 2; *Journal of the Telegraph,* 10 (April 16, 1877), p. 114.

66. Edward S. Holden, "On the Distribution of Standard Time," in *Popular Science Monthly,* II (June 1877), pp. 174–182. Holden denied that the Naval Observatory signals interfered or conflicted with any other observatory's. It is not clear what the Naval Observatory gained from the relationship besides the free transmission of some messages. The Observatory may have hoped, by strengthening its position as the source of time signals, to increase its annual appropriation. The enormous political and economic power of Western Union may have been persuasive as well.

67. Langley to Edward Pickering, April 9, 1877, quoted in Obendorf, "Samuel Langley," p. 25.

68. *Pittsburgh Commercial,* Feb. 17, 1870.

69. It must be pointed out that Observatory staff, with few exceptions, never profited personally from time sales. On the other hand, time services freed astronomers from having to scare up funds and earned money for research. Langley profited from his service, which made over $60,000 during his tenure, in that it freed him to pursue the solar researches that made his reputation. The point is not personal greed—most were hardly venal men—but the use of time as a commodity and the attempt to standardize it. On the relationship between science and business, see Bruce, *The Launching of Modern American Science,* passim.

70. Truman Abbe, *Professor Abbe and the Isobars* (New York, 1955), passim.

71. *Annual Report of the Director of the Cincinnati Observatory* (Cincinnati, June 1870). Abbe directed the Cincinnati Observatory.

72. Abbe, *Professor Abbe*, p. 145. The most complete record of these scientists' work, and of American time reckoning habits before 1883, appears in the *Proceedings of the American Metrological Society*, 1–5 (New York, 1889). The Society should not be confused with the American *Meteorological Society*. For a detailed recounting, see Ian R. Bartky, "The Adoption of Standard Time," in *Technology and Culture*, 30 (January 1989), pp. 25–56.

73. Cleveland Abbe (?), "Standard Time in America," in *Science*, 22, n.s. (Sept. 8, 1905), pp. 315–318; American Metrological Society, *Standard Time Circular Number Two* (Mar. 1, 1881), in *Proceedings of the AMS*, II (New York, 1880), p. 181.

74. *Proceedings of the AMS*, II, pp. 308–311; Abbe to William F. Allen, June 14, 1879, in AP, v. 1, p. 2.

75. *Proceedings of the AMS*, pp. 308, 181. For the Signal Service, uniform Greenwich time facilitated national and international weather bulletins and scientific and military dispatches while preserving the time services established by individual observatories. Their time, determined by the clearinghouse plan, was to be more accurate and hence "better."

76. *New York Times*, Dec. 24, 1881, p. 1; Feb. 20, 1882, p. 4; *New York Herald*, Dec. 24, 1881; Jan. 7, 1882, p. 4.

77. *Congressional Record*, (hereafter *CR*), July 27, 1882, pp. 6578–6579. The Observatory, like Western Union, pronounced itself in opposition to uniform time standards for the general public. Its service was to apply only to shipping and transport.

78. Obendorf, "Samuel Langley," p. 26.

79. *Science*, 22, n.s. (Sept. 8, 1905), p. 317; *CR*, July 27, 1882, p. 6579. *House Report*, no. 681 (Mar. 9, 1882), "Meridian Time and Time Balls on Customs Houses." Its failure is somewhat mysterious. It was killed by the unstated objections of eleven congressmen, and never revived. This is mostly speculation on my part, but it probably had something to do with the railroads, who strongly opposed any government legislation affecting their operations and were by then at work on standard time systems of their own (see Chapter Three).

The Signal Service, through the American Metrological Society, strongly opposed the bill as well. See *Proceedings of the AMS*, II (May–December 1881), p. 310.

80. See *Papers in the Matter of the Controversy Between the United States (Signal Bureau) and the Western Union Telegraph Company* (New York, 1874).

81. *Journal of the Telegraph*, Feb. 16, 1882, p. 52.

82. Pittsburgh, Commission on the City Hall, *The City Hall* (Pittsburgh, 1874), pp. 41, 36.

83. Leonard Waldo, "The Distribution of Time," in *North American Review*, 131 (December 1880), p. 530; Holden, "On the Distribution of Standard Time," p. 175.

84. *New York Tribune*, Feb. 3, 1870, p. 6; Mar. 3, 1877, p. 4. The *Tribune* rightly pondered the ambiguity in Western Union's time service circular. Did it propose Washington time for the nation, or both Washington and local time?

85. Waldo, "Distribution of Time," in *North American Review*, 131 (December 1880), p. 528.

86. Ibid.

87. State of Connecticut, *Twenty-Eighth Annual Railroad Commissioners' Report* (January 1881), p. 57.

88. *Annual Report of the Board of Managers, Yale College Observatory, 1881* (November 1879–May 31 1881), pp. 6–22. Detailed accounts of the Bureau's work appear in the first through fourth *Annual Reports of the Director in Charge of the Horological and Thermometric Bureaus of The Winchester Observatory of Yale College* (1880–84), photocopies on file in the Division of Engineering and Industry, National Museum of American History, Washington, D.C. Thanks to Carlene Stephens for sharing these. The Bureau dealt mostly with other corporations. The newly formed Waltham Watch Company, for example, sent some of its products to Waldo for testing. Its business declined rapidly after the first year.

89. State of Connecticut, *Journal of the House of Representatives*, January Session, 1881, pp. 60–61. See House bill no. 11. The bill made no provisions for enforcement.

90. *Annual Reports, Yale Observatory, 1881–1882,* Appendix, p. 16; Connecticut, *Journal of the House of Representatives,* March 1, 1882, House Joint Resolution no. 95.

91 State of Connecticut, *Twenty-Eighth Annual Railroad Commissioners' Report* (January 1881), p. 58.

92. Ibid., pp. 57, 59.

93. Marx, *The Machine in the Garden,* p. 194, testifies to the popularity of the phrase.

94. Waldo, "Distribution of Time," p. 529; William F. Allen in *Proceedings of the American Railway Association,* 1 (1893), p. 690.

95. *Annual Reports, Yale Observatory* (1884–1885), p. 8.

96. Ibid., 1886–87, p. 6. The Standard Time Company disappeared from New Haven city directories after 1885. It may have been absorbed into Western Union's time service.

97. Ibid,. p. 6; and "Leonard Waldo in Reply to Certain Questions Addressed to Him by Members of the Corporation at their Meeting April 18th 1884." Thanks to Carlene Stephens for showing me a photocopy on file in the Division of Engineering and Industry, National Museum of American History, Washington, D.C.

III
The Day of Two Noons

1. Hamlin Garland, *Main Traveled Roads* (New York, 1891), pp. 55, 62.

2. *Proceedings of the American Railway Association,* I (1893), Appendix, pp. 681–682; Stewart H. Holbrook, *The Story of American Railroads* (New York, 1947), p. 356; Ian R. Bartky, "The Invention of Railroad Time," in *Railroad History,* 148 (Spring 1983), p. 13. Similar conventions had met before, under less specific names.

3. Above and two letters in the William F. Allen Papers, Manuscript Division, New York Public Library (subsequently referred to as AP). See William F. Allen to Albert Fink, Sept. 5, 1882 (AP, v. 1, p. 44); and Allen to P. D. Cooper, Aug. 30, 1882 (AP, v. 1, p. 43). The papers are organized into letterbook volumes and numbered boxes with subject folders.

4. William F. Allen, "Railway Operating Associations: An Address Delivered Before the Graduate School of Business Administration, Harvard University, Jan. 11, 1909," p. 5. Information on Allen from the *Dictionary of American Biography* and William F. Allen, *History of the Adoption of Standard Time. Read Before the American Metrological Society, on December 27, 1883* (New York, 1884), pp. 10–11.

5. Allen, *History of the Adoption of Standard Time*, pp. 8–9. See Chapter Two for examples of the need for these guides. Other guides include *Dinsmore's Railroad and Steam Navigation Guide* (1853–63); *Appleton's Railroad and Steam Companion* (1848), and *Appleton's Illustrated Railway and Steam Navigation Guide* (1858–77).

6. Charles F. Dowd, *A Paper Read Before the American Metrological Society, December 27, 1883* (Saratoga Springs, NY, 1883), pp. 5–9. Allen, *History of the Adoption of Standard Time*, p. 9. Frederick T. Newberry, letter to *Travelers Official Guide*, April 1882, reprinted in *Proceedings of the American Railway Association*, I (1893), pp. 684–685.

7. See Chapter Two.

8. *Annual Reports of the Smithsonian Institution, 1882* (Washington, D.C., 1883), pp. 321–322. American Society of Civil Engineers, *Standard Time for the United States of America, Canada, and Mexico* (New York, 1882). Fleming suggested either adopting the twenty-four-hour notation now used in the military and in Europe, or labeling AM and PM with numbers and letters, or using letters to designate standard and numbers to designate local time.

9. *Standard Time: Replies to Questions Submitted by the Special Committee of the American Society of Civil Engineers* (Ottawa, 1882), in AP, Bx 2, fl. 2.

10. *Senate Reports*, 4 (July 18, 1882), Report no. 840.

11. *Proceedings of the American Association for the Advancement of Science*, 30 (August 1881), p. 5. Several members of this group later adopted the American Metrological Society's plan.

12. Association for the Reform and Codification of the Law of Nations, Committee on Standard Time, *Views of the American Members of the Committee as to the Resolutions Proposed at Cologne Recommending a Uniform System of Time Regulation for the World* (New York, 1882), pp. 5–7.

13. Abbe to Allen, June 14, 1879 (AP, v. 1, p. 2); *Proceedings of the American Metrological Society,* II, 1878–79 (New York, 1880), p. 29. Allen, *History of the Adoption of Standard Time,* p. 11.

14. Allen, *History of the Adoption of Standard Time,* p. 8. On regional time standards, see Chapter Two and below.

15. On Connecticut, see Chapter Two and *Hartford Courant,* Jan. 25, 1881, p. 2; Feb. 17, p. 2; Feb. 25, p. 1; Mar. 4, p. 1. On the Signal Service, see Chapter Two and *New York Times,* Dec. 24, 1881, p. 1; Feb. 20, 1882, p. 4; *New York Herald,* Dec. 24, 1881; Jan. 7, 1882, p. 4.

16. "General Von Moltke on Time Reform," in Canada, Parliament, *Documents Relating to the Fixing of a Standard of Time and the Legislation Thereof* (Ottawa, 1891), pp. 25–28. See also Howse, *Greenwich Time and the Discovery of the Longitude* (Oxford, 1980), p. 120; and Stephen Kern, *The Culture of Time and Space* (Cambridge, MA, 1983), pp. 12–16.

17. Howse, *Greenwich Time,* p. 131.

18. Malcolm M. Thompson, *The Beginning of the Long Dash: A History of Timekeeping in Canada* (Toronto, 1978), pp. 33–35.

19. Howse, *Greenwich Time,* pp. 134–138.

20. Association for the Reform and Codification of the Law of Nations, *Views of the American Members,* pp. 14–15. International Meridian Conference, *International Conference Held at Washington for the Purpose of Fixing a Prime Meridian and a Universal Day. October, 1884. Protocols of the Proceedings* (Washington, D.C., 1884), pp. 209–212. The best primary account of the movement toward international standard time can be found in *Proceedings of the American Metrological Society,* 1–5, 1873–88 (New York, 1889). A good summary appears in Ian R. Bartky, "The Adoption of Standard Time," in *Technology and Culture,* 30 (January 1989), pp. 25–56.

21. Howse, *Greenwich Time,* pp. 116–152. Quote from David S. Landes, *Revolution in Time: Clocks and the Making of the Modern World* (Cambridge, MA, 1983), p. 286. On time and World War I, see Kern, *The Culture of Time and Space,* pp. 259–289.

22. See Chapter Two and *Twenty-Ninth Annual Report of the Railroad Commissioners of the State of Connecticut* (Hartford, 1882).

23. Allen, *History of the Adoption of Standard Time*, pp. 12–13; *Traveler's Official Guide*, April 1882. Allen summarized the various plans briefly.

24. Allen, *History of the Adoption of Standard Time*, p. 13.

25. For an example, see Allen to Charles Pugh, Mar. 31, 1883 (AP, v. 1, p. 68).

26. Allen, *History of the Adoption of Standard Time*, pp. 16–21. The first map, badly faded, is now on file in the Division of Engineering and Industry, National Museum of American History, Washington, D.C. Numerous copies of the second remain in the Allen Papers. Allen paid special attention to asking the least possible exertion from the railroads. Most of the lines in the Northeast used New York, Boston, or Philadelphia time, and the differences between the three were relatively slight. The real problem came in east-west movement. By using existing breaks, Allen avoided most of these. Charles Dowd had come up with a similar plan in 1877, but by then he had lost the railroads' attention. See Charles F. Dowd, *The Railway Superintendent's Time Guide* (Saratoga Springs, NY, 1877), and *The Traveler's Railway Time Adjuster* (Saratoga Springs, NY, 1878).

27. *Proceedings of the American Railway Association*, I (1893), pp. 690–691.

28. See replies of M. E. Mathews (n.d.), J. J. Phano, Oct. 1, 1883, and L. F. Dutton, Sept. 12, 1883 (AP, Bx 1, fl. 3); George Crocker to Allen, Oct. 8, 1883 (AP, v. 2, p. 97); E. M. Reed to Allen, Sept. 3, 1883 (AP, v. 1, p. 127). Allen's reply to Reed, Sept. 4, 1883 (AP, v. 1, p. 153), and reply of J. D. Layng, Sept. 7, 1883 (original missing from AP—photograph of circular on file in the Division of Engineering and Industry, National Museum of American History, Washington, D.C.). Allen addressed most objections either in personal meetings or in correspondence which he did not preserve. A sample circular appears in Allen, *History of the Adoption of Standard Time*, pp. 19–21.

29. Allen to H. B. Ledyard, Oct. 4, 1883 (AP, v. I, pp. 292–293).

30. Allen to Connecticut Railroad Commissioners, April 18, 1883 (AP, v. I, p. 85). The legislature, however, had resolved not to take on any new business that session and would not hear the measure. See George P. Utley to Allen, May 2, 1883 (AP, v. I, p. 93). The question was decided automatically when New York City adopted the seventy-fifth meridian on Nov. 18.

31. W. H. Barnes to Allen, Sept. 8, 1883 (AP, v. I, p. 137); John Adams to Allen, Oct. 2, 1883 (AP, v. II, p. 68). Allen assured them that the observatories would follow the railroads, while privately taking care to see to it that they would. Allen to Barnes, Sept. 10, 1883 (AP, v. I, p. 170); Allen to Adams, Oct. 4, 1883 (AP, v. I, p. 299).

32. Abbe to Allen, Oct. 1, 1883 (AP, v. I, p. 272). Pickering favored standard time but believed that the demand for it should come from the public. See *Annual Reports of the Director of Harvard College Observatory, 1882–1883* (Boston, 1884), pp. 12–13.

33. Allen, *History of the Adoption of Standard Time*, pp. 23–24, 47–49. Edmands to Allen, Oct. 8, 1883 (AP, v. II, p. 29). Edmands to Allen, Nov. 6, 1883 (AP, v. IV, p. 32).

34. *Boston Evening Transcript*, Oct. 15, 1883; Oct. 29, 1883.

35. *Boston Globe*, Oct. 14, 1883; Nov. 17, 1883; *Daily Advertiser*, Oct. 25, 1883; City of Boston, *Report of the Committee on Standard Time*, Document 161 (Boston, 1883), pp. 2–7.

36. *Boston Daily Advertiser*, Nov. 3, 1883, p. 4.

37. Unidentified newspaper clipping, with letter dated Dec. 19, 1883, in AP, v. V, p. 64. See also *Boston Herald*, Jan. 9, 1884, p. 2.

38. Boston, *Report of the Committee on Standard Time*, pp. 5–7; *Boston Daily Advertiser*, Nov. 3, 1883, p. 4; Nov. 15, 1883.

39. *Proceedings of the ARA*, pp. 698–699, and Allen, *History of the Adoption of Standard Time*, pp. 58–59. Allen to J. Rowan, Oct. 6, 1883 (AP, v. I, p. 304).

40. Allen, *History of the Adoption of Standard Time*, pp. 24–25. The Convention met October 11, 1883. Nowhere does Allen or anyone else give a reason for choosing Nov. 18, except that Sundays usually saw less traffic, thus minimizing the potential for accidents.

41. Allen to J. M. Toucey, Oct. 4, 1883 (AP, v. I, p. 288).

42. Allen to Eckert, Sept. 14, 1883 (AP, v. I, p. 195).

43. Allen to Pugh, Sept. 28, 1883 (AP, v. I, p. 249); Pugh to Allen, Oct. 1, 1883 (AP, v. II, p. 64); Bates to Allen, Nov. 17, 1883 (AP, v. IV, p. 120).

44. See Allen, *History of the Adoption of Standard Time*, pp. 26–27, especially reprints of Mayor Edson's letter and the board of aldermen's

report on pp. 44–47; and the numerous articles in the New York newspapers the week before and after the change.

45. Baltimore and Ohio Railroad Co., *Circular No. 200*, Nov. 14, 1883. Photograph of circular on file in the Division of Engineering and Industry, National Museum of American History, Washington, D. C.

46. Quote from *St. Louis Globe-Democrat*, Nov. 18, 1883, p. 1; see also *New York Herald*, Nov. 19, 1883, p. 1; *New York Times*, Nov. 18, 1883, p. 3; *New York World*, Nov. 19, 1883, p. 1; *Chicago Tribune*, Nov. 19, 1883, p. 1; Pittsburgh *Dispatch*, Nov. 19, 1883, p. 2; and *Washington Post*, Nov. 18, 19, 1883, p. 1.

47. *St. Louis Globe-Democrat*, Nov. 19, 1883, p. 2; see also *New York Herald*, Nov. 19, 1883, p. 6; *New York Times*, Nov. 19, 1883, p. 5.

48. *New York Times*, Nov. 19, 1883, p. 5; *Chicago Tribune*, Nov. 14, 1883, p. 6. Western cities generally paid little or no attention to the change. San Francisco noted it with approval.

49. *Chicago Tribune*, Nov. 19, 1883, p. 1; *St. Louis Globe-Democrat*, Nov. 19, 1883, p. 2.

50. *Washington Post*, Nov. 18, 1883, p. 1.

51. *Indianapolis Sentinel*, Nov. 19, 1883, p. 8; *New York Times*, Nov. 19, 1883, p. 5.

52. *Chicago Tribune*, Nov. 14, 1883, p. 6, offers a detailed look at how cities obtained time before 1883. See also Nov. 19, p. 1; Nov. 20, p. 6.

53. *Bangor Daily Whig and Statesman*, Nov. 20, 1883, p. 1, Benedict Bros. to Allen, Nov. 19, 1883 (AP, v. IV, p. 133); *Atlanta Constitution*, Nov. 17, 1883; *St. Louis Post-Dispatch*, Nov. 19, 1883. See also *St. Louis Globe-Democrat*, Nov. 18, 1883.

54. *Atlanta Constitution*, Nov. 18, 1883.

55. Ibid., Nov. 20, 1883.

56. *Omaha Daily Republican*, Nov. 21, 1883, p. 4.

57. *New York Times*, Nov. 18, 1883, p. 3; *Pittsburgh Dispatch*, Nov. 19, 1883, p. 2; *St. Louis Globe-Democrat*, Nov. 18, 1883, p. 1; *Boston Daily Advertiser*, Nov. 14, 1883, p. 1.

58. Anyone looking up accounts of the invention of standard time would be surprised to find Dowd getting most of the credit. Thanks largely

to his own efforts, Dowd was often cited as the inspiration for the plan, while other accounts wrongly named F. A. P. Barnard. Annoyed, Allen threatened to resign from the American Metrological Society, and so Allen and Dowd were each invited to present that body with their own versions. They compromised, dividing the credit — Dowd for originating the idea of zones, Allen for working out the details and implementing the plan. Privately, Allen resented Dowd's intrusions. "The old crank," he wrote later, "would be amusing if he did not make himself so annoying" (AP, v. I, p. 654). Both men preserved the relevant papers to protect their claims. Ironically, Dowd died in 1904, struck by a train while crossing the railroad tracks near his home. The train was late and making up lost time. On the priority of invention, see Ian R. Bartky, "The Invention of Railroad Time," in *Railroad History*, 148 (Spring 1983), p. 22, notes 16 and 17.

59. *Harper's Weekly*, Dec. 29, 1883, p. 843.

60. *Proceedings of the American Railway Association*, 1 (1893), p. 703. On the International Meridian Conference and its effects, see Eviatar Zerubavel, "The Standardization of Time: A Sociohistorical Perspective," in *American Journal of Sociology*, 88 (July 1982), pp. 12 – 17; and Stephen Kern, *The Culture of Time and Space*, (New York, 1983), passim. The conference had no binding authority, and World Standard Time was only gradually adopted. Congressional attempts to formalize it by law failed until 1918.

61. William Graham Sumner, *What Social Classes Owe to Each Other* (1883), quoted in Richard Hofstadter, *Social Darwinism in American Thought* (1944; reprint ed. New York, 1955), p. 8.

62. *The Old Farmer's Almanac*, 1885 (Boston, 1884), p. 1; *Cincinnati Commercial Gazette*, Nov. 22, 1883, p. 4.

63. Though the case was occasionally cited as precedent over the next decades, a diligent search of both state and regional law reports and Holmes's private papers turned up no transcripts of his decision. The record of the case (*Clapp* vs. *Jenkins*, no. 1171) is now in the State Archives Building, University of Massachusetts, Boston. The case was a single Justice sitting of the Supreme Court and in such cases records were often not kept, according to the Clerk of the Suffolk County Courthouse. For reports of the case, see *Boston Daily*

Advertiser, Dec. 5, 1883, p. 2; *Boston Globe,* Dec. 5, 1883; *New York Times,* Dec. 5, 1883, p. 4.

64. *Bangor Daily Whig and Statesman,* Nov. 13, 1883, p. 3.

65. *Railway Age,* Nov. 29, 1883, p. 753; *Boston Journal* quoted in *Bangor Daily Whig and Statesman,* Nov. 15, 1883, p. 2.

66. *Railway Age,* Dec. 13, 1883, p. 787. *Railway Age* first called Cummings "A. Dogberry." Some of the few subsequent historical accounts of standard time missed the joke.

67. Arnold A. Lasker, "Standard Time Had a Rough Time in Bangor," in *Maine Historical Society Quarterly,* 24(2) (Fall 1984), pp. 276–277. Augusta *Journal* quoted in *New York Times,* Mar. 30, 1884, p. 14. See Allen's denial in the *Times,* April 1, 1884, p. 2, and a rebuttal from Maine, also in the *Times,* April 13, 1884, p. 2. See also Payson Tucker to Allen, Oct. 6, 1886 (AP, v. VI, no. 2A); Tucker to J. H. Manley, Oct. 4, 1886 (AP, v. VI, p. 1). Allen described his wooing of the Maine legislature in the *New York Tribune,* Jan. 1, 1887, p. 5. He referred to an "extensive correspondence" on the subject but did not preserve these letters.

68. See, for example, *Chicago Tribune,* Nov. 20, 1883, p. 6. Many other papers reprinted the story. On standard time in the District of Columbia, see *CR,* Mar. 13, 1884.

69. *New York Times,* Nov. 13, 1883, p. 3; *CR,* Mar. 10, 1884, pp. 1760–1763. A bill to fix a national time standard rose and fell very briefly in 1891.

70. Letter, response, and editorial in *Louisville Courier-Journal,* Nov. 22, 1883, p. 4. *New York Times,* June 28, 1884, p. 3; *Rochester German Ins. Co.* vs. *Peaslee,* June 13, 1905 (87 SW 1115). The case involved the time of expiration of an insurance contract.

71. *Wheeling Daily Register,* April 1, 1887, p. 4; Letter to Allen, Oct. 4, 1886 (AP, v. V, p. 161); *Pittsburgh Dispatch,* Dec. 28, 1886, p. 4; Jan. 1, 1887, p. 1. Thomas Schlereth tells me that as late as the 1950s, before the Vatican II reforms, Pittsburgh Catholics joked that the period of fast before taking Communion actually began at twelve-twenty by the clock, not midnight, since eastern time was twenty minutes ahead of the Pittsburgh meridian.

72. See the *Savannah Morning News,* Nov. 16, 1883, p. 2; Nov. 23, 1883, p. 4; Nov. 26, 1883, p. 3.

73. Ibid., Mar. 22, 1888, p. 8; *Augusta Chronicle,* April 30, 1888.

74. *Henderson* vs. *Reynolds,* Dec. 16, 1889 (10 SE 734).

75. *Indianapolis Daily Sentinel,* Nov. 21, 1883, p. 4; *Indianapolis Journal,* Nov. 21, 1883, p. 3.

76. *Charleston News and Courier,* Nov. 26, 1883, p. 1; *Natchez Daily Democrat,* Nov. 27, 1883, p. 1.

77. Quotes from *Cincinnati Commercial Gazette,* Nov. 24, 1883, p. 4; Nov. 22, 1883, p. 4; Nov. 18, 1883, p. 4; Feb. 20, 1890, p. 3.

78. Reprinted in the *Columbus Dispatch,* Nov. 27, 1883.

79. *Bellmont Chronicle,* Feb. 7, 1889, p. 1; *Wheeling Daily Register,* Feb. 22, 1889, p. 4; *New York Times,* Feb. 23, 1889, p. 1.

80. Letter to Allen from the Cleveland, Columbus, Cincinnati and Indianapolis Railway, Feb. 21, 1884 (AP, v. V, p. 106).

81. *Cincinnati Commercial Gazette,* Nov. 17, 1883, p. 7; Doris Chase Doane, *Time Changes in the U.S.A.* (San Francisco, 1973), p. 83; Henry Ford, *My Life and Work* (Garden City, NY, 1922), p. 24; Charles F. Dowd, "The Twenty-Four Hour Notation Leading to a Single Standard of Time and a Universal American Day" (2nd ed., n.d.) in the Dowd Papers, Manuscript Division, Boston Public Library, 19.9, no. 20. Dowd tried presenting this plan to the General Time Convention in 1884, but was denied a hearing.

82. Letter to Allen from the Cleveland, Columbus, Cincinnati and Indianapolis Railway, Feb. 21, 1884 (AP, v. V, p. 106); Mendenhall to Allen, Jan. 7, 1890 (AP, v. VI, p. 46); *Eleventh Annual Report of the Ohio Society of Surveyors and Civil Engineers* (Columbus, 1890), pp. 66–67; Ohio, *Journal of the House of Representatives,* Feb. 7, 1893, p. 222.

83. *Jones* vs. *German Ins. Co.,* Dec. 15, 1899 (81 NW 188).

84. See *Searles* vs. *Averhoff* (44 NW 873); *Rochester German Ins. Co.* vs. *Peaslee* (87 SW 1115); *Globe and Rutgers Fire Co.* vs. *Moffat,* NY, 1917 (254 FED 13). Additional examples include *Ex Parte Parker,* TX, 1895 (29 SW 480); *Texas T. & C. Co.* vs. *Hightower,* TX, 1906 (96 SW 1071); and *Walker* vs. *Terrel,* TX, 1916 (189 SW 75).

85. *State* vs. *Johnson*, MN, 1898 (71 NW 294); *Orvick* vs. *Cassleman*, ND, 1905 (105 NW 294); *Salt Lake City* vs. *Robinson*, Utah, 1911 (116 PAC 442); *Goodman* vs. *Caledonian*, NY, 1917 (118 NE 524); *Bank of Fruitvale* vs. *Fidelity, etc., Co.*, CA, 1917 (35 CAL APP 666).

86. *Globe and Rutgers Fire Co.* vs. *Moffat*, NY, 1917 (254 FED 13); *The National Economist*, April 19, 1890, and W. Scott Morgan, *History of the Wheel and the Alliance and the Impending Revolution* (1891), p. 88.

87. *National Economist*, Mar. 14, 1889, p. 9. The article quoted ran as part of a weekly series under the theme "history repeats itself."

88. Nelson A. Dunning, *The Farmer's Alliance History and Agricultural Digest* (Washington, D.C., 1891), pp. 462 and 140, respectively.

89. Morgan, *History of the Wheel and the Alliance*, pp. 677 and 209, respectively; explanation of "the wheel," p. 62.

90. *Proceedings of the American Railway Association*, 1 (1893), pp. 732–733. Introduced in 1884, the regulations were offered as a model in the wake of the new time. They were not formally adopted by the Convention and may never have been applied on any railroad in precisely this form.

91. *Indianapolis Journal*, Nov. 16, 1883, p. 5.

92. *Cincinnati Commercial Gazette*, Nov. 18, 1883, p. 1.

93. Unidentified newspaper clipping dated Nov. 25, 1883, probably from the *New York* or *Boston Herald*, in AP, v. V, p. 12.

IV

Keep a Watch on Everybody

1. *New York Herald*, Nov. 19, 1883.

2. *New York Daily Tribune*, Dec. 10, 1895, p. 2. Thanks to Grace Palladino for this reference.

3. Lawrence W. Levine, *Highbrow/Lowbrow. The Emergence of Cultural Hierarchy in America* (Cambridge, MA, 1988), pp. 171–200; *Boston Daily Advertiser*, Jan. 1, 1884, p. 4.

4. *Music*, 2 (July 1892), pp. 253–254. Thanks to Lawrence W. Levine for this reference.

5. *McGuffey's Fifth Eclectic Reader* (1881; reprint ed. New York, 1920), pp. 161–163.

6. *McGuffey's Third Eclectic Reader* (1881; reprint ed. New York, 1920), pp. 72–74.

7. *Harper's New Monthly Magazine*, 68 (January 1884), p. 327. Warner never mentioned standard time or even clocks—he focused his complaints on the larger divisions of months, days, and years. But its appearance less than two months after the invention of standard time suggests a connection.

8. George M. Beard, *American Nervousness: Its Causes and Consequences* (1881; reprint ed. (New York, 1972), pp. 104–105. As an alternative to the public world of time pressure, Beard favored "rest cures" that isolated the patient from time constraints.

9. Late nineteenth- and very early twentieth-century advertising is notoriously hard to find, since ads were often cut out of magazines before binding for library storage. Regrettably little survives today. I have relied heavily on a few periodicals and on the outstanding collections of advertisements and trade catalogues in the Business Americana Collection, Archives Center, National Museum of American History (BAC); and the files of the Section of Mechanisms, Division of Engineering and Industry, also at the Museum of American History (DEI).

10. See *Main Features of P. H. Dudley's Electrically Controlled System of Railroad and City Time Service* (New York, 1882), and another example, *The Electric Signal and Time Register Co.* (New York, 1882), pamphlets on file in BAC, "Clocks and Watches," Bx 1. Dudley drew his signals from the Washburn Observatory in Wisconsin. See also *New York Tribune*, Feb. 7, 1885, p. 8, "Time Furnished Like Gas or Water," for another example. As Chapter Two related, the Naval Observatory took pains to get the Signal Bureau's competing time service suspended by the Secretary of the Navy. The Secretary's order made the Naval Observatory the only federally sanctioned source of time. Again, standard time, and the railroad meridians, never received any official government endorsement. Theoretically,

"Naval Observatory time" meant time by the meridian of Washington, D.C., not the seventy-fifth meridian, the eastern zone standard.

11. Application for Time Service by Standard Yarn Co. of Oswego, New York, April 10, 1889, in the Western Union Archives, Archives Center, National Museum of American History (BAC). The Self-Winding Clock Company seems to have held the position of exclusive hardware supplier for the Western Union time service. Applications for the service admitted that other clocks, properly prepared to receive the time signal, might be used. But they discouraged substitutions.

12. *Jeweler's Circular and Horological Review,* 21 (February 1890), p. 91. Hiero Taylor, "The United States Government System of Observatory Time," in *What Is Standard Time?* promotional pamphlet of the Self-Winding Clock Company, in DEI.

13. *Scientific American,* 69 (July 29, 1893), p. 69. The service was available for home use but cost too much for most homes. The time signals were relatively inexpensive, but the clocks themselves were not.

14. Catalogue of the Electric Signal Clock Company, 1891, p. 5. In BAC, "Clocks and Watches," Bx 3. The Autocrat was a master clock that could be made to ring bells automatically.

15. Catalogue of the Blodgett Signal Clock Company, 1896, p. 2. Photocopy in National Association of Watch and Clock Collectors (NAWCC) Library, Columbia, PA.

16. Catalogue of the Electric Signal Clock Company, p. 12.

17. Catalogue of the Blodgett Signal Clock Company, p. 2.

18. Ibid., p. 1.

19. For an intriguing and important discussion of the relationship between machines, efficiency, and individuality in this period, see Walter Benn Michaels, "An American Tragedy, or the Promise of American Life," in *Representations,* 25 (Winter 1989), pp. 71–98. Michaels argues that only standardization and machine models made it possible for individuals to find a niche, to free themselves from the organic ties of sentiment and tradition and take their place in world where their individual attributes would be studied and utilized

to the full. Standardization, in other words, harmonizes the notion of the individual with the realities of machine culture.

20. Neil McKendrick, "Josiah Wedgwood and Factory Discipline," in *The Historical Journal*, IV (1961), pp. 30–55; A. G. Bromley, "Charles Babbage and the Invention of Workmen's Time Recorders," in *Antiquarian Horology*, 13 (September 1982), pp. 442–447. The base of the lamp reads "Pat. Applied For," but there is no patent number or record of the inventor's name. Consequently, it is difficult to tell how widely the device was used.

21. Alan Sayles, "A Short History of Dial Recorders," in *Bulletin of the National Association of Clock and Watch Collectors*, 9 (1961), pp. 941–942. In Bundy's system the keys were kept on a board or in a cabinet next to the clock.

22. *The Bundy Time Recorder*, n.d. (ca. 1893), pamphlet on file in BAC, "Watches and Clocks," Bx 1. Later models usually included windows, to allow the workers to see if their time had been recorded properly.

23. 1914 Catalogue of the International Time Recording Company (ITRC), p. 7; letter from S. H. Chamberlain to the Peace Dale Manufacturing Company, Feb. 1, 1913; International Time Recording Company, "Time: The Gateway to a Better Business," 1916, p. 4. All in DEI.

24. 1914 Catalogue of the ITRC, p. 9. In DEI.

25. *Factory: the Magazine of Management*, 6 (January 1911), p. 6. See also Adrian Forty, *Objects of Desire: Design and Society from Wedgwood to IBM* (New York, 1986), p. 122.

26. 1918 catalogue of the ITRC, p. 1. In DEI. Recall the description of the Lowell Mills that ended Chapter Two. Here, ending the process begun at Lowell, the mechanical clock has completely replaced paternal authority, and rebuilt the bonds between employer and employee.

27. 1914 catalogue of the ITRC, p. 9. In DEI. Samuel Haber, *Efficiency and Uplift: Scientific Management in the Progressive Era* (reprint ed. Chicago, 1973), p. ix.

28. See Haber, *Efficiency and Uplift*, passim.

29. On the tension between individual and system in scientific management and the Progressive era, see Michaels, "An American Tragedy," pp. 71–98. On Taylor as a system builder, see Thomas P.
Hughes, *American Genesis: A Century of Invention and Technological
Enthusiasm* (New York, 1989), pp. 184–248.

30. Frank B. Copley, *Frederick W. Taylor, Father of Scientific Management*
(New York, 1923), p. 52.

31. On Taylor and his disciples, see Copley's largely uncritical *Frederick
W. Taylor*; Haber, *Efficiency and Uplift*; Daniel Nelson, *Frederick W.
Taylor and the Rise of Scientific Management* (Madison, WI, 1980);
Hugh Aitken, *Taylorism at the Watertown Arsenal: Scientific Management
in Action, 1908–1915* (Cambridge, MA, 1960); Milton Nadworny,
Scientific Management and the Unions (Cambridge, MA, 1955); and the
discussions of Taylor in Daniel T. Rodgers, *The Work Ethic in Industrial America, 1850–1920* (Chicago, 1974). On rationalization in
the home, see Catherine Beecher, *A Treatise on Domestic Economy*
(1841; reprint ed. New York, 1970), p. 42 and the discussion of
Beecher in Chapter One. Taylor's obsession with work came from
his mother, not his father, who was said to have been "born retired."
Women seem to have borne most of the burden of socializing their
children to hard and efficient work. Dolores Hayden's *The Grand
Domestic Revolution: A History of Feminist Designs for American Homes,
Neighborhoods, and Cities* (Cambridge, MA, 1982) explores the long-
standing emphasis, among American feminist reformers, on conservation of time and motion. See discussion of time in the home below.

32. Frederick W. Taylor, "Shop Management," in *Transactions of the
American Society of Mechanical Engineers*, 24 (1902–03), pp. 1391–
1406 (reprinted, slightly revised, as *Shop Management* [New York,
1911], pp. 100–122). See also Aitken, *Taylorism at the Watertown
Arsenal*, pp. 13–34.

33. Hughes, *American Genesis*, pp. 184–248; Aitken, *Taylorism at the
Watertown Arsenal*, pp. 28–29, 97; Haber, *Efficiency and Uplift*, p. 24;
Taylor, *Shop Management*, pp. 102–103; *Principles of Scientific Management* (New York, 1911), pp. 124–125; Copley, *Frederick W. Taylor*,
vol. 1, pp. 358–370.

34. Copley, following one of Taylor's several versions, put the date as
1883, while Nelson's more careful review disclosed several alter-

native dates. See Nelson, *Frederick W. Taylor*, p. 41. As Nelson and others have pointed out, Taylor's memory was often conveniently faulty.

35. U.S. Congress, *Special Committee to Investigate the Taylor and Other Systems of Shop Management*, 3 vols. (Washington D.C., 1912). Testimonies of Orrin Cheney, vol. 1, p. 31; Richard Stackhouse, vol. 1, p. 295, 308–309; W. T. Probert, vol. 1, p. 757; and Olaf Nelson, vol. 1, p. 507. See also Rodgers, *The Work Ethic in Industrial America*, pp. 166–168.

36. Aitken, *Taylorism at the Watertown Arsenal*, p. 72. *Special Committee to Investigate the Taylor and Other Systems of Shop Management*, testimony of Joseph R. Cooney, vol. 1, 255.

37. Taylor, *Shop Management*, pp. 153–154.

38. A concise account is given in Aitken, *Taylorism at the Watertown Arsenal*, pp. 144–150. See also *Special Committee to Investigate the Taylor and Other Systems of Shop Management*, vol. 3, pp. 1888–1891. The molders misunderstood how Taylor's time was determined, and assumed that Taylor's man had simply lied. Twenty-four minutes represented the ideal time—under Taylor's standard formulas, premium pay rates would begin at any time under forty minutes.

39. *Special Committee to Investigate the Taylor and Other Systems of Shop Management*, testimony of Olaf Nelson, vol. 1, p. 508; testimony of John R. O'Leary, vol. 1, p. 18.

40. E. P. Thompson, "Time, Work-Discipline, and Industrial Capitalism," in *Past and Present*, 38 (December 1967), p. 86.

41. *CR*, Feb. 23, 1915, p. 4352.

42. It is sometimes claimed that officers were issued watches for the first time in the Civil War, but I have found no evidence to support this. It is true, however, that soldiers attached great prestige to owning a watch and that watch trading seemed to have been a popular pastime. On Waltham, see Charles W. Moore, *Timing a Century: The History of the Waltham Watch Company* (Cambridge, MA, 1945), passim. On the American watch industry, see Michael C. Harrold, *American Watchmaking: A Technical History of the American Watch Industry, 1850–1930* (1981), a supplement to the *Bulletin of the National Association of Watch and Clock Collectors*, 14 (Spring 1984), and the

concise account of David S. Landes, *Revolution in Time: Clocks and the Making of the Modern World* (Cambridge, MA, 1983), pp. 290–320.

43. Quoted in Landes, *Revolution in Time,* p. 307.

44. Landes, *Revolution in Time,* p. 318; Moore, *Timing a Century,* p. 53; National (Elgin) Watch Company, *Illustrated Almanac, 1871* (New York, 1870).

45. John G. Cawelti, *Apostles of the Self-Made Man: Changing Concepts of Success in America* (New York, 1965), p. 118.

46. Henry Ford, *My Life and Work* (Garden City, NY, 1925), p. 24. Watch clubs described in Boris Emmet and John E. Jeuck, *Catalogues and Counters: A History of Sears, Roebuck and Company* (New York, 1950), p. 28. For a rural example, see ad of J. C. Saunders and Co. in the *Bonham* (Texas) *News,* July 12, 1889–"A man working for a salary has no excuse for not owning a watch," the ad claimed.

47. Waterbury Watch Company, *Tick Tock Tick and Other Rhymes,* dated "ca. 188?" in Library of Congress.

48. Waterbury Watch Company, *Round and Round the Wheels Go Round* (New York, 1887), pamphlet in BAC, Bx 6, "Waterbury Watch Co." folder.

49. *New Haven Evening Register,* Mar. 1, 1887, p. 4.

50. *Round and Round the Wheels Go Round* (BAC, Bx 6, "Waterbury Watch Co." folder).

51. Harold Wentworth and Stuart Berg Flexner, eds., *Dictionary of American Slang* (New York, 1960), p. 518; and Flexner, *I Hear America Talking: An Illustrated History of American Words and Phrases* (New York, 1976). Thanks to Tom Schlereth for the information about Phi Beta Kappa, and to Mark Meigs for help with these ideas.

52. Reverend Alfred Taylor, *The Watch and the Clock, Number Thirty-Seven of the Home College Series* (New York, 1883), p. 13; U.S. Bureau of Standards, *Circular No. 51: Measurement of Time and Test of Timepieces* (Washington, D.C., 1914), pp. 18–19.

53. *The Waterbury,* 1 (October 1887), p. 62; *Harper's New Monthly Magazine,* 39 (July 1869), pp. 169–182.

54. *The Waterbury,* 2 (August 1888), p. 28.

55. Waterbury Watch Company, *Keep a Watch on Everybody* (New York, 1887) (BAC, Bx 6, "Waterbury Watch Co." folder).

56. National (Elgin) Watch Company, *Illustrated Almanac, 1875* (New York, 1874).

57. Lewis Mumford, *Technics and Civilization* (1934; reprint ed. New York, 1963), p. 14.

58. *The Waterbury*, 2 (December 1888), p. 91; 2 (January 1889).

59. *The Waterbury*, (February 1888), p. 121; *Collier's*, 44 (November 6, 1909), p. 5.

60. *Cleveland Gazette*, Nov. 3, 1883. The watch is billed ahead of the fifty dollars, though probably worth at the very most about half that. The ad reinforces the value of the watch as a universal status object, and the reference to "stem-winding" associates the watch with the aggressive man on the rise.

61. Boris Emmet and John E. Jeuck, *Catalogues and Counters: A History of Sears, Roebuck and Company* (New York, 1950), pp. 25–35.

62. Sears, Roebuck and Co., *1897 Catalogue* (reprint ed. New York, 1968), p. 369; *National Economist*, Oct. 18, 1890, p. 83. The ad is for Sears as "The Warren [Sears's middle name] Company."

63. Sears, Roebuck and Co., *1897 Catalogue*, p. 369.

64. Emmet and Jeuck, *Catalogues and Counters*, p. 33. Montgomery Ward and Co., *1895 Catalogue and Buyers Guide* (reprint ed. New York, 1969); Sears, Roebuck and Co., *1897 Catalogue*. Though the mail-order catalogues emphasized pastoral scenes more than more urban icons, it would be wrong to ignore the general popularity of rural scenes in other decorative arts of the period—in jewelry, for example. It might easily be argued that the general popularity of rural scenes as a decorative motif indicates a widespread ambivalence about machine production and industrialization. I only hope to call attention to the particularly striking juxtaposition of pastoralism with the pocketwatch, an unmistakably industrial machine, and the ambivalence about time and technology it suggests.

65. Ward and Co., *1895 Catalogue and Buyers Guide*, p. 144.

66. Dolores Hayden, *The Grand Domestic Revolution: A History of Feminist Designs for American Homes, Neighborhoods, and Cities* (Cambridge, MA,

1982); Beecher, *A Treatise on Domestic Economy* (1841; reprint ed. New York, 1970), p. 171.

67. See Susan Strasser, *Never Done: A History of American Housework* (New York, 1982); and Ruth Schwartz Cowan, *More Work for Mother: The Ironies of Household Technology from the Open Hearth to the Microwave* (New York, 1983); Daniel Rodgers, *The Work Ethic in Industrial America, 1850–1920* (Chicago, 1978), pp. 182–209.

68. Cowan, *More Work for Mother*, pp. 12–13.

69. On the ideology of separate spheres, see Katherine Kish Sklar, *Catherine Beecher: A Study in American Domesticity* (New Haven, 1973); Nancy Cott, *The Bonds of Womanhood* (New York, 1977); and Strasser, *Never Done*, pp. 181–201.

70. Catherine Beecher and Harriet Beecher Stowe, *The American Woman's Home* (New York, 1869), p. 372; Todd S. Goodholme, *Goodholme's Domestic Encyclopedia* (New York, 1878); Frank and Marion Stockton, *The Home: Where it Should Be and What to Put In It* (New York, 1873), pp. 76–77.

71. Hayden, *The Grand Domestic Revolution*, p. 128.

72. Quote from Maria Parloa, *Home Economics* (New York, 1906), p. 48. On cooking and recipes, see Laura Shapiro, *Perfection Salad: Women and Cooking at the Turn of the Century* (New York, 1986); Sidney Morse, *Household Discoveries* (New York, 1908), pp. 767–770; Ruth A. Beezly and Annie Gregory, *The National Course in Home Economics* (New York, 1917), frontispiece.

73. Quote from Thetta Quay Franks, *The Margin of Happiness* (New York, 1917), pp. 79–80. On scientific management in the home, see Cowan, *More Work for Mother*, ch. 6; Strasser, *Never Done*, pp. 213–219; Forty, *Objects of Desire*, pp. 114–120. For examples, see Martha Bensley Bruere and Robert W. Breure, *Increasing Home Efficiency* (New York, 1912), and Christine Frederick, *Household Engineering: Scientific Management in the Home* (Chicago, 1920).

74. Rodgers, *The Work Ethic in Industrial America, 1850–1920*, pp. 94–99.

75. Mrs. Henry Ward Beecher (Eunice White Bullard), *The Home: How to Make It and Keep It* (Minneapolis, 1883).

76. Elsie DeWolf, *The House in Good Taste* (New York, 1913), p. 5. The extreme example of personality expressed through consumer goods

would of course be Dreiser's Sister Carrie, the woman who literally makes herself over in the consumer marketplace. For a discussion of personality in home furnishings, see Forty, *Objects of Desire*, pp. 104–115 esp.

77. See Warren Susman, " 'Personality' and the Making of Twentieth Century Culture," in *Culture as History: The Transformation of American Society in the Twentieth Century* (New York, 1984), pp. 271–285.

78. De Wolf, *The House in Good Taste*, pp. 3, 300–306.

79. Examples of clock design drawn from trade catalogues on file in DEI, including Waterbury Clock Company, *Catalogue Numbers 154* (1908–09) and *156* (1910–11); F. Kroeber Clock Company, *Illustrated Catalogue, 1888–1889* (reprint ed. Kansas City, 1983); Ansonia Clock Company, *Catalogue of the Ansonia Clock Company, 1886–1887* (reprint ed. Ironton, MO, 1978); *1904–1905* (New York, 1904), and *1914* (reprint ed. Benicia, CA, 1983); and the survey of American clock design in Anita Schorsch, *The Warner Collector's Guide to American Clocks* (New York, 1981).

80. De Wolf, *The House in Good Taste*, p. 3. On the splintering of private time and its connection to public standardization, see Stephen Kern, *The Culture of Time and Space* (Cambridge, MA, 1983), pp. 10–30.

81. *Saturday Evening Post*, Nov. 4, 1916, p. 40.

82. Ibid., April 15, 1916, p. 39.

83. Michaels, "An American Tragedy," in *Representations*, 25 (Winter 1989), pp. 71–98. Michaels argues that in the early twentieth century individuality could only exist within mechanical social systems — that becoming a cog in Taylor's machine, or wearing standardized clothing styles, granted the individual a "place," a degree of individuality and autonomy not found in "organic" society.

84. *Saturday Evening Post*, Oct. 7, 1916, p. 39.

85. Ibid., Oct. 14, 1916, p. 47.

86. Ibid., Jan. 27, 1912. Thanks to Charles McGovern for this reference.

87. *Ladies' Home Journal* (December 1915), p. 74. Thanks to Miriam Formanek Brunell for this reference.

V

Therbligs and Hieroglyphs

1. Robert Bartlett Haas, *Muybridge: Man in Motion* (Berkeley, CA, 1976); Kevin McDonnel, *Eadweard Muybridge: The Man Who Invented the Moving Picture* (Boston, 1972); Gordon Hendricks, *Eadweard Muybridge: The Father of the Moving Picture* (New York, 1975): Craig Zabel, "Capturing Time: Muybridge and the Nineteenth Century," in David Robertson, ed., *The Art and Science of Eadweard Muybridge* (Carlisle, PA, 1985); and Robert Sklar, *Movie-Made America: A Cultural History of American Movies* (New York, 1975), pp. 3–9.

2. On the relationship between American art and scientific management, see Cecelia Tichi, *Shifting Gears: Technology, Literature, Culture in Modernist America* (Chapel Hill, NC, 1987); Stephen Kern, *The Culture of Time and Space* (Cambridge, MA, 1983); and Donald M. Lowe, *History of Bourgeois Perception* (Chicago, 1982).

3. Lary May, *Screening Out the Past: The Birth of Mass Culture and the Motion Picture Industry* (Chicago, 1983), p. 25; David A. Cook, *A History of Narrative Film* (New York, 1981), pp. 61–62.

4. Cook, *History of Narrative Film*, pp. 7–8; Gordon Hendricks, "The Kinetoscope: Fall Motion Picture Production," in John L. Fell, ed., *Film Before Griffith* (Berkeley, CA, 1983), pp. 13–21.

5. May, *Screening Out the Past*, pp. 36–37. On early American film makers, see Charles John Musser, "Before the Nickelodeon: Edwin S. Porter and the Edison Manufacturing Company" (Ph.D. diss., NYU, 1986), and his forthcoming book; John L. Fell, *Film and the Narrative Tradition* (1974; reprint ed. Berkeley, CA, 1986); David Bordwell, Janet Staiger, and Kristin Thompson, *The Classical Hollywood Cinema: Film Style and Mode of Production to 1960* (New York, 1985); and Kemp R. Niver, *The First Twenty Years* (Los Angeles, 1968).

6. Sklar, *Movie-Made America*, p. 17. Movie exhibitors apparently felt free to alter the films. Musser, "Before the Nickelodeon," calls the exhibitors of the period "co-creators" of the audience's experience, and sees their construction of film programs as an antecedent of movie editing.

7. *The Nation*, Aug. 28, 1913, quoted in May, *Screening Out the Past*, pp. 35–36. See also Sklar, *Movie-Made America*, pp. 18–19.

8. *The Independent*, Feb. 6, 1908, pp. 307–308.

9. *Harper's Weekly*, 51 (Aug. 24, 1907), p. 573; *The Independent*, 69 (Sept. 29, 1910), p. 715. See also C. Francis Jenkins, *Animated Pictures* (Washington, D.C., 1898), pp. 102–106.

10. *Survey*, June 5, 1909, pp. 355–365; *Harper's Weekly*, 51 (Aug. 24, 1907), p. 573.

11. *The Dial*, 57 (Sept. 1, 1914), p. 127.

12. *Scientific American*, 100 (June 26, 1909), p. 476.

13. Georges Méliès, *The Clockmaker's Dream* (New York & Paris, 1904), Paperprint Collection, Motion Picture, Television and Sound Division, Library of Congress. The film had a very smooth continuity; it had a narrative flow, but no real story. Méliès's films were so often copied that in 1903 he finally opened a New York office to control distribution and deter felonious American rivals. On film and magic, see Eric Barnouw, *The Magician and the Cinema* (New York, 1981).

14. For a general description of film structure and content in this period, see John L. Fell, "Motive, Mischief, and Melodrama: The State of Film Narrative in 1907," in Fell, ed., *Film Before Griffith* (Berkeley, CA, 1983), pp. 272–285.

15. *Harper's Weekly*, 57 (Jan. 18, 1913), p. 20.

16. Cook, *History of Narrative Film*, pp. 32–33. For examples of recent scholarship, see Musser, "Before the Nickelodeon," and the various essays in Fell, ed., *Film Before Griffith*.

17. *Survey*, 22 (June 5, 1909), pp. 355–365. See also *Harper's Weekly*, 54 (July 30, 1910), pp. 12–13; and Roy Rosenzweig, *Eight Hours for What We Will: Workers and Leisure in an Industrial City, 1870–1920* (Cambridge, MA, 1985). Lawrence W. Levine, *Highbrow/Lowbrow. The Emergence of Cultural Hierarchy in America* (Cambridge, MA, 1988), points out that this kind of audience behavior was disappearing.

18. Rosenzweig, *Eight Hours for What We Will*, p. 201; *Harper's Weekly*, 61 (Dec. 11, 1915), p. 574.

19. *Scientific American*, 112 (May 15, 1915), pp. 454–455.

20. *American Magazine*, 76 (September 1913), p. 60; *Harper's Weekly*, 57 (January 18, 1913), p. 20.

21. *Survey*, 32 (June 27, 1914), p. 337. Detailed discussions of movie censorship can be found in May, *Screening Out the Past*, ch. 3; Sklar, *Movie-Made America*; Rosenzweig, *Eight Hours for What We Will*; and Kathy L. Peiss, *Cheap Amusements: Working Women and Leisure in Turn-of-the-Century New York* (Philadelphia, 1986).

22. Conflicting prints of the film survive. Though the version described is now generally regarded as the "original" as Porter released it, some believe the repeated action of the last scenes was often recut in a more modern form. See Musser, "Before the Nickelodeon," pp. 265–272; and Cook, *A History of Narrative Film*, pp. 18–20.

23. André Gaudreault, "Temporality and Narrativity in the Early Cinema," in Fell, ed., *Film Before Griffith*, pp. 316–319.

24. David Wark Griffith, "The Fatal Hour" (1908), Paperprint Collection, Motion Picture, Television and Sound Division, Library of Congress. Thanks to Charles Musser for bringing the film to my attention.

25. *The Independent*, 69 (Sept. 29, 1910), p. 714.

26. *Harper's Weekly*, 61 (Dec. 11, 1915), p. 573.

27. Between 1910 and 1919, New York newspapers give a mixed picture. Major features or special presentations of news started at precise times, but many theaters simply listed the names of new films, or major stars, with no show times. Obviously, the transition to feature films proceeded slowly; the one-reel format lasted into the twenties in some cases. On the other hand, many more films were produced and shown than advertised. Most theaters, counting on neighborhood patronage, may simply have posted starting times outside and assumed that customers would note the times on their way by.

28. *American City*, 7 (Sept. 12, 1912), pp. 234–38; *Literary Digest*, Aug. 5, 1916, p. 508.

29. *The Policy and Standards of the National Board of Censorship of Motion Pictures* (New York, 1914), pp. 10–11, passim. Thanks to Kathy Piess for loaning me a copy of this document.

30. *Current Opinion,* 63 (October 1917), p. 251. For examples of different ad formats, see *New York Tribune,* Nov. 13, 1916, p. 3; and Nov. 13, 1916, p. 7.

31. See Bordwell, Staiger, and Thompson, *The Classical Hollywood Cinema,* pt. 3.

32. *Survey,* 23 (Aug. 27, 1910), p. 740. See also Randolph Bourne's critique of a similar film in *New Republic,* 3 (July 3, 1915), p. 233.

33. *Good Housekeeping* (Aug. 10, 1910), pp. 184–185.

34. *Lippincott's,* 84 (October 1909), p. 455.

35. Seymour Chatman, "What Novels Can Do that Films Can't (and Vice Versa)," in W. J. T. Mitchell, ed., *On Narrative* (Chicago, 1981), p. 126 and passim, makes some related points.

36. Noël Burch, "Porter, or Ambivalence," in *Screen,* 19 (Winter 1978–79), p. 104.

37. Hugo Münsterberg, *The Photoplay: A Psycholocial Study,* 1916 (quoted in Dover reprint ed., retitled *The Film: A Psychological Study,* (New York, 1970), pp. 74, 95.

38. *Lippincott's,* 84 (October 1909), p. 455.

39. Münsterberg, *The Photoplay,* p. ix; *Psychology and Industrial Efficiency* (Boston, 1913), pp. 37–56; *American Problems: From the Point of View of a Psychologist* (1910; reprint ed. New York, 1969), pp. 25–43.

40. Münsterberg, *The Photoplay,* p. 94.

41. *Scientific American,* 56 (Jan. 13, 1917), p. 56.

42. *Harper's Weekly,* 58 (June 6, 1914), p. 21.

43. Leslie T. Peacocke, *Hints on Photoplay Writing* (Chicago, 1916), pp. 21, 28–29; *Colliers,* 52 (Nov. 1, 1913), pp. 24–26; Frederick A. Talbot, *Moving Pictures: How They Are Made and Worked* (Philadelphia, 1914), pp. 146–147; *Moving Picture World* quoted in Janet Staiger, "Dividing Labor for Production Control: Thomas Ince and the Rise of the Studio System," in *Cinema Journal,* vol. 18, no. 2 (Spring 1979), p. 19. See also *Harper's Weekly,* 56 (Sept. 7, 1912), p. 13.

44. *Saturday Evening Post,* 188 (May 13, 1916), p. 14. See also *New York Times,* Sept. 28, 1919, sec. IV, p. 5.

45. On Ince, see Janet Staiger, "Dividing Labor for Production Control: Thomas Ince and the Rise of the Studio System," in *Cinema Journal,* vol. 18, no. 2 (Spring 1979), pp. 16–25; and her chapters on "The Hollywood Mode of Production to 1930," in Bordwell, Staiger, and Thompson, *The Classical Hollywood Cinema,* pp. 85–142. See also the account of Ince's career in Lewis Jacobs, *The Rise of the American Film* (New York, 1939), pp. 204–206. Jacobs claims Ince stamped his scripts "produce this exactly as written!" in order, like Taylor, to disempower his employees and eliminate their input into the manufacturing process.

46. Bordwell, Staiger, and Thompson, *The Classical Hollywood Cinema,* p. 162.

47. *Survey,* Sept. 13, 1913, p. 724.

48. *Survey,* Sept. 6, 1913, pp. 684, 691.

49. Frank B. and L. M. Gilbreth, *Applied Motion Study* (1916; reprint ed. Easton, PA 1973), p. 203. The Gilbreths' "One Best Way" turned into a sort of Benthamite calculus of good. An innovation's worth, they insisted, depended on the number of "happiness minutes" it produced. On the lives of the Gilbreths, see Edna Yost, *Frank and Lillian Gilbreth: Partners for Life* (New Brunswick, NJ, 1949).

50. *Current Opinion,* 55 (September 1913), p. 206.

51. L. M. Gilbreth, *The Psychology of Management* (New York, 1914); Münsterberg, *American Problems,* pp. 25–33; and *Psychology and Industrial Efficiency,* p. 164. Münsterberg visited the Gilbreths' laboratory and cited their work in the latter.

52. On Gilbreth's relationship with Taylor and his disciples, see Daniel Nelson, *Frederick W. Taylor and the Rise of Scientific Management* (Madison, WI, 1980), pp. 131–136; Samuel Haber, *Efficiency and Uplift: Scientific Management in the Progressive Era, 1820–1920* (Chicago, 1973), pp. 37–42; and Milton Nadworney, "Frederick Taylor and Frank Gilbreth: Competition in Scientific Management," in *Business History Review,* XXXI (Spring 1957), pp. 23–34.

53. Gilbreths, *Applied Motion Study,* pp. 65–70.

54. Frank and Lillian Gilbreth, "Abstract of the Effect of Auto Micro-Motion Study on Educational and Industrial Methods" (Nov. 23, 1916), in a set of microfilm reels, "Frank B. Gilbreth, Selected

Papers, ca. 1910–1924," from the Gilbreth Library, Purdue University Libraries, Lafayette, Indiana (hereafter referred to as GP), Reel 1.

55. Gilbreths, *Applied Motion Study*, p. 119, See also Frank and Lillian Gilbreth, *Fatigue Study* (1916; reprint ed. Easton, PA, 1973), p. 126.

56. Adapted from chart in GP, Reel 1.

57. Vachel Lindsay, *The Art of the Moving Picture* (1915; reprint ed. New York, 1970), pp. 172–173. In his 1922 revision of the book, Lindsay commented on America's "hieroglyphic civilization." Advertisements, cartoons, photography, and the movies "make us into a hieroglyphic civilization far nearer to Egypt than England," pp. 21–22.

58. Quotes from Lindsay, *Art of the Moving Picture*, pp. 65–66; Gilbreths, "Abstract of the Effect of Auto Micro-Motion Study," p. 4 (GP, Reel 1). Thanks to Michael Rogin for help with these points.

59. *The Independent*, 69 (Sept. 29, 1910), p. 713.

60. *Scientific American Supplement*, 80 (May 22, 1915), p. 323; *The Bookman*, 47 (May 1918), p. 238.

61. Lindsay, *Art of the Moving Picture*, p. 54.

62. Recent scholarship on Griffith downplays both his originality and the idea that he "invented" the modern film vocabulary. For examples, see Michael P. Rogin, "The Sword Became a Flashing Vision: D. W. Griffith's *The Birth of A Nation*," in *Ronald Reagan, The Movie, and Other Episodes in Political Demonology* (Berkeley, CA, 1987); Bordwell, et al., *The Classical Hollywood Cinema*, part 3, passim; Cook, *A History of Narrative Film*, pp. 59–92; and Tom Gunning, "Weaving a Narrative: Style and Economic Background in Griffith's Biograph Films," in *Quarterly Review of Film Studies*, 6 (Winter 1981), pp. 12–25.

63. Rogin, *Ronald Reagan, The Movie*, pp. 199–200. I am greatly indebted to Michael Rogin for his many provocative discussions of Griffith and American film.

64. Lindsay, *Art of the Moving Picture*, p. 49.

65. *St. Louis Mirror* quoted in *Current Opinion*, 64 (May 1918), p. 332.

66. Wilson quoted in Rogin, *Ronald Reagan, The Movie*, p. 192.

67. Woodrow Wilson, "After-Dinner Remarks in New York to the Motion Picture Board of Trade," Jan. 27, 1916, reprinted in Arthur Link, ed., *The Papers of Woodrow Wilson* (Princeton, NJ, 1985), vol. 36, pp. 16–17.

68. *Current Opinion*, 63 (December 1917), pp. 346–347. Despite his optimistic words, Griffith's romantic vision of war collapsed after he visited the trenches. *Hearts of the World* made money, thanks to the era's superheated patriotism. But the film lacked the narrative continuity and simulacrum of history that distinguished *Birth*. Griffith was unable to connect the atrocities he had seen in Europe with any grand, romantic principles of crusade, and the film's narrative trajectory led toward disgust, cynicism, and disillusion. Wilson apparently found the film repellent, and after seeing it he severed his friendship with Griffith permanently. See Russell Merritt, "D. W. Griffith Directs the Great War: The Making of Hearts of the World," in *Quarterly Review of Film Studies* (Winter 1981), pp. 45–65.

69. Wilson quoted in Rogin, *Ronald Reagan, The Movie*, pp. 97, 94.

70. Larry Wayne Ward, *The Motion Picture Goes to War: The U.S. Government Film Effort During World War One* (Ann Arbor, MI, 1985), pp. 17–18; Terry Ramsaye, *A Million and One Nights: A History of the Motion Picture Through 1925* (New York, 1926), p. 728.

71. Münsterberg, *The Photoplay*, p. x.

72. Ward, *The Motion Picture Goes to War*, pp. 34–43. The films apparently do not survive.

73. On World War I motion pictures generally, see the detailed accounts in Ward, *The Motion Picture Goes to War*, pp. 10–19; David H. Mould, *American Newsfilm, 1914–1919: The Underexposed War* (New York, 1983); Michael Isenberg, *War on Film: The American Cinema and WWI, 1914–1941* (Rutherford, NJ, 1981); and Craig W. Campbell, *Reel America and World War One* (Jefferson, NC, 1985).

74. Although Wilson condemned the excesses and anti-German hysteria of the period he never took any strong action against them, and as the war went on the CPI's productions became increasingly virulent. On anti-German hysteria and the Wilson administration's contribution to it, see David M. Kennedy, *Over Here: The First World War and American Society* (New York, 1980).

75. *World Outlook* (November 1918), p. 8.

76. George Creel, *Complete Report of the Chairman of the Committee on Public Information* (Washington, D.C., 1920), p. 47.

77. George Creel, *Rebel At Large: Recollections of Fifty Crowded Years* (New York, 1947), p. 138; *Washington Herald,* July 19, 1918; *Washington Times,* July 19, 1918; clippings in Papers of George Creel, Manuscript Division, Library of Congress, Washington, D.C. (hereafter CP), Box 5.

78. See Creel to Charles Hart, June 6, 1918, in record group RG 63, Records of the Committee on Public Information, 1917–1919, CPI 1-A1, National Archives, Washington, D.C.; Creel to North Carolina Press Association, July 25, 1918, in CP, Bx 5. See also Creel to Wilson, undated memorandum asking Wilson to allay theater managers' fear of competition from four-minute men, CP, Bx 2. On the four-minute men, see James Mock and Cedric Larson, *Words That Won the War* (Princeton, NJ, 1939), pp. 113–126; Ward, *Motion Picture Goes to War,* p. 129.

79. *New York Times,* July 29, 1917, p. 8.

80. Creel, *How We Advertised America,* p. 5.

81. Charles S. Hart to Bruce Barton, Mar. 28, 1918, CPI 10A-A1.

82. Mould, *American Newsfilm,* pp. 268–272.

83. Howard Herrick to George Newland, April 19, 1918, CPI 10A-A1.

84. Creel, speech at premier showing of *America's Answer,* July 29, 1916, CPI, Bx 5.

85. *Variety,* Aug. 2, 1918, p. 38, quoted in Mould, *American Newsfilm,* p. 266.

86. *Fortnightly Review,* 113 (May 1920), p. 718.

87. Terry Ramsaye, *A Million and One Nights,* p. 784. On the Signal Service photographers, see Mould, *American Newsfilm.*

88. Charles S. Hart to James Hoff, April 5, 1918, CPI 10A-A1.

89. Gilbreth to O. O. Ellis, Jan. 14, 1918, pp. 4–5, GP, Reel 4.

90. Gilbreth to Ellis, Feb. 12, 1918, GP, Reel 4.

91. Frank Gilbreth to Lillian Gilbreth, Jan. 15, 18, 1918, GP, Reel 3.

92. O. O. Ellis to Margaret Hawley, Dec. 5, 1928, quoted in Margaret Hawley, "The Life of Frank Gilbreth" (M.A. thesis, University of California, Berkeley), p. 92.

93. Following Gilbreth's stay at Fort Sill, the Army hired animation expert J. R. Bray to produce a second series of training films. Bray combined actual footage with animated cross sections and slow-motion close-ups that showed the principles of the object under study. *Literary Digest,* 60 (Feb. 22, 1919), pp. 25–26.

94. *The Bookman,* 47 (May 1918), p. 238.

95. *Current Opinion,* 64 (January 1918), p. 404.

96. *The Bookman,* 47 (May 1918), p. 239.

97. *Current Opinion,* 64 (January 1918), p. 404.

VI
The Golf Stick and the Hoe

1. Thorstein Veblen, *The Instinct of Workmanship* (New York, 1914), pp. 311–319.

2. Noah Webster, *An American Dictionary of the English Language* (1828); reprint ed. (New York, 1970), vol. II; William Cragie and James Hulbert, eds., *A Dictionary of American English* (Chicago, 1946), vol. IV; *Oxford English Dictionary* (Oxford, 1934), vol. XII.

3. On the transformation of attitudes about leisure time and its use, see Lewis A. Erenberg, *Steppin' Out: New York Nightlife and the Transformation of American Culture, 1890–1930* (Chicago, 1981); Lawrence W. Levine, *Highbrow/Lowbrow. The Emergence of Cultural Hierarchy in America* (Cambridge, MA, 1988); John Kasson, *Amusing the Millions: Coney Island at the Turn of the Century* (New York, 1978); Lary May, *Screening Out the Past: The Birth of Mass Culture and the Motion Picture Industry* (Chicago, 1983); Kathy Piess, *Cheap Amusements: Working Women and Leisure in Turn-of-the-Century New York* (Philadelphia, 1986); Daniel Rodgers, *The Work Ethic in Industrial America, 1850–1920* (Chicago, 1974); and Roy Rosenzweig, *Eight Hours for What We Will: Workers and Leisure in an Industrial City, 1870–1920* (Cambridge, MA, 1985).

4. *CR,* Aug. 19, 1919, p. 3994.

5. *Cleveland Plain Dealer,* April 16, 1914, p. 13. Georgia and Florida were also particularly dissatisfied with standard time.

6. *Literary Digest,* 31 (Dec. 15, 1900), p. 725.

7. *American City,* 15 (September 1916), p. 277; *American Review of Reviews,* 54 (August 1916), pp. 208–209.

8. Franklin, "An Economical Project" (1784), in Albert Henry Smyth, ed., *The Writings of Benjamin Franklin* (New York, 1970), vol. IX, pp. 183–189. See also *The Autobiography of Benjamin Franklin,* in Smyth, ed., *Writings of Benjamin Franklin,* vol. I, p. 385. Decadent Parisians, Franklin noticed, rose late and conducted their affairs by candlelight. In an anonymous letter to the *Journal of Paris,* Franklin feigned astonishment, on "accidentally" awakening before noon one day, at the sunlight streaming through his hotel window. Awaken all of Paris at sunrise with ringing bells or booming cannons, he conjectured, and her citizens would soon be doing business by daylight, saving 96 million livres in the cost of candles. Franklin proposed waking people at sunrise, not at any specific hour of the clock. An interesting precursor to daylight saving appeared in the *Connecticut Journal,* Feb. 20, 1827, p. 2. The writer noted that some New Haven churches rang their morning bells an hour earlier in the summer, and suggested that if this custom were adopted by the city as a whole, "many thousand dollars" would be saved, in addition to "increased health and vigor to the constitution."

9. Willett's pamphlet is reprinted in Donald de Carle, *British Time* (London, 1947), pp. 151–160; and discussed in *The Washington Post,* Mar. 28, 1909. On time in Cleveland and Detroit, see *American Review of Reviews,* 54 (August 1916), pp. 206–208; Cleveland Chamber of Commerce, *Annual Reports,* 1914, 1915, 1916, pp. 145–148, 108–109, 85–86, respectively; *Cleveland Plain Dealer,* April 16, 17, 1914, p. 8; April 30, p. 1; May 2, p. 1; City of Detroit, *Journal of the Common Council,* April 27, 1915, pp. 714–715; *Detroit Free Press,* May 13, 1915, pp. 4, 13; May 16, 1915, pp. 1, 4.

10. *Cleveland Plain Dealer,* May 1, 1914, pp. 1, 7.

11. *Cleveland Plain Dealer,* May 2, 1914, p. 1; April 16, 1914, p. 13; Cleveland Chamber of Commerce, *Annual Reports,* 1914, p. 147.

12. United States, Senate, Committee on Interstate Commerce, *Standardization of Time,* May 26, 1916 (Washington, D.C., 1916).

13. *Engineering Record*, 73 (June 10, 1916), p. 759; *Literary Digest*, 52 (June 3, 1916), p. 1644; *Literary Digest*, 52 (Aug. 5, 1916), p. 300; *Saturday Evening Post*, July 29, 1916, p. 22.

14. *The Independent*, 86 (June 12, 1916), p. 430; *Engineering Record*, 73 (June 10, 1916), p. 759.

15. *New York Times*, May 8, 1916, pp. 6, 10.

16. *The Independent*, 86 (June 12, 1916), p. 430. For the most extreme example of daylight saving as a curb on nightlife, see George Patrick, "The Psychology of Daylight Saving," in *The Scientific Monthly* (November 1919), pp. 385–396.

17. *Scientific American*, 114 (June 10, 1916), p. 614; 115 (Aug. 12, 1916).

18. *New York Times*, May 8, 1916, p. 6.

19. *New York Times*, May 4, 1916, p. 16; May 6, 1916, p. 10.

20. *New York Times*, May 30, 1916, p. 5; Jan. 31, 1917, p. 9.

21. Several stacks of these cards, held together by cloth tapes, remain in the records of the Committee on Interstate Commerce in the National Archives. For documents in the Archives relating to daylight saving in this period, see H.R. 64A-H11.7 through H.R. 66A-H10.2.

22. Boston, Chamber of Commerce, Special Committee on Daylight Saving Plan, "An Hour of Light for an Hour of Night." The pamphlet is undated, but must have been issued sometime in late 1916. It was reprinted as a supplement to *Current Affairs*, March 19, 1917.

23. United States, Senate, Committee on Interstate Commerce, *Daylight Saving and Standard Time for the United States*, May 3, 10, 1917 (Washington, D.C., 1917), pp. 4–8, 26–27.

24. Senate, Committee on Interstate Commerce, *Calendar No. 53, Report No. 46: Daylight Saving* (May 25, 1917). The Committee concluded that by the time the bill passed in 1917, its period of greatest usefulness would be largely over.

25. *New York Times*, Jan. 14, 1917, p. 7; Jan. 16, 1917, p. 7; May 18, 1917, p. 7; June 5, 1917, p. 15; *The Automobile*, Feb. 8, 1917, p. 336; July 5, 1917, p. 33; *The Outlook*, 115 (Feb. 19, 1917), p. 293.

26. *New York Times*, Jan. 23, 1917, p. 11; Resolution of Pennsylvania Senate, May 16, 1917. In NA, H.R. 65A-H6.4.

27. Few examples of these posters remain. Until 1976, the New Jersey Historical Society had copies of at least five, but these were sold at auction in that year. The two posters cited were reproduced in *American City*, 18 (March 1918), p. 218, and James R. Beniger, *The Control Revolution: Technological and Economic Origins of the Information Society* (Cambridge, MA, 1986), p. 328 (thanks to Steven Reber for the latter). See also New Jersey Historical Society, *Collection of World War I Posters* (Newark, NJ, 1986), p. 30. Each of these posters bears the legend "National Cigar Stores Company." Since the themes and style of the posters are nearly identical to the National Daylight Saving Association's mailing cards, I am assuming that this company sponsored the posters in cooperation with Marks's organization. But I have no idea how many were produced or how widely they were disseminated, or if other companies sponsored similar posters.

28. For editorials favorable to daylight saving, see the *Survey*, 39 (Jan. 12, 1918), p. 420; *Scientific American*, 118 (Jan. 26, 1918), p. 82; *American City*, 18 (March 1918), pp. 217–218; *The Outlook*, 118 (Mar. 13, 1918), p. 396; *Literary Digest*, 56 (Mar. 30, 1918), p. 20.

29. Joshua Burley and Co. to H. H. Dale of New York, Mar. 11, 1918; same letter dated Mar. 12, 1918, from Schwartz and Jaffee Boys and Juvenile Clothing, both in NA, H.R. 65A-H6.4. The same letter was also entered into the *Congressional Record* by Rep. Moore of Pennsylvania on Mar. 15, 1918 (p. 3575). I do not know who originated this letter, but suspect it to be either Marks's organization or the United States Chamber of Commerce under A. Lincoln Filene. These two organizations were the most active on the bill's behalf.

30. *CR*, 56:4 (Mar. 15, 1918), pp. 3564–3584; Hoover's endorsement, p. 3579.

31. *CR*, p. 3571. Although at least two other congressmen mentioned this article, I have been unable to find a copy of it. It certainly seems too ridiculous to have been a real proposal.

32. *Appendix to the Congressional Record*, 56:4 (Mar. 18, 1918), p. 225. Hereafter *ACR*.

33. *CR*, 56:4 (Mar. 16, 1918), p. 3595. *New York Times*, Mar. 29, 1918, p. 8; Mar. 31, 1918, sec. iv, p. 14; Apr. 1, 1918, p. 11; May 9, 1918, p. 12.

34. *Current Opinion*, 64 (May 1918), p. 366; *Survey*, 41 (Oct. 26, 1918), p. 105. The bill officially expired on October 27, but it proved so popular in some circles that Congress considered extending it to apply all year long. Even its most vocal partisans pointed out that keeping daylight saving in winter made no sense, and in fact only increased the number of morning hours spent in darkness. The bill was allowed to expire on October 27, which of course made it necessary to pass an entirely new bill next year.

35. *Literary Digest*, 59 (Nov. 9, 1918), p. 12.

36. *Survey*, 41 (Nov. 9, 1918), p. 171.

37. Interstate Commerce Commission, *No. 10122. Standard Time Zone Investigation* (Washington, D.C., Oct. 1–Oct. 24, 1918), pp. 278–279, 281.

38. *Literary Digest*, 60 (Feb. 1, 1919), pp. 23–25.

39. Petition from Citizens of New Britain, Connecticut, to Senator MacLean, Feb. 27, 1919. See also Minnesota State Vegetable Growers to Schall of Minnesota, Feb. 14, 1919; Diamond State Grange of Stanton, Delaware, to Albert Polk, Feb. 10, 1919, all in NA, H.R. 65A-H6.4. This latter file contains the fullest account of opposition to daylight saving. Until recently, most of the letters from this time related to daylight saving were being kept at the Department of Transportation. When I called that department in fall of 1986, however, I was told the letters had been destroyed the year before.

40. *New York Times*, Feb. 22, 1919, p. 8; Feb. 23, 1919, p. 8; *Scientific American*, 120 (Mar. 8, 1919), p. 220; *New York Times*, Feb. 27, 1919, p. 17.

41. An exhaustive account of the arguments against daylight saving appears in House of Representatives, Committee on Interstate and Foreign Commerce, *Repeal of Section Three of the Daylight Saving Act* (Washington, D.C., June 2–3, 1919), pts. I–III; and in the *Congressional Record* and *Appendix* throughout the summer months, especially June 18, 1919, pp. 1304–1335. Congressmen reprinted a considerable number of letters and petitions from their constituents in *CR*, and many examples of these survive in the National Archives, especially record group H.R. 66A-H10.1.

42. *CR,* 58:2 (June 18, 1919), p. 1320.

43. *ACR,* 58 (June 18, 1919), p. 8885. See also *CR,* 58:2, pp. 1322–1323.

44. *ACR,* 58 (June 18, 1919), p. 8887. For an early example of these objections, see Petition from the Farmer's Club of Enfield, Connecticut, June 20, 1917, in NA record group H.R. 65A–H6.4.

45. *CR,* 58:2, p. 1305.

46. *CR,* 58:2, p. 1305; 58:3, p. 2843, 3505; and *Literary Digest,* June 14, 1919, pp. 16–17.

47. *CR,* 58:2, p. 1317; 58:3 (Aug. 1, 1919), p. 3509. It also put some places closer to the local sun time than they had been before daylight saving, assuming, of course, that standard and not local time prevailed. Longitude, and a community's location within a zone, greatly affects the period of daylight. In the South, daylight saving is less drastic than in the North, where the variation in the length of the day from summer to winter is much greater. For a description of the effects of daylight saving in different regions, see Ian Bartky and Elizabeth Harrison, "Standard and Daylight-saving Time," in *Scientific American,* 240 (May 1979), pp. 46–53.

48. Extension of Remarks of Thomas Schall of Minnesota, June 24, 1919, in *ACR,* 58, p. 8891.

49. Extension of Remarks of William Boies of Iowa, June 18, 1919, in *ACR,* 58, p. 8876.

50. *CR,* 58:2, pp. 1332–1334.

51. Wilson's first veto message is reprinted in *CR,* 58:3 (July 12, 1919), p. 2492; his second veto, dated Aug. 15, 1919, is in the NA, record group H.R. 66A–H10.

52. *CR,* 58:3 (July 12, 1919), p. 2835.

53. *CR,* 58:3 (Aug. 1, 1919), p. 3507; "Extension of Remarks of William Boies of Iowa," June 18, 1919, in *ACR,* 58, p. 8876; *CR,* 58:2 (June 18, 1919), p. 1313; *CR,* 58:2 (June 18, 1919), p. 1321.

54. *ACR,* 58, p. 8875.

55. *Literary Digest,* 60 (Feb. 1, 1919), p. 24; 62 (Sept. 6, 1919), p. 18. See also *Outlook,* 122 (June 25, 1919), p. 320–321; *Scientific American,* 20 (June 21, 1919), p. 648; *American Review of Reviews,* 60 (August 1919), p. 121; *The Review,* 1 (Sept. 6, 1919), p. 357; *New*

York Times, Aug. 21, 1919, p. 10, Aug. 22, 1919, p. 10, Aug. 25, 1919, p. 10, Oct. 6, 1919, p. 16; and the numerous letters included in *CR* during the summer of 1919.

56. This fact still holds true today. Ride any city's mass transportation system at six o'clock in the morning, and the patrons are largely black and Hispanic, dressed casually or in work clothes. Two hours later, the riders are nearly all white, and wearing suits.

57. See summary of arguments in House Committee on Interstate and Foreign Commerce, *Report No. 42: Repeal of Daylight Saving Law* (June 13, 1919), pp. 2–3.

58. *New York Times,* Aug. 22, 1919, p. 10.

59. American Federation of Labor, *Proceedings of the 39th Annual Convention,* 39 (June 10, 1919), p. 185. See also *New York Times,* June 11, 1919, p. 17. For other evidence of worker opposition, see testimony in hearings on daylight saving in House of Representatives, Committee on Interstate and Foreign Commerce, *Repeal of Section Three of the Daylight Saving Act* (Washington, D.C., June 2–3, 1919), esp. pp. 9–17, 34–39, 44–45.

60. See letter from Marks in *The American City,* 21 (September 1919), p. 212; also 21 (November 1919), pp. 432–433; *American Review of Reviews,* 60 (December 1919), pp. 647–648; *Literary Digest,* 63 (Nov. 1, 1919), pp. 17–18; 61 (April 10, 1920), pp. 30–31.

61. *Massachusetts State Grange* vs. *Benton, United States Supreme Court Reports,* 272 (1926), pp. 525–529. For a summary of changes in time since 1919, see United States Department of Transportation, *Standard Time in the United States: A History of Standard and Daylight Saving Time in the United States and an Analysis of the Related Laws* (Washington, D.C., 1970).

62. *New York Times,* Mar. 19, 1918, p. 12.

63. *New York Times,* Apr. 2, 1918, p. 15.

64. See "Statement of Edward King," in House of Representatives, Committee on Interstate and Foreign Commerce, *Repeal of Section Three of the Daylight Saving Act,* pp. 40–42, and *CR,* 52:8, pp. 1332–1334.

65. *New York Times,* Aug. 9, 1919, p. 7.

66. Scrap of film in my possession, undated but approximately 1915–19. The scrap, on highly unstable nitrate film stock, is all that remains of a longer film, which would have been used to introduce a feature, or as filler between one-reelers. Thanks to Andrea Kalas of the UCLA Film Archives, Los Angeles, for finding and sending me this fragment, and to Helena Wright of the Division of Graphic Arts at the National Museum of American History, Washington, D.C., for confirming the dating.

67. Harold B. Franklin, President, Fox West Coast Theaters, to E. B. Duerr, Pathé Studios, May 17, May 26, June 20, 1930; Franklin to George Young of the *Los Angeles Examiner*, May 23, 1930, all in Margaret Herrick Library, Academy of Motion Picture Arts and Sciences, Beverly Hills, CA, Pathé Exchange Collection, folder 11, "General Matters No. 2." See also editorial in the *Los Angeles Examiner*, May 23, 1930.

68. Fern S. Chapman, "Business's Push for More Daylight Time," in *Fortune*, 110 (Nov. 12, 1984), p. 149.

69. Telephone conversation between the author and James Benfield, Bracy, Williams and Co., 1000 Connecticut Ave. NW, Suite 304, Washington, D.C., 20036, November 1986.

70. *The Independent*, July 12, 1919, p. 51.

71. *New York Times*, Apr. 2, 1919, p. 10.

72. Orville H. Platt, "Invention and Advancement" (1891), reprinted in Henry Nash Smith, *Popular Culture and Industrialism, 1865–1890* (New York, 1967), pp. 40–41.

73. *Scientific Monthly* (November 1919), pp. 385–396.

74. Responses to relativity described in Lawrence W. Levine, "The Unpredictable Past: Reflections of Recent American Historiography," in *American Historical Review*, 94 (June 1989), p. 677.

75. Robert and Helen Merrell Lynd, *Middletown: A Study in Modern American Culture* (New York, 1929), pp. 253–254, 258.

76. *The American Mercury*, VI (October 1925), p. 160. In *Anti-Intellectualism in American Life*, *The Paranoid Style in American Politics*, and *The Age of Reform*, Hofstadter linked fundamentalism to what he saw as a long tradition of delusional thinking on the American political margins. His view deprives fundamentalists of their historical

uniqueness and, worse, characterizes their objection to modernism as pathological and paranoid largely because it failed. See also Peter Novick, *That Noble Dream: The "Objectivity Question" and the American Historical Profession* (Cambridge, MA, 1988), pp. 337–341.

77. Ernest R. Sandeen, *The Roots of Fundamentalism: British and American Millenarianism, 1800–1930* (Chicago, 1970). My understanding of fundamentalism has been greatly influenced by George M. Marsden, *Fundamentalism and American Culture: The Shaping of Twentieth Century Evangelism, 1870–1925* (New York, 1980). Marsden points out that Sandeen's emphasis on Millenarian thinking fails to account for the larger fundamentalist movement.

78. Samuel Harris quoted in Jon H. Roberts, *Darwinism and the Divine in America: Protestant Intellectuals and Organic Evolution, 1859–1900* (Madison, WI, 1988), p. 9.

79. For American responses to Darwin, see James R. Moore, *The Post-Darwinian Controversies: A Study of the Protestant Struggle to Come to Grips with Darwin in England and America, 1870–1900* (Cambridge, 1979); Roberts, *Darwinism and the Divine.*

80. Quoted in Ray Ginger, *Six Days or Forever? Tennessee v. John Tyler Scopes* (1958; reprint ed. Chicago, 1969), p. 15. The quotation reflects common-sense realism's approach to science, in that it relates religion to the natural world—observe the natural world "scientifically" for examples of the proper use of time.

81. On the history of the week, see Eviatar Zerubavel, *The Seven-Day Circle* (New York, 1985).

82. For geology's impact on ideas about time, see Stephen Jay Gould, *Time's Arrow, Time's Cycle: Myth and Metaphor in the Discovery of Geological Time* (New York, 1986), and for examples of the problems geology posed, see Henry Adams's chapter on Darwinism in *The Education of Henry Adams.* The notion that instead of "progress" evolution only gave evidence of change greatly upset Adams. He marveled at the discovery of two prehistoric fish, *terabratula* and *tserapsis,* which appeared to have survived unchanged from antiquity. If there was no progress, thought Adams, then history and time were ultimately just meaningless records of change.

83. Richard Hofstadter, *Social Darwinism in American Thought* (1944; reprint ed. Boston, 1955), p. 58. For examples of social Darwinist

thinking, see Stephen Jay Gould, *The Mismeasure of Man* (New York, 1981). For the connection between evolution, machines, and modernist culture, see Cecelia Tichi, *Shifting Gears: Technology, Literature, Culture in Modernist America* (New York, 1987), p. 34.

84. Norman F. Furniss, *The Fundamentalist Controversy, 1918–1931* (New Haven, 1954), pp. 23–25.

85. Quoted in Lawrence W. Levine, *Defender of the Faith: William Jennings Bryan: The Last Decade* (New York, 1965), p. 280.

86. On Darrow, see Ginger's uncritical *Six Days or Forever?* pp. 47–68.

87. Levine, *Defender of the Faith*, p. 339.

88. This is pure speculation on my part. According to Leslie H. Allen, *Bryan and Darrow at Dayton* (1925; reprint ed. New York, 1967), p. 157, Raulston's watch was fifteen minutes fast on the last day of the trial. Fifteen minutes error was probably too great to have been accidental. Dayton was then located in the far east of the central zone, and central standard time would have been about fifteen minutes slower than local time by the Dayton sun. If Raulston set his watch by a sundial, or by a local clock set to mean local time, he would have been about fifteen minutes fast of standard time.

89. Quoted in Ruth Miller Elson, *Guardians of Tradition: American Schoolbooks of the Nineteenth Century* (Lincoln, NE, 1964), p. 16.

90. This is according to Ray Ginger, *Six Days or Forever?* p. 170. The nearly complete transcript of the Bryan-Darrow confrontation given in Leslie H. Allen, *Bryan and Darrow at Dayton*, does not record any mention of the specific time of creation, but does record it given as part of the scientific testimony read earlier in the trial. The comment about "eastern standard time" may have occurred then.

91. Audience reaction quoted in L. Sprague DeCamp, *The Great Monkey Trial* (New York, 1968), p. 403.

92. The 1960 movie, directed by Stanley Kramer, is oddly obsessed with time as well. It opens with a shot of the clock over the town courthouse approaching 8:00 a.m., then moves to a shot of three local citizens, all looking at their watches. Across the square they meet a fourth, also looking at his watch. In the trial scenes the judge sits before an open window, through which the camera shows a building with the painted sign "Traveler's Time." At one point in his cross-

examination of the Bryan character, Spencer Tracy refers to foes of evolution as "clock-stoppers." Kramer seemed to pick up the theme of natural time versus industrial, clock-based, standardized time.

93. Marsden, *Fundamentalism and American Culture,* p. 214.
94. Quoted in Leslie H. Allen, *Bryan and Darrow at Dayton,* p. 190.
95. Ibid., p. 195.

Epilogue

1. Standard time was first made federal law in 1918. The Uniform Time Act of 1966 extended the federal government's authority over time and established penalties for failure to conform to standard time.

2. For a discussion of the relation between the internal, biological clock and social structures, see Michael Young, *The Metronomic Society: Natural Rhythms and Human Timetables* (Cambridge, MA, 1988).

Index

Page numbers in *italics* refer to illustrations.